The Secular Miracle

The Secular Miracle

Religion, Politics and Economic Policy in Iran

Ali Rahnema and Farhad Nomani

Zed Books Ltd
London and New Jersey

The Secular Miracle: Religion, Politics and Economic Policy in Iran was
first published by Zed Books Ltd, 57 Caledonian Road, London N1
9BU, and 171 First Avenue, Atlantic Highlands, New Jersey 07716, USA
in 1990.

Cover designed by Sophie Buchet.

Typeset by Photosetting and Secretarial Services, Yeovil, Somerset.

Printed and bound in the United Kingdom
by Biddles Ltd, Guildford and Kings Lynn.

British Library Cataloguing in Publication Data

Rahnema, Ali
  The Secular Miracle : religion, politics and economic policy in
Iran.
  1. Iran. Politics
  I. Title II. Nomani, Farhad
320.955

ISBN 0-86232-938-8
ISBN 0-86232-939-6 pbk

Contents

Acknowledgements

We wish to thank all those who helped and prompted us to finish this book. Valuable research material was provided by the Center for Iranian Documentation and Research, Hedayatollah Matine-Daftary and Mohammed Khame. A special debt is acknowledged to Anne Enayat who commented extensively and provided sound advice on earlier drafts. Rosalind Sykes and Mark Baldock deciphered our handwritings and typed the many drafts of the manuscript, cheerfully and accurately. We would like to thank Mike Pallis of Zed Books for his helpful suggestions and encouragement. Special thanks to Mariam, whose presence and help, in her own special way, was indispensable.

May 1990

1. The People's Revolution

The events in Iran between November 1977 and February 1979 with their extensive political consequences will remain a subject of interest, investigation and controversy for historians in the future. The Iranian revolution upset and challenged certain well-established assumptions about the long-term stability of the régime which had ruthlessly repressed all attempts at armed struggle, stifled all forms of political dissent and co-opted certain outspoken members of the radical opposition. By all standard political yardsticks, the régime was doing well. It enjoyed the highest (GNP) growth rate in the world in 1974, financial viability and an awe-inspiring regional military power. One month before the outbreak of demonstrations, President Carter hailed Iran as an 'island of stability'. There were no signs to prove the contrary. The régime had come to power with the overt aid of the United States and enjoyed its close support. The Shah had also appeased his northern neighbour, through a cordial economic agreement: Iran provided gas and, in exchange, the Soviet Union built a steel mill in Isfahan. The Shah's military machine was strong enough to stretch out across the Persian Gulf to ensure the security of Oman.

The manner in which the Iranian revolution was fought presented revolutionary movements with a new approach to destabilization. It proved that it was possible to nibble away at the basis of power of a mighty régime with all the means of protest short of armed struggle. What Mao and Giap had contributed to guerrilla warfare and Guevara had put into practice in terms of the vanguard foco in Bolivia was now surpassed by a new insurrectionary method, one that would have seemed foolish wishful thinking had it only stayed on paper.

The revolution in Iran employed open action rather than clandestine activity, relied on mass participation and mobilization rather than the action of a small revolutionary vanguard and appealed to a broad section of the population, cutting across class barriers, rather than to a specific class. The tactics of the revolutionaries included mass demonstrations and strikes, unarmed provocations and psychological war against the soldiers who patrolled the streets of every major city.

That an anti-autocratic revolution can recruit supporters even from traditionally non-revolutionary classes was demonstrated by the Iranian revolution. The exclusion of the bourgeoisie (the designated beneficiaries of the Shah's administrative capitalism) from real political participation placed them shoulder to shoulder with the workers, intellectuals and the dispossessed, in the ranks of the anti-autocratic movement. None of the property owning classes fought against the revolutionary upsurge. Some even supported the religious elements of the revolution with financial backing. The bureaucratic arm of the régime, namely the ministries, was among the first to join the revolution. Only the army as an institution resisted, but even it did not fight back in the military sense of the word. Towards the end of the revolution a number of high-ranking generals even collaborated with the revolution.

Yet the collapse of the house of cards was by no means due to the anti-autocratic nature of the revolution only. A catchy slogan 'Death to the Shah' distinguished the revolutionary from the non-committed. The firm and unswerving leadership of Ayatollah Khomeini, with his saint-like reputation and a past record of outspokenness against the Shah, Zionism and US intervention in Iran, gave credibility to the movement. He was a spiritual leader in the eyes of the believers, a die-hard opponent of the Shah's arbitrary rule to those who wished for the implementation of the constitution and an anti-imperialist to all nationalists, socialists and communists.

Social tolerance became an outstanding feature of the anti-autocratic stage of the revolution as no one was excluded on the basis of class or political conviction. A people who had become deeply immersed in the impersonal human relations of urban life during the Shah's reign suddenly discovered solidarity with and compassion for their fellow country-persons. No political or social group had a monopoly over the movement at this stage. Consequently, the movement imposed its own code of conduct on the participants: respect for the democratic rights of all who struggled for the overthrow of the monarchy. The revolution encompassed all with their differences, never attempting to whitewash or deny those differences. Dialogue, discussion, pamphlets and books became the means of settling immediate disputes and comparing different ideological perceptions of the future.

A sense of responsibility and restraint was demonstrated in the revolution by the masses. Once the power was in the hands of the people, individuals did not take it upon themselves to try, pass judgement and punish those who had resisted them or committed crimes against them. The myth of mass hysteria, mass rage and thus mass brutality was shattered by the conduct of the Iranians during the short period in which the people held power.

The revolution was the rebirth of a nation. A sense of national identity and pride that was the result of a common struggle prevailed. For once, this was the people's Iran and not the Shah's Iran. Nationalism, which was the Shah's monopoly during his international interviews, was now truly socialized. The world marvelled at a relatively bloodless revolution, which was neither the result of a self-righteous army coup wanting to impose law and order or to defend 'democracy', nor the result of 'generous' aid of one or another 'friendly' power. The people had imposed their will with the minimum destruction and blood-letting.

Yet the revolution in Iran was rich in all aspects. It taught the world how to create an exemplary revolution, then showed what could become of it when the people forfeit power to a dictatorial minority who pretend to deliver everything to everyone.

The theocracy's linguistic distortions

During the past years, the political conduct of the post-revolutionary clerical leadership in Iran has constantly brought under question even the most well-established political and social tendencies or laws. An observer of the Iranian political scene must decode, translate and put into the correct context the leadership's language otherwise their words and the acts that follow would seem so divorced that the analyst would have to declare the leadership schizophrenic, which it definitely is not.

Revolution as a radical type of social change which imposes the will of the majority over that of a dictatorial minority is considered progressive and liberating. The outcome of the Iranian revolution would seem to challenge this assertion; the nature, however, and objectives of the revolutionary struggle should be distinguished from those of the post-revolutionary leadership.

In the case of Iran, the revolutionary movement envisioned a non-despotic society in which all that had been denied to the people, namely democratic rights – social, political and economic – would be made available. For the post-revolutionary leadership, the word *democratic* was utterly meaningless since a corresponding entry for it could not be found in their doctrine. The first move of the post-revolutionary leadership was to channel the power of the people into the hands of a lumpenproletariat whose economic, social and political interests in no way corresponded to that of the people's or even to the immediate interests of any particular social class. Thus a movement which had started as a democratically oriented, progressive revolution turned into an anti-democratic, regressive, theocratic dictatorship.

In the case of Iran, change led to the emergence of an anachronistic régime. This created an unprecedented communication disorder both among Iranians and between post-revolutionary Iran and the rest of the world. Well-established concepts which had a common meaning to all suddenly obtained other meanings. Hiding behind the smoke-screen of linguistic confusion, the Islamic leadership could claim itself to be the vanguard of the struggle of all the oppressed people nationally and internationally.

The terminology used by the Islamic leaders had roots in Islamic tradition and was not readily applicable to the modern world. It was given a latter-day interpretation and used to demonstrate the common ground between the ideas of this new revolutionary force and the old concerns of the two major world ideologies: communism and capitalism. Each camp found elements in the Islamic discourse which suited its broad political interests.

The theocratic leadership's slogan of 'Neither the East, Nor the West' struck a familiar note. Here was a revolutionary country which was calling all oppressed people to join a third force at a time when the non-aligned movement was losing its appeal. Islam's anti-communism promised the western world that 'Neither the East, Nor the West' was more anti-communist than anti-capitalist. Soon western political analysts turned their wishful thinking into geo-political theories of 'the green Islamic belt' encircling the Soviet Union. Taking their cue from 'revolutionary Islam' in Iran, the naïve cold-warriors rejoiced at the idea of all Moslem regions revolting and seceding from the Soviet Union. Thus the containment policy suddenly found a potent weapon: Islam. The old protectors of the status quo suddenly became ardent revolutionaries, thanks to the Iranian revolution.

On the other hand, the movement's anti-imperialist tone promised the left – inside and outside Iran – that Islam's 'Neither the East, Nor the West' was the battle-cry of a new anti-colonial force which would spread to the rest of the Moslem world like wildfire, thus further isolating and weakening the imperialist camp.

The theocracy's anti-imperialism

The post-revolutionary régime was, for the want of a better word, anti-imperialist. In reality, the clerical leadership was anti-non-Islamic. It made no difference if the non-Islamic state was a truly proletarian, democratic, imperialist or fascist state. Relations of production, the ownership of the means of production and the need to expand overseas due to domestic accumulation of capital were not considered relevant criteria in an assessment of imperialism.

So xenophobia, rooted in a fear of and a revulsion towards all non-Islamic states, suddenly became synonymous with anti-imperialism. The post-revolutionary régime was fearful of any outside influence, social, cultural, political or economic. Such influences were considered corrupting and contaminating. Society had to be closed, cleansed and then opened up in order to export the revolution. Political analysts, taking words and acts at their face value, argued that since the movement was nationalist in character it was logical that it would be anti-imperialist as well. They jumped to the wrong conclusion that the post-revolutionary leadership had to be anti-imperialist, given that the leadership was the continuation of the movement and had acted in an anti-imperialist manner on the international scene.

The theocratic leadership provided a clearer definition of an imperialist state as time went by. Even some Islamic states came to be considered as stooges of imperialism, not necessarily because of any economic or political relations with imperialism, but because their interest differed from those of the theocratic leadership. The rule of thumb was simple: any country which opposed Islamic Iran was imperialist or in league with imperialism and any country which supported it was anti-imperialist. The linguistic distortion was taken to its logical consequence when, at one point, all socialist and Marxist groups came to be considered as creations of one or another imperialist power.

The linguistic counter-revolution carried out by the theocratic leadership created utter confusion. Even in 1987, seven years after the Islamic government's official declaration of war against Marxist organizations and their subsequent systematic repression and annihilation, there were still Marxist groups and organizations which considered the régime to be anti-imperialist and therefore worthy of support by the left.[1] The use of the term *anti-imperialism* by the post-revolutionary régime took away the concept's socio-economic significance. The failure of the left to unveil this linguistic distortion meant giving support to a régime which intended to disarm it. The clerical leadership usurped the theoretical tools of the revolutionary left, stripped them of their significance and practical application and, finally, used them to silence all opposition. The left's support facilitated the régime's campaign against democratic rights and freedoms at home. The left's lack of theoretical analysis not only played into the hands of the clerical leadership, but provided it with a breathing space to prepare for the eventual liquidation of the left itself.

The Islamic Republic and democratic rights

In an interview with foreign journalists on 9 November 1978, Ayatollah Khomeini was asked: 'You are in favour of an Islamic Republic, but will such a Republic ensure *democratic rights for all*, will the Marxists be given the right of free expression?' Ayatollah Khomeini responded: 'An Islamic republic is a democratic state in the true sense of the word and . . . everyone can voice his own opinion . . . and the Islamic state will respond with logic to all the arguments put forward'.[2]

To those who read these words, the future was clear, since 'democratic rights' should have no other meaning than that which it implies. Yet to the clerical leadership, democratic rights applied to and were accorded to all Iranians who were within the circle of the faithful. In this case, the faithful were not even determined by their adherence to Islam, but according to obedience to the arbitrary decisions and rules of the leadership. It did not take very long for most people to discover the meaning of democratic rights according to the post-revolutionary leadership.

Less than twenty days after the victory of the revolution, in a referendum on the country's form of political system, the people were faced with a strange choice: Islamic Republic, Yes or No? In the heat of the excitement, barraged with misinformation on what an Islamic Republic meant, fearful that a no vote would mean support for the monarchy and given no other choice, the Islamic Republic was voted in by an overwhelming majority.

While despotism was quietly defacing all democratic rights, socialist and Marxist-oriented groups and parties hid their heads in the sand and justified their support for the régime by counting the democratic rights that still existed. The left's wishful thinking and refusal to call the régime what it truly was facilitated the leadership's manoeuvring. One by one, the rights of those who were outside the clearly defined circle of the faithful were violated. In this task, the régime used the 'people'. It was the people who had had enough of the 'liberal propaganda' of a certain newspaper. It was the people who wielded their clubs, threw stones and bashed heads in imposing its will. Newspapers were closed by the 'people' for the benefit of the people and the régime extended its gratitude.

It was enough to allude to the 'people' and all democratic and left-leaning groups became disarmed and speechless. The dilemma was that if it was the 'people' who were attacking and taking away society's newly won democratic rights, then maybe these were not truly democratic rights after all. Some jumped to the conclusion that the régime was ushering in the dictatorship of the proletariat and so bourgeois rights had to be sacrificed. Thus, the right of the accused to an open trial became too bourgeois to be a concern of progressive elements.

The régime had put across the idea that the lumpenproletariat that supported it were the real representatives of the people; unfortunately, the left were taken in by this. Each group went over to the opposition as its turn came to be discarded and repressed. The revolutionary forces were so concerned with winning social rights that they overlooked the fact that they were losing all the individual and private rights that had existed even during the Shah's régime. Thus the Shah's despotic rule was replaced by a despotic quasi-totalitarian state which penetrated, controlled and directed every aspect of social, political, economic, cultural and private life, in order to impose its anachronistic uniformity.

Revolutionary language in the service of the counter-revolution

The régime's greatest accomplishment in politically duping the left was to play on two concepts that they held as dear as anti-imperialism. The leadership spoke of itself as the representative of the *Mostazafin* (disinherited). The left took this to mean the toiling classes – the workers and the peasants. Now, if the régime considered itself the representative of the disinherited, then obviously it included latent Marxist-Leninist elements. In due time, the progressive elements would shed their turbans and cloaks and hoist high the red flag. Such a progressive régime had to be supported. But the disinherited that the régime referred to were not the workers and the peasants, they were simply the lumpenproletariat who were the régime's crutch, in addition to those elements who supported it in its vendetta against anything that was non-Moslem. If democracy, human rights and socialism were non-Islamic categories, they had to be removed, along with western cultural imperialism. The régime used the

Mostazafin to break into and evict the true representatives of the workers from their trade union headquarters.

The second concept which duped the left for a long time was the régime's intention of creating an army of 20 million. This, again according to the books, was the characteristic of a progressive régime. If the leadership created a militia and armed the people, then the people would never allow imperialist powers to intervene. On this account, the régime was true to its promise. First, everyone was asked to return the arms they had taken from the army's arsenals, which they did. The exception was those directly involved in political groups with a paramilitary wing. Then the régime set up training sessions in which the use of light arms was taught. This lasted but a few months. Once again, the left took this to mean that everyone would be armed. To its dismay, it found that the régime limited training to 'dependable elements' only. None but the immediate supporters of the régime were trained and even they were not all armed. In contrast, the armed paramilitary groups which emerged after the victorious revolution who were extentions of the mosque committees had been organized into structured establishments to reduce the power of the army and to act as the obedient repressive arm of the theocratic leadership. It was these same 'popular militia' groups which ultimately hunted down, captured or killed members of the opposition groups.

A brief anatomy of the Iranian revolution

The trajectory of the Iranian revolution and a socio-economic exposition of the participants in each phase of the movement will facilitate a better understanding of why the post-revolutionary régime differed so fundamentally from the aspirations of the majority of those who took part in the revolution.

The Iranian revolution can be divided into three distinct phases. The first and third phases were short, but determining. The first phase broke the ice; a long period of political inactivity and apathy came to an end. The third phase transformed the unarmed struggle of the people into a mass, armed uprising. The second phase was clearly the period in which all forms of protest and struggle, short of armed resistance, were employed to paralyse the régime economically, discredit it politically and disarm it psychologically. The sudden disintegration of the army was, in reality, the result of a long war of nerves between the people and the soldiers on the streets during this second phase. When the decisive hour came for the soldiers to fight against their armed countrymen or defect, they chose the latter course.

In dividing the revolution into three phases, we shall examine: the events which initiated each phase of the protest; the role and social background of the participants in each phase; the instruments of struggle and protest and the manner in which the régime reacted in each phase.

Phase one: the intellectual challenge

In response to the pressure brought to bear by the Carter administration for an improvement in Iran's human rights record, the Shah slightly eased the rigid controls which he had maintained on social and political expression. The new period came to be called, 'the period of political relaxation'.

In May 1977, the Iranian intelligentsia and the professionals were the first to take advantage of the new opening in the political atmosphere in order to press for freedoms that were unheard of before. The intelligentsia wielded the weapon it was most accustomed to: the pen. The first part of this phase involved an open-letter campaign to the Shah and his prime minister criticizing the absence of constitutional liberties, such as the freedom of political parties, press, speech and so on. The intellectual and professional campaign was stepped up with the formation of various committees and organizations for the defence of human rights, intellectual freedoms and academic and judicial independence.

This phase culminated in the ten evenings of poetry readings at the Goethe Institute in Teheran. During these nights in October 1977, the Iranian intelligentsia indulged in unprecedented public criticism of the government's undemocratic practices. The audience, which was made up of students, middle-class intellectuals and professionals, enjoyed a given degree of freedom and was motivated to press for more. The mere act of criticizing the régime without suffering immediate and grave retribution gave the audience the courage to stand up when the occasion for mass protest arose.

The state apparatus was not used to such situations. In the past, such events would have been suppressed immediately. However, because of the period of 'political relaxation', the old repressive measures were no longer applicable. The Iranian security apparatus's lack of knowledge about how to deal with the intellectual opposition without using physical force was very pronounced throughout this phase. The régime reacted to the challenge of the intelligentsia by throwing fire bombs at the homes of certain prominent founders of the Human Rights Association in Iran. This amateurish act backfired. The media coverage of this event disseminated the news that professionals and intellectuals were challenging and criticizing the excesses of the régime. The despised security service SAVAK became the target of a new round of abuse and criticism. Soon the régime abandoned this type of approach.

The clergy were caught off guard. Ayatollah Khomeini instructed them to follow the general manner of protest. In a letter in late August, the Ayatollah said

> today we are faced with an opportunity [an opening] in Iran and you should take advantage of it. If this occasion had not arisen, this situation would not have resulted. . . . Today members of various parties find fault and voice their criticism in signed letters to the Shah and the

government. You should write too and a few of the learned members of the clergy should sign also . . . write about the problems and hand it to them; others have done so and we have witnessed that they have said a lot but nothing has happened to them.[3]

The nature of this first phase of the revolution was such that the clergy could have had no input. The legal framework of the intellectual opposition's criticism required subtlety, legal knowledge of the constitution and restraint. The intellectuals knew that their demands would fall on receptive ears among the majority of the professionals, civil servants and educated youth who wished for a free political atmosphere. Yet the clergy were not sure who would respond to their appeal, especially since the Islamic movement had become divided between the revolutionary ideology of Ali Shariati, a French-educated intellectual, and the traditional outlook of the conservative clergy.

Phase two: the tacit anti-Shah popular front

The second phase of the revolution involved the first street demonstrations on a relatively small, but politically significant, scale. This stage was launched by the Qum seminary students as a response to a provocative article written in one of Iran's leading newspapers about Ayatollah Khomeini in January of 1978. The government thought that, in the midst of the period of 'political relaxation', it too could settle intellectual scores with the ayatollah. The purpose of the article was to discredit an old foe of the régime and neutralize his future influence upon the movement by exposing certain details about his life. This proved a grave and irreversible error on the part of the government, as it became quite clear that it was unaware of the people's sensitivities.

The seminary students took to the streets of Qum. Their slogans defended Khomeini and denounced the article and those who had published it. The police panicked and their shootings resulted in a number of deaths.

Demonstrations, mourning ceremonies and riots spread like wildfire from January 1978 to February 1979. This second phase of the revolution was carried out through three different, yet complementary, methods: large peaceful street demonstrations which showed the numerical strength of the opposition; strikes in ministries, banks, public services, factories and the oil industry and street skirmishes with and riots against the police and the army.

This stage was marked by the absence of military operations and an armed struggle by the people. The security services and the military proved themselves incapable of coping with a situation where unarmed people took to the streets to chant anti-Shah slogans. A psychological war of attrition was being fought by the people who had become used to armed soldiers in the streets. Their presence, with no regular pattern of bloody repression, had broken the atmosphere of fear that the régime wished to impose. Blood on the streets and shots in the air became everyday sights and sounds.

The régime was caught in a dilemma. On the one hand, it feared that an all out brutal repression would completely alienate the conscript soldiers imposing martial law and lead to a breakdown in the hierarchical chain of command, culminating in mass fraternization with the people. On the other hand, it was aware of the fact that by simply keeping the soldiers on the streets without using their fire power, the people would end up regarding martial law as a paper tiger. By zigzagging between heavy-handed policies and no action, the régime brought the two things that it dreaded most upon itself: the soldiers began to question their role and identified more with the people, while the people became bolder in the face of martial law's irresoluteness. The rapidly expanding scale of the movement and the everchanging protest tactics employed by the people led to total confusion in the top echelons of the political and military decision-making apparatus. No one knew how to deal with an amorphous movement which took all shapes and used every avenue of opposition except the one that the régime wanted: an armed struggle.

The peaceful demonstrations and the street skirmishes eroded the combativeness of the army, the strikes brought the country to a standstill and the régime was rapidly losing its grip. The second phase demonstrated that the régime had no support, popular or class based. What had started as a reformist movement was soon transformed into a fully-fledged revolution. Demands for the implementation of the constitution soon gave way to that of the overthrow of the Shah.

In contrast to the first phase where the professionals and intellectuals had taken the anti-régime initiative, the second phase was marked by the entrance of the clergy, the working class, the commercial bourgeoisie – bazaar merchants, the lumpenproletariat and the broad participation of students.

The clergy
The clergy's power to organize and mobilize the people was embedded in their control over the mosques and the spiritual and social respect which they enjoyed among the masses. The activities of each neighbourhood were organized by its own neighbourhood committee – a co-operative organizational form which had arisen due to the scarcity of certain goods during the strikes. The neighbourhood committee was, in turn, responsible to and took its lead from the local mosque. The local mosque acted as the organizational brain of the closely knit network. It organized and co-ordinated the activities of a whole neighbourhood on the basis of the instructions it received from the national organizers of the religious movement. They, in turn, received their general directives from Ayatollah Khomeini who was abroad. These directives came in the form of widely circulated letters and tapes. However, the tactics used by the people, such as going to the roof tops at night and chanting anti-Shah slogans to demoralize the soldiers, were quite spontaneous.

In the second phase of the revolution, the clergy played a key role in organizing peaceful demonstrations by using the mosque as a sanctuary for agitation and mobilization against the régime. In this phase, the

Islamic movement converted its weakness into strength by incorporating both wings of Islam and thus appealing to a broader public. The politicized revolutionary Islam which was articulated by Shariati had alienated the traditional conservative clergy, but appealed to young people. Shariati's invitation to (martyrdom) in the fight against tyranny and injustice presented a new revolutionary Islam which soon gained support. However, his sharp criticism of passive and unpoliticized Islam led to caustic counter-criticisms from the traditional clergy. Ayatollah Khomeini's leadership incorporated both Shariati's revolutionary aspect of Islam and Islam's traditional appeal which was based more on its rituals and practices.

Throughout the second phase of the revolution up to its final victory, Khomeini aimed his criticisms and denunciations at the monarchy and the Shah. His case against the Shah revolved around certain central themes which he developed and conveyed to the people in a popularly comprehensible language. He accused the Shah of having adopted policies which were against the interests of the Iranian people. Khomeini appealed to the people's sense of: nationalism; respect for liberty and freedom; economic well-being and cultural heritage and self-respect, referring to Islam as the guarantor of each. On the issue of the Shah's foreign policy, Khomeini reiterated the United States' role in returning the Shah to power in 1953 and gave detailed accounts of how the Shah had conceded capitulatory rights in 1964 and acted in the interest of the United States by betraying the Palestinian cause and siding with Israel. On the issue of domestic policies, he condemned the Shah's record of human rights, the absence of political rights and the inhuman treatment of political prisoners. On economic policies, the ayatollah referred to Iran's ruined agriculture and accused the Shah of reducing industry to an appendage of foreign corporations, auctioning oil and rich mineral resources to foreigners and spending huge sums on building up Iran's army. Thus the welfare of the Iranian people was forsaken for the material and geo-political benefit of foreigners. On the cultural policies of the Shah, Ayatollah Khomeini derided him for allowing cultural imperialism to corrupt Iran's women and youth. He assailed the so-called humiliating fate to which Iranian women had been subjected by their transformation into 'pretty western dolls'. He abhorred the prevalence of permissive western habits and fashions which, in his opinion, acted as the opium of youth. He spoke of Iran's lost Islamic culture, one which would bring back self-respect and salvation to all Iranians.

Khomeini presented an extremely black picture and everyone found some truth in at least one of the arguments he presented. He promised something to every social group. No one was excluded from the ayatollah's promises, all who were Iranian, be they capitalists, workers, merchants, land owners or peasants, were promised something by the adoption of Islam. Even the régime's generals and politicians were promised clemency. During this phase, the ayatollah refrained from any allusions which might alienate any segment of the population. As far as his plans for the future of the country's domestic policies were concerned, he spoke in broad terms and left his statements for individuals to interpret themselves. He left the particulars of his programme to the future, but made it clear that it would be based on Islam and anti-imperialism.

The working class

During phase two of the movement, the organization and mobilization of the Iranian working class gained momentum. Certain important points characterized this group's participation and methods of struggle. The Iranian working class had been denied the right of organization and representation through authentic trade unions or councils. Whatever unions did exist under the Shah were mere façades, designed by those at the top. The workers never found themselves in a position to bargain over wages or press for better working conditions or shorter hours. The right to strike did not exist; strikes were usually repressed whenever they occurred.

The working class entered the revolutionary movement with the hope of winning the rights which it had been denied. This would have enabled it to defend and assure its own class interests. It was thus on its way to gaining trade union consciousness. Time was needed for the working class to organize its own autonomous political organization. It was neither prepared organizationally, nor equipped politically to lead the revolution. The alternative was to press for, and defend, democratic rights and accept the leadership of a democratic united front. This option, however, was denied to the working class when the Islamic leadership imposed its hegemony.

The Iranian working class was cautious about taking action, but when it found that the régime was too confused to react forcefully, it used its most potent weapon – the strike – to bring the régime to its knees.

In February 1978, two thousand workers went on strike at Teheran's tobacco factory. This first strike had economic and welfare objectives rather than political ones. On 5 September 1978, two important events reflected the emerging militant posture of Iran's factory workers. The National Workers' Union demanded the expulsion of redundant foreign workers. At the Ahwaz steel factory, four thousand workers went on strike to protest against the plunder of Iran's wealth by foreign and domestic capitalists.

From 25 September, workers in the service sector and those in governmental offices and ministries joined the strikes. Blue and white-collar workers brought the country to a virtual economic halt. The country lived through a period when blackouts became a norm, post office workers worked a few hours a day, banks closed their counters during most of the week, the popular newspapers of the country refused to print, the dock workers refused to load and, finally, the workers at the oil refinery shut down the plants.

The objectives of the working class coincided with that of the clergy at one stage, but differed from it during the next. Having realized the power of strikes, the working class wished to accelerate the revolution and topple the monarchy. Yet in toppling the monarchy, it foresaw an active role for itself and its organized arm, namely free and powerful unions and workers' councils. The clergy, on the other hand, wished to see workers' organizations subjected to its directives and operating according to the imperatives of the Islamic state. However, while the common struggle against the Shah was on the agenda, differences were put aside and the Islamic forces paid lip service to the tacit democratic united front.

The students

Iranian universities had always been some of the most active and politicized centres of anti-Shah agitation. Right from the first phase of the revolution, Iranian students opposed the Shah's iron-fisted censorship policies and his political straitjacket and participated actively in the revolutionary movement. Their initial demands centred on political, organizational and democratic rights. Large-scale street demonstrations by the students started in Teheran in solidarity with political prisoners who had gone on a hunger strike in two of Teheran's prisons. This political demonstration soon spread to Isfahan, Tabriz and other large cities.

It was the high-school students who defied the martial law soldiers every day by chanting anti-Shah slogans, building barricades in the streets, burning tyres and challenging the bullets that were shot at them. Again, it was these youngsters who took to the streets at night to break the curfew set by martial law. The students played a major role in eroding the self-righteousness and will of the army. They were partly mobilized by the mosque, influenced by Shariati's revolutionary Islam and partly by their own politicized organizations, influenced by different shades of Marxism-Leninism. The revolutionary movement had become a school in its own way. The students gained practical experience in confronting, provoking and escaping the soldiers. They read all that was put on the reading list of their political organizations and reflected on what they had learnt on the walls. This social category was maturing and becoming politicized in its one and a half years of urban unarmed struggle against a well-armed army. The irony of it was that the best of arms seemed incapable of matching the determination, voluntarism and the fun of challenging the Shah's authority and gaining an alternative education.

The traditional commercial bourgeoisie

The traditional merchant class which held on to its old bastion of power, the bazaar, was well in the foreground of the movement. The closure of the bazaar or central market, had important political significance. In the last years of the Shah, the traditional merchants had been constantly threatened by the role of powerful export-import companies and the ever-expanding role of monopolistic chain stores which threatened the financial viability of small stores and their suppliers, namely the bazaar wholesalers.

The traditional merchants demanded a return to the *laissez-faire* economics that existed prior to the emergence of highly subsidized state and private monopolies. Import substitution industries and joint ventures with foreign concerns were high on the Shah's list of priorities in his quest for rapid economic growth. Therefore, as the competitive output of these concerns increased, the bazaar had to accept a dwindling share of the market. So for the merchants, the anti-Shah and anti-imperialist movement was a return to the pre-monopoly period, which, in turn, meant a return to the old profitable years. The commercial bourgeoisie's acceptance of the democratic united front was simply because it hoped to gain what domestic monopolies and foreign companies had denied it. It would be simplistic to assume that the commercial bourgeoisie's anti-imperialism, at this point, was in any way related to anti-capitalism.

So the bazaar too resorted to its old weapon: that of closure. The merchants in Tabriz were the first to close their shops in protest against the death of a university student at Tabriz University on 12 April 1978. This symbolic closure was immediately copied in other big cities.

The traditional commercial bourgeoisie had long-standing strong ties with the clergy. The merchants were one of the few remaining social categories among which one could find members who still paid their religious dues – *khoms* and zakat – to the clergy. Many among this class helped the religious movement with generous financial contributions throughout the revolution.

The lumpenproletariat

Marx described the lumpenproletariat as a 'disintegrated mass', comprising *'ruined and adventurous offshoots of the bourgeoisie, vagabonds, discharged jailbirds etc.'* upon whom Louis Bonaparte relied in his struggle for power.[4] For Marx, the lumpenproletariat were social elements that could not be categorized as peasants or workers. Poverty was their major characteristic, yet their poverty was not comparable to that of the worker or the poor peasant. The lumpenproletariat did not usually come into contact with the forces of production and did not enter into the work-force on a permanent basis. They had neither the skills nor the capital that was required in the productive process. They were neither workers, artisans nor peasants.

In many of the world's great cities, the lumpenproletariat lead a marginal and parasitic life with no defined social, economic or political interest. The rapid rate of rural-urban migration has swollen up the urban centres of developing countries. From Sao-Paulo to Jakarta, the capital cities of developing countries are surrounded by slums and shanty towns. The rapid penetration of the capitalist mode of production and exchange, on the one hand, and the expansion of mechanical farming, on the other, is forcing the peasants out of their rural surroundings and into the cities in search of higher incomes and better social services. This large number of migrants has created a social category which is much more politically significant today than it was in Marx's days.

Iran was no exception to this general tendency, even though its oil revenue provided an economic rent unavailable to many other developing countries. The rate of rural-urban migration was greater than the absorptive capacity of the Iranian economy. Between 1956 and 1976, 4.3 million people migrated from the rural areas to a few urban centres. By 1977, 2.15 million had migrated to Teheran itself. So nearly half of Teheran's population of 4.5 million was made up of rural migrants who had come to the city during the previous twenty years.[5]

This large migrant population had certain characteristic features. Economically, it made up the urban poor who lived in the slums and shanty towns which had cropped up around Teheran. For the most part, they were underemployed. Those who found employment were engaged in part-time or seasonal jobs in the construction sector, petty vending and commerce and menial private and public services. Some had started work as unskilled labourers in food processing, canning and the tobacco industry as part-time labourers. This social category had no particular skills that were marketable in an urban setting, except its raw labour power. Sociologically, the migrants reacted to their urban surroundings in two ways. Either they found the westernized city life both attractive and unattainable or they viewed it as too shamelessly modern and secular for their tastes. In either case, they resented it and the social position to which they had been relegated. The permissive opulence of big cities necessitated a minimum of financial resources which this large social group did not possess.

The lumpenproletariat had not been recently involved in Iranian politics, nor had they any long-term cohesive political aspirations.[6] Yet social and economic deprivation had provided the migrants with a primitive consciousness and a gut hatred. Hatred for a régime which denied them a fair share of the wealth so glaringly possessed by some and hatred for those who humiliated them with their wealth, education and well-paid jobs. At the same time, they identified with those who spoke their language and referred to their problems and promised to solve them. The migrant population rushed under Khomeini's flag. Islam provided an identity which returned to the lumpenproletariat the self-respect they had lost ever since they had left their villages.

The second phase of the revolution had provided this social category with organizational and combative experience. In the poorer neighbourhoods, the everyday activities of rioting, demonstrating and distributing rationed goods, such as kerosene, water and other basic necessities, were carried out by these young zealots. The revolution had given them an identity, society had found some use for them. As long as the condition of crisis and social disintegration fostered by the revolution lasted, the lumpenproletariat had a social role to play. During this stage of the revolution, this social category co-operated with other anti-Shah social groups only because the order of the day coming from religious leaders was based on unity and solidarity.

Phase three: the armed insurrection

This last phase differed from the first two in relation to the tactics of struggle employed. During the last two days of the revolution, the military apparatus started to disintegrate. The Shah's departure had decapitated the army's organizational and decision-making hierarchy. On 10 February 1979, at an airforce training base, a clash took place between conscript soldiers and enlisted officers. From there, the fighting spread to the rest of Teheran and by the next day, the High Military Command met to declare its neutrality, while deserted and abandoned army barracks and police headquarters were sacked by the people. All pockets of armed resistance succumbed in the two days of fighting. On 12 February, power was in the hands of the people. The tacit anti-Shah popular front had achieved its objective and it was, therefore, automatically doomed to abolition.

The third phase of the revolution armed the lumpenproletariat and subsequently assigned them a role which they did not want to give up easily. The position and power achieved during the second phase could be buttressed and maintained by the weapons taken from the army's arsenals during the third phase. However, if the social conditions were to normalize under either a capitalist or socialist social order, what would become of this social category which had come to consider itself as the true flag bearer of the revolution? Production under socialism or capitalism needed skill, expertise, discipline, social organization and a minimum of education. The modern lumpenproletariat lacked all these attributes. With the adoption of any known economic system which sought to produce efficiently, the lumpenproletariat would have been denied its newly acquired social status.

While all the other participants in the revolutionary movement did benefit and would have continued to benefit from the maintenance and defence of democratic rights, the lumpenproletariat would have gained nothing. They were not concerned with social, political or economic freedoms because they were marginal to the social productive process. However, they could maintain the power they had attained through: becoming an important element in the organizational network of the clergy; playing an active role in the revolution and becoming the armed functionary, propagator and protector of the theocratic leadership's ideology.

When the revolution ended on 12 February 1979, it brought to power a clerical régime which had the overwhelming support of elements whose future social position and power were directly related to the survival of a theocratic system.

The social and political system favoured by the clergy was clearly different from the old social order; this was why the lumpenproletariat supported it. At the same time, the clerical leadership elevated the lumpenproletariat to the position of executioner, supervisor and guardian of their decisions and policies. The theocratic leadership had nothing to fear since the social expectations of this social category were in no way contrary to the socio-political system the theocracy wished to impose. Furthermore, the co-operation of the lumpenproletariat gave the régime a semblance of having a popular base. Thus the lumpenproletariat were placed in a position to revenge the shame and humiliation they had been subjected to under the old régime. The society which had denied them a position, a role, a job and an identity in the past had to pay and answer for its sins.

This social category set out to create a society in the image outlined by the theocratic régime. These groups had two things in common: they despised the ancient régime and the rules by which it was conducted; they believed only in their own righteousness as devoted Moslems with a civilizing mission. The 'white man's burden' was now transformed into the 'Moslem's burden'. Having been relegated to a marginal position in the meritocratic past, the lumpenproletarians were not going to give up their social, political and economic status without a fight.

Their mission implied that society at large had to be disciplined, non-Moslem organizations had to be dismantled, conventional social discipline had to be mutilated and classes had to be broken down into individuals participating in a uniform Moslem mass. A collaborating capitalist was a good *Haj Aqa*, one who had carried out all his religious obligations, and was thus acceptable among the circle of the faithful. A militant trade union worker faced a fate worse than that of a western spy while an obedient communist party member was a brother at the Friday congregational prayers. A radical Moslem group, however, which dared to challenge the interpretations of the ruling clergy was viewed as heretical.

The régime's annihilation campaign – sometimes physical and sometimes psychological – was non-exclusive. It was aimed at all political, professional and artistic groups; women; religious and national minorities and even proclaimed Moslems, including religious leaders, supporters of the revolution and close associates of Ayatollah Khomeini. In sum, anyone who voiced an opinion different from that of the monolithic theocracy was silenced.

Conclusion

It was not long before the contours of the new Iran became clear. Ideologically, it was rooted in Ayatollah Khomeini's conception of the way an Islamic state should be run.

Iran was to be governed according to *Velayat-e Faqih* (Guardianship of an Islamic jurist or jurists). The most crucial aspect of the government, according to the *Velayat-e Faqih*, was that the Islamic state had to be run on the basis of Qur'an's teachings. Those teachings could only be interpreted by the Faqih who was supposed to be the most knowledgeable in Islamic law and who was supposed to be just. Once the Islamic state was put into operation, the clergy's role was to assist the Faqih in his administration of the state. All the affairs of state were to be placed under the scrutiny of Islamic jurists. The type of state to ensue depended on the omniscient Islamic jurist, who was none other than Ayatollah Khomeini himself.

Given the theocratic structure of the government, all that was needed was the active arm of the clergy to implement the Islamic state. Without zealous militants who were to administer the change and carry out the revolutionary orders, the Islamic state would have remained a dream.

Once the revolution was over, all those who had gone on strike went back to work. The white-collar staff returned to their offices, the blue-collar workers to their factories, the merchants opened up their shops in the bazaar and the students returned to schools and universities. They had all developed political sympathies either on the basis of their class origin or on their class identification. Yet they all went back to what they did before the revolution. All except the lumpenproletariat who were to become the militant functionaries, administrators and transformers of the new state. They had nothing to go back to and thus became the powerful, repressive arm of the theocratic state. For them, this elevated status and new-found power was the achievement of the revolution, not the abolition of a dictatorship or a repressive political system, as they had nothing to gain from the antitheses of dictatorship: freedom and democratic rights. The revolution which had started with anti-Shah, democratic and anti-imperialist aspirations turned against those very people who had fought for it and brought it victory.

Notes

1. See *Marxist Review : The Monthly Theoretical Journal of the Workers Revolutionary Party,* Vol. 2. No. 8 (1987).
2. Imam Khomeini, *Nedaye Haq* (Paris, 1357), p. 82.
3. From an open letter circulated in Teheran in the form of a leaflet. Dated 'Zihadjeh of 1397' and signed by Ayatollah Khomeini.
4. T. Bottomore, *A Dictionary of Marxist Thought* (Basil Blackwell, 1985), p. 292.
5. F. Hesamian, G. Etemad and M-R Haeree, *Shahr Neshini dar Iran* (Teheran, Agah, 1363), pp. 85, 115, 116.
6. The last time the lumpenproletariat were used in Iranian politics was during the 1953 American-staged coup against the nationalist government of Dr Mohammed Mossadeq.

2. The Role of the Islamic System in the Iranian Revolution

Shi'i and Sunni Islam

For Iranian *'i* Moslems, the overwhelming majority of whom do not know Arabic, the Qur'anic verses and injunctions only come to life and obtain practical applicability through the Persian interpretation and solutions of the Islamic experts, the *mojtaheds*.

Shi'i trace their disagreements with the Sunnis to the guardianship of the Islamic community after the death of Mohammed the Prophet. According to the *Shi'i*, the Prophet's cousin and his son-in-law, Ali ibn-Abu Taleb, was his rightful successor. Basing themselves on the *hadith*, one of the main sources of Islamic knowledge and practice, the *Shi'i* argue that all the evidence indicates that Ali should have succeeded Mohammed. He was the first man to believe in Mohammed and the faith of Islam and was reputed to have known the Qur'an by heart. Furthermore, he was aware of the precise context and circumstances under which each verse of the Qur'an was revealed to the Prophet.[1] It is reported that when Prophet Mohammed agreed to the marriage of his daughter, Fatima, to Ali, he told her:

> I am making you wife to one who is a saint in this world and a saint in the next. He was the first follower of Islam, wisest of all Moslems in respect of his knowledge and the greatest of them in his forbearance and patience. Ali and I were born of one light and that is the light of God.[2]

The *Shi'i* refer to Sura 33:33 in the Qur'an (when the people of the Prophet's house are informed that God wants to cleanse them) to prove that apart from the Prophet, only Ali, his wife Fatima and their sons Hassan and Hossein, were infallible and sinless, thus, worthy of leading the Moslems. Finally, the *Shi'i* maintain that the Prophet stopped at Ghadir Khom on his way back to Medina from his last pilgrimage to Mecca. There, raising Ali's hand, he declared him his successor and

Amir-al-Mu'menin (the Commander of the Faithful).

When the Prophet died, while Ali was involved with performing the proper Islamic burial ceremonies, an election was held for the leadership and Abu-Bakr, a father-in-law of the Prophet, was chosen as the commander of the faithful and the first caliph (the successor of Mohammed and chief civil and religious leader). After Abu-Bakr, Omar and Othman were chosen and Ali became the fourth caliph. The Sunnis believe that Ali was rightfully the fourth caliph, while the *Shi'i* maintain that Ali's right was unjustly usurped by Abu-Bakr. This constitutes the essential political difference between the *Shi'i* and the Sunnis.

As the *Shi'i* consider Ali to be the first imam and the principle of *imamat* (the institution of the rule of the imams as vicegerents of the Prophet) to be strictly limited to Ali's family, after Ali's sons, the *Shi'i* believe in nine more imams. The *Shi'i* believe there are fourteen *maasums* (infallible souls) worthy and capable of leadership: Mohammed, Fatima, Ali and their eleven descendants.

The last Imam is believed to have gone into occultation in AD 874, at the age of nine. The *gheybat* (absence) of the Twelfth Imam – Imam al-Zaman, the ever-present Imam – created a spiritual and leadership vacuum among the *Shi'i*. From AD 874 to the late 1700s, mainstream *Shi'i* religious thought held that the absence of the last infallible imam blocked the path to religious knowledge since only through the medium of the Prophet and the imams could such divine knowledge be obtained.

The religious experts of this period were known as the *Akhbariyoun*, or the supporters of the Akhbari school. This Akhbari school maintained that all necessary religious edicts and laws had been promulgated by the Prophet and the imams and such rulings provided sufficient bases for the religious experts to apply in all cases that emerged. Religious experts were thus prohibited from passing any independent judgements. The *Akhbariyoun* believed that the role of the religious expert during the occultation of the Twelfth Imam was simply to report on and transmit the word of the Qur'an and the judgements made by the Prophet and the imams, which provided examples of how different cases had to be dealt with from an authentic Islamic perspective. It was argued that if a problem emerged for which a ruling could neither be found in the Qur'an nor the *hadith*, the religious expert was still prohibited from making an independent judgement because such a situation heralded the reappearance of the Hidden Imam. The reopening of the fountain of Islamic knowledge and the announcement of new rulings were thus relegated to the reappearance of the infallible Imam al-Zaman, who was expected to return 1,000 years after his disappearance. So the *Shi'i* religious experts expected the return of the Imam in the 1700s.

Even though the *Shi'i* were expecting the reappearance of the Twelfth Imam towards the end of the eighteenth century, a prominent *Shi'i* clergyman, Akhund Mulla Mohammed-Baqer-e Behbehani, challenged the mainstream Akhbari position and founded the Usuli school of *Shi'ism*. Behbehani argued that no one other than God was aware of the Twelfth Imam's date of reappearance, therefore it was harmful to leave the faithful without proper guidance during the Imam's occultation which could be very long.

The Usuli argued that precisely because of the absence of the Twelfth Imam, *mojtaheds* (erudite, learned and qualified Islamic experts) were obliged to engage in independent reasoning in order to guide and lead the faithful in their private and social lives. It was argued that by pronouncing a definite and authoritative opinion, the *mojtaheds* could end the conflicts that were arising due to the vacuum in proper Islamic arbitration during the Imam's absence.

Behbehani's ideas revitalized *Shi'i* Islam since, until his time, the *Shi'i* believed that government was the sole right of the *maasums* (infallibles) and thus concluded that all governments in the absence of the Twelfth Imam were unjust and usurpatory. Consequently, the *Shi'i* and their clergy refused to consider even Islamic governments formed during the Imam's occultation as legitimate, even though they did not oppose them.[3] Behbehani's revisionist position opened the path for the active involvement of the clergy in politics. If the absent Imam did not reappear soon, then the Islamic scholars, or *mojtaheds*, were the best positioned to govern, due to their mastery of religious laws.

It has been argued that Khomeini's concept of the government of the jurisconsult, or the rule of the most learned religious scholar, is fundamentally rooted in the Usuli school. In his book *Revealing the Secrets*, Khomeini emphasized the Usuli position and reiterated that, the 'gate to Islamic knowledge was open' and, therefore, *mojtaheds* were free to pass independent judgements on the basis of their religious knowledge and their *aql* (reason).[4] In his second book *The Islamic Government*, Khomeini concluded that since the Twelfth Imam had been absent for some one thousand three hundred years and that he might not reappear for another thousand years, Islamic laws could not be left unattended and unimposed. He argued that God's laws were not limited to the two hundred years during which the imams were alive and, therefore, had to be imposed on society in the absence of the Twelfth Imam. Khomeini thus called upon the learned jurisconsults to create an Islamic government in which religious laws would rule the land.[5] The Usuli analysis led to a view of society in which believers were either categorized as *mojtaheds*, in which case they guided the *ummah*, the Islamic community, and participated actively in adapting religion to the needs of changing times, or they were not *mojtaheds*, in which case they became the followers of the *mojtaheds* or *moqalids* (those who imitate).

With the domination of the Usuli position over that of the Akhbari, *taqlid*, or following the guidance of one more learned than oneself in the absence of the Imam, became a cornerstone of *Shi'i* Islam. The principle of *taqlid* fosters a tie based on leadership. In other words, a Moslem who is not a *mojtahed* and, subsequently, not well steeped in religious laws is bound to follow a *mojtahed* unless he practices *ehtiyat* (caution) which itself requires a thorough knowledge of all Islamic practices, laws and edicts. Apathy towards or abstention from entering such a relationship becomes inconceivable, since it would imply that the abstaining person is a *mojtahed*, one who, when faced with problems for which no clear-cut answer can be found in the original sources, is capable of finding an Islamic solution. The victory of the Usuli position placed considerable social, political and economic power in the hands of the *mojtaheds*. On the triumph of the Usuli position over the Akhbari, Shahrough Akhavi points out that

> The Usuli school, affirming the need for *mojtaheds* to exercise independent judgement on matters of law, advanced *agl* (reason) as the source for the development of Islamic jurisprudence. In thus keeping open the gates of *ijtihad*,[6] then, the Usuli efforts have issued in the active participation of men in shaping their existence.[7]

Even though Akhavi suggests that the triumph of the Usuli 'issued in the active participation of men in shaping their existence', it would probably be more correct to say that it allowed the *mojtaheds*, who only constituted a very small part of the population, to shape the lives of others. This development meant that the great majority of the people who were *moqalids* (imitators or followers), had to forfeit their right of decision making whenever their *mojtahed* took a position on an issue. The victory of the Usuli position presented a permanent and irrevocable mandate to the *mojtaheds* during the absence of the Twelfth Imam, to lead or demand action from the *moqalids*, if and when they took a position or made a pronouncement.

The concentration and centralization of power in the hands of religious authorities went even further with the concept of the *marja-e taqlid*, or source of emulation, or supreme authority on Islamic law. The *marja-e taqlid* is an erudite, pious and just *mojtahed* to whom other *mojtaheds* pay allegiance. On the process of selection of the *marja-e taqlid*, Michael Fischer points out that: 'Although it is admitted that, beyond the certification of *mojtahed* status, the question of who is the most learned of all is merely a matter of opinion, the theory holds that a consensus slowly emerges'.[8]

On the one hand, Moslems are free to choose a *marja-e taqlid* according to their individual preferences and reasoning and with a view to the *marja*'s reputation, qualities, proclamations and writings. This aspect of finding a source of emulation is non-coercive and based on the individual's initiative. On the other hand, once the medium or channel to a pious and Islamic life is chosen, then whatever the *marja-e taqlid* decrees has to be accepted without hesitation or questioning and the execution of his *fatva* (authoritative pronouncement on religious issues) becomes a religious obligation from which there is no escape. The principle of *taqlid*, or following, established a well-organized hierarchical system of command, through which all followers could be moved or incited to action by the proclamation of a *marja-e taqlid*. The *marja* does not need to explain his position, since his wisdom gives him the right to pronounce an independent opinion and the *moqalid* and *mojtahed* relationship requires obedience. This vertical structure provides a powerful tool for those *maraje-e taqlid* (plural for *marja-e taqlid*) who wish to use the popular base that they command in order to introduce or resist change.

Algar emphasizes the importance of the outcome of the Usuli and Akhbari debate in terms of contemporary events by pointing out that:

> One may say that the revolution in Iran, at least the particular shape that it has taken, the form of leadership that it has enjoyed and continues to enjoy, would also be unthinkable without this triumph of the Usuli position in this apparently technical dispute in the eighteenth century.[9]

It was the independent effect and appeal of pronouncements made and positions taken by different *mojtaheds* in Iran that allowed Islam to act as a rallying ideology for the majority of Iranians during the last stages of the revolutionary movement and ensured the maintenance of power by the Islamic Republic.

The appeal of Islam during the revolution

By the end of 1978, it had become evident that the revolutionary movement in Iran was significantly influenced, if not totally overshadowed, by its dynamic Islamic component. The mass demonstrations and marches organized during this period attracted huge numbers of participants from all walks of life, under the banner of Islam. The number of participants in the Tassua and Ashura marches of 10 and 11 December 1978, the diversity of class composition of the demonstrators, the Islamic convictions of the official organizers of the march and, finally, the resolution read at the end of the march, all provide proof for the fact that the popular, heterogeneous, multi-class-based movement had acquired an Islamic character during its final stages. The number of reported participants varies from one to three million,[10] but there is a general consensus among all observers that 'a giant wave of humanity swept the capital'.[11] Such a popular show of force was unprecedented in the modern history of Iran. The eye-witness report of the British ambassador to Iran described the demonstrations in the following words:

> From 9 a.m. until lunchtime on each morning [December 10 and 11] I stood at my window while serried ranks of marchers passed up Ferdowsi Street on their way to join the processions. The street is wide but it was filled from pavement to pavement and from top to bottom as far as the eye could see for a period of three to four hours. It was only one of the many feeder roads to the main procession route. The popular estimate of one to one and a half million people on each day cannot have been an exaggeration.[12]

On the issue of class diversity and the heterogeneity of the participants too, there is a general consensus. Most analysts, observers and eye-witnesses agree that the marches which symbolized the opposition movement included professional middle-class people, the traditional petty bourgeoisie, artisans, the *bazaaris* (traditional merchants), intellectuals, students, urban workers, migrant workers, segments of the bourgeoisie and civil servants.[13]

The plurality of political groups that participated in the marches is another indication of the diversity within the revolutionary movement. Two main groups were instrumental in inviting the people to take part in the demonstrations. First and foremost were Ayatollah Taleqani and the Association of the Militant Clergy of Teheran who represented the Islamic tendency of the movement. Second were Karim Sanjabi's National Front and Mehdi Bazargan's Iran Freedom Movement, along with the Iranian Association for the Defence of Freedom and Human Rights which had called for a march on 10 December on the occasion of the International Day for Human Rights. This second group essentially represented the middle and upper-middle classes, both religious and secular. The radical and revolutionary organizations of the Mojahedeen-e Khalq-e Iran and the Marxist-Leninist Fadaian-e Khalq-e Iran participated in the marches, chanting their slogans and distributing their leaflets, but did not officially invite their members to participate in the marches. At the end of the Ashura demonstrations a seventeen-article resolution was read and ratified with the acclamation of the participants. The first three articles show clearly how the participants had consciously or otherwise paid their allegiance to the Islamic character and leadership of the movement.

Article 1: Ayatollah al-uzma [the supreme *mojtahed*] Imam Khomeini, is the leader of the *ummah* [the religious community] and his demands are those of the whole people. This march, is once again a whole-hearted vote of confidence in him and a sincere expression of gratitude of Iran's Moslem and struggling people put towards the highly esteemed *maraje* [the supreme authorities on Islamic law].

Article 2: An end should be put to the absolutist monarchical system and the Shah should be overthrown. An end should be put to all types of foreign domination and colonialism which are closely linked to internal despotism and power should be transferred to the Moslem and struggling people of Iran.

Article 3: A just Islamic government should be established on the basis of universal suffrage and the maintenance and protection of Iran's national sovereignty and independence. The provision of individual and social freedoms within an Islamic framework and according to Islamic criteria should be assured.[14]

Articles 1 and 3 are clear indications of an unchallenged acceptance of Ayatollah Khomeini as the leader of the revolution and Islam as its predominant ideology.

In this chapter, it will be argued that shortly prior to the 1979 revolution and for at least two years after the revolution, Islam as an ideology could provide such a diversity of discourses that it offered something of interest to just about everyone. The historical feat of uniting the overwhelming majority of a socially stratified society under the banner of Islam can only be explained by Islam's multidimensional and multifarious appeal. In this lies the key to understanding the success of the 'Islamic' revolution.

For Islam, the line is drawn between the believer (*mu'men*) and the disbeliever (*kafar*). The difference between faith and infidelity can be bridged by the utterance of the simple phrase: 'There is but one God and Mohammed is his Prophet.' From Islam's point of view, the door to becoming a *mu'men* is always open and there is always room left for even the oppressor to go through a psychological inner revolution and join the party of God. It can be argued that this flexible reputation of gaining membership within the Islamic flock prevented the early formation and emergence of a dedicated and vengeful opposition to Islam's emergence as a dominant ideology. An Islamic government was viewed by the majority as a system which only expected individuals to be believers, without imposing any particular social, legal or political system. The general belief that Islam was an individual matter was rooted in the public's ignorance of the real implications of a clerically ruled Islamic state. It would be safe to say that in the collective consciousness of the Iranians in 1978, Islam was more or less concerned with:

> The struggle between the covenant of God and the seduction of Satan, between faith and infidelity, between righteousness and falsehood, between guidance and going astray.[15]

Prior to the victory of the revolution and the entrenchment of the Islamic Republic, most secular Iranians did not feel threatened because of this preconception. Who would not consider him or herself as a righteous person? Who would consider him or herself as seduced by and under the influence of Satan? In Islam, one does not find a regular and repeated pattern of discrimination against any social group or class as long as they are believers. For Islam, any individual, irrespective of his social class or political position, can join the ranks of the believers without much economic sacrifice and thus stay on the safe side. This non-antagonizing quality of Islam shown in the pre-victory stages of the Iranian revolution and shortly afterwards, played a determining role in pacifying those social groups which would have opposed the revolution had it been led and organized according to a different ideology.

The main object of our study is to provide an explanation for the success of the clerical leadership both during and after the revolution. Iranian society during the end of the Shah's reign was a well-stratified, class-ridden, heterogeneous society which was typical of all growing, less-developed economies. Within the Iranian social and economic formation, one could also detect 'the remnants of earlier stages of economic development',[16] side by side with specificities of early and mature capitalism. One could thus speak of a social formation in which the capitalist mode of production constituted the dominant mode.[17] As such, any ideology appealing to one group or class and antagonistic or threatening to another would have divided Iranian society into struggling camps during and immediately after the revolution.

In our analysis, we will examine Islam as a force that came to the foreground due to its diversity of discourse and also due to the weakness of the competing classes within Iran's social formation regarding taking the political lead and governing. Even though the absolutist monarch and the royal bureaucracy had lost its *raison d'être*, the bourgeoisie and 'the working class had not yet acquired the faculty of ruling the nation'.[18]

The policies, positions and conduct of the Islamic leadership immediately after its ascendance to power managed to maintain the support of a great majority of the people and did not precipitate the immediate formation of any large-scale social and political resistance or challenge to its rule, except among Kurds. As pockets of discontent and resistance began to take shape, they were repressed with the explicit and implicit help of future victims.

Shi'i Islam as an ideology constitutes a system of ideas and principles, fragmented as they may be, on economics, politics, jurisprudence, philosophy and morality. It depends primarily on the interpretations of religious experts and preachers in order to popularize and communicate its doctrine. Different experts can develop different interpretations, emphasizing greatly one aspect at the cost of others. Such a practice leads to the emergence of lopsided or even one-sided accounts of what *Shi'i* Islam ought to be. Each one of these specific accounts and interpretations, which rallies a segment or a class of believers around its main ideas and arguments, constitutes a subsystem of the main system of *Shi'i* Islam. The origin of Islamic subsystems can be traced to an important point made by Motahhari, whom Ayatollah Khomeini considered to be one of the few contemporary knowledgeable experts on Islam. Motahhari said:

> It is evident that Islam is neither a theory of society nor a philosophy of history. In the sacred book of Islam, no social or historical problem is dealt with in the technical jargon of sociology and philosophy of history. In the same way no other problem, ethical, legal or philosophical is discussed in the Qur'an, either in the current terms or according to the traditional classifications of sciences. However, these and other problems related with various sciences can be deduced from the book.[19]

Even though the subsystems share the principles and basic tenets of *Shi'i* Islam, they can adopt particular positions on social, political hilosophical issues which differentiate them from other *Shi'i* subsystems.

The Islam of each subsystem, in turn, appeals to one specific social group. These subsystems, however, form a unified whole under the general rubric of *Shi'i* Islam, even though they may be at odds with one another. The key to the success of Islam as the mobilizing ideology of the Iranian revolution lies in the attractive characteristics of its subsystems. While each subsystem aims at and attracts one social group in the name of Islam, it necessarily repels another social group. The antagonized social group will not necessarily turn away from or against Islam because it can be wooed and attracted by another *Shi'i* subsystem which is responsive to its needs. The Islamic view of this second subsystem can assimilate the social group which was antagonized or disillusioned by the first subsystem. Each subsystem has a legitimate and justified claim to orthodoxy by tracing its position to the Qur'an and *hadith* and, therefore, uses certain verses to buttress its positions. The coexistence and attractive aspect of subsystems under the general umbrella of Islamic ideology is only possible in the short run. In the longer term, they will tend towards greater competition for a greater following and finally one, or a merger of these subsystems, will exert its hegemony in the name of authentic Islamic ideology. The process of moving from a multiplicity of subsystems to a hegemonic one is concomitant with chasing out, marginalizing, branding as infidels, repressing and, finally, liquidating the followers of the weaker Islamic subsystems.

As each subsystem comes to represent one social group or class, the struggle between the subsystems can be traced to the on-going class struggle within the society. The competing subsystems are forced, through the process of struggle for hegemony, to further clarify their positions and, by doing so, become even more associated with the economic interests of one class or another. The process which begins with the independence of the state and the flourishing of *Shi'i* subsystems in order to attract the greatest majority of the people, ends up with class rule both in terms of the economy and the government. In its initial stages, this class rule cannot be as pure and stark as that in dictatorships in less developed countries, since the government still seeks the support of the people and is thus committed to slogans and talk of principles that involve social justice and equality. This verbal commitment allows for uncontrollable challenges and accusations from members of the defeated subsystems to which the ruling class continues to be sensitive. Finally, members of the dominating class cannot rule the economy with an iron hand, since they continue to be at the mercy of the unpredictable acts of the government that result from favourable reactions to sporadic challenges by the defeated subsystems. For example, even though the property-owning classes will benefit from the hegemony of a subsystem which defends their interest with the appropriate Islamic interpretations, they will not, by any means, enjoy the predictability and security that is provided in systems officially based on the private ownership of the means of production and the market system as the economic co-ordinator of production, consumption and distribution.

The *Shi'i* system

In order to understand the subsystems of *Shi'i* Islam which will be examined in the next chapter, it is important to construct and present the contours of the *Shi'i* system.

First, *Shi'i* Islam constitutes a system in which: believers as individuals, socio-economic groups and classes interact as equals before God and are merit-worthy only according to their degree of piety and conviction. Individuals are further differentiated in accordance with their religious expertise between *mojtaheds* and *moqalids*. Religious agents of varying status, from a simple preacher to an ayatollah, interact with members of the community through distinct religious institutions. A variety of religious institutions such as the mosque, the *hosseinieh*, the *hey'at* and the Islamic associations perform different religious purposes with varying degrees of formality.

Second, the set of rules and principles that co-ordinates the acts and behaviour of all participants within the system can be broken into two types: *usul-e din* and *foru-e din*. *Usul-e din* refers to the principles of the faith, while *foru-e din* constitutes the duties of the believer. According to the *Shi'i* doctrine, there are five religious principles in *usul-e din*. The first three are also shared by other Moslems, for example, the Sunnis. These principles are: *towhid* (unity of God); *nabuwaat* (prophethood); *ma'ad* (resurrection day); *imamat* (belief in the Twelve Imams who are the viceregents of the Prophet) and *adl* (belief in the justice of God).

Foru-e din is made up of the following duties: *namaz* (prayers); *ruze* (fasting); *khums* (income tax); zakat (wealth tax); *hadj* (pilgrimage to Mecca); *jihad* (holy war); *amr-e be ma'aruf* (commanding others to do what is commanded by God); *nahy-e az monkar* (forbidding others from that which is prohibited by God); *tavalla* (loving and supporting God, the imams and their followers) and *tabarra* (hating and fighting the enemies of God and the imams).[20]

Third, Islam provides two categories of incentives and disincentives to believers for following its principles: worldly and spiritual. Within the worldly category, Islam presents an individual as well as a social or collective incentive system. On an individual basis, believers are motivated to act according to the precepts of Islam and become pious, righteous and enlightened God-fearing individuals, in order to give God satisfaction and obtain his mercy. Wealth, power and success are all favours that God bestows. Therefore, in order to attain them, individuals have to follow a straight path. The believer is also given a social role and a collective incentive: God has promised that the earth will be inherited by His righteous servants and, in order for this to happen, society has to move towards the establishment of God's order on earth. The path to such an order goes through the implementation of the words of the Qur'an. So the Moslem has to perform a social role too, he has to forbid others from that which is forbidden by God and command them to do that which is commanded by Him. Within the spiritual category, the faithful are rewarded by a place in heaven and the disbelievers and wrongdoers are condemned to the eternal fire of hell. The incentive system described leads to two basic views of what should motivate Moslems: an individualistic view of Islam which promotes and supports practising the faith for private salvation and redemption and a social or collectively oriented view of Islam within which the whole society has to change in order to benefit from the collective incentives promised to the *ummah* which has successfully established God's order.[21]

Finally, we come to the fourth part of the system. The ultimate objective of the Islamic system is to provide harmony and total felicity for all mankind through the observance of the divine order with the application of *Shari'a* (Law of Islam).

Islam, as a system, presents itself as a comprehensive universal whole which possesses the means of solving man's basic problems, leading him along the straight path to piety and enlightenment and providing him with security in this life and the other. As a total ideology, all private and public life in the Islamic system is religious. Islam does not intervene in people's lives, since it is itself the clay of which the people in the system are made. The function of life within the system is the realization of the universal objective of the whole: to serve God by implementing and following the *Shari'a* which presents His concrete description of the divine order on earth.[22]

The Islamic system, as we have outlined it, could not have been sufficient to appeal to all the diverse social groups that existed in Iran, because as a broad outline it did not deal with specific contemporary issues on which different classes take different positions. As long as the particular policies of the Islamic system remained ambiguous, various groups and classes could not rally against it and, at the same time, the policy of non-commitment to anything but Islam allowed Khomeini who represented the system to keep out of squabbles with any of the social groups and classes who were participating in the movement. However, at the same time, the subsystems were allowed to function and present more specific policies and positions, thus creating the mass base of support for the revolution and the initial stages of the Islamic Republic. While the subsystems were appealing to specific social groups and classes and repelling others, Ayatollah Khomeini refused to give any cause to any group for disagreement or a confrontation with Islam. In an interview with an Egyptian journalist he clearly demonstrates the argument:

Interviewer: Some people maintain that you do not have a clear programme and indulge in simple slogans.

Ayatollah Khomeini: We do have a precise and clear programme. Islam's programme is both clear and precise.

Interviewer: May we know its main guidelines and contours?

Ayatollah Khomeini: Not yet. You must go, study and then grasp the main outlines. We will in the future announce all political, economic and cultural policies.[23]

On the basis of the *Shi'i* Islamic system outlined, it is possible to deal with an often used categorization which is employed in dealing with the revolution in Iran and the Islamic Republic. The word 'fundamentalism' has now become a household expression which is supposed to specify a specific type of Islam. Reporters, newsmakers and academics have categorized different Islamic groups on this basis. It is important to explain the weakness, if not the inappropriateness, of this concept as a differentiating term that should explain the difference between a fundamentalist Moslem and a non-fundamentalist Moslem. Bernard and Khalilzad define fundamentalists thus:

Fundamentalists regard the religious authority as the primary one and the state, at best as its instrument. They are radical, expansionist, and totalistic in their approach to foreign and domestic affairs. Unlike the traditionalists, they do not want a designated part of the government, they want to be the government and to shape society in all its aspects.They refer to tradition as evidence that such conditions are envisioned by original Islam, but their claim rests on an idealised distant past rather than on the actual tradition of their society. To traditionalists an Islamic policy is one in which Islamic precepts are followed in the life of the community. To fundamentalists, it is above all necessary that the government be Islamic and the leadership religious.[24]

If fundamentalism is characterized by regarding religious authority as primary and Islam as 'totalistic'; the desire 'to shape society in all its aspects'; respect for 'original Islam'; and the necessity of Islamic leadership, then Islam as a system is fundamentalist. As it was pointed out, the ultimate objective of Islam is to provide total felicity for all mankind through the observance of the divine order. As long as society ultimately serves God by following the precepts of the *Shari'a* then there will be no difference between the traditionalists and the fundamentalists.

Distinguishing between different types of Islamic tendencies or what we have called subsystems on the basis of their view towards the ultimate objective of Islam or the implementation of the divine order is misleading. It would be difficult, if not impossible, to find a Moslem who would disagree with the principle that the only way to deliverance and absolution is through abiding by the *Shari'a*, Again, shaping society in all apsects is another manifestation of establishing the divine order, with which no Moslem can disagree since it is the road to salvation.

An overview of *Shi'i* Islamic subsystems

The competing Islamic subsystems that emerged and acted as the centripetal force of the revolution have to be explained at two levels: their relation to the system and the process by which they gain legitimacy from it, and the distinguishing feature of each subsystem in relation to others. A subsystem is a natural consequence of the process of adaptation or relation of the system to changing conditions and emerging challenges to the system itself. In order for the system to survive as a viable and functional organism, it needs to remain responsive to the changing needs of its participants and as the different participants give rise to different demands, the system gives birth to various subsystems, each of which gains its legitimacy through its connection with the system and, in turn, provides the system with acceptability and support through its newly adapted or revised content.

The content of the subsystem has a dual aspect. First, a part of it remains faithful to certain immutable features of the system and, as such, it is based on the fundamentals of the system. A second part of the content of the subsystem is composed of adaptations and mutations which, even though they are not alien to the parts of the original system, present a new and different variation, with a different emphasis.

In reference to the Islamic system that was presented in the previous pages, it can be argued that each one of its four elements: its unit of analysis; set of rules and principles; incentive and disincentive systems and the ultimate objective of the system, could differ among different Islamic subsystems.

In relation to the first element of the system, the one according to which the interaction among social participants themselves and between social participants and institutions is categorized and described, the only relevant attribute of the participant is his or her status as a believer. The question of whether the unit of organization is the individual, clan, tribe or class is left open. The Qur'an addresses the individual believer (*mu'men*) as well as social groups or communities of believers. The absence of any specific injunction on this issue has led to the adoption of different positions by different subsystems.

Each religious position ultimately gives birth to varying and contradictory political positions. One subsystem can choose the individual as its unit of analysis, explaining social change through the transformation of the individual psyche and the merits of the Islamic system through its impact on the individual. Another subsystem can base its analysis on a class approach, using a terminology and classification which explains and interprets all social interaction on the basis of class polarization, interest and conflict. Even though each subsystem would develop and attract a different political constituency and hence represent varying political interests, each would continue to remain within the system. In terms of the relationship between the people and the religious institution (*ruhaniyat*) there is no clear-cut indication as to how it should be organized or if the system needs a deep-rooted hierarchical institution to obtain its objectives. One subsystem can maintain that the proper implementation of an Islamic society is simply impossible without the guidance and leadership of the clergy as the medium through which Islamic knowledge is transmitted. Another subsystem can argue that the spiritual value of the clergy does not provide any justification for their rule, since the Qur'an and the *hadith*, the real sources of Islamic knowledge, are ever present. Furthermore, it could be argued that no clerical institution ever existed during the time of the Prophet or Imam Ali, so why should one exist after them? Related differences can also exist in the importance that each subsystem attaches to various forms of locations where the faithful assemble and religious ceremonies are held. One subsystem can emphasize the importance of the mosque as the formal location of religious congregation, while another can underline the informal and specifically *Shi'i* location of a *hosseinieh*, where popular preachers move the people by primarily giving an emotional account of what happened to Imam Hossein in Karbala where he was martyred.

The second element of the system, which co-ordinates and defines the behaviour of believers is enunciated in the *usul-e din* and *foru-i din*. These principles and duties of the faith are accepted by all subsystems; however differences emerge in the method of implementation. One subsystem could argue that the observation of religious duties is a social obligation and that the Islamic state has the responsibility of enforcing public conformity, while another subsystem could view such duties as a personal responsibility, for which the individual is accountable only to God.

The incentive mechanisms which encourage and discourage individuals to respect and observe the principles of the faith constitute the third element of the Islamic system. The adoption of each one or a combination of spiritual rewards, individual worldly rewards, or collective worldly rewards could lead to a different mode of social action and interaction. One subsystem can base itself entirely on individual worldly rewards as the inducement mechanism of an Islamic society. Private acquisitiveness in such a subsystem becomes not only desirable in relation to enhancing one's title to wealth, but it will also come to reflect the favour and grace of God towards the successful individual. The Qur'an informs us that no one's position in life is without the consent of God. Clearly, the philosophical basis, and subsequently the economic structure, of one subsystem developed on the grounds of individual worldy rewards, would be different from another subsystem basing itself exclusively on spiritual rewards. In the latter subsystem, the selflessness of the individual and his sense of self-sacrifice, to the point of martyrdom, for the advancement of the Islamic cause becomes the eternal recompense, one that surpasses all worldly enclosures.

The fourth element of the system consists of believing in the *Shari'a*, the Islamic way, as the path towards total felicity. The social realization of the *Shari'a* ultimately presents itself as the final objective of the *Shi'i* Islamic system and all its satellite subsystems. Even though all subsystems remain loyal to the idea of the ultimate implementation of the Islamic law, differences emerge in the mode of administering the *Shari'a*. One subsystem can argue that compliance with the laws of God should be imposed through coercion, if necessary. This type of position maintains that only the fear of heavy retributions would induce proper conformity with the Islamic order. Another subsystem, basing itself on the Qur'an, can reject all notions of force and argue that the role of Islam is that of inviting people to observe God's law and the most effective means of popularizing Islamic principles is through setting individual examples worthy of imitation by others. Subsequently, two Islamic subsystems could end up with two diametrically opposed practical policies, without deviating from fundamental canons of the system.

The dynamic aspect of the exercise of the Islamic law should be kept in mind with the interpretive role that the Usuli *Shi'i* assign to the *mojtahed*. The degree to which *mojtaheds* are allowed to exercise their freedom in interpreting Islamic law is debatable. Yet, it is important to realize that the role and the margin of freedom that is extended to the *mojtahed* in each subsystem can itself become a source of variation. If the *mojtahed* is viewed as the catalytic agent who is supposed to bridge the gap between the laws that pertained to past historical conditions and circumstances, on the one hand, and the demands and requirements of the evolving modern world, on the other hand, then the *mojtahed* himself can become the source of numerous innovative and revisionist rulings, providing he continues to remain faithful to the basic principles and objectives of the system.

In order to put the concept of subsystems into practical use, a hypothetical Islamic subsystem can be constructed. The unit of analysis in this subsystem is assumed to be social class within the Islamic community (*ummah*). The ideal organizational structure is a non-hierarchical and unregulated relationship between the believers. All Islamic institutions that exist, such as the mosque or the *hosseinieh* are assumed to play only one role and that is to mobilize and conscientize the people through a call to Islam (*da'vat*). The rules and duties of Islam are to be observed with an emphasis on their symbolic roles. Let us say that fasting is presented as a means of experiencing the predicament of the dispossessed. Our subsystem places a great deal of emphasis on the circumstances and the historical conditions in which the Qur'anic dictums were made. The theoreticians of this subsystem come to the final decision that the letter of the Qur'an, for example, on polygamy was not only justified but the only correct solution to several other problems at the time of the Prophet, but that it is no longer applicable to the present conditions. Basing their arguments on the Qur'an, they question the legitimacy of the right to polygamy. The motivating force of the believer is a combination of spiritual and collective worldly incentives. The *mu'men* (believer) is encouraged to change his society and the world around him in order to arrive at the ideal condition of the rule of God. The collective worldly reward system views the collectivity as the unit of reward and thus adopts strictly egalitarian economic policies. The final objective of Islam, which is the realization of all mankind's felicity, is guaranteed by this subsystem through the implementation of the social aspects of the *Shari'a* which is believed to guard against modern social ills, such as imperialism, exploitation, despotism and alienation.

The above hypothetical construction is similar to one of our Islamic subsystems, that of Ali Shariati, which was very active during and after the revolution and became that attractive pole of Islam which appealed to the students and the intellectuals, who needed a progressive and dynamic Islam to identify with. The significance of a constellation of subsystems, as was pointed out, was and continued for a while to be the source of Islam's appeal to different interests and social groups and of its ability to unite a highly differentiated body under the umbrella of Islam.

In order to grasp the political influence and importance of the various subsystems which operated under the shelter of Islam, it is important to understand and analyse the most important of these subsystems. Even though the competition between them after the victory of the Islamic Republic resulted in the castigation of certain subsystems, the discourse, ideas and tools of operation of each one of these subsystems remain as a potent weapon in the hands of the policy makers of the Islamic Republic.

The eclectic policies of the Islamic Republic have their roots in the different and, at times, contradictory solutions that it borrows from the different subsystems. This approach allows the régime to ride over crises in the short term. However, arbitrary use of different policies which were originally conceived by different subsystems to satisfy the particular interest of their specific constituents will result in alienating and antagonizing a large majority of society. The source of unity – the different policies and recommendations of the different subsystems – evolves into the source of disequilibrium and instability.

Four *Shi'i* subsystems which we believe are of great importance will be closely studied to demonstrate the source of the Islamic Republic's eclectic policies, both domestic and international. As Sayyed Qutb correctly observed:

> The Islamic system has room for scores of models which are compatible with the natural growth of a society and the new needs of the contemporary age as long as the total Islamic idea dominates these models in its expansive external perimeter.[25]

The factor that Sayyed Qutb overlooks is the destabilizing role that each of these competing models would eventually play, once a system of government based on Islam came to power. Even though Islam claims to remain independent of class conflicts, in a class-ridden society and in the long term Islam would be used by the majority classes in society to secure their interests.

Notes

1. Zainolabedin Rahnema, *Translation and Interpretation of the Qur'an*, Vol. 1 (Teheran), p. 34.

2. Zainolabedin Rahnema, *Payambar*, 22nd edn (Teheran: Amir-kabir, 2536), p. 258.

3. Meraat Khavari, *Naqd ketabe Kashf al-asrar* (Paris: Alam Forouz, Ordibehesht, 1364), p. 28.

4. Imam Khomeini, *Khasf al-asrar*, p. 316.

5. Imam Khomeini, *Hokomat Islami*, p. 27.

6. *Ijtihad*: exercise of reason in the interpretation of Islamic law.

7. Shahrough Akhavi, *Religion and Politics in Contemporary Iran: Clergy-State relations in the Pahlavi Period,* (Albany: State University of New York Press, 1980), p. 121.

8. Michael M. J. Fischer, *Iran. From Religious Dispute to Revolution* (Cambridge: Harvard University Press, 1980), p. 88.

9. Hamid Algar, *The Islamic Revoltion in Iran* (London: The Open Press, 1980), p. 6.

10. Estimates of the participants vary from the ridiculously low figure of 300 to 400 thousand claimed by the military-controlled Iranian radio and television to one million by the Persian language programme of the British Broadcasting Corporation and the Federal Republic of Germany. Suroosh Irfani, *Revolutionary Islam in Iran* (London: Zed Books, 1983), p. 142. Mehdi Bazargan refers to two million people in Mehdi Bazargan, *Enqelab-e Iran Dar Do Harekat* (Teheran, 1363), p. 36. Akbar Khalili refers to an estimation of over three million people calculated by 'a group of students and professors at Teheran University'. Akbar Khalili, *Gam be Gam ba Enqelab* (Teheran: Soroosh, 1360), p. 113.

11. T. Allway, 'Iran Demonstrates', *Christian Science Monitor* 12 December 1978.

12. Anthony Parsons, *The Pride and the Fall. Iran 1974-1979* (London: Jonathan Cape, 1984), p. 110.

13. Analysts, depending on their political commitment, tend to reduce or emphasize the presence of one or another group. Mehdi Bazargan's description of the participants of the 10-11 December 1978 demonstration is more or less a realistic one:

'Members of the urban middle class, especially young high school and university students, constituted the majority of the participants, next came the Bazaaris (craftsmen and tradesmen), shopkeepers and civil servants who were also numerous. The workers and peasants who were present formed a very small minority. Religious students (*talaba*) and clergymen did participate but in proportion to their number in society at large, they were less represented. Young women . . . were present, without the veiled ones having the majority'. Mehdi Bazargan, op. cit. p. 39.

14. This seventeen-article resolution is signed by 'The Organising Committee of the Tassua and Ashura Marches', dated 19 and 20 Azar 1357.

15. Yvonne Haddad, 'The Quranic justification for an Islamic Revolution: The view of Sayyed Qutb', *The Middle East Journal* Winter 1983, Vol. 37, No. 1, p. 18.

16. See D. Ross Gandy, *Marx and History* (Austin: University of Texas Press, 1979), p. 151.

17. Maurice Godelier writes:

'It is often the case that a certain society is organised on the basis of several modes of production all interconnected in a specific way and dominated by one; therefore in order to describe these connected wholes and modes of production, we have the notion of "economic and social formation"'. Maurice Godelier, *Perspectives in Marxist Anthropology* (Cambridge: Cambridge University Press, 1977), p. 18.

18. In explaining absolutism and Bonapartism as two forms of the independent state, in which the state gains independence from the classes, Marx maintained that in:

'the seventeenth and eighteenth centuries . . . the absolute monarchy gained independence from the classes. Neither the rising bourgeoisie nor the weakening aristocracy was strong enough to govern. The king played the two classes against each other and built up his power. By divine right he ruled through the royal bureaucracy and the army, responsible only to God'.

In relation to Louis Napoleon's dictatorship over France in 1851, which formed the basis of his model of Bonapartism, Marx says: 'In reality it was the only form of government possible at a time when the bourgeoisie had already lost and the working class had not yet acquired the faculty of ruling the nation'. Cited in R. Gandy, Ibid. p. 133.

19. Murtada Motahhari, 'Sociology of the Quran' Motahhari translated from the Persian by Mahliqa Qara'i, *Al Tawhid*, Vol. 1, No. 3, Rajab 1404 (April 1984), p. 139.

20. See Fischer, Ibid. p. 280 and the introduction to *Nahjul Balagha*. (Rome: European Islamic Cultural Centre, 1984) pp. vii-ix. It is interesting to note that in the second source which is published by the Islamic Republic, there is no mention of *tavalla* and *tabarra*, since they emphasize a historical bone of contention between the *Shi'i* and Sunni schools, which the Islamic Republic wishes to play down on the international scene.

21. For a Qur'anic justification of the arguments presented in this part see the following references which are by no means exhaustive:

The Koran, trans. J. M. Rodwell (London: J. M. Dent and Sons Ltd., 1983) Sura 3:25 p. 388, Sura 3:108 p. 396, Sura 3:127 p. 398, Sura 3:136 pp. 398-9, Sura 3:103 and 106 p. 396, Sura 6:125 p. 329, Sura 39:74 p. 261, Sura 21: 105 p. 158.

22. Abdul Ala Mawdudi says:

The *Shariat* is a complete scheme of life, an all embracing social order where nothing is superfluous and nothing lacking. Abdul Ala Mawdudi, *Islamic Law and Constitution* (Lahore: Islamic Publications, 1967), p. 53.

23. Imam Khomeini, *Nedaye Haq: Majmu'aeh-i az payamha, mosahebeh ha va sokhanrani ha ye Imam Khomeini dar Paris* (Etehadiyeh Daneshjouyan dar Europa va America) Bahman 1357, pp. 92-93.

24. Cheryl Bernard and Zalmay Khalilzad, *The Government of God – Iran's Islamic Republic* (New York: Columbia University Press, 1984), p. 33.

25. Cited in Yvonne. Y. Haddad, 'Sayyed Qutb: Ideologue of the Islamic Revival'. In John L. Esposito, *Voices of Resurgent Islam* (Oxford: Oxford University Press, 1983), p. 71.

3. Roots of the Islamic Republic's official policies

The ability of the clerical leadership to maintain and consolidate its power against enormous odds prompts an analysis of the underlying causes of their political success. To invoke the Islamic Republic's policy of ruthless repression begs the question, since before attaining the power to repress, the Islamic tendency within the revolutionary movement enjoyed widespread popularity. It was this initial popularity which provided it with the necessary power to later apply repression against the opposition. The capacity of the Islamic forces to grow and gain increasing support during the revolution rested on the diversity of their socio-economic interpretations and subsequently programmes. Once in power, the clerical leadership combined pragmatism with repression to hold on to the reigns of power.

Failure to grasp the flexibility which the adoption of different aspects of various subsystems offers to the clerical leadership leads to erroneous categorizations such as Islamic modernists, traditionalists, fundamentalists, moderates, extremists, etc. Each subsystem provides its own particular economic, political and social tools which can be used to implement a specific view of Islam. The clerical leadership which hopes to set itself above the subsystems can draw on the entire range of these tools, as expediency dictates. The positions and statements of prominent figures of the clerical leadership can oscillate and differ according to changing political circumstances and national moods. Western inability to grasp the logic and ease with which religious leaders could swing from one position to a diametrically opposed one, yet remain within the general framework of the Islamic system, has its roots in a failure to recognize the existence and importance of *Shi'i* subsystems.

James Bill, who is considered to be a knowledgeable analyst of Iranian affairs – one who was interested in Iran well before the revolution – categorizes Hojatolislam Ali-Akbar Hashemi-Rafsanjani and Ayatollah Mahdavi-Kani as political extremists:

Individuals who take an unflexible, hard line stance of a profoundly

> conservative nature on most social and political issues . . . The
> extremist mullah is a true believer who is generally lacking tolerance
> of other opinions and world views.[1]

The statement lacks precision and clarity. The categorization does not
provide any basis for consistent prediction of these individuals' probable
acts in the face of changing circumstances. Making categorical statements like these about members of the leadership based on a position that
they took at one time and translating that position in to extremism,
moderation or fundamentalism, is static and leads to mistakes. Ayatollah
Mahdavi-Kani whom Bill categorizes as extremist has close ties with
Mehdi Bazargan – the Islamic Republic's first prime minister – who has
criticized the leadership and its policies for its disrespect for democratic
freedoms (freedom of the press, speech, assembly, elections, association
etc.). Mahdavi-Kani has also made public declarations justifying differences of opinion and has indirectly supported Bazargan's right to dissent.[2]
Hashemi-Rafsanjani who is once again categorized as an extremist by
Bill is known to be in favour of improvement in relations with the West.[3]
In the Irangate affair he proved flexible enough not only to bargain with
the United States, but to close his eyes on the deal with Israel over the
purchase of arms. Analysts have referred to him as the 'moderate'
alternative in Iran. So Bill's fundamentalist of 1982 becomes the 'moderate' alternative of 1987.[4]

In order to provide a basis for understanding the policies of the Islamic
Republic ever since its establishment and shed some light on what might
be expected of it in the future, four subsystems will be studied. Each
subsystem will be described and constructed on the basis of the writings
of one renowned Iranian religious and political figure. Once the content
of each major subsystem is examined and the manifestation of parts of
each is demonstrated in the policies of the Islamic Republic, the confusion over the nature of the Islamic Republic will be reduced. It should
become easier to decipher Mehdi Bazargan's statement that:

> Even though our present dominant system possesses elements and
> signs of all systems (despotism, clergyocracy, democracy, theocracy,
> socialism, fascism, anarchism, Islamic order) it is neither consistent
> with nor equivalent to any one of them.[5]

Subsystem I: According to Ayatollah Motahhari

Ayatollah Morteza Motahhari can be considered as one of the most
prominent contemporary intellectual figures among the Iranian clergy.
Motahhari's impressive record of publications on Islamic issues which
comes to some 33 books of between 70–100 pages is witness to this fact.
Motahhari went through the traditional seminary school of Mashhad and
then to Qum where he was a student of a number of the *maraje-e taqlid*
(the supreme authorities on Islamic law), including Ayatollah Khomeini.

Upon his graduation from the seminary school of the holy city of Qum he entered Teheran University and taught at the faculty of Theology. Motahhari's firsthand experience and interaction with students at Teheran University enabled him to assess the strength and appeal of Islam among Iran's intelligentsia. His observations convinced him that Islam's philosophical content had to be systematically addressed, revitalized and presented in a lucid fashion to the young. The inroads that dialectical materialism and Marxism were making among Iranian youth had to be countered with a methodical Islamic critique of materialism as a philosophy; the role of the clergy in relation to the people, the traditional educational system of the seminary schools and the organizational network of the clergy were all in need of reform.

Motahhari realized that traditional Islam, which expressed itself mainly in the religious ceremonies and practices of the believers, did not respond to the demands of educated young people, a majority of whom were from practising Moslem families. In a society where the value of any belief or ideology was measured by the tools that it could offer to solve and redress the pressing social and political contradictions of the country, the reputation of traditional Islam was marred by superstition, parochialism and conservatism, if not retrogression. The task that Motahhari undertook was a difficult one. He wished to reform the traditional image of Islam and improve the organizational structure and quality of the clergy, in order to protect it from those anticlerical revolutionary Islamic currents which were becoming popular among the youth. He set out to confront those who maintained that an 'authentic Islam' was not in need of an intermediary in the shape of the clergy. Motahhari's reformism introduced an element of renovation which was not to the taste of the traditional clergy, who were quite comfortable with the prevalent social and political conditions of the country, including their own status in society, and who were more concerned with the practice of religious ceremonies than with the socio-political role of Islam.

Motahhari's theoretical contributions and his role not as a militant revolutionary but as an Islamic scholar who was highly esteemed by Khomeini earned him a position as one of the official theoreticians of the Islamic Republic. As one of Khomeini's confidants, Motahhari was a key member of the Revolutionary Council.[6] The Council was responsible for the co-ordination and implementation of the anti-Shah activities of the Islamic opposition forces during the revolution and was given the responsibility of acting as the nation's legislative body after the revolution, until the time when a new constitution was adopted and a parliament convened.[7] During the revolution and after the establishment of the Islamic Republic, Motahhari continued to act as the theoretician and spokesperson of the Islamic ideology which would become the guiding light of the new leadership. His role became even more important as it became his duty to distinguish, point out and argue against 'un-Islamic tendencies, currents and concepts' which were being used as Islamic categories. During the initial stages of the Islamic Republic, Motahhari's statements and positions were generally considered as a reflection of the official line that the Islamic Republic sought to follow.

On 1 May 1979, ten weeks after the fall of the monarchy, Motahhari was assassinated in Teheran. A group called Forqan accepted responsibility for the assassination and claimed they were disciples of Ali Shariati. Forqan carried out its assassination in the name of an Islam without *Akhunds* (a slightly derogatory term for the clergy). It is ironic that Motahhari and Shariati were initially close collaborators in running and politicizing the Islamic centre of *Hosseinieh-e Irshad* which became the most influential and dynamic centre for propagating Islam among the youth in the early 1970s. Later, however, Motahhari fell out with Shariati, whose view of Islam was too radical and anticlerical for Motahhari's taste. The fanatic disciples of Ali Shariati never forgave Motahhari and Bazargan for the letter of castigation and condemnation that the two men were said to have written and circulated against Shariati.

Ayatollah Khomeini's message on Motahhari's assassination is a clear indicator of the importance and significance that Khomeini attached to Motahhari's theoretical contributions to Islam and the revolutionary movement. Khomeini referred to Motahhari as 'the highly esteemed martyr and the venerated sage, philosopher and faqih' (expert in Islamic law) who 'spent his noble and fruitful life in attaining the holy objectives of Islam and fought relentlessly against all deviations and aberrations'. Khomeini called him, 'A man who was unique in his knowledge of Islam, the Qur'an and various other Islamic skills' and said, 'I (Khomeini) have lost a very dear son and I am mourning his death, since he was the product of my own life'.[8] A year later Khomeini said,

> Motahhari has rendered great services to Islam and the sciences and it is a great loss that murderous hands took away this fruitful tree from the religious and scientific centres and denied his contributions to us all ... Now I have heard that through their anti-Islamic propaganda the opponents of Islam and counter-revolutionary groups are in the process of detaining our dear university students from reading the books written by this learned faqih. I encourage students and committed intellectuals to safeguard the books of this dear teacher and prevent them from being forgotten through anti-Islamic plots.[9]

Even though Khomeini presented Motahhari's theoretical contributions as the correct interpretation of Islam and the approach that ought to be followed in order to arrive at a truly Islamic outlook of life, our examination of the Islamic subsystem propounded by Motahhari will reveal the extent to which the practices and positions of the Islamic Republic came to differ from Motahhari's own preferences.

Motahhari's unit of analysis

From Motahhari's point of view, the unit of analysis, the main social actor and the entity to whom religious rights and obligations belong is the individual. It is the individual to whom Islam addresses itself. God establishes his relation with individuals or with a people. The criteria according to which the individual is judged are his or her piety, trust in God and the individual's resignation to the will of God.[10] Consequently, individuals cannot attain felicity unless they become pious. The transformation from corruption and profanity to faith, trust and devotion is deemed to be the prerequisite of good fortune.

> We are usually lamenting the fact that God has given a handful of Jews, military, economic and political superiority and dominance over seven hundred million Moslems . . . God will not change his law, we have to change ourselves. We are submerged in religious ignorance and are deeply inflicted with moral corruption and still we expect God to be our friend and our aid.[11]

According to Motahhari, social transformation is a function of each individual's own development in society. Such a betterment can only result from an internal psychological revolution. Motahhari argues that Satan can only influence an individual by penetrating his mind. Whether Satan comes to exert authority over an individual's thoughts and acts depends on whether that individual submits to Satan's temptations or not.[12] The individual is therefore considered as the master of the relationship that develops between himself, God and Satan. Submission to Satan, irrespective of class position, leads to the enchainment of one's humanity. Even an oppressor will have an oppressed inner self. The individual liberates his oppressed inner self by accepting the invitation of Islam and its road to salvation. It is assumed that all individuals are capable of appreciating divine values and possess within themselves aspects of God's nature. Motahhari's analysis cuts across classes and takes a forceful stand on the issue that neither piety nor profanity are class specific. Intent on neutralizing the class arguments of radical Moslems, Motahhari maintains that no specific class has a monopoly over faith, devotion and piety. On this basis Motahhari argues that Islam's invitation is also extended to those who are oppressors (*estezafgar*). He says,

> From an Islamic world outlook, every oppressor and every pharaoh (symbol of oppression) has also enchained a human being within himself. According to Islam's logic the pharaoh has not only enslaved the Israelites but has also enslaved a human being within himself.[13]

As long as man has the potential of liberating himself from his inner enslavement caused by Satanic temptations, he can trigger off an inner psychological revolution. This concept of individual volition to attain piety is emphasized by Motahhari to refute the Islamic validity of the class-divided society depicted by the radical Moslems. Motahhari refers to the Pharaoh's wife and points out that even though she belonged to the ruling class, once she learnt about Moses' invitation to faith she liberated herself and then revolted against the Pharaoh.[14] If any individual is capable of spiritual and moral transformation, class analysis as a tool of scientific inquiry loses its significance. Motahhari argues that according to the Qur'an the individual is not determined by his class and therefore can move from one class to another while his conduct, thoughts and mannerisms remain unaltered.[15] The two examples provided by Motahhari are Imam Ali and the Prophet who both had humble backgrounds, rose to become 'the most influential people of the Islamic lands' but never changed their thoughts and conduct. Motahhari argues that by accepting the notion that the nature of the individual is determined by his class, man will be denied the potential of liberating himself from the moral corruption and spiritual degradation that might be associated with a specific class. He rejects the idea that:

> Commitment to a particular class is the measure and test of all things . . . of being materialists and not Moslems.[16]

Motahhari's position on the decisive role and power of the individual as the agent who is capable of transforming himself into a pious believer leads him to conclude that Islam *does not* consider that the oppressed and the disinherited *mostazafin* constitute the social origin of divine movements. Motahhari argues that, unlike Marxism, Islam maintains that divine movements will benefit the disinherited, but will not entirely depend on them; nor will the disinherited become the movements' sole beneficiary. After the victory of the revolution, Motahhari seeks to draw a clear line of demarcation between his own view of Islam and what he considers to be a dangerous and deviationary interpretation. He says,

> during our time, the emphasis on the class origin of revolutions has become very popular and even those who speak of Islamic concepts and consider themselves to have an Islamic culture, place too much emphasis on concepts such as: the disinherited (*mostazafin*), oppression (*estezafgary*) and being oppressed (*estezafshodegi*). This overemphasis has led to a kind of deviation and misrepresentation.[17]

Motahhari seeks to cleanse Islam of all allegations of radicalism or proximity to Marxism. He presents a critique of those whom he accuses of deceitfully propagating Marxism under an Islamic guise. He argues that, first, according to the Qur'an, society is not polarized between those who exploit and those who are exploited. On the contrary, believers and the pious can be found among all classes and that on numerous occasions the Qur'an refers to groups of the disinherited and exploited as infidels and disbelievers. He concludes that no economic class has a monopoly over piety as the Islamic radicals maintain. Motahhari argues that through the Qur'an, God addresses all the people, not a particular class. He rejects the notion that the movement of history, according to the Qur'an, is in the direction of imposing the hegemony of the dispossessed classes.[18]

Motahhari's deep respect for the market system based on private property and its corollaries removed the anxieties of property-owning classes during the revolution. The wave of expropriations that swept across the country after the victory of the revolution and the anti-property owning rhetoric that was widely employed and played upon by the clerical leadership was clearly unacceptable to Motahhari. In spite of his identification with Motahhari's subsystem, Khomeini abandoned its tenets temporarily in order to secure the support of the dispossessed masses at the time when he moved forcefully against dissenting opposition groups and parties. Khomeini who had invited all Moslems to unite as brothers against the Shah, expediently proclaimed that the Islamic government had to implement and assure the rule and government of the dispossessed and the exploited over that of the exploiters and the possessors.

Individual freedoms and democracy

Motahhari's antagonism towards a social analysis based on class conflict which would subsequently employ policies that would exclude the property-owning classes and impose the will of the dispossessed does not qualify him as a pluralist or a partisan of individual freedoms in the liberal sense of the word. Motahhari supports the interests of the propertied classes but rejects all legal, political and cultural concomitants which have been traditionally associated with a capitalist mode of production in the West. Cautious not to alienate all those who opposed the Shah because of his refusal to respect democratic freedoms, Motahhari flirts with and even pays tribute to a conditional and thus mutilated concept of freedom of thought. On the one hand he argues that, 'in the Islamic Republic, there will be no limitation on the freedom of thought and that all should be free to present their authentic ideas'. In the same breath, Motahhari says, 'I have to warn against conspiracy and duplicity which is different from the presentation of authentic ideas'. The final verdict exposes the contradictory nature of these two positions. Motahhari concludes that, 'conspiracies are prohibited but people are free to present their thoughts'.[19]

The contrast between Motahhari's Islamic concept of freedom and the classical liberal version of the term is stressed by Motahhari himself in his philosophical discourse on the distinction between freedom of thought and freedom of opinion or belief. Motahhari argues that freedom of thought is the prerequisite for the development and evolution of mankind. But he adds that not all ideas or opinions are correct and therefore that freedom of opinion could be harmful both to the individual and society. He refers to Abraham smashing the idols and in the end convincing the people that they should worship only God. Motahhari maintains that even though Abraham did not respect the people's freedom of belief or opinion he liberated them from their ignorance and alienation.[20] The fact that Abraham's act furthered the cause of monotheism is sufficient proof for Motahhari that the idol worshippers had no right to their belief. The limit of freedom is determined by the ultimate objective of the Islamic system which is total felicity through the implementation of the Islamic law. Clearly if the will or opinion of the people and the Islamic rules interpreted according to those who are in power clash, it is the former that has to yield in an Islamic state.

Even though Motahhari pays lip service to the freedom of all political parties including those with non-Islamic opinions, in practice he condones their suppression, which is viewed as beneficial to the Islamic cause. Khomeini's position on the freedom of opinion is free of all ambiguities found in Motahhari. Khomeini says, 'as for those who oppose us because of their opposition to Islam, we must cure them by means of guidance, if it is at all possible; otherwise we will destroy these agents of foreign powers with the same fist that destroyed the Shah's régime'.[21]

On the issue of democracy, Motahhari's position is no less ambiguous. He argues that, 'when it is claimed that democracy does exist in Islam, we mean that Islam wishes to provide Man with genuine freedoms'. However, Motahhari immediately qualifies his statement and adds that, 'in other words, Islam strives to imprison Man's animal instincts and liberate his human instincts'.[22] Islamic democracy, according to Motahhari, follows a well defined and clear path, along which Man evolves towards his spiritual perfection. The roadmarks of this path are provided by the Qur'an and the *Shari'a* and in order to ensure his safe progress along this path, Man has to be protected and guided. Man is thus only free to traverse *this path* to felicity.

Motahhari criticizes political democracy since it replaces divine laws with man-made laws and gives priority to the will of the majority over the will of God. It is argued that as long as Man is not guided by God, he may well go astray and head for disaster. The elevation of the majority principle, which constitutes the foundation of democracy, to the position of an inalienable right and an indispensable axiom, is viewed as detrimental to the creation of an authentic Islamic society. Motahhari tries to expose what he considers to be the pitfalls of democracy and says, 'What is the basis of the laws promulgated in Western democracies? The will of the majority. And it is on this basis that homosexuality becomes legalised. This is the outcome of respecting democracy and the opinion of the majority. From Islam's point of view, such freedom reflects the downfall of human freedom. It exemplifies the liberation of bestiality and the bondage of humanity'.[23]

Therefore, even though Motahhari's unit of analysis and focus is on the individual, his view of the individual is completely shaped by what he should be and become according to the Qur'an. Concepts such as individual freedoms and political democracy based on the conviction that individual happiness and pleasure constitute the purpose of life can not be applied to Islam. The building block of the Islamic system is the *mu'men* or the individual who has embraced the faith, while the cornerstone of liberalism is the individual, pure and simple. The two individuals are very different; the societies that are constructed upon them and the laws that rule them are also very different.

It is interesting to observe that while in exile, Ayatollah Khomeini spoke about the establishment of a democratic Islamic Republic. His ambiguous references to democracy were for foreign consumption and the appeasement of the middle class, professionals and intellectuals at home. In an interview with Danish television he said,

> The government that will replace the tyrannical régime of the Shah will be a just government, the like of which does not exist in the West. It is possible that our ideal democracy will be similar to those democracies in the West. But the democracy we wish to create does not exist in the West. Islamic democracy is more complete than western democracy.[24]

Once he came to power, his declarations, positions and acts clarified the issue. Political democracy is not compatible with an Islamic interpretation similar to Motahhari's. Islamic democracy as explained by Motahhari shows total disdain for the four essential principles of political democracy: the majority principle, popular control, fundamental political freedoms and universal suffrage.

The role of the clergy

The relationship between the people and the clerical institution (*ruhaniyat*) plays an important role in Motahhari's subsystem. Motahhari's views on this subject are in harmony with those of Khomeini. His attitude towards the clergy can be viewed at three levels: his opinions regarding the organizational and educational problems of the clergy before the revolution; his defence of the clergy and the *ruhaniyat* in face of Ali Shariati's 'Islamic protestantism'; his views on the role and place of the clergy after the revolution.

Motahhari begins his analysis by arguing that since the *ruhaniyat* occupies a position of leadership in relation to the affairs of Moslems, any and all reform in the affairs of Moslems has to be initiated by this institution. In an important and revealing passage Motahhari says,

> If we assume that a reformist and religious movement is initiated by an individual or a group of people, this movement will not be very successful in a situation where the institution of the clergy remains unprepared and uncoordinated.[25]

From Motahhari's point of view the source of the problem of the clergy is the manner in which they are financed. Before dealing with this major issue he points to the other weaknesses in the clergy's education. The students in the theological schools who aim to become *mojtaheds* one day do not take an entrance exam and since in the theological schools students are not examined as they go from one level to another, they might end up unprepared for their task. In Motahhari's opinion, there are those who become members of the clergy who have neither adequate knowledge nor faith and these people put the *ruhaniyat* to shame. Motahhari finally argues that Arabic literature is not properly taught and even though students learn the grammar they remain incapable of writing or speaking Arabic fluently. In order to correct the above problems, Motahhari addresses the issue of the manner in which theological students are financed. The Islamic tax, *khums*, which is an obligation on all Moslems constitutes the basis of these finances. Half of the *khums* is called the *Sahm-i-Imam* (the Imam's share) and is spent in the manner which the *maraje-e taqlid* (sources of imitation) who receive it see fit. Motahhari argues that the method of financing the clergy, which depends entirely on the people and not on the government, has positive aspects. It provides the clergy with independence, on the basis of which they can stand up to governments and fight against their excesses and their cruelty. On the other hand, he argues, because of their dependence on individual contributions, the clergy have to be responsive to the demands and directives of the people and have subsequently become static and conservative. In a revealing account of the common people (*avam*) Motahhari laments their conservatism and says,

> Due to the fact that our clergy is under the spell of the common people, it can never take the lead and become the vanguard, it is always forced to follow the common people. A characteristic of the common people is that they are closely tied to the past and the traditions which they have become accustomed to. They cannot distinguish between right and wrong . . . They are against anything which is new and they are the defenders of the status quo.[26]

Motahhari concludes that the clergy have no other option than to remain docile and inert since this is what the common people want. In his opinion, the solution to the problem lies in centralizing all the money that is paid by Moslems in a common fund which would then belong to all the *maraje* (sources of imitation). Consequently, no individual member of the clergy would be directly dependent upon the people. The money collected in the common fund would be allocated to the highest ranking *maraje-e taqlid* who would distribute it to other *mojtaheds* and the theology students. Motahhari argues that such a scheme frees the clergy from the conservative clutches of the common people and allows the *ruhaniyat* to regain its postion of leadership.

There are a number of important elements in Motahhari's analysis. Firstly, he shows his utter disdain for the masses whom he describes as,

> people who are usually faithful, dedicated and true believers, but who are ignorant, unaware and decadent and are, as a result, against reforms.[27]

Secondly, he is concerned with breaking the conservative spell of the common people on the clergy. Motahhari realizes that the clergy must address issues such as, 'the equitable distribution of income, social justice and national sovereignty' which he considers to be directly related to Islam. If they fail to do so opponents of the *ruhaniyat* who represent another Islamic subsystem (Ali Shariati's) could attract a large following and further undermine the position and significance of the *ruhaniyat*. Thirdly, he is preoccupied with the fact that the *ruhaniyat* has to lead without needing to worry about its source of livelihood. Even though Motahhari realizes that the *ruhaniyat* is being supported by what he calls ignorant and decadent common people, he seeks to create a religious institution that will be responsive to reform-minded intellectuals and professionals who do not necessarily have any faith in the clergy as a progressive body. An important force that directs Motahhari towards reforming the clergy and its image is the competition that Ali Shariati's subsystem presents. Motahhari is forced to threaten the clergy by saying,

> Our highly esteemed religious figures should realise that the sustenance and existence of the clergy and Islam in this country depends on the deep rooted reforms that our religious leaders have to initiate. Today we are faced with a half awoken people who become more and more awake every day . . . If Islam and the *ruhaniyat* does not respond to their needs and feelings, they will turn to those newly born shrines.[28]

During the late 1960s and early 1970s, Motahhari witnessed the rise of a religious awareness among Iranian intellectuals which was essentially anticlerical. The increasing popularity of Shariati's Islamic subsystem based on an Islamic movement completely independent of the clergy threatened the credibility and *raison d'être* of the *ruhaniyat*. Capitalizing on the revived religious interest among Iranian youth, Motahhari was concerned with subjecting the wave to clerical leadership. Brushing aside non-clerical leaders such as Shariati, Motahhari argues that a movement which has an Islamic nature and an Islamic objective is in need of a leadership knowledgeable about the ideology of Islam, its moral, social and political philosophy. Motahhari says,

> It is evident that only those who have been brought up and are steeped in an Islamic culture and who are thoroughly familiar with the Qur'an, the Sunnah (the tradition of the Prophet's and the Imams' practices), Fiqh (religious laws) and Islamic epistemology, can occupy the position of leadership and thus it is only the *ruhaniyat* (the clergy) who can lead such a movement.[29]

Motahhari maintains that in a movement led by the clergy their main responsibility is to prepare for the post-revolutionary period. In his opinion the post-revolutionary period necessarily ushers in an atmosphere in which the clash of ideas and debates on different philosophies becomes the norm. 'At this time, swords would not further our cause, the suitable weapon is the book, the pen and our lectures.'[30] Motahhari feels that the *ruhaniyat* needs to be strengthened, unified and organized in order to guide the people along Islamic lines and to fight against all deviations. The Mosques, he argues, having served the movement very well during the revolution, should continue to be used and made attractive to the people. Even though Motahhari supports and encourages the formation of an Islamic party and centres of Islamic studies, along with religious programmes made for the radio and television, he warns that 'if all these institutions ever come to replace the Mosque, then we will be faced with disaster.'[31] For Motahhari, Islam as an ideology requires its own means of dissemination of information. The Mosque as the traditional centre for propagating Islam is the physical emanation of Islam, the presence and vitality of which is considered as a witness to the omnipresence of Islam itself. He cautions against the erosion of the power of the Mosque even to the benefit of an Islamic party. The source of Motahhari's anxiety lies in the fact that the organized power of Islam reflected through a party can very well slip into the hands of the non-clergy. The party, as a non-Islamic entity, cannot assure the dominance of the *ruhaniyat*, but the power that is wielded through the Mosque can be harnessed only by the clergy. In the final analysis Motahhari envisions an Islamic society with the clergy as the ultimate decision makers and is alarmed and distressed at the possible political ascension and domination of Islamic intellectuals. In a caustic passage, Motahhari informs the Islamic intellectuals that 'they have woken up a bit late', since 'the old guardians and custodians of this huge reservoir of energy and force (Islam) have already demonstrated that they are well aware of how to tap and make use of this source'. He concludes that the clergy will not allow anyone else to 'expropriate' it.[32] Even though the revolution places the clergy in the position of leadership, Motahhari warns against the possibility of the intellectuals taking over the leadership and predicts that if this happens, 'after one generation, Islam will undergo a metamorphosis and become completely distorted and mutilated.'[33]

Motahhari's concern with the leadership of the clergy and his dislike for 'Islamic intellectuals' is shared by Ayatollah Khomeini who uses the same terminology as Motahhari when he attacks the concept of an Islam without the *ruhaniyat*. Motahhari calls it a 'colonialist thesis' and points out that 'nothing can replace our clergy'. Ayatollah Khomeini says:

> Islam without the clergy is treason. They want to do away with Islam so first they have to do away with the clergy. First they say we want Islam but we don't want the clergy. If the clergy is excluded, there will be no Islam left. Islam has reached this point due to the hard work of the clergy . . . This thesis denies Islam. Be aware, I warn you against this great danger.[34]

The incentive systems

In dealing with the incentive system in Motahhari's subsystem it is important to remember that for him the unit of analysis is the individual. Employing individual worldly incentives, Motahhari bases his formulations on the Qur'an and argues that once individuals become pious and God-fearing, God will find a solution for their problems and He will provide for them in ways that they would never suspect.[35] Thus, individual piety is rewarded in this world.

In a discussion of social justice, Motahhari deals with the issue of ownership in Islam, which is directly related to his view of worldly individual rewards. From Motahhari's point of view, private property, which generates private rewards, is acceptable. He points out, however, that ownership of property should be maintained within certain limits. These limits are neither specifically nor approximately defined. He argues that all types of ownership cannot be categorized as exploitative. On the contrary, if different people with different capabilities and capacities and therefore different levels of productivity are taxed proportionately by the government and the government then distributes the social product according to the needs of people in society, this constitutes an injustice to some members of society. Motahhari argues that since the product of each person's labour belongs to that person, the act of taking away by force a part of his product, even if it is due to the fact that someone else is much more in need, is an act of injustice and exploitation. Motahhari concludes that sharing in material wealth is only justified when individuals voluntarily participate in such a scheme.[36] It can be argued that Motahhari's approach to the topic of private or individual worldly incentives played an important role in attracting the property owning classes to his subsystem and to the Islamic system. In an interesting analysis, he compares the Iranian revolution to the events after the death of Usman, the Third Caliph, and the people's invitation to Ali to become the Fourth Caliph and says,

> The revolution of the Moslem people in those days was very similar to today's revolution in Iran, since both were popular revolutions comprising all the people. In other words not only the poor people, but *also the rich people had revolted*.[37]

By claiming that even Ali came to power with the support of the property owning classes, Motahhari seeks to undermine and diffuse the anticapitalist rhetoric prevalent after the victory of the revolution.

Motahhari's approach is classical in the sense that he considers life on earth to be a period of cultivation, while life after death is one of harvesting what has been cultivated on earth. So, on earth, people act and in life after death they are judged. The judgement that is passed after death is strictly a private one. Motahhari argues that in the other world, it would be impossible to share in the judgement that is passed on someone else's action. One is neither rewarded nor punished for someone else's acts. In the other world, each individual is judged according to his own deeds.[38]

Motahhari's emphasis on individual rewards both at the worldly and the spiritual level led partisans of a *laissez-faire* philosophy to look favourably upon his subsystem. Motahhari's subsystem does not negate the right to property, the share of the property owning classes in the revolution, the right of inheritance, the right to accumulate wealth and capital within an unspecified limit and contractual freedoms, or any of the fundamentals of a *laissez-faire* economic system.[39] On the contrary Motahhari repeatedly lashed out against those who spoke of expropriation and confiscation as a policy which had Qur'anic justifications. Furthermore, Motahhari's anti-communism both at a philosophical level and a socio-economic level assured both the traditional bourgeoisie and the petty bourgeoisie of his commitment to an Islamic *laissez-faire* system. As far back as 1962, Motahhari had spoken of 'communism and Zionism' as the two great dangers which threatened Islam and 'functioned like two blades of a pair of scissors which intended to cut out the roots of Islam'.[40]

From a socio-economic point of view, Motahhari's subsystem did not emphasize or discuss the practical aspects of how Islamic laws and precepts would be enforced. It was understood that the Islamic government would enforce the *Shari'a* (religious laws), but less clear whether the government would enforce the observation of such laws at the micro or macro level. According to Islam the use of alcoholic beverages is forbidden. Now if the incentive and disincentive system is constructed on an individual basis, the consumer of alcoholic beverages in his own home is guilty of a sin for which he will be punished in the other world. As far as the state is concerned, his freedom of consumption in public is curtailed by the *Shari'a* which is the law of the land, but his private freedom to consume is a separate matter. In terms of such a subsystem, the *Shari'a* regulates the activities and practices of the public domain while the private domain is left to the individual. Motahhari's emphasis on individual responsibility gives the impression that his subsystem does not envision the implementation and enforcement of all and every article of the *Shari'a* in every household. Whether he would have supported the systematic intervention of the Islamic state in the private affairs of the faithful we cannot say. In any case, for the supporters of Motahhari's subsystem, the traditional bourgeoisie and the petty bourgeoisie, the problem did not arise, since even in private they either observed or pretended to observe the Islamic laws.

Motahhari's subsystem naturally appealed to a great majority of the clergy who were being promised an important role in guiding and leading the country. During the rule of the Shah only a small number of the clergy such as Ayatollahs Taleqani, Montazeri, Lahooti, Rabani-Shirazi and Hojatolislams Anvari, Saeedi and Ghaffari had chosen an openly confrontationist approach. The majority of the clergy remained passive. When the debate on the role and significance of the clergy was opened up by Ali Shariati, the majority of the clergy remained intellectually defenceless. It was the theoretical contributions and arguments of Motahhari and the circle around him that shielded the clergy against Ali Shariati's use of a vocabulary that only a few of the clergy could understand in order to criticize. It thus becomes understandable why the majority of the clergy in the leadership, including Khomeini, refer to Motahhari's work as the source of right and proper Islamic guidance. Even though Motahhari had probably never read Marx or any primary sources on Marxism, he had at least addressed it and developed an Islamic critique of it. Suroosh Irfani's passionate attachment to Ali Shariati leads him to say that:

To neutralize Shariati's image as the architect of the Islamic Revolution, the clerical régime began projecting its protégé, Ayatollah Motahhari, a well read clergyman and lifelong employee in the Pahlavi régime's Ministry of Education, as the ideologue of the Islamic Revolution.[41]

Motahhari had responded to Shariati's theories well before the revolution; the subsystems were already at odds, drawing their social power from different social strata. There was no single ideologue of this revolution in which several social groups and classes participated. It is undoubtedly true that Ali Shariati was one of the ideologues of the revolution, but it is too simplistic to claim he was the only one, especially in view of what happened to the revolution after the consolidation of power by the Islamic government.

Motahhari's subsystem appealed to all those who lamented the erosion of Islamic values. Like Shariati, Motahhari argued for a return to an Islamic identity. Motahhari maintained that the penetration of Western culture and values was most dangerous since it was the Trojan horse of political colonization. He argued that cultural colonialism involved mesmerizing the people with such 'deceiving concepts as freedom, democracy, socialism, civilization, modernization, progress, etc'.[42] Motahhari argued that once the Islamic people had become disillusioned with 'Western Liberalism and Eastern Socialism', they had 'started searching for their real and authentic identity', which was none other than Islam.[43] Motahhari's invitation to throw away all that which was Western and adopt all that which was Islamic appealed to those members of the traditional middle class who were witnessing an ever widening gap between their own style of life and those of their children. The 'individual freedoms' which were provided by the Shah's régime, and admittedly well received by the urban youth, were generally viewed by these traditional and religious parents as immoral, corrupting and vulgar. Furthermore, the anti-Western but pro-capitalist discourse of Motahhari's subsystem provided a favourable economic perspective for the national bourgeoisie who had increasingly come under pressure from international competition and who harboured typical mercantilist views.

Subsystem II. According to Ali Shariati

Ali Shariati has been hailed as the Rousseau and the Voltaire of the Iranian revolution.[44] His concept of Islam was both novel and unorthodox. In a way, he was the logical product of an Iranian society which was leaving behind its traditional cultural values, basically summed up in its Islamic heritage and was striving towards an undefined and unclear future. Shariati, born in Khorasan, a north-eastern province of Iran, and raised in a religious family, received a Bachelor of Arts degree from the University of Mashhad at the age of 26 and went to Paris a year later. As the Shariati-type trajectory became more prevalent in an Iran which could afford to educate its youth at home and abroad, the search for a distinguishing identity intensified among the young. On the one hand, the Shariati-type youth were proud of and closely attached to their Islamic culture and roots, on the other hand, they were well aware of Islam's inability, as it existed in Iran, to find a solution to the economic, political, social and cultural plight that they found themselves in.

Shariati's experience with the positive role of Islam in the Algerian revolution and his correct understanding that the language of Islam provided the most dependable means of communication with believers, led him to embark on the development and presentation of an Islamic subsystem. This subsystem played a determining role in the Iranian revolution. The question always poses itself whether Shariati was simply using Islam in order to attain certain specific political objectives or whether he believed in Islam as an ideal social system? Without direct reference to Shariati, Motahhari draws a distinction between the 'Islamic Revolution' and 'Revolutionary Islam'. He says the objective of the 'Islamic Revolution' is the implementation of Islam and its values, while the revolutionary struggle that precedes it is only a means which should be immediately dispensed with once the revolution has succeeded. Motahhari maintains that for those who believe in a 'Revolutionary Islam', the revolutionary struggle was the main objective and Islam constituted an instrument.[45] According to Hossein Dabbagh, Motahhari confided in him that: 'Shariati was an instrumentalist in the sense that he used religion as an instrument for his political and social objectives'.[46] As long as Shariati's subsystem remains within the main framework of the *Shi'i* Islamic system, the issue loses its relevance. Shariati bases his views and arguments on the sources used by all Moslems: the Qur'an, the *hadith,* and the Sunnah, with an emphasis on Imam Ali's *Nahjul Balagha.* Shariati's proclamation of faith in *Shi'i* Islam is clear:

> The true and scientific *Shi'ism* belongs to those who understand Islam – the religion which was brought to us by Mohammad and those principles which can be deducted from the Qur'an – on the basis of five principles. I who am a believer of Imam Ali's *Shi'ism* understand Islam on the basis of *Towhid* (unity of God), *Nabuwaat* (prophethood), *Maad* (resurrection), *Imamat* (belief in twelve Imams) and *Adl* (God's justice).[47]

Even though Shariati's interpretations and deductions disconcerted the clergy, he was never officially pronounced as an unbeliever or 'excommunicated' by any of the prominent *mojtaheds* in Iran.

Shariati was not a *mojtahed*. He had received his doctoral degree in medieval Iranian philology.[48] However Shariati, who was interested both in Islam and sociology, dedicated himself to the study of Islam in an all encompassing manner. Before his departure for Paris, Shariati was greatly influenced by the Islamic atmosphere in which he grew up. His father, Mohammed Taqi Shariati, was very familiar with the Qur'an and had written a book on its interpretation. Taqi Shariati's expertise in Islamic studies helped Shariati overcome the shortcomings that existed in his mastery of Islamic knowledge. The close intellectual collaboration between the two men provided Shariati with constructive comments and criticisms on Islamic issues, usually before he presented his ideas in his lectures and classes. On issues where Shariati thought his interpretations were as valid as his father's, he would present both interpretations.[49] According to the *ulama*, Shariati made mistakes in terms of Islamic dogma and doctrine, but he moved swiftly to revise and reformulate his errors.[50]

Shariati and politics

Shariati's interpretation of Islam addressed the major universal themes that faced the intellectuals of the post-World War II period. The decline of Europe's transparent stage of colonialism before World War II had given way to the United States' opaque policy of economic hegemony and political manipulation after the war. Shariati had witnessed the fall of Dr Mohammed Mossadeq's popular government and the subsequent denationalization of Iran's oil due to the United States' imperialistic posture towards Iran. He was arrested in 1957, four years after the coup against Mossadeq, for his participation in the activities of the Mossadeqist National Front.[51].

Shariati's experience in Iran and the influence of the 'third worldist' neo-Marxism of the 1960s demonstrated an appropriate course of action for Iranians. The subjugated and dependent countries had to break with the imperialist powers which perpetuated their underdevelopment. The confrontation between the centre and periphery, or the imperialist and underdeveloped countries, became the principal contradiction of the epoch. The tools of analysis, categories and means of waging the anti-imperialist struggle, were rooted in Leninism. The world revolution and liberation were believed to hinge on the anti-imperialist struggle of the developing countries. Inherent in the 'third worldist' outlook was a return to all that which was endogenous. This implied the use of culturally specific means and methods of struggle. Shariati's experience in Iran and his exposure to radical western intellectual circles had convinced him that the prosperity, welfare and cultural development of his country were only possible through an anti-imperialist movement. Anti-imperialism was theoretically inconceivable without a struggle against capitalism, the economic system which facilitated and perpetrated the underdevelopment of the developing world, on the one hand, and the development of the imperialist western economies, on the other hand. Finally, an anti-imperialist struggle had to become an anti-despotic movement, since it was the domestic and indigenous allies of the imperialists who maintained the status quo in the underdeveloped countries for the benefit of the centre and the ruling classes of the peripheral countries.

Shariati's achievement was the utilization of Islam as a socially applicable and easily communicable form of presenting a content which could be considered as essentially Leninist. Islam had no direct references in relation to imperialism, capitalism and despotism, yet the corpus of *Shi'i* Islamic theory provided fertile grounds for the deduction and presentation of a dynamic and revolutionary ideology, posing itself as a culturally suitable alternative to Marxism-Leninism. Shariati was greatly impressed by the non-aligned movement and its quest for an alternative road to political and economic sovereignty and welfare. His attempt to provide an Islamic response to the crucial social, political and economic problems of his epoch fits well within the pattern of theorizing which attempted to steer a so-called independent path away from capitalism and distinct from Soviet Communism. The presentation and discussion of anti-imperialism, anti-capitalism and anti-despotism in Islamic terms and on the basis of evidence found in Islamic and *Shi'i* theory, made good tactical sense in generating and propelling a mass movement, the participants of which were culturally and traditionally attached to Islam. However, on a theoretical level it was clear that concepts such as anti-imperialism or anti-capitalism were borrowed from a Marxist-Leninist system of thought. Shariati was aware of his indebtedness to Marxism-Leninism as a dominating trend in his sociological approach to the problems of subjugated and colonized countries. Yet, he became subject to the illusion that he was really showing a third way, just because he was veiling his borrowed theories in Islamic jargon and evidence. Shariati says:

> The socio-economic system of Islam is the same as that of scientific socialism except that it is based on faith in God. This system holds a middle ground between the two corrupt systems of capitalism and communism.[52]

The importance of Shariati lies in his popularization of a radical and revolutionary Islamic subsystem. Shariati's subsystem appealed to the university students who had always constituted a forceful centre of opposition to the Shah's régime. To those university students who had come from mainly provincial traditional families in which it was natural to be a believer, Shariati provided an ideal and an identity that they could be proud of and defend. While these students were embarrassed by the fetishistic, superstitious and petty religious practices that were common among believers and considered as obligations of all Moslems, they came from traditional religious backgrounds and so found themselves disoriented by the secular values and relations of the university and, most important, humiliated and overshadowed by the theoretical formulations and arguments of the Marxist-Leninist or simply secular students who questioned the basis of their faith and looked down upon them as conservative and reactionary elements. Shariati's Islamic subsystem provided a novel redefinition of a Moslem, one who was free of all superstition and fetishism, yet conscious of social problems and prepared to change society armed with the culturally familiar weapon of Islam. In addition, Shariati's attack on westernization gave greater credence and legitimacy to his followers who could strike back at the ultimately western source of inspiration of the left and the non-believers. To those who had once embraced Marxism-Leninism, Shariati presented an endogenous version which was simpler to comprehend and internalize, since its history was a part of the people's everyday life and its heroes were such celebrated characters as Ali and Hossein who were always present in the social memory of the people. His change-oriented world-view chose the older generation whether secular or religious as one of its main targets of criticism, accusing them of passive collaboration with the status quo. His subsystem proceeded by whipping up enthusiasm for and interest in politics and social reflection, presenting an ideal to those who chose to become actively engaged in politics. Finally, it provided the activists with an internally consistent method of struggle in order to attain the ideal: martyrdom (*shahadat*) or open criticism of the status quo.

The Shah's régime could not depend on any substantial segment of Iranian youth to defend its modernization and westernization drive. The westernization that was exercised by the régime was essentially reflected in the implementation of a dependent capitalism, along with the prevalence of an imported western culture and its corollary of vulgarized western values and morals. Yet the political liberties, democratic institutions and respect for human rights which are supposed to form the cornerstone of all western democracies were absent in the Shah's Iran. Those who had come to enjoy the secularization of society could not defend the régime's corruption, disrespect for political freedoms and human rights, and disrespect of social justice and equality. The autocratic character of the Shah's régime and its harsh reaction in the face of political dissent, along with its self-proclaimed aim of westernization, led to the conclusion that a repressive political system was part and parcel of westernization. It became very difficult for individuals to distinguish between potential positive aspects of an authentic westernization and the negative aspects of such a policy, such as alienation, social and individual disorientation and anomie. Finally, westernization, as it existed in Iran, became a symbol of the negative and undesirable: political repression, economic exploitation, cultural alienation and moral corruption. Anti-western discourse became synonymous with an attack against the Shah and the totality of what he stood for. Thus, Shariati presented westernization as the Horse of Troy which would finalize the complete domination of the Shah's brand of government in Iran. This type of analysis led to many anti-monarchists adopting anti-western modes of life to resist the despotic political conditions. For Shariati's young followers, the veil, for example, became a symbol of anti-westernization.

Shariati did not live to see the revolution, the seeds of which he had undoubtedly sown among the youth. On 19 June 1977, he died in England at the age of 44. The mysterious circumstances of Shariati's death have led his followers and many analysts to believe that SAVAK, the Shah's secret police, was involved. If this were true, silencing the 'great teacher', as he was called by his disciples, did not save the monarchy from the volcanic energy that Shariati had generated. The religious uprising of 1963 led by Ayatollah Khomeini failed, while the 1978 movement, which accepted the leadership of Ayatollah Khomeini only in its final stages, succeeded in overthrowing the Shah. Hamid Algar explains that:

It seems to me that the most important factor in the process of preparation for revolution was the work of Dr. Shariati. Whatever one may think of this or that statement or doctrine of Dr. Shariati's, his achievement that cannot be denied is that he led back a large part of the alienated middle-class generation to an identification with Islam. Maybe their understanding of Islam needs refining, and in some cases correcting, but the commitment is there, and in many cases it is the single-handed work of Dr. Shariati.[53]

As great as Shariati's influence and imprint on the revolution were, it would be too simplistic to view him as the sole source of inspiration for all the participants. His subsystem, closely examined below, provided a set of categories, concepts and, consequently, a jargon and language which attracted a social strata who had never been interested in Islam as a tool for action. Shariati's appeal to youth and intellectuals convinced a great number of these social groups of the progressive nature and revolutionary character of the Islamic leadership. Shariati's subsystem broadened the social basis of the revolution and strengthened the Islamic Republic during its initial stages.

The framework of Shariati's subsystem
In his description of the nature of the individual, based on his understanding of the Qur'an, Shariati stresses the contradictory essence of man, who was created by God to become His inheritor on earth. Man is constantly torn between two innate contradictory forces. He is half-God and half-Satan. One force pulls him towards the base and ignoble element that he is made of: mud and earth, while the opposite force pushes him towards the highest and most noble of ideals which have been revealed to him by God. Shariati argues that since Man has been endowed with free will and volition by God, he is capable of choice and is thus responsible for his acts.[54] In Shariati's subsystem, the individual is a socially responsible actor whose decisions affect society at large: 'With every decision, it is as if a new law is promulgated for all humanity'.[55] The individual that Shariati outlines is both an existentialist being with all the anguish that accompanies it and a Promethian man with all the power that it implies. The individual is not a private being, but a public figure whose slightest gesture creates ripples among all mankind and contributes to the state of intellectual maturity of society. Consequently, the condition in which individuals find themselves and the political system which governs them are the direct consequences of their own actions. Based on the conviction that individuals are masters of their own fates, Shariati rejected fatalism and determinism, which were long associated with traditional Islam. The idea that man's position in life is determined by the will of God is viewed as the fabrication of those who wish to maintain the exploitative and oppressive status quo, because they benefit from it. Shariati lashes out against the upholders of the Islam which invites the believers to resignation and acceptance of their fate in life. The pacifying Islam which avoids confrontation at all costs and thus turns a blind eye to social injustices is

considered as polytheism, or *shirk*, concealed and veiled behind monotheism, or *towhid*.

In Shariati's subsystem, the individual is a socially conscious, untiring
revolutionary who either speaks out and raises the consciousness of the
people against injustice or takes up arms and fights. The ultimate model
is Imam Hossein, the *Shi'i* Third Imam:

> He has remained alone with empty hands. But the heavy burden of all
> these responsibilities rests solely upon his shoulders. . . . He is alone but
> in this school, a person who is alone is still responsible. In this school,
> a person who is alone also has responsibility to oppose oppressive
> absolute rule which determines the fate of the people, because respon-
> sibility is born from awareness and faith, not from power and
> possibility. Whoever is more aware, is more responsible and who is
> more aware than Hossein?[56]

Well aware of the outcome of his decision to fight singlehandedly against
injustice, Imam Hossein chooses to sacrifice himself and thus seeks martyrdom.

In contrast to Shariati's concept of human kind, Motahhari suggests
that all occurrences are subject to God's will. If an individual subjects
himself to danger and becomes injured, what occurs is in compliance with
God's wishes. If the individual avoids danger and saves his own life, that,
too, is according to God's will and his law.[57] Within Motahhari's
framework, the individual can choose according to his interests and since
social responsibility is not emphasized he can remain passive and
resigned. His social and political passivity does not come into conflict
with his status as a good Moslem. Furthermore, according to Motahhari's
subsystem, the individual who is responsible for correctly regulating his
relations with God and Satan is only expected to repudiate Satan and
embrace God.

For Shariati, however, being a believer is not sufficient since true convictions are tested only in times of action. Imam Hossein is powerless and
alone and the enemy is most powerful and ruthless, yet he cannot accept
the situation as God's will because he has a collective responsibility to
fight against injustice, oppression and exploitation. Shariati points out
that Imam Hossein accepts the challenge, even though 'All of the
custodians of intelligence and religion, advisors of divine law and
common law expediators – seekers of goodness and logic, all say "no"'. [58]
The criterion of assessment of the individual in Motahhari's subsystem
is faith in God, but for Shariati it is the praxis of the individual.
Pronouncing oneself a Moslem and performing the practices and ceremonies of Islam in private, which is considered as the fulfilment of the
individual's responsibility in Motahhari's subsystem, is not sufficient
proof of being a Moslem in Shariati's subsystem. Shariati's believer is a
committed political activist who fights for the attainment of an ideal: a
society based on Islamic equity, or *qest*.

In examining the relationship between the participants in his subsystem, Shariati refers to the individual and his role, but does not limit his analysis to the individual. It is argued that the Qur'an does not speak of the individual or one person, but it always addresses itself to the people.[59] Shariati argues that the trajectory of humankind's history on earth is predetermined. History is moving towards the realization of God's promise and will. God's promise is made to the oppressed and the dispossessed classes. Thus, according to Shariati's interpretation of Islam, social analysis has to be based on the examination and interrelation of classes. It is maintained that:

> Allah promises that He will rescue and liberate the victims of oppression. . . . The class of people who were always and everywhere deprived of their human rights will inherit the palaces of power, the treasuries of wealth and the fortunes of education.[60]

The concept of class as it is used by both Shariati and Motahhari is different from the Marxian usage. Neither uses the term to mean a concept determined by the direct relation between the owners of the means of production and the direct producers. Instead, for them, class determination is based on a wide spectrum of classifications: wealth, political power, social status, education, religious conviction and cultural tendency.[61]

In Shariati's subsystem, class struggle occupies an important position since the *mostazafin*, or oppressed and dispossessed, are promised to inherit the earth. Shariati does not specifically define the *mostazafin* as the workers or peasants, but uses the term in relation to all those who are not members of the property owning classes, in other words, for the masses. Echoing Marx's statement in the Communist Manifesto: 'The history of all hitherto existing societies is the history of class struggle', Shariati writes:

> The philosophy of history represents the eternal struggle of two contradictory forces, each determined by its class. . . . This historical class struggle – or historical dialectic – which started with Abel and Cain continues indefinitely.[62]

For Shariati, the dominant class monopolizes: the spiritual power in society, through the control of the 'official' religion and the clergy; the economic power in society, through the ownership of assets; the political power in society, through the control of governmental posts. Those who possess all these powers are the *mostakbarin*, or the oppressors and the proprietors. The struggle against the *mostakbarin* had been historically led by Prophets, who were socially conscious leaders. It is argued that such revolutions against injustice, despotism and exploitation 'will change the class relations and the "people" will come to power'.[63] By dividing Moslem society into two antagonistic classes, Shariati undermines the justification and legitimacy of Motahhari's appeal for a movement based on the participation of all social groups and classes.

Shariati's argument is clear: since society is divided into opposing classes with conflicting interests, the oppressors can never fight on the same side as that of the oppressed, irrespective of the cause.

Motahhari's argument is also clear: since society is divided between believers and disbelievers, all believers, irrespective of their social positions, can unite for the implementation of Islam. The two different political positions represent different philosophical foundations, one rooted in the primacy of class struggle and the other in social harmony among the believers. The one position which remains ambiguous, from a theoretical viewpoint, is that of Khomeini, since he invokes both positions within a short period of time. Prior to the victory of the revolution and during the initial stages of the Islamic Republic, Khomeini's most important leitmotivs were: 'All together' and 'Advance together with a single voice and a single purpose'.[64] In his declaration upon his arrival at Mehrabad Airport in Teheran, he says:

> I offer my thanks to all classes of the nation: to the religious scholars . . . to the students . . . to the merchants and traders . . . to the youths in the bazaars, universities, and *madrasas* [seminaries] of the country . . . to the professors, judges, and civil servants; to the workers and peasants. You have triumphed because of your extraordinary efforts and unity of purpose.[65]

Therefore, it would be logical to assume that Khomeini adheres to Motahhari's subsystem in relation to its view of the relationship between the participants of the system. The emphasis on a 'single voice' and 'unity of purpose' at the national level is not compatible with Shariati's view of a polarized society with two diametrically opposed voices and purposes. Yet Khomeini abandons Motahhari's subsystem relating to this issue and makes verbal use of Shariati's, even though the two subsystems are contradictory on theoretical grounds.

Shariati's Islamic justification for this radical position on class struggle in society is essentially based on the two concepts of *imamat*, or the vicegerency of the twelve imams after the Prophet, and *adl*, or the justice of God, the two principles of the faith that were formulated and upheld by the *Shi'i* as their distinguishing attributes. It is argued that with the incorporation of these two principles, *Shi'i* Islam assures that society under the leadership of the vicegerents, or imams, will be guided towards the establishment of justice and equity, or *qest*. Shariati refers to the example of Imam Ali, the Fourth Caliph of Islam and the First Imam of *Shi'i* Islam, as the principal theoretician of class-oriented Islam. According to Shariati, Imam Ali says:

> I accepted the Caliphite because it enabled me to return to the oppressed that which had been taken away from them, and it allowed me to put an end to the injustices perpetrated by the oppressors.[66]

Imam Ali's Islam is portrayed as a populist challenge to all vested interests and an invitation to rise and struggle for the establishment of an equitable social system. Shariati argues that Imam Ali's outlook and position cannot be considered as a manifestation of his private taste, but that of his thorough understanding of the Qur'an. It is argued that Imam Ali's interpretation of the Qur'an cannot be contested, since he was judged by the Prophet to be the most knowledgeable teacher of the Qur'an. Finally, to provide suffcient Islamic justification for his subsystem, Shariati refers to the Sura of Al Imran verse 21 in the Qur'an which says:

> Those who believe not in the signs of God and unjustly slay the Prophets and enslave those men who support justice are all similar and shall be punished.[67]

'Prophets' and 'men who support justice' are considered by Shariati to be those who are engaged in a class struggle against the oppressive and property owning classes, who do not heed the promise of mastery that God has made to the oppressed and the dispossessed. The imams and their successors have the responsibility of keeping the struggle in permanence until the principle of justice, *adl*, which includes equity and freedom, is thoroughly established in society. In Shariati's subsystem, the *mostazafin* constitute the class which stands to benefit from a society based on Islamic justice and, therefore, Shariati appeals to this class though, as it will be demonstrated, he does not have much respect for it or its decisions. In terms of the *mostakbarin* or *motrefin* (the oppressors or the proprietors), Shariati views their demise and destruction as a natural consequence of the rule of the *mostazafin*.

Initially, Khomeini adopted Motahhari's view, including all believers irrespective of their class in the ranks of the revolutionaries. Even non-believers who participated in the anti-monarchist stage of the revolution were considered as friends. During the aftermath of the Iranian revolution, Khomeini gradually realized that his appeal to all social classes could not be sustained, since implementation of Islam according to himself was alienating the middle-class professions, civil servants, the bourgeoisie and segments of the students, all of whom he had flattered and thanked on his arrival. Therefore, Khomeini adopted Shariati's language and began to use the class-oriented *mostazafin* and *mostakbarin* dichotomy. In his attempt to retain the support of his cultural power base, Khomeini referred to the *mostazafin*, or the dispossessed, as the main pillars of the revolution. He proclaimed the 'message of Islam' as 'the realization of the rule of the *mostazafin* over the *mostakbarin*'.[68] In a more revealing statement, Khomeini ignored Motahhari's statement that 'too much emphasis on the class origin of the revolution and the concept of *mostazafin* is deviationary and unorthodox',[69] and said:

> All heavenly ordinances which have descended have the deliverance of the oppressed as their objective. The *mostazafin* of the world should unite, rise and expel the oppressors from the stage, since the world

belongs to God and the *mostazafin* are his inheritors.[70]

Khomeini, the supraclass symbol of national unity, suddenly declared himself a partisan of the cause of the dispossessed class. Thus he seems to abandon Motahhari's position and embrace Shariati's. However, the terms coined by Shariati are abstracted from their internally consistent subsystem. The rule of the *mostazafin* implied an anti-capitalist economy for Shariati, even though he was never very clear about the practical specifics of his economic system. Khomeini's position on property and the rule of the *mostazafin* could not have been what Shariati had in mind. As far back as 1943, Khomeini had made his position clear on the topic of property and capitalism. He had gone as far as saying:

> You have justice when everyone is permitted freely to dispose of the property they have acquired by legitimate means and injustice when someone is allowed to transgress the property and rights of others.[71]

Khomeini uses the *mostazafin* and *mostakbarin* dichotomy to express his moral and spiritual support for the dispossessed. Yet he finds himself bound by the traditional Islamic interpretation of society as presented by Motahhari and is incapable of espousing Shariati's revolutionary subsystem which claims to hold as its model Imam Ali's economic system, explained as 'an absolute and authentic collectivist economy'.[72] Khomeini's emphasis on the *mostazafin* as the inheritors of the revolution was effective in maintaining the support of the urban poor and lower middle classes who were at least being addressed by the leadership, although not much was being done to improve their material conditions. Certain Marxist-Leninist and Maoist organizations welcomed Khomeini's terminology and interpreted it as his radicalization, since for them the *mostazafin* referred to the workers and peasants.

In Khomeini's book *Islamic Government*, which according to Hamid Algar was written between 21 January and 8 February 1970 (three years after Shariati had started his lectures and had introduced his interpretations), he addresses the issue of freeing the oppressed and deprived. It is interesting that he too describes society as being divided between the oppressors and the oppressed, but he does not use the words *mostazafin* and *mostakbarin*, which are used in the Qur'an and to which Shariati gives an economic colouring. Khomeini's analysis of the social policies of the Islamic state in this book, which is considered to be his programme of action, is very limited. He says: 'We must support and defend the oppressed and be an enemy of the oppressors'.[73] Mehdi Bazargan suggests that Shariati popularized the class-oriented concepts of *mostazafin* and *mostakbarin* which were alien to Islam. In an interview with Hamid Algar, Bazargan maintains that Khomeini was influenced by Shariati's use of the concept of *mostazafin* and adopted his terminology.[74] The adoption and widespread invocation of the cause of the *mostazafin* by Khomeini and the members of the leadership of the Islamic Republic is a clear example of how part of the subsystem is replaced by another when political expediency dictates. The eclecticism of the leadership becomes more transparent when Khomeini's deep-rooted differences with Shariati are explained. As Bazargan correctly asserts, Khomeini was neither very fond of Shariati, nor did he consider Shariati's ideas as totally Islamic.[75] Yet it is the pragmatism of the Islamic Republic's leadership that allows it to remain in power by co-opting, integrating and utilizing any momentarily suitable idea that is offered by Islam's subsystems.

Shariati and the clergy: monotheism versus polytheism

In order to understand the nature of a *Shi'i* subsystem in relation to the interaction of its participants, organized within institutions, it is necessary to examine Shariati's position on the clergy (*ruhaniyat*). Shariati addresses the issue of institutional religion and the clergy at four interconnected levels. He examines the theoretical position of the clergy in Islam; the type of Islam which the clergy created and continued to support; how the Islam of his time differed from what it should have been and the possibility of reconciling these two types of Islam.

From Shariati's position, in Islam, no special place has been designated for a mediator between God and man. Through the removal of the intermediary body, it is argued that Islam has freed itself from its subjection to an official religious institution. It follows, therefore, that Islam is not a hierarchical religion and that the performance of religious duties does not need the supervision or mediation of a specific official body. Shariati argues that because of division of labour and specialization, people could not afford time to learn all of the Islamic precepts which pertained to their everyday lives, so, consequently, the emergence of religious experts became a necessity. However, Shariati argues that official monopoly over religious matters, along with a concomitant centralization of religious power, creates the necessary and sufficient condition for the emergence of a 'religious and clerical despotism'.[76] He argues that a 'religious aristocracy' will inevitably lead to ossification and resistance to change. To maintain its own social position, such an institution will lend support to oppression and reaction. Shariati refers to the important role that the clergy can play in revitalizing Islam, but it is evident from his writings that he visualizes an Islam without the monopolized position of the clergy on religious inspiration and interpretation.

For Shariati, the clergy had actively participated in the creation of a religion which he considered to be polytheism, but masked under monotheism. He argues that an Islam which concerns itself solely with spiritual retreat, asceticism and mechanical religious practices which have become divorced from their intended social and political contexts is a polytheistic Islam. Even if it wages *jihad*, or holy war, and conquers in the name of Islam, builds mosques and holds prayers in them and upholds Islamic practices it can remain a fraudulent creed.[77] Shariati argues that polytheistic Islam as it is practised through the Iranian clergy provides a religious justification for the inequalities and the injustices that prevail in society. The clergy are accused of driving society towards the abandonment of its historical goal of attaining justice and equity. In this respect, they undo what the prophets and imams strove for. In the name of religion, people are assured that the status quo is ordained by God and it should be accepted as such. Polytheistic Islam is resigned and deceitful while monotheistic Islam or the authentic Islam encourages a critical social outlook. Shariati's monotheistic Islam is action oriented, aggressive and revolutionary, it has an ideal and provides a mission for committed Moslems. Polytheistic Islam is viewed as another state institution serving to secure the rule of the Shah.[78] To Shariati, the clergy were collaborators in the depoliticization of an essentially revolutionary doctrine: *Shi'i* Islam.

Monotheistic Islam can come into existence only when: 'oppression, capitalism and hypocrisy have been overthrown'.[79] In outlining his concept of Islam, Shariati begins with the causes of polytheism, which have to be eliminated if his model is to be realized. Shariati considers the root of polytheistic Islam to be in the absence of equity (*qest*). According to Shariati's interpretation, *qest* is related to the economic substructure and to attain a monotheistic Islam based on it, 'a social revolution in the system of ownership has to take place'.[80] To distinguish between *adl'* (justice) and *qest* (equity), Shariati indicates that justice belongs to the superstructure and reflects the legal codes which govern society. He uses an example to explain both justice and equity which form the basis of monotheistic Islam. If a factory owner hires a worker for an eight-hour day for twenty Tomans (an Iranian unit of account) and pays him his agreed wage at the end of the day justice has been observed. Shariati argues that *qest*, however, has not been respected, since contractually his wage is twenty Tomans, but the real value of his work is fifty Tomans. The worker's legal wage has been paid, but his real right has been usurped, since his wage is not equal to the real value of his work. Shariati says *qest* requires that another thirty Tomans be paid to the factory worker; *qest* is the worker's real share.[81] It is clear that Shariati is greatly influenced by Marx's theories of labour power, surplus value and rate of exploitation. In his simplistic and primitive outline of *qest*, a very rudimentary understanding of Marx's theory of surplus value can be detected. Shariati pretentiously claims that:

> The principle of *qest* is the same as that which Marxists think that they have discovered in sociology and that which socialists advocate. . . .
> It is clear that *qest* has deep religious roots and its realization is in accordance with God's will and all Prophets have sought to implement it.[82]

So the abolition of private property signals the implementation of *qest*. Shariati is by no means clear on what he implies by private property, whether it applies to all means of production or whether it could also apply to consumer goods. Shariati's knowledge of Marxism becomes more suspect when he assumes that monotheism, which seems to be the Islamic equivalent of a communist society, can be implemented at any historical period, irrespective of the stage of development of the forces of production. In this sense, Shariati's concept of monotheistic Islam is quite ahistorical, as much as he wishes to introduce historical materialism into his formulations.

In order to implement a monotheistic Islam, the revolution in the economic base has to be accompanied by a revolution in the political and ideological or religious realms. The political system which Shariati formulates as his ideal model will be addressed in detail separately, but on a more general basis, Shariati calls for the overthrow of 'despotism, militarism and fascism'.[83]

In describing the hypocrites who are considered as the third pillar of polytheism, Shariati refers to the: 'so-called spiritual leaders who consciously or unconsciously mislead people instead of guiding them'.[84] By identifying the spiritual leaders as a crutch which supports polytheism, Shariati prepares the ground for the introduction of his Islamic protestantism. Shariati argues that the two Islams, monotheist and polytheist, are antagonistically contradictory and cannot be reconciled. Subsequently, he calls for an Islamic renaissance through which the actually existing religious mode of thought will be subjected to purification. The object of such a movement would be to develop and present a socially problem solving Islam which would not be rejected by the intellectuals and the youth as an outmoded, superstitious and reactionary doctrine practised only by those who have no interest in the socio-political world around them, let alone a desire to change it. Thus as a self-proclaimed expert on Islam, Shariati calls for: 'the destruction of the religion which has ruled until now'.[85] Disregarding and ignoring the clergy and the *ulama* (the learned men of Islamic jurisprudence), Shariati appeals to the intellectuals to fight against the religion which has undermined the ultimate Islamic objectives of equity and justice. He argues that in the absence of an Islamic renaissance, the young generation which is already caught between the two unsatisfactory alternatives of a superficial imported western culture and an old-fashioned static religion would become further disoriented and succumb to the more attractive western doctrines.

Shariati's call for an Islamic reformation led by the intellectuals, with the objective of undermining the capitalist system, the conservative religious establishment and the despotic rule of the Shah, fell on the receptive ears of the Iranian youth who flocked to attend the lectures of 'the great teacher'. Shariati's popularity among the students increased to the extent that when Ayatollah Alameh Tabatabaie, a close intellectual collaborator of Motahhari, made a public announcement about his disagreement with Shariati's interpretations, they are said to have removed Tabatabaie's books from their library at Teheran University with the intention of burning them.[86] The clergy, who rightly felt threatened by Shariati's theories, reacted with a volley of accusations which ranged from calling him a Sunni to the questioning of his unorthodox and so-called Marxist-inspired sociological interpretations.

Shariati's view of the clergy is radically different from that of Motahhari and Khomeini who were both concerned with the position of the clergy in Iran and felt that it had to be reformed to successfully carry out its religious and political responsibilities. They were convinced and confident that only the clergy had the power, knowhow and ability to lead a social movement which would culminate in the implementation of an Islamic government. In his major political work, *The Islamic Government*, Khomeini criticizes the clergy for being constantly preoccupied with prayers and religious discussions which pertain to the trivial technicalities of Islamic duties. Khomeini's criticism is more of an invitation to dissent and outspokenness against what he considers to be policies that undermine the existence of Islam. Khomeini encourages the clergy to overcome their insecurity and apathy and to dare to overthrow the system because:

> Even though the foreigners tell us to stay away from politics and concern ourselves with religious affairs . . . you, the clergy, have to become the masters of all mankind, don't ever forget that you too can administer this country.[87]

Khomeini's criticism of the clergy is similar to that of a concerned father who wishes to see the ultimate success of his son. This type of criticism cannot be compared to Shariati's. Khomeini wishes to ensure the leadership of the clergy while Shariati seeks to prove that they are incompetent and can, therefore, have no claim to leadership. Khomeini's response to the threat of replacing the clergy with the intellectuals as the vanguards and administrators of a social movement based on Islam is clear:

> We need the Ulama [the clergy] until the end. Islam needs the Ulama. Without the Ulama, Islam will disappear since they are the Islamic experts and have maintained Islam until now. . . . Islam cannot remain safe with the intellectuals.[88]

Khomeini and Motahhari's disagreement with Shariati is not only on the issue of the role and significance of the clergy, but also on Shariati's anti-capitalism as the most important prerequisite for the realization of monotheistic Islam. The revolutionary aspects of Shariati's subsystem, such as his anti-capitalist, anti-colonialist and anti-reactionary discourse, which appealed to youth and broadened the Islamic base of the anti-Shah movement, displeased the institutional clergy. Ironically, however, it was the dedicated and voluntaristic high school and university students who became the instruments with which the clergy were able to overthrow the Shah's régime and establish the Islamic government.

Shariati's concept of revolutionary leadership and democracy
In his definition of monotheism, Shariati argues that 'despotism, militarism and fascism' have to give way to a political system which represents their antithesis. His concern and anxiety in relation to intellectual repression, indoctrination and unchecked political power exercised by

the Shah's régime, could lead analysts to the assumption that the political model that would stem from Shariati's subsystem would be based on respect for individual rights and political democracy. One could conclude that the antidote for despotism is participatory democracy, if one assumed that an anti-despotic movement would have to be democatic by definition. However, as it will be demonstrated, Shariati's deeply felt fascination with the implementation of an ideal Islamic model based on justice and equity (which to him presents universal and ethical principles of the highest order, which have to be imposed on society) pushes him towards an ideologically determined egalitarian dictatorship in the political realm. Shariati's political formulations are based on his assessment of two factors: the condition of the Islamic society as it existed and the responsibilities of the leadership which has to transform society into the ideal Islamic community.

Shariati's arguments are constructed on a sociological and religious basis. From a religious perspective, it is argued that the imams, who are the vicegerents of the Prophet after his death, have a clear ideological mission which has to be accomplished through the shortest route and at the most rapid pace possible. Their mission is to construct an ideal Islamic society 'as it ought to be'. Shariati does not provide details about this ideal Islamic society, other than that it is based on justice and equity The imam who is to lead society towards the preconceived ideal is neither elected nor appointed. Shariati argues that leadership or *imamat*:

> is an innate right which is the consequence of the nature of the imam himself . . . whether he is elected or not, or appointed or not, *he will be the Imam*, since he has all the virtues of being an imam. It is immaterial if he becomes the choice of all members of society or that of only a few.[89]

Through his description of the necessary conditions for becoming a leader, or imam, Shariati severs all the ties that exist between an elected leader and his constituency. The leader of the Islamic community is neither in need of the people's consent, nor is he, as a result, responsible to them. The imam is guided by the vision of a perfect society and equipped with a maximum programme which is based on a clearcut Islamic ideology. The imam's sole responsibility is to God. Shariati argues that in the process of reaching the ideal society, the imam is not responsible for the provision of welfare, happiness and contentment for the members of his society.[90] Yet he is directly responsible for the functioning and administration of the state and, as such, is in command of the economy, foreign and domestic affairs and the army. In sum, he is the head of the government, the chief ideologue and the national leader, with no accountability to the people. All sacrifices are argued to be necessary during the transition period. The goal has to be attained 'at all costs'. Based on his theological studies of *Shi'i* Islam, Shariati presents a totalitarian model of the political system which he holds necessary for the implementation of his version of Islam. According to his formulations, Islam as a universal truth acts as a totalistic ideology which has its own specific prescriptions and responses in relation to all aspects of life. Consequently, all individual and political rights must be subjected to the edicts and requirements of Islam to attain the predetermined state of humankind's perfection.

The totalitarian 'transitional government' that Shariati conceives of as necessary for the attainment of a monotheistic Islam is very similar to Khomeini's concept of an Islamic government. For Khomeini, too, the establishment of the rule of the *faqih* (the Islamic jurisprudent) obliges all members of society to accept his leadership.[91] The religious leader, according to Khomeini, has total control of all political, economic and social levers of power, without being responsible to the people.[92] The religious leader is placed in a position of responsibility because, in the absence of the Prophet, a religious figure who is knowledgeable about Islam's jurisprudence and is also just has to assure the implementation of laws which are in accordance with Islam. Khomeini adds that in an Islamic government people do not make laws and so political representation becomes meaningless, since God's laws are already available through the Qur'an. An Islamic government is based on the rule of God over men, co-ordinated and administered by the Islamic ruler.[93]

Shariati's sociological argument against democracy is primarily based on the experience of the newly independent countries after World War II. He refers to the Bandung Conference of the leaders of the non-aligned nations in 1955 and contends that the merits of democracy for developing countries were questioned at that forum. His argument reflects an elitist and paternalistic position in relation to the people, which does not tally with his populist pronouncements. It is argued that the masses in all underdeveloped and poor countries of Africa, Asia and Latin America are unaware, ignorant, conservative and decadent.[94] It is, consequently, deduced that such a backward mass would not be attracted by a progressive leadership concerned with the total transformation of society's old modes of thought, concept and ways. If the people were to vote under such circumstances, Shariati argues that their vote would be for ignorant and conservative leaders like themselves. Therefore, the principle of democracy is considered to be in contradiction with the principle of revolutionary change, progress and leadership. Shariati describes democracy not only as a weak political system but as dangerous and counter-revolutionary.

Shariati's contempt for democracy has its roots in: his analysis of the masses; his view of the mission and goal of the ideal Islamic society and the experience of post-revolutionary countries such as the Soviet Union and China. Both Khomeini and Motahhari share Shariati's disdainful view of the masses. Khomeini believes that 'the masses are handicapped, incomplete, and incapable of looking after their own affairs'.[95] Shariati takes Khomeini's statement a step further and says 'the brain of the masses is as developed as that of a primitive Neanderthal man'.[96] It is difficult to reconcile Shariati's elitist, one can even say, colonialist position – the intellectual's burden rather than the white man's – with his emphasis on the revolutionary potential of the masses. Either the masses are revolutionary or they are counter-revolutionary. For both Khomeini and Shariati, the masses are revolutionary as long as they are engaged in the struggle to overthrow the Shah's régime, but become conservative and even counter-revolutionary as soon as they bring the new leaders to power. This rapid change in the nature of the masses, which neither man attempts to explain, necessitates a rigid and non-democratic post-revolutionary régime which would guide or forcefully direct the masses along the 'correct' path.

In presenting a Leninist justification against political democracy, Shariati points out that the classes who have endured the real burden of oppression and exploitation do not have any patience for free elections and a pluralist democracy, which is the objective of affluent liberal intellectuals.[97] On the one hand, Shariati rejects democracy because it might interfere with the implementation of the Islamic ideal due to the decadence and ignorance of the masses. On the other hand, he invokes the will of the same toiling masses to reject political democracy. As contradictory as the two positions are, they are used to support an anti-democratic conviction. The goal of imposing the Islamic system irrespective of the will of the people is far too important to be compromised by the concern for political democracy and individual rights.

Finally, Shariati refers to Lenin's and Mao's experiences and seeks justification for his anti-democratic position by referring to their political decisions. Firstly, Shariati points out that once the revolution succeeds, a strong hand is necessary to: crush the counter-revolutionaries; destroy the old social relations and purify the moral and ethical fabric of society, through a 'brainwashing' campaign.[98] Secondly, Shariati claims that Marxism as a revolutionary ideology is, by its nature, against political democracy and finding solutions through elections and the vote.[99] Once again, Shariati's reference demonstrates his very limited knowledge of Marxian concepts. For Marx, the historical development of the forces of production determined the majority classes or class in society. The social relations in society were altered as new majority classes, fostered by the developing forces of production, made a social revolution possible and indispensable. Social revolutions are impossible without the participation of the majority classes. Even if a new set of progressive social relations is imposed on a society in which the interests of the majority classes require a historically inferior set of social relations of production, such a political act could, according to Marx, only attain the objectives of the social classes which make up the majority. Furthermore, Marx considered political democracy as a great advance over absolutism, since it allowed for a greater participation of the people in the administration of the state. Marx's respect for the vote and the majority principle which he always held is well reflected in his statement that:

> But universal suffrage is the equivalent of political power for the working class of England, where the proletariat forms the large majority of the population.[100]

Furthermore, when Shariati claims that one cannot leave the fate of the revolution in the trembling hands of democracy when the votes of the ignorant masses can be bought with a simple meal,[101] he thinks that a Marxian position would concur with his. Shariati overlooks the fact that for Marx, the Paris Commune of 1871 represented the model of a transitional society. Engels proclaims that the Paris Commune represented the functioning of the 'dictatorship of the proletariat'. It was the Paris Commune that held elections immediately after it had attained power and in the midst of civil and national war handed the power, which had been attained through a revolution, to the elected representatives of the people. Furthermore, the commune did not elect reactionary or conservative representatives, but individuals who reflected the progressive and revolutionary character of the majority who had participated in the revolution.

In explaining Shariati's subsystem, it is important to examine his view of the incentive system which motivates the participants to interact and function in order to attain the final objective of the subsystem. As a logical consequence of his position on the social character and responsibility of the individual in life, Shariati's incentive mechanism is, fundamentally, a collective one. This incentive mechanism plays a determining role within Shariati's socio-political framework. Shariati's primary concern is to fuse spiritual incentives with material ones. These two were traditionally separated by the clergy. The customary view that concern with worldly material life was unimportant, since it was the hereafter which counted, is considered by Shariati as an aspect of polytheistic Islam. It is argued that the philosophy of *ma'ad*, or the Islamic hereafter, does not negate the pursuit of material life in this world. On the contrary, the judgement that is passed on individuals in the other world is held to be closely related to their endeavours and activities in this world. Therefore, those religious figures who invite the poor and the deprived to accept their lifestyles as the price for attaining eternal well-being in heaven are considered to be deceiving and betraying the masses. Such religious teaching is viewed as an abuse of Islam for the benefit of the economic and political ruling classes. Shariati argued that inviting people to accept their destitute positions in life as God's will, God's test of their endurance and faith, or even God's love, purposefully diverts their attention from the injustice and inequity that exists within society. Within Shariati's subsystem, all are equal participants in society and are equally entitled to the material wealth of society.

Shariati's criticism is directed at such members of the clergy as Motahhari who argue that people should be content and thankful in face of difficulties and hardships, since those who are confronted with misfortunes are exceptionally favoured by God.[102] Through such an argument, Motahhari justifies social hardship and difficulties as conditions which are willed by God and recompensed with His favour in the hereafter. According to Motahhari, poverty cannot be associated with absolute misfortune, since so often wealth is said to have led to misfortune and poverty has bred well-being.[103] The orthodox argument, that the dispossessed should not seek to alter social conditions, since they will be well compensated in the hereafter, is in harmony with Motahhari's subsystem, which appealed to the traditional property owning classes who were satisfied with an Islamic justification of income and wealth disparities in society.

For Shariati, however, in a society where poverty, hunger and destitution exist, all members are directly responsible. The claim of not belonging to the exploiting classes does not absolve one. As long as the non-exploiting members of society refrain from struggling against those who are directly responsible for poverty and hunger, they, too, collaborate with the exploiters and uphold the system of injustice.[104] Shariati's concept of collective responsibility and his collective incentive mechanism express the rights and obligations of the individual in his subsystem. As much as the benefits derived from the establishment of a society based on Islamic justice and equity are collective and act as an incentive for the realization of such a system, the responsibility of establishing such a society through a struggle against all the forces that oppose it is collective as well: 'Because the way of Allah is the way of the people, it should be pursued collectively and not individually'.[105]

On the spiritual front, Shariati derides those pious religious figures who view Islamic practices as individual acts which get individual rewards for those immersed in their private relationships with God. According to Shariati, Islam has expressed its concept of collective responsibility through one of the most important duties of a believer. *Amr-e be ma'aruf* and *nahy-e az monkar*, which mean commanding others to follow God's instructions and forbidding them from what God prohibits respectively, direct Moslems to adopt active and vigilant roles in their community's life. Shariati argues that these inescapable obligations are Islam's answer to the passive and apathetic philosophy of those who invoke private obligations and incentives and hide behind the statement that: 'socio-political issues are none of our business'. This type of position is argued to be the main cause of social decadence, since it overlooks and undermines the collective responsibility of implementing social justice and the ideal equitable Islamic society.[106]

Shariati's revolutionary prescription for those who live in societies dominated by oppression, exploitation and underdevelopment is derived from his concept of a collective incentive and responsibility mechanism. The individual's choice is limited to martyrdom, or open and active intellectual dissent. The responsible and faithful Moslem, who cannot remain blind to his adverse and inhuman social environment, can either adopt armed struggle as a means to liberation or can disseminate the message of the revolution. The individual who chooses neither is regarded as an accomplice of the oppressors and exploiters and is, consequently, viewed as the enemy. For Shariati, the history of *Shi'i* Islam provides the best symbols of revolutionary struggle. Imam Hossein sought martyrdom and Zeinab, his daughter, took it upon herself to carry on the struggle through preaching about Imam Hossein's revolutionary actions and inviting Moslems to pursue his cause. The name and legacy of *Shi'i* heroes such as Imam Hossein and Zeinab, ingrained in the Iranian psyche through being an integral part of upbringing, was revitalized and given a new and more palpable meaning through Shariati's formulations. The factor that distinguished Hossein and Zeinab from others in the *Shi'i* world was not their piety, but their active participation in the revolutionary struggle. Shariati unearthed the heroes that had always existed, redefined their characteristics in modern terms, demonstrated their paths and offered them as a model. Shariati maintains that believers are on a par with disbelievers and ascetics with criminals once they refrain from participating in the constant battle between truth and falsehood. Shariati points out that Imam Hossein is present in every age and living among all generations, consequently, it is the responsibility of the conscious revolutionary vanguard to join in the battle and turn the tides.[107]

It is noteworthy that Khomeini's view of the role of the believer and his social responsibility in what he calls a 'corrupt environment' is identical to Shariati's. Khomeini explains the role of the believer as such:

A believing, pious, just individual cannot possibly exist in a socio-political environment of this [corrupt] nature and still maintain his faith and righteous conduct. He is faced with two choices: either he commits acts that amount to the antithesis of Islam and contradict righteousness, or, in order not to commit such acts and not to submit to the orders and commands of the *taghout* [symbol of despotism], the just individual opposes him and struggles against him in order to destroy the environment of corruption. We have in reality, then, no choice but to destroy those systems of government that are corrupt in themselves and also entail the corruption of others, and to overthrow all treacherous, corrupt, oppressive and criminal regimes.[108]

Khomeini, like Shariati, intends to jolt the people out of their slumber and encourage them to revolt by confronting them with a clear choice: if you do not fight against the status quo which represents the corrupt enemy, then you are collaborating with them. Shariati's use of this tactic was far more effective initially, since his audience were the easily influenced youth who were moved to action by such ethical blackmail. Once the Islamic Republic became well entrenched, it used the same tactic – presenting the people with a single political choice. Individuals, groups and parties either supported the Islamic government and its policies or were considered as its deadly enemy; there were no shades in between. This position was clearly geared towards the implementation of a totalitarian ideology which could not tolerate dissent and intended to rapidly separate 'the devotees' from 'the rest' in order to deal with 'the rest' appropriately.

The final objective of Shariati's subsystem is the creation of an 'exemplary community' based on *towhid*, or monotheism, where 'the structure of polytheism in human consciousness and in society is eradicated' and 'the three powers of "ownership", "sovereignty" and "divinity" are all found and invested 'in almighty God alone'. Such a condition allows the establishment of 'a society based on equality and oneness of mankind'.[109]

In his quest for the theoretical outline of an ideal Islamic society, Shariati indulged in a number of unorthodox interpretations which are worth referring to. Some of his controversial interpretations remain unaccepted by the majority of practising Moslems. Shariati does not believe that only the clergy has a monopoly over the explanation and interpretation of the Qur'an and the Sunnah. He explains that *ijtihad*, or independent judgement in the interpretation of Islamic law, allows for independent and unfettered research on religious issues, in order to arrive at new religious interpretations which are in accordance with and adapted to modern times.[110] Shariati argues that Islam has always been against blind obedience and imitation. He thus opens the way to free interpretation of Islamic law, disregarding the practice of receiving a religious education at the traditional seminary schools and writing a religious thesis, known as a *tagrirat*.

Following his own interpretation of the Qur'an, Shariati takes two very controversial positions. He argues that polygamy in Islam was conceived of as a solution to a social problem which existed at the time of the Prophet. The conditions for marrying more than one wife have been made so difficult by the Qur'an itself that if a man wishes to strictly follow its letter, polygamy will become impossible. It is argued that Islam allowed for polygamy because in the days of the Prophet, homeless single women and fatherless children would have become corrupted, if someone did not take care of them. Islam thus encouraged polygamy in order to prevent the moral degeneration and corruption of society. Furthermore, Shariati argues, the Qur'an clearly shows that if a man is incapable of establishing absolute justice between his wives, he should not marry more than one. The Qur'an says: 'Since you cannot establish justice, one wife will suffice'.[111] Shariati concludes that today the practice of polygamy is distasteful and worthy of condemnation and denunciation.[112] On this issue, Shariati clearly differs from just about all Islamic experts, who hold that polygamy is clearly and unambiguously allowed in Islam and the Prophet's practice proves this point. To the egalitarian and modernist Shariati, not only is polygamy worthy of condemnation, but so is the veil. He explains that 'the veil is a chain that imprisons and humiliates our women'.[113] However, Shariati does not seek to find justifications in the Qur'an in support of his position on the veil.

In Shariati's subsystem, the Islamic socio-economic elements that would assure an egalitarian and just society are far more significant than the everyday practices of Islam which are abstracted from their socio-political context. As such, it was natural that Shariati's subsystem should appeal to youth and intellectuals who sought an endogenous, radical and progressive ideology. His language and his concepts were too alien and, ironically, too westernized to be understood and absorbed by the labouring masses for whom he wished to create the exemplary community of justice and equity and in whom he had no faith or trust. It is not surprising that the political organizations and groups that adopted his subsystem were overwhelmingly student organizations. It was these same students who battled relentlessly with the army and the police in the streets of all the major Iranian cities, gradually eroding the soldiers' willpower and morale and realizing the Iranian revolution.

Yet Shariati's revolutionary Islam provoked hostile reactions from some of the orthodox custodians of Iranian *Shi'i* Islam. Much of this reaction was against: Shariati's so-called socialism and his position against property owning classes, with whom the traditional clergy had always had amicable relations; Shariati's anti-clericalism and his scornful attitude towards asceticism and non-socially-committed Moslems. Along with the orthodox clergy, the property owning and ruling classes had no sympathy for Shariati, who was educating and inviting his audience and students to revolt against the Shah's régime. In Hamid Enayat's succinct words:

> Whatever reservations one might have about the legitimacy of this [Shariati's] kind of eclecticism, one can have scant doubt that Shariati's potent mixture of dialectic and Islamic, especially *Shi'i*, ideals of social justice, have done more than any other form of religious indoctrination to make Islam the sole ideology of struggle in contemporary Iran for vast numbers of militant young people, who would have been otherwise attracted to secularist, left-wing doctrines.[114]

The contribution of Shariati's subsystem to broadening the Islamic base of the Iranian revolution and his introduction of terms and concepts that were later used by the Islamic government, when it shifted to verbal radicalism, undoubtedly played a most significant role in disarming and duping the left and allowing the Islamic government to adopt a pseudo-leftist posture when expediency dictated. The availability of the Shariati subsystem, and the Motahhari subsystem, allowed the Islamic government to borrow and utilize aspects of both subsystems to overcome the different problems that it faced.

Subsystem III: According to Navab-Safavi

Sayyed Mujtaba Mir-lowhi, better known as Navab-Safavi, has played an important role in the contemporary political history of Iran. His name and the name of the conspiratorial organization which he founded – the *Fadaian-e Islam* or Devotees of Islam – are associated with a series of political assassinations during Iran's stormy period from 1945–56. Unlike Motahhari, Shariati and Bazargan, the effect of his ideas and acts on any particular social class are not easily distinguishable or measurable. No major and visible social or political organization claimed allegiance to Navab-Safavi during the revolution. While Shariati's speeches and writings were being illegally published and sold by the thousands and Motahhari and Bazargan were articulating their ideas in speeches or published articles and books, the volumes of printed matter which surfaced rarely referred to Navab-Safavi. The dearth of Navab-Safavi's theoretical contributions based on Islamic research and free interpretation was compensated for by his resolve in applying terroristic Islamic justice, in order to pave the way for the establishment of a society functioning on the basis of the *Shari'a* (the religious laws). Access to Navab-Safavi's ideas is only possible through a short book called *The Revolutionary Program of the Fadaian-e Islam* and the numerous declarations and proclamations that were circulated under the name of the *Fadaian-e Islam*.[115] Navab-Safavi was a non-intellectual voluntarist who believed that when Islam was in danger, it was not scholastic arguments or debates which could save it. In his opinion, only the application of so-called revolutionary terror against the enemies of Islam would return society to its righteous path towards salvation.

Contrary to Shariati and Motahhari, who used scholarly concepts which required their own sophisticated terminology, Navab-Safavi's message was clear, simple and prosaic. The language he used was unrefined and fiery and, as such, it appealed to the common people (*avam*), who shared his concern for Islam and his anguish over the direction in which Iranian society was developing. Navab-Safavi articulated the anxieties and frustrations of a transitional class which was being uprooted from its traditional environment and transplanted in alien surroundings, where it was unable to adapt itself to the new socio-economic conditions and, consequently, remained incapable of identifying with the aspirations of any one of the established social classes. The customary model of life of this uprooted social group along with its social and individual code of conduct was being rapidly replaced by a dynamic capitalist system which imposed its own conditions on all aspects of life. Condemned to change, but unprepared for it, the *déclassés* sought refuge in the only sanctuary with which they could identify – Islam. Suspicious of change in general and of state-promoted change in particular, the agricultural workers and peasants of yesterday who had become the *déclassés* of today, constituted the main partisans of a formalistic and superstructural Islam. This type of *Shi'i* Islam was quite unlike the *Shi'i* Islam of Motahhari, Shariati and Bazargan. Their Islam apppealed to those members of society who had a fairly clear view of their own positions and interests and who, subsequently, identified with an established social class. The Islam of Navab-Safavi was change resistant, while the subsystem of the other three aimed at adapting Islam to the needs and interests of one or more different social classes which capitalism had generated.

Navab-Safavi's disciples were moved and excited to a frenzy by his dramatic accounts of how Islam was being trampled upon through the spread of corruption and immorality and of how it was the responsibility of all good Moslems to resist and roll back the onslaught of apostasy. The *déclassés*, who found themselves confronted with a multitude of complex and confusing issues in their new environment, welcomed an analysis which would focus on a single uni-dimensional factor as the cause of their misfortune. Navab-Safavi argued that social misfortune, corruption and vice were the natural consequences of a society which did not base its conduct on the teachings of Islam.

In his subsystem, the focus was on the un-Islamic practices that had come to prevail in the Iranian society and the danger they posed to Islam. The solution was to purge society of individuals who perpetrated un-Islamic and counter-Islamic practices. The key figures responsible for the de-Islamization of society were considered as sources of corruption and, therefore, had to be condemned to death. Although sympathetic accounts of Navab-Safavi's life, written after the revolution, have tried to present him as an anti-despotic, anti-monarchist and anti-imperialist revolutionary, the activities and positions of Navab-Safavi and his organization were not motivated by any of the above political considerations.[116] At various periods of his life, he took positions which could be construed as anti-monarchist or anti-imperialist, yet Navab-Safavi never sought to be anything but a warrior for his concept of Islam. The political positions that such a path imposed on him or the labels that others attached to such positions neither inhibited nor encouraged him. The pursuit of what he considered to be the objectives of Islam led him along different paths, which might seem contradictory to an outsider. It has to be remembered, however, that Navab-Safavi's simultaneous adoption of a monarchist and an anti-monarchist position seems contradictory only to those who view the individual's approach to the monarch as a central political issue. Clearly, for Navab-Safavi, despotism, monarchy and imperialism did not constitute fundamental issues. His attack on the Shah was not rooted in anti-monarchism as a principle, but, as will be shown, it resulted from the Shah's failure to fulfil the Islamic role which Navab-Safavi expected from an Islamic head of state. A genuinely Islamic Shah would have been just as dear to Navab-Safavi as a fellow clergyman. In his theoretical apparatus, no other criteria but Islamic orthodoxy determines the desirability or undesirability of individuals and ideas. In this sense, Navab-Safavi's subsystem is purely doctrinaire, since it is completely immune to the type of exogenous principles that crept into Shariati's and Motahhari's subsystems.

In Navab-Safavi's *Shi'i* subsystem, the unit of analysis is the individual, the Moslem. The individual is said to be confronted with two opposing forces in everyday life. Caprice and desire push the individual towards sin by justifying all that is evil. Wisdom acts as the guardian angel, reminding the individual that if he or she commits a sin they will be punished by God and condemned to eternal damnation. The individual is argued to be in need and in search of a spiritual force to depend on and have faith in. This spiritual force is God and the individual does not find inner peace unless the correct path, leading to the ultimate awareness of God, is taken. According to Navab-Safavi, the correct path to God is none other than Islam.[117] So, in order to prepare the individual and ensure the attainment of inner peace and felicity, Islamic laws and rules are required, to be applied along with the punishments that Islam imposes on various crimes. Navab-Safavi says:

The source of all decadence and misfortune is the absence of faith and an Islamic education. Iran would become a heaven on earth if faith and an Islamic educational system would come to reign in this country.[118]

According to Navab-Safavi, the only variable capable of transforming the Iran of the 1950s into a heaven would have been the implementation of Islamic laws and an Islamic educational system. This formula does not specify any particular economic or political system as the only one which is compatible with Islam. The imposition of Islamic laws on any socio-political system would be acceptable for Navab-Safavi.

In his writings, Navab-Safavi compares the Shah with the father of a family and urges him to acquire the qualities and attributes expected of the family head. He advises the Shah to act as a father figure to the Iranian people. A father to the Iranian people has to be a *Shi'i* Moslem and he should use the Islamic laws as a blueprint to rule and serve his people justly. Navab-Safavi concludes that: 'All the people of the world need such a father figure, whatever his name may be. Yes! the Shah must act as a father in order to assure his own sustenance'.[119] Navab-Safavi promises to support the Shah wholeheartedly on the condition that the Shah submits to the implementation of Islamic laws. If, however, the Shah refuses to enforce Islamic laws, Navab-Safavi threatens to kill him immediately. He never proclaimed that his concept of Islam was at odds with the institution of the monarchy. During the sensitive political period of late 1952 and early 1953, when the monarchy was under great pressure and Dr Mossadeq's nationalist government was in power, Navab-Safavi cautioned all political parties against any anti-monarchic agitations and activities and threatened that the *Fadaian-e Islam* would suppress and destroy all rebellious elements.[120]

In a similar way, Navab-Safavi's attacks on the ruling class were rooted neither in his enmity towards property ownership, nor in his anti-despotism. In an article on 'Islam and Economics', published in the weekly organ of the *Fadaian-e Islam*, *Manshoor Baradari*, the private accumulation of capital is viewed as necessary for society and it is maintained that as long as capital remains in circulation through investment or trade, profit accrued from it is justified and legitimate. It is further argued that all individuals are free to receive the fruits of their innovations.[121] Exalting the money-making mentality of shopkeepers, Navab-Safavi suggests that the frugal manner in which the grocer manages his store and accumulates capital should become a model for Iran's minister of economy.[122] However, he virulently attacked men of wealth and power for their moral corruption, decadence and disrespect for Islam and its teachings.

In Navab-Safavi's subsystem, lust and sexual immorality constitute the major elements which undermine the Islamic foundations of society. His argument presented is a simple one and the conclusions drawn from it are even more elementary. He maintains that sexual desire is an ever-present sensation which is constantly active among individuals. Every single part of a woman's body is believed to excite men's sexual desire. On the primacy of sexuality in the individual's psyche, Navab-Safavi does not differ from Freud, whom he had most certainly not read. For both men, the libido or sexual energy constituted the 'prime motor of psychic life'. Navab-Safavi postulates that the perpetual quest for satisfying one's lustfulness weakens men's nervous systems and reduces their capacity to fulfil their socially necessary responsibilities. The sexually exciting parts of a woman's body distract men and, as a result, it is argued, their intellect ceases to function correctly. Navab-Safavi concludes that men's mental systems are disrupted by the display and movement of women's bodies. If they are not protected from this evil, men will gradually lose love for their families, and will be driven to savagery and capriciousness. Then, with the destruction of the family nucleus, men and women will follow their animal sexual instincts and society will collapse into anarchic immorality, corruption and decadence.[123] Navab-Safavi presented a simple formula: public display of a woman's body is synonymous with moral perversion and social degeneration. Convinced that western societies were undergoing a critical stage of moral and social degeneration, he sought to protect Moslem Iran by speaking against the evils of westernization.

In order to uproot the causes of corruption and immorality, Navab-Safavi urges the use of Islamic laws which deal with the 'problem' of sexual desire at two levels. Firstly, once women are clad in an Islamic veil, which covers the entire body from the head to the ankle, leaving visible only the face, men's sexual desire will no longer be aroused. In Navab-Safavi's writings, unveiled women are referred to as nude women. Secondly, *Shi'i* Islam allows men to have as many temporary wives as they can afford. The Islamic institution of temporary marriage allows men to have numerous legal concubines in addition to their long-term wife or wives. The most important characteristic of a temporary marriage is that the duration of companionship is limited and determined by a contract approved by the partners. A couple can agree to any time period, from an hour to several days, weeks or months. Navab-Safavi maintains that temporary marriages would eliminate the cause of adultery and suggests that, according to the holy laws of Islam, respectable offices should be inaugurated in all Iranian towns and cities where noble and pure men and women can go to become temporarily married by conscientious members of the clergy.[124] His recommendations reflect his concern for a formal moral order in which puritanical appearances are pushed to the foreground as the solid proof of a virtuous Islamic society. With the application of the veil, an attempt is made to restrict and suppress sexuality. Yet, through the legalization and encouragement of temporary marriage as an institution, men's sexual desire is given unlimited scope for manifestation and realization. Navab-Safavi's ideal Moslem society is based on a duality: on the one hand, sexuality is repressed in public, while on the other, a social institution is created to give it free and unlimited reign within the privacy of the home. The observance of this double standard is viewed by Navab-Safavi as the key to maintaining a social order based on morality and decency. The moral crisis of western society can be avoided if the acceptable sexual relations of the private or clandestine realm can be prevented from overflowing into the public realm. Navab-Safavi does not for a moment doubt the validity of his assumption that men are perpetually obsessed with sex. The discriminatory nature of the veil and its implied injustice to women escape him completely, since the concepts of sexual discrimination and female sexuality do not even enter into his intellectual universe. Finally, the fact that temporary marriage is not very different from adultery or concubinage, except that the former recieves Islam's blessing, does not strike him as dubious or hypocritical. Navab-Safavi's logic is founded on the simple precept that whatever is ordained by Islam is, by its nature, beyond doubt or debate and the implementation of such ordinances is obligatory.

In Navab-Safavi's subsystem, the relationships are based on rigidly defined, sexually segregated models. It is argued that the most important functions of women are to procreate, rear the children in the best Islamic tradition and run the home. However, faced with the rapid spread of a capitalist economy which breaks the privacy of the home and lures women into the workplace, Navab-Safavi seeks to protect them from non-intimates (*namahram*). He stipulates that if women wish to work in factories or offices, an all-female place of work, devoid of men, should be established, where they can get down to serious work.[125] The same plan must apply to schools, where girls should be taught only by women and boys by men. Navab-Safavi maintains that all: 'fraudulent and deceitful excuses for the mixing and co-operation of sexes in all private and public establishments is motivated by lustfulness and immorality', and as such, 'it should be rejected and outlawed'.[126]

In his pursuit of a return to a moralistic Islamic society, Navab-Safavi holds that men and women should be segregated in all public places where the possibility of mingling exists. For example, he suggests sexual segregation in Islamic theatres and on bus lines.[127] His obsessive preoccupation with the role of sexuality in Islamic society cannot be found in any of the other subsystems analysed here. In his subsystem, the Islamic code of individual conduct, of which the women's dress code is one of the most important topics, is given a central and determining place. From this perspecitve, Islam intervenes and regulates the conduct of the individual, down to the smallest details, in private and in public.

While Shariati, Motahhari and Bazargan tried to adapt Islam to the newly evolving needs of a changing society, Navab-Safavi intended to stop the direction of change and lead society back to its closed and introverted pre-capitalist past. The resort to terrorism and violence reflected the frustration of the subsystem's adherents in the face of social and economic forces which were constantly relegating religiously dominated or related solutions and practices to the background. Navab-Safavi's subsystem represents a violent and reactionary Islam which contains many of the necessary attributes of a totalitarian system.

In his description of the ideal Moslem society, Navab-Safavi draws up an elaborate list of outlawed practices. He laments the proliferation of stores selling alcoholic beverages, adding that: 'One should spit on the European, American and the progressive Westerner, as the ignorants call them, whose non-stop use of this dangerous poison is an expression of their intelligence, progress and civilization'.[128] He then concludes that anybody who produces, distributes or sells alcoholic beverages should be punished according to Islamic laws, so that not even a drop of one of these drinks could be found in Iran. Opium, tobacco and cigarettes are also considered individually and socially dangerous by Navab-Safavi and he demands that their production, distribution and sale be stopped for good and that consumers of these products be punished. Gambling and gambling houses, too, are proclaimed illegal, since Islam forbids them. In Navab-Safavi's subsystem, novels, poetry, films, theatre and music are deemed instrumental in awakening sexual desire so they should be banned.[129] The only form of music that can be permitted in an Islamic society is the recitation of the Qur'an and the only films allowed are those which portray the history of Islam or have a scientific content.

In the ideal Islamic society envisaged by Navab-Safavi, life is divided between work, attending to the family and performing religious duties. It is argued that Islamic pursuits should permeate the workplace and, obviously, the home. Therefore, life in the multiplicity of its aspects becomes the perpetual experience of Islam. In one of his edicts aimed at transforming the un-Islamic society into an Islamic one, Navab-Safavi recommends building a mosque in every office building and factory, where communal prayers can be held.[130] In this manner, work is fused with religious pursuits. The remaining time at home with the family is also supposed to be spent on the religious education of children. For Navab-Safavi, a lifestyle which leaves extra time over and above that spent at work, with the family and in performing religious duties is dangerous. Leisure frees the imagination and allows the individual to speculate, question and pose problems. Navab-Safavi maintains that free periods in schools should not be used for fun and games, but for the teaching of Islamic studies, Islamic morals and ethics and the life of the Prophet. His subsystem is squarely based on a traditional pastoral or agricultural society in which the household awakens with the first rays of the sun and retires when the sun sets. In such societies, economic conditions do not allow much time for leisure. As long as religious practices and mobilizations occupy the short respites, people will be left with only one source of cognitive nourishment, that is, Islam. Since leisure and reflection could ultimately breed the seeds of agnosticism, a relentless drive to mobilize the masses around religious concerns during their free time becomes a practical necessity.

The appeal of Navab-Safavi's subsystem

According to Navab-Safavi's subsystem, Iran like all other underdeveloped countries was confronted with the scientific and technological power of the West, as well as its cultural values.[131] Navab-Safavi believes that if science were simplified and taught to students who had first received a thorough Islamic education, Iran would become self-sufficient and independent of foreigners. His xenophobia, like that of Khomeini, is primarily rooted in a hatred of epistemological competitors which might replace Islam. While Shariati faced the challenge of new ideas by incorporating some of their arguments into his concept of Islam, Navab-Safavi did not possess the necessary knowledge of the competing epistemologies to harness them; he, therefore, set out to destroy them. In a revealing passage, Navab-Safavi expresses his frustration and rage in the face of the challenge of Western ideas:

> You who are a misguided son of Islam. You who have seen Europe. You who are a mathematician. You who are weak and ignorant, you felt inferior to the Europeans as soon as you saw the colorful and deceptive appearances of the Europeans, you forgot all the illuminating teachings of Islam and all human virtues, you forgot all that the Prophet had done for you and all the sacrifices and the hard work that your Moslem predecessors had undertaken in order to keep the holy flag of Islam hoisted in the civilized world. You betrayed the memory of our Moslem forefathers who had freed the world of barbarism and ignorance. Why did you forget your heritage? Was it because of the novelty of the Gillette razor blade, the hair cream, the tie, the bowtie, the Western-style hat, or the word 'merci'; did the naked and lustful body of a Western woman mesmerize you or did you forget God who created you and Europe and all which is beautiful on earth just as soon as you were confronted with Parisian prostitutes who walk along the Champs-Elysees?[132]

In Navab-Safavi's subsystem, the model individual is one who mechanically rejects all that is non-Islamic or un-Islamic through blind faith and total devotion to Islam and to the clergy – the custodians of Islam. The blind rejection or imitation which is demanded is clearly not arrived at through a critical understanding of non-Islamic practices, since knowledge about alternative world outlooks could cause an attraction to them. Navab-Safavi was suspicious and distrustful of intellectuals, because their methodology was based on speculation and a thirst for knowledge, irrespective of its origin or tendency. The intellectuals' supposedly open approach to new ideas was the antithesis of Navab-Safavi's closed and xenophobic *Shi'i* subsystem, the legitimacy of which could only be defended by violence and the destruction of competitors. In describing the educated members of society, Navab-Safavi demonstrates his anti-intellectualism. He writes:

> Undoubtedly, three-quarters of all the educated members of society who are bureaucrats or professionals, are completely void of any respectable human virtues and they all possess the most despicable and vile human vices.[133]

Clearly, Navab-Safavi did not intend to appeal to the intellectuals.

In his assessment of social groups, Navab-Safavi considers the peasantry to be the most virtuous class in Iran and argues that they have not yet been polluted or corrupted and are yearning for the day when an

Islamic government based on the Qur'an is established. Modest shop-keepers and grocers are also considered the least corrupt of all classes. Navab-Safavi believes the the social actors least exposed to the social and economic relations imposed by capitalism are the purest Islamic ele-ments. As such, his subsystem appealed to those who were distrustful of the unfamiliar and alien socio-economic relations and morals imposed by the new ascending mode of production in the cities. As long as the peasants continued to live in rural isolation, they remained good Moslems, but they could not witness the gradual prevalence of un-Islamic ideas and practices in the cities and, consequently, they could not be mobilized into political activity against change. In order to become potentially active supporters of Navab-Safavi's subsystem, the insulated peasantry had to be pushed onto the urban stage, where they would confront the un-Islamic qualities that Navab-Safavi deplored. The significant wave of rural-urban migration that took place between 1966 and 1976 ended the socio-economic and cultural innocence of those who had been protected by geographical isolation. The migrant workers who had been brought up in religious rural families, operating under predominantly feudal relations of production, found themselves in a different environment along with a different set of exigencies. The small minority of migrants who were able to thoroughly adapt themselves economically and culturally to the system joined the rushing tides of change. Those who were not co-opted into the system found it and the classes which benefited from it repug-nant. Their ultimate goal, like that of Navab-Safavi, became the return to an Islamic society and the defence of Islam against all non-Islamic tendencies. The four basic principles of Navab-Safavi's programme provide a clear indication of his concept of a purely Islamic state. They are: the application of Islamic law in its entirety; the administration of punishments, or *qisas* according to Islamic rules and edicts; the imme-diate abolition of all un-Islamic laws passed in the Iranian parliament and an end to man-made law making; and the immediate prohibition of alcoholic beverages, cigarettes, gambling, prostitution, music, films, cabarets, nightclubs and 'nudity' (unveiled women).[134] In his testament before he faced a firing squad, Navab-Safavi said:

> In the pursuit of His cause, I tried to impose the reality of Islam on the whole world and free Islam and all Moslems from the clutches of ignorance, lust and oppression. I tried to realize the enlightened rules and edicts of Islam, and I tried to disseminate Islamic culture and knowledge to bring life to today's dead souls.[135]

The objectives of Navab-Safavi's subsystem, the realization of which implied an anachronistic, backward social transformation, on the one hand, and his conviction about the absolute truth and universal applica-bility of these objectives, on the other hand, necessitated conspiratorial and violent tactics. His fear of the spread of new ideas forced him to abandon all methods of conflict resolution, save the physical liquidation of opponents. Assassinations put an end to all those whom Navab-Safavi considered to be 'spreading corruption on earth', while dialogue and debate would have helped the dissemination of corrupt ideas. According to Navab-Safavi, anyone who stood in the way of implementing the Islamic code of conduct or who opposed Islam had to be assassinated immediately. He argued that all believers were responsible for the realization of an Islamic society and were, consequently, obliged to destroy and eliminate all those who opposed Islam. He supported his argument for the assassination of Islam's enemies and usurpers of the Islamic government by claiming that God condoned such acts, since their objective was the implementation of God's rule on earth. In an interview with a journalist who asked him whether terrorism was necessary for the implementation of Islamic laws, Navab-Safavi said:

> The word terrorism does not apply to what we do, since the social and individual sacrifices of the children of Islam who are willing to stake their lives for God and Islam are a defensive holy war [*jihad*] and we hope that soon there will be no more thorns left in the path of implementing the holy edicts of Islam and when such a day comes there will be no need for what you call terrorism.[136]

Thus, according to Navab-Safavi's subsystem, once a *mojtahed* gave an authoritative opinion, or *fatva*, proclaiming that an individual was a threat to Islam and that the shedding of his blood helped the cause of Islam, assassination and terrorism were not only justified, but became a religious obligation. Islamic punishments administered in the form of assassination became the cornerstone of this subsystem which held that vengeance in the name of God constituted a religious duty. The summary trial of individuals *in absentia* and the swift execution of the death penalty provided the 'defenders of the faith' with a power which grew out of the fear and insecurity they sowed among their enemies. In addition, those who died in the line of religious duty, by, for example, destroying an enemy of Islam, were considered martyrs worthy of emulation.

The politics of Navab-Safavi's subsystem

From Navab-Safavi's perspective self-sovereignty through the government of the people by the people is the outright negation of the sovereignty and government of God. The existence of Islamic laws renders law making by representatives of the people futile. Navab-Safavi argued that man-made laws can never be as correct and appropriate as those of God and that, therefore, the legislature should refrain from promulgating laws. He points out that parliament must become an Islamic parliament: the people's representatives consult only on the choice of the best Islamic solution on the basis of the Qur'an and the Sunnah. In other words, the legislature is forbidden to seek solutions which do not have some precedence in Islamic law, since all solutions are believed to be available in the *Shari'a* Navab-Safavi maintains that:

> The type of law which is the product of the rotten mind of a member

of parliament has no legitimacy in an Islamic country such as Iran, since it is in contradiction to science, wisdom and the holy principles of Islam.[137]

Navab-Safavi attacks the Iranian Constitutional Movement and considers it a fraud and an inauspicious plot. In explaining the manner in which the Islamic parliament should function, he maintains that elections for representatives should be free. However, he immediately adds that only *Shi'i* Moslems can stand for election. The choice is further narrowed by Navab-Safavi's stipulation that the candidates be 'honest', too. The decision as to who is 'honest' is probably left to the clergy, who have the knowledge and insight to pass correct judgements. Navab-Safavi does insist that: 'members of parliament should never utter a word against the interests of the Islamic country of Iran and their activities in parliament have to be supervised and controlled by the clergy (*ruhaniyat* and the *ulama*). Navab-Safavi's fear of discussion and the airing of new ideas forces him to demand a sealed-lip parliament, whose candidates are selected by the clergy and whose performances and activities are also placed under the clergy's control. Therefore, the contents of the discussions held by such an institution and of its recommendations remain totally Islamic. For Navab-Safavi, a theocracy is the only obvious political system which is compatible with a society which intends to impose the rule of God. He, like Motahhari and Shariati, adopts an anti-democratic position. All three men believe in one absolute truth. For them, the approval or opposition of the majority in relation to the teachings of Islam does not confirm or alter the justness of Islam. They view the opposition of the majority to the implementation of Islam as merely a reflection of the ignorance of the people.

Navab-Safavi's disrespect for the people's views and his justification of such a position is similar to Shariati's. He, too, argues that people who have been under the yoke of foreign cultures for decades are not in a position to distinguish what is to their benefit and what is not. Consequently, these people should be ruled according to the edicts of Islam, which will put them on the proper path to a healthy and ethical life.[138] On the value and significance of majority opinion, Navab-Safavi and Khomeini take an identical position, which, interestingly enough, is also worded in a similar fashion. Khomeini argued that if the whole world agreed on an issue which the clergy determined to be incongruent with Islam, the clergy had the responsibility of standing up to the whole world, since the legitimacy of the absolute truth – Islam – did not depend on the consent of the majority. Navab-Safavi took Khomeini's argument a step further, saying that just because Islamic countries have become strongly influenced by foreign ideas and have deviated from the correct Islamic path, committed Moslems should not passively stand by and watch the unfolding of events. Resignation before misguided majorities was not the practice of prophets; so, Navab-Safavi argued, Moslems should be ready to sacrifice their lives to oppose this majority.[139]

In his outline of the responsibilities of an Islamic press, Navab-Safavi does not even bother to pay lip service to a free press. In his direct and candid manner, he lists what the press should not do. It is forbidden to publish: dishonourable and sexually provocative stories, fables, humourless jokes, sexually provocative photographs and not so much as a word against Islam and Islamic ethics.[140] A tightly controlled press which would be managed by the clergy and thus become purely Islamic in content complements Navab-Safavi's drive to fill in all of an individual's possible weekly period of respite with Islamic ideas, practices and activities.

Navab-Safavi's foreign policy once again reflected his fear and dislike of foreign ideas. He, therefore, supported the formation of an Islamic bloc which would first protect itself from foreign intrusion and then proceed to spread Islam to foreign lands. In pursuit of his policy of insulating Moslems from the negative influence of foreigners, Navab-Safavi advocated reducing to a minimum all interaction between Moslems and foreigners. He maintained that Iranian students should not be sent abroad to study and that Iranian travel abroad had to be curtailed as much as possible. If certain conditions necessitated the departure of Iranians abroad or the arrival of foreigners to Iran: 'they had to be placed under close scrutiny and surveillance'.[141] In a passage on foreign policy, Navab-Safavi addresses the United Kingdom, the United States and the Soviet Union in the same tone, accusing them of having common interests and of acting against the welfare of other countries. Navab-Safavi's anti-foreign sentiments were not rooted in an economically based anti-imperialist position. He argues that since all three of these oppressive countries are controlled and conditioned by lust and worldliness their influence on others can only be negative and detrimental.[142] It was argued that widespread international relations had already damaged Moslem countries, through the spread of non-Islamic principles. Therefore, Navab-Safavi called on the rulers of these Islamic countries to purge their societies of un-Islamic elements, before aspiring to spread Islam.[143]

The ideas of Hasan al-Banna, the founder of the Moslem Brotherhood, or *Ikhwan al-Moslemin*, in Egypt greatly influenced Navab-Safavi. To familiarize the Iranian public with Banna's ideas, a translation by Navab-Safavi of one of Banna's articles appeared in Teheran's newspapers, along with a preface by Navab-Safavi. Although the terms 'imperialism' and 'colonialism' had been household words since the early 1950s, during Iran's struggle with the British over the nationalization of the oil industry, Navab-Safavi uses the word '*zede ajnabi*' (anti-foreign) when referring to Banna's movement. Navab-Safavi admires Banna's courage and strong will in his struggle for the glory of Islam, which led to his martyrdom. An important passage of the article written by Banna and translated by Navab-Safavi provides a clear presentation of both of their positions on the supposed threat to Islam and of their prognoses for the future of their respective movements:

> We Moslems firmly believe that Islam will undoubtedly be the victor and that Islamic governments and people will be liberated from the

destructive and ruinous clutches of the present civilization. A movement will be initiated by Islamic countries which will realize the
mission of the Prophet and will renew the grandeur and rule of Islam
all over the world.[144]

The most pressing issue from Navab-Safavi's perspective was the
launching of a two-tier movement which would first fight the wave of
apostasy which the present civilization had forced on Moslem countries
and then retrieve and reconstruct the grandiose and glorious Islamic
Empire of the past. Ideological purification within and expansionism
abroad constitute the building blocks of Navab-Safavi's subsystem. The
instruments to be used in obtaining such objectives were not important
to him, as long as the ultimate control remained in the hands of the clergy.
During his meeting with King Hussein of Jordan, Navab-Safavi reminds
him of his historical task as a Moslem. Contrary to the manner one would
expect from a 'revolutionary' addressing a king, Navab-Safavi's tone and
words were friendly and cordial, if only because the king was a descen-
dant of the Prophet:

> My dear cousin, safeguard and protect yourself, your religion and your
> people. Islam has to reach the glory and splendour that characterized
> the epoch of your revered great-grandfather, the Prophet.[145]

In 1954, in order to prepare the conditions for a return to the glorious
Islamic past, Navab-Safavi presented all Moslem countries with a plan
to strengthen the unity of all Islamic states. In this plan, he envisaged an
international council of all Islamic countries. Its duty was to supervise
and ensure proper implementation of the Islamic laws accepted by both
Shi'i and Sunni Moslems. It was to act as the defender of the rights of
all Moslems and was to become the nucleus of future industrial and
military co-operation.[146]

Iran's intention of joining the Baghdad Pact was opposed by Navab-
Safavi who warned against a military alliance in which the United States
and United Kingdom played central roles. He argued that instead of
entering into an alliance with non-Islamic countries, it was in the interests
of all Moslems to establish a defence and military pact among themselves. In a declaration, Navab-Safavi spoke categorically against joining
either of the two military blocs and defended the idea of an independent
Islamic alliance system. In supporting his 'Neither the East, Nor the
West' position, he argued that a powerful Islamic military alliance would
be able to act as a balancing force between the two major blocs and thus
assure an enduring peace.[147] The Shah, who had been restored to power
through the US backed coup against Mossadeq, did not heed Navab-
Safavi's warnings and under US pressure declared his intention of joining
the Baghdad pact. One day before his departure to Baghdad to finalize
Iran's membership, an attempt was made on the life of Iran's prime
minister, Hossein Ala. The assailant was Mostapha Zolqadr, a *Fadaian-
e Islam* member and ardent disciple of Navab-Safavi.

The traditional clergy who followed Ayatollah Mohammed Hossein Borujerdi condoned Iran's membership of the Baghdad Pact, unlike Navab-Safavi whose messianic voluntarism led to his separation from and final abandonment by the traditional clergy. As a clergy member his violent methods and unrealistic religious aspirations compromised the official institution of the clergy, which did not wish to provide the government with an excuse to limit or take action against its accepted activities, role and social status. Ayatollah Borujerdi, the highest Islamic authority of the time, was first and foremost concerned with attaining a respectable and prominent position for the clergy. He kept his distance from politics and was considered a proponent of the separation between politics and religious affairs. Navab-Safavi's infatuation with his own Islamic subsystem led him, and, consequently, *Fadaian-e Islam*'s members, to criticize the passivity and apathy of the clergy in general. They even pointed an accusing finger at the *marja-e taqlid*, who was Ayatollah Borujerdi. In the 'Revolutionary Programme of the *Fadaian-e Islam*, it is written.

> You who are the highest ranking *Shi'i* clergy [Ayatollah Borujerdi], whatever time you have spent for the cause of Islam, you have spent more than a thousand times over to secure your own position as leader and the highest source of imitation. If you feel the slightest threat against your own privileges and position, you will resist and make authoritative religious declarations, even if they end up being to the detriment of Islam. But if they burn and destroy the products of all the hard work and sacrifices of the Prophets before your eyes, you will not bother to move the slightest finger, unless your own position is threatened.[148]

Even Shariati had not made such accusations against the highest ranking clergyman in Iran. Navab-Safavi's vehement attack on a fellow clergyman of far higher rank was unprecedented. It was not until the Islamic Republic's denunciation campaign (carried out after the revolution with Ayatollah Khomeini's consent) against Ayatollah Shariatmadari, who was also a *marja-e taqlid*, that such an incident was to repeat itself. Neither Navab-Safavi nor Khomeini were concerned with, or sensitive to, the much-emphasized feeling of professional solidarity and hierarchical respect within the *Shi'i* religious community, especially wherever the observance of such matters detained them from doing what they perceived to be in the interests of the Moslem community.

Less than two weeks after the attempt on Hossein Ala's life, eight key figures in *Fadaian-e Islam* were arrested and charged with a series of assassinations of prominent Iranian politicians and with conspiracy to assassinate at least four others. Ayatollah Borujerdi expressed his dislike for Navab-Safavi and his subsystem by keeping absolutely silent during the arrest, imprisonment, de-robing (a most humiliating act when applied to a clergyman, as he is forbidden to wear the religious garb and the turban) and trial of Navab-Safavi and his disciples. If Borujerdi had intervened and pleaded for a pardon for Navab-Safavi as a member of the clergy, the Shah might have commuted his death sentence. Borujerdi's silence was a sign of his tacit approval of the sentences delivered by the military court and Navab-Safavi and three of his comrades were executed by a firing squad on 17 January 1956.

The socio-economic base of Navab-Safavi's subsystem

Navab-Safavi's subsystem appealed to the non-intellectual rural migrants who, as first or second generation city dwellers, could witness the economic and cultural transformations of a society which they could neither identify with nor benefit from. His simple message fell on the receptive ears of those who had been exposed only to a popularized set of Islamic values and ideas and who viewed apostasy and the abandonment of traditional orthodoxy as a cause of their own marginalization. All the elements of Navab-Safavi's subsystem had their roots in a common cultural past, in which religious formality held a position of eminence in society. His subsystem was characterized by: its unswerving intention of implementing the letter of the *Shari'a*, or religious laws; its call to all Moslems, irrespective of their class or political rank and position, to unite and rid society of all foreign influences, ideas and tendencies; its collective spiritual incentive system, in which every Moslem who sought martyrdom for the benefit of Islam was assured of God's love and eternal felicity in heaven; its collective worldly incentive system which guaranteed the welfare of all members of society once the law of God was imposed and its aim to return to the glorious Islamic Empire of the past, which had been initiated by the Prophet. The realization of each of these constituent elements required a historical retrogression and a thorough reorganization of society away from the gradual advances that were being made in the direction of plurality, tolerance and heterogeneity, towards a traditional straitjacket of uniformity, intolerance and homogeneity.

For Navab-Safavi, Islam was a totalitarian system, in the sense that it provided precise and inflexible instructions for the proper conduct of private, social, national and international life. The methodology employed in his subsystem to obtain the desired ideological objectives was in perfect harmony with the subsystem's unilateral and uni-dimensional world outlook. If the attainment of the objectives of Navab-Safavi's subsystem hinged on the cleansing of society of heretics and infidels, then victory could only be secured through the use of terror, intimidation and force. Force was viewed as a necessity, since time was on the side of the powers of apostasy and only decisive acts of terrorism could bring the progressive de-Islamization of society to a halt. The assassination of those who had acted as corruptors on earth was believed to plant the fear of God in the hearts of 'wrong-doers'.

The revolutionary, administrative, judicial and military organizations which came to power after the revolution functioned in a manner which reflects the degree to which those who participated in them were influenced by Navab-Safavi's subsystem. As was argued in Chapter 1, after the victory of the revolution, the great majority of those social classes which actively participated in the economy went back to their old employments, while the students went back to their classes. Only those who had not had secure jobs or specific skills were available to fill the countless vacant positions which were created by new post-revolutionary organizations. While the managerial and decision-making positions went to the clergy, which was gradually spreading its network of control over the whole of society, those who had constituted the socio-economically marginalized during the Shah's régime became the vengeful executive arm of the clergy. An understanding of the development of this vast source of bigoted militancy may be traced to the rural-to-urban migration trends of the thirty years preceding the revolution.

The characteristics of the rural migrants, their social and economic life in the cities, their acquired urban consciousness of inequality and injustice and the existence of Islam as their sole source of collective identity and weapon of defence against the inhospitable conditions of city life allowed for the effective mobilization of an obedient urban mass easily moved by religious leaders. This social group, in turn, enjoys the power it wields and uses it to destroy the awe-inspiring and intimidating gods of social, political and economic modernizatioin which capitalism imposes on a developing nation.

Julian Bharier suggests that between 1956 and 1966, the net rural-to-urban migration figure came to 1.68 million individuals.[149] On the basis of official government figures, Farhad Kazemi points out that from 1966 to 1976, 2.11 million individuals migrated from rural areas to cities.[150] Only a few major cities, such as Teheran, Isfahan, Mashhad, Tabriz, Shiraz and Abadan absorbed the great majority of these migrants. Kazemi concludes that: 'In 1966 about 40 per cent of Teheran's population was of migrant origin. By the 1970s the number of migrants living in Teheran exceeded 50 per cent'.[151] The flow of migrant workers into cities introduced an exogenous factor which, on the surface, seemed compatible with the interests of the emerging capitalist class which was in need of cheap labour. The maintenance of a reserve pool of unskilled and unemployed or, at best, a seasonally employed work-force made good neo-classical economic sense, as long as this pool did not become the means of overturning the whole apple cart. The migrant worker did not automatically become a member of the proletariat, since the rate of urban immigration outstripped the rate at which the manufacturing sector could create jobs.

The great majority of rural migrants were aged between 18 and 22 and were landless peasants or farm labourers. In 1976, the under-15 age bracket in Iran constituted 44.5 per cent of the total population. The migrants brought no skills or know-how with them which could be in any way useful in the city, or helpful in terms of securing jobs. Since only 20 per cent of Iran's rural population was literate in 1976, one can assume that a great proportion of the migrants was illiterate. Teheran's rural migrants can be categorized as either squatters who lived in shacks, hovels or active and inactive brick kilns, or non-squatters who lived in rented or owned dwelling units in low-income areas. Kazemi characterizes most of these communities as 'slums by common standards'.[152] The socio-economic position of the rural migrants was characterized by their irregular employment and their subsistence-level earnings. The great majority of the migrants who were unskilled and uneducated earned their living as construction workers, pedlars, petty street vendors, domestic servants or in menial positions in private or government offices. These activities, in general, fall under the labour-intensive, capital-poor, small-scale and unskilled informal sector, which forms a most important part of economic life in third world urban centres. The illegal side of the informal sector includes activities such as dealing in stolen goods, drug pushing, smuggling, prostitution and petty theft. It can be argued that the first generation rural-to-urban migrants found their employment in the legal informal sector, since entrance into the illegal informal sector required greater familiarity with city life values, morals and human relations.

According to Farhad Kazemi's study, in 1977, 48.2 per cent of the non-squatting migrants 'worked in various low level jobs in the private sector'.[153] He does not describe the type of employment in this sector, but it would be safe to assume that the activities of the majority in this group fall within the informal sector. Kazemi categorizes 7.5 per cent of his sample as 'unemployed or unable to work', 12.1 per cent as government or public agency workers or labourers, 13.3 per cent as government or public agency employees or minor civil servants, 17 per cent as independent workers and 10.9 per cent as foremen.[154] The only categories which can be considered to be comprised of fairly regular wage earners are those of government employee, independent worker and foreman. These groups constitute 32.2 per cent of the non-squatting migrants, who are employed as semi-skilled masons, house painters, office doormen, couriers and so on. It would be safe to classify 67 per cent of the non-squatting rural migrants as a fluid work-force without regular or secure jobs, scraping a living at the margins of society. Farhad Kazemi says: 'Compared with the squatters, these [non-squatting] migrants are better off both occupationally and in terms of their earned incomes. Their lifestyles, however, are not above the subsistence level'.[155]

As long as the poor rural migrants remained outside the mainstream of economic activity, they were unintegrated within the social classes which were taking form and expanding in Iranian cities, they were: 'Living on the crumbs of society, people without a definite trade, vagabonds, *gens sans feu et sans aveu*'.[156] The free-floating, amorphous body which Marx called the lumpenproletariat found its recruits among the poor rural migrants and the informal sector. The material and psychological conditions of the rural migrants, characterized by poverty, deprivation, inaccessibility to urban services, social and economic marginalization, low literacy levels, low political awareness, envy of the 'haves' and hatred for all those individuals and institutions which denied them access to an equal share of social wealth, transformed this social group into a potent and lethal socio-economic force. While the Shah's government viewed independent professional, social and political associations and organizations as a threat to the stability of the nation and moved to disband or co-opt them, the poor rural migrants established and strengthened their ties through religious associations called *hey'ats*. It can be argued that of all the social groups that sought to organize themselves during the revolution, ironically enough, only the loosely defined lumpenproletariat had effectively participated in organized associations, such as *hey'ats*, under the Shah's régime.

Shi'i Islam provided the only refuge for those who where largely rejected and atomized both economically and socially. Finding themselves in an alien cultural environment, the migrant workers maintained their sanity by organizing around Islam – their sole source of identification. Arranged on the basis of common geographical or ethnic origin, *hey'ats* became the poles of attraction for all migrant workers, new and old, first generation and second generation. In these religious associations, members listened to religious sermons, participated in religious discussions and raised religious questions about their everyday concerns and duties. These associations, which met regularly, were a means of socialization. Furthermore, the *hey'at* safeguarded dearly cherished rural customs against urban apostasy. The more established migrant workers kept in touch with and helped new migrants who came from the same geographical regions or villages as themselves. Through the *hey'at* rural relations and values were reproduced as much as possible in urban surroundings. The highlight of the *hey'ats'* activities was the performance of a ritual during the month of Moharram when each demonstrated its geographically or ethnically specific manner of mourning the martyrdom of Imam Hossein in Karbala in AD 680. The *hey'ats* in Teheran usually dispatched their mourning groups (*dasteh*), in a procession to the streets and particularly to the main bazaar of Teheran, where each group chanted religious hymns and songs, while they flagellated themselves in Imam Hossein's memory. The show of force demonstrated by the mobilization, organization and passionate zeal of the members of different religious associations during the days of Ashura and Tassua inspired awe even under the Shah's régime. Many parts of these ceremonies, such as cutting one's scalp with long knives followed by bleeding and, sometimes, fainting, were outlawed, and the duration of these rites was reduced to the two days of Ashura and Tassua and took place under tight police control and supervision.

These religious associations provided the ideal channel through which the clergy could mobilize the rural migrants. While the Islamic propertied classes were reached through mosques and, consequently, in Motahhari's subsystem the mosque remained the most effective communication channel, in Navab-Safavi's subsystem the *hey'at* became the means of establishing an institutional bridge between the poor rural migrants and *Shi'i* Islam. It should be remembered that for Shariati's subsystem, the *hosseinieh* constituted the institutional platform from which *Shi'i* Islam was disseminated. The *hey'at* presented a potentially powerful political fulcrum, since, ironically enough, the rural migrant members were generally devoid of any political awareness and believed in the righteousness and wisdom of the clergy who addressed their problems and soothed their anguish. Through the *hey'at*, the political force of the rural migrants was harnessed by the clergy. In return for the spiritual service which the clergy rendered to the rural migrants, they received the unquestioning and wholehearted political support of a relatively impoverished mass that had nothing to lose and everything to gain from an Islamic revolution. In a 1974 interview, a 21-year-old man, from a family living in a squatter settlement, provides a clear explanation of the political importance of *hey'ats*:

> Nothing brings us together more than our love for Imam Hossein. My personal view is that these *hey'ats* have a positive aspect in uniting us and keeping us informed about each other's affairs. But gatherings alone are not enough. I told our *hey'at*: 'What is the point of killing Imam Hossein every year and then mourning his death? We also have Mohammed and Ali whose words are worth billions.' I gave examples from our religous books, *Nahaj al-Balaqih* and *Nahaj-al-Fasahih*, and pointed out that they should follow their orders.[157]

Against the secular, decadent, unequal, competitive and intimidating social and productive relations of the dominant capitalist system, the *hey'at* provided a safe Islamic defence mechanism. Under the protection of the Islamic shield, however, the poor rural migrants learnt to view the implementation of Islamic laws as the only solution for their socio-economic and psychological problems. Many of the Islamic Republic's present prominent political figures were speakers and performers at these *hey'ats*. In 1971, Hojatolislam Hashemi-Rafsanjani, who is today one of Iran's most powerful politicians, used to address the *hey'at* of the '*Ansar al-Hossein*' on Fridays.[158]

The rural migrants shared Navab-Safavi's dislike of the dominant western culture which rendered them foreigners in their own country. For them, the choice was between Islam, to which they were accustomed, and cultural isolation accompanied by social marginalization. Once the clergy in the *hey'ats*, who had the confidence of the rural migrants, argued that the Shah was not a Moslem, since he had committed 'atrocities' against Islam and was responsible, along with his entourage of un-Islamic characters, for social decadence and the economic poverty of the masses, the urban poor responded favourably to what was expected of them. Challenging the authority of the Shah in the name of Islam, among those for whom Islam was an undisputable universal truth, unleashed the blind zeal which had moved these same people to engage in self-flagellation and the cutting of their own scalps. This social group's zeal and sense of vengeance became instrumental in shaping and directing the revolution. From this rich source of manpower, the Islamic régime recruited its dedicated shock troops, who repressed all dissent at the order of the ruling clergy.

Navab-Safavi's call for rapid and categorical Islamic justice was echoed in the performance of the post-revolution Islamic revolutionary courts. He wrote:

> Yes, Islamic law pertaining to punishments has to be implemented to
> the last detail. The hands of the common thief have to be amputated,
> the adulteress has to be whipped in public, and every criminal has to
> be dealt with according to the laws of Islam, so that crime and
> corruption can be uprooted and destroyed. All should be summoned
> to the Great Islamic Court without exception, and their records should
> be examined without exception. The Holy Islamic Laws should judge
> the Shah, the ministers, the porter, the roadsweeper, the judge and the
> minister of war.[159]

The quick and indiscriminate meting out of death sentences by the
Islamic revolutionary courts can, to a large extent, be accounted for by the
prevalence of Navab-Safavi's concept of swift and exemplary physical
elimination of Islam's enemies. As Hamid Enayat points out: 'the
judicial philosophy of the revolutionary regime of the Islamic Republic
of Iran can be put down in no small measure to the Devotees' [*Fadaian-
e Islam*] concept of Islamic justice'.[160]

The influence of Navab-Safavi's subsystem on prominent leaders of
the Islamic Republic is particularly noteworthy. It can be argued that the
similarity, on certain issues, of Khomeini's and Navab-Safavi's views,
makes allegiance to both men very easy. Shaykh Sadeq Khalkhali was
appointed by Khomeini as the first prosecutor-general of the Islamic
revolution. Khalkhali, who made a name for himself as the hanging
judge, has always taken great pride in his summary style of sentencing
and executing. His many victims were called 'corruptors on earth'; they
had to be put to death in order to purify Islamic society. Khalkhali claimed
the support of the poor and the dispossessed, who, in his opinion, eagerly
awaited the 'revolutionary' punishment and execution of all wrong-
doers. After the revolution, the *Fadaian-e Islam* began their political
activities and Khalkhali proclaimed himself the new leader of the
organization. Thus the most instrumental post-revolutionary judicial
position was placed in the hands and under the direct influence of an
individual who considered himself a disciple of Navab-Safavi's subsystem. Khalkhali's religious justifications and his self-righteous attitude
towards successive executions transformed murder into a virtuous act of
Islamic justice. The marginalized and unfavoured social groups were
moved to a frenzy by Khalkhali's morbid horror show and thus became
indirect accomplices in an unprecedented blood-letting, to which the
revolutionary left gave its explicit support. In a revealing statement,
Khalkhali explained his method of administering Islamic justice:

> In the revolutionary courts, we worked around the clock and sent the
> 'corruptors on earth' before firing squads. I knew that this wave [of
> mass hysteria] would recede and that they would limit our activities,
> therefore while we had the opportunity and the time, I did not heed to
> anyone and with the decree that I had [from Khomeini] I executed them

all for their crimes. According to the letter of the Qur'an they were 'corruptors on earth' and had to be killed.[161]

Mohammed Ali Rajaee, who became the second prime minister and later the second president of the Islamic Republic, was always candid about his close affinity with the ideas of Navab-Safavi and *Fadaian-e Islam*. Rajaee, whose prime ministership was the result of a long struggle between President Bani-Sadr and the Islamic parliament, was the candidate of the Islamic Republic Party (IRP), which dominated parliament. Rajaee's lifestyle and the reasons for his attraction to the ideas of the *Fadaian-e Islam* provide an interesting example of the pattern by which poor rural migrants gravitated towards Navab-Safavi's subsystem. Rajaee was born in Qazvin in 1933. He came to Teheran at the age of 13 to earn a living. Rajaee recalls that: 'As a result of abject poverty, I worked as a street vendor, selling aluminium goods in the poor squatter districts of Southern Teheran'.[162] He came into contact with the *Fadaian-e Islam* during the 1950s and continued his collaboration with them even when he worked in the imperial airforce as a low-ranking technician. Rajaee writes:

> I became familiar with and attracted to the ideas of the Devotees of Islam [*Fadaian-e Islam*], and I can say that the religious ideas that are being pronounced today in the highest religious circles were developed and disseminated by the Devotees of Islam in those days. It would probably interest you to know that one of their slogans was the call for the immediate implementation of Islamic laws, down to their finest detail.[163]

Later, after Navab-Safavi's death and the suppression of the *Fadaian-e Islam*, Rajaee joined Mehdi Bazargan's Iran Freedom Movement. As will be shown in the last part of this chapter, Mehdi Bazargan's Islamic subsystem differs considerably from Navab-Safavi's. The influence of Navab-Safavi's passionate Islamic message is clearly echoed in Rajaee's vision of an ideal Islamic society, in which social relations and individual behaviour are co-ordinated and regulated according to Islamic laws and ordinances. Rajaee symbolized the devoted Moslem leader who had risen from the poor rural migrants. He represented the simplicity, hatred, intolerance and preoccupations of this social group and consequently benefited from its support, since they saw in him what they themselves could eventually become in the Islamic Republic, something which was impossible in the Shah's régime. Rajaee's xenophobia and his populist statements about the threat posed by non-Islamic ideas to the creation of an Islamic society endeared him to those who were undergoing a social and economic rebirth as first-class citizens, due to the needs and policies of the Islamic Republic. Rajaee revived Navab-Safavi's old objectives, saying:

We are the devotees of Imam Khomeini and members of the Islamic community. If the realization of Islam and the goals of the Islamic revolution require the sacrifice of our lives, then death will become our greatest hope and desire.[164]

The last issue which must be addressed in relation to Navab-Safavi's subsystem is the noteworthy similarity that exists between the ideas expressed within that subsystem and those voiced by Ayatollah Khomeini. It was not accidental that Rajaee and Khalkhali, who considered themselves devoted disciples of Navab-Safavi, were given sensitive positions which led to their control of the judiciary and the executive.

In 1943, two years before the conspiratorial organization *Fadaian-e Islam* was officially born, Khomeini made his views public in a book called *Kashf al-Asrar* (Revealing the Secrets). In the book, he deals with three important issues in which his opinions seem to be identical to those of Navab-Safavi. Firstly, Khomeini argues that a government becomes legitimate when it accepts the rule of God: 'Whose every act is just and whose right is to rule over the whole world and all the particles of existence'.[165] The manner in which the law of God can be established is through the implementation of the *Shari'a*. Khomeini argues that all laws contrary to the *Shari'a* should be proclaimed null and void, because 'it is only the law of God that will always stay valid and immutable in the face of changing times'.[166] Once Islamic laws were enforced: 'everyone in the country would unite in harmony and the country would move forward with the speed of lightening'.[167] Thus, according to Khomeini, the political form of government, whether it was a monarchy, republic, democracy or dictatorship, was not a crucial point, as long as the *Shari'a* was implemented. It would be safe to say that Khomeini, like Navab-Safavi and Motahhari, would have accepted the monarchy and the Shah had the latter agreed to the implementation of the *Shari'a*. The same thing cannot be said of Shariati.

Secondly, Khomeini is very clear about the Islamic society which he envisions. The community's purification of all tendencies and traits alien to Islam is explicit in his formulations. As with Navab-Safavi, the imposition of Islamic laws provides an ideal excuse for Khomeini to mould society in the shape and form that he wishes. For both men, Islam represented a totalitarian force which subordinated every aspect of the citizen's material and spiritual life to a preconceived straitjacket. Khomeini points out that the implementation of the *Shari'a* will usher in the ideal Islamic state, since it will put an end to 'lechery, treachery, music, dancing and a thousand other varieties of corruption'.[168] Khomeini, too, holds foreigners responsible for leading Moslems astray. He accuses them of 'stealing from the misled Moslems their reason and intelligence'. For Khomeini, the abandonment of the traditional way of life and the embracement of any aspect of Western civilization presents a threat to Islam, which constitutes the most important cornerstone of Iranian traditional life. Khomeini lashes out at those who adopt a Western style of dress and in a tone resembling Navab-Safavi's he condemns those who wear 'European-style hats'. Khomeini's attack is directed against secularism. He scorns the intellectuals for popularizing Western ideas and renouncing their own Islamic culture. He argues that: 'intellectuals think that if we abandon religion, we will advance and catch up with Europe, but they do not realize that what Europe has to offer is not civilization but savagery'.[169] Navab-Safavi's anti-intellectualism is well paralleled by Khomeini's dislike and distrust of intellectuals. Both men view intellectuals as proponents of non-Islamic ideas, the spread of which would ultimately undermine the Islamic value structure of the people. Thirdly, Khomeini warns that these:

> idiotic and treacherous rulers, these officials – high and low – these reprobates and smugglers must change in order for the country to change. Otherwise you will experience worse times than these, times so bad that the present will seem like paradise by comparison.[170]

As much as Khomeini might have wished to pass a verdict on these 'treacherous rulers', he refrained from condemning them to death until much later. It was some thirty years later that he finally wrote, in his book *The Government of God*: 'Corruption on earth has to be eradicated and its perpetrators should meet their fate'.[171]

It was not until after the victory of the revolution that Khomeini demonstrated the degree to which he was in agreement with Navab-Safavi's opinion that all those who stood in the way of Islam had to be executed. It is important to understand that the *Fadaian-e Islam* must have been highly respected by all those doctrinaire Moslems who wished to see Iranian society purged of all the key figures who supported the secularization and westernization drive. Khomeini found that he shared more than a few characteristics with Navab-Safavi and that this endeared Navab-Safavi to him. Both men detested secularization, intellectuals and foreign ideas that challenged the universal truth and applicability of Islam; both were genuinely concerned with the implementation of a predominantly superstructural Islam; both were dogmatic about their religious ideas and intolerant of dissent and 'deviation'; both were courageous in defending their ideas and both derived their strength from their decisiveness which was, in turn, rooted in their uni-dimensional world outlook.

Khomeini wrote his book, *Revealing the Secrets*, in 1941, to challenge and refute a book called *The Thousand Year Old Secrets* written by Ali-akbar Hakamizadeh. It is believed that Hakamizadeh belonged to Ahmad Kasravi's reformationist movement, which attacked religious superstition and the clergy's conservative role in misguiding the public. Navab-Safavi left his religious studies in Najaf and returned to Iran in order to organize the assassination of Ahmad Kasravi, who became the first victim of the *Fadaian-e Islam*. Both men considered Kasravi to be a deviationist and a heretic who was polluting the minds of believers and ultimately obstructing the implementation of the *Shari'a*. Mohammed Khorassani writes: 'Certainly one of those ardent supporters of the Devotees of Islam [*Fadaian-e Islam*] was Imam Khomeini, who maintained his relation with them away from the eyes of the public and in an inconspicuous manner'.[172]

Subsystem IV: According to Mehdi Bazargan

On 1 February 1979, Iran entered a transitional and unstable period of dual power. Shahpour Bakhtiar, the Shah's last prime minister, based his claim to legitimacy on the mandate he had received from parliament and on the support of the army, which had remained loyal. Khomeini, however, was impatient to see his broad-based popular support transformed into legal state power and, in a political move aimed at forcing Bakhtiar to relinquish the fulcrums of state power, he appointed Mehdi Bazargan as prime minister of the provisional government. In a decree addressed to Bazargan, Khomeini wrote:

> On the basis of the trust that I have in your resolute devotion to the doctrine of Islam and the information that I have concerning your past Islamic and nationalist struggles . . . I appoint you as the prime minister of the provisional government so that you may proceed with: administering the country; holding a referendum which would appeal to the popular vote of the whole nation in order to transform the political system of the country into an Islamic Republic; the creation of a constitutional assembly which would ratify the new constitution and the new system; and finally the election of the representatives of the people to the Parliament, on the basis of the new constitution.[173]

Bazargan was no newcomer to the Iranian political scene. In 1952, as the first president of the board of directors of the nationalized Iranian Oil Company, Bazargan made a name for himself as an honest and capable nationalist. After the fall of Mossadeq's government in the same year, Bazargan joined the National Resistance Movement (NRM), or *Nehzate Moqavemate Melli*, which had been formed to pursue the goals of Mossadeq's nationalist movement. The NRM sought to reinstate national sovereignty, continue the struggle against British, Soviet and US colonialism and to oppose puppet régimes and their corrupt elements.[174] It was a broadly based coalition composed of different Mossadqist parties and an influential religious wing which had remained faithful to Mossadeq. It has even been argued that the Islamic tendency within the NRM was hegemonic and that the majority of its organizers, supporters and activists held firm Islamic convictions.[175]

In the aftermath of the coup against Mossadeq which brought the Shah back to power, all voices of dissent were silenced and all opposition parties and newspapers were outlawed. It was under these conditions that the NRM invited the people to change their resigned and apathetic stance. The NRM intended to transform the atmosphere of political reticence that prevailed by informing the people through its clandestine publications, by encouraging them to participate in the political process by voting in elections and by mobilizing them by calling strikes. However, the NRM never rejected the Iranian constitution, which legitimized the position of the Shah. It maintained that while the government's actions were illegal, its own activities were perfectly legal. In 1955, the police uncovered the NRM's clandestine press, and Bazargan, along with a group of other NRM activists, was arrested and imprisoned.

In the late 1950s, although the opposition had been thoroughly muzzled, domestic economic problems persisted. Between 1953 and 1957, the United States provided a total of US /366.8 million in economic and financial aid. In 1961 alone, US /107.2 million in aid came from Washington.[176] The US influence in Iran grew substantially, since: 'Iran had become the recipient of one of the largest quantities of American economic aid outside the NATO alliance in the post-war period'.[177] Nevertheless, the Iranian economy showed no signs of improvement. During the 1960s, the economy fell into a recession, with: 'high rates of inflation, worsening balance of trade, and a dramatic drop in the general level of productivity and economic activity'.[178]

The Shah, who viewed the strengthening of his domestic position as a function of his subordination to and friendship with the United States, was feeling disoriented with the changes in US domestic policy. In May 1961, Ali Amini, towards whom the Shah had never felt much sympathy, became prime minister, in order to prevent Iran from 'going down the drain'. Ali Amini was said to be Washington's choice. His premiership 'symbolised the height of American influence in Iranian politics, and the Shah's submission to American pressure clearly indicated that the Iranian-US relationship had indeed developed very asymmetrically in favor of Washington'.[179]

Amini's premiership and the presidency of John Kennedy in the United States, signalled a period of liberalization on the Iranian political scene. In order to foster a mood of national reconciliation, the government promised free elections and political liberties. In view of its overtures, a number of political organizations which had become inactive during the post-1953 period of repression reappeared in the domestic political arena.

On May 15 1961, Medhi Bazargan, Hojatolislam Mahmood Taleqani, Yadollah Sahabi, Rahim Attai, Hassan Nazih, Abbas Sami'i and Mansour Attai' founded the Iran Freedom Movement (IFM). As the successor to the NRM, the IFM provided a platform for all those who were struggling against the Shah's autocracy. Its political stance was clearly outlined in its statute, which read:

1) We are Moslems and convinced that religion cannot be separated from politics.
2) We are Iranians, but our love for Iran and our nationalism is irreconcilable with racism.
3) We respect the constitution and will not allow its fundamental principles to be violated. We consider these fundamental principles to be freedom of opinion, press and assembly, the independence of the

judiciary, the separation of powers, and finally, free elections.

4) We are the followers of Mossadeq and consider him as the only head of state in Iran's history who was popular among the people and authentically elected by the majority of the people.[180]

Less than two years after its establishment, the IFM was outlawed and Bazargan was again imprisoned. It was not until 1978 that the IFM was to make a true political comeback. The premiership of Bazargan was, in reality, Khomeini's affirmation that the Iranian revolution would only approve an honest broker who was acceptable to not all, but the majority of the Iranians. Before the revolution, Bazargan as an individual and the IFM as a political organization were well known among students, merchants, professionals and civil servants.

Bazargan possessed four qualities which, combined in various ways, gave him legitimacy in the eyes of different segments of the urban population. Firstly, he was viewed as a true follower of Mossadeq which made him an honest nationalist, a legalist and a liberal democrat. Secondly, he had firm Islamic convictions and believed that the teachings of Islam provided a basis for social organization. Thirdly, Bazargan was a reputed educated scientist, who taught thermodynamics at the National University of Teheran. Fourthly, Bazargan had a long history of opposing the Shah's autocratic rule and had paid for it by serving numerous prison terms. His influential role in the NRM and later in the IFM lent him credibility both as an activist and as an opposition politician. These characteristics provided him with a vast and complex network of socio-political connections and bonds.

As a Mossadeqist and a good Moslem, Bazargan appealed to the traditional bourgeoisie which, although it had lost its political weight during the Shah's régime, continued to play a determining economic role. For the secular professionals and civil servants, who were dissatisfied with the political repression of the Shah's régime, Bazargan was the rational physics professor who had always struggled for political freedom. He had always been intent on cultivating and maintaining ties with professionals and civil servants. Since 1941, he had been involved in the establishment of various professional Islamic centres. By 1961, thirteen different Islamic groups, centres and associations had their first national congress in Teheran. This nucleus of Islamic engineers, doctors, teachers and students continued to function, though in a diffused manner, during the Shah's rule and acted as a bridge between professional interests and political objectives which were disguised in religious wrappings. Bazargan's preoccupation with blending Islam and science was derived from his greater concern with the formulation and enunciation of a modernized Islam which would be acceptable to the intellectuals and the educated.

Even the national bourgeoisie saw Bazargan as a nationalist, a professional and a legalist, with whom collaboration based on clearly defined and mutually respected principles was not only possible, but, perhaps preferable to a collaboration with the Shah. The Shah's rule was characterized by dependence upon foreign interests and arbitrary and uncertain internal policies. Bazargan's ties with students and Iranian youth in general date back to his teaching years at the National University of Teheran. The students' respect for the university branches of the NRM and the IFM further strengthened these ties. When Marxism (from the late 1960s onwards) became the prevailing ideology in the universities, the IFM was still able to attract both Mossadeqist and Moslem students.

The IFM gave birth to two very important tendencies. Ali Shariati had joined its overseas branch while in Paris and, upon his return to Teheran, collaborated closely with Bazargan in launching the popular *Hosseinieh-e Irshad* lecture series, which drew great numbers of students. Although Shariati's roots were in the IFM, his ideas about Islam's role and developing an ideal Islamic society had evolved to a point where he shared no common theoretical, political or tactical grounds with Bazargan. Each man represented the universal values of a different period. Political democracy, which at the time of Bazargan's stay in France, between 1927 and 1934, was considered to be the most progressive political doctrine, seemed obsolete and faulty to Shariati. While Bazargan tried to blend Islam and liberal democracy, Shariati combined Islam with revolutionary egalitarianism and anti-imperialism. As Shariati invited his followers to emulate the martyred Imam Hossein in a revolt against tyranny, another IFM outgrowth emerged, with armed struggle and martyrdom as its chosen means to liberation. This was the *Sazeman-e Mojahedeen-e Khaleg-e Iran*, or People's Mojahedeen Organization. Its founders, Mohammed Hanif-nejad, Saeed Mohsen and Ali Asghar Badi'-Zadegan, belonged to Islamic student associations affiliated with the IFM and it was the IFM which had exposed them to the idea of Islam as a potent political force, which could be used to overthrow the Shah. However, by the time the Mojahedeen was carrying out its military operations, in 1971 and 1972, it, too, had diverged from the IFM's platform. Bazargan continued to address them as his children, but the Mojahedeen's theoretical and tactical approach soon led to a fundamental rift, though they retained their respect for a man who had persistently struggled against authoritarianism. It was not until 1984 that the Mojahedeen began to subject Bazargan to verbal abuse and slander.

Bazargan's clerical connections were varied and divergent. Since 1930, he had been a close friend of Ayatollah Taleqani, with whom he founded the IFM; their friendship was to endure until Taleqani's death. Also, Bazargan collaborated extensively with Ayatollah Motahhari. For Taleqani, Islam was a revolutionary ideology which could be used to overthrow the Shah's régime. Furthermore, he believed that the correct interpretation and application of Islamic rules would inevitably bring about a harmonious society based on equality, social justice and fraternity. Although an ardent Moslem and an activist, Taleqani was known to be tolerant and the strength of his convictions did nothing to weaken this quality. The overwhelming majority of Moslem activists, as political prisoners, avoided all contact with Marxist activists, but Taleqani was the exception. It is said that he actually respected 'true communists', for their devotion to the improvement of the lot of the toiling masses.[181] What distinguished Taleqani from the rest of the so-called progressive clergy who for a time held the support of one or another Marxist-Leninist or Maoist group, was probably what endeared him to Bazargan. His tolerance and understanding was not limited to the left, to which one of his sons belonged; many said that, after the revolution, Taleqani's house became a sanctuary for those against whom he had struggled for years. He requested permission to attend the trial of General Nasser Moqadam, the last SAVAK head, to plead for his case, it was claimed, because of Moqadam's role in minimizing blood-letting during the revolution. Taleqani was not, however, invited to assist at the trial, and Moqadam was convicted and executed. Taleqani's objections remained unanswered. Taleqani was an outspoken critic of political monopoly and an advocate of the right to dissent and of pluralism. He and Bazargan shared this democratic methodology, which is clearly reflected in Taleqani's denunciation of those who try to monopolize power and control society:

Nobody has been given the right to impose his will on the people or suppress them and exert control over society. Even prophets were not given this right. Similarly, no single individual or party has any right to impose his self-righteous control over others. Control and leadership are two different things. In the Islamic system of government, it is possible for a person to be in a position of leadership, but he has no right to control and dominate people.[182]

That Bazargan had ties with both Taleqani and Motahhari, who were different from one another in many ways, might seem difficult to understand; yet he shared much with each man. His collaboration with Motahhari dates back to the late 1950s and early 1960s, when the two men contributed to the Monthly Religious Society Lectures.[183] In 1959, Motahhari, Bazargan and Taleqani were among the founders of the Islamic Association of Teachers. Motahhari again joined Bazargan and Taleqani to organize the first and second National Congress of Islamic Associations. However, due to his conservatism, Motahhari preferred not to participate in the gatherings, since Taleqani and Bazargan regularly attacked or humoured the Shah in their speeches.[184] According to Bazargan, some time in 1974 to 1975, Motahhari, Taleqani and Sayyed Ali Khamenei (who became president of the Islamic Republic after Rajaee's assassination) formed a clandestine group whose aim was the drawing up of an Islamic world outlook; their project was interrupted, however, when SAVAK discovered their index cards in a house in Mashhad.[185]

Seldom did Ayatollah Khomeini praise individuals in the declarations he made and the circulars he distributed before or after the revolution. It was customary for him to praise those who had contributed greatly to the Islamic cause only after their deaths. This tradition, however, was broken at least once in relation to Bazargan and Taleqani. Their Islamic credentials must have been solid and irreproachable, if they motivated Khomeini to issue a circular in which he unreservedly supports them for having defended: 'Islam and the constitution'. Referring to the arrest of Bazargan and Taleqani in 1962, Khomeini wrote:

> I was scared that if I were to write something about the injustice which has been committed against Hojatolislam Taleqani, Mr. Bazargan and our other friends, their sentences would have been prolonged from ten to fifteen years. Now that the final sentence has been delivered I have to express my regrets about the situation in Iran in general and the conditions under which the judiciary functions in particular.[186]

In addressing Bazargan and other members of the IFM as 'our friends', not only did Khomeini reveal his awareness of Bazargan's activities, but he acknowledged a tacit alliance between the IFM and his own forces in the Qum seminary school.

Hamid Rouhani, the author of an officially approved biography of Khomeini, says:

> The support that was accorded to the Iran Freedom Movement by the Great Leader [Khomeini] was a positive and fruitful step towards an alliance between all Islamic and anti-colonial forces on the one hand, and the closer association of the struggling forces at the University and those at the seminary schools on the other.[187]

Rouhani adds:

> Although the Qum seminary school had very close and systematic ties with the leaders of the IFM and Taleqani, in the aftermath of this supportive declaration relations with the IFM were deepened and cemented on the basis of a more organized and co-ordinated type of association.[188]

The Qum seminary school was regularly engaged in duplicating and distributing the declarations and circulars of the IFM and its leaders and was also responsible for making available the text of the IFM leaders' defence as presented at their trial.[189] It is interesting to note that the text of Bazargan's defence, which was considered revolutionary at the time and was duplicated and distributed by the clergy of the Qum seminary school, was presented as proof of his monarchist tendencies after his fall from grace. The Qum seminary's lower ranking clergy, who were predominantly Khomeini supporters, showed their solidarity with Bazargan when the latter's mother passed away. Fifty-five of them signed a letter of condolence addressed to Bazargan and sent it to official newspapers for publication. Once the newspapers had refused to publish it on orders from SAVAK, the letter was published, duplicated and distributed by the Qum seminary school. At the bottom of the letter, the signatories condemned the repressive régime which had prevented them from publishing the text in the country's newspapers.[190] The list of these signatories is a veritable Who's Who of the present Islamic régime.

Bazargan's disagreement with Khomeini on the manner in which an Islamic state should be governed led to his resignation after nine months of premiership. Pushed out of power by the rapid unfolding of events, Bazargan gradually moved from a position of disagreement with the conduct of the Islamic Republic to one of opposition to it. Though he and his organization, the IFM, and, recently, the Society for the Defence of Freedom and the Sovereignty of the Iranian People (SDFSIP), are regularly harassed by various civil and paramilitary forces of the Islamic Republic, he continues to be tolerated. His connections within the leadership of the Islamic Republic plays an important role in his relative freedom of expression, despite his intransigence. In the absence of Khomeini and during a return to normality, only a figure such as Bazargan could play a determining role in a government of national reconciliation. Furthermore, Bazargan has never completely crossed the Rubicon in the Islamic Republic.

On 10 June 1981, the National Front, which considered itself the true inheritor of Mossadeq's legacy, invited the Iranian people to a demonstration against the *qisas* bill, or the Islamic code of penalties and retributions, which was to be presented to and ratified by parliament. The circular was signed by Dr Mehdi Azar, who belonged to the leadership of the National Front and was very well versed in Islamic studies. The ratification of the *qisas* bill meant that Islamic laws and penalties would come to co-ordinate and regulate the conduct of individuals in society. The opposition forces, which viewed the legalization of the Islamic code of penalties as a dangerous development which would negate their individual freedoms, were unanimous in their hostility towards the *qisas* bill. It was considered inhuman and regressive; for example, it stipulated the amputation of the arm of a thief and the stoning to death of an adulteress. It was, therefore, expected that all opposition forces would participate in this demonstration. The denuciation of the bill by Sayyed Abolfazl Zanjani, a well-known clerical figure, added to the importance of the National Front's position. None of the major political organizations declared their intention of joining the demonstration openly, but their supporters were instructed to attend. On the morning of 10 June, Khomeini confronted the opposition with an unexpected counter-attack. He declared that:

the National Front is condemned to apostasy from today onwards, they have proclaimed God's decree as inhuman and have invited the people to rebel against the Qur'an. . . . The IFM however has to clarify its position . . . I used to like these people and I still like some of them. What are we to do with them? You have to clarify your position . . . I am sure that you [IFM] are not in agreement with the National Front. Why do you remain silent?[91]

By early afternoon, an announcement by Bazargan was read over the radio in which he declared that the IFM had never intended to participate in the demonstration organized by the National Front.

Bazargan's repentance came at a very opportune moment. From 15 June 1981, leaders, members and sympathizers of all shades of the opposition were gradually imprisoned, killed in street fighting, faced the firing squads or fled the country. Although their newsaper, *Mizan*, was outlawed, only Bazargan and the IFM were left unmolested to constitute the single opposition group in the Islamic Republic. It is important to note that Bazargan's criticism of the republic surpasses the intensity and depth of his criticism of the Shah's régime. He survives an ongoing struggle between competing subsystems. Bazargan's subsystem is of particular importance, since he constructs an Islamic model which could be considered democratic.

The essence of Islam

Bazargan's analysis of Islam is primarily based on the Qur'an. He argues that Moslems can avoid deviations and misunderstandings only by returning to and understanding the Qur'an without interjecting into it ideas derived from outside sources.[192] In his model, Bazargan clearly defines the unit of analysis, the principles of the faith and the ultimate objectives of *Shi'i* Islam, as well as the incentive and disincentive system which ensures member participation. What distinguishes Bazargan's subsystem from those considered thus far is its romantic view of God in Islam and of Islam as a religion. From verses 182 to 186 of the Sura of Baqarah, and verse 24 of the Sura of Anfal in the Qur'an, Bazargan deduces that:

> God is both the source and object of love. This source of love is a world of life and generosity who is not in need of anyone yet who gives everything to those who are enamoured of Him. He has created heaven and earth for us and made us its masters.[193]

For Bazargan, God is the source of love and Islam is the doctrine which invites all individuals to unison through the observation and exercise of God's edicts. The content of these edicts, however, cannot have its source in anything but love and affection. Thus, not coercion and fear, but the attraction and satisfaction produced by loving and being loved are the only forces which can induce an individual to enter into a unison co-ordinated by the rules of God. Bazargan quotes Imam Mohammed Baqer who says that 'religion is nothing but love and affection'.[194] The emphasis on 'love and affection' as the cornerstone of Islam is an important feature of Bazargan's subsystem which influences the other aspects of his model.

Bazargan argues that in the Qur'an, God addresses the people without any discrimination on the basis of social, economic or political position. Islam's unit of analysis is neither geographically nor racially specific. God establishes his relationship with human beings as individuals and not as members of social groups, classes or communities. According to Bazargan, the principle of inviting the people to follow the path to salvation and felicity, the mission of every prophet, is based on this invitation being extended to everybody. Islam holds that individuals are endowed with rights and values as human beings. These rights and values apply to believers, as well as to infidels, disbelievers and hypocrites.[195] Unlike Shariati's subsystem, in which an individual's value and his proximity to God are determined by his class position, Bazargan views Islam as a non-discriminatory religion in which the most rewarding act in the eyes of God is to serve the people whom He has created: 'God reminds us that people [whether believers or not] are members of His family and anyone who serves them more is closer to Him'.[196] Bazargan's Islam is not a religion of exclusion in which the 'other' (a capitalist, for example, in Shariati's subsystem, or an unveiled woman in Navab-Safavi's) must be castigated or seen as a corruptor on earth, and thus condemned to death. By his inclusion of the 'other' in God's family, Bazargan singles out tolerance as a foundation of Islam. To substantiate his vision of Islam, he refers to this passage taken from Imam Ali's directive to Malek-e Ashtar, who was appointed Governor of Egypt by the Imam:

> Replenish your heart with love and affection for your subjects and do not cease your kindness towards them. Be careful not to shed their blood like a wild beast, since your subjects are of two types: they are either your religious brothers or they are your equals in creation. You must pardon their sins and be forgiving.[197]

In Bazargan's subsystem, individuals are ranked as equal in the eyes of God and worthy of equal respect. As such, the common people, or *avam*, cannot be looked down upon as either ignorant and decadent, as Motahhari assumed them to be, or as non-revolutionary and reactionary, as Shariati deemed them. Since individuals constitute the basis of society, it is through the awareness, purification and transformation of these individuals that society is transformed. It is thus argued that, according to the Qur'an, the individual has priority over the collective and individual transformations are of greater importance than social ones.[198] Bazargan's emphasis on individual transformation as a basis for social transformation is similar to Motahhari's position on this issue. The two men differ, however, on the way in which individuals are to experience this 'inner revolution'. While Bazargan maintains that this consciousness may be attained only through a voluntary process of self-analysis and self-transformation, Motahhari believes that Islamic society itself will impose such a process.

According to Bazargan, Islam does not coerce any individual into compliance with its rules. Following the premise that Islam addresses the individual, it is argued that the rules and edicts affirmed in the Qur'an are private and enunciated for the purpose of indicating the goals which should be attained through the self-development of the individual. Bazargan argues that ordinances which are essentially private and left to the individual to adopt or reject have been made into social laws which have to be observed by the whole society.[199]

The whole question of whether Islamic ordinances are social maxims that ought to be followed by all members of an Islamic society or private values, the pursuit of which is left to the individual, lies at the root of the Islamic incentive and disincentive system. If they are viewed as private, then society cannot impose punishments, since their observation is a private choice. For Bazargan, the observation and implementation of Islamic ordinances are private matters that are left to the individual, since God willed individuals to be free in their judgements and decisions.[200] The disincentive is, therefore, primarily a private and spiritual one.

The ultimate objective or the final destination of individuals in Islam is the hereafter. Bazargan argues that prophets invite people to live in such a way that they would feel closer to God who is the source of real love and, consequently, become prepared for the real eternal life of the hereafter.[201] Concern for worldly life and the individual's conduct in it is neither abandoned nor forgotten. Although man's worldly life is viewed as a transitory existence in which the individual sows the seeds which he will harvest in the hereafter, Islam does not neglect the pursuit of material life. Bazargan refers to the Sura of Loqman, Verses 13 and 14 and *Qesas,* Verse 77 to show that God expects man to enjoy the fruits of his life and as long as man does not engage in waste and corruption his satisfaction in life is God's will.[202]

The importance attached to the worldly life of individuals makes necessary a set of worldly disincentives, which serve to curb man's excesses. It is on this basis that Bazargan argues that Islam acts as both the motor of and the brake on humankind's actions.[203] Since God knows humankind better than it knows itself, Bazargan says, He has imposed constraints upon its instincts. The ordinances dealing with punishment and retribution have been formulated to control humankind's wrath and vengefulness. Thus the disincentive system exists to prevent cruelty, not to cause or perpetrate it. God has ordered us to act with kindness and forgiveness in the face of aggression and viciousness and it is only when we feel ourselves incapable of such humane responses, that vindictiveness, harnessed within the limits set by Islamic ordinances, is a recourse.[204] But those who apply Islamic penalties are not endeared to God: 'God's mercy and blessing belongs more to those who are charitable than to those who resort to the use of retribution'.[205] The Qur'an, according to Bazargan, is adamant about reducing tension and differences between individuals and communities through reconciliation. The settlement of ideological disputes is consigned to the hereafter, so there may be less discord in this world.[206] While for Shariati, Islam was an aggressive ideology which was to jolt the resigned out of their submission and urge them to fight and defeat the oppressors, Bazargan's Islam is a school of *détente* and dialogue, in which kindness and forgiveness will transform vice to virtue and the vengeful adversary into the most loyal of friends. Although reconciliation constitutes an important aspect of Bazargan's subsystem, he does not belong to the group of religious figures who chose to avoid confrontation with the Shah's régime. Passiveness based on the

Shi'i concept of *taqiyeh*, or dissimulation of belief, common among many religious figures, was criticized by Bazargan as far back as 1962.[207] Providing total felicity through the implementation of the *Shari'a* – the ultimate objective in all *Shi'i* subsystems – is a principle which also applies in Bazargan's subsystem. However, Bazargan's introduction of freedom of choice breaks the unilinearity found in the other Islamic subsystems. For him, the implementation of the *Shari'a* does not constitute an Islamic society or system, although it is the final objective of such a society. Only a society which has consciously and freely chosen the *Shari'a* as its guide can be an Islamic society. Within this later society, however, individuals who have not yet accepted the *Shari'a* can conduct their lives as they see fit. God has willed individuals to be free.[208] The principle that God's relation with humankind is based on freedom, is given priority over the imposition of the *Shari'a* or the observation of religious rituals. Bazargan argues that God does not wish to impose His view of what is good on individuals, since coercion would negate their God-given freedom of choice.[209] Individuals are confronted with the choice of doing right or doing wrong; their fates depend on their choices: 'God not only leaves Man free to be either grateful or to do evil, but He helps the believer as well as the disbeliever in the path that they have chosen'.[210]

Bazargan further argues that man is given a period of respite during which sinning is permitted.[211] God, he says, even gave Satan a respite period, until judgement day, in which he was free to tempt humankind to evil and to deceive it. Humans, then, may choose between God's invitation and Satan's temptation. Freedom is considered God's divine gift to man, who is His successor on earth.[212] In Bazargan's subsystem, the implementation of the *Shari'a* is readily sacrificed if this is at the expense of freedom. Furthermore, the kinds of conviction, faith and piety which are acceptable to God must be the results of individual free will and decision.[213] Individual freedom is so indispensable that Bazargan suggests that even those who deny the necessity of essential Islamic practices, such as fasting and prayers, may still be considered Moslems. As long as an individual does not go so far as to negate monotheism, he will not be branded an apostate.[214]

Bazargan asserts that though praying is obligatory in Islam, no one can be forced to do it.[215] This obligation, he says, is a personal one and cannot be imposed either by religious authorities or by a government acting in the name of Islamic values. Bazargan supports his view that the exercise of religious practices should be forfeited when a conflict between freedom and religious obligations arises, with a reference to a letter written by Imam Ali to a tax collector. Despite the fact that paying zakat, wealth tax, is one of a believer's duties, Imam Ali gives the following directives to the collecting agent:

> When you enter a community . . . inform them that you have been sent by me to collect that part of their wealth which belongs to God. Then ask them whether any part of their wealth is God's share. If anyone

answers in the negative you must accept his answer and pursue the matter no further. If someone answers in the affirmative, go with him, take whatever he gives you without causing him anguish or prying into his affairs.[216]

Bazargan thus shows that in Islam, zakat is paid according to the free will of individuals and that coercion cannot be applied for its receipt. He does not present a similar argument for each of the ten duties of believers, the *Foru-e din*, but his reasoning applies to all of them. If Bazargan's argument regarding the absence of coercion in the performance of duties is accepted, it would be logical to claim that, according to his subsystem, an Islamic state is not empowered to punish those who do not carry out their religious obligations.

Bazargan maintains that his emphasis on freedom of choice does not conflict with the fact that God and His messengers have continually encouraged individuals to be pious and warned them against sin.[217] Freedom should not be misconstrued as indifference to vice and virtue. If one chooses to sin, one is aware of the consequences. Sinners will be punished in part during their time on earth and will receive the longer and heavier remainder of their punishments in the hereafter.[218] Bazargan concludes that:

God's only intervention is in the form of sending messengers to put forward solutions and illuminate paths towards felicity. To offset the negative effects of the freedom that God has given to individuals, He has endowed them with intelligence and has sent them prophets to act as their guides.[219]

On the role of the prophets

In order to construct his model of the Islamic state and set a framework for Islamic social relations, Bazargan analyses the mission, and thus the responsibilities of the prophets. He contends that the prophets' conduct and the responsibilities God has entrusted them with should provide an ideal model for someone wishing to create a state based upon religious foundations. But along with the rights granted to prophets, to be exercised upon the people they are sent to guide, God imposes certain limitations. Bazargan's implicit assertion is that if God places restraints upon the prophets He has chosen, then such restraints must also apply, but with greater force and rigidity, to those who wish to establish a state in the name of God.

According to Bazargan, the prophets' mission comprised two separate stages, each distinguished by a different kind of activity. Firstly, they were responsible for inviting people to follow the divine path, for presenting their world outlooks and values and for offering guidance.[220] Bazargan argues that the five responsibilities of Mohammed the Prophet during this first, or 'guidance', stage, are clearly enumerated in the Qur'an.[221] The Prophet has been sent to: act as a model and be a witness;

spread the good news about heaven and the joyful rewards of piety, faith and good deeds; warn against sinful acts and their tormenting consequences; invite people to go towards God in His own tradition; and, finally, act as a lighthouse which illuminates the path and allows people to reach their destinations.[222] During this first stage, the Prophet is responsible only for informing, guiding, educating and consciousness raising; he must not impose his views. Even if the Prophet encounters strong resistance on the part of disbelievers, he must abide by God's command that: 'there can be no coercion in religion'.[223] Bazargan maintains that this fundamental Islamic principle is applicable to opinions, ideas, acts and even to religious practices.[224] Bazargan's God is not only compassionate and tolerant, but, most important, He is patient, for He considers time to be on His side. During the first stage of his mission, Mohammed the Prophet is confronted with the disrespect and derision of disbelievers, and loses heart. God reminds him that He could have willed all people to become believers, had he wanted; therefore, the Prophet's sole responsibility is to continue informing the people.[225] Bazargan concludes that since God does not wish to impose His way through coercion and is not impatient for the immediate destruction of disbelievers, but is content to wait while they learn from their mistakes, then no one can use coercion in His name.[226]

An important characteristic of the first stage of the Prophet's mission is that he does not need to consult anyone or obtain anyone's consent. His acts are for a divine cause and he is guided by the Almighty. During the propagation of his doctrine, he cannot impose his will upon people nor does he need their support. No one is allowed to interfere with the content of a Moslem's prayer, the fasting period of a Moslem or that which the Qur'an deems forbidden (*haraam*), or allowed (*halaal*), in a Moslem's comportment.[227] The form, content and objectives of divine ordinances are incontestable and the Prophet does not allow individuals to tamper with them. They can be accepted or rejected, but never modified.

During the second stage of their mission, prophets are assigned a specific task. According to Bazargan, Mohammed's mission consisted of the first stage of guidance and the second stage of government (*velayat*).[228] The governing of a people is a worldly act which aims at reforming and saving them. Mohammed was assigned the task of leading a people, which involved: promulgating laws; social, economic and administrative management; the formulation of foreign policy; and control of such matters as war and peace.[229]

Bazargan argues that as soon as the Prophet is appointed to govern the people, God orders him to: 'consult with the people on issues and policies' that will concern their lives.[230] God informs the Prophet that although he is acting in the name of a divine cause, he will be expected to govern democratically and on the basis of consultation, with the use of councils, or *shoura*. The Qur'an states that: 'the government of the people is possible through consultation with them',[231] and it is argued that leadership implies compliance with the wishes of the led. Bazargan holds that to govern according to Islamic precepts, even the most base elements in society, those who need to be pardoned for their sins, for example, must be included in the consultation process, which should take place before any policies are officially formulated. Consultation need not be on the basis of a participatory, or direct, democracy and can occur within the framework of a representative democracy.[232]

Bazargan develops the notion of the Prophet having been entrusted with two distinct missions. It is from the particular nature of these missions that he derives the foundation of his democratic subsystem. The Prophet's first mission is to preach what God has revealed to him. He is the messenger and his responsibility is to inform. The second mision entitles the Prophet to rule, but obliges him to abide by the will of his subjects. In neither case, according to Bazargan, does Islam encourage or even permit coercion.[233] He maintains that:

> In the consultative system of the Qu'ran it is individuals who as a whole . . . choose the government and rule over the government. One thousand years before the emergence of the concept of democracy in the West, the government of the people by the people was practiced in the days of the Prophet. . . . If the ruler or the government is to be appointed by God or a high-ranking religious, scientific or political personality, and the people are left unconsulted in the affairs of the government of their own nation, the principle of freedom and individual responsibility will be negated and distorted.[234]

In analysing the Catholic church of thirteenth- and fourteenth-century Europe, Bazargan points out that it imposed its doctrines on Europeans, since it saw itself as the official repository of Christian truth. Armed with the Bible, the church felt itself superior to and responsible for the common people, who were compelled to blindly accept all of its declarations. Bazargan recognizes that a clerical leadership which treats the common people as invalids, incapable of directing their own affairs, will inevitably end in autocratic despotism, where people are denied the rights of expression and dissent.[235] He attempts to prove that although a theocratic system of government can lead to despotism, this can be prevented by adhering to Qur'anic methodologies. The functioning of a democratic Islamic government will further be ensured if the following Qur'anic directives are consistently observed: let there be no coercion in religion and government of the people is possible through consultation with them. A state which does not practise democratic rights and freedoms could not be considered an Islamic state, since it would not be respecting the letter of the Qur'an. According to a popular *hadith* (report of the Prophet's, or imams' sayings or actions), a country and its government can survive with *kufr*, the sin of disbelief, but it cannot last if there is oppression. From Bazargan's perspective, an Islamic government cannot take any other form than that of a divine democratic state based on a system of councils.[236]

Bazargan's object in reviewing the mission of the Prophet is clear. If the Messenger of God who received revelations from Him had to comply with the ordinances which instructed him not to force Islam upon anyone and to consult people, it was incumbent on those who ruled in his name and used the Qur'an as their guiding torch to rule accordingly. Bazargan does not hide his liberal democratic orientation. On the contrary, he tries to show that liberalism is compatible with his concept of Islam. Based on his understanding of the Qur'an and the Sunnah, Bazargan distinguishes four relationships which characterize his subsystem.[237]

The first relationship is that which an individual establishes with God. God does not need man's piety and this is demonstrated, says Bazargan, by God's emphasis on the absence of coercion in religion. Furthermore, it is God's will that freedom of choice should be the co-ordinating mechanism between Himself and individuals.[238] In Bazargan's opinion, the kind of relationship envisaged by Islam between God and man is one based on the principles which constitute liberalism.[239]

Second is the individual's relationship with himself, in which his desires and instincts may not have free rein. From Bazargan's stance, Islam expects the individual to restrain himself from committing forbidden acts. Since man has freedom of choice, only his faith, his willpower and his convictions can induce him to voluntarily limit his own freedoms, or sacrifice his wealth or even his life, for the love of God. In Bazargan's subsystem, then, the individual is the only one allowed and invited to impose limitations on himself. The individual's relation to himself, it is argued, is organized around a personal sense of his growing awareness.[240]

The third relationship individuals enter into is with others. In this context, Bazargan argues that, although God foregoes His own rights in relation to individuals, He will not allow the rights of any one individual to be violated by another. It is argued that the Islamic principle which states that: 'No one can do damage or harm to any other person and no one can be subjected to damage or harm by any other person', settles the manner in which individuals should relate to one another in an Islamic society.[241] Bazargan points out that in this relationship, individuals cannot deny or violate the liberties and rights of others. Here his arguments are very similar to those of western philosophers of the liberal tradition.

Finally, individuals find themselves in daily relationship with the state. The principle which regulates this is clearly stated in the Qur'an, says Bazargan, where rulers are instructed to govern in consultation with the people. This axiom ensures a democratic system of government in which the democratic rights necessary to gauge the different views of the people are respected and upheld. In such a system, the state cannot commit injustices against individuals, since individuals are vigilant and instrumental in the affairs of the state. According to Bazargan, the Islamic society insures itself against despotism by exercising the fundamental Islamic principle of: 'inviting to do good and cautioning against wrong-doing'. The individual, thereby, has the obligation to disagree with and criticize the government. Bazargan asks:

How could it be possible to respect and practice *amr-e be ma'aruf* and *nahy-e az monkar* [inviting to do good, and cautioning against doing wrong] in an Islamic society and at the same time violate freedom of opinion and expression, along with political and judicial rights?[242]

The Islamic political system formulated by Bazargan is an Islamic version of a liberal democracy. The important thing, however, about his *Shi'i* subsystem is that the evidence and arguments used for its validity are all rooted in either the Qur'an or the Sunnah.

The methodology of Bazargan's subsystem

In Bazargan's subsystem, tolerance is viewed as the cornerstone of an Islamic code of conduct. It is argued that the conduct of the Prophet and of the imams is witness to the fact that Islam is a religion of compassion and tolerance. The Prophet is said to have debated with those who opposed him and with disbelievers.[243] This openness to opposing views was not limited to the period when Moslems were contending for power. Even during the time of the imams, when an Islamic government had been established, athiests were free to pose their questions and voice their opinions.[244] Islamic tolerance is not a result of weakness or apathy, but is rooted in the belief that sinners, disbelievers and athiests can be led to the path of God. While others can educate and invite, the individual must undergo the inner transformation which leads to faith. Bazargan offers this Qur'anic directive as evidence to refute the common description of Islam as dogmatic and aggressive: 'If a polytheist comes to you and seeks asylum, accept him so that he will hear God's word and provide him safe conduct to wherever he is going. Realize that they are ignorant people'.[245] If Islam was not tolerant of non-Moslems and intended to destroy them, Bazargan maintains, God would have ordered Moslems to befriend the polytheist only if he accepted the faith and to behead him if he refused.[246] It is important to realize that Bazargan's *Shi'i* subsystem is based not only on tolerance, but on social change. The combination of these two forces gives rise to a reformist Islam with little in common with any other subsystem. Although Bazargan acknowledges that he cannot claim to be a revolutionary, his political career bears witness to a lifelong reformist struggle for political and democratic freedoms, with the exception of a few occasions during his premiership.[247]

The major themes of Bazargan's political discourse which shed light upon the methodology in his subsystem can be identified by analysing the principles to which he has remained steadfast during different periods of his life. In 1961, his beliefs were well reflected in the basic tenets of the IFM. These can be summarized as: respect for the constitution; respect for democratic and political freedoms; and democracy on the basis of majority rule. In a lecture given in 1962, to the Second National Congress of Islamic Associations of Iran, Bazargan said: 'In the final analysis, government ought to be a government on the basis of councils [*shoura*] and the struggle is a struggle by the people against arbitrary rule'.[248] Later, Bazargan was arrested and tried by a military tribunal for his political activities, and he used the same principles in his own defence.

He declared that: he had always respected the constitution and acted according to it; he condemned the violation of the constitution through the autocratic and arbitrary rule of one person (the Shah) and he believed in the political and democratic freedoms stipulated in that constitution. Some fifteen years later, following his appointment in 1979 as prime minister of the provisional government, Bazargan emphasized, in his first official public address, the following points: our Republican Islamic government is a democratic republic since Islam is based on true democracy; Iran's government does not belong to any particular class; in an Islamic government, the exercise of freedom is not only a right but an obligation; and that until a new constitution is drawn up the government would respect the old constitution, minus the monarchy.[249] Finally, after his resignation from the premiership, Bazargan wrote: 'But on the manner in which the country should be governed, the participation of the people through a system of councils and their self-sovereignty is a well-documented fact in the Qur'an and it constitutes an indisputable deduction'.[250]

The gradualism, or 'step-by-step' strategy used by Bazargan during his premiership, became the target of those political groups which saw the revolution as a justification of the hegemony of their own constituencies, real or imagined. For Bazargan, the victory of the revolution meant the immediate imposition of the rule of law, since his antagonism towards the old régime was a result of its arbitrariness and disrespect for the law and constitution. The old theme of all Mossadeqist militants pivoted around the illegitimacy of the Shah due to his despotism. Legalism was an important consideration for those who believed that the Iranian revolution was a mere anti-despotic revolution. Political democracy, legalism, political and democratic freedoms and the immediate restoration of law and order have, theoretically, constituted the ultimate objective of anti-despotic revolutions. Iran was no exception to this rule, except that there were numerous political groups which viewed the revolution as one which was more than a simple anti-despotic one. For these groups, victory had ushered in a transitional phase which had to give way to some other form of government. For the left, Bazargan's government represented the bourgeois democratic stage of the revolution which had to be immediately succeeded by the dictatorship of the proletariat. With the exception of Taleqani, the clergy in the Revolutionary Council viewed the provisional government as a necessary compromise which had to be replaced with a purely clerically controlled government as soon as the social conditions would permit. Thus, neither the left nor the clerical right had any interest in supporting Bazargan. On the contrary, each sought to confront the provisional government with grave social, political and economic problems to undermine its authority, prove its incapacity to rule and pave the way for their own ascension to power.

Bazargan accepted the impossible role of reconciling the various demands of the divergent political forces which had participated in the revolution. Not only did his appointment provide the clergy with the much-needed time to consolidate its forces, but it forced the traditional reformist forces to reckon with a multitude of post-revolutionary national problems. Instituting law and order required iron-fisted policies directed at those who were threatening the government. Clearly, Bazargan was not the ideal candidate for such a task. The clergy, who had expected him to ruthlessly repress the left while giving free reign to the paramilitary groups under its control, instead found Bazargan apprehensive about an unprovoked repression of the left and about the arbitrary power of the revolutionary institutions. While the left regarded the provisional government as the repressive arm of religious reaction, the anti-democratic clergy saw Bazargan as the protector of 'counter-revolutionary' leftist groups.[251] Bazargan found himself fighting on too many fronts: restoring order and introducing political and democratic rights and liberties; controlling the excesses, the violence and the vengefulness of the armed revolutionary committees and the Islamic courts, which were supposedly subordinate to the provisional government; and responding to the demands and accusations of various political organizations. As long as Khomeini was supporting him, Bazargan thought it worth while to continue despite the pressure, because he knew that between himself and Iran's middle classes, a steadily increasing bond was developing.

With Bazargan 'in power' the forcible imposition of any given issue or system proved problematic; his allegiance to democratic rights and freedoms meant that no illegal and violent action could be carried out unnoticed by the people. The freedom enjoyed by the ever-growing press ensured that people would be informed. While Bazargan himself rejoiced at the closure of the opposition newspaper *Ayandegan* by the order of the revolutionary prosecutor, declaring that: 'fortunately *Ayandegan* which never ceased to heap insults [upon the government and its members] was banned', the means of informing the people of such an undemocratic act and of organizing a co-ordinated response was still available.[252] Bazargan's policy of transparency and the absence of iron-fisted action permitted the people to respond to the closure of *Ayandegan* by staging the second most important demonstration since the revolution's victory (the most important being that held by women after Khomeini stated that they should wear the veil). Bazargan was unwilling to abandon his policy of providing freedoms and in response to critics who accused him of being too lenient with those who criticized, provoked or plotted against the government, he said: 'We could not have arbitrarily banned newspapers and parties'.[253]

During Bazargan's premiership, those who had participated in the revolution, but who had returned to their ordinary lifestyles once it was over, were becoming ever more sensitive to the assault on individual and political freedoms by the most ardent of Islamic revolutionary institutions, the committees of the Islamic revolution and the Islamic courts, which fell under the jurisdiction of the Office of the Prosecutor of the Islamic Revolution. Bazargan's relationship with these institutions was an enigmatic one. While they were supposed to facilitate the provisional government's task of imposing the central government's authority (through respecting the former's decisions and by pursuing and ultimately punishing those who violated the law) Bazargan accused them of being the source of his government's problems. With respect to the committees of the Islamic revolution, Bazargan condemned: the atmosphere of intimidation and terror they created; their disobedience and disrespect for the decisions and decrees of the provisional government; and their interference with and obstruction of government policies.[254] As for the Islamic revolutionary courts, Bazargan denounced their spirit of vengefulness and their unwillingness to forgive, reflected in the wave of arrests and executions. Less than four months after the revolution, in the provisional government's report to Khomeini and the Revolutionary Council, Bazargan wrote:

> The arrests, the harsh treatments and, possibly, the insults and the ruthlessness which are occurring under the order of the revolutionary courts, or in their name, has not only created an aura of terror, insecurity and discontent among certain classes of society, but it has distracted the revolution and the government from its most urgent programmes and policies. It has furthermore generated numerous problems for the government and has weakened it.[255]

Bazargan, however, knew full well that it was Khomeini who had created a dual system of power after the victorious revolution. The provisional government could not introduce any change or exert any control without the approval of the Revolutionary Council, which was dominated by the clerics who were sympathetic to either a pure or a combined version of Motahhari and Navab-Safavi's subsystems. It was the Revolutionary Council's clerical component which controlled the Islamic revolutionary courts, which dealt with all offences categorized as counter-revolutionary, past and present, political and moral. These clerics also controlled the revolutionary guards and the committees of the Islamic revolution, which had, in effect, replaced the police and the gendarmerie. Despite, therefore, Khomeini's appointment of Bazargan as prime minister and his implicit support of Bazargan's subsystem, he had, in fact, set up an institutional structure which balanced this subsystem with others which were more to his taste. The frustrating state of confusion and arbitrariness which resulted from what Bazargan called 'the city with one hundred sheriffs' was exactly the optimal equilibrium of power between competing subsystems that Khomeini had envisaged. When, regardless of the position of his government, certain policies were adopted and imposed and he was left to justify them to the people, Bazargan realized that he was governing in name only and decided to resign.

In his last televised interview, Bazargan offered the following explanation for his resignation:

> The Shah has left. The main despot has gone, but the mini-despots remain. And when I say mini-despots I do not mean those who are still attached to the SAVAK or the court or those who are mercenaries. Who knows, maybe I too have become a despot. I am talking about the

spirit of despotism, the ideas of despotism.[256]

Bazargan laments the mini-despots and rightly questions his own credentials as a militant for a liberal democratic Islam which assures individual rights and political liberties. His rejoicing at the violation of the freedom of the press, his claim that: 'the majority of those who were executed deserved to be executed' and his accusation that the left was in collusion with counter-revolutionaries because they engaged in 'unneccessary obstructionism and criticism', are probably some of the reasons which led Bazargan to question his old convictions.[257] His statement regarding the justness of executions is the only statement he has made to this effect. In all his other references to the matter, he has condemned the undemocratic procedure used in the Islamic revolutionary courts.[258] Yet in giving up his leadership, Bazargan demonstrated his awareness of the predicament he had found himself in as prime minister. In his letter of resignation, he wrote: 'I present my resignation so that the Ayatollah [Khomeini] will be able to bring all the affairs of the state under his control and leadership or appoint volunteers with whom co-ordination and harmony is possible to form a government'.[259]

By presenting a verbally tolerant and pluralist Islam, Bazargan's subsystem played a crucial role in the initial stages of implementing the Islamic Republic, but it was evident that his policies and the gradual Islamization which he supported were incompatible with the approach of the Revolutionary Council's clerical members. As long as the beneficiaries of the Islamic Republic could be kept mobilized and in a state of revolutionary frenzy, the supporters of non-democratic Islamic subsystems could gain legitimacy by claiming to have the approval of 'the Moslem people of Iran'. As the middle classes grew sceptical and weary of the infringements upon their rights and liberties, they pressed for a slowing down of the Islamization process. In theory, Bazargan's subsystem represented the only alternative to an autocratic Islam. His tendency to form an independent social base of power posed a real threat to proponents of an autocratic and totalistic Islam. Khomeini's support of Bazargan would have established Bazargan's subsystem at the expense of the others. Most important, Khomeini would have been overshadowed by and restricted to one subsystem and its tools, thus losing his absolute authority as the grand architect of an Islamic system without blueprints, whose every element was a result of his improvisation. The refusal by the middle class and by the left to accept the immediate implementation of Islamic measures, forced the Revolutionary Council to mobilize 'the Moslem people of Iran' into omnipresent shock troops which would crush all resistance. The flagrant violation of rights and freedoms to rapidly impose Islamic measures was clearly incompatible with Bazargan's subsystem and in harmony with others. Bazargan's departure, however, did not mark the demise of his subsystem, but rather its temporary retirement until, once again, a liberal democratic Islam, or aspects of such, proves to be the indispensable solution for the maintenance of an Islamic Iran.

Bazargan's subsystem in comparison with other subsystems

In many respects, Bazargan's subsystem is similar to Motahhari's. Both view the individual, rather than class, as the unit of social analysis. Consequently, worldly and spiritual incentives and disincentives are applied to individuals, who are responsible for their individual acts. Bazargan also resembles Motahhari in his emphasis on the primacy of psychological revolutions as the correct path towards piety and deliverance. The threat of Marxism as an alternative ideology which attracted youth and undermined religious sentiments in society was of great concern to both Motahhari and Bazargan. Modernizing Islam and increasing its capacity to address the pressing socio-political issues confronting youth became the aim of both men. Yet Bazargan's subsystem differs from Motahhari's on two essential issues.

Firstly, while Motahhari believed that freedom and democracy were the precursor of laxity and incompatible with Islam, Bazargan maintained that these constituted the functional basis of Islam. Rejecting the view of those, such as Motahhari and Navab-Safavi, who condemned freedom because it leads to corruption and bestiality, Bazargan says:

> The opponents of freedom and those who condemn it have always tampered with and misused the concept of freedom either out of ignorance or malevolence . . . corruption is not specific to democracies and has existed and will exist on earth until the return of the hidden Imam. . . . Freedom is for the purpose of ridding people of the bondage and tutelage that rulers impose and in turn subjecting them to the rule of law. Now if there are any problems, they would be in relation to the laws that are promulgated and not because of freedom.[260]

Secondly, while Motahhari was distrustful of intellectuals and believed that the clergy should impose its leadership on the revolutionaries, Bazargan, who had always argued for a more active political role for religious figures, makes this subtle distinction: 'We had always supported the thesis that politics should take its lead from religion, not from the clergy (*ruhaniyat*)'.[261] As far back as 1962, Bazargan warned that an unlimited integration of religion and politics could become an imposing monolith.[262] He argues that once the clergy places itself above the people and considers itself the guardian of the people, it will violate individual and social liberties and undermine the government of the people by the people:[263] 'The government of religion and religious leaders cannot accept freedom of opinion and expression and the right to protest'.[264] For Bazargan, religion provides a set of values through which man can attain felicity, but as soon as the spectre of forceful imposition of those values by the clergy looms, he is the first to denounce it. He implicitly questions Khomeini's concept of guidance by religious experts, *Velayat-e Faqih*, when he argues that:

> if a source of emulation who has all the qualities for guiding a people wishes to interfere with the affairs of a people and forces them to

comply according to religious instructions, without their consent or
demand to do so, he will be tampering with the principle of man's
freedom and responsibility.[265]

On the issue of clerical leadership, Bazargan and Shariati share a common
view, while Motahhari and Navab-Safavi believe that social leadership
can be exercised only by the clergy.

Bazargan's subsystem differs from Shariati's in four important ways.
Firstly, Shariati sees the use of force as necessary after the victory of a
revolution, whereas Bazargan is theoretically averse to coercion, regardless of its object. Secondly, Shariati mocks democracy as: 'a weak
political system' which would ultimately lead to the election of change-
resistant and ignorant leaders; Bazargan points to pluralism, freedom of
speech and democracy as the modern manifestations of an Islamic
government based on consultation. A third difference is clearly illustrated in Bazargan's simple response to Shariati's belief that a monotheist
Islam should implement the Islamic principle of economic equity and
justice, or *qest*: 'One should not expect the easy victory of justice and
equity over oppression and tyranny before the appearance of the hidden
Imam, but neither should one give up hope'.[266] Finally, the two men differ
on polytheism. For Shariati, this concept is inseparable from social and
economic inequity; his solution to the problem is a class war which would
restore to the exploited what had been expropriated from them. Bazargan
accepts the status quo, maintaining that any action which excludes a
segment of the population is a polytheistic act, since God invites us to act
as a unified body.[267] Elsewhere, Bazargan extends the definition of
polytheism to include those who mix Islamic principles with Marxist
ones and his target clearly becomes Shariati's subsystem.

The most important characteristic of Navab-Safavi's subsystem, emphasizing the forceful imposition of all Islamic ordinances on society, is
entirely incompatible with Bazargan's subsystem. Navab-Safavi's ideal
Islamic state is a homogeneous society in which dissent has been weeded
out and in which all members are blindly unanimous about and thus
subjected to an Islamic world outlook defined by the clergy. Bazargan
castigates such a model as un-Islamic. According to the Qur'an, it is
argued, God will inform and guide those who respect and promote
freedom of expression and the exchange of opinions, since only in such
a community can all ideas be voiced and the most suitable ones chosen.[268]
In Bazargan's view, leaders and systems which require blind obedience
from their people are challenging the will of God and would be considered oppressors and corruptors, *taghout*.[269]

Ever since his resignation, Bazargan has hammered away at one
essential theme. If, he says, freedoms had been respected after the
revolution as stipulated by the constitution, and the clergy, *ruhaniyat*,
had not monopolized every political lever and channel, repression and
despotism would not have taken root. Bazargan accuses the Islamic
government of violating the constitution which is its own creation. He
blames the developing crisis in Iran on the absence of freedom of opinion,

assembly and expression, but most of all on the absence of free elections.[270] Bazargan reminds those who violate democratic and individual
freedoms of a statement on freedom made by Khomeini in the summer
of 1978, a retort to the Shah's declaration that he had granted freedom to
the people. Khomeini said:

> The law has given freedom to the people, God has given freedom to
> the people, Islam has given freedom to the people and the constitution
> has given freedom to the people. What nonsense to say that we have
> been granted freedom. Who are you to grant freedom?[271]

Nationalism and communism

The blending of Iranian nationalism with Islamic internationalism has
always posed a problem for political movements which have tried to
harness both forces. In Bazargan's subsystem, nationalism constitutes an
essential pillar. During his inauguration speech for the IFM in 1961,
Bazargan proclaimed: 'We are Moslems, Iranians and Mossadeqists'.[272]
For Bazargan, the relationship between Islam and Iran is clear: the
objective is 'serving Iran through Islam'.[273] Unlike Navab-Safavi's
subsystem, in which all aspects of social and cultural life are subordinated
to the Islamic mode of life to the extent that Iranian characteristics lose
all identity as they are submerged in Islam, Bazargan seeks to raise Islam
to the position of a principal, though by no means does he wish it to be
the only one. The unconditional adoption of Islam as the sole principle
implies the subordination of national interests to the greater supranational interests of Islam, should the two conflict. For political activists
like Bazargan, who fought primarily for the cause of national sovereignty
and the satisfaction of national interests, the abandonment of a national-
istic platform in favour of any other ideology, even Islam, is difficult to
accept. Yet, as Bazargan himself points out, all of his social and political
activities, all that he does with the aim of serving Iran, has been inspired
by his faith in Islam.[274]

Khomeini's belief in the absolute primacy of Islam over nationalism
conflicted with Bazargan's attempt at combining the two. For Khomeini,
the Iranian people was the means and Islam was the end.[275] His encouragement of the view that the Iranian people had given their lives for the
cause of Islam was an attempt at inculcating the idea that the sole object
of the Iranian revolution was the implementation of an Islamic system.
The consolidation of this concept, by calling the revolution the Islamic
Revolution, facilitated the popularization of the idea that Iran should
serve Islam and therefore abandon its narrower national interests for a
greater cause. The argument was that since the Iranian people had
demonstrated that they had not been led to revolt by their sense of
nationalism, Islam was the sole impetus for the revolution and thus
serving Islam could be its only aim.

The clergy's argument that Iran and Iranians are only a means for
serving Islam has resulted in relentless attacks against all nationalist
manifestations and tendencies. Nationalism is attacked as a sign of

polytheism, since it is said to ascribe a degree of importance to national ideas, culture and tradition which properly belongs only to Islam. Thus nationalists are accused of worshipping a second god, the nation. The Islamic government has attempted to efface all historically or nationally significant signs of the Iranian heritage and replace them with Islamic ways and customs. One of the few traditions that have been maintained are the new year celebration and the holiday on the thirteenth day of the new year. The government's campaigns against national customs and rituals have provoked a nationalist backlash which, combined with the Iran-Iraq war, has created a deep sense of nationalism among Iranians. During the reign of the Shah, young Iranian women showed their opposition to the leader by wearing the veil; today, in the Islamic Republic of Iran, the observance of national traditions and customs is a symbolic act of resistance and opposition.

In defending nationalism and its compatibility with Islam, Bazargan argues that the Qur'an permits holy war, or *jihad*, only when a people must defend its country against aggressors.[276] Thus, he says,

> one cannot separate love for Iran and its people from being a Moslem, and view Islam as anti-Iranian and anti-nationalistic. Without this country and its people, there will be no one and no place left to conclude the revolution for the benefit of Islam and of the disinherited of the world.[277]

With regard to communists in Iran, Bazargan's subsystem is similar, yet not identical, to those of Navab-Safavi and Motahhari. Bazargan sees himself as the champion of the Iranian middle class. He believes that 'humane qualities' are most often found among the middle class, since its members are neither poor, nor extremely rich. Those at the extremes of the spectrum, he argues, are prone to enter into a destructive kind of competition to improve their situations and in this process, humane and religious considerations are overlooked.[278] In the economic sphere, Bazargan favours a mixed system in which the government irons out the problems the private sector cannot cope with. He cites the edict given by Imam Ali to the governor of Egypt as a desirable economic framework:

> Improvement in the general condition of the people is dependent upon the activities of merchants, salesmen and craftsmen who create markets and establish productive units in search of profits. Others cannot perform their task. But the needy and impoverished classes whose condition injures the heart should also be helped. Each one of these classes has been allocated a specific reward by God, and the governor has an obligation to each class according to its social contribution and its enterprise and art. . . . Merchants and tradesmen are the pillars of the economy. Always accept their demands and inform your functionaries to provide them with unlimited help . . . they are all the source of profit and economic prosperity. . . . Be aware that many of them engage in hoarding and in order to make greater profits,

charge any price that they desire. This is detrimental to the welfare of the people. Therefore prevent them from hoarding. Exchange has to be just and prices should not be damaging to either party. Punish those who continue to hoard after you have cautioned them but do not become indulgent in your punishments.[279]

Bazargan wishes to create a socio-political atmosphere in which all members of society are able to conduct their affairs peacefully and legally. The communists, he believes, are by the nature of their ideology, violent and hostile. In his writings, it is this confrontational and destructive aspect of communism which is attacked. Bazargan condemns Marx's philosophy for its pessimism and destructiveness and holds the left responsible for all the excesses practised after the revolution.[280] His obsession with Marx and Marxism leads him to make statements the coherence and validity of which are clearly suspect. To prove that violence and hatred constitute the essential pillar of Marx's system, Bazargan writes: 'The labour theory of value which is considered to be Marx's greatest economic masterpiece was essentially formulated for inciting hatred and revolutionary agitation'.[281] Bazargan's ignorance about Marx and his formulations is not surprising when one recalls that even Shariati, who was deeply influenced by Marx, had never been seriously educated in Marxism. Bazargan's weakness, in terms of providing an unemotional analysis of the role of Marxists during and following the revolution, leads him to assertions which are both erroneous and misleading. He argues that the spirit of vengefulness and brutality which came to dominate the post-revolutionary period was due solely to the influence of the left. The executions, the witch-hunts in the guise of purging non-zealous employees, the spiteful allegations, the spread of intolerance, all this, says Bazargan, was the contribution of the left.[282] He goes as far as saying that: 'it was the rapid penetration of leftist ideas and goals among the religious and doctrinaire groups' that led to the reign of terror.[283]

Bazargan is well aware that the executions were controlled and administered by the clergy and as Khalkhali, the revolutionary prosecutor, candidly acknowledged, it was he who, having received a written decree from Khomeini, rapidly undertook to exercise Islamic justice by executing the 'corruptors on earth'. Blaming the left entirely for the violence committed after the revolution shows ignorance not only with regard to Marxism, but also about Navab-Safavi and Shariati. The categorical violence preached and extolled by Navab-Safavi, to be unleashed when Islamic ordinances were disregarded, was far closer to the hearts of young rural migrants turned revolutionaries than was any concept of class hatred formulated by the revolutionary left.

Bazargan's approach to communism and the left is so tempermental that it undermines his commitment to democratic principles. On the one hand, he criticizes the government's purge of non-zealous employees from the civil services, calling it a witch-hunt which settles old scores and creates a distrustful, vindictive atmosphere. He is adamant about the incompatibility of such acts with Islam.[284] On the other hand, Bazargan invites his audience, during a speech made in Zanjan, to pray with him to God to: 'purge all Marxists from the civil services and the revolutionary institutions and replace them with honest people'.[285] The argument that purges, or 'purification campaigns', are evil and non-Islamic except when they are used against Marxists, casts a sombre shadow of doubt over Bazargan's respect for democracy.

On the occasion of the arrest of the leaders of the Tudeh Party of Iran (the traditional pro-Soviet communist party), the IFM published a pamphlet congratulating the authorities for their enterprise. It contains an alarming statement which reflects the IFM's intolerance of Marxist tendencies. The Islamic authorities are warned that:

> we should not be content with these arrests and thus limit ourselves to them, since even though the members of this group [the Tudeh Party] have been arrested, the poisonous residue of their ideology still remains in this country and it exerts its hegemony. The time has come for us to cleanse and purify once and for all the home of the revolution from the spider-webs of Marxism. We have to wash away and cast out from the dominant political outlook the Marxist culture, dialectical contradictions and Stalinist methods which are the end result of this group's [the Marxists] propaganda.[286]

As long as Bazargan continues to treat Marxists as an exceptional group to which democratic benefits need not, and should not, be applied, even the most democratic of Islamic subsystems will fall short of fulfilling the requirements of qualifying as politically democratic.

Notes

1. James A. Bill, 'Power and Religion in Revolutionary Iran', *The Middle East Journal*, Vol. 36, No. 1, Winter 1982, p. 36.

2. Mehdi Bazargan, *Azadi az do didgah.* (Teheran: Nehzate Azadi Iran, Dey 1362), p. 17. Bazargan refers to Ayatollah Mahdavi-Kani and Ayatollah Montazeri as two influential authorities who have repeatedly asserted that disagreeing with certain acts or ideas of those in the ruling circles is neither illegal nor against the religious laws, but on the contrary it is a common feature of any and all human, Islamic and free systems.

3. The *Economist*, 9–15 May 1987, p. 43. The *Guardian Weekly*, 1 February 1987, p. 8.

4. The *Guardian Weekly*, 29 March 1987, p. 15. Amir Taheri, *The Spirit of Allah* (London: Hutchinson 1985), p. 292.

5. Mehdi Bazargan, *Enqelab-e Iran Dar Do Harekat*, op. cit., p. 197.

6. S. Bakhash, Ibid. p. 51. Amir Taheri presents an unsubstantiated thriller type scenario in which in December 1977, upon the receipt of a message from Ayatollah Khomeini to prepare for *jihad*, Ayatollah Motahhari invites Ayatollahs Beheshti, Mohieddin Anvari and Golzadeh Ghaffouri. 'All four had been designated by Khomeini himself as members of a special secret committee charged with the task of "supervising the defence of the faith" under Motahhari himself.' Taheri, Ibid., p. 183.

7. Bahonar, 'Karnameh-e Shoura-e Enqelab', *Ettelaat*, 14 September 1980. In an interview with Hamid Algar, Bazargan says that the Revolutionary Council was supposed to act as the Majlis (The Parliament) and the government was to carry out the task of the executive. In *Mavaze' Nehzat-e Azadi Dar Barabare Enqelab-e Islami*

(Teheran: Nehzat-e Zanan-e Mosalman, 1361), p. 132.

8. Dr Abdol Karim Soroosh (ed.) *Yadnameh Ostad Shaheed Morteza Motahhari* (Teheran: Sazeman Entesharat va Amoozesh Enqelab-e Islami, 1360), p. 3.

9. *Kalam Imam*, Daftar Panjom, Shakhsiyatha (Teheran: Entesharat Amir Kabir, 1361), p. 53.

10. M. Motahhari, *Adl Elahi* (Teheran: Entesharat Sadra), p. 133.

11. Ibid., p. 127.

12. Ibid., p. 81.

13. M. Motahhari, *Piramoone Enqelab-e Islami* (Teheran: Entesharat Sadra), p. 38, Herafter referred to as *Piramoone*.

14. Ibid., p. 39.

15. M. Motahhari, *Naqdi bar Marxism* (Teheran: Entesharat Sadra, 1363), p. 124.

16. Motahhari, *Sociology of Qur'an*, op. cit., Tawhid, p. 161.

17. Motahhari, *Piramoone*, op. cit., p. 32.

18. Motahhari, *Jamee va Tarikh* (Teheran: Entesharat Sadra), pp. 162–70.

19. Motahhari, *Piramoone*, op. cit., p. 11.

20. Ibid., p. 7-10.

21. Imam Khomeini, *Islam and Revolution, Writings and Declarations* trans. Hamid Algar (London: RKP, 1985), p. 269.

22. Ibid., p. 103.

23. Ibid., p. 101.

24. M. Bazargan, op. cit., *Enqelab-e Iran Dar Do Harakat*, p. 52.

25. M. Motahhari, *Moshkellat Assasi Dar Sazeman Ruhaniyat* (Teheran), p. 4.

26. Ibid., pp. 22–3.

27. Ibid., p. 21.

28. Ibid., p. 35.

29. M. Motahhari, *Nehzathaye Islami dar Sad Saleh Akhir* (Teheran: Entesharat Sadra), p. 71.

30. Motahhari, Piramoone, op. cit., p. 182.

31. Ibid., p. 184.

32. Motahhari, *Nehzathaye Islami dar Sad Saleh Akhir,* op. cit., p. 84.

33. Motahhari, *Piramoone,* op. cit., p. 184.

34. Speech to the women of Qum. Khordad 1358, Cited in A. Abolhassani (Manzar). *Shaheed Motahhari* (Teheran: Daftar-e Entesharat-e Islami, 1362), pp. 43–4.

35. Motahhari, *Adl Elahi,* op. cit., p. 131. The sura is: Divorce, *The Koran*, ibid., p. 429.

36. Motahhari, *Piramoone,* op. cit., p. 149–51.

37. Ibid., p. 145.

38. Motahhari, *Adl Elahi,* op. cit., p. 233.

39. See his speech on 'Independence and Freedom', Motahhari, *Piramoone,* op. cit., p. 163.

40. M. Motahhari, *Dah Goftar* (Teheran: Entesharat Hekmat), pp. 236–7. Similar references can be found in Motahhari, *Piramoone,* op. cit., p. 124.

41. S. Irfani, *Revolutionary Islam in Iran* (London: Zed Press, 1983), p. 217.

42. Motahhari, *Piramoone,* op. cit., pp. 84–5.

43. Ibid., p. 160.

44. Ali Mazrui, 'Ideological Encounters of the Third World', *Third World Book Review*, Vol. 7, No. 6, 1986, p. 10.

45. Motahhari, Piramoone, op. cit., p. 57.

46. Hamid Algar, *The Islamic Revolution in Iran,* (London: Open Press, 1980), p. 47.

47. Dr Ali Shariati, *Collected Works, Vol. 26* (Teheran: Entesharat Niloufar, Bahar 1362), p. 409.

48. John L. Esposito, op. cit., p. 194. In the biographical sketch that is provided in the English translations of Shariati's works such as *Martyrdom* and *Hajj,* it is mentioned that he had received 'two Ph.D's in the fields of sociology and the history of religions'.

49. A. Shariati, op. cit., p. 596. Ali Shariati presents his father's opinion as well as his own, on whether it was Imam Ali's right or the people's right that was denied, when

Imam Ali did not become the first Caliph.

50. Fischer, op. cit., p. 168. Fischer presents a table of Shariati's mistakes in dogma.
51. N. R. Keddie. (ed.), *Religion and Politics in Iran: Shi'ism from Quietism to Revolution* (New Haven: Yale University Press, 1983), Shahrough Akhavi, p. 125.
52. A. Janzadeh, *Dr Shariati* (Teheran: Entesharat Hamgam) cited in op. cit. Ali Abolhassani Manzar, p. 288.
53. Hamid Algar, *The Islamic Revolution in Iran* (London: Open Press, 1980) p. 47.
54. Dr Ali Shariati, *Collected Works, Vol. 30* (Teheran: Entesharat Niloufar, 1362), p. 109.
55. Dr Ali Shariati, *Pedar, Madar, Ma Motahamim* (Teheran, Hosseinieh-e Irshad, 1350), p. 116.
56. Dr Ali Shariati, *Martyrdom.* trans. Laleh Bahktiar and Husayn Salih (Teheran: Abu Dharr Foundation), pp. 54–5.
57. Motahhari, *Adl Elahi,* op. cit., p. 132.
58. Shariati, *Martyrdom,* op. cit., p. 56.
59. Dr Ali Shariati, *Hajj,* trans. by Ali Behzadnin and Najla Denny (Houston: Free Islamic Literatures Inc. 1980), p. 76.
60. Ibid., p. 77.
61. Among Shariati's numerous definitions of class the one that comes closest to a Marxian definition is: 'A group of people who share similar types of work, lifestyle or income'. Shariati, *Collected Works Vol. 26,* p. 490.
62. Shariati, ibid., pp. 237-8.
63. Shariati, Collected Works Vol. 26, op. cit., p. 244.
64. Imam Khomeini, *Islam and Revolution,* op. cit., p. 244.
65. Ibid., p. 252.
66. Shariati, Collected Works Vol. 26, op. cit., p. 293.
67. Ibid., p, 290.
68. Ayatollah Khomeini, *Khat Imam, Kalam Imam* (Teheran: Entesharat Noor, 1360), p. 183.
69. Motahhari, *Enqelab-e Islami,* op. cit., p. 32.
70. Ayatollah Khomeini, *Khat Imam . . .* op. cit., p. 102.
71. Imam Khomeini, *Islam and Revolution,* op. cit., p. 170.
72. Shariati, *Pedar, Madar . . .* op. cit., p. 70.
73. Nayibal-Imam Khomeini, *Hokomat Islami* (Teheran), p. 37.
74. *Mavaz-e Nehzat Nehzat-e Azadi Dar Barabare Enqelab-e Islami* (Teheran: Nehzat-e Zanan-e Mosalman, 1361), pp. 143-4.
75. Ibid., p. 144.
76. Shariati, Collected Works Vol. 30., op. cit., p. 25.
77. Dr Ali Shariati, *Mazhab Alieh Mazhab* (Takseer as Anjoman Islami daneshjouyan dar Amrika va Canada), p. 42.
78. Shariati, Collected Works Vol. 26, op. cit., p. 471.
79. Shariati, *Hajj,* op. cit., p. 101.
80. Dr Ali Shariati, *Tarikh Adyan* (Teheran: Entesharat Taheri), p. 334.
81. Ibid., p. 332.
82. Ibid., p. 334.
83. Shariati, *Hajj,* op. cit., p. 103.
84. Ibid., p. 103.
85. Shariati, *Mazhab Alieh Mazhab,* op. cit., p. 25.
86. Ali Abolhassani (Manzar), *Motahhari,* op. cit., p. 99.
87. Khomeini, *Hokomat Islami,* op. cit., p. 167.
88. A speech to the clergy 18, 6, 1360.
89. Shariati, Collected Works Vol. 26, op. cit., p. 577.
90. Ibid., p. 521.
91. Khomeini, *Hokomat Islami,* op. cit., p. 55.
92. Ibid., pp. 79–80.
93. Ibid., p. 46.
94. Shariati, Collected Works Vol. 26, op. cit., pp. 601, 624.
95. Khomeini, *Islamic Government,* op. cit., p. 41.

96. Shariati, Collected Works Vol. 26., op. cit., p. 626.
97. Ibid., p. 502.
98. Ibid., pp. 620, 627.
99. Ibid., pp. 501–2.
100. Karl Marx, *Surveys from Exile*, (ed.) D. Fernbach (London: Penguin Books, 1977), p. 264.
101. Shariati, Collected Works Vol. 26, op. cit., p. 624.
102. Motahhari, *Adl Elahi*, op. cit., pp. 178, 184.
103. Ibid., p. 185.
104. Shariati, *Mazhab Alieh Mazhab*, op. cit., p. 51.
105. Shariati, *Hajj*, op. cit., p. 29.
106. Shariati. Collected Works Vol. 26, op. cit., p. 38.
107. Shariati, *Martyrdom,* op. cit., p. 106.
108. Imam Khomeini, *Islam and Revolution,* op. cit., p. 48.
109. Shariati, *Hajj*, op. cit., p. 144.
110. Shariati, Collected Works Vol. 30, op. cit., p. 62.
111. Ibid., p. 544.
112. Ibid., p. 534.
113. Ibid., p. 513.
114. Hamid Enayat, *Modern Islamic Political Thought* (London: Macmillan Education Ltd., 1982), p. 158.
115. Enayat, op. cit, p. 204. H. Khoshneiyat, *Sayyed Mujtaba Navab-Safavi* (Teheran: Entesharat Manshoore Baradari, 1360), p. 59.
116. See Khoshneiyat, ibid., p. 129 and Reza Golesorkhi, 'Fadaian-e Islam aghazgar-e jonbesh mosallahaneh dar Iran', *Ettelaat* no. 15843, Ordibehesht 10, 1358 (30 April 1979).
117. Navab-Safavi, *Barnameh Enqelabi Fadaian-e Islam* (Teheran), p. 71.
118. Ibid., p. 3.
119. Ibid., p. 52.
120. Ibid, p. 80., Khoshneiyat, op. cit., pp. 107, 124.
121. Khoshneiyat, op. cit., p. 238.
122. Navab-Safavi, op. cit., p. 34.
123. Ibid., pp. 6–8.
124. Ibid., pp. 30–31.
125. Ibid., p. 8.
126. Ibid., p. 54.
127. Ibid., p. 28.
128. Ibid., p. 9.
129. Ibid., pp. 10–11.
130. Ibid., p. 20.
131. Ibid., p. 19.
132. Ibid., p. 6.
133. Ibid., p. 34.
134. Khoshneiyat, op. cit., p. 127.
135. Ibid., p. 202.
136. Ibid., p. 93.
137. Navab-Safavi, op. cit., p. 56.
138. Khoshneiyat, op. cit., p. 210.
139. Ibid., p. 211.
140. Navab-Safavi, op. cit., p. 21.
141. Ibid., p. 45.
142. Ibid., pp. 81–83.
143. Ibid., p. 84.
144. Khoshneiyat, op. cit., p. 141.
145. Ibid., p. 139.
146. Ibid., p. 149.
147. Ibid., pp. 156–7.
148. Navab-Safavi, op. cit., p. 83.

149. Julian Bharier, *Economic Development in Iran: 1900-1970* (New York: Oxford University Press, 1971), p. 30.
150. Farhad Kazemi, *Poverty and Revolution in Iran* (New York: New York University Press, 1980), p. 30.
151. Ibid., p. 30.
152. Ibid., pp. 46, 49.
153. Ibid., p. 55.
154. Ibid., p. 56.
155. Ibid.
156. Karl Marx: *The Class Struggle in France: 1848-1850* (New York: International Publishers, 1972), p. 50.
157. Kazemi, op. cit., p. 126.
158. H. Akhavan Towhidi, *Dar Passe Pardehe Tazvir* (Paris, 1364), p. 266.
159. Navab-Safavi, op. cit., p. 25.
160. Enayat, op. cit., p. 95.
161. Keyhan Sal. Doreh jadid (Teheran: Jeld Aval, 1364), p. 13.
162. Mohammed Ali Rejaee, *Gozideh Sokhanan Raies Jomhoor* (Teheran: Nashre Saberin, 1360), p. 13.
163. Ibid., p. 14.
164. Ibid., p. 31.
165. Imam Khomeini, *Islam and Revolution, op. cit.,* p. 170.
166. Ruhollah Khomeini, *Kashf al-Asrar*, p. 274.
167. Imam Khomeini, op. cit., p. 171.
168. Ibid.
169. Ruhollah Khomeini, op. cit., p. 6.
170. Imam Khomeini, op. cit., p. 173.
171. Khomeini, *Hokomat Islami,* op. cit., p. 35.
172. Soroosh, *Yadnameh,* op. cit., p. 339.
173. Abdol Ali Bazargan, *Moshkelat Va Masael Avalin Sale Enqelab* (Teheran: 1362), p. 1.
174. *Asnade Nehzate Moqavemate Melli* (Teheran: Nehzate Azadi Iran, 1938), p. 10.
175. Bazargan makes this assertion in Bazargan, *Bazyabi-e Arzeshha,* Vol. 2 (Teheran, 1361), p. 171.
176. *U.S. Office of Statistics and Reports, International Administration, Foreign Assistance and Assistance from International Organizations* July 1, 1945 through June 30, 1966, p. 12. Cited in: Amin Saikal, *The Rise and Fall of the Shah* (New Jersey: Princeton University Press, 1980), p. 52.
177. Saikal, op. cit., p. 52.
178. Ibid., p. 73.
179. Ibid., p. 76.
180. Sayyed Jalel-e-din Madani, *Tarikhe Siyasi Moasere Iran* (Teheran: Daftar Entesharat Islami, 1361, Jeld Aval), pp. 354-5.
181. Afrasiabi, B and S Dehqan, *Taleqani va Tarikh* (Teheran, 1359), p. 372.
182. Ibid., p. 403.
183. Akhavi, op. cit., p. 222.
184. Abdol Karim Soroosh, *Yadnameh Ostaad Shaheed Morteza Motahhari* (Teheran: Sazeman Entesharat va Amoozesh Enqelab-e Islami, 1360), p. 364.
185. Nehzate Azadi Iran, *Shesh Nameh-e Sar Goshadeh* (Teheran, 1362), p. 43.
186. Hamid Rouhani, *Barrasi va Tahlili az Nehzate Imam Khomeini* (Teheran, 1361), p. 692.
187. Ibid., p. 693.
188. Ibid.
189. Ibid.
190. Ibid., p. 694.
191. *Mavaz-e Nehzat-e Azadi Dar Barbare Enqelabe Islami* (Teheran: Nehzat-e Zanan-e Mosalmen,1361), pp. 177-8.
192. Mehdi Bazargan, *Bazyabi-e Arzeshha,* Vol. 1 (Teheran, 1362), p. 56.
193. Mehdi Bazargan, *Bazyabi-e Arzeshha,* Vol. 3 (Teheran, 1362), p. 149.

194. Ibid., p. 148.
195. Ibid., p. 27.
196. Bazargan, *Bazyabi-e Arzeshha,* Vol. 2, op. cit., p. 137.
197. Ibid., p. 142.
198. Bazargan, *Bazyabi-e Arzeshha,* Vol. 3, op. cit., p. 28.
199. Ibid., p. 29.
200. Bazargan, *Bazyabi-e Arzeshha,* Vol. 1, op. cit., p. 132.
201. Bazargan, *Bazyabi-e Arzeshha,* Vol. 3, op. cit., p. 32.
202. Ibid., p. 32 and Vol. 1, p. 143.
203. Bazargan, *Bazyabi-e Arzeshha*, Vol. 2, op. cit., pp 93–4.
205. Ibid., p. 25.
206. Ibid., p. 26.
207. Mehdi Bazargan, *Mazhab dar Eurupa* (Teheran: Bongahe Matbuati Iran, 1344), pp. 126–7.
208. Bazargan, *Bazyabi-e Arzeshha*, Vol. 3, op. cit., p. 109.
209. Ibid., p. 110.
210. Bazargan, Bazyabi-e Argeshha, Vol. 1, op. cit., p. 67.
211. Ibid.
212. Ibid., p. 68.
213. Ibid., Vol. 3, p. 109.
214. Ibid., Vol. 1, p. 78.
215. Ibid., Vol. 3, p. 118.
216. Ibid., p. 30.
217. Ibid., p. 110.
218. Ibid., Vol. 1, p. 87.
219. Ibid., Vol. 3, pp. 110–11.
220. Ibid., p. 10.
221. Ibid., p. 11. Bazargan's argument is based on the *Sura* of *Ahzab*, Verse 21.
222. Ibid., p. 12.
223. *Sura* of *Baqarah*, Verses 256–7.
224. Bazargan, *Bazyabi-e Arzeshha,* Vol. 3, op. cit., p. 35.
225. Ibid., p. 36 and Vol. 1, p. 66, based on the *Suras* of: *Youness*, Verses 88-99; *Qashiyeh*, Verses 21-2; *Anaam*, Verse 107.
226. Ibid., Vol. 1, p. 67 and Vol. 3, p. 35, based on the Sura of *Hojr*, Verse 3.
227. Ibid., Vol. 3, p. 12.
228. Ibid., p. 11.
229. Ibid.
230. Ibid., p. 12, based on the *Sura* of *Al Omran*, Verses 153-9. See also: A Rahman I. Doi, *Shariah: The Islamic Law* (London: Taha Publishers, 1984), pp. 15–19.
231. Ibid., Vol. 1, p. 73, based on the *Sura* of *Shoura*, Verses 36–8.
232. Ibid.
233. Ibid., Vol. 3, p. 116.
234. Ibid., p. 117.
235. Ibid., Vol. 1, p. 63.
236. Ibid., p. 74.
237. Ibid., Vol. 2, p. 118.
238. Ibid., p. 109.
239. Ibid., p. 118.
240. Ibid.
241. Ibid., p. 113.
242. Ibid., Vol. 1, p. 85.
243. Ibid., p. 77.
244. Ibid.
245. Ibid., p. 36, based on the *Sura* of *Tobeh*, Verse 6.
246. Ibid.
247. Ibid., p. 123.
248. Bazargan, *Mazhab dar Eurupa*, op. cit., p. 136.
249. Bazargan, *Moshkelat Va Masael . . .* op. cit., pp. 73, 74, 79.

250. Bazargan, *Bazyabi-e Arzeshha*, Vol. 1, op. cit., p. 73.
251. *Mavaze Gorouhha Dar Qebal Enqelab-e Islami* (Teheran: Vezarte Ershad Islami, 1360), p. 41.
252. Bazargan, *Moshkelat Va Masael* . . . op. cit., p. 226.
253. Ibid., p. 228.
254. Ibid., p. 131.
255. Ibid., p. 33.
256. Ibid., p. 282.
257. Ibid., pp. 112, 208.
258. See ibid., p. 98.
259. Ibid., p. 67.
260. Bazargan, *Bazyabi-e Arzeshha*, Vol. 3, op. cit., p. 71.
261. Ibid., p. 45.
262. Bazargan, *Mazhab dar Eurupa*, op. cit., pp. 124-5.
263. Bazargan, *Bazyabi-e Arzeshha*, Vol. 1, op cit., p. 62.
264. Ibid., p. 63.
265. Ibid., Vol. 3, pp. 115–16.
266. Ibid., Vol. 2, p. 228.
267. Ibid., p. 141.
268. Ibid., Vol. 3, p. 77.
269. Ibid., p. 76.
270. *Bohran, Tahlili az Vekhamat Ozae Keshvar,* Nehzate Azadi, 1361, p. 19.
271. Bazargan, *Enqelab-e Iran Dar Do Harekat*, op. cit., p. 92.
272. Bazargan, *Bazyabi-e Arzeshha*, Vol. 2, p. 117.
273. Ibid., p. 118.
274. Ibid., p. 120.
275. Ibid., p. 119.
276. Ibid., pp. 21–22.
277. Ibid., p. 22.
278. Ibid., Vol. 1, p. 18.
279. Ibid., pp. 137–8.
280. Ibid., p. 20.
281. Ibid., Vol. 2, p. 183.
282. Bazargan, *Enqelab-e Iran Dar Do Harekat*, op. cit., p. 171.
283. Ibid., p. 94.
284. Bazargan, *Bazyabi-e Arzeshha*, Vol. 2, op. cit., p. 16.
285. Ibid., p. 53.
286. *Piramoone Dastigirie Sarane Hezbe Khaeen Tudeh* (Teheran: Nehzate Azadi, 1362), p. 6.:

4. The Economic Subsystems of *Shi'i* Islam

Introduction

In Chapter 2 we said that *Shi'i* Islam: 'presents itself as an arbiter, a broker which could successfully satisfy the aspirations of all different groups and classes'. To examine this appeal of *Shi'i* Islam as an ideology and a tool for action in the Iranian revolution, chapters 2 and 3 presented the interpretations and socio-political positions of major religious authorities and activists. Our objective was to provide an ideological explanation for the ability of the Islamic leadership to gain hegemony over the revolution, to ride out different crises and to continue to remain in power in the class-ridden, heterogeneous Iranian society. However, the economic thoughts and positions of the individuals who were identified with these subsystems were barely touched upon. This is because most of those whose socio-political views were discussed did not always write on economic matters and, if they did, their writings are scanty and too general to enable a meaningful study of their ideal Islamic economic systems. Nevertheless, the emphases they placed on certain important aspects of the Islamic economic system, for example, their positions on the legitimacy of private ownership and its limitations and on the economic role of the state in the operation of the system, makes it possible to associate them with specific shades in the spectrum of the *Shi'i* Islamic economic school. Therefore, in this chapter, we will examine the main economic thoughts of those who have either tried to present the goals, institutions and structure of an ideal Islamic economy as a system distinct from capitalism or socialism, in a more or less systematic manner or have, to some extent, presented their views on the Islamic economic model. Though our major objective is to show the source of the historical eclecticism and pragmatic approach of the leaders of the Islamic Republic regarding economic policies (which will be studied in Chapter 6), the following study illuminates the ideal economic system envisioned by the major contemporary *Shi'i* writers.

Our references

The main references for our discussion in this chapter are the basic economic ordinances and studies of: Ayatollah Khomeini; Ayatollah Taleqani, Ayatollah Baqer Sadr; the professors of the Qum seminary school and the lectures and articles of Ayatollah Azari-Qumi and Hojatolislam Hashemi-Rafsanjani. This list basically represents all the important economic tendencies within the government of the Islamic Republic of Iran.

Parts of Khomeini's economic ordinances and judgements have been translated from Arabic and have been collected in *Resaleh-e Nouvin* (*New Treatise*).[1] The second volume of this collection was translated and edited by A. Biazar-e-Shirazi and received the approval of Khomeini's secretarial office. It covers his religious judgements in *Tahrir al-vassileh* (*Elaboration on Means of Salvation*) on Islamic taxes, transactions, contracts and ownership.

The core of Taleqani's *Islam va Malekiat* (*Islam and Ownership*), which was first published in Teheran in 1965, is presented in *Society and Economics in Islam*.[2] *Islam and Ownership* is one of the first serious attempts to discuss the Islamic economic system from a *Shi'i* perspective although one could say that to some extent the forerunner to Taleqani's effort is the Fadaian-e Islam programme, first published in 1950.[3]

Mohammed Baqer Sadr's *Eqtesad-e Na* (*Our Economics*)[4] is another important effort by a *Shi'i* theologian to present the Islamic economic system. Sadr was an influential writer whose works dealt with Islamic jurisprudence, philosophy, logic and economics. He was a politico-religious activist in Iraq, where he was born in 1930 and executed in 1980. *Our Economics* was translated into Persian and was first published in Teheran in 1971. The main arguments of *Our Economics* and *Islam and Ownership* on the sources and limitations of ownership in Islam are basically similar, as is the repeated critical evaluation of capitalism, socialism and the role of the Islamic state found in both works, although Sadr discusses a wider range of economic problems and phenomena. The principal aim of *Our Economics* is to prove that the economic teachings of Islam constitute a 'school of economics' and an economic system. The first volume of the book is exclusively a criticism and refutation of Marxism and to some extent, capitalist political economy.[5] This book has had a great influence on the Islamic economic thinking and position of Ayatollah Beheshti, who was one of the influential leaders of the Islamic government after the revolution.[6]

In 1982, Hashemi-Rafsanjani held teach-in sessions for Islamic Republic Party members, explaining the party's positions as presented in its platform, which was written mainly by Beheshti, Hojatolislam Khamenei and Bahonar after the revolution. The economic positions of this programme were explained by Rafsanjani in ten sessions and were published in a book called *Siyasat-e Eqtesadi* (*Economic Policy*) in 1984.[7]

The interpretation of the ideal Islamic economic system which most resembles Khomeini's outlook is presented in *Daramadi Bar Eqtesad-e Islami* (*An Introduction to Islamic Economics*).[8] The basic economic positions in this book are in harmony with those of Motahhari, Ayatollah Montazeri in recent years, the influential Ayatollahs and the founder of the daily journal *Resalat* (*Mission*). To some extent, Bazargan's vision of some Islamic aspects of the economic system is also represented in this book. However, the book, written between 1981 and 1983 by the professors of the influential Qum seminary, is subtly critical of the more romantic approach taken by Sadr and Taleqani and of their radical phraseology. In fact, although the book contains some references to Sadr's works, Taleqani's are not mentioned.

This important work is the brain-child of many religious authorities and, since the revolution, has received the undeclared backing of many well- and lesser known religious politicians in Iran, so a brief history of its 'creation' may be useful. The need arising during the 'cultural revolution' for the 'reconstruction of social sciences',[9] with the purpose of lending them a religious flavour, led to the book's preliminary draft. This concentrated on the means of establishing a closer relationship between the Qum seminary and the universities. It was prepared by a professor at the seminary, Hojatolislam Mesbah-e-Yazdi, and approved by the Society of the Seminary Instructors (then headed by Azari-Qumi) and by the Office of the Cultural Revolution. The execution of the programme was the responsibility of the Committee of Seminary and University, which was formed by the Society of the Seminary Instructors. In the summer of 1981, this committee created the Office of the Co-operation of the Seminary and the University, which aimed to reconstruct the five social science branches of economics, sociology, law and political science, psychology and education. The office included twenty elected seminary and university professors, whose task was the 'purification' of the social sciences. The two volumes of *An Introduction to the Islamic Economy* were the product of the working group on Islamic economics within the office. The introductory chapters of the first volume are concerned with the behavioural aspect of human beings under the Islamic system, the objectives of the Islamic economic system and sources and methodology of Islamic economics; the succeeding chapters deal with ownership (the rights, forms and limits of ownership and disposition), production, distribution and consumption in the Islamic economy. Each chapter also discusses the Islamic economic laws and the ideal behaviour of economic agents in an Islamic system. Thus the textbook is not really an analytical study of Islamic economics, but simply economic jurisprudence classified and categorized according to some basic modern economic nomenclature.[10]

As we will see, the economic views of the writers mentioned constitute two converging tendencies. The views of Sadr and Taleqani can be considered as a more or less radical interpretation of Islamic economic positions, while those of the seminary professors, including Azari-Qumi, are conservative and *laissez-faire* oriented. Khomeini's economic views as presented in his pre-revolution writings are in line with the latter, although he sometimes played with both tendencies.

Their sources and methodology

One would search in vain for a theoretical economic framework in the works of any of the aforementioned writers. This is because *Shi'i* Islamic political economy does not explain the objective laws governing the processes of production and distribution in real societies. Islam is considered to be a universal vision or truth, an ideology, which is to provide a moral framework for timeless, ahistorical economic and other social relations. Sadr explicitly addresses this problem by saying that: 'Islamic economy represents a just system of economic life, but it has nothing to do with the scientific discovery of the economic relationship as it actually exists'.[11] The Qum seminary professors accept Sadr's differentiation, even though they seem more aware of the need for an economic theory for the 'efficient' functioning of the Islamic economic system.[12] This may be because their economic viewpoint had been influenced by collaboration with the economics professors of the universities.

The timeless and universal Islamic principles which govern the entire code of life, including the economic activities which form the foundation of Islamic economics, apply to the past, the present and the future. They are based on the primary sources, the 'revealed knowledge', or injunctions and precepts in the Qur'an, the practices and sayings of the Prophet and the twelve *Shi'i* Imams in the Sunnah and *hadith*, for example, and on the secondary sources, or the subsequent analogical deductions, interpretations and consensus of the theologians, such as *ijma*.

The process of deducing new verdicts and ordinances from the original texts of the Qur'an, authenticated Sunnah and *hadith* was claimed to involve a high degree of reasoning and interpretation and is known as *ijtihad*, or independent judgement. However, *ijtihad* is only possible when it is not in conflict with the Qur'an or the Sunnah. The *mojtahed*, a person who exercises this independent judgement, must deduce these laws and regulations only for new events which could not have been known to his predecessor. This leads to another principle, a well-known tenet of the Usuli school of twelver *Shi'ism*, the *taqlid*, which enjoins the Moslem to imitate the living *mojtaheds*.[13] A strong emphasis is placed on taqlid, since without it, *ijtihad* would have divisive effects and because there is concern about the corrosive effects of foreign concepts and ideas and about protecting the 'cause of righteousness'. Referring to young Moslem radicals who demand quick socio-economic reforms, the Qum seminary professors defend the 'complicated' process of *ijtihad* in the following manner:

Some simpletons are of the opinion that the process of deducing ordinances can not be so difficult and say, what did Abuzar do? What about Salman and Meqdad?[14] Did they sit and discuss and spend a lot of time on these things? You are making the work of deducing ordinances unduly difficult.[15]

The devices employed by the jurists and *mojtaheds* to deduce new rules and regulations are numerous. Basically, deductive or inductive logic is used, or a combination of both. Principles of the Islamic economic system are deduced from the primary sources; historical precedents in the primary sources are also referred to in the inductive process of finding solutions to current economic problems.

Shi'i interpreters of the ideal Islamic economic system are all of the opinion that the Islamic state and economy have not yet been instituted, except for two brief periods, one at the time of the Prophet and another at the time of Imam Ali, the first *Shi'i* Imam. It is believed that during these periods, Islamic economic institutions and precepts were, in fact, implemented, an experience which provided the *Shi'i* Moslems with the sayings and practices of the Prophet and Imam Ali. It is also believed that the methods they used as patrons and rulers of the community, and the conduct of the people in economic activities, had their approval: 'The system derived from any of these sources must have the Islamic form and label'.[16] However, these sayings and practices basically reflected a socio-economic context which was traditional, rural, and in some urban areas, commercial. Ownership of the means of production at the level of the individual workshop was widespread and petty commodity production was the rule in major urban areas. Given this concrete setting, the Qur'an and the Sunnah could not, obviously, say anything more on the subject of a developed, complex and dynamic economic system.[17] Nevertheless, it is claimed that the Qur'an and the Sunnah set certain principles and approve or condemn the workings of certain institutions, from which *Shi'i* theoreticians develop a conceptual framework to explain past economic behaviour, present economies or expected socio-economic relations of the future.

This creates a problem for Islamic economic writers and interpreters. The writers whose views will be discussed, excluding Shariati, are or have been *mojtaheds*. As such, they have had to reconcile economic reality with the teachings of the *Shari'a*, or sacred laws. However, their economic ideology reflects the contradictory nature of a doctrine which emerged from a more or less heterogenous, traditional, petty commodity production and commercial society, which was then adapted by the classic Islamic jurisconsults to fit the more developed, feudal or pre-capitalist economy of the middle eastern societies of the Middle Ages and which now attempts to fit the present capitalist economies, while at the same time trying to safeguard its creed and influence. Some of these interpreters, like Shariati, do not bother to be 'authentic' and dare to make their own radical interpretations, which are more in line with existing modern socio-economic outlooks. But the *mojtaheds* do not enjoy this kind of freedom. They are prisoners of their own dogmas to a larger extent than the non-*mojtahed* Moslems. To avoid doctrinal difficulties, they

make a distinction between Islamic economy and the science of economics: 'Islam has not come to discover the phenomena of economic life and
their causes. That is not its responsibility'.[18] The *mojtaheds* do like to
draw a line between what is 'just' and what is not. When they do this, they
are confronted with historically developed socio-economic phenomena,
for instance, labour, capital and capitalist rent, within the ahistorical
framework of the *Shari'a* and the interpretations of the classical jurists.
In addition, they must always handle economic questions within the
context of the kinds of contracts involved in transactions. Both the former
and the latter problems, which constitute a juridical approach to economic activity, are distinct features of scholasticism and create many
contradictory situations for the *mojtaheds*. We will see, for example, that
while they staunchly condemn interest, they must justify trade, private
ownership and profit.[19]

In order to educate non-initiated Moslems and to encourage them to
embrace their faith, *motjaheds* launch political and philosophical attacks
on Marxism and to a lesser degree on other 'western ideologies'.
Sometimes, in the efforts to politically refute Marxism, Islamic laws and
traditions are interpreted in such a way as to make them appear revolutionary. Conservative *mojtaheds*, however, do not want to sound revolutionary. Therefore, they are able to take care of the problem by merely
attacking the so-called 'materialistic foundation' of capitalism and
socialism, although they, too, engage in analytical criticism of Marxist
and capitalist economies. Despite the fact that the *mojtaheds* want to
avoid examining economics as a positive social science, they are sometimes obliged to debate economic laws such as the law of value, but this
is rarely done in a rigorous, analytical way. Finally, when discussion of
certain socio-economic problems would not suit their purposes, it is
simply avoided. This tactic was used by Khomeini who, as the supreme
jurisconsult, was expected by believers to translate his verbal condemnation of unbridled capitalism and socialism, corruption, *estekbar* or arro-
gance, and class differences into a scheme of systematic reform, which
he has always refused to do. In the past, before the revolution, Khomeini
did not hesitate to give his legal opinion on petty matters, such as whether
or not alms tax could be levied on women's necklaces.[20] Faced with the
stalemate in socio-economic reforms after the revolution, some of his
closest followers, including Rafsanjani, publicly begged Khomeini to
offer guidance and make use of his uncontested prerogatives in order to
break the economic impasse strangling the disinherited, or the *mostazafin*,
which he verbally eulogized. For a long time his response was to observe
a nobly ambiguous silence, or to offer a prayer for their salvation.

One reason offered for Khomeini's silence on economic matters after
the revolution, is that his opposition to any 'Islamic eclecticism' (*Islam-
e elteqati*) made him fear that he could get himself involved in reconciling
Islam with modern economic ideas.[21] However, as we will see, the more
important reason is that Khomeini's economic views were basically
traditional and conservative, which, if implemented, could at best give
rise to a primitive Islamic market-oriented economic system. Khomeini

could manoeuvre populist political methods to implement his views and objectives, as he did before and after the revolution. But as a traditional *mojtahed* of the school of twelver *Shi'ism*, he knew very well that his commanding position as *faqih*, or jurisconsult, required him to make the *Shari'a* the only law of the land. The *Shari'a* excludes man-made laws, no matter how wise and proper they are. The basic economic institutions and ordinances which have been approved by the *Shari'a* regarding the legitimacy of private ownership and market transactions, for example, are inflexible. It is no wonder that we never find Khomeini using populist phraseology when dealing with economic issues. In fact, during the first year of Islamic power in Iran, concerned by the demands of the masses for earthly, concrete economic reforms, Khomeini dismissed the problem by stating that: 'economics is for the donkey'.

Philosophic foundations of Islamic economics

All of the contemporary writers on *Shi'i* socio-economic views make the point that Islam can accept neither capitalism and its ideology, nor Marxism and its ideal socio-economic system. This is stressed in every radical interpretation of the Islamic outlook, such as Shariati's, as well as in those of traditional-conservative *mojtaheds* from the Qum seminary, such as Azari-Qumi. All agree, therefore, that Islam must 'offer an alternative programme consistent with its own outlook' to guide the Moslem community.[22] While 'western theories' of capitalism and Marxism are 'materialistic theories', Islam will ensure 'the fulfilment of the material and moral needs of mankind'.[23] For these writers, Islam is the only ideology with dimensions covering life in this world and in the hereafter: 'It is only Islam that looks after both [spiritual and temporal] aspects of human life, whereas all other social systems are confined to social and economic aspects only'.[24] Islam alone, they claim, teaches us how to lead a moral and fruitful life in poverty and in wealth. They conclude that since this unity of spiritual and temporal affairs exists only in an Islamic society, Islamic beliefs, customs and ethics make of its citizens: 'a big motivating and constructive force for the purpose of organizing the economy and economic life along correct lines'.[25] To this end, Islam must change the materialist concept of life and this is the system's major objective: to combat the material concept of existence and the universe and to provide a conceptual basis for society in which 'neither is the individual an automatic tool in the service of society, nor is society a body formed for the sake of the individual'.[26]

Nevertheless, the individual remains the basic unit of society, playing the role of vicegerent of God on earth, with the aim of obtaining Allah's blessing on earth and in the hereafter. The utilitarian concepts of pain and pleasure used in neo-classical economics are transformed into the pleasure of Allah and avoidance of the pain resulting from God's wrath. A Moslem will: 'make the pleasure of Allah the criterion of all his deeds throughout his life'.[27] The present world prepares the individual for a:

'journey towards the eternal world where there will be no affliction or pain'.[28] The presence of this moral criterion prevents the individual from considering all personal interests as lawful and everything involving an individual loss as unlawful. Self-love and egoism are guided and controlled and the interests of the individual are reconciled to the collective interest of the Islamic society.

With respect to economic freedom, we are told that in Islam the entire *Ummah* (Moslem community, owners and workers) is guaranteed security and private ownership is incorporated in the social system without any contradiction.[29] Social security based on alms taxes provides peaceful cohesion in Islamic society and the individual Moslem submits to the public good when it requires surrender of part of the individual's freedom.

The ideal socio-economic system envisaged by our 'authentic' *Shi'i* writers, then, is an ideological society like that of the ancient Israelites, or medieval Moslem and Christian societies, in that the avowed objective of such a system is to serve God and obey his precepts. It happens that in Islamic society, these precepts also include the temporal organization of society.

Common features of the ideal *Shi'i* economic system

Without discussing, for the moment, the important question of whether or not the system presented by these contemporary writers does, in fact, constitute a distinct economic system, we can identify the features common to their different versions of this ideal economy, using familiar conventional terminology.

As mentioned before, the Islamic faith, with its constant awareness of the hereafter, supposedly makes individuals and their social behaviour different from those in a 'valueless' secular society. Obedience to Allah and to the *Shari'a* is equated with real freedom and the Moslem's purpose in life is to fulfil his role as the vicegerent of God on this earth and to be successful in that role. His success, however, depends on the acquisition and allocation of the resources which are held in trust.

A Moslem, in the spirit of submission to Allah, follows the path of Islam by taking the *Shari'a* and using it to solve his economic problem. This rational and altruistic Islamic behaviour is supposedly built into the Moslem character. The Moslem will follow the *Shari'a* and the *motjaheds'* and jurists' interpretation of it, with regard to consumption, production and distribution decisions. Thus, the Moslem will not produce or consume forbidden goods and services, such as wine, pork or books which propagate secular or un-Islamic ideas, or music which incites lust; the Moslem will be neither wasteful nor spendthrift. The Moslem will shun gambling, lotteries, speculation, monopolistic practices and receipt of interest. On the other hand, the Moslem is permitted to accept a just return from any financial, industrial or service activities engaged in; to hire labour and to enter into lawful contracts and transactions in the market. The Moslem may even own human beings, although this is rarely mentioned nowadays. Zakat and *khums* taxes will be paid and charitable contributions will be made.[30]

All these activities take place within the market, where prices are determined for the factors of production and for goods and services; thus, resources are allocated based on private ownership of the means of production. The Moslem individual can participate fully in market activities provided the precepts and other Islamic constraints are observed. The Islamic government also has a regulatory role to play in the structure and operation of the economy, the objectives and the extent of which are a matter of dispute among our writers. Nonetheless, all agree that the Islamic government shall receive taxes, for example, zakat, and will spend them on welfare and other projects.

No discussion of the Islamic economic system's fiscal and monetary policy is to be found among the writings. One can infer, however, that in this economic system based on small-scale ownership and market, the authors would claim that social behaviour would conform automatically to the Islamic behaviour described above. Apparently, in a truly Islamic society, unemployment, low economic growth, inflation and unequal distribution would not exist. The simplistic answers implicit in these writings, unaccompanied by an analytical discussion, are the following: everyone will receive his fair share in the production process; personal incomes cannot give rise to accumulated wealth due to ethical rules, the institution of zakat and the Islamic inheritance law; income earned is spent either in lawful consumption or for investment purposes; the economy will not be subject to ups and downs or cycles, since there are no leakages from the macrosystem; savings are always available for investment and keep employment continually high. Hence, the rich are free to engage in gainful, lawful activities and the poor are taken care of; all this is mainly through Islam and its economic institutions, such as zakat, small-scale ownership and the prohibition of interest.[31] We are then told that as a result of these institutions and norms: 'Islam has a doctrine which is quite different from the theories of capitalism and Marxism, and as such should be regarded as a third school of economics along with them'.[32] We will see whether this is so or not when we examine in detail some of the major institutional and structural aspects of their economic systems.

It is clear that a third school of economics is not as easily formulated, intellectually or practically, as our writers make it out to be. Not one *mojtahed* or Islamic economist in Iran has provided the Iranian people, even in scant detail, with a reasonable integrated structure of ideas and policies of Islamic economics. No *Shi'i* Moslem intellectual has ever paid serious attention to the micro- and macroeconomic implications of Islamic injunctions and regulations within the Islamic market economy. The material which is presented as economic analysis is often based on illusory conceptions, such as the one which maintains that in an Islamic economy the market: 'in the capitalist sense . . . cannot govern exchanges'[33] or resource allocation, and that: 'goods are offered and made available to the extent required to satisfy the necessities of life'.[34] It is not enough to discard the difficulty by saying that since *Shi'i* Islamic economics has not yet been applied, it cannot provide us with an Islamic science of economics.[35] The social and economic costs of such an attitude in today's modern, complex and dynamic world would be immense, as we will see in chapters 6 and 7 when we look at Islamic economic practices in Iran.

What is, however, clearly spelled out in the writings of our *Shi'i* authors, are their ideas about the important institutional and structural aspects of their ideal economy and the common and differing emphasis of these aspects. We have seen the common features of the ideal *Shi'i* economic system; now we can look at the differences. These differences are due to varying interpretations of some of the Qur'anic and traditional statements and precepts and to different degrees of stress placed on this or that precept or saying to support a particular socio-economic outlook. This is possible because so many views within the framework of Islam are expressed in the above sources. Basically, these differing interpretations revolve around the extent of and limitations imposed on property ownership and wealth, the operation of the market and the Islamic government's role in the operation of the Islamic economy.

The institution of property and property ownership

According to *Shi'i* economic writers, the nature and scope of ownership in the Islamic economic system distinguishes it from all other existing systems, notably capitalism and socialism. Sadr asserts that the problem of property: 'is the basic point of contention between various schools of economics'.[36] The professors of the Qum seminary tell us that by: 'knowing the form and scope of ownership in any economic system one can find the position of that economic system with respect to other economic issues'.[37] The writers consistently stress that in Islam, God has 'real ownership', while man merely holds property in trust and that, therefore, man is accountable to God and must follow His various injunctions relating to property, laid down in the *Shari'a*. According to the Qur'an: 'His, whatsoever is in the Heavens and whatsoever is in the Earth, and whatsoever is between them both, and whatsoever is beneath the humid soil'.[38] Or, in other words: 'All that is in the Heavens and all that is on the Earth is God's': and God encompasseth all things'.[39]

The concept of 'real or absolute ownership' cannot be used as an economic or legal criterion and is a matter relegated to Islamic philosophy. It is interesting to note that the Qum seminary professors reject the use by young Moslem radicals of the 'God's ownership principle' as a guide for land reform.[40] If God is the real or absolute owner, His vicegerent can own the riches of this world only in a nominal or relative form which is subject to a moral obligation to be discharged through voluntary effort. Having said this, all the 'authentic' *mojtaheds* affirm that: 'in the view of Islam, property ties . . . are bound up with the pattern of thought and with human sentiments and instincts'.[41] Nevertheless, the *Shi'i* writers' differences on the subject of ownership focus on two main points: the legitimacy of private ownership and the degree of social control of private ownership, or its limitations.

Legitimacy of private ownership

Of the authors whose economic views are discussed in this chapter, Shariati is the only one who explicitly rejects the legitimacy of private ownership in an ideal economic system. According to his theory of history and social evolution, the ideal social system of Islam is based on equity and the people's common ownership. This ideal society is a revival of the 'system of Abel', a society of 'human equality and thus also of brotherhood – the classless society'.[42] This is the fundamental principle of Shariati's ideal Islamic society, 'whose infrastructure is economy', but not its objective. This last point distinguishes his ideal society from 'western socialism', which 'has retained the [materialistic] world view of the Western bourgeoisie'.[43]

Shariati's view is not shared by the *mojtaheds,* since they accept the Qur'anic precept which recognizes the existence of different classes, the legitimacy of ownership, the benefits derived from it and the ownership 'instinct'. According to the professors of the Qum seminary: 'private property has an innate natural root. Islam has confirmed this ownership in accordance with the nature of man and has set limits and regulations for it'.[44] In one of his books, Khomeini refers to the *hadith* which states that: 'people have dominance over their property' and that 'the rule of respect for the belongings of Moslems is derived from the rule of reign over belongings, because the owner of the object rules over it and has all rights concerning its disposition'.[45] Khomeini then cites the Prophet's statement, made during his last pilgrimage: 'Your blood and your belongings are forbidden to each other.'[46] It is natural, then, to hear Rafsanjani claiming that 'individuals can own water, land, machines and the like privately'.[47] Sadr, recognizing the legitimacy of private owner-ship and absolving the institution of private ownership, blames all the deplorable consequences of a capitalist system on materialism, rather than on private property:

> In capitalism it is not private property that is the source of troubles and tragedies. . . . It was not private property that threw millions of workers out ot private property that compels the capitalists to destroy large quantities of their products to keep the prices stable. . . . Lastly it is not private property that impels the capitalists to arrange new markets for themselves even at the cost of the sovereignty and rights of other nations. . . . It is materialism . . . that allows the capitalists to indulge in all sorts of evil practices and unjust transactions.[48]

Contemporary Islamic writers are fond of separating private property, and greed and acquisitiveness, defending one and rejecting the others; this is all done within a market-oriented system which is an inseparable aspect of their ideal economic system. However, they fail to realize that the philosophical position of capitalism justifies private property on the basis of the assumption that the individual is in perpetual pursuit of self-interest or greed. When this capitalist philosophical argument is taken away, what is left is an altruistic behavioural explanation which is typical of all scholastic approaches, including that of the *mojtaheds*. Based on this outlook, the Islamic Republic's constitution recognizes private property as one of the legitimate forms of ownership.[49] The other categories mentioned in the constitution are state and co-operative ownership.[50] The latter cannot be found in the primary or secondary sources of Islam, but neither does it contradict the *Shari'a*.[51] The *mojtaheds* classify ownership in Islam in three categories: imam (Islamic state) ownership, public ownership by Moslems and private ownership.[52] State ownership includes all natural resources which have not been previously owned and all forms of wealth whose proprietors are unknown. They are called *anfal* : 'Say: the spoils [*anfal*] are God's and the apostle's. Therefore, fear God, and settle this among yourselves'.[53] The difference between public and state ownership does not have much operational meaning for contemporary societies. The terms were not even applied in the Middle Ages,[54] so it is no wonder that they are not mentioned in the Islamic Republic's constitution. For all practical purposes, then, the line between state and private ownership is clearly drawn.

Limitations on the right of ownership and disposition[55]

All those who recognize the legitimacy of private ownership in the Islamic economic system stress that since God is the absolute owner of everything, private ownership of wealth and property is 'relative'. The right of ownership and disposition is limited by Islamic rules and regulations. These limitations are not imposed to deny the legitimacy of private ownership, but to 'prevent the undesirable effects of unlimited private ownership. . . . For if private ownership is denied, society will not be able to realize [its] valuable consequences'.[56] However, elegantly classified 'moral' and 'legal' constraints in no way weaken the institution of private property. In addition, some of these constraints are much more inhumane than the corresponding practices of capitalism, which the *Shi'i* writers call deplorable. Moral constraints based on the Qur'an and the Prophet's advice encourage Moslems to avoid ostentatious goods, to help the needy and not to be spendthrifts or prodigal. Wealth is good, if it leads to virtuous living.

The legal limitations on the right of ownership and disposition in Islam are discussed with respect to three categories: individuals, ordinances and the Islamic government. In Islam, certain individuals are not allowed to own anything:

The obvious example is the case of *mortad-e fetri* (innate apostate). He is one whose parents have been Moslem and he himself has accepted Islam after puberty, and then has abandoned the sacred religion of Islam. Such an individual loses the right to own anything . . ., and if he works or if he has an activity, he can't own anything and his belongings will be divided among his Moslem heirs.[57]

Another legal limitation concerns the *kafar-e harbi* (war infidel) who is either engaged in war or has a peace treaty with Moslems. This individual can retain ownership of his property and engage in transactions, but the property may be considered as spoils of war by Islamic jurists. The property of infidels who are not at war with Moslems (*kafar-e zammi*), and some other categories of apostates, such as *mortad-e melli* or national apostates (those whose parents are infidels, but who have rejected Islam after being Moslem for a while), men and women, must be respected in the Islamic system under various restrictive conditions. Islamic ordinances forbid the ownership of: certain animals; instruments of gambling; amusements, such as chess; the buying and selling of pork; wine and so on. These are limitations on the right of ownership and disposition, as is the Islamic government's right to collect *zakat* and other taxes.[58]

Taleqani and Sadr are more subtle in their designation of these limitations, especially regarding non-Moslems. According to Taleqani: 'Mature individuals governed by faith and having moral responsibility are free to dispose of their property as they are free in other matters; they may possess and profit by properties not subject to the claims of others'.[59]

A favourite subject of the *mojtaheds* regarding limitations on the right of ownership is the source of the right of priority in ownership. According to the *mojtaheds*, labour can justify the right to ownership of unused natural resources. This is claimed to be an important point, differentiating Islamic economy from all other economic systems.

Ownership may be primary (original), or transferal (contractual). Primary ownership exists when an individual becomes the owner of an object not owned by anyone before, for example, a precious stone found or firewood gathered in the forest. Transferal ownership refers to the ownership of an object or property which has had a previous proprietor. Labour is claimed as the justification for both kinds of ownership at all stages of the process of production, distribution and exchange, even in the case of transfer of ownership due to inheritance. In the case of contractual ownership, it is said that the labour is not 'the labor of the recipient but the labor of the transferer'.[60]

Taleqani and Sadr, whose views on normative issues are to some extent more radical than those of the professors of the Qum seminary, especially regarding land ownership, place more emphasis on the role of labour in ownership. Even in their discussions, however, the definition of labour is so vague and general that almost any activity, such as buying and selling, is covered. This could not be otherwise, since in the Qur'an and the Sunnah, commerce is a venerable activity.

According to Sadr and Taleqani: 'those who actively work with natural resources have prior claim to these resources and the materials derived from them and are, in the first instance, their owners'.[61] Nationalization of land is, therefore, ruled out, but a kind of land reform is implicitly advocated. Its principles are that, firstly, natural resources, including land, are supervised by the imam or Islamic ruler.[62] Lands may be owned by Moslems who have obtained them 'through the ways specified by jurisprudence, as well as those that persons have taken as fief or by unlawful means'.[63] Secondly, the cultivation of land creates the right of priority, ownership and disposition, provided cultivation continues. The Islamic ruler can levy land tax (*kharaj*) on cultivated land and alms tax on income derived from that land. Thirdly, usable wastelands and uncultivated lands must be granted free of charge to those who wish to cultivate them. The honouring of the prior ownership of villages and fields must apply to cultivated lands only, along with their frontages. In this case, however, 'the right to sow seed should be given to the peasants'.[64] The peasants are allowed to own the harvest and pay rent to the land owner. The majority of existing *mojtaheds* in Iran do not favour this kind of land reform, proposed by a reformist *mojtahed* like Taleqani, although it is less radical than the Shah's land reform of the 1960s. After the revolution, this issue was a matter of serious controversy; finally, after much implicit and discreet alteration by Khomeini, the land reform programme, like many other programmes, was shelved for good.

The jurisconsults have problems regarding waged labourers; for example, can these workers, and not the owner-employers, become the owners of whatever they fish, mine or till? This problem is tackled within the context of the different kinds of just and unjust contracts. Hiring people is a contractual activity and jurisconsults consider the hiring of wage labour for work on natural resources to be lawful. In this case, workers may not claim ownership of the product.[65] Some jurisconsults distinguish between *hiazat* (gathering - as in gathering firewood in a forest, or catching fish in a river) and *ehya-e mavat* (reclaiming dead land or a dead mine, for example). Hiring wage labour is lawful in the former case, since the workers do not labour to create the object; it is unlawful in the latter, because the product reaped from the reclaimed object belongs to those who directly and originally worked on it. However, Sadr, Taleqani and Beheshti believe otherwise. For them, hiring labour is unlawful for both *hiazat* and *ehya-e mavat*, even though the use of wage labour by the state for the same activities is permitted.[66] Khomeini solved the dispute in the 1950s by introducing the concept of *qasd* (intention), whereby if the worker and employer declare their intentions before the work begins, the worker receives his wage, but has no claim on the product he creates.[67] Furthermore, Khomeini states – contrary to the opinion of other jurisconsults such as Mohaqeq Helli and Sadr – that the person reclaiming the land can claim ownership of it and the product culled from it. Before the revolution, Khomeini explicitly asserted that private ownership of explored oil was lawful, as was the hiring of wage labour in private workshops.[68] Being the supreme jurisconsult of the land, Khomeini's verdicts were the ruling ones and Rafsanjani and the Qum seminary professors find these rulings to be in accordance with their own tastes.[69]

Interestingly, the Qum seminary professors, concerned by the undesirable conclusions reached by potential young radicals respecting ownership, offer their own definition of labour. They say labour refers to any kind of economic activity and that a worker's labour should not be considered more meritorious than a merchant's. In fact, a merchant's work should be seen as preferable, since the fifth imam says earning one's living from wage labour is abominable.[70] The right of ownership justified by labour is extended to exchange and ends at death. In commerce, the 'disposition' of products is considered a productive act:

> The reason is that the productive act is not confined to obtaining natural resources and preparing goods, but encompasses subsequent useful acts such as making the goods available to those in need of them. The rights of middlemen must also be taken into consideration.[71]

However, 'useful acts' do not include those transactions which are either forbidden or judged abominable by the *Shari'a*, for example, all 'usurious' and 'quasi-usurious' *mu'amala* (transactions), 'going to meet a caravan and buying up its goods before it reaches the city' and all aleatory contracts.[72] Therefore, the activities of producers, middlemen, merchants and consumers of forbidden goods are not legitimate.

Another limitation on the right of ownership is the rule concerning the disposal of wealth after death. A third of one's wealth must be set aside, to be used upon one's death, for settling the claims of family members, for the Islamic government, charitable undertakings or for beneficiaries whose share of the bequest is not sufficient to meet their needs. The remaining amount must be divided among the heirs according to well-defined laws. If sons of the deceased are alive, the widow will receive one-eighth of the bequest and each daughter will receive one-half the share of a son. These inheritance laws are set forth in the Qur'an, but have rarely been strictly observed.

Some *mojtaheds* feel that the deceased's wishes should be ignored. Here, again, Khomeini and the seminary professors are flexible. Khomeini says, with the heir's consent, freedom should be granted with respect to the division of two-thirds of the bequest.[73] Sadr opts for strict observance of the laws for the entire amount of the bequest. . . . including the freedom of disposing of the one-third, although he does not consider this advisable.[74]

The mandatory inequality of men's and women's shares in Islamic inheritance laws is explained by Taleqani in this manner: 'Since the man is responsible for the protection of the woman and is, generally speaking, the agent through whom wealth is put to work, for every class of heir the man's claim is twice that of the woman's'.[75]

Economic and non-economic transfer of ownership
Transfer of ownership from one individual to another can be non-

economic (compulsory) or economic (voluntary), according to the judicial discussions, which are considered to comprise yet another aspect of the *Shari'a*'s limitations on the right of ownership and disposition. We have already seen examples of compulsory ownership transfer, such as the verdicts pronounced against various apostates and infidels. However, after the revolution in Iran, *Shi'i mojtaheds* faced a problem which had not been dealt with by classical or contemporary jurisconsults: they had to decide whether or not confiscating the property of Moslem officials and close associates of the Shah's régime was according to Islamic law. In the autumn of 1979, Khomeini indirectly approved the confiscations, warning against excesses and unauthorized confiscations:

> If ownership is legitimate, it will be respected, but not in the sense that anyone can do what he wants to do. . . . The legitimacy of ownership means that it must be based on the *Shari'a* standards, it must not be usury. . . . The properties of those who have usurped the people's belongings must be confiscated, but this confiscation must be lawful. If individuals decide on their own about confiscation, it will be anarchy, and there must be no anarchy. Islam has its own limitations . . . Islam doesn't recognize properties that are illegitimately acquired. . . . Thus, even though the sacred *Shari'a* respects ownership, *Vali-e Amr* [imam] can delimit this legitimate ownership when it is contrary to the interest of Moslems and Islam.[76]

The professors of the Qum seminary discreetly correct Khomeini's use of the concepts:

> In Islam there is no such thing as confiscation. If one sees the phrase 'confiscation of property' used in the declarations of the revolutionary prosecutors, it is because this phrase is known and is commonly used. . . . What has been done after the Islamic Revolution with regard to the properties of the *taghotian* [socially undesirable categories] is something other than political confiscation. . . . This was repossession of usurped properties.[77]

The same professors then warn against the Islamic officials' misunderstanding when they talk about the confiscation of the goods of commodity hoarders. In these cases, it is claimed, goods must be offered by the government in the market at a just price and the government must return the proceeds of sales to the owners of the goods. The government cannot confiscate the goods and is permitted only to fine the hoarder or administer a corporal punishment.[78]

The economic means of transfer of ownership include all economic transactions, for example, exchange, rent, hiring, share-cropping, profit sharing. According to Islamic jurisprudence, any mature individual 'governed by faith' and 'having moral responsibility'[79] can acquire ownership and transfer it by means of one of the accepted transactional contracts. All these contracts, especially *muzara'a* and *musaqat*, were quite common in pre-capitalist socio-economic formations. Some of them, for example, *muzaraba* or *qiraz*, are pre-Islam and the Prophet himself, as well as some of his companions, were partners in *muzaraba* contracts.[80] Despite some difference on minor points, these contracts are unanimously considered legitimate, at least among *Shi'i* jurisconsults and economics writers. A brief explanation of some of the most important contracts is useful since Islamic jurisconsults always handle economic questions within the context of the kinds of contracts involved in transactions. Their justification of these contracts is based on the Qur'anic verses and the Sunnah.[81] In addition, the canonical conception of market behaviour as a moral issue emerges within this context.

Muzaraba, or profit-sharing, is a contract between the supplier of money capital and the industrialist or merchant, who is considered the working partner. Where capitalist economies exist in Islamic countries, *muzaraba* is the act of transferring money assets into capital, as a result of a joint activity between two or more parties. The resulting profit is to be shared as an agreed, fixed percentage of profit. The possible loss is to be absorbed by the investor's capital and the working partner can only demand the value of his labour. In case of a dispute between the capital investor and the working partner about the amount of profit or loss, the working partner's word takes precedence. However, if there is no evidence of the working partner's share in the contract, the investor's word takes precedence.[82]

Islamic interest-free banking can use various techniques and methods of investment, such as *muzaraba* and *murabaha* (cost plus) contracts, in which banks can trade in a certain commodity according to their clients' specifications and deliver the commodity on the basis of sharing an agreed fixed-profit percentage. Banks can make direct investments, deal in foreign exchange markets and real estate and provide services such as consulting. They may also deal in other banking service operations such as letters of credit and letters of guarantee and receive service charges provided this 'is not substituting for interest'. According to Khomeini, banks can award prize money to savers to encourage them to open accounts with them and can engage in lotteries for this purpose. They may not pay interest to account holders, but 'can give them something extra without any predetermined agreement'.[83] Khomeini is also lenient concerning the payment of extra sums of promisory notes, if it is not called interest.[84]

Individuals are permitted to engage in most of the above activities and to invest either directly or on the basis of *muzaraba*, *murabaha* and in participation with Islamic banks and other credit institutions.

Khomeini and other jurisconsults maintain that *muzaraba* is not possible in agricultural activities. *Muzara'a*, however, is legal in this domain.[85] *Muzara'a* in Islamic jurisprudence is a contract between landlords and peasants (nowadays, peasant farmers) wherein the product from the land must be divided between the landlord, the peasant and other partners who have provided part of the means of production, such as seeds or draught animals. This must be done as a ratio: 'eg. 1/2 and 1/2 or 1/3 and 2/3',[86] in money or in kind. Historically, peasants who were de facto dependent on land or landlords were exploited in the institution of *muzara'a*.[87] This is why some well-intentioned Moslem radicals reject *muzara'a* as illegitimate, even though they do not question the legitimacy of private ownership in general. Sadr and Taleqani set more restrictive conditions for *muzara'a* than Khomeini does, but they do accept the institution's authenticity. For example, Taleqani states that: 'water, fertilizer and other requisites, as well as seed [according to the preferred interpretation], are to be provided by the landowner'.[88]

The *musaqat* contract is similar to *muzara'a*, but is applied to plantations. Here, peasants share the product of the orchard with the landlord in certain fixed ratios.[89] The argument concerning the *ja'ala* contract is based on a verse in the Qur'an: 'We miss, said they, the prince's cup. For him who shall restore it, a camel's load of corn! I pledge myself for it'.[90] Therefore, *ja'ala* is a unilateral promise on the part of an employer to provide remuneration for a job upon its completion. In this contract, the work performed need not take place within a certain period of time. However, according to Khomeini: 'if the worker stops working, he does not deserve any payment'.[91] *Ijara* (rent and hire) is either a contract to carry out a job, or a contract for the use and exploitation of the benefits of a property, within a fixed period and for a fixed sum of money.[92] *Ja'ala*, *ijara*, *muzara'a* and *musaqat* are all important juristic bases of the Islamic labour laws in the Islamic Republic of Iran. It is worthwhile to cite one of Khomeini's verdicts on the subject of *ijara*:

If the work of babysitting and breast-feeding hinders the husband of a woman from sexual gratification, employment of another woman for babysitting or breast-feeding . . . for a fixed period of time is permissible, and in this case the permission of the wife is not necessary.[93]

In conclusion, private ownership is legitimate in the ideal Islamic economic system. The right of ownership would be limited, since injunctions are promulgated or interpreted by jurisconsults. However, moral constraints were also imposed on the right of ownership and disposition in the interpretations of Christian theologians of the Middle Ages and they were sometimes more restrictive.[94] For them, private property was a natural phenomenon and wealth was good only if it led to pious living. Unlike the *Shi'i* jurisconsults, Christian theologians thought trade neither natural nor good, although permissible, provided it was used for household maintenance or for the benefit of the country. To lend respectability to the economic practices being engaged in all around them, they set moral and ethical rules. For example, a seller was obliged to notify a buyer of any defects in his commodities, insofar as he knew of them, just as the Islamic jursiconsults had ordained. In the words of St Thomas Aquinas: 'trading for the sake of trading is a shameful thing because it promotes the love of lucre, which knows no limit'.[95] One activity which the Christian theologians ruled absolutely illegal, in 1311, was usury. The Christian principle laid down in the New Testament was that 'the laborer is worthy of his hire'; the Old Testament demanded prompt payment of wages.[96] These principles are reiterated in the writings of the Islamic jurisconsults.

Existing mature capitalist economies, too, have all kinds of legal limitations and regulations regarding the right of private ownership and market operation. Anti-trust laws exist in countries with these economies, even though they have been unable to prevent the increasing concentration of ownership. There are many direct and indirect means of government intervention, so many in fact that they would be considered unfair to the private owners by the majority of *mojtaheds* and ideal by the more reformist among them. Thus, juristically, no religious justification exists to weaken private property or to create uncertainty for property owners in the Islamic economy. In fact, since in many areas a definite legal distinction has been made between private and state ownership, the manoeuvrability of more reform-minded religious politicians with respect to the government's role in economic development is quite limited. If before and after the development of capitalism in Islamic countries - and currently, in Iran - the institution of private property has lacked the strong independence of private property in western capitalism, it is not due to Islamic religious principles *per se*. Rather, it is due to the socio-historic and political conditions of these countries' development.

Income distribution: profit, rent, interest and wage

From the discussion of the legitimacy of private ownership, it is clear that profit and rent are lawful and that interest income is forbidden. Furthermore, legitimacy of private ownership goes hand in hand with a return on that ownership and in the ideal Islamic economic system, owners of natural resources - including land and capital, no matter how these concepts are defined - are to receive a share of the output and income. All *Shi'i mojtaheds* and jurisconsults recognize the legitimacy of profit and rent. Khomeini claims that rent and profit may be earned from many kinds of activity which, while not subject to others' claims, are subject to Islamic moral and legal rules.[97] According to Taleqani, profit and rent can be derived from all Islamic transactions and contracts.[98] The same view is held by Sadr.[99] *Shi'i* economics is undeveloped. However, the views expressed about what constitutes the factors of production can be seen to bear upon the writers' opinions about income distribution.

At the time of the Prophet and the twelve imams, capital and labour in the modern sense were almost non-existent. The urban economy was dominated by simple commodity production and merchant capital and rural areas had a pre-capitalist mode of production based on the work of *de facto* dependent peasant households. Thus, the economic formulation of the concept of capitalist rent and profit could not have been possible and the role of modern production factors could not have been reflected in the economic discussions of classical jurisconsults. This makes it difficult for contemporary *Shi'i* economic writers, whose arguments are based on these classical writings, to form a clear and consistent idea of these phenomena. Thus, their only concrete point of reference is small-scale and traditional agricultural, industrial and commercial activity, for example, the rent received by a small water-mill owner. Nevertheless, today these writers define factors of production on the basis of the conventional tripartite categorization: land, labour (including management) and capital.[100] This list is endorsed by them, since the existence of contracts such as *muzara'a*, *muzaraba* and *ijara* justify rent, profit and wage. However, capital and labour are necessarily considered as eternal attributes of a natural order and not as the creations of a process of historical development, such as the rise of capitalism. Temporal and spatial conditions are not to affect the socio-economic explanations. This problem necessitates a brief look at the writers' ahistorical view on factors of production within its timeless moral and ethical framework, as loosely laid down in the *Shari'a* and by contemporary writers faced with the emergence of socialist movements and the western-capitalist intellectual challenge.

It is claimed that in an Islamic economy land, labour and capital are to be utilized according to the *Shari'a*. Both the Qur'an and the Sunnah condemn the waste of land. The *Shari'a* puts limits on what employers can do with their labour, for example, certain professions are forbidden or to be avoided, such as being a publisher of books which propagate ideas contrary to the *Shari'a*. In addition, employees are morally responsible for protecting the interests of employers. Workers and capitalists must not exploit one another. Employees are to do their jobs faithfully and not to engage in wage bargaining through their trade unions, which are considered exploitative. Since labour must work within just *ja'ala* and *ijara* contracts established with the capitalists, trade union activity would be frowned upon as unnecessary and abominable. Therefore, the relation between labour and capital in an Islamic economy is based on co-operation. It is said that Islam neither recognizes the exploitation of labour by capital, nor approves of the elimination of landlords and capitalists. Landlords, capitalists and workers have a happy partnership because, according to the ethical commands of the Qur'an and Sunnah: 'The servant shall do his work faithfully and to the best of his ability and the master shall pay him fully for the service rendered'.[101] It is always emphasized that 'exploitative profits' resulting from monopolistic activities: hoarding, holding back products from the market in expectation of a price rise or usury, are forbidden.[102] Thus, Islam supports normal profit, which in the conventional micro-economic theory of perfect competition refers to that level of profit at which no tendency exists for new firms to enter or for old firms to exit a given trade. As far as labour is concerned, workers 'are free in their person and in their work; their livings are secured in a measure commensurate with their freely performed labour and their needs'.[103]

Capital is to be interest free and will be able to increase despite this, since Islam allows profit which acts as an incentive to save. Although profit allows capital to grow, however, it will not give rise to an 'un-Islamic' concentration of ownership and prodigal consumption, thanks to Islamic taxes like zakat and moral rules. This kind of unworldly capital accumulation supposedly leads to 'appropriate consumption', increased output and future consumption, justifying the existence and role of capital in the production process. According to the professors of the seminary: 'by accepting . . . different kinds of contracts, such as partnership, *muzaraba, musaqat, muzara'a* . . . Islam has paved the way for the formation of capital'.[104] For an economic system which is upheld as a model of equity, equality and justice, it would be interesting to seek the Islamic justification for sources of economic inequality, such as profit and rent. In fact, the justification is not so different from the explanation provided by conventional economic theory in capitalist economies. Both consider the owners of capital and land to be on the same level with labour: capital is regarded as productive, in the sense that when it is combined with labour more is produced than when it is not; the share of capital in output (income) is recognized to the extent of its contribution to output and the institution of private ownership creates a claim for the owner of the machines and equipment. Sadr writes: 'Capital has value because of the service it renders for man . . . and it is due to this fact that its supplier receives a reward'. [105]

It must be pointed out that Sadr and other *Shi'i mojtaheds* who accept the above justification of profit do not consider 'risk' to be a factor of production and, therefore, do not see profit as a reward for taking risks.[106] Capital is the product of labour – is, in fact, labour embodied, resulting from the operation of this factor. Rent is also justified with reference to labour applied to land which originally resulted in property ownership and so is commercial capital.

According to Taleqani: 'Capital is the product of the original work that has been applied to products of nature . . .'.[107] This description is not different from Wicksell's definition of capital as a single mass of saved-up labour and saved-up land which is accumulated in the course of years.[108]

Regarding commerce, the following argument is usually provided:

> [The] productive act is not confined to obtaining natural resources and preparing goods, but encompasses subsequent useful acts such as making the goods available to those in need of them. The rights of middlemen must also be taken into consideration. Thus, to the extent that exchanges [in commerce and trade] are based on useful work, the rights of middlemen [merchants and tradesmen] are natural and lawful.[109]

Therefore, profit results 'from the joining of additional instances of labour to the original instances'[110] and the share of the owners of the means of production (land and capital) out of output (income) is to compensate and reward their services: 'This is what the producer owes to the owner of the means of production'.[111] In the case of land, rent is also explained as a reward for a service offered. It is said that although output produced by a farmer is owned by him, he must pay a share of it for the services of the landlord: 'The owner of land can only demand his rent'.[112]

After all, whoever owns the equipment, machines and buildings which support labour during the process of production, controls capital and earns whatever share of the output earned as a factor of production. In other words, no matter how one explains the nature of capital, where private property is legitimate, earning from it is legitimate. This has been the practice even for interest, which is the only return explicitly prohibited in the Qur'an and, therefore, rejected by all *Shi'i* and Sunni economic writers.

Islam 'disallows interest, but allows the charge of water-mill, keeping in view the principle of economic freedom'.[113] This, as previously noted, is not an originally Islamic idea. Usury, defined as charging for the use of money lent, was forbidden to clergy in AD325 and to the European laity by the end of the twelfth century. In 1311, at the Council of Vienna, it was considered absolutely illegal. The arguments against usury in the scriptures, the Greek philosophers' works and those of Christian and Moslem theologians, are the same: a payment in excess of the loan itself exploits the poor. The function of capital in these arguments was not clearly understood, since in the Middle Ages opportunities for profitable investments were few and borrowers were usually the needy and the poor. The Islamic jurisconsults and economic writers describe *riba* (usury) as any interest charged on loans, not just 'excessive' interest rates. In addition, they make no distinction between real and nominal interest rates. Some Islamic writers include the element of risk in their arguments, as a justification for profit, but Sadr and Taleqani reject this approach. Taleqani explains the justification for the prohibition of interest, as opposed to return in profit sharing and other contracts, in the following manner:

> should capital have no motive factor and fail to combine with labor, in the view of Islam it has no profit [as is the case with usury]; so, for instance, in a contract of *muzaraba*, to set a fixed profit for the capital would not be permitted and would be unlawful, because the transactions would take the form of usury . . . a profit is derived from fixed and motiveless capital. In the case of the rental [*ijara*] of immovable properties and lands, although the capital is set [as with usury], because it undergoes depreciation, the rental money is made lawful. In the case of usury . . . the capital proper has neither motive nor depreciation.[114]

Khomeini, as has been mentioned, offers something of a solution to this problem, at least with respect to banks and promissory notes. For example, he proposes paying an extra sum which is not to be determined at the time a savings account is opened or a promissory note is made. This sum, of course, is not to be called interest. The other possibility for circumventing the problem is to give a prize to the customers.[115] These measures have already been adopted by Islamic banks in the Islamic Republic of Iran.

The institution of the market and price

It is obvious, then, that the institution of the market is the basic institution which allocates resources, combines and processes resources for the production of goods and services, determines the amount of goods and services to be produced, distributes them and determines what provision is to be made for the future growth of per capita income in the ideal *Shi'i* Islamic society. However, this market is to be regulated by Islamic injunctions against speculation, the creation of artificial scarcities and monopolistic practices, on the supply side, and guided by Islamic ethical and legal precepts, on the demand side. The principle that must oversee the operation of the market, and which is emphasized by all the *Shi'i* economic writers, is that of 'non-detriment to others' (*la zarar va la zerar*). All the jurisconsults discuss this principle in a rather vague fashion, using as its point of reference only one authentic example taken from the Prophet's verdicts. Basically, the principle holds that individuals must act in such a way as not to injure others in economic and non–economic matters. Each *mojtahed*, however, has interpreted it according to his own social and political interest. Khomeini's discussion of non-detriment is basically political, in that he justifies the role of the *Vali-e Faqih* as the guardian of the observance of the principle in the period of occultation.[116] A more radical economic interpretation is offered by Taleqani, who states that rights of ownership:

> are upheld only in so far as they do not injure the general welfare, because resources and materials in their natural state belong to the public, and the private right to dispose of them is limited by the public right to them.[117]

Conservative *mojtaheds* could interpret the principle as a Pareto optimality which asserts that production and distribution cannot be reorganized to increase the utility of one or more individuals, without decreasing the utility of others. Thus, any policies directed at the redistribution of income and wealth could be opposed on the grounds that they would ultimately deny benefits to those who have been denied their original share.

The role of the market in the Islamic economy
All the *Shi'i* economic writers assert that the observance of the *Shari'a* would lead market participants to behave in a way which would eliminate all the vices found in a capitalist market. However, none of them has yet offered a formal analysis of the operation of this unworldly institution. They discuss either the justification for the existence of the market, or the necessary Islamic modifications which they favour for it. For example,

although the professors of the Qum seminary are quite clear on their staunch defence of the market, they fail to analyse the microeconomic and macroeconomic implications of the Islamic moral and legal constraints upon market performance. In other words, it is not known whether or not the market with the Islamic injunctions (provided they are not circumvented) would adjust more slowly than a capitalist market. After all, with the prohibition on interest, the information cost to potential investors is likely to be high. Under such conditions, savers have to evaluate the performance of many firms gathered in the banks in order to invest properly in *muzaraba* contracts. Although it can be claimed that marginal rates of return on capital can be used in such circumstances, these rates would be less clear than the market rate of interest. The question arises: would the elimination of interest within a private economy lead to lower aggregate saving? If so, would the Islamic government supply the desired level of investment to supplement lack of sufficient saving? We will see shortly that the seminary professors favour a free market economy with minimum government intervention. Further, the prohibition of interest means that money holders would lose if inflation occurred. In such a situation money might well change hands rapidly, increasing inflationary pressures, especially if at the same time the Islamic government had a budget deficit. Are Moslems ready to give interest-free loans to the government for the financing of its deficit? If not, would not this lead to the printing of money by the government? In addition, would not the absence of flexible interest-rate mechanisms, combined with a fixed rate for almstax, decrease the Islamic government's ability to engage in counter-cyclical monetary and fiscal policy? Given the possible instability of the macro-economic system in Islamic society, which is based on private ownership and the market, what instruments of economic stabilization are available to an Islamic government?

Questions arise regarding the microeconomic implications of the Islamic economy. Given the idealistic assumptions about the behaviour of market participants, would individual prices be more unstable if the operation of a futures market and the holding of inventories are considered speculative and are successfully forbidden? Would firms and merchants really hold their prices in spite of rising demand when there is a shortage? How would they then ration goods between their customers? Would not the uncertainty facing businessmen under such circumstances be higher, leading to prices that would include a high-risk premium? The *Shi'i* writers do not discuss the economic implications of the doctrine, claiming that Islamic economics is not their responsibility, and that they are concerned only with economic moralizing. This has not prevented them, however, from taking positions for or against free-market or socialist economies. Although they condemn these systems morally, they engage in superficial theorizing or uncritical acceptance of the basis of existing economic theories. For example, after writing several hundred pages on the moral, ethical and legal virtues of the Islamic economic system, the professors of the Qum seminary, who support Islamic *laissez-faire*, get to the gist of the problem in the following manner:

> [The] price mechanism is the result of the material propensities in pro-
> duction, exchange and consumption of goods and services. . . . The
> price mechanism provides for the most efficient form of the allocation
> of resources, since it leads to the highest level of satisfaction for the
> consumer, producer and supplier of factors of production.[118]

One may infer from these statements, taken from a straightforward competitive model of nineteenth-century marginalist economists, that in an
Islamic *laissez-faire*, market-oriented system, income earned is automatically spent, either for Islamic consumption or Islamic investment.
There are no economic fluctuations, since supply creates its own demand.
Any deviation from full-employment equilibrium is eliminated by the
competitive economy's self-correcting Islamic and non-Islamic forces.
Thus, the maximization of the producer's profit, or in the professors'
words, 'producer's satisfaction', and the consumer's satisfaction are
accompanied by the most efficient use of scarce economic resources and
the principle of 'non-detriment to others', or the Pareto optimality rules.
However, no attention is given to the fact that when this model was
developed in the nineteenth century, it did not allow for the complications
created by the external diseconomies of rapid economic growth and in-
dustrialization, the producers' market power and the other dynamic
aspects of the market. The model is static and its institutional, 'moral',
'ethical' and 'legal' assumptions and parameters are certainly not 'Islamic'. In addition, in the real world it led to large inequalities in income
and wealth and economic fluctuations, as well as to extensive class,
racial, sexual and national conflicts and discrimination. Since the 1940s,
some of these limitations and deficiencies have even led the supporters
of this model, who still use it as a heuristic device, to abandon it as a
realistic model and to modify it drastically. The Qum seminary professors, however, who have benefited from the advice of some secular
economic professors of the Iranian universities, concede only that the
model contains some possible: 'inelasticities and immobilities of the
factors of production'. Furthermore:

> Free fluctuation of prices within the framework of Islamic rules . . . will
> increase the efficiency of the economic system and in cases where
> natural factors create obstacles to this fluctuation, Islam has provided
> appropriate solutions. For example, inelasticities and immobilities of
> factors of production, unavailability of information about the existing
> possibilities and prices, inappropriate market structure, directly, and
> the unavailability of certain factors . . . indirectly, reduce the efficiency
> of price mechanism.[119]

To solve this problem, the professors recommend minimal planning, but
this is to be used only in the elimination of the obstacles to free fluctuation
of prices:

> within the limit of permissible [Islamic] activities and with the

possibility of planning for the removal of the natural obstacles to free fluctuation of prices, general stabilization of prices is not needed. . . . the necessary stabilization will be realized automatically by the price mechanism.[120]

According to the professors, the stabilization policy leads to higher costs and more bureaucracy. Planning will not be able to predict all needs, nor take into consideration all production and commercial possibilities.[121] 'Appropriate planning with the objective of removing obstacles to the free movement of prices, rather than planning for stabilization of prices, can be more effective'.[122] It seems, then, that the professors' concern to enforce religious economic rules and regulations is simply a discussion of the necessity and the means of removing obstacles to the free operation of the market in the Islamic economy. There is clearly no substantial difference between this argument and those presented by staunch supporters of *laissez-faire* capitalist economy in the West.

While Taleqani and Sadr disagree with the views of the Qum seminary professors, their analytical claims about the operation of the 'Islamic' market are unrealistic and romantic. According to Taleqani: 'the principle of supply and demand – in the capitalist sense – cannot govern exchange' in an 'Islamic' market.[123] He asserts that while income and willingness to purchase determine the demand for goods and services in capitalism, in an Islamic market, demand arises from need: 'Accordingly goods are offered and made available to the extent required to satisfy the necessities of life. The market is not to become the plaything of greed'.[124] Both consumers and suppliers are considered to be pious and self-sacrificing Moslems. Nevertheless, even Moslem customers and suppliers might sometimes be misled by Satan and therefore 'intervention of the pious state and governor in matters of commerce is permissible and at times necessary'.[125] The Islamic government 'may fix prices for goods that are needed or subject to the greed of speculators'.[126]

Such interventions are not uncommon in existing capitalist systems and are, in fact, more extensive than what the more social-minded *mojtaheds* could enforce or even dream of in a bazaar-type economy. There is nothing distinctly 'Islamic' about them. The Islamic economic system is based on the institution of private ownership of the means of production and the market, which are the most important characteristics of any capitalist system. Market forces determine the prices of goods and services, of the factors of production, land, labour and capital, despite the talk of 'Islamic prices' and 'equitable wages', and about wage, rent and profit being proportional to the labour performed. Indeed, contemporary *Shi'i* economic theorizing often lacks even the insights of the great Islamic sociologists of the Middle Ages, or of the classical jurisconsults' explanations of economic categories.

Theory of price

In the Middle Ages, Islamic classical jurisconsults living in urban regions, where the economy was based on commodity production and trade, had to justify merchants' profits. They did this by developing the idea that the trader added to commodities a value proportionate to his labour and costs. Starting from the tradition of Aristotle, who distinguished value in use from value in exchange, the explanation given by the jurisconsults came close to being an objective theory of value. In other words, their starting point was production and production cost, rather than a subjective evaluation of satisfaction or utility derived from a commodity's consumption. 'Just price' basically corresponded to production cost and it was usually identified with the current market price. The jurisconsults did not question the right of the Islamic government to set and regulate prices under special circumstances; just price was the price which ruled at the moment. In these traditional economies of the Middle Ages, wage income was not predominant and, therefore, if it was discussed at all, the concept of justice was invoked. Usury was forbidden, although it must have happened. The renting of land was seldom mentioned, although it constituted the main source of income of the secular and religious ruling class. Rent did not have the same distinctive characteristic it has in capitalism, because it was mixed in with the many different dues that were imposed on peasants.[127]

All of the *Shi'i* economic writers follow the tradition of classifying value into use value and exchange value. However, the contemporary writers base exchange value upon satisfaction of wants, asserting that labour does not determine the value of commodities. Taleqani and Sadr emphasize the role of labour in justifying ownership of objects and property and justify rent and profit in terms of the benefits or services provided by the labour of merchants, landlords and capital owners.[128] The Christian scholastics did likewise centuries ago,[129] however, neither their utility value theory, nor the price theory of the *Shi'i* Islamic writers, makes use of the concept of diminishing utility to explain why demand for quantities of goods and services at a given price is satiable. For the *Shi'i* economic writers, price ratios are proportional to total utility ratios and not to marginal utility ratios. In this subjective evaluation, it is not even possible to provide an answer to the basic question: why is the price of water or bread less than that of a luxury item, such as a diamond?

Hashemi-Rafsanjani states that: 'We accept neither the formula of Western capitalism that uses supply and demand as the criterion of the value of a commodity, nor the Marxist principle that believes that the value of a commodity is determined by the labour embodied in the commodity.'[130] His alternative solution is both confused and subjective:

> Our view is that the source of exchange value is . . . the usefulness of and the demand for a commodity . . . not supply and demand, but the psychological state and the amount of usefulness and the demand for the commodity in society. . . . In addition, the newness of the goods will have a role to play in their exchange value.[131]

Of all the explanations of exchange value and price offered by the *Shi'i* economic writers, Sadr's is the most systematic. After rejecting the

Marxist theory of value, he develops one of utility-cum-scarcity. All goods are valued in relation to the satisfaction of wants and their utility is related to their relative scarcity:

> The relationship between usefulness and value is quite clear from a psychological vantage point, since usefulness is the base of utility, and utility is the criterion of value and its general source. . . . Utility has an inverse relationship with the possibility of acquiring goods. . . . However, it is clear that the possibility of acquiring goods is a function of their scarcity or abundance.[132]

Labour is the source of ownership of fishermen, merchants, craftsmen, land owners, real estate owners and so on, but it is not the source of value according to this view: 'value of any material is the result of its general social utility. . . it is private ownership which is based on labor'.[133] We have already mentioned that there is nothing particularly Islamic in this view, except that it is discussed by *Shi'i* writers with the contemporary challenges of capitalism and socialism in mind. The similarity of the whole argument to the views of the Christian scholastic thinkers, especially those of St Thomas Aquinas, is striking. With the growth of trade, the market and, simultaneously, that of capitalism, the scholastic doctrine lost its effectiveness and influence. The doctrine is fundamentally medieval and was unable to adapt to important changes which affected all aspects of life.

The economic role of the Islamic state

Economically, the Islamic state is to be a welfare state and can hold considerable economic power. It owns property, organizes and disposes of state and 'public' properties and revenues and receives various taxes. Since the point of reference for all of these institutions is the time of the Prophet and the Islamic conquests, there is little controversy among *Shi'i* economic writers when it comes to recognizing the Islamic government's economic power. Rather, their dispute focuses on the extent and means by which the government can interfere in the operation of the private sector.

The professors of the Qum seminary, like the other *Shi'i* writers, regard the Islamic government's economic power as an important aspect of Islamic might and as necessary for the defence of Islam:

> The greatest economic power in society is in the hands of the Islamic government and it manifests itself either by the domination of a great part of the resources, such as *anfal* and *khums*, or by the supervision of the remaining part of the society's resources, such as public properties . . . the use of zakat.[134]

Besides wielding this economic power, the *Shi'i* government, which is a variant of the figure variously known as imam, *vali* and *khalifah* (caliph) or derives its authority from this figure, naturally enforces the all-encompassing *Shari'a*. Sadr is thus led to say that Islam: 'proclaims the principle of dual property. It believes both in private and public property and puts them on an equal footing'.[135] In his view, the state's power can surpass even the *Shari'a*: 'When the Ruler prohibits something by nature permissible, it becomes forbidden, when he orders that it be done, it becomes permissible'.[136] For example, in the case of land reclamation which is normally lawful, 'if necessary the government can prevent it'.[137]

Sadr affirms that the maintenance of a 'social balance' refers not to income levels but to standards of living, for which he allows moderate differences between classes. Since this condition would lead to small-scale private enterprises, Sadr stipulates that the activities of large-scale enterprises must be undertaken by the Islamic government.[138] In Sadr's model then, the government not only enforces the *Shari'a*, but regulates and guides economic and non-economic life in affairs not covered by the *Shari'a*, as the need arises due to changed conditions.[139] Taleqani's view on the role and objectives of the Islamic government is similar:

> [The Islamic government] has priority in disposing of property and exists, moreover, to establish equity; therefore, for the sake of public welfare and the precedence of public interests over private ones [where the rights of the individual and those of society are in conflict], it is empowered to limit individual ownership to a greater degree than the law may authorize.[140]

As for the Qum seminary professors, their views on the appropriate extent of the Islamic government's intervention have already been discussed in the previous section. They dislike the extensive government intervention in economic affairs advocated by Sadr and Taleqani, although they do not object to its religiously oriented, political and social interference in Islamic society. Nevertheless, the Shi'i economic writers all agree that in times of trouble and in extraordinary circumstances, the *Vali-e Amr* (Guardian of the Cause) can invoke a secondary or governmental ordinance to distinguish public welfare from accepted rights. In this case, they all accept price fixing or further government intervention.

According to Khomeini: 'The Imam . . . and the ruler of Moslems can practice whatever is in the interest of Moslems, for example set a fixed price, register an industry or delimit commerce, etc.' by means of secondary or governmental ordinances.[141] The professors of the Qum seminary and Khomeini, in his early writings, stress, however, that these ordinances are to be exceptional, not permanent and that they must not apply to all, or even many, commodities. In the summer of 1987, Khomeini activated this right. Faced with the Islamic Republic's continual inflation and serious shortages of many foodstuffs and other goods, he allowed the government to interfere in the market and to control the prices set by enterprises in the public and private sectors, as well as those set by retailers. This incited the founder of the daily newspaper *Resalat*,

Azari-Qumi (an influential Qum seminary professor and former head of the Society of the Professors of the Qum Seminary) to write a series of articles warning against the government's misinterpretation and abuse of the ordinance. According to Azari-Qumi: 'Some of the authorities . . . believe that fixing prices of goods can be generalized and is of a permanent nature. However, it must be noted that fixing prices for all goods requires the Imam's permission' and must be a temporary measure only, invoked under abnormal conditions:'[142]

> Price fixing has been rejected in the sayings of the immaculate Imams, and the Prophet, peace upon him, has said that the ups and downs of the prices are God's will. The great jurisconsults have also emphasized this verdict and the rate and the price of goods are left to supply and demand . . . in their juristic books.[143]

To substantiate his argument, Azari-Qumi makes reference to a *hadith* of the Prophet, cited by Imam Ali: 'The Prophet confronting some hoarders, ordered them to offer their goods in the market. . . . They told the Prophet that it would also be better if he set the price of those goods. The Prophet, peace upon him, became quite angry . . . and then said . . . "price fixing is in the hands of God, if He wills it, it will go up and down"'.[144]

Azari-Qumi's argument is apparently not favoured by the other ruling faction in the Islamic government. However, he says he will speak out despite the fact that: 'some individuals or even some of the authorities accuse us and continuously agititate against us and *Resalat* . . . and don't let others listen to us'.[145] Azari-Qumi and his followers among the Qum professors, in the bazaar, the Islamic parliament, the bureaucracy and in other walks of life, are accused of being pro-proprietors and pro-*Mostakbarin* (the arrogants).

In the light of the explicit provisions concerning taxes in the *Shari'a*, all the *Shi'i* economic writers devote some discussion to the public finance of the Islamic economy. This is rarely analytical, or at least it fails to analyse the macroeconomic and microeconomic implications of zakat and *khums*. The discussion consists mostly of a juristic presentation of the coverage, rates and disbursement of zakat revenues, which are claimed to be the centrepiece of Islamic public finance. The contemporary writers, however, have a difficult task in that their basic reference for discussion of many modern forms of wealth and income is the classical jurisconsults, who could not have dealt with forms of wealth not in existence at the time of the Prophet and in the Middle Ages. For example, it is not clear whether zakat (tax on wealth, income or both, with a variable rate in excess of a minimum or *nisab*) and *khums* (a per capita tax of twenty per cent on wealth, income or both) are to be applied to current income, wealth or net wealth. Khomeini and the other jurisconsults are quite vague about this. Another problem is that some objects are subject to zakat and *khums* simultaneously. These difficulties lead Khomeini and other jurisconsults to stick primarily to objects of wealth which existed at the time of the Prophet, such as livestock, grain, gold and silver, while not much is said about shares, securities, savings in the form of insurance premiums, machinery and other capital goods. Generally, the problems involved are so numerous that even the Islamic Republic does not concern itself with them, except in the seminary discussions. Here again, one finds that much ado is made about nothing. Taleqani, Sadr and the Qum seminary professors state that the cure for market vices and ills is the institution of zakat, which improves the standard of living of the poor, finances public activities and investment and is a distinctive feature of the Islamic economy. None of them, however, provide an operationally meaningful framework of analysis for this tax or similar recognized taxes, nor do they explain how they differ from modern taxes which exist in all capitalist economics:[146]

> Zakat represents the general approach of Islam as a system . . . it is a part of the plan to introduce a common standard of living and not a mere moral exhortation. It is definitely a step towards creating a school of economics.[147]

Khomeini puts compulsory Islamic taxes into two categories: fixed direct taxes and secondary or provisional taxes. The former include zakat, *khums*, *kharaji* (land tax) and *jazieh* (per capita tax levied on non-Moslem believers). The latter is not to be levied under normal conditions, has a rate which is not predetermined and is changeable and is considered an indirect tax. When the independence of the Islamic state is in danger: 'the Islamic government has to take away all the belongings of the people above what is considered as a necessity for them'.[148]

Zakat is sometimes interpreted as an income tax, for example, ten per cent may be levied on produce of non-irrigated land and five per cent on produce of agricultural commodities irrigated through wells or motor pumps. It is sometimes considered as a wealth tax, levied as a certain percentage on the excess of a minimum level of wealth called *nisab*.[149] Whether or not the rate can be varied and whether or not the tax can be applied to physical, financial wealth or luxury durables is also unclear. Khomeini, for example, states that if gold and silver are coined and transacted, zakat can be applied to them. However, 'the coins that women use as ornament will not merit zakat'.[150] If one lends coins, one can avoid paying zakat on them.[151]

Khomeini is of the opinion that other taxes can be deduced from zakat, but the minimum level of wealth is to be determined before this deduction.[152] However, due to the scholastic and ahistorical nature of his discussion, it is not clear whether the market value of the asset is the basis of valuation or the purchasing price, or whether zakat applies to the production units or the owners of the enterprise. No matter how zakat is defined, it has not always been paid and is not enforced in the Islamic Republic.

According to Khomeini, *khums* (one-fifth tax) applies in seven cases: the spoils of war; mines; treasure; jewellery derived from the sea; household income in excess of its expenditure; land bought by a non-

Moslem believer and money associated with an activity which is considered forbidden.[153] The proceeds of *khums* is distributed among the *mojtaheds*, the poor relatives of the Prophet and the needy.

Shi'i economic writers in Iran have presented no serious economic discussion of fiscal, monetary or income policy, their implications for the stabilization policy or of their relative effectiveness. This is partly because they avoid discussing economics altogether and believe there would be no serious problems in an ideal non-inflationary no-crisis Islamic economy.[154] Such claims lead Moslems nowhere and platitudes such as the following can not give rise to a programme of independence, freedom and welfare for Moslems:

> [In the Islamic economy] man will not become a fattened animal or a machine like he is in capitalism and socialism, but he will become dominant over himself, his path, his life and objectives.[155]

Is the Islamic economy a non-capitalist system?

> Islam has given us general principles and detailed laws which can be turned into a full-fledged economic system having distinctive Islamic features.[156]

> On this basis . . . Islam does not fit in the framework of capitalism, socialism and communism.[157]

Yet, based on what has been shown so far, it is clear that no matter how one brings together Islamic economic institutions and Islamic moral, ethical and financial laws, the position of a contemporary ideal Islamic economy is not different from that of a capitalist one. If the Islamic moral and financial laws and institutions are implemented, there will be some modification in terms of the structure and functioning of the capitalism and the system will have an Islamic flavour. However, if capitalism as a mode of production is generalized commodity production, based on private ownership of the means of production, the Islamic economy, as described by the authors studied, is still capitalist. A commodity is a good or service which is bought and sold in the market. Under capitalism, people work according to a contract for a wage or salary. These same people are separated from ownership or control of the means of production, such as factories, machines, farms and banks, which are privately owned. Goods and services, including the capacity to work or labour power, are traded in the market. This translates into generalized commodity production, a definition of capitalism which both its supporters and critics could agree upon.

Despite the contrary view held by the contemporary *Shi'i* economic writers and despite their differences, what they propose is Islamic capitalism as a variation of capitalism. In the West, there are several models of capitalism, each with its own distinctive features - the social democratic variety of Scandinavian countries, for example, or that found in the regulated, mature economies of North America. All of these are capitalist in economic content, that is, in their fundamental economic relations and institutions.

The contemporary, 'authentic' *Shi'i* economic writers maintain that: private ownership of the means of production is legitimate and respectable; that wage-labour is a natural institution, within which one may hire a horse, a mill, a house, a machine and skilled or unskilled labour; that trade and commerce are encouraged, even favoured; that rent and profit are legitimate and that the market is the basic economic institution for the provision of the needs of the Islamic community. Their vision, however, is of a religious, and in that sense, ideological system, the objective of which is to serve God on earth. Therefore, the above-mentioned institutions and processes must be structured according to and operate within the framework of the *Shari'a* and then within the different institutional emphases and interpretations favoured by an author. Our writers claim that in Islam private ownership and disposition are relative and conditional and conclude that private property is not weakened by such constraints. It can be said that the Moslem state holds a *dominium eminens* over land, as do other states in the existing capitalist system. The clear lines drawn between state and private ownership by jurisconsults ensure that no misunderstanding on the part of young radical Moslems will arise.

Certain commercial practices which are fraudulent or involve religiously forbidden objects are prohibited. Accumulation of capital, however, is legitimate, provided zakat and *khums* are paid and moral obligations and inheritance laws are observed. The institution of zakat will ostensibly prevent a high concentration of wealth, but it must not discourage enterprising activities, which are preferable to the hiring out of one's labour.

Although there are disagreements about the state's role in this market-oriented system, all the *Shi'i* writers stress the importance of its economic and non-economic power in the ideological Islamic society. However, regarding the private sector, one view calls for a supervisory and regulatory government role, while another demands a more active role.

Finally, a favourite topic for the *Shi'i* economic writers is Islamic economic justice. They consistently assert that 'Islamic economy represents a just system of economic life',[158] or that:

> Islam has defined the limits of justice and has laid down general laws for social life in the various fields of production, distribution of wealth and mutual dealings. It has described any violation or neglect of these laws and commandments as injustice and transgression.[159]

Once more, there are similarities between the views of the *Shi'i* economic writers and those of the Christian scholastics. Both schools identify two kinds of justice: distributive and commutative. The domain of the former is the distribution of wealth and income based on the recognition of social differences, while the latter's concern is the dealings of individuals with one another. The former is covered by zakat, the latter by just prices and wages, prohibition of *riba* and monopolistic activities, Islamic contracts and so on. Though there are differences between the Qum professors' interpretation of equity and Taleqani and Sadr's understanding of it, none of them advocates a class-free society. This is because the Qur'an has already recognized class differences: 'See how we have caused some of them to excel others!', or 'It shall be no crime in you if ye seek an increase from your Lord'.[160]

The *mojtaheds* consider that the ideal economic system based on Islamic justice is the one which existed at the time of the Prophet. It is neither homogeneous nor classless:

> We have the perfect example for Islamic society and government in Muslim public life and governmental relations as they took shape at the time Islam first appeared and after the migration of the Holy Prophet and the Muslims around him to Medina.[161]

Notes

1. Abdol-Karim Biazar-e Shirazi (ed. and trans.), *Resaleh-e Nouvin: Masael-e Eqtesadi*, Vol. 2 (Teheran: Nashr-e Farhang-e Islami, 1363). Hereafter cited as *Resaleh*.

2. Sayyid Mahmud Taleghani, *Society and Economics in Islam*, trans. R. Campbell (Berkeley: Mizan Press, 1982). Hereafter cited as Taleghani.

3. Navab-Safavi, op. cit.

4. Mohammed Baqer Sadr, *Eqtesad-e Ma*, Vol. I, trans. Mohammed-Kazem Bojnordi (Teheran:Entesharat-e Borhan, 1350). Mohammed Baqer Sadr, *Eqtesad-e Ma*, Vol. II, trans. Abdolali Espahbodi (Teheran: Entesharat-e Islam, 1357). Hereafter cited as Sadr, Vol. I or Vol. II.

5. It is interesting to note that the translator of the first volume of *Eqtesad-e Ma*, himself an Islamic activist and former deputy in the Islamic Consultative Assembly, finds himself obliged to insert his own comments in several footnotes concerning Sadr's mild criticism of capitalism that sometimes sounds apologetic, especially when he refutes Marxism. For example, see Ibid., Vol. I, p. 235 f.n. 1.

6. See Hashemi-Rafsanjani, *Siyasat-e Eqtesadi* (Teheran: Hezb-e Jomhouri-e Islami, 1362), p. 16. Hereafter cited as Rafsanjani.

7. Ibid.

8. Daftar-e Hamkari-e Hozeh va Daneshgah, *Daramadi Bar Eqtesad-e Islami* (Teheran: Salman Farsi, 1363). Hereafter cited as *Eqtesad-e Islami*.

9. Ibid., pp. 9 and 10.

10. The outline of the book is basically similar to that of Sadr's *Eqtesad-e Ma*, Vol. II.

11. Ayatullah Baqir al-Sadr, *Islam and Schools of Economics*, trans. M. A. Ansari (Accra: Islamic Seminary Publications, 1982), p. 149. Hereafter cited as *Islam and Schools of Economics*. There seems to be some confusion among Moslem writers on this problem. Some regard Islamic economics as a 'system', some as a 'science' and some as both. See M. A. Mannan, *Islamic Economics: Theory and Practice* (Cambridge: The Islamic Academy, 1986), pp. 14-15. Hereafter cited as Mannan.

12. *Eqtesad-e Islami*, op. cit., pp. 14-15.

13. Ibid., pp. 57-69, Sadr, Vol. II, op. cit., pp. 21-60 and Taleghani, op. cit., pp. 49-50.

14. Abuzar, Salman and Meqdad were the Prophet's companions and are *Shi'i* idols.

15. *Eqtesad-e Islami*, op. cit., p. 71.

16. *Islam and Schools of Economics*, op. cit., p. 155. See also Taleqani, op. cit., p. 58.

17. Out of the six thousand verses in the Qur'an, only two hundred and forty five are about different aspects of social legislations, including seventy on civil and financial affairs, ten on economic affairs and seventy on personal affairs (see *Esposito*, op. cit., Al-Sadiq al-Mahdi, p. 233).

18. *Islam and Schools of Economics*, op. cit., p. 149.

19. Note that the schoolmen of thirteenth-century Europe had the same kind of problem in reconciling the theological dogma with actual conditions in economic life. They, to, tried to codify temporal laws and rules which were to guide men in their economic relations. To do this, they used deductive and inductive methods and syllogistic reasoning by citing biblical teachings and dogma to present their doctrine. The precepts so derived were to guide men in correct living (see Joseph A. Schumpeter, *History of Economic Analysis* (London: George Allen & Unwin Ltd., 1963), pp. 73-115. Hereafter cited as Schumpeter.

20. *Resaleh*, op. cit., p. 89.

21. James P. Piscatori (ed.), *Islam in the Political Process* (Cambridge: Cambridge University Press, 1983), Hamid Enayat, p. 175.

22. *Islam and Schools of Economics,* op. cit., p. 130.

23. Ibid., p. 131.

24. Ibid., p. 35.

25. Ibid., p. 33. According to Sadr, and similarly to all the other writers, the basic human aim in capitalism is the pursuit of pleasure and the acquisition of wealth. This leads to disastrous consequences. The Marxian solution to this problem of 'materialism' is even worse. They are 'mere heretics', who have transformed the theory of materialism into a philosophy 'while capitalism has no philosophical base at all' (ibid., p. 85).

26. Ibid., p. 90.

27. Ibid., p. 91.

28. Ibid.

29. Ibid., pp. 88-90 and 118. We will see later that Shariati does not consider private ownership of the means of production to be legitimate, so excludes it from his ideal Moslem society. However, his philosophic views on the basic axioms of Islam and his tolerance of personal and political freedoms, as we saw in Chapter 3, are similar to the views presented in this section.

30. See *Revolutionary Program of Fadaian-e Islam*, op. cit., for a complete list of injunctions favoured by *Shi'i* Moslems as a typical example. Of course, almost all of these injunctions are taken from the Qur'an and the traditions. For example, according to the Qur'an: 'be not prodigal, for God loveth not the prodigal' (*The Koran*, op. cit., p. 330) and 'God hath abounded to some of you more than to others in the supplies of life; yet they to whom He hath abounded impart not thereof to the slaves whom their right hands possess, so that they may share alike'(Ibid., p. 205).

31. See for example Taleghani, op. cit., p. 50 and *Islam and Schools of Economics*, op. cit., p. 161.

32. *Islam and Schools of Econimics*, op. cit. p. 161.

33. Talqani, op. cit., p. 31.

34. Ibid.

35. Sadr, Vol. I, op. cit., pp. 402-8.

36. *Islam and Schools of Economics*, op. cit., p. 160.

37. *Eqtesad-e Islami*, op. cit., p. 79.

38. *The Koran*, op. cit., p. 94.

39. Ibid., p. 424.

40. *Eqtesad-e Islami*, op. cit., p. 100. Some *Shi'i* jursiconsults (*faqihs*) are of the opinion that God can also have nominal ownership of objects and property, e.g., one-fifth (*khums*) of spoils of war belong to God and the Prophet (see for example, Ibid., p.

101). See also Rafsanjani, op. cit., p. 43.

41. Taleqani, op. cit., p. 26.

42. Ali Shariati, *On the Sociology of Islam*, trans. Hamid Algar (Berkeley: Mizan Press, 1979), p. 119.

43. Ibid.

44. *Eqtesad-e Islami*, op. cit., p. 109. Note that this statement sounds like the twentieth-century version of Aristotle and St Thomas Aquinas that the holding of private property is in accordance with natural laws (see Schumpeter, op. cit., p. 92). See also *Resaleh*, op. cit., p. 293.

45. *Resaleh*, p. 292.

46. Ibid.

47. Rafsanjani, op. cit., p. 43.

48. *Islam and Schools of Economics*, op. cit., pp. 80–81.

49. *The Constitution of the Islamic Republic of Iran* (Teheran: Islamic Propagation Organization,), Article 47. Hereafter cited as *The Constitution*.

50. Ibid., Article 44.

51. See Rafsanjani, op. cit., pp. 56-7 on this point.

52. *Eqtesad-e Islami*, op. cit., pp. 99–104, *Taleghani*, op. cit., p. 47 and Sadr, Vol. II, op. cit., pp. 63-117.

53. *The Koran*, op. cit., p. 375. See also *Resaleh*, op. cit., p. 12 for *anfal*.

54. See Farhad Nomani, *Takamol-e Feudalism dar Iran*, Vol. I (Teheran: Kharazmi, 1358), pp. 145-236 for the actual development of landownership in Iran during and after the Moslem conquests. It must be emphasized that the concrete origin and point of reference of state ownership in Islam lies in the early Islamic conquests. Hereafter cited as Nomani, *Feudalism*.

55. The verbal noun translated here as disposition is *tassarruf kardan*. As a theological term, it means God's power to do with His creation whatever he wishes. Here, it primarily implies man's power to control his property.

56. *Eqtesad-e Islami*, op. cit., p. 257. Again, one observes the similarity of the argument with that of Thomas Aquinas and other Christian scholastics who considered production under private ownership desirable and that order is better preserved under private ownership (see Schumpeter, op. cit., pp. 92 and 119).

57. *Eqtesad-e Islami*, op. cit., p. 259. In fact, according to the Islamic laws an innate apostate is to be sentenced to death. The example is based on Khomeini's juristic justments and is quite authentic.

58. Ibid., pp. 190-99, 259-60 and 187. See also Sadr, Vol. II, op. cit., pp. 79–99 and *Resaleh*, op. cit., pp. 232–37.

59. Taleghani, op. cit., pp. 27-8. Italics are ours.

60. *Eqtesad-e Islami*, op. cit., p. 272.

61. Taleghani, op. cit., p. 34. See also Sadr, Vol. II, op. cit., pp. 146-59.

62. Khomeini is of the opinion that *anfal* are under the supervision of the imams and that his permission for the use of natural resources is required. However, some other jurisconsults doubt this verdict, especially at the time of the occultation of the twelfth imam (see *Eqtesad-e Islami*, op. cit., pp. 104–5).

63. Taleghani, op. cit., p. 36.

64. Ibid., p. 36 and *Islam and Schools of Economics*, op. cit., p. 156.

65. *Eqtesad-e Islami*, op. cit., p. 141 and *Resaleh*, op. cit., pp. 195-213.

66. Sadr, Vol. II, op. cit., pp. 94 and 127.

67. *Eqtesad-e Islami*, op. cit., pp. 117 and 274.

68. *Resaleh*, op. cit., pp. 208-9.

69. See Rafsanjani, op. cit., pp. 28-36 and *Eqtesad-e Islami*, op. cit., p. 274.

70. *Eqtesad-e Islami*, p. 301.

71. Taleqani, op. cit., p. 30.

72. Ibid.

73. *Resaleh*, op. cit., p. 157.

74. Sadr, Vol. II, op. cit., pp. 195-8. See also *Eqtesad-e Islami*, op. cit., p. 187 and Taleghani, op. cit., p. 39.

75. Teleqani, op. cit., p. 40.

76. *Resaleh*, op. cit., pp. 299-300.

77. *Eqtesad-e Islami*, op. cit., p. 189. In fact, the Prophet took away the properties of two clans as *anfal*, but the word used in that respect is spoil and not confiscation (see *Resaleh*, op. cit., p. 37).

78. *Eqtesad-e Islami*, p. 189. See also the similar verdict by Khomeini, in *Resaleh*, op. cit., p. 237.

79. Taleghani, op. cit., p. 27.

80. Khurshid Ahmad (ed.), *Studies in Islamic Economics* (London: The Islamic Foundation, 1981), p. 66.

81. *Resaleh*, op. cit., p. 252.

82. Ibid., pp. 253-5. See also Taleqani, op. cit., p. 65.

83. *Resaleh*, op. cit., p. 137 and see pp. 136-9 for verdicts by Khomeini on banking.

84. Ibid., p. 142.

85. Ibid., p. 253.

86. Ibid., p. 197.

87. See Nomani, *Feudalism*, op. cit., pp. 257-83, on the origin and development of *muzara'a* in the history of agrarian relations in Iran.

88. Taleghani, op. cit., p. 65. See also Sadr, Vol. II, op. cit., pp. 226-7 and *Eqtesad-e Islami*, op. cit., p. 338. It is obvious that the contract can now be held between a landlord and the share-cropper. It is claimed that the share-cropper is likely to do his job with greater interest than the hired labourer, even though the latter contract is also legal.

89. *Resaleh*, op. cit., pp. 199-201 and Taleghani, op. cit., p. 65.

90. *The Koran*, op. cit., p. 236.

91. *Resaleh*, op. cit., p. 212 and see Taleghani, op. cit., p. 65.

92. *Eqtesad-e Islami*, op. cit., p. 212 and *Resaleh*, op. cit., pp. 202-7.

93. Resaleh, op. cit., pp. 208-9.

94. Schumpeter, op. cit., pp. 92-4.

95. Quoted in John Fred Bell, *A History of Economic Thought* (New York: The Ronald Press Co., 1967), p. 44.

96. Ibid., p. 45. See *Resaleh*, op. cit., pp. 208-11, 283-7 and Taleghani, op. cit., p. 27 for similar ideas.

97. *Resaleh*, op. cit., pp. 76-117, 131-42, 189-265.

98. Taleqani, op. cit., p. 66.

99. *Islam and Schools of Economics*, op. cit., pp. 155-61. See also *Eqtesad-e Islami*, op. cit., pp. 235-9. Only Shariati, whose view on the legitimacy of private ownership is not 'authentic', equates profit with exploitation.

100. Ibid., p. 297 and Sadr, Vol. II, op. cit., p. 66.

101. Mannan, op. cit., p. 88. See also *Resaleh*, op. cit., pp. 233 and 289. Khomeini says that: 'the wage (the workers) receive is for their work. Therefore, if they work less, they are violating the religious laws' (Ibid., p. 289). See also Ibid., p. 211.

102. Taleghani, op. cit., p. 45.

103. Ibid., p. 44. Khomeini explicitly states that collective income derived from collective labour is forbidden (*Resaleh*, op. cit., p. 289).

104. *Eqtesad-e Islami*, op. cit., p. 308.

105. Sadr, Vol. II, op. cit., p. 219 and also pp. 207-8.

106. Ibid., p. 257-60.

107. Taleghani, op. cit., p. 46.

108. Bell, op. cit., p. 649.

109. Taleghani, op. cit., p. 30.

110. Ibid., p. 46.

111. Sadr, Vol. II, op. cit., p. 208.

112. Ibid., p. 214, citing a saying of the Fifth *Shi'i* Imam. Jurisconsults and *mojtaheds* have always found themselves in a paradoxical position with reference to rent. Historically, they have always enjoyed the rent received from *waqf* (religious endowment) lands and received considerable sums of money and crops as rent in money and in kind without 'labour' (see Nomani, *Feudalism*, op. cit., pp. 187-95 and 257-83 for the origin and development of *waqf* lands and rent in Iran before and after the Islamic

conquests).
113. *Islam and Schools of Economics*, op. cit., p. 161.
114. Taleghani, op. cit., p. 66.
115. *Resaleh*, op. cit., pp. 87–8.
116. See Khomeini's interpretation of this principle in Ibid., pp. 302–4.
117. Taleghani, op. cit., p. 29.
118. *Eqtesad-e Islami*, op. cit., p. 353.
119. Ibid., pp. 353–4.
120. Ibid., pp. 354–5.
121. Ibid., p. 355.
122. Ibid. See also Azari-Qumi's editorial in *Resalat* for a similar view.
123. Taleghani, op. cit., pp. 30–31.
124. Ibid., p. 31.
125. Ibid., p. 61.
126. Ibid., p. 66.
127. Nomani, *Feudalism*, op. cit., pp. 237–55.
128. See Taleghani, op. cit., p. 30, Sadr, Vol. II, op. cit., pp. 207–8 and 219, and *Eqtesad-e Islami*, op. cit., pp. 333 and 353–5.
129. See Schumpeter, op. cit., pp. 97–9.
130. Rafsanjani, op. cit., p. 30.
131. Ibid., pp. 30–32.
132. Sadr, Vol. I, op. cit., pp. 230–1.
133. Ibid., p. 430.
134. *Eqtesad-e Islami,* op. cit., p. 268.
135. *Islam and Schools of Economics,* op. cit., p. 160.
136. Sadr, Vol. II, op. cit., p. 348. The authority of the Islamic government, *Vali* (Guardian) or imam is derived from the following verse in the Qur'an: 'O ye who believe! Obey God and obey the apostle, and those among you invested with authority' (*The Koran*, op. cit., p. 417).
137. Sadr, Vol. II, op. cit., p. 347.
138. Ibid., pp. 340–1.
139. Ibid., pp. 338–50.
140. Taleghani, op. cit., p. 28.
141. *Resaleh*, op. cit., p. 272.
142. *Resaleh*, 4 Shahrivar, 1366, p. 1.
143. Ibid.
144. Ibid., 13 Mordad, 1366, p. 12.
145. Ibid., 11 Mordad, 1366, p. 11.
146. See Sadr, Vol. II, op. cit., pp. 320–450, Taleghani, op. cit., pp. 36, 38 and 48.
147. *Islam and Schools of Economics*, op. cit., p. 159.
148. *Resaleh*, op. cit., p. 66. See also Ibid., pp. 67–8 and 78–92.
149. Ibid., p. 87.
150. Ibid., p. 89.
151. Ibid., p. 90.
152. Ibid., pp. 86–7 and 93.
153. Ibid., pp. 104–17.
154. For example, see *Eqtesad-e Islami,* op. cit., pp. 305 and 411.
155. Rafsanjani, op. cit., p. 116.
156. *Islam and Schools of Economics,* op. cit., p. 131.
157. Ibid., p. 130.
158. Ibid., p. 149.
159. Ibid., p. 157.
160. *The Koran,* op. cit., pp. 166 and 359.
161. Taleghani, op. cit., p. 58. See also *Islam and School of Economics*, op. cit. pp. 154–5 for a similar view.

5. Domestic Policies

Rise and demise of democratic rights and freedoms

On 19 August 1953, Iran's short-lived experiment with democracy came to an abrupt end as the rightist army generals supported externally by the United States and internally by royalist sympathizers, a few religious leaders and their followers and finally the hired lumpenproletariat (*chagu keshan*) ousted Dr Mohammed Mossadeq. In the twenty-six years that followed, the Iranian people witnessed the erosion of their democratic rights as the Shah steadily concentrated political power in his own hands. The irresolute foreign-backed Shah developed into an effective dictator who not only silenced all opposition, but succeeded in forcing the traditional aristocracy, which considered itself as a partner in political power, into a position of obedient subservience. The Shah exercised his dictatorial rule on the basis of the support that he received from the state security organs: the army, the gendarmerie, the police and the infamous Iranian Secret Police – SAVAK. Although he made attempts at securing popular support to stabilize his régime and add credibility to his rule, the Shah's preoccupation with the absolute control of policy-formulation at all levels was incompatible with an atmosphere conducive to popular participation at the national level. Mossadeq had no control over the army, gendarmerie or the security forces and hence relied on the power of the people to control the circumstances. The Shah's fear of the people who had once dethroned him forced him to base his power on the terror sown by the security forces.

Between the summers of 1960 and 1963, the Shah toyed with the idea of democratization, but realized that this would ultimately strip him of his powers, if not dethrone him. By the spring of 1963, when new elections were held, all pretence of free elections were dropped. Instead of rigging the ballots, sifting through the undesirable candidates and pulling out the loyal elements, a hand-picked and dependable election list was compiled of peasants, workers, members of guilds and people from all walks of life. When the Shah was asked about the charge that members of the Majlis had been 'hand-picked' by the government-supported Congress of Free Men and Women, the Shah replied: 'So what. Was it not better that this organization do it than that it be done by politicians for their own purposes?'[1]

The economic success of Iran in terms of spectacular growth rates varying between 4.5 and 15.3 per cent, fuelled by Iran's growing oil income, between 1963 and 1973, allowed the Shah to substitute consumerism and hedonism for political participation. The Iranian people were encouraged to enrich themselves in any way that they could. Bribes, petty theft, fraud and embezzlement, along with connections (*party bazy*) determined the final financial position of those who were willing to benefit from and had access to such mechanisms. The policy of encouraging economic acquisitiveness and discouraging citizens from any meaningful political action or participation led the majority of urban dwellers to self-indulgent life-styles. Frustrated intellectuals were either forced into armed resistance or a cynical and latent confrontationist coexistence with the régime. The Shah's emphasis on modernization from above required the co-operation of professionals, experts and members of the growing bureaucratic machine who were capable of realizing his dream. As the size of the modern sector grew, the self-esteem of its members grew with it. The Shah failed to realize that the increasing importance of the modern sector provided its members with the justification and need for greater participation. Capitalism without political representation and participation had reached its limits in Iran.

On 10 October 1977, when the ten nights of poetry reading at the Goethe Institute in Teheran began, the intellectuals relieved themselves of fourteen years of pent-up rage against a repressive political system which had denied them the rights of free self-expression, association and press. Had the majority of technocrats, bureaucrats and professionals not felt the need to attain the democratic rights which gave a real meaning to their self-seeking life-styles, Iran's revolution might have never taken place.

Khomeini's genius was in realizing that by criticizing the greatest defects of the Shah's régime as perceived by a large majority of the people – the absence of democracy and freedom; overt dependence on and alignment with the United States and widespread corruption – he could gain the widest base of support possible. Bani-Sadr claims to have advised Khomeini to adopt democratic principles as the cornerstone of his discourse.[2] If Bani-Sadr's contention is true, then he should be credited for having masterfully masked Khomeini's genuinely anti-democratic principles, with the populist, libertarian and freedom loving 'Paris discourse'. Iran's revolutionary slogan chanted by millions all across the country became, '*Esteqlal – Azadi – Jomhouri-e Islami*' (Independence – Freedom – Islamic Republic).

The incompatibility of freedom with Khomeini's concept of Islamic government was only evident to those who had studied his book. Khomeini's anti-democratic discourse is based on two interrelated notions. Firstly, the presumed immaturity and infancy of the people, which he calls 'minors' and secondly, the 'superiority' of the governing jurisconsult over 'other men'.[3] Infants and minors are incapable of independent thought and lack proper judgement, so, as Khomeini argues forcefully: 'the existence of a holder of authority, a ruler who acts as trustee . . . and a vigilant guardian of God's creatures; who guides men to the teachings, doctrines, laws and institutions of Islam and who prevents the undesirable changes that atheists and enemies of Islam wish to introduce, is a necessity'.[4] The relation between the leader, the governing jurisconsult and the people is also clearly defined and leaves no room for suspecting Khomeini of democratic or libertarian tendencies. Khomeini argues that:

> Just as God Almighty set the Most Noble Messenger (peace be upon him) over the Muslims as their leader and ruler, making obedience to him obligatory, so, too, the just jurisconsults must be leaders and rulers.[5]

The relation between the inept masses and the just and enlightened jurisconsult cannot be anything other than blind obedience and Khomeini exhorts this. Believing that ordinary people, or non-jurisconsults, are forever incapable of sound judgement and, subsequently, unable to alter their state of mental incapacity, Khomeini adds that: 'the *Ulama* of Islam [the learned men of Islamic law] have been appointed by the Imam (upon whom be peace) to the positions of ruler and judge and these positions belong to them in perpetuity'.[6] Democracy, in the sense of the rule of the people by the people and for the people, is, therefore, in contradiction with Islam and unjustifiable in Khomeini's political scheme, since he would argue that such a system of government would be similar to leaving a lost herd in hostile territory without a shepherd. On the issue of the people's relation to the Islamic leader, Khomeini's position is identical to that of absolute monarchs for whom benevolent despotism towards their subjects was the only just posture conceivable.

Islamic ordinances, especially as they are interpreted by Navab-Safavi or Motahhari, do not leave much room for freedom. Once a choice is made by a religion or an ideology for the people and attempts are made to impose it on society, the discussion of whether individual freedoms exist in such a society or not becomes formalistic. It can be argued that a rigid interpretation of Islam, such as that of Navab-Safavi's, which views the forceful imposition of the *Shari'a* as the sole mission of an Islamic society, is intrinsically intolerant of and hostile to individual freedoms. It is only within Bazargan's Islamic subsystem that, conceptually, Islam and individual freedoms need not be contradictory. Even Taleqani, whose position throughout the revolution and genuine concern for the administration of the nation through peoples' councils set him apart as one of the few progressive and democratic clergymen, would choose the authoritarian approach whenever the will of the majority opposed the *Shari'a*.

In an interview with foreign journalists on 18 March 1979, Taleqani was asked what would happen if, for example, a religious leader thought that abortion was forbidden while Bazargan (the prime minister) thought that it should be made legal? Taleqani answered that if abortion is forbidden on the basis of an Islamic ordinance, then clearly Bazargan should obey it. The journalist posed an interesting hypothetical question which delved into the depths of the epistemological problem of an Islamic concept of democracy: Taleqani was asked what he would do if after the inauguration of the Iranian parliament, the majority of the members voted in favour of legalizing abortion? His answer was most revealing:

> Such a parliament would never be convened. It is like saying the parliament would legalise the consumption of alcoholic beverages but that is *haraam* – forbidden by the *Shari'a*. No such parliament can be convened. We would reject such a parliament and throw it away.[7]

By hammering at the idea that 'our Islamic government will be based on the will and vote of the people' in his interviews, Khomeini sought to reassure the Iranian people of his democratic intentions and, at the same time, obtain international respectability.[8] Khomeini pledged the creation of: 'a democratic government in the form of an Islamic Republic, in which a Parliament composed of the true representatives of the people would administer the affairs of the state'.[9] Undoubtedly, his Paris advisors such as Bani-Sadr, Yazdi and Qotbzadeh who had spent most of their politically active lives in democracies, played a major role in coaching Khomeini on the political necessity of paying lip service to democracy. On the issue of democratic freedoms, Khomeini had to make promises in which he obviously did not believe. Again, the Iranian people had to be reassured that they were not dethroning one despot to replace him with another. Asked whether the Islamic Republic would assure democratic freedoms and whether Marxists would be able to express themselves freely, Khomeini replied: 'The Islamic government is a democratic one in the true sense of the word . . . everyone can express his opinion and Islam has the responsibility of responding to those ideas. The Islamic government will use logic to respond to all ideas'.[10]

Even though Khomeini did not deviate from his authentic views on individual liberties, he camouflaged them in such a manner that they did not seem too provocative to his Iranian and foreign audience. When Liz Thurgood of *The Guardian*, one of the very few knowledgeable foreign correspondents on Iranian politics, asked Khomeini whether: women would be able to choose freely between western style clothing and the *chador* (veil); cinemas would be allowed to function and, if so, what kind of films would be permitted, and whether alcoholic beverages would be forbidden once Islamic laws were implemented, Khomeini explained that the implementation of Islamic laws required the realization of a series of complex preconditions and prerequisites.[11] He said that while women would be free to choose their work and their garb, they would have to comply with certain standards. He asserted his opposition to films that corrupted youth and were harmful to Islamic culture, but added that he was in favour of educational films that were beneficial to the healthy and scientific growth of society. Only on the issue of alcoholic beverages did he provide a precise and unconditional answer: 'the use of alcoholic beverages and other intoxicating substances harmful to society will be prevented'.[12]

Making the enforcement of Islamic laws conditional upon the realization of a series of preconditions was a classical evolutionary argument which has its equivalents in all ideologies. While he did not deny his intention of enforcing the *Shari'a*, Khomeini sought to assure a large section of the Iranian population who had become fond of their individual rights that Islamization would be a gradual process and, therefore, there should be no cause for alarm. Bazargan probably took this position at its face value, as did many other wishful thinkers who desperately sought to reconcile Khomeini's Islam with an open Islamic society.

The role of the Hezbollah

On 16 January 1979, the Shah left the country. For a majority, the Shah's presence symbolized the rule of repression; his departure, therefore, created an atmosphere of euphoria only to be found at the end of wars and the fall of despots. The news of his departure coincided with an ominous event which continued to shape the political scene of Iran for another two and a half years. During the reopening ceremonies of the universities throughout the country, in the second week of January, the demonstrations and speeches inaugurating a new democratic era were systematically interrupted and disrupted. A small, yet vocal and violent group entered the universities, tore up all secular pamphlets and literature along with the posters of non-Islamic heroes and forced the participants to break up their meetings. The same mysterious group chanted '*Hezb Faqat Hezbollah, Rahbar Faqat Ruhollah*' as it went about its destructive activities. This chant, which later became the battle cry of the *Hezbollahis* (the supporters of the Party of God) asserted that there was and could only be one party; the Party of God, and that there was and could only be one leader: Ruhollah Khomeini. This amorphous group, the Islamic shock troops who came to constitute a determining political force in the hands of the clerical leadership, adopted the name Party of God to convince the naïve Moslem masses that their acts and positions were truly Islamic. The Hezbollah had no official leaders, no official headquarters or even a newspaper. Yet they appeared whenever the Islamic status quo was questioned, criticized or challenged. Nearly a month before the victory of the revolution, the Islamic pressure groups attacked the universities chanting 'Death to Communism'.[13]

The activities of the Hezbollah in Iran were closely related to what was going on in Paris. The growing influence of the left in Iran was receiving wide coverage in the western press. Khomeini was constantly questioned about the size and significance of communists and leftists in Iran. Although he brushed them off as 'an insignificant force' which 'did not pose a serious problem', he had realized that democratic conditions would certainly not reduce their force or appeal.[14] The Hezbollah was ordered into action to prove that, irrespective of the left's political power in Iran, the spontaneous and popular reaction of concerned Moslems would not allow them to exert any real power over Iran's future domestic and foreign policy. Thus the United States was reassured that the fall of the monarchy would not lead to communist rule in Iran.

In the first phase of the Hezbollah's activities, during which Khomeini wished to maintain a democratic appearance, they attacked and curbed the activities of Marxist-Leninist forces, saving Khomeini the embarrassing task of publicly condemning them even before he came to power. Two days after the Hezbollah's attack on Teheran University, Khomeini tried to present himself as an honest broker, pretending to be totally uninformed about the operations of the Islamic shock troops at home. He told a Lebanese newspaper that: 'Marxists will be free to voice their demands but they will not be free to conspire against the country'.[15] While Marxist-Leninist forces benefited from the open political environment which had been created due to the breakdown of the old régime's security forces, they continued to remain the target of the Hezbollah's ever-increasing and intensifying violence. During this first phase, the Hezbollah consistently attacked leftist assemblies, demonstrations and book exhibitions. On 20 January 1979, a march organized by democratic and leftist teachers was attacked by the Hezbollah. Posters of non-Islamic personalities, including Mossadeq, were torn up and paint was thrown at unveiled women. This incident resulted in a number of injuries among nationalists, as well as leftists. The activities of the People's Mojahedeen also came under attack. The slogan of 'death to the hypocrites' referring to the Mojahedeen was used by the Hezbollah as early as mid-January of 1979.

After the victory of the revolution, on 20 February 1979, the Marxist-Leninist organization of the People's Fadaian called on all revolutionary compatriots who had fought for a free and democratic Iran to join them in a march towards Imam Khomeini's place of residence. The march was announced to be in support of Imam Khomeini and was intended as a demonstration of the People's Fadaian's allegiance to the leader of the revolution. The second phase of the Hezbollah's activities started after Khomeini refused to accept the People's Fadaian. In a radio message, Khomeini invited the general public not to co-operate with the Fadaian because: 'the organizers of this march are not Moslems and are hostile toward Islam'.[16] An information bulletin published by Imam Khomeini's Office of Propaganda cautioned the people not to participate in the Fadaian's march, since the organizers were communists.[17] Subsequently, the People's Fadaian, perplexed at Khomeini's open rebuff, cancelled the march.

By publicly discouraging the people from co-operation with left organizations and by labelling the communists as hostile forces to Islam, Khomeini provided the Hezbollah with the ideological justification it needed to enter into a more violent phase of confrontation with the left. In this second phase, the Hezbollah not only attacked leftist organizations, but all non-clerically endorsed parties. It is important to point out that since the key clerical figures had gathered in the Islamic Republic Party (IRP), non-IRP supported parties and organizations became synonymous with non-clerically approved parties. The scope of the Hezbollah's operations went well beyond the boundary of curbing the activities of parties without clerical support. They systematically assailed all non-IRP approved demonstrations, assemblies, bookshops, photo exhibitions and speeches with knives, blades, bricks, clubs and knuckle dusters. The invisible clerical leadership of the Hezbollah hoped to intimidate and terrorize the increasing number of supporters of non-clerical political organizations, by arousing a lynch mentality amongst angry Moslems who wished to silence the opposing atheists.

In a speech on 27 February, Khomeini singled out the Moslem people's targets of wrath. Referring to those who had sown the seeds of dissent, disunion and sectarianism, Khomeini invited the people not to participate in their assemblies. He also warned the press not to deviate from the proper path of the Islamic Revolution by publishing provocative articles.[18] Khomeini's policy for confronting the opposition during this phase was based on a formal support of democratic freedoms, along with public statements concerning his personal dislike of communists and dissenters. The real objective of his political strategy was to have the opposition silenced by devoted and active Moslem masses who would take their lead from the 'Imam's' pronouncements. Khomeini was carefully cultivating an image of a closely reciprocal relationship with the Moslem masses in which he supposedly followed the signals he received from the masses and proceeded to represent and voice their aspirations as state policies. The Hezbollah movement, which was organized and controlled by the clerical leadership, was held up as an example of Khomeini's brand of spontaneous popular Moslem democracy, in which the true majority would crush the opposing minority. The Hezbollah was supposed to represent this zealous Islamic mass.

According to Bani-Sadr, Khomeini was well aware of the Hezbollah's violent campaign against democratic freedoms. Bani-Sadr recalls that on one occasion when he requested Khomeini in the presence of a clerical member of the Revolutionary Council to publicly condemn the acts and methods of the Hezbollah, either Khomeini or the cleric present (Bani-Sadr does not recall who) responded that these groups should be left alone to carry out their duty and that the non-Islamic political groups should be swept away by the club wielders.[19] The political polarization of society into clerically approved organizations and the rest simplified the Hezbollah's task.

The organization of the Mojahedeen of the Islamic Revolution: the legal front of the Hezbollah

On 4 April 1979, the Islamic paramilitary organizations, *Towhidi-Saff*, *Mansourin*, *Fallah*, *Movahedin*, *Falaq*, *Towhidi-Badr* and *Omate Vahe-*

deh, formed a coalition of the Islamic forces loyal to Khomeini. The new body was called the Organization of the Mojahedeen of the Islamic Revolution (OMIR). A few of these organizations, such as *Towhidi-Saff*, *Falaq* and *Mansourin*, had been active in Iran, Syria and Lebanon prior to the revolution. Certain members of these groups were in touch with Khomeini in France and awaited his order of *jihad* (holy war) against the Shah's régime. Although the order never came, these armed political groups trained and organized their members for the eventuality. The unification of these seven paramilitary political groups is reported to have been at the initiative of Behzad-Nabavi and Mohammed-Ali Rajaee who were members of *Towhidi-Saff* and *Mansourin*. The two men were, however, encouraged by Beheshti and Rafsanjani, founders of the IRP (Islamic Republic Party), who wished to see a unified command.[20] The IRP was in need of a paramilitary organization capable of supporting the legal actions and positions of the party, as well as organizing and carrying out illegal acts of harassment, intimidation and assault against its rivals.

The new organization's choice of name revealed another purpose of the OMIR. In the contemporary political history of Iran, Mojahedeen was always associated with the People's Mojahedeen organization, but the OMIR intended to break this tradition by establishing itself as a viable political alternative. The choice of name was further intended to sow confusion among the people as to which organization was the real successor of the Mojahedeen's active revolutionary past. Clearly, the IRP viewed the People's Mojahedeen as one of its main political rivals within the Islamic spectrum of political forces and thus encouraged the OMIR's creation. It is reported that Jalal-e-deen Farsi, who was a member of the IRP and later became IRP's unsuccessful presidential nominee, had said that: 'the OMIR is a part of us, we shall push out the People's Mojahedeen from wherever they are and replace them with the Mojahedeen of the Islamic Revolution'.[21] The prime objectives of the OMIR became: the organization and control of club-wielding Islamic shock troops, the Hezbollah; the harassment, intimidation and physical assault of all opposition political forces and the establishment of itself as an alternative force to the People's Mojahedeen.[22]

Certain prominent members of the *Towhidi-Saff* and *Mansourin*, such as Mohsen Rezaee, who later became the commander in chief of the Corps of the Islamic Revolutionary Guards (CIRG) and Mohammed Gharazi, who later became minister of oil and minister of post, telegraph and telephone, established themselves as influential figures in the CIRG and thus extended the OMIR's sphere of influence. Other influential members of the OMIR such as Rajaee, Behzad-Navabi, who later became minister of heavy industries and Mohammed Salamati, who later became minister of agriculture, took control of key positions in the Islamic Revolutionary Committees, creating another bridge with post-revolutionary paramilitary institutions. The OMIR's influence within CIRG and the committees allowed it to tap the manpower and armed resources of legal institutions, as well as their information-gathering services, in order to repress all opposition without directly involving the state.

In a declaration announcing its creation, the OMIR maintained that: 'it was dedicated to the struggle against elements, tendencies, governments and superpowers which acted against the realisation and expansion of the Islamic revolution'.[23] The OMIR threatened that it would 'conduct an ideological and political struggle against Imperialist powers of the right and left, Zionist aggressors and internal hypocrites, deviationists and opportunists and would reserve the right of full-fledged military operations against such forces if such action became necessary'.[24]

With the creation of the OMIR, the clerical leadership strengthened its power structure. The OMIR's surrogate role allowed the IRP to keep out of political disputes which compromised its position as a respectable democratic party. While the OMIR carried out the dirty work of mud slinging, name calling, baiting, assault and battery, the IRP's strongmen, such as Beheshti and Mofatah, could continue to publicly praise political freedoms and denounce any attempt at the monopolization of power by political groups. Gagging of all political forces opposed to the IRP proceeded, while the IRP tried, with some success, to keep its hands clean. The IRP shielded Khomeini so that the 'Imam's' image as an honest broker would not become tarnished by the unfolding of events and the OMIR protected the IRP. This complex, yet efficient, machine intended to put all power into the hands of the clerical leadership. Its structure was such that it took the majority of people a long time to peel off the layers of protection around Khomeini and identify him as the mind behind all major state policies.

The OMIR proved efficient at provoking crisis situations which were intended to lure the opposition into open confrontation with the Islamic government. Their tactic of baiting the opposition was well illustrated in the abduction of Taleqani's sons, master-minded by them. The illegal arrest and abduction of Mujtaba and Abol-Hassan Taleqani were planned and carried out by Mohammed Gharazi, Ali-Reza Aladpoush and Asgar Sabaghian, all prominent members of the OMIR and key decision makers in the CIRG. The object of this operation was to humiliate Taleqani whose independence, wisdom and distaste for authoritarian methods rendered him too popular for Khomeini's liking. Khomeini viewed Taleqani as a powerful rival who had none of the weaknesses and shortcomings of his other clerical rivals. Arresting Mujtaba on the charge of being a Marxist was also intended as a warning to Marxists. If Taleqani's Marxist son could be arrested arbitrarily, then all Marxists could be rounded up at will. Furthermore, the People's Mojahedeen considered Taleqani as their spiritual father. The OMIR hoped that by humiliating Taleqani, it would be able to provoke the People's Mojahedeen to react rashly and thus provide sufficient excuse for their military repression and annihilation.

The Taleqani affair triggered off a wave of public condemnations of those who were responsible for the abduction. Even after the release of Abol-Hassan Taleqani, spontaneous protest marches against the abductors mushroomed all over Teheran and spread to the provinces between 15 and 18 April 1979. The demonstrators, who numbered up to five thousand people at a time chanted 'Death to reaction, the enemy of our people' and 'Taleqani, Taleqani you are the anti-reactionary'.[25] The People's Mojahedeen who were instrumental in organizing the sporadic demonstrations, especially among the students, refused to officially call for a demonstration in favour of Taleqani. The OMIR, which had created the crisis but was not successful in bringing the People's Mojahedeen out into open confrontation and was being subjected to a backlash which made Taleqani more popular than ever, called for a march with the object of 're-emphasising Imam Khomeini's leadership and supporting Taleqani'.[26] Clearly, the OMIR wished to control the runaway situation and assert Khomeini's leadership in face of Taleqani's rising popularity, while it still hoped to provoke the Mojahedeen into open conflict. Khomeini, who must not have expected such a great degree of support for Taleqani, opted for double talk and lashed out against those who had staged protest marches, without referring to their cause. Khomeini refrained from mentioning Taleqani's name and invited the CIRG to combat the conspiracy of those groups which: 'did not believe in Islam and wished to sow disunion among the people'.[27] Khomeini's reference was both to the People's Mojahedeen which systematically criticized the reactionary and schismatic actions of certain elements in the Islamic government and to the many thousand-strong demonstration organized by the National Democratic Front of Iran and disrupted by the Hezbollah.

The OMIR's demonstration resembled a semi-military parade. Groups of demonstrators were escorted with columns of armed men on foot and jeep loads of armed men came from behind. In reality, the OMIR's demonstration was a military parade involving the CIRG and the revolutionary Islamic committees. Obviously, the demonstration was not interfered with, since it was the Hezbollah itself that was staging the march. In the declaration that was read at the end of the march, the leadership of Khomeini was emphasized and blind obedience to all his suggestions and decrees was categorically demanded. Point nine of the declaration posited that:

> we believe that all opportunistic, schismatic, hypocritical, deviationist and atheistic activities are aimed at reviving the interests of Imperialists and Zionists and therefore we condemn them 'vigorously'.[28]

The OMIR, which was unsuccessful at obtaining its original objective, used the crisis it had created to label and condemn the People's Mojahedeen and other democratic or Marxist forces as agents of imperialism and Zionism. Exactly two weeks after the referendum which legally established the Islamic Republic, the clerical leadership made it extremely clear that anyone or any political organization which did not thoroughly approve of its policies and positions was considered an enemy, a lackey of imperialism and Zionism and would be dealt with accordingly.

The freedom of the press and expression

It was natural that after many years of rigid control over the press and publishing in general, the revolutionary conditions would break the past culture of silence, especially in politically related fields and produce a spectacular period of literary renaissance. Books that were not allowed publication in the past were sold by the tens of thousands. The revolution had created its own brand of books. They were called 'white covers', reproduced books that were obviously printed without the permission of the author and sold in every corner of the city. The black tarmacs of the sidewalks around Teheran University changed to white as vendors sold white-covered books. The books that appeared and were devoured by the people had one common characteristic; they were prohibited under the Shah's régime. Shariati and Bijan Jazani (one of the ideologues of the Marxist-Leninist People's Fadaian guerilla organization) had both written books that sold two hundred thousand copies, while Taleqani and Samad Behranghi (a hero of the left) each sold one hundred thousand copies.[29] The literary renaissance of a few months before the victory of the revolution and a short month afterwards was thoroughly pluralistic. At the same time, every party, organization or group which felt like voicing an opinion published a newspaper. A bare four months after the revolution, one hundred and five newspapers were coming off the press in Teheran.[30] The majority of these newspapers, however, had non-Islamic tendencies. The clerical leadership suddenly found itself confronted with a popular press which took itself seriously and acted as a vigilant watch-dog of the policies and positions of the leadership. The newspapers and weeklies that appeared on the news-stands were generally unfavourably inclined towards the officials and authorities of the Islamic Republic.

Finding the press unco-operative and outside its control, the clerical leadership set out to threaten and intimidate it. Once threats failed to secure the desired type of printed material, the leadership resorted to force. On the heels of Khomeini's 27 February 1979 speech against newspapers that deviated from the proper path of the Islamic Revolution, the Hezbollah embarked on a campaign of punishing dissenting and deviationist newspapers in Isfahan, Qum, Zanjan and a number of other cities. *Keyhan*, *Ettelaat* and *Ayandegan*, the country's three main newspapers, were taken off the news-stands by force and ripped up. In other cities, the newspaper kiosks were forcefully prevented from selling the newspapers. The Hezbollah's attack against the freedom of the press was so flagrant and premature, even by clerical standards, that Khomeini was forced to harness their activities temporarily. Khomeini did not reprimand the Hezbollah personally, but his son, Ahmad Khomeini, announced that his father: 'did not condone the tearing up of newspapers'.[31] The game of inciting the Hezbollah to attack democratic freedoms, on the one hand, and public invitations to restraint and moderation, on the other hand, became a distinct feature of Iran's political scene during the first six months of the revolution. The leadership could wash its hands of all excesses committed by the Hezbollah, while the Hezbollah's violent activities went unchecked.

Bookstores in provinces became the Hezbollah's main target of attack only days after the victory of the revolution. Where intimidations and threats against bookstores which sold leftist books did not work, the bookstores were set on fire. On 28 March 1979, Pejvak bookstore in Ahwaz was set on fire. The weekly *Zaban Ashayer* (Voice of the Nomads) provides a vivid description of how five bookstores in Khoramabad, capital of Luristan, were burned down. Four of them sold leftist books and one belonged to supporters of the People's Mojahedeen:

> The crowd which chanted 'Allah-O-Akbar' [God is Great] set fire to the bookstores while the fire engine moved behind the crowd as if it knew what the crowd was there for. All along the route of the crowd, vigilant Islamic Revolutionary Guards observed the activities [of the Hezbollah] but did not make the slightest move to restrain them.[32]

In Tabriz, the so-called deviationist bookstores were warned twenty-four hours in advance to rectify their political tendencies. Once the bookstores refused to comply, they were set on fire. The representative of Tabriz's Council of Publishers and Bookstores met with Ayatollah Madani Khomeini's representative in Tabriz and sought his help. Madani responded that: 'as long as you refuse to burn all communist books, despite our efforts to restrain the people, they will continue to burn them. If you agree to burn these books yourselves, we are ready to fully reimburse you'.[33] The clergy's animosity towards Marxist literature was partly due to the threat that it felt due to the popularity of such literature among students and to a far lesser degree among workers and partly due to Marxism's fundamentally atheistic philosophical position.

As the harassment against leftist bookstores, printing houses and publishers increased, the publication of such books dwindled. The wave of political repression, arrests and executions, which reached its zenith after 20 June 1981, created an atmosphere in which the possession of a leftist book could be used as evidence of the owner's attachment to a leftist organization and could finally provide the basis for the reader's execution as an individual at war with God. According to a publisher who continued to publish leftist books in spite of all the pressure, the clerical leadership had succeeded in dissuading readers from buying such books: 'consumers are so frightened of being seen with leftist books that they look at them on the shelves but do not dare buy them. How long can publishers go on providing unsold goods?'[34] Pressure on opposition newspapers which criticized the policies and proposals of the clerical leadership and published news of opposition activities began during the last week of April 1979. *Peyghame Emrouz*, a newspaper which campaigned for the defence of freedom and independent political thought, was subjected to regular harassment. In a letter to the prime minister, Reza Marzban (*Peyghame Emrouz*'s editor) complained about regular attacks against the newspaper's offices, intimidation of its workers and

editors, the arrest, ill treatment and physical assault of its sales representatives in the provinces, the tearing up of its newspapers at news-stands
and threats of setting fire to its printing house.[35] Marzban requested the
government to take action against 'the mercenaries or soldiers of reaction
and fascism' and to defend the freedom of the press. *Peyghame Emrouz*
and *Ayandegan* were both left-leaning publications and were, subsequently, the main targets of the clergy's efforts to purge the press.
Ayandegan posed a greater problem. Its growing daily circulation was
already reported to be above one hundred thousand copies, which made
it, by far, the most popular newspaper in Iran. *Ayandegan*'s critical
reporting, debates over sensitive issues such as the form of the post-
revolutionary government, the Constituent Assembly or the Assembly of
Experts, the Constitution and its shortcomings, democratic freedom and
the question of nationalities, on top of the newspaper's relative indifference to the speeches and statements made by Khomeini and other
religious figures, angered the clerical leadership.

On 1 May 1979, Motahhari was assassinated. *Forqan* claimed responsibility. Khomeini accused the United States, the communists and
members of the old régime of the assassination and said: 'they are
mistaken if they think they can gain anything with these assassinations'.[36]
Motahhari's funeral was turned into a rally against the left and the
People's Mojahedeen. The large crowd of hundreds of thousands chanted:
'Death to the Communists' and 'Death to the Hypocrites'.[37] Barzargan
claimed that Motahhari had been assassinated by counter-revolutionaries
because of his many years of ideological struggle against Marxism.[38]
Rafsanjani, too, held the left responsible for the assassination.[39] The
whole affair seemed orchestrated to justify an attack against the left.

Ayandegan invited the public to help reveal the real identity of *Forqan*
and clarify the confusion. On 10 May, based on the documents sent to the
newspaper by *Forqan*, it published a well-researched report and concluded that, contrary to Khomeini's statement, *Forqan* was an Islamic
organization. *Ayandegan* revealed that *Forqan* was a *Shi'i* organization which believed that its ideology and practice were rooted in the
teachings of Dr Shariati. It was reported that following in Shariati's
footsteps, *Forqan* believed in an Islamic system in which the clergy did
not play a role and further considered the enemies of Shariati as its own
enemies. *Ayandegan* referred to a leaflet published by *Forqan* and
reported that, according to that document, Motahhari was assassinated
because of a letter which he and Bazargan had written against Shariati.
Forqan had condemned both men to death for: 'betraying the monotheistic movement of the dispossessed Islamic people of Iran during the
Shah's régime'. It also condemned Motahhari for his membership of the
Revolutionary Council.[40] *Ayandegan*'s report reduced the anti-left hysteria which was being cultivated over Motahhari's assassination. Furthermore, it defied Khomeini and publicly exposed the sensitive issue of
inter-Islamic disagreements and feuds which had led to Motahhari's
physical liquidation. The last thing Khomeini wanted the public to be
told, less than three months after the revolution, was that deep-rooted

conflicts existed among different *Shi'i* subsystems. *Ayandegan's* theme of Islam against Islam shattered the image of Islamic unity which Khomeini was presenting as the only force capable of guiding and serving the people.

One day before its report on *Forqan*, *Ayandegan* published a letter addressed to an Islamic Revolutionary Guard called Jahanshah Panahi. In this, the author made the following pertinent points:

> 1 – The people ask why the Hezbollah never attack or disrupt the Islamic Republic Party's (IRP) meetings and demonstrations? Is Hezbollah really the same organisation as the IRP?; 2 – the people wonder why these small groups (Hezbollah) consider themselves to be one and the same with Islam and consequently consider any criticism of them as counter-revolutionary and anti-Islamic; 3 – the people think that the anti-Communist hysteria is only an excuse to cover up the real internal disputes and the power struggle between the clerics themselves; 4 – the people wonder why 120 per cent of the population voted in favour of an Islamic Republic.[41]

The letter referred to sensitive issues which the clerical leadership wished to hide from the public. For the first time, the Hezbollah was being directly associated with the IRP, the fairness of the referendum was being questioned and the internal disputes among the clerics were being exposed.

Khomeini's office published a statement refuting the validity of *Ayandegan's* report on those responsible for Motahhari's assassination and added that the 'imam' had said that he would never read *Ayandegan* again, since it had always played a deviationary role which was against the interests of the Moslem people of Iran.[42] At the end of the statement, it was emphasized that the dedicated and pious workers of *Ayandegan* should be distinguished from the editorial board. The statement was an attempt at driving a wedge between the editorial board and the rest of the staff. The provocative statement by Khomeini's office was broadcast regularly and elaborated upon by the Islamic Republic's radio and television network. Pressure groups began their activities. In Isfahan, authorities at the airport prevented *Ayandegan's* representatives from taking delivery of newspapers flown in; in Shiraz, the newspaper's offices were occupied by an armed group; in Bushehr, its offices were burnt down; in Dezful, the names of those who bought the paper were registered. Following a day of harassment and threats, *Ayandegan* published a one-page statement declaring that it could not continue its work under the conditions that had been imposed on it.[43] The one-page paper sold over one hundred and fifty thousand copies and various organizations, parties and dignitaries condemned the measures employed against *Ayandegan*.[44] The National Democratic Front of Iran organized a meeting in solidarity with *Ayandegan*. The success and widespread support for the meeting persuaded the editorial board and workers to resume publication. After nine days, *Ayandegan* reappeared and stated that:

> Among the Iranian people and among those who are steadfast support-
> ers of a free press, there is a group which reads *Ayandegan* and wants
> it. Small or large and irrespective of their profession, political thought
> and ideology this group considers it to be its right to demand the
> publication of this paper. The unity and resolute decision of *Ayande-
> gan*'s writers, workers and staff, along with the support of its readers
> will make this task possible.[45]

Although *Ayandegan* managed to ride out this first storm, *Keyhan*, which
had published *Ayandegan*'s protest statement announcing its suspension,
fell in to the trap set for *Ayandegan*. *Keyhan* was by no means an
opposition newspaper. Certain elements of the editorial board were later
found to be members of the Tudeh Party, but until its suppression in 1983,
the pro-Soviet Tudeh was a devoted follower of 'Imam' Khomeini and,
in many cases, more catholic than the Pope.

Khomeini's strategy of putting the workers and staff of a newspaper
against the editorial board worked well in the case of *Keyhan*. The
imposition of clerical rule started with an assembly of *Keyhan*'s workers
and staff protesting at its publication of *Ayandegan*'s statement. They
argued the newspaper should serve the Islamic revolution by adopting a
more conciliatory posture towards the government. The kind of absolute
harmony with the clerical leadership which they sought implied the
sacrifice of the newspaper's professional independence. Following two
days of protests and sit-ins against the editorial board, twenty of the most
experienced journalists on the paper were laid off. The authority which
made this decision was unidentified, so the twenty journalists continued
to come to work. They were refused entrance to the newspaper's office.
In solidarity with them, up to one hundred other journalists went on
strike.[46] *Keyhan* appeared with four pages, two of advertisements and
two filled with announcements by various governmental institutions and
a long speech by an IRP ideologue.

The next phase in the Islamization of *Keyhan* was a visit by the
rebellious workers and staff to Khomeini. Khomeini commended these
devoted Moslem workers and said: 'I hope that the press in general
rectifies itself as you did in *Keyhan*, the first issue of the newspaper that
was brought out by you is exactly what the people want'.[47] Khomeini's
support of the arbitrary action of a group of workers who had resorted to
force and violence to impose one rigid line of thought gave the go-ahead
signal. Any zealous Islamic workers at other papers and weeklies could
expel anybody who sought to maintain their independence and professional integrity.

Ayandegan, too, had to be silenced. The elections for the representatives to the Assembly of Experts which were boycotted by seventeen
political organizations and parties took place under overt and covert
pressure from the IRP.[48] Even those newspapers under the direct control
of the clerical leadership reflected the fact that the elections were neither

free nor honest. The minister of the interior spoke of irregularities even at the polling stations in Teheran, where he was present. He acknowledged similar irregularities in large cities, such as Tabriz, Mashhad and Boroujen.[49] As the flood of protests against the unfairness of the elections started to pour in from various political organizations, *Ayandegan* alone gave wide coverage to the reported cases of fraud, manipulation, illegality and outright cheating. On 6 August 1979, *Ayandegan* dedicated a number of its pages to a thorough piece of investigative journalism, exposing the scale and extent of the clerical leadership's manipulation of the elections. The issue that most enraged the clerical leadership was the newspaper's report of protests not only by the leftist and nationalist organizations, but also by well-known clerical figures, such as Ayatollah Mahalati who protested against the elections in Shiraz.[50]

On 7 August 1979, the public prosecutor general of the Islamic revolutionary courts announced that *Ayandegan* was established with the aid of SAVAK, the CIA and Israel; that the publication's objective was to criticize and condemn the Islamic revolution in Iran. Therefore, it was to be banned for counter-revolutionary activities.[51] Having successfully sent their candidates to the Assembly of Experts the clerical leadership moved swiftly and forcefully to silence all opposition newspapers. However, no other newspapers apart from *Keyhan* had fallen to the régime's divide and rule tactics. New measures were called for. This time *Ayandegan*'s head office was occupied by armed IRG men, its printing machines were sealed and locked and thirteen members of its editorial board were arrested and imprisoned.[52]

Ali Qoddoussi, the public prosecutor general, warned that if newspapers and weeklies deviated from the correct path of the Iranian people's struggle for the implementation of Islam, according to the 'Imam's' directive, they would be forcefully dealt with.[53] By 21 August 1979, three lists of banned newspapers and weeklies in Teheran and the provinces had been published, bringing the total figure of closed newspapers and weeklies to seventy-three.[54] In a parallel move, the activities of the foreign press were also curbed. Journalists working for the BBC, *Financial Times*, *Daily Express* and two West German papers were given notice to leave the country immediately.[55] The closure of the offices of the Associated Press followed on 5 September. The only Islamic newspaper that suffered was Mohammed Montazeri's newspaper called *Payame Shaheed* (Martyr's Message). The order to close down the paper after a week of publication came from Teheran's prosecutor general. The paper was accused of criticizing Bazargan, Yazdi and the commanders of the army.[56] Since it was already embroiled in a large-scale military campaign against Kurdistan, the clerical leadership freed itself from the constraints imposed by a free press. With a docile and homogeneous press, the task of drafting an acceptable constitution which included the concept of the governance of the jurisconsult was made far easier. Discussions and embarrassing revelations about the activities of people's representatives in the Assembly of Experts could be kept to a manageable minimum. This monopoly over the propagation of information was an essential step in the proper imposition of a totalitarian state. However, as disputes and disagreements within the Islamic subsystems erupted after the cleansing of the movement of non-Islamic tendencies, more newspapers were closed down. After the closure of the Islamic Republic Party of the Moslem People of Iran (IRPMPI) which was associated with Ayatollah Shariatmadari in December 1979, the IRPMPI's newspaper, *Khalq-e Mosalman* was also closed down.

The second wave of attacks against the freedom of the press resulted from the IRP-Bani-Sadr conflict. On 3 March 1981, the People's Mojahedeen's organ, the *Mojahed* and sympathizing newspapers were closed down by the prosecutor general of the Islamic revolutionary courts. By this time, the People's Mojahedeen had intensified attacks against the IRP and its monopolization of power. Seventeen other newspapers, the majority of which sided with Bani-Sadr in his dispute with the IRP, were also closed down.[57]

Three months later, as the conflict between the IRP and Bani-Sadr intensified, the prosecutor general completed the final stage of purging the press of all opponents of the IRP. On 24 May 1981, Bani-Sadr's newspaper, *Enqelab Islami*, Bazargan's newspaper, *Mizan* and the National Front's paper, *Jebhe-e Melli*, along with three other papers sympathetic to Bani-Sadr, were banned.[58] Now that the Navab-Safavi subsystem had defeated Bazargan's subsystem, it denied its adversaries the right to express their Islamic views. Authentic Islam, as conceived by the IRP and supported by Khomeini, could not tolerate the dissenting voices which demanded Islamic pluralism. However, although Khomeini was instrumental in this inter-Islamic dispute, he did not completely abandon the tools of the other two subsystems. On the contrary, he asked their representatives to repent and return to the flock.

By 1985, over eight hundred of the one thousand and two hundred or more dailies, weeklies, bi-weeklies and monthlies that appeared after the revolution, were closed, banned or suspended.[59] From a total of sixty government-associated publications, 46 were distributed free. The majority of the remaining publications had an average circulation of less than one thousand and five hundred, some circulated as few as one hundred and fifty copies.[60] The repetitive and overlapping content of the Iranian publications after the major purges eventually led Khomeini and Montazeri to call for further press cuts, simply to save on unnecessary costs.

Political organizations and parties

In the aftermath of the revolution, a variety of parties and political organizations came into being. Some remained on paper, some never extended beyond a circle of friends and relatives. A few, which had a history of political or armed activity, or both, attracted the majority of politicized Iranians. The novelty of a free political atmosphere was so great that, across the country, small circles of intellectuals published declarations announcing the appearance of new political groups or simply stating their views of how things should be. Never in its contemporary history had Iran witnessed the publication of such a large volume of political pamphlets, declarations, manifestos, organizational charters or constitutions. As the intital excitement of experiencing the newly won freedoms subsided and the pressure groups of the clerical leadership mounted their repressive campaigns of intimidation, political organizations began to wither away. Soon, the survival of the fittest became the rule governing Iran's political arena. Numerical strength and the devotion of party members and sympathizers became the determining guarantee against political extermination. For the IRP which planned to become the sole political party of the nation, all organizations which did not accept its absolute hegemony constituted barriers which had to be knocked down. The timing and excuse for the Hezbollah's attack on various organizations differed. In some cases, a general directive by Khomeini or the IRP was issued against a specific or group of organizations which had committed some grave error, such as systematically criticizing the clerical leadership. Sometimes, the IRP or the OMIR judged that a group had insulted or questioned the integrity of those historical figures revered by the Islamic government as pioneers of the Islamic movement. Occasionally, basing themselves on a general directive, the regional Hezbollah thought it appropriate to attack specific groups based on its own evaluation of the balance of power in the region.

Among the dozens of parties that appeared, one was the Republican Party of Iran (RPI), which probably remains unknown even to a large majority of Iranian experts on Iran. The RPI declared itself in favour of freedom of expression, freedom of trade and the imposition of the rule of law and order. The founder of the RPI, Abol-Hossein Baqaee-Kermani, warned against repressive pressure groups engaged in clandestine activities. At first sight, the activities, ideology and political weight of this party seemed too insignificant to attract the attention of the Hezbollah. In one of the Baqaee's declarations, in reference to the referendum, he purposefully drew a line between the Islamic Republic and the Islamic Republic Party. Baqaee explained that Khomeini's instruction to the people to vote for the Islamic Republic should not be misconstrued as the 'Imam's' injunction to vote for and support the IRP. In his declaration, Baqaee attacked those trying to curb freedoms of expression and association and promised to reveal their identity. Every time the RPI organized a meeting for its members and supporters, it was disrupted and the club-wielding assailants took over the microphones and prevented the speakers from addressing the crowd. In vain, the RPI officially requested protection for its meetings from the police and the CIRG. Islamic forces responsible for the maintenance of public peace did not arrest a single one of the assailants, although one young man pulled a gun on Baqaee and tried to assassinate him. The Hezbollah, insulted by Baqaee's back-handed comment about the IRP and angered by his repeated threats to disclose the identity of: 'those who wish to impose a one-party system', silenced the RPI. This demonstrated that the Hezbollah was very well informed about the activities of political organizations and their position in relation to the government and that it was determined to quell the opposition voice of even the weakest political forces.

On 5 March 1979, Ahmad Abad, a small village close to Teheran, where Mossadeq spent the last years of his life in exile, witnessed the greatest assembly of non-clerical political forces since the victory of the revolution. On the twelfth anniversary of Mossadeq's death, all the non-clerical political forces and organizations of significance officially announced their intentions to participate in the ceremonies commemorating the leader of Iran's nationalist movement. Among others, the participants included the Marxist-Leninist People's Fadaian Organization, the Tudeh Party (the pro-Moscow communist party of Iran), the Islamic, yet by no means clerically approved, People's Mojahedeen Organization, the traditional Mossadeqist political organizations of the National Front, *Bakhtar Emrooz*, *Hezb Iran* and groups such as the Association for the Defence of the Freedom of the Press, the Iranian Bar Association and the National Organization of Iranian University Members. The presence of Taleqani, one of the very few clerical figures who remained faithful to Mossadeq in the latter's dispute with Ayatollah Kashani, symbolized the convergence of all the anti-reactionary forces which believed in the participation of all political forces in the administration of the country.

In the gathering, which was reported to have assembled more than one million people, Hedayatollah Martine-Daftari, the organizer of the meeting, announced the creation of the National Democratic Front in Iran (NDFI).[61] The new organization tried to distinguish itself from the traditional National Front, yet it hoped to benefit from the National Front's long record of national struggle and resistance. In the tradition of Mossadeq's National Front, the NDFI hoped to create a democratic body in which all major anti-reactionary and anti-imperialist political organizations could participate. As such, in Article 1 of its demands, it called for the dissolution of all those forces which prevented the free expression of opinions in an attempt to impose their own ideas through intimidation, harassment and other anti-democratic means. In Article 2, the NDFI further demanded the creation of a Co-ordinating Council of the Revolution, composed of representatives of blue- and white-collar workers, various guilds and other progressive social strata, which would supervise the activities of the provisional government. Concern for the defence and extension of democratic freedoms reappeared in articles 1, 6, 9 and 10.

The nation-wide observance of commemoration ceremonies for Mossadeq and the enthusiastic participation of a very large number of people indicated that non-clerical forces could become a sizeable force. Khomeini, who viewed Mossadeq's nationalism as a threat to his own transnational Islamic outlook, was always suspicious of political organizations and forces that held Mossadeq as the founder of the Iranian resistance movement which culminated in the revolution. The gathering at Ahmad Abad, especially given Taleqani's presence, upset the clerical leadership. They saw it as a show of force of the major opposition organizations challenging the clerical hegemony.

Khomeini's sensitivity to the NDFI grew as this political organization, despite its limited membership, continued to oppose proposals he felt constituted essential elements of his ideal Islamic government. Khomeini had repeatedly invited, pleaded and ordered the people to vote for an Islamic Republic in the referendum to determine Iran's post-revolutionary form of government on 1 April 1979. The People's Fadaian and the NDFI defied Khomeini who had said: 'even the communists should want an Islamic Republic' and announced that they would not participate in the referendum.[62] The two organizations criticized the biased form of the referendum which only provided a yes or no vote choice to an Islamic Republic, refusing to allow people to choose their preferred political system. They argued that the socio-political content of the Islamic Republic remained undefined and vague and, therefore, people were being asked to vote for an unknown system.[63]

During the Taleqani affair, the NDFI was the only political organization which called for a march in support of Taleqani. The resolution read at the end of the march called on the government to: guarantee and safeguard the freedoms of speech, opinion and assembly; punish those responsible for repressing such freedoms and imposing censorship throughout the country and to immediately arrest those responsible for the abduction of Taleqani's sons.[64] The NDFI's protest march, which attracted thousands of people who wished to show their concern about the disquieting course of events, was attacked a number of times at different points on its itinerary by groups of the Hezbollah carrying Khomeini's portrait and hurling insults. The march left behind a number of injured participants and an angry Khomeini who said:

> Do not be swayed by these groups who are participating in demonstrations when they are not allowed to do so. If these groups are concerned with the welfare of the people, why then did they boycott the referendum. . . . Those satans who are amongst the people and disrupt the public peace are lackeys of the U.S. and if they succeed we will revert to our pre-revolutionary situation and lose our independence and our freedom.[65]

The NDFI's persistence in warning the people about an oncoming wave of repression against freedoms and the imposition of a régime many times more despotic than the previous one enraged the clerical leadership.[66] Khomeini, who had refrained from publicly attacking any political organization, warned those who talked about being democratic to behave themselves, otherwise he would have to issue a religious decree concerning them.[67]

While the Islamic government was gradually eroding the democratic freedoms which were the left's only assurance of survival, the left was caught in limbo. On the one hand, it did not wish to provoke the government and compromise its newly won freedom of legal activity and on the other hand, it was genuinely impressed with the Islamic government's anti-imperialism and its heavy handed policies in relation to members of the old régime. While the clerical leadership was steadily eliminating and repressing the left, the radical and non-clerical Moslems and the democratic forces, the People's Fadaian and the People's Mojahedeen rejoiced at and complimented the régime for its execution of members of the old régime.[68] Even the NDFI, which considered itself as, primarily, a democratic force, declared its unconditional support of the decisions and rulings of the Islamic revolutionary courts in their trial of those whom the NDFI accused of having killed and tortured the people for twenty-five years.[69] Progressive Iranian opposition forces were too haunted and conditioned by the spectre of the past to develop a lucid picture of the present and a common programme of action to guarantee their own survival. Negligent attitudes towards the fundamental right to life were justified as revolutionary revenge. The quest for some common grounds with the clerical leadership made the progressive opposition forces abandon major principles.

Upon Khomeini's announcement that he would no longer read *Ayandegan*, the editorial board suspended publication. Subsequently, the NDFI announced that it would hold a meeting on the anniversary of Mossadeq's 100th birthday. Using the occasion as an excuse to mobilize the people against the relentless violation of freedoms by the clerical leadership, the NDFI dubbed the day as one of freedom of thought, speech and press.[70] In view of the gravity of the situation, important political organizations such as the People's Fadaian and Mojahedeen, along with a number of other organizations, participated in the meeting. The crowd was estimated between tens of thousands and 100 thousand.[71] Although the Hezbollah made sporadic attempts to disrupt the meeting, the number of participants was greater than it could handle. The final resolution of the meeting warned against the spread of anti-democratic practices by certain hegemonic groups which, if left unchecked, would finally impose fascism. The resolution condemned the fascist groups which attacked meetings and burnt books and newspapers. It further demanded the immediate republication of *Ayandegan*, condemning all types of interference with the freedom of the press. The resolution protested against the government's policy of silence in relation to the activities of those who were imposing an atmosphere of repression and intimidation.[72]

Ayandegan resumed its publication on the day after the NDFI's meeting. Khomeini, who had personally interfered to put an end to *Ayandegan*, found himself confronted with a united opposition, which, through its concerted show of force, had challenged successfully the 'Imam's' incursion against the freedom of the press. The issue which preoccupied the clergy most was the outcome of the ongoing debate about having a Constituent Assembly and a small Assembly of Experts. Khomeini feared that the opposition's success in the republication of *Ayandegan* would give it the momentum to mobilize large sections of the population in favour of a large Constituent Assembly. Consequently, Khomeini decided to set aside all ambiguity and publicly attacked the weakest link in the opposition.

The NDFI, which considered itself the rightful heir of Iran's democratic revolution, was the only secular political organization of significance born after the revolution. Its membership, however, was relatively small, its organization loose and its partisans were not combative. It possessed no paramilitary organization and depended heavily on attracting the sympathizers of other well-established political organizations at its meetings. NDFI's concern for democracy and the rights which should be respected within such a system did, however, appeal to a growing audience as the clerical leadership continued its anti-democratic campaign. After NDFI's meeting, Khomeini voiced his anger by candidly saying that:

> Those who cry out for democracy are pursuing the wrong path. . . .
> They are against Islam and hide behind a nationalist figure [Mossadeq]. . . . We want Islam and we are not going to give it up just because someone nationalised our oil. . . . Recognize your enemies. I am giving my last warning to those who are conspiring.[73]

A day later, he became more specific and said:

> A few days ago those parties which speak of democracy and never say a word about Islam, had a big meeting. All they said in their meeting was against Islam. Muslim people should not co-operate with these groups and should distance themselves from them. . . . They are conspiring against Islam and our people will not tolerate this.[74]

Khomeini's references were directives for the Hezbollah.

A month later, on 22 June 1979, the NDFI's meeting in support of the Constituent Assembly was attacked, the participants were assaulted and dispersed by the Hezbollah. Symbolically, the crowd shouted 'Death to Fascism' as it retreated before the onslaught. Even though the NDFI had requested protection from the police, the Corps of the Islamic Revolutionary Guards (CIRG) and the Islamic revolutionary committees, the so-called 'forces of peace', did not intervene and not one of the assailants was arrested.

Once the idea of an Assembly of Experts was imposed on the people, the clerical leadership's main concern became the exclusion of candidates belonging to non-clerically approved political parties. To this end, they conducted a systematic campaign in favour of clerical candidates, exerting pressure on voters at the polls to vote for clerically approved candidates, rigging the election results and, finally, silencing the opposition newspapers which informed the people of the wrongdoings during the election.

Khomeini incessantly reiterated that the Assembly of Experts' candidates should be experts in Islamic law and, consequently, they had to be of the clergy. The people were asked not to vote for non-Islamic candidates, which meant non-clerically approved candidates. Concomi-

tantly, the Hezbollah, with the aid of the Islamic revolutionary committees and the CIRG, was free to disrupt the activities of the opposition
forces. Campaign meetings of the People's Fadaian and Mojahedeen
were assaulted by the Hezbollah both in Teheran and the provinces.
Militants of these organizations distributing campaign leaflets and
posters were beaten up and arrested by armed men who introduced
themselves as members of the Islamic revolutionary committees. Even
the election campaign meetings of small Marxist groups, such as the
Trotskyist Socialist Workers' Party, were attacked and dispersed.[75]

A newly born organization, the Movement for the Defence of the
Islamic Revolution (MDIR), warned that counter-revolutionary elements had hired groups of thugs to attack meetings, bookstores, political
headquarters and press offices. MDIR reminded the authorities that
negligence in combating these mercenary groups would constitute an act
of treason towards Islam, the Qur'an and the ideals of the Iranian people.[76]
As the election day approached, the MDIR accused groups of pseudo-
Moslems, whom it called the mercenaries of certain power-hungry
political forces, of tearing up the posters, leaflets and pamphlets of
various political groups and beating up young men and women engaged
in legal political activities. MDIR maintained that these pseudo-Islamic
shock troopers were well trained and equipped with motorcycles, knives
and guns.[77] Although no one dared to publicly accuse the IRP and OMIR
of organizing and controlling the Hezbollah, everyone knew what was
meant by 'power-hungry political forces'.

After *Ayandegan* had provoked the clerical leadership in to closing it
down before more was exposed about the irregularities of the Islamic
Republic's first so-called free elections, the NDFI called for a protest
march against the repression of freedoms and democratic rights. It
accused the ruling class of arbitrary press censorship and invited all anti-
reactionary parties, groups and organizations to join the fight against
repression.[78] Once again, the NDFI was challenging the monopoly of
power exercised by the IRP and the clerical leadership. Psychologically
uplifted by its success at the polls, the clerical leadership felt defiant and
powerful enough to withdraw the freedoms which were hindering its
absolute rule. The OMIR congratulated the public prosecutor for this
correct 'yet belated' decision to close down *Ayandegan* which it called
'the illegitimate child of a treacherous union between the Left and the
Right'.[79] The themes elaborated by the OMIR in its harsh declaration
against *Ayandegan* were encapsulated in the slogans chanted at the
Friday congregational prayers: 'We support the closure of *Ayandegan*,
the mercenary of foreigners', 'the closure of *Ayandegan* was a gift to the
people by the Public Prosecutor' and 'Mercenary journalists must be
executed'. The people were being prepared for the crushing of any
attempt to reinstate the freedom of the press. While all political organizations and parties except the IRP and the OMIR condemned the closure
of *Ayandegan*, a previously unknown political party, *Hezbe Towhidi*,
suddenly made a transient yet spectacular appearance on the Iranian
political scene. The spokesman of the *Hezbe Towhidi* warned those who

intended to participate in NDFI's protest march in support of *Ayandegan* and invited people not to join the march, since the 'Imam' had forbidden marches and demonstrations. 'Committed Moslems will prevent such activities', said their spokesman and added that *'Hezbe Towhidi* had ordered its members to counter all conspiracies'.[80] The OMIR declared the march an act of animosity towards the revolution which fulfilled the interests of imperialism and Zionism. It asked the people to refrain from any type of confrontation with the demonstrators.[81] The day before the NDFI's march, the new public prosecutor general warned that 'any type of conspiracy against the Islamic Revolution of Iran will be severely suppressed and crushed'.[82]

Even though opposition political organizations and parties of stature did not officially announce their participation in the NDFI's march, a crowd of 500,000 was reported.[83] The People's Fadaian and Mojahedeen either considered the closure of *Ayandegan* too small a detail or their reticence was due to their reservations about openly challenging the Islamic Republic. However, despite their official abstention, their supporters had been given the go-ahead to participate in the march. The opposition was divided as to whether they should abandon all hope of restoring democracy and, therefore, pursue a confrontationist policy or whether they should act as a legal opposition and hope to put pressure on the clerical leadership for democratic rights, without resorting to force. For political organizations with a large following, such as the Fadaian and the Mojahedeen, any move towards direct armed confrontation necessitated elaborate planning and careful consideration for the security of their members and sympathizers.

On 12 August 1979, Hezbollah activities entered a new phase which was marked by open street fighting involving large numbers of people. The assault on the NDFI's march was well planned and prepared. Before the march started from the University of Teheran, a large group of the Hezbollah gathered on the campus of the university and demanded the execution of *Ayandegan*'s editorial board. Once the march started, the Hezbollah followed the protestors out of the university and attacked them with stones, rocks and bottles that had been delivered to the spot by an ambulance and two vans. The protestors, however, were able to repulse the Hezbollah because of their numerical superiority. At two other points along their route to the prime minister's office, the protestors were attacked by groups of the Hezbollah armed with knives, clubs and whips. The IRG fired tear gas at the crowd which had finally made it to the prime minister's office and was listening to the resolution read by the organizers of the march. In Teheran's bloodiest street fighting since the days when the people clashed with the Shah's soldiers, the government announced that at least 270 people had been hospitalized.[84] Ayatollah Azari-Qumi, the public prosecutor of Teheran, gave his own version of the street fighting: 'The People's Fadaian, intellectuals and members of SAVAK [the Shah's security forces] surrounded our Moslem people and according to a pre-planned plot, attacked them with stones, clubs and knives injuring 300 of them'.[85]

The growing membership of the opposition organizations, especially the People's Mojahedeen and Fadaian, alarmed the clerical leadership who had long wished to close down these organizations' headquarters, thereby denying them visibility and the ability to spread their ideology. The Hezbollah-provoked confrontations during the NDFI's march were used by the régime as proof of the opposition's use of violent means to settle political disagreements. Harnessing the anti-opposition mass hysteria that was whipped up after the bloody clashes of 12 August, the wrath of the Hezbollah was efficiently co-ordinated and directed. Attacks against the political headquarters of the People's Fadaian and Mojahedeen in the provinces started after Khomeini's 27 February 1979 speech in which he invited the people to curb the activities of dissident organizations. Ayatollah Mohammed Saddouqi, the religious strongman of Yazd, followed Khomeini's advice immediately and announced that: 'any type of opposition to the decisions of the Islamic government, under any pretext, will be considered as intriguing against the revolution and will be repressed forcefully'.[86] On the day of Saddouqi's announcement, the People's Mojahedeen's headquarters in Yazd, Kashan and Torbate-Heydarieh were attacked, their occupants were beaten up and evicted and the documents in the headquarters were either removed or set on fire. The pattern of closing the headquarters of the Mojahedeen continued in many major towns such as Ahwaz, Isfahan, Khoramabad, Qum, Bushehr and Tabriz. The headquarters of the People's Fadaian were similarly attacked and sacked in provincial cities. In Abadan, Sari, Oroomieh, Tabriz and many other cities, the Fadaian were evicted from their offices.

On the heels of the attack on the NDFI's march, the People's Fadaian's headquarters in Teheran were attacked and invaded at 11 a.m. by 200 club-wielding members of the Hezbollah. The place was immediately handed over to the revolutionary committee of the fourth district. At around noon, another group tried to attack the headquarters of the pro-Soviet Marxist-Leninist Tudeh Party, but was dispersed by the CIRG. The Tudeh Party had always followed the clerical leadership's political line and had never criticized or opposed their acts. It is reported that the Hezbollah, which intended to attack the headquarters of the Tudeh Party, was armed with knives and left peacefully after some discussions without causing any damage to the offices. In the afternoon of the same day, the People's Mojahedeen who had received news that the Hezbollah was going to attack its headquarters, rushed 5,000 of its members to protect their offices.

A week after the Hezbollah failed to occupy the People's Mojahedeen's headquarters, Azari-Qumi, ordered the CIRG to surround the building and gave the Mojahedeen a forty-eight hour notice to evacuate its offices.[87] The Mojahedeen's offices were occupied by the CIRG on 22 August 1979. Within fifteen days, from 7 to 22 August, the clerical leadership used all the means of repression available to it, legal and illegal, to impose its power over an opposition which was only taking advantage of the democratic conditions that came to prevail after the victory of the revolution.

The Kurdish Democratic Party of Iran

As long as the opposition could operate and propagate its ideas from areas which were not under the firm control of the central government, it continued to challenge the clerical leadership. Kurdistan remained a stronghold of non-clerically approved political organizations and its long history of armed struggle against the central government in Teheran threatened the clergy's complete monopolization of power. Khomeini's speeches during August 1979 clearly indicated his intentions and plans. On 18 August, in the heat of the Hezbollah's assault on political freedoms, he said:

> Had we outlawed these corrupt parties and set up the hanging poles to punish their leaders these problems would not have occurred. . . . Had we been revolutionary we would not have allowed any party or front to operate, we would have outlawed them all and allowed only one party, the Hezbollah.[88]

Khomeini's reference to the Hezbollah as the only acceptable political organization was revealing in view of the Hezbollah's activities, especially during August. On 19 August, history repeated itself. Twenty-six years ago on that day, the army's coup put an end to Iran's short-lived democracy under Mossadeq. On 19 August 1979, Khomeini declared that: 'We will approve one or two political parties and proclaim the others illegal. . . . This is in the interests of Islam'.[89] Khomeini's word was the living law; Ali Qoddoussi, the public prosecutor general of the Islamic revolutionary courts warned that: 'any act or step against Iran's Islamic Revolution will be firmly punished by the Revolutionary Courts'.[90]

In order to impose the absolute rule of the clergy right across the country, all pockets of resistance had to be crushed. The arena of confrontation was thus shifted from Teheran to Kurdistan. On 18 August 1979, the central government used the excuse of confrontations in Paveh to launch a major military offensive against the Kurds. The Paveh crisis started when the demand of a great majority of the people for the dismissal of the non-indigenous commander of the CIRG, Zolfaghari, was not complied with by the authorities. A large number of Paveh's citizens decided to stage a sit-in in an area outside the town called Qori Qaleeh. According to the commander of the Kermanshah region's gendarmerie:

> the confrontation and bloodletting in Paveh occurred over the negligence of the authorities to consider the eight reasonable and applicable demands of those who had taken refuge in Qori Qaleeh. After giving a 48-hour grace period to the authorities, these people took up arms since their demands were not met. . . . Had the authorities negotiated with them and complied with their demands for the implementation of developmental and welfare projects in the region, such a bloody confrontation would have never resulted.'[91]

The Kurdish Democratic Party of Iran (KDPI), the most influential Kurdish political organization, which at the time had a 34-year-old tradition of struggling for the autonomy of Kurdistan, placed the responsibility of the bloodshed on the central government. A member of the KDPI explained that instead of listening to the demands of the people of Paveh, the local authorities requested military help from Kermanshah. According to the same source, the night before the confrontations, the Islamic Revolutionary Guards (IRG) attacked and fired upon the people who had taken refuge in Qori Qaleeh, forcing them to fire back.[92] The governor of Kermanshah gave no explanation for the clashes and simply stated that: 'the supporters of the KDPI who had taken refuge in Qori Qaleeh had attacked and occupied the headquarters of the Islamic Revolutionary Guards and the gendarmerie before laying siege to the city of Paveh'.[93] The governor added that counter-revolutionary elements and political agitators were present among the 2,000 men who had attacked Paveh.

The clerical leadership accused the Kurds of harbouring secessionist aspirations. Dr Abdol Rahman Qassemlou, secretary general of the KDPI, had repeatedly rejected the central government's accusation. The KDPI's strategic slogan of 'securing autonomy for Iranian Kurdistan within the framework of a democratic Iran' threatened the régime, which viewed Kurdistan as a prospective pocket of resistance for democratic rights within Iran. The free activity of armed left, democratic and Sunni forces in Kurdistan was intolerable for a clerical leadership determined to impose its own uncontested rule. The fact that the Kurdish resistance had become a grass-roots movement was even more disquieting, especially since according to one account, 400,000 armed men lived in Kurdistan.[94]

The Paveh crisis proved that the IRG alone was incapable of imposing Teheran's Islamic rule on the Kurds. The authorities then instructed the army and the airforce to intervene. The clerical leadership hoped that the campaign against Paveh would be the first in a series of offensives which would lead to the complete defeat of the Kurdish resistance. After the initial setbacks of the IRG, in an outburst of rage, Khomeini issued a decree as the commander in chief of the armed forces. He ordered the army and the gendarmerie to move towards Paveh fully equipped to crush the Kurds. Khomeini threatened that: 'If I do not receive positive results within 24 hours, I will hold the Commanders of the Army and Gendarmerie responsible'.[95] On the same day, an F-4 phantom jet of the Islamic Republic's airforce and an army helicopter were shot down over Paveh. The impressive list of forces dispatched to Paveh and reported in the press indicated the scale of the operations: a battalion of the 55th brigade of the rangers stationed in Shiraz; 150 members of the marine corps and 100 members of the 92nd division stationed in Kurdistan and dispatched by Admiral Madani; a column of tanks from the 81st armoured division; 200 soldiers from the Nowhed brigade; an unspecified number of paratroopers; nine Cobra helicopters; an unspecified number of tanks and armoured vehicles of the 71st armoured division; three C 130 planes full of CIRG members from Teheran; regular missions flown by F-14 fighter planes over the region; 1,000 IRG's from Mashhad, Hamedan and Isfahan; the elite corps of the 81st armoured division of Kermanshah.[96]

After three days of intense fighting, the government announced that the IRG, with the co-operation of the army and the gendarmerie, had taken full control of Paveh. The number of casualties announced by the government was put at approximately four hundred, three hundred of whom were Kurds.[97] As the army moved towards Sanandaj, Saqez, Bookan and Miandoab, the Islamic revolutionary courts dispatched Khalkhali to execute suspicious elements in the cities where the central government had succeeded in imposing its rule. In Teheran, the Revolutionary Council announced the dissolution of the KDPI on the grounds that it had received support from foreigners and that it had incited the Kurds to revolt against the central government, with the intention of separating Kurdistan from Iran. In the midst of the central government's military campaign against Kurdistan, Khomeini pronounced what had become the clerical leadership's policy towards Kurdistan and the left in general. He said:

> Those who have deceived our youth, those who wish to corrupt and annihilate our country in the name of democracy and democrats, have to be forcefully repressed and our people will crush them. . . . Those who are linked with foreigners and are traitors to this country wish to institute a Communist system in Kurdistan, they would like to efface Islam from Kurdistan. . . . There is no Kurdish problem, there is a Communist problem.[98]

Khomeini hoped that the Islamic Republic's military forces would be able to defeat the Kurdish resistance. After four months of military engagement and thousands of casualties, Khomeini realized that a military solution was impossible in Kurdistan. Thus from 17 October 1979, the central government, through Daryoush Forouhar, entered negotiations with the KDPI. The objective of forcing Kurdistan to surrender remained as central as in the past, but time had to be bought. Excluded from legal political activity by the Islamic Republic, the KDPI continued its guerilla war in the region. Despite the central government's concerted efforts, Kurdistan remains the only region where the clerical leadership has proved unable to impose its absolute control.

Islamic Republic Party of the Moslem People of Iran

On 25 February 1978, the Islamic Republic Party of the Moslem People of Iran (IRPMPI) launched itself as a new Islamic force. Soon, it became clear that the IRPMPI had been created at the behest of Shariatmadari, one of Iran's most prominent *maraje-e taqlid*. Khomeini's popularity and his firm control over the Islamic movement disturbed the other high-ranking clerics who did not fully accept his religious dominance. It has always been said that after Khomeini's arrest on 5 June 1963, Shariatmadari's letter to the authorities was instrumental in saving Khomeini from death. In that letter, Shariatmadari argued that according to the Constitution, the highest ranking *ulema* (clergy) were exempt from arrest, imprisonment or exile. He demanded Khomeini's release.[99] Khomeini's meteoric rise to political power overshadowed the religious stature of clerical dignitaries such as Shariatmadari, Marashi-Najafi and Golpayegani. Shariatmadari, however, was the only one of them who had a real social power base. It was in Azarbayejan, where he was acknowledged as the *marja-e-taqlid* of the majority of the people. As the highest ranking member of the clergy during the Shah's rule and as the head of the Dar al-Tabligh (a parallel religious institution to the Qum seminary school), Shariatmadari controlled and distributed large sums of money among theology students and middle-ranking clergy. Shariatmadari's followers thus extended beyond his Azari power base, estimated to be around 14 million, and included an influential network of clerics.

The IRPMPI followed Shariatmadari's moderate political tendency. On numerous occasions, Shariatmadari had come down strongly in favour of a democratic political system for Iran. He had defined democracy: 'as a political system in which the people of one country could freely elect their representatives to administer their affairs'.[100] The primacy that he accorded to the people's choice, at least in theory, contrasted sharply with Khomeini's condescending view of the will of the ordinary people. Basing his analysis on the classical notion of the government of all the people, Shariatmadari and the IRPMPI adopted positions in relation to the clerical leadership's policies. From its inception, it became clear that the IRPMPI and the clerical leadership were on an inevitable collision course. Both sides, however, tried to postpone a bloody showdown due to the Islamic nature of their adversary. Whether Shariatmadari genuinely believed in pluralism and the freedom of expression, or simply found it to be the most convenient and popular issue around which opposition forces could be assembled, is difficult to ascertain. His political record after the revolution does, however, show that Shariatmadari consistently adopted a political position which stressed the people's freedom of political choice.

On certain crucial political measures that were strongly supported by Khomeini, the successful completion of which assured the final imposition of an absolute clerical leadership, Shariatmadari dissented from the clerical mainstream position. Regarding the referendum on Iran's post-revolutionary political system, Khomeini argued that the voters should be limited to a yes or no option on the Islamic Republic's form of government. Shariatmadari opposed limiting the people's choice and called for an open question on the people's desired form of government.[101] On the issue of the size of the Constituent Assembly, Shariatmadari and the IRPMPI disagreed with Khomeini's insistence on a small Assembly of Experts. Khomeini labelled the opponents of the Assembly of Experts as conspirators against the Islamic revolution. Nevertheless, Shariatmadari and the IRPMPI insisted that the drafting of the Constitution which was to act as the rudder of the future system of society needed lengthy deliberation by experts who were also the people's representatives. Shariatmadari told the press that: 'a Constituent Assembly should be convened and the failure to do so would constitute a grave error'.[102] The IRPMPI's decision to call for a meeting in support of fundamental freedoms and the necessity of a Constituent Assembly won the approval of the NDFI and the Trotskyist Socialist Workers' Party, among other organizations. The affinity that certain secular and Marxist organizations came to feel with the IRPMPI over its democratic positions provided an excuse for the IRP and the clerical leadership to question its Islamic credentials. Over the *Ayandegan* affair, Shariatmadari and the IRPMPI once again demonstrated their rejection of the clerical leadership's attempt to silence all opposition. Khomeini's statement to the effect that he would no longer read *Ayandegan*, which had provoked the first wave of repression against the paper, was obstinately responded to by Shariatmadari. In response to a telegram dispatched by a group of progressive intellectuals and organizations, requesting Shariatmadari's opinion on the movements against the freedom of the press, he announced that:

> the occupation of newspaper offices, the use of pressure, threats, intimidation, vandalism and arson does not correspond to an Islamic and humane logic; anyone who does not like to read a newspaper can choose not to read it, but the decision to close down or publish a newspaper is the responsibility of the government.[103]

Shariatmadari's consistent positions against the hegemony of Khomeini's brand of Islam pushed the IRPMPI closer to the nationalist, secular bourgeois-democratic and certain left organizations. Ironically, even the left, which categorized Shariatmadari as a conservative who would have even settled for a constitutional monarchy, was forced by the Islamic Republic's anti-democratic policies to obtain his support. Given the inflexible theoretical framework of the traditional left, Shariatmadari was an enigma. Economically, he was viewed as the representative of the large land-owning classes and the commercial bourgeoisie and was thus categorized as an antagonist. Yet this advocate of capitalism acted as a strong and outspoken champion of democratic rights and freedoms. The simplified political formula adhered to by most left organizations that only anti-imperialists could be democrats suddenly lost its practical usefulness as a concept.

The closure of numerous independent newspapers and the limitations imposed on the activities of non-Islamic political organizations and parties after 22 August 1979 led to the emergence of the IRPMPI's weekly meetings on Fridays as a pole of attraction for different shades of opposition. The well-guarded meeting place of the IRPMPI in the heart of Teheran and the proclaimed Islamic nature of the party shielded it for a while from attacks by the Hezbollah. The IRPMPI's newspaper, *Khalq-e Mosalman* (The Moslem People), became a vociferous mouthpiece of those individuals and organizations who actively resisted the total control of political life by the clerical leadership. The People's Mojahe-deen and the People's Fadaian did not openly collaborate with the IRPMPI, but their positions, declarations and demands were regularly reflected in *Khalq-e Mosalman*.

The Assembly of Experts' decision to grant the governance and leadership of the nation to a jurisconsult gave rise to considerable controversy. If the content of the Constitution drafted by the Assembly of Experts was officially endorsed by the public, the continued leadership position of the clergy would have been assured by the application of the Constitution. Furthermore, Article 110 cemented the indisputable authority of the jurisconsult by granting him unlimited powers. Predictably, the left and the bourgeois democratic forces objected to and resisted the legalization of clerical dictatorship. Khomeini, in return, accused them of ignorance about Islam, if not outright antagonism towards it. Referring to their opposition to the Islamic Republic as a sign of anti-Islamic convictions, the clerical leadership could convince the masses that non-Islamic forces threatened the survival of the Islamic Republic and therefore had to be silenced and excluded. Khomeini's emphasis on the notion that only the enemies of Islam were against the inclusion of the concept of the jurisconsult's governance in the Constitution was difficult to reconcile with the fact that a very high-ranking member of the clergy such as Shariatmadari openly disagreed with the legalization of this concept in view of the powers and responsibilities that accompanied such a position. Shariatmadari argued that the principle of the governance of the jurisconsult contradicted the principle of the sovereignty of the people. He said:

> The governance of the jurisconsult is a valid concept, yet it applies to conditions where legal institutions are absent in a country. After the revolution we did not have a Parliament or a government and therefore the Provisional Government was appointed by the governing jurisconsult. But this concept does not imply the negation of national and popular sovereignty and the delegation of all responsibilities to the jurisconsult, it does not mean dictatorship.[104]

The potent blade of labelling the opponents of the new Constitution as enemies of Islam was blunted by Shariatmadari's intervention. The second highest ranking clerical figure of the land could not be brushed aside as an enemy of Islam or an atheist. The once unifying Islamic subsystems were deploying their forces against one another.

The weekly meetings of the IRPMPI provided the best forum for the critique of the new Constitution. The participants emphasized the points that were articulated by Shariatmadari against the manner in which the Constitution had dealt with the concept of the governance of the jurisconsult. During the sixth weekly meeting of IRPMPI, one of the speakers pointed out that: 'not all of the eminent sources of imitation [*maraj-e taqlid*] were in favour of the concept of the governance of the jurisconsult'.[105] From Khomeini's point of view, dissent and disagreement among the clergy over an issue which he had forcefully presented as an evident and paramount religious theme presented a grave danger to his position. His religious authority and his political leadership were closely intertwined; any doubt cast on his religious authority influenced his political future. Furthermore, the clerical leadership viewed the ratification of the new Constitution, which was going to be put to a referendum, as the most important stage in the realization of their uncontested power. Shariatmadari, who had always belonged to that group of clerics who advocated the non-involvement of the clergy in political affairs, became one of Khomeini's major opponents.

On 26 November 1979, the IRPMPI announced that it would participate in the referendum on the new Constitution only if certain alterations were made to its content. The IRPMPI referred to and deplored the fact that the wide range of powers attributed to the jurisconsult effectively violated national and popular sovereignty. The direct attack on Article 110, which listed the responsibilities of the governing jurisconsult, was left to Shariatmadari who publicly announced his refusal to participate in the referendum unless Article 110 was modified.

The clerical leadership had three options: to ignore the challenge and accept the risk of a growing broad opposition; to make an attempt to discredit Shariatmadari before the referendum; or to deal with him after the referendum. Confronting Shariatmadari was obviously hazardous, since it pitted the authority of two eminent *marja-e taqlids* against one another creating the possibility of an open conflict between *Shi'i* brothers. Irrespective of the outcome, the *Shi'i* monolith which was the source of power of the religious forces would have shattered. A head-on confrontation with Shariatmadari was risky, since it could involve the country in another regional conflict, if not a civil war. The occupation of the American embassy and the hostage crisis had mobilized a large segment of the population in Khomeini's favour. Capitalizing on his popularity as the anti-imperialist hero who had brought the United States to its knees, Khomeini accepted the risk of confronting and discrediting Shariatmadari after the referendum.

Three days after the new Constitution was passed, the process of Shariamadari's exclusion was put into motion. On 5 December 1979, a demonstration in support of the new Constitution was organized in Qum. The demonstrators gradually moved towards Shariatmadari's house, chanting insulting remarks.[106] The house guards dispersed the crowd, but the ensuing shooting led to the death of a guard and the injury of nine other people. The IRPMPI immediately accused Khalkhali and his armed bodyguards of inciting and co-ordinating the attack.[107] The incident, which constituted an insolent affront to Shariatmadari's followers, sent waves of anger and emotion across Azarbayjan. The IRPMPI invited all supporters of freedom and popular sovereignty to a rally against the monopolization of power and the attack on Shariatmadari's house. It continued to demand the modification of Article 110. After the IRPMPI's rally in Tabriz, the radio and television buildings were occupied by Shariatmadari's supporters. Normal programmes were interrupted and an-

nouncements by the IRPMPI, airforce personnel, the army, the gendarmerie and the police in support of Shariatmadari's position were broadcast.
Tabriz radio demanded the immediate departure of the authorities sent to
Azarbayjan by the central government. Madani, Khomeini's representative, Mohammed Qarani, the governor of Azarbayjan and the director of
Tabriz radio and television, were called on by name to leave Tabriz as
soon as possible. The IRPMPI's announcement broadcast on the 'liberated' Tabriz radio publicly condemned the new Constitution as the basis
on which the new régime could construct its dictatorship.[108] Tabriz radio
demanded the departure of all non-indigenous members of the CIRG and
of Islamic judges who were appointed by Teheran. The uprising in Tabriz
was so serious that Khomeini condemned the attack on Shariatmadari's
house, invited the people to calm down and sent a high-powered
committee composed of Ahmad Khomeini, Bazargan, Hashemi-Rafsanjani,
Yadollah Sahabi and the powerful Mahdavi-Kani to meet and consult
with Shariatmadari. The clerical leadership who had not expected such
a violent reaction, set out to appease Shariatmadari and to buy time, in
order to prepare for a major and final assault against him and the IRPMPI.

Two days after the occupation of Tabriz's radio and television stations,
the IRG dispatched to Tabriz along with a group of Khoemini's supporters and took back the buildings. On the same day, the clerical leadership
found an efficient solution to the Shariatmadari problem. It attacked the
IRPMPI as a party which had been penetrated by 'anti-Islamic foreign
agents' and avoided direct confrontation with Shariatmadari. The face-
saving door of disassociation from the IRPMPI was left open to Shariatmadari. A letter was written to Shariatmadari by 15 clerical figures, only
two of whom were of any stature. It requested him to order the dissolution
of the 'anti-Islamic' IRPMPI.[109] Following this letter, a flood of requests
from all over Iran poured in demanding the dissolution of the 'pro-Zionist
and pro-imperialist party'. Resisting the pressure, Shariatmadari retorted
that:

> the IRPMPI is an independent party whose founding members are
> good Moslems whom I support. The dissolution or continuation of the
> party depends on the party and its members who are said to be between
> 2 to 3 million. I hope this country does not have that many Zionists and
> imperialists.[110]

The IRPMPI responded to the increasing pressure against it by organizing rallies in Tabriz, which reportedly attracted up to a million Shariatmadari supporters, reportedly asking the Ayatollah to give them the order
of *jihad* (holy war).
To break the stalemate, Khomeini intervened directly and said:

> Today we are faced with the hypocrites. It is far more difficult to deal
> with these people than it was with the Shah or Hoveida, since these
> people claim to be Moslems but are in reality against Islam. . . . They
> are holy people who claim to be serving the interests of Islam. . . . Yet

they are supporters of the West.[111]

Shariatmadari was left with the choice of either calling on his followers to fight, or to concede. Adverse to blood-letting, Shariatmadari chose the easy way out. On 15 December 1979, the IRPMPI announced the temporary closure of all its offices and the suspension of all its activities.

Exactly one month after the attack on Shariatmadari's house in Qum, forty bus loads of IRPMPI supporters went on the rampage in the city of Qum, attacking pro-Khomeini supporters, tearing up Khomeini posters, pinning up Shariatmadari posters and, finally, making their way towards Khomeini's house. The assailants chanted: 'Our leader is Shariatmadari and long live Shariatmadari'.[112] The crowd left Qum after it was driven away from Khomeini's house. Shariatmadari, who had already decided not to put up a fight, declared that: 'If, contrary to the past decision of the party to close its offices, the party resumes its activities it would no longer have my support'.[113] The day after Shariatmadari's declaration of disassociation, a 400-strong group called 'The Dedicated Moslem Youth' occupied the offices of the IRPMPI in Teheran. Bloody conflict and street fighting continued in Tabriz which left at least 15 dead and 100 injured, according to the government.[114] Shariatmadari had abandoned the struggle, but the momentum of the IRPMPI was considerable enough to keep the anti-Khomeini movement alive and dynamic. The Tabriz uprising was finally put down by the IRG, dispatched from Teheran and other cities. The revolutionary court started rounding up IRPMPI members and, according to official figures, 15 were executed, 4 of whom were officers in the army.

It was not until April 1982 that Shariatmadari's name reappeared. He was implicated in a plot against the Islamic Republic, masterminded by one of Khomeini's closest collaborators and the republic's former minister of foreign affairs, Sadeq Qotbzadeh. After confessing on television that Qotbzadeh's organization had contacted him and that he had conceded to give his blessing to the new government, if the coup succeeded, Shariatmadari asked Khomeini for forgiveness. It was commonly believed that he had asked for forgiveness to save his son-in-law who had been arrested and was in danger of being executed. Qotbzadeh, however, refused to repent and was executed on 15 September 1982. Shariatmadari died under house arrest on 3 March 1986 in Qum.

The consolidation of power

After the defeat of Shariatmadari and the IRPMPI, the clerical leadership felt strong enough to further restrict the range of permissible political organizations. The National Front of Iran (NFI) which, due to its historical prestige, could have become a contending force in the division of power after the victory of the revolution, accepted Khomeini's leadership. This followed Dr Karim Sanjabi, the NFI leader, taking a trip to Paris. In the provisional government of Bazargan, Sanjabi became minister of foreign affairs and Daryoush Forouhar became minister of labour. Relations between the NFI and the clerical leadership deteriorated as it became clear to the NFI that its national figures, such as Sanjabi and Forouhar, were being used to give respectability to the clerical leadership. Initially, the active political participation of the NFI with its social-democratic political tendency assured the middle and upper-middle classes that the revolution was being managed by people amenable to their interests. Gradually, the NFI realized that in the clerical leadership's long-term plans, no genuinely independent position was envisaged for secular political organizations such as theirs. As the clerical leadership used the Hezbollah to strike blows against independent political organizations and even independent clerical figures such as Taleqani, the NFI chose to join the opposition. Sanjabi resigned from the government in protest against the illegal abduction of Taleqani's sons and the inability of the government to do anything about it. In an interview, Sanjabi criticized the anarchy that reigned after the revolution and held the armed committees of the Islamic revolution and their activities responsible for the prevailing conditions.[115]

The NFI's cautious opposition to the clerical leadership's attempt at imposing its preconceived model of Islam led to a rupture between Forouhar and the NFI. Forouhar remained as minister of labour, criticized the NFI's unco-operative posture towards the Islamic Republic and announced his resignation from the NFI. The NFI tried hard not to antagonize the clerical leadership; nevertheless, Sanjabi's emphasis on respect for democratic freedoms and democratic procedures, on the one hand, and his attacks against dictatorial, fascistic and one-party rule, on the other, placed the NFI among the opposition political parties. The clerical leadership used all means possible to efface the achievements and contributions of the Mossadeq-led nationalist movement. Mossadeq's role was belittled, while the whole oil nationalization issue was made out to be the result of Kashani's activities. Even the politically prudent NFI could not countenance a large-scale defamation campaign aimed at its historical *raison d'être*. Sanjabi noted that:

We believe that a monopolising and reactionary force is taking shape in this country. This force cannot ignore and deny Iran's past history. It cannot negate Mossadeq or the significance of the oil nationalisation movement. It cannot ignore the importance of pluralism and the freedom of the press. Accusations and intimidations are the manifestations of this fascist and reactionary tendency. The National Front of Iran has the responsibility of resisting reaction and dictatorship.[116]

The NFI's position became more radical when it openly declared that: 'the country is being directed towards a form of fascism'.[117]

On the night of 18 July 1980, the offices of the NFI and its newspaper were attacked and sacked. The assailants left the premises the next day, accompanied by armed members of the committees of the Islamic revolution.[118] The following day, the Hezbollah attacked and occupied the NFI's buildings. Despite protests and legal measures taken by the NFI, the Islamic judicial system neither provided an explanation, nor acted to evict the illegal occupants. One day after the expropriation of the NFI's buildings, Haadi Ghaffari, who was renowned for his leadership and mobilization of the Hezbollah and who later became an influential member of parliament, made an important speech at the NFI's occupied club:

> We have not yet acted as Fascists, but from now on we will. As I said earlier, the people have decided not to be intimidated and embarrassed by being labelled as despots. We have decided to close down the offices of all those organisations who do not follow the Imam's line of thought [*Khate Imam*] within a month. The members and supporters of the National Front of Iran should know that after 2,500 years we intend to rule this country and we will not give up the opportunity.[119]

Not only did the outspoken Ghaffari publicly announce the IRP's political plans, he openly defended the activities of the Hezbollah, since its objective was said to be the enforcement of Khomeini's line of political thought.

The IRP, which, except in Kurdistan, had successfully crushed all opposing political organizations within two years of the victory of the revolution, now had to contend with its only major defeat, the presidential election. Bani-Sadr remained an obstacle who could not be removed by sending in the Hezbollah to occupy his buildings. The presidential palace housed the highest official in the country after Khomeini. The clerical leadership committed the mistake of repeatedly using a method which had proven successful in the past; Hezbollah attacks against the gatherings of this popular president, who was gradually becoming the most vocal opponent of the IRP and its leaders and was supported by the well-disciplined, dedicated and numerous sympathizers of the People's Mojahedeen, were a monumental blunder.

The elimination of the People's Mojahedeen and the Left

Pressure against the People's Mojahedeen was applied from the victory of the revolution. During the first anti-Mojahedeen phase, the clerical leadership tried to provoke the Mojahedeen into open conflict by abducting Taleqani's sons and arranging attacks on its headquarters by the Hezbollah. On 22 August 1979, the second phase of the IRP-orchestrated anti-Mojahedeen campaign culminated in the closure of its headquarters in Teheran. The Mojahedeen's versatility allowed it to renew its public activities through offices known as 'relief centres' established in all major Iranian cities. Its decision not to vote in favour of the Constitution provided the grounds for the third phase of the attack against it. The Mojahedeen, along with all parties and organizations of the left save the Maoist *Ranjbaran* Party, opposed the new Constitution drafted by the clerically dominated Assembly of Experts. In a telegram to the Assembly of Experts, the People's Mojahedeen demanded the inclusion of a clause that would respect the people's sovereignty in the Constitution.[120]

After Khomeini disqualified Masoud Rajavi, the People's Mojahedeen's presidential candidate, the political conduct and position of the organization gained a wide range of support, not only among the youth, but among the professionals, civil servants and intellectuals who viewed it as a viable democratic alternative to the clerical leadership. The Mojahedeen's emphasis on the defence of democratic rights and their daily confrontations with the IRP, the OMIR and the Hezbollah, increased its popularity. By portraying itself as an innocent victim of an IRP-orchestrated vilification and extermination campaign, the Mojahedeen stirred up widespread sympathy for itself. The clerical leadership correctly viewed the organization as the only real threat to its power and, therefore, sought to deny it access to power through legal channels.

During its campaign for parliamentary elections, the People's Mojahedeen used its usual tactic of requesting democratic fair play, while threatening those who denied it its democratic rights. In an election meeting of the People's Mojahedeen, held at the Teheran University and attended by tens of thousands of people, Mehdi Abrishamchi of the central committee said:

> At this stage, we are experiencing democracy along with and side by side with the people. We try to obtain seats in the parliament through legal and democratic means and we hope to use our presence in parliament to combat reaction and imperialism. But it will be up to the ruling political forces to create a conducive atmosphere for the participation of revolutionary forces.[121]

In a well-planned campaign, the IRP's newspaper *Jomhouri-e Islami*, published an article against Masoud Rajavi and the People's Mojahedeen. The IRP argued that since the People's Mojahedeen had not participated in the referendum on the new Constitution, it had rejected it and, therefore, could not legally run for the parliament stipulated by that same Constitution. Following the article in the IRP's newspaper, demonstrations and electoral meetings of the People's Mojahedeen and its relief centres were again disrupted and attacked by the Hezbollah. Consequently, on 21 and 22 February 1980, approximately a year after the clerical leadership's first wave of attacks against the People's Mojahedeen, its supporters and opponents clashed in Teheran and at least ten other major cities, including Shiraz, Tabriz, Sari, Ghaem-Shahr, Gorgan and Hamedan. According to official reports, during the two days of street fighting, more than 2,000, the great majority of whom were Mojahedeen sympathizers, were injured and at least 1 person was killed.[122] In Gorgan, the army had to intervene to restore order and in Ghaem-Shahr, the Hezbollah was openly aided by the IRG in the evacuation of the People's Mojahedeen's relief centres. After the physical harassment and systematic repression, Mousa Khiabani, the People's Mojahedeen's second in command, warned that:

> Our supporters have not yet reacted or resorted to violence in face of regular attacks against us, but we cannot continue to control our supporters who are systematically assaulted; even our patience has limits. . . . By condemning such acts of Fascism, the Imam can easily put an end to these attacks.[12]

Khomeini, however, never condemned such acts.

The widespread attacks against the People's Mojahedeen during the first parliamentary elections were not only aimed at discrediting and excluding their candidates. They were also intended to suppress the call for a single-ballot majority system, as demanded by the People's Mojahedeen along with all political parties and organizations which were not associated with the IRP. The Revolutionary Council had adopted a double-ballot majority system, in which members of the National Consultative Assembly – Majlis – were to be elected on the basis of obtaining an absolute majority of over 50 per cent of the votes. From among those candidates who did not receive an absolute majority, twice as many as the number of required representatives in each district would participate in a second round, during which only a relative majority sufficed. The double-ballot system was a further guarantee that non-IRP-supported candidates, who might have succeeded in a single-ballot system based on a relative majority, would be permanently excluded. Once the IRP got its own candidates elected during the first round, it could engage in electoral coalitions with smaller parties to get an IRP-supported candidate elected to the assembly. Despite widespread opposition to the double-ballot system, the IRP-dominated Revolutionary Council finally re-endorsed it on 28 February 1980.[124]

The first parliamentary election of the Islamic Republic was marked by unprecedented IRP pressure to ensure the election of its candidates to the Majlis. The extent of wrongdoing was so widespread that even Khomeini's elder brother, Ayatollah Passandeadeh, protested about the elections in Khomein and wrote:

> Threats, intimidation and harassment were used by Revolutionary judges and prosecutors to ensure the election of IRP-endorsed candidates . . . I am sorry to say that never before has anything similar occurred. People did not expect such outrageous injustice from the Islamic government.[125]

Even under such conditions, Masoud Rajavi, the People's Mojahedeen's candidate from Teheran, qualified for the second round, though he lost in the elections.

All legal channels of participation in the country's process of effective decision making were illegally closed to the People's Mojahedeen. At this stage of Iran's political development, it had come to command a great deal of respect. The Mojahedeen continued to avoid direct confrontation with the clerical leadership and concentrated on conducting a verbal and theoretical campaign against the anti-democratic nature of the IRP in the open, while it gradually moved underground. The Mojahedeen's anti-IRP campaign made this organization ever more attractive, as the IRP's intervention and control in every aspect of social, political and economic life became increasingly pronounced.

The anti-Mojahedeen campaign carried out by the Hezbollah, for whom no member of the clerical leadership took responsibility, entered a new phase once Khomeini started to condemn the Mojahedeen directly. Aware of its growing popularity on 26 July 1980, Khomeini lashed out against it and said:

> I might keep on repeating the name of Islam, I might keep saying I am a Devotee of Islam [*Fadaee Islam*] or a devotee of the people [People's Fadaee] or that I am a People's *Mojahed* [a warrior of the people's cause]. Even though I utter such words, if you look closely at my deeds you will discover that I have done the opposite right from the start. . . . These people [the People's Mojahedeen] want to destroy us with the Qur'an and the *Nahjul balagha* and then destroy the Qur'an and the *Nahjul balagha*.[126]

The IRP, which had come to view Bani-Sadr and the Mojahedeen as its two main enemies, sought to incite anti-Mojahedeen hysteria by accusing it of communism, corruption and subversive activities in Kurdistan. In Qum, Hojatolislam Bahonar, an IRP strongman who later became prime minister for a short time before he died in a bomb explosion, roused the people to participate in an anti-Mojahedeen march. In Behshahr, Fakhreddin Hejazi, an old member of Navab-Safavi's *Fadaian Islam* who later became a member of parliament, moved the public by his anti-Mojahedeen oratory to attack the Mojahadeen and their offices. Hojatolislam Khazali became the roving anti-Mojahedeen cleric. Charging it with Marxism, promiscuity, murder of revolutionary guards and armed struggle in Kurdistan, Khazali told his audience in Mashhad that: 'even if the Mojahedeen hide in a mousehole we will drag them out and kill them. . . . We are thirsty for their blood'.[12]

The clash between the Hezbollah and the supporters of Bani-Sadr and the Mojahedeen on 6 March 1981, in Teheran University, proved to be the IRP's second-most serious defeat after Bani-Sadr's election to the presidency. The huge meeting which he called to commemorate Mossadeq's death was attacked by several groups of the Hezbollah. Clearly, the IRP wished to intimidate Bani-Sadr whose supporters were not believed to be combative enough to respond to the provocations of around three hundred and fifty members of Hezbollah. The meeting, however, was also attended by a large number of the Mojahedeen's well-disciplined and hardened militia. On Bani-Sadr's request from the people to evict the Hezbollah from the meeting, fighting broke out and more than seventy members of the Hezbollah were arrested.[128] For the first time since the revolution, the identification cards carried by the Hezbollah members proved they belonged to the IRG, committees of the Islamic revolution, IRP and various ministries and organizations related to the IRP.[129] Bani-Sadr's newspaper, *Enqelab Islami*, published the identification cards of the arrested members which, to the embarrassment of the government, revealed the close ties which existed between the club-wielding Islamic shock troops and the Islamic organs of the state. The IRP was even more concerned with the political and organizational proximity of Bani-Sadr with the Mojahedeen, a combination which posed a very real threat to its future.

The IRP used the tacit alliance between Bani-Sadr and the Mojahedeen to discredit him in the eyes of Khomeini who always disliked the Mojahedeen. It accused the Mojahedeen of plotting against the Islamic Republic and thus prepared public opinion for a final wave of repression against it. The clerical leadership's attitude towards the Mojahedeen and other political opponents was well reflected in a classification of political parties by the Rajaee government's spokesman, Behzad Nabavi. Nabavi divided political parties into four types. The first two categories were those which supported the Islamic Republic: the first group was composed of those organizations which were ready to sacrifice the lives of their members for the Islamic government, while the second group were not. The third group was made up of parties which opposed the government, but did not 'cause the government any damage'. Nabavi believed that these groups pretended to defend the interests of the masses; however, as long as they did not resort to armed struggle they were allowed to have offices and newspapers. The fourth group were those which were 'directly at war with the Islamic government, these included *Komeleh* [Revolutionary Organization of the Kurdish Toilers of Iran], the Kurdish Democratic Party of Iran (KDPI), the People's Fadaian [minority group] and the People's Mojahedeen. Nabavi only elaborated on the People's Mojahedeen organization and accused it of being 100 per cent hypocritical because it was: 'on the one hand allied to Qassemlou [leader of the KDPI] and wished to propagate its destructive Marxist ideology and on the other hand allied to American groups'.[130] Nabavi concluded that: 'We have to prepare for a final confrontation and disarm the Mojahedeen as soon as possible'.[131] His first category referred to the IRP and its allies, the second category probably referred to a prominent and powerful clerical group called the *Hojatiyeh* Society which had philosophical differences with Khomeini's religious interpretations. The third category referred to the Tudeh Party and the People's Fadaian (majority group) which supported the clerical leadership's political line.

It was rapidly becoming clear that either the Mojahedeen had to join the organizations in Nabavi's third category and accept the clerical leadership while it awaited the clergy's final assault, or it had to declare outright war against the Islamic Republic. The tactical alliance between Bani-Sadr and the Mojahedeen meant a common fate for both. In a last attempt at reconciliation with Khomeini on 2 May 1981, the Mojahedeen asked to visit him in private. It was ten days later that Khomeini responded:

> You have threatened us with armed struggle, how can we reach an agreement with you? If you return your arms which you hold illegally and voluntarily disarm yourselves, then we will treat you even better than you wish. . . . We wish to see all those who have been misled return to the Islamic flock. . . . However, if I thought there was a one-in-a-thousand chance that you would repent I would have accepted a visit with you, I would have even come to visit you myself. . . . In the end I advise you to return the arms that you have stolen from the people. But if you revolt against the Islamic government, you will be swept aside by an immense popular wave.[132]

Faced with a choice of disarming and surrendering to the clerical leadership, or armed resistance, the Mojahedeen chose the latter and hoped to overthrow the régime with the aid of Bani-Sadr's political popularity. On 18 June 1981, the People's Mojahedeen effectively announced their decision to use armed resistance in the face of increased violent attacks against them. Following Bani-Sadr's dismissal from the presidency and the hardening of the clerical leadership's position, on 20 June 1981, the Mojahedeen organized demonstrations in Teheran and other major cities. This resulted in a number of deaths and more than one hundred wounded in Teheran. Following this clash, left organizations such as the *Peykar* and the People's Fadaian (minority group), the Communist Union and the *Ranjbaran*, which had always supported the government, embarked upon an armed offensive against the clerical leadership. Iran was in the throes of a civil war in which the majority of the people chose to remain as concerned bystanders. After the signing of a covenant between Bani-Sadr and Rajavi, the two men fled to Paris where they announced the formation of the National Council of Resistance (NCR).

In Iran, the Mojahedeen implemented its three-phase insurrectionary strategy for the overthrow of the régime. First, it sought to exterminate the apex of the pyramid of political power, the decision-making core of the clerical leadership, by assassinating prominent individuals. It was hoped that once the nervous system of the régime was disrupted and destabilized, the Mojahedeen would be able to organize armed street demonstrations, in which it would confront and defeat the IRG, creating conditions in which the people would shed their fear and join in with the demonstrations. Finally, the Mojahedeen assumed that this second phase would lead to a mass uprising, similar to the one which brought down the Shah.

Its first phase started with a continuous string of predominantly successful assassinations. On 28 June 1981, two powerful bombs transformed the headquarters of the IRP into rubble, killing at least seventy-two members attending a party meeting. Mohammed Beheshti, the founder of the IRP and Iran's second-most powerful person after Khomeini, was among the dead. The toll included four cabinet ministers, six deputy ministers, twenty-seven Majlis deputies and scores of other officials. According to the intelligence unit of the IRG, the bombs were meticulously placed by a 22-year-old member of the Mojahedeen, Reza Kollahi.[133] On 5 August 1981, Dr Hassan Ayat, the ideologue of the IRP and the man who, according to Hashemi-Rafsanjani should be credited for the inclusion of the concept of the governance of the jurisconsult in the Constitution, was shot in front of his house.[134] The string of assassinations continued with the deaths of President Rajaee; the prime minister and new IRP chairman, Bahonar; the chief of the national police, Dastjerdi and the powerful public prosecutor general of the revolutionary courts, Qoddoussi. In the provinces, key clerical figures who conducted the Friday congregational prayers became targets. In Tabriz, Yazd and Kermanshah, devoted disciples and confidants of Khomeini were assassinated. The speed, accuracy and boldness of the Mojahedeen's attacks surprised the leadership. The vacuum created by the death of Beheshti and men close to him led to the abandonment of all policies, save the ruthless application of state terror in order to eradicate the Mojahedeen. In spite of the insecurity and vulnerability of the ruling circles, the clerical leadership withstood the shock and the decimation of its ranks. On 11 August 1981, Khomeini issued a religious edict and asked the people to spy and inform on the clandestine activities of the Mojahedeen. He said:

> If someone plans to kill a Moslem, you should report that person to the authorities, otherwise you are a party to the crime. The people all over the country should be careful. They should observe what is going on in their neighbourhood and they should watch and see who frequents their neighbour's house; if they are suspicious characters, the people should immediately inform the Revolutionary Guards, the members of the Committees or the police stations.[135]

The Mojahedeen's second phase was launched in September. Members organized into groups of 100 to 200, well guarded by armed militia, took to the streets chanting 'death to Khomeini' and invited the people to join them. On a few occasions, the people participated, but the second phase proved generally unsuccessful and the armed members of the Mojahedeen ended up engaging the IRG in lengthy street battles. The Mojahedeen abandoned all hope for a mass uprising and modified its strategy by returning to the assassination of what it called the 'body and base' of the pyramid of political power. In this third phase, which continued well into 1982, it carried out assassinations of low-ranking members of the IRP, the revolutionary institutions, various information gathering and repressive organs of the régime and ordinary activists of the Hezbollah. While the activities of the first and second phase of their insurrectionary strategy met with the inactive support of a large number of Iran's urban dwellers, the assassination of rank and file supporters of the Islamic government was met by the people's apathy, if not antipathy.

The clerical leadership used the IRG members of the committees of the Islamic revolution and the revolutionary courts to counter and ruthlessly suppress the Mojahedeen's uprising. Based on what was popularly known as the '36 million-strong Intelligence Agency' (the information provided by devoted Moslems) as well as on confessions extracted from tortured prisoners, the 'safe houses' of the Mojahedeen were identified, and attacked with whatever fire power was necessary to overcome their resistance. Conducting an armed urban uprising forced the guerilla organizations to depend heavily on hideouts and bases in the middle of the cities. The concentration of manpower in these safe houses, organized on the lines of military barracks, made them vulnerable. From June 1981, the fall of each safe house constituted a serious blow to the armed opposition. From February to April 1982, the security organizations of the Islamic Republic launched a common operation called *Daheye Fajr* (The 10 days of dawn) during which numerous safe houses were identified and destroyed. The IRG inflicted important losses. Mousa Khiabani, the Mojahedeen's commander in chief in Iran and Rajavi's first wife, Ashraf Rabiee, were killed, along with a number of other high-ranking members.[136] The pattern of discovering safe houses and killing or arresting their members repeated itself in all major cities. During April, at least 10 safe houses and bases were identified and destroyed, while 5 members of the central committee and 61 high-ranking members were arrested and killed.[137]

By 1982, it had become clear that the Mojahedeen's strategy for overthrowing the clerical leadership was ineffective. Contrary to Rajavi's prediction that: 'with the death of 60 per cent of the IRP leaders, a Medieval régime cannot survive', the Islamic régime neutralized the immediate threat of the Mojahedeen to its power.[138] The Mojahedeen suffered enormous losses and its urban guerilla activities waned considerably in 1983. Gradually, it was forced to move its theatre of operations to Kurdistan. In October 1987, the Mojahedeen published a detailed list of 14,028 political executions that the government was said to have had carried out since June 1981. It reported 140,000 political detainees who were said to have been regularly tortured.[139]

The political organizations which had participated in the revolt against the Islamic government were also attacked. The Marxist-Leninist organization of *Peykar Dar Rahe Azadi Tabaqee Karegar* (Struggle for the Liberation of the Working Class), which opposed the Islamic Republic from its inception and had called for transforming the Iran-Iraq war into a civil war, found its organization completely dismantled after the June uprising. Its entire leadership, along with its high-ranking members, were either arrested or killed in the IRG raids against fifty-three of its bases and hideouts in Teheran and Shiraz.[140]   In these raids, all the internal documents, correspondence, conference documents, along with the underground arsenal and communications and logistics equipment were confiscated. More than 380 members of *Peykar* were arrested, of whom 246 were executed.[141]

The Marxist-Leninist People's Fadaian splintered into a minority and majority faction in April 1980. The majority faction, which later splintered further over the issue of joining forces with the pro-Soviet Tudeh

Party, remained in loyal opposition to the Islamic government until it was suppressed in February 1983. The minority faction took up arms against the government after June 1981. In an extensive operation, called *Mersad*, launched by the IRG, the minority faction came under severe attack. In the first phase of the operation, Siyamak Assadian (who was reported to be a member of the central committee and in charge of the military wing of the organization) along with the leaders of the Teheran and provincial committees of the Fadaian were killed, while one hundred and twenty-five members and cadres were arrested in Khoramabad. In the second phase of operation *Mersad*, safe houses were discovered and attacked and 8 members were killed and 40 were arrested. At the end of this operation, the organization's entire stock of printing equipment was confiscated. Towards the end of April 1982, more than 10 safe houses were discovered and attacked in Sistan and Baluchestan and a number of other cadres were killed or arrested.[142] As a result of these persistent blows, the urban guerilla activities of the People's Fadaian (minority) virtually dried up after 1982 and they, too, concentrated their manpower in Kurdistan.

After the June revolts, beside the IRP and its political allies, only the pro-Soviet Tudeh Party, the Fadaian (majority) and Bazargan's Iran Freedom Movement were tolerated by the government. The Tudeh Party, which formally came into existence in October 1941, was Iran's oldest Marxist-Leninist party. After the revolution, it became a firm supporter of the Islamic government and considered itself a true follower of Khomeini's line. According to its analysis, the progressive anti-imperialist leadership of 'Imam' Khomeini had to be accepted full heartedly. The Tudeh Party thus became a close associate and ally of the clerical leadership, aiding it in its confrontations with Bazargan, the Mojahedeen and the radical Marxist-Leninist groups who viewed the Islamic government as reactionary, petty bourgeois and anti-democratic. The Tudeh Party succeeded in placing its members in relatively important bureaucratic positions and it was even successful in penetrating the revolutionary institutions and the armed forces.

The arrest of Nooreddin Kianoori, the general secretary of the Tudeh party, together with numerous other senior party leaders, on Saturday 5 February 1983, caught the party by surprise. The Islamic Republic accused the Tudeh Party of plotting to overthrow the government and of spying for the Soviet Union. The real reason behind the suppression of the party is reported to be linked with the defection to the United Kingdom of Vladimir Kuzichkin, a soviet diplomat and KGB major stationed in Teheran.[143] The list of several hundred Soviet agents operating in Iran provided by Kuzichkin is reported to have been forwarded to the Iranian authorities by the British. In a widely publicized campaign, the highest ranking members of the Tudeh Party, along with its ideologue, Ehsan Tabari, appeared on television and confessed to crimes committed by the party, since its establishment. The issue of espionage was, however, given more coverage than the party's other offences. Following the dissolution of the party, Mohsen Rezaee, the commander in chief of the IRG corps, reported that more than 1,000 high-ranking members and cadres of the Tudeh Party had been arrested. After the prosecutor general of the revolutionary courts ordered party members to identify themselves and report to the nearest CIRG office, there were waves of Tudeh members turning themselves in. Captain Bahram Afzali, the commander of the Iranian navy, confessed to his membership of the party and was executed for high treason. In August 1984 in Tabriz, Azim Mohaqeq, a party member who had risen in the ranks of the CIRG to the sensitive post of director of intelligence gathering in Azarbayjan, was also executed. The high dignitaries of the party such as Kianoori, Behazin and Tabari were spared.

The connection between the Kuzichkin affair and the clamp-down on the Tudeh Party became even more evident following the Tudeh leaders' confessions and the Iranian ministry of foreign affairs reaction. In a televised confession, Kianoori said: 'We used to send reports on political and military matters to the Soviet Union. . . . This was the greatest offence on our part, an act of treason. This indubitable treason of ours was the mother of all offences'.[144] On 4 May 1983, 4 days after Kianoori's confession, 18 Soviet diplomats were expelled for interfering in the internal affairs of the Islamic Republic. Never in the post-revolutionary history of Iran had such a well-disciplined and informed political organization collapsed like a house of cards. The Tudeh Party of Iran, which was partly dismantled by the CIRG and partly disbanded by its own members, fell without a whimper or a volley.

The purge of Islamic political forces loyal to the 'Imam's line'

By mid-1983, after four years of bloody and incessant struggle, the clerical leadership had effectively freed itself of the existence and intervention of all religious or secular forces which openly opposed, or had the ideological potential to oppose, the absolute rule of the governing jurisconsult. The remaining parties and forces were instrumental in forging the political system which prevailed. However, as the external liberal or Marxist threat to the clerical leadership's vision of Islam subsided, the inner contradictions of the leadership, reflected in competing subsystems, surfaced. Khomeini's solution to the emerging tug of war between political forces loyal to him was either to allow one subsystem to prevail temporarily, at the cost of generating enmity and alienation among his other disciples, or to completely remove the arena of political and theoretical competition, by dissolving the political body or organizations in which factions representing subsystems could compete, for example. In an attempt to restore political stability and a semblance of unity, Khomeini did not solve the problem of competing subsystems, but chose to minimize the eventual struggle by removing the classical political mechanisms for conducting such a struggle. He correctly perceived that even thoroughly Islamic political organizations would, by their nature, breed discussion and debate among members of different socio-economic classes. Such debates would lead to factions and, as the members became hardened in their convictions, their differences would emerge in public and eventually destabilize the régime. Khomeini seems to have concluded that the long-run survival of the Islamic government, as it existed, was guaranteed best by a political climate free of political parties or organizations. The fate of Khomeini-approved political organizations and parties between 1983 and 1987 bears witness to this contention.

The Anti-Bahai Society or the *Hojatiyeh Mahdaviyeh* Society

The *Hojatiyeh Mahdaviyeh* Society (Anti-Bahai Society) was established in 1953 by Ayatollah Mahmood Zakerzadeh Tavallaie, better known as Halabi. The society focused on combating the growing influence of the Bahai faith in Iran. The Bahais believed that Mirza Hossein Ali (*Baha Ullah*) who proclaimed himself the Messiah in 1863 was the twelfth or hidden imam of the *Shi'i* faith. In Iran, Bahais were viewed by the *Shi'i* majority as heretics whose leader *Baha Ullah* (Glory of God) was a fraudulent imposter and whose religion was no more than the fabrication of a worldy being. During the Shah's régime, the Anti-Bahai Society was given free rein, since it provided a safe outlet for religious activities that could have otherwise become subversive. The Anti-Bahai Society renounced participation in political affairs and concentrated on infiltrating Bahai organizations, winning back the Bahais to *Shi'i* Islam, conducting a propaganda campaign against the Bahais and, finally, confronting them in all the non-violent ways possible. One of the most well-known campaigns reportedly linked with this society was that of boycotting Pepsi-Cola which was owned by Sabet-Pasal, a Bahai. The *fatva*, or religious opinion, against the consumption of Pepsi-Cola, however, was said to have come directly from the highest *Shi'i marja-e taqlid*, Ayatollah Borujerdi.

The *Hojatiyeh* Society, attracted a very large number of adherents, though the exact number is difficult to determine, since its activities were shrouded in secrecy. It maintained close relations with the merchants and shopkeepers of the bazaar who paid a considerable part of their religious dues to its spiritual leaders.[145] There were also many followers in the armed forces. The outbreak of the revolution placed the organization in an awkward position. As a non-violent and non-political society, it feared that Khomeini would mix religion with politics, the end result of which it expected to be the failure of the Islamic movement and the ultimate establishment of a communist system. For the *Hojatiyeh*, a *Shi'i* monarchy was far preferable to an atheist communist system. Theoretically, too, the *Hojatiyeh* believed that only after the reappearance of the 12th imam from his occultation could a just Islamic government be established. They argued that the 12th Imam would resurge only once sin and evil had completely prevailed in the world, and before that time, whoever pretended to establish a just Islamic state was a liar and an imposter. Therefore, the *Hojatiyeh* did not look upon the Islamic movement very favourably and it is reported that even during the revolution the members of *Hojatiyeh* opposed Khomeini and even insulted him.[146]

After the revolution, the society continued and its large number of professional and educated cadres gained access to sensitive positions, due to their religious records. At this time, the *Hojatiyeh*, fearing the growing influence of the left, embarked on a virulent anti-communist campaign. Based on their close ties with the bazaar, the *Hojatiyeh* were in favour of a totally private economy and opposed any tampering with the free play of the market system. Consequently, they opposed the left and the radical Islamic organizations, such as the People's Mojahedeen, on both political and economic grounds.

During the debates over the Constitution and the religious validity of the concept of the governance of the jurisconsult, the society, once again, found itself in a delicate position. The *Hojatiyeh* could not, theoretically, accept the governing of the jurisconsult, since they believed that the responsibilities of the jurisconsult as stipulated in the Constitution could only be expected of a *maasum* (one who is infallible and who has never sinned).[147] The *Shi'i* believe that there are only fourteen *maasums*, the Prophet, twelve imams and Fatima; the only one to come is the twelfth imam. Probably exercising *Taqiyeh* (dissimulating one's true beliefs when in danger), which is encouraged in *Shi'i* Islam, Halabi issued a directive to all members of the *Hojatiyeh* Society to participate in the referendum on the Constitution and vote in favour of it.[148] The *Hojatiyeh* Society publicly supported the governance of the jurisconsult.

On the sensitive issue of the Iran-Iraq war, the *Hojatiyeh* adopted a position contrary to that of Khomeini and the government. Halabi argued that only a *maasum* imam had the credentials to proclaim war against another Islamic nation.[149] The prerequisite of being a *maasum* immediately disqualified Khomeini from making such decisions and led to the *Hojatiyeh*'s old argument that only the twelfth imam who was a *maasum* could make such decisions. The increasing involvement of the state in economic activities, the rumours of the Tudeh Party's growing influence in the state apparatus and the general administration of the Islamic state led to increased criticism by *Hojatiyeh* members who had come to occupy important positions in the bureaucracy and even in the cabinet.

Aware of the disputes within the clerical ranks and convinced that the reflection of such differences in the cabinet would weaken the Islamic government, Khomeini made an indirect attack against the *Hojatiyeh* Society. On 13 July 1983, Khomeini said:

if our grumblings become complaints and complaints become opposition, we will face a catastrophe. If you oppose the people your hands and legs will be broken. . . . Those who believe that we should allow sins to increase until the twelfth imam reappears should modify and reconsider their position. . . . Those who grumble about the predicament of the faith under the Islamic Republic and say that this Islam is useless are saying that the Shah's Islam was correct. That Islam was correct in which all the streets were full of prostitution . . . alcoholic beverages were consumed and Islamic retributions were absent. Those who criticise us today never criticised the Shahanshahi Islam.[150]

Khomeini's attack led to the publication of a circular by the *Hojatiyeh* Society. Dated 23 July, it criticized the government and pointed out that since the society was informed that Khomeini's statement of 13 July referred to them, they preferred to discontinue their activities. They purposefully included a statement expressing the hope that their thirty years of service had been to the satisfaction of God and the Twelfth Imam. As many of their critics emphasized later, the *Hojatiyeh* intended to stress that activities unsatisfactory to Khomeini could well be satisfactory to God and the Twelfth Imam, thus pushing a wedge between Khomeini's Islam and that of the Twelfth Imam.

In a passionate speech in the Islamic parliament, Khalkhali demanded the official dissolution of the society, rather than the cessation of its activities.[151] Ayatollah Taheri of Isfahan accused them of neither believing in the Islamic revolution nor in the governance of the jurisconsult.[152] In a most vehement attack, Hojatolislam Hamidzadeh, a member of parliament, demanded the trial of the chief members of the society.[153] After two weeks, the anti-*Hojatiyeh* campaign, which was originally launched by the Tudeh Party, subsided and the society continued its existence and its internal activities. The *Hojatiyeh*'s brand of *Shi'i* Islam was too well rooted among segments of the bazaar, the clergy and the army to be eradicated. Among those said to have had close relations with the *Hojatiyeh*, if they were not members of it, were: Ayatollah Khazali, Shaykh Mohammed-Taqi Falsafi; Ali-Akbar Parvaresh, the former minister of education; Hojatolislam Nateq-Noori, the former minister of interior; and Colonel Salimi, the former minister of defence. Khomeini only wished to bully the *Hojatiyeh* into silence. He did not wish to open a can of worms over the correctness of his or the *Hojatiyeh*'s interpretation of Islam. As far as Khomeini was concerned, their *Taqiyeh* was enough to keep the country out of Islamic confrontation.

The dissolution of the Organization of the Mojahedeen of the Islamic Republic (OMIR)

The Organization of the Mojahedeen of the Islamic Republic which, as we showed, emerged as an efficient sword in the hands of the IRP to silence and suppress all opposition forces, faced internal conflicts as soon as all external threats were removed. The OMIR could not remain immune to the epidemic factionalism that infected the remaining Islamic organizations and parties which considered themselves as devoted followers of Khomeini. The self-righteous claim of each faction to constitute the true disciples of Khomeini aggravated their conflicts and differences. The development of these factions, more or less representing different subsystems, gradually surfaced, breaking the initial unity which characterized all Khomeini-approved political organizations.

Three factions developed inside the OMIR.[154] The first faction was led by Rajaee, Nabavi and Salamati. This group represented a variant of Shariati's subsystem, believing in a dynamic Islam which ranked social justice high on its list of priorities. Consequently, the Rajaee-Nabavi faction suppported the imposition of limitations upon property and a greater degree of government intervention in the economic sphere. The second faction, led by Jalal-e-deen Farsi, believed in an unfettered market system and based its economic outlook on the Qum seminary school's traditional view of Islam (*Fihe Sonati*). This second faction was a variant of the Motahhari subsystem. The third faction tried to steer clear of the infighting between the first two groups and by claiming itself to be under the absolute command of the 'imam' remained friendly with both groups. Their leader was Mohsen Rezaee, the commander in chief of the CIRG.

The internal disputes of the OMIR forced Khomeini to appoint a representative as the organization's spiritual leader. Ayatollah Raasti-Kashani, who was a firm believer in an unregulated market system and was reported to have had close ties with the *Hojatiyeh* Society, purged the OMIR of the members of the interventionist faction. Nabavi and his colleagues resigned and confined themselves to their activities in the government. The pro-bazaar faction, which had prevailed under the auspices of Raasti Kashani, published a pamphlet on developments in the OMIR and advised all parties concerned to seek advice from the clerics of the Qum seminary school for the formulation of their ideology. Clearly, the reference was an attack on the interventionist faction which had attempted to develop a theory of egalitarian social justice.

In 1985, the free-market-oriented *Resalat* Foundation was founded by four prominent conservative clerics, Ayatollah Azari-Qumi, Khazali, Raasti-Kashani and Hojatolislam Share'i. The group published a pro-bazaar and anti-interventionist daily newspaper, *Resalat*, from 9 January 1986. Raasti-Kashani's links with both the *Resalat* group and the OMIR meant that the two organizations became very close.

The OMIR found an outlet for its positions in the *Resalat* newspaper, in which Jalal-e-deen Farsi wrote frequently, and the *Resalat* group benefited from the support of a well-organized body, such as the OMIR. The OMIR, however, had served its purpose of suppressing the opposition. After the expulsion of the interventionist faction and its quasi-merger with *Resalat*, there was no need for a separate organization, since most of the OMIR's members were well integrated in the revolutionary institutions and the government bureaucracy. Furthermore, OMIR's links with the CIRG provided the *Resalat* group with possible paramilitary support which was frowned upon by Khomeini. The strengthened anti-interventionist forces disturbed the balance of power to the detriment of the interventionists centred around Prime Minister Mir-Hossein Moussavi. Khomeini, who viewed the weakening of the government as a threat to the whole Islamic system, sought to destroy the concentrated force of the market-oriented Islamic tendency which agitated against the government. Furthermore, he was intent on an apolitical CIRG, one which would remain unattached to the competing subsystems and obedient only to himself.

On 29 August 1986, Raasti-Kashani requested Khomeini to accept his resignation from the OMIR and suggested that, since a large number of the OMIR's members had gone to the war front on Khomeini's orders and others were on their way, the organization be dissolved.[155] Five days later, Khomeini commended Raasti-Kashani for his services and accepted his request to dissolve the OMIR.[156] By de-institutionalizing the disputes, Khomeini felt that they could be more effectively contained. The subtle manner of dissolving the OMIR, over which Khomeini had total control, differed considerably from the manner in which parties opposed to Khomeini were banned and dissolved.

The dissolution of the Islamic Republic Party

Ayatollah Mohammed Beheshti should be given the lion's share of the credit for the IRP's creation and its success in becoming the most powerful political organization in the Islamic Republic. In a revealing interview, Beheshti was asked by *Keyhan*'s correspondent whether he preferred the Islamic Republic Party to the Islamic Republic. He responded: 'the party is important and useful to us so long as it serves the interests of the Islamic Revolution and ensures the survival and blossoming of the Islamic Republic'.[157] Initially, Beheshti intended to create an all-encompassing corporate party which would bring members of all social classes under the giant umbrella of Islam. Bani-Sadr points out that the IRP: 'intended to attract a large social spectrum including intellectuals of the left, conservative clerics, capitalists, workers, peasants, progressives and reactionaries'.[158] Even though the party proved incapable of attracting left and bourgeois democratic elements, it became a true melting pot of various shades of Islamic orientations and factions. The party's programme remained unspecific in all aspects, except in its objective of creating a potent political power which held its allegiance only to the clergy as the sole guiding force in society. The primary task of the party thus became the defeat of all those forces that refused the clergy's leading role and their concept of an ideal society. As long as the party was combating anti-religious, anti-Islamic and anti-clerical forces, the common external enemy forced the diverse social components of the party to overlook their differences. One can speculate that had Beheshti remained alive, the victory of the IRP in purging all opposition forces would have led to an internal purification campaign, resulting in the final hegemony of one faction over others. Beheshti would have probably favoured an Islamic orientation for the party on the lines of Motahhari's subsystem.

The decimation of the party's leadership, during the summer of 1981, had left the IRP, which effectively controlled all levers of power, disoriented. After the bloody repression of 1981, there were no more threatening 'other' political forces to rally and campaign against, there were no more threatening demonstrations or marches to whip up the Hezbollah's rage, but, at the same time, there was no clear vision in the party as to where the country should be directed after the acquisition of total power. The party's lack of a clear programme began to hurt. It seemed as if it had developed into a self-destructive machine. There was nothing more to destroy but the Islamic forces. As Hashemi-Rafsanjani looked back on the party in 1987, he said: 'in the beginning the mission of the party was to combat those who opposed the Islamisation of the country. Gradually as the opposition faded away, so did the mission of the IRP'.[159] As the country operated on an *ad hoc* basis during this period, so did the party. The absolute hegemony of the corporate party carried the seeds of its disintegration, as the class interests of its diverse members began to surface in the absence of a common external foe. So, on 10 May 1983, the party decided to hold its first party congress, four years after its creation, to settle differences between the representatives of the different subsystems. This was the party's first and last congress. It was supposed to: ratify the party statutes; ratify the party principles; draft a two-year party programme; draft the necessary internal regulations; elect members of the central committee and elect members of an arbitration committee.[160]

The party had become more or less polarized into two major factions, one representing Motahhari's free-market, clergy-dominated subsystem and the other representing certain economic aspects of Shariati's social justice and class-oriented Islam. The interventionist or statist versus non-interventionist or *laissez-faire* dichotomy had come to permeate the society at large and the IRP represented the conflict in a microcosm. This clash of interests was presented as a clash between variants of Islam. It was a public acknowledgement of dissent within Islam that was repugnant to Khomeini, yet, ironically, he never forcefully repressed differences of Islamic opinion among his loyal clerical followers.

Incapable of solving any major problems, or even of drafting a preliminary programme, the party ratified a pamphlet entitled 'Our Positions' which was drawn up by Beheshti before his death.[161] The congress elected President Sayyed Ali Khamenei as its general secretary and the composition of the new central commitee reflected a shift in power in favour of the pro-bazaar *laissez-faire* faction. The party congress ended its deliberation in four short days. The attempt by the *laissez-faire* faction to monopolize all levers of power and especially the government, led to a tug of war within the leadership.

On 10 February 1987, in a party meeting of the leaders and cadres of the IRP, President Khamenei who supported the *laissez-faire* faction, lashed out against Prime Minister Moussavi and accused him of being incompetent. Following Khamenei's re-election in 1985, Khamenei did not wish to introduce Moussavi as prime minister, but he was forced to do so, since Khomeini viewed a change in government as a sign of the

Islamic leadership's weakness. The brawl between Khamenei and Moussavi at the IRP meeting was, therefore, not surprising. Khomeini's response to the spreading dispute among the leadership was to threaten both sides with reprisals. Incriminating anonymous letters against President Khamenei and Prime Minister Moussavi's government started circulating inside parliament and were then leaked out to the public. On 14 March 1987, Khomeini said:

> When everyone is out to get us, we sit and fight amongst ourselves. . . . One group should not plan to undermine the Revolutionary Guards, neither should the other group plan to get rid of the government. . . . If I ever see such a thing developing I will stop it with every means possible. Even if I have to sacrifice one or a group of people, I will do so for the people.[162]

Once again, Khomeini threatened but did not purge the members of any one subsystem.

Khomeini's warning was a clear indication of his intention to put an end to the disputes. While the high-ranking members of the party, who were also in the leadership, could have reached a provisional agreement halting all attacks against one another, they were sceptical of the reactions of lower echelon members who attacked their adversaries in order to maintain their petty bureaucratic positions. The fear of an all-out uncontrolled factional war within the Islamic forces, especially the military and paramilitary forces, convinced the leadership to disband the IRP. It is significant that the party whose mission was the destruction of the forces opposed to the Islamization of Iran was itself becoming instrumental in the destabilization of the so-called Islamic monolith.

In a letter to Khomeini, President Khamenei and Majlis speaker Hashemi-Rafsanjani, pointed to the outstanding services of the party to the Islamic Republic and wrote:

> Now that the Republic's institutions are well entrenched and the high level of consciousness and political perception of the people have rendered the revolution unassailable . . . while the plots of domestic counter-revolutionary forces and the designs of world arrogance [imperialism] have been defused, it is felt that the existence of the party does not have the usefulness that it initially possessed and on the contrary now it may have become a focus for controversy and polarisation, posing a threat to unity among the people and wasting the potentially productive energy of the people in confronting and neutralising one another. Therefore as we have repeatedly said in the past, the central committee has unanimously decided to dissolve the IRP and discontinue all its activities.[163]

On 1 June 1987, Khomeini agreed with the dissolution of the party and added that: 'insulting any Moslem, irrespective of his membership of the IRP is contrary to Islam and counts as breeding dissent, which is at this time the greatest of sins'.[164]

Close to six years after purging society of all parties that stood in its way, the IRP bowed out of the Iranian political scene, leaving behind a handful of Islamic political groups essentially representing two major factions. The *laissez-faire* faction combined forces around the *Resalat* group, while the interventionists grouped themselves around the newly created *Ruhaniyoun Mobarez* (Militant Clerics) and accused the former of representing an American brand of Islam or capitalist Islam. Though Khomeini welcomed the dissolution of the IRP, he left the members of the competing *Shi'i* subsystems loyal to his own leadership intact and unmolested.

The fate of individual liberties

The Iranian revolution was so very much concerned with the attainment of political freedoms which it assumed as a natural consequence of the Shah's fall that it completely neglected the maintenance of the basic individual liberties it had come to possess. Individual liberties, such as the freedom to choose one's attire, the freedom to socialize with individuals of the opposite sex, freedom of access to artistic or leisurely entertainment of one's choice, freedom to select the educational institution of one's preference and freedom to engage in the job of one's choice all existed during the Shah's reign. Of course the extent to which individuals benefited from them depended on individual purchasing power. However, prior to the revolution, such individual liberties gradually became the target of attacks by both the Islamic and progressive forces. The traditional Moslem believers viewed these individual liberties as the catalyst which threatened the customary network of family life. Principal targets of criticism were the so-called westernized promiscuous 'painted women'.

Islamic intellectuals, as well as a large number of secular bourgeois intellectuals, engaged in the extremely fashionable and politically non-hazardous exercise of criticizing cultural imperialism and its social manifestations. Lamenting the loss of Iran's authentic Islamic or Iranian identity, they poured virulent abuse on whatever came from the west. For the great majority of secular bourgeois intellectuals, this was a safe way of remaining 'revolutionary'. Islamic intellectuals, such as Shariati, sought to present a political model of what the truly liberated Islamic man or woman should be.

The existence of choice for sons and daughters of traditional Moslem families broke the umbilical cord between the present and the past. Various tyrannical aspects of the traditional family hierarchy were rejected and defied. The gradual erosion of patriarchal power was an unwelcome consequence of the spread of individual liberties which went hand in hand with Iran's capitalist development. The traditional merchant class and the evolving petty bourgeoisie, who were predominantly second- and third-generation rural migrants, perceived such liberties as immoral and corrupt. Khomeini soothed concerned fathers who grieved at the possibilities that westernization provided for their daughters. He lashed out at the corrupting influences of individual rights and said: 'This [the Shah's] government seeks to corrupt our youth, they have propagated all types of corruption to keep our youth out of the universities in order to fill the night clubs and bars'.[165]

The left, which witnessed the proliferation of self-indulgent western cultural norms in Iran's urban societies, also developed a dislike for individual liberties, which were considered as the Shah's means of de-politicizing and pacifying Iranian youth. Influenced by Mao's invitation to simplicity and uniformity in the choice of attire, numerous Maoist groups developed puritanical views of individual liberties, similar to those of the Islamic forces. The Stalin-inspired Iranian left, which viewed the Soviet Union as the model of communism, encouraged a rigid and stoic life-style for its supporters and partisans, based on life in the early 1950s in the mother country. Such organizations shared the Islamic forces' disdain for extroverted, colourful and fun-loving individuals and life-styles, believing that the enjoyment of individual liberties distracted individuals from total commitment to ideological and political work. Mountain climbing, which was one of the few acceptable sports, was endorsed more as a physical fitness programme than a leisurely activity. The left, as defenders of the proletariat, viewed the demand for individual liberties as a concern of the upper and middle classes and, therefore, did not prioritize such 'bourgeois' considerations. Statements such as: 'toiling women do not want unrestrained looseness under the name of liberation, but genuine equality of women and men' simply facilitated the Islamic authorities' attacks on individual liberties.[166]

The Islamic Republic's first impingement upon individual liberties was aimed at women. Less than a month after the victory of the revolution, in words literally identical to Navab-Safavi's, Khomeini addressed the issue of women's attire and said: 'Women should not go naked in Islamic Ministries. Women can work there, but they have to wear the *hejab* [The Islamic Veil]'.[167] Ironically enough, Khomeini's speech was delivered on 7 March, one day before the International Women's Day for which numerous women's organizations had prepared meetings and demonstrations. From 8 to 12 March 1979, Teheran witnessed huge demonstrations, resembling those against the Shah. Under heavy snow, women took to the streets protesting against Khomeini's statement. They stopped work in government offices and ministries and debated the issue of *hejab*. Girls' high schools were effectively closed and the girls took to the streets. In a large number of state hospitals, nurses refused to work, but stayed on the premises. While tens of spontaneous demonstrations crippled the city, on 8 March 15,000 women, accompanied by a number of men who had gathered in Teheran University, marched towards the prime minister's office and were finally dispersed by the IRG firing shots in the air.[168]

The demonstrations against *hejab* were countered by groups of 20 to 200 of the Hezbollah who attacked veilless women with stones, clubs and knives. The Hezbollah, whose slogans usually rhymed very well in Farsi, chanted: '*Ya roosari ya toosari*' (Wear a head garment or receive a smack on the head). While the women battled in the streets, Khomeini continued his campaign against what he called the 'corrupt morals' of the *ancien régime*. He called for the reform of learning institutions, which he branded as 'centres of prostitution'.[169] Meanwhile, the minister of health announced that abortion was illegal in the Islamic Republic. First Taleqani and later Bazargan intervened, to assure Iranian women who were against the *hejab* that the Islamic veil was not compulsory and the 'Imam's' statement had been misconstrued.

The truth, however, was that Khomeini had meant every word he uttered. The compulsory Islamic veil was an integral part of the Islamic system he envisaged. On this issue, he was supported by a relatively large section of the urban population. Even during the Shah's reign, Teheran was geographically divided into veil wearing areas and non-veil wearing areas. The female members of the traditional petty bourgeoisie, the bazaar, the working classes and the rural migrants were predominantly veiled. Therefore, on 17 March, 10 days after the outbreak of demonstrations against the veil, a million-strong demonstration was organized in which the participants voiced their support for the Islamic veil and called on all women to abide by Khomeini's statement. In the months that followed, women who refused to wear the veil and women's organizations which condemned the forced imposition of the veil were intimidated, insulted and attacked in Teheran and the provinces. On 9 August 1979, the minister of justice declared that according to Islam women could not become judges and those that had been trained for this purpose would be given other responsibilities.[170]

The process of imposing the veil, which was initiated by Khomeini, gradually picked up momentum. In certain provincial towns, stores refused to sell goods to veilless women. Khomeini's representatives threatened not to admit veilless girls to school and, finally, on 28 June 1980, as a part of Khomeini's decree for an 'administrative revolution', the Islamic veil for women in government offices became compulsory. Effectively, from July, the *hejab* became obligatory for all women in public and the clerical leadership sought to impose its desired dress code by force. The Islamic government argued that the refusal to strictly observe the *hejab* in the cities was not simply a question of spreading immorality, but that it was a political counter-revolutionary act. President Khamenei said:

> Those who opposed this revolution have focused their counter-revolutionary activities on the development of moral laxity and decadence among women. . . . This is a movement designed by world politicians. . . . In our present society there are those who wish to return the condition of women to the past. Clearly we will not stand for such agitations.[171]

On 16 June 1984, a special patrol called *Gashte Mobareze ba Monkerat*

(Anti-vice Patrol) was created. This newly created repressive arm was responsible for combating all types of immorality and what Islam considered as vice and corruption. The anti-vice patrols were composed of two cars, one occupied by armed 'brothers' of the anti-vice squad and the other by 'sisters' belonging to the same organization. Depending on the sex of the offenders, the respective patrol cars give advice and guidance; in the event of resistance, they would arrest the offenders. On their first day of activities, Hojatolislam Moqtadaee, the spokesman of the Supreme Judicial Council, said:

> Those counter-revolutionary elements who refuse to observe the Islamic veil and code of conduct and continue to engage in vice and immorality despite our warnings should be reminded that depending on their crime they can be judged as corruptors on earth and executed.[172]

The most important function of the anti-vice patrols was to assure that women covered their whole body while they were in public. While the use of make-up was encouraged at home, the patrols removed lipstick, nail polish and any kind of make-up used by women in public. Men were prohibited from wearing short-sleeved shirts. The Islamic uniform designed for school girls imposed the use of sombre material in dark brown, navy blue or black, in addition to the *maqnaeh* (a hooded garment which completely covers the hair). The crackdown on those who are 'not properly veiled' has been extremely cyclical. Depending on the domestic political situation, the vice patrols are at times extremely tolerant or even absent from the streets, while during other periods they can become highly efficient, intolerant and brutal.

The issue of sexual segregation became an important topic during the summer of 1979. In a key speech, Khomeini said:

> The Westerners are afraid of the Islamic Republic and so they should be since Islam opposes lustfulness, Islam will not allow people to go swimming in the sea naked. . . . Islam will not permit men to go swimming naked with women. . . . Western civilisation wants naked men and women to go swimming. This was the civilisation that the Shah's régime imposed on this country. . . . If the government does not stop them, the people will.[173]

Immediately after Khomeini's speech, in numerous seaside resorts clashes occurred between groups of the Hezbollah and ordinary people of both sexes bathing in the sea. Male and female holiday makers were effectively denied the right to go swimming together and, subsequently, a complicated system of dividing the use of the Caspian Sea in to different hours for the sexes prevailed. Gradually, sexual segregation was imposed on all types of sport. The ski slopes of the Alborz mountains were divided between male and female slopes, preventing families from skiing together. Even religious minorities had to introduce sexual segregation.

Armed members of the Islamic revolutionary committees closed down the swimming pool at the Armenian Club in Teheran, explaining that since the Armenians were living in an Islamic country, they had to abide by Islamic laws.[174] The Islamic government has made attempts at instituting sexual segregation in buses, demanding the front door of the bus to be used by women and the rear door by men, but the project has failed. Various attempts are still made by zealots who continuously try to separate men and women queuing in public.

The Islamic Republic successfully proceeded to introduce sexual segregation in preliminary, middle and high schools. At university, due to the absence of qualified professors, co-educational classes were permitted, but students were segregated within the classroom. The arrest, intimidation and whipping of couples, who could not prove they were married or next of kin, became prevalent during the second and third years of the revolution. Couples were arrested and interrogated in parks, which were closed for a time as centres of prostitution, in cars driving from one point to another, in restaurants or even on the side walks. A handshake or a kiss on the cheek between people of opposite sex became a punishable offence.

On 23 July 1979, Khomeini said that:

> One of those things which intoxicates our youth is music. After a while, music leads to the inactivity of the listener. . . . There is no difference between music and opium. . . . If we wish to have an independent country our radio and television should become entirely educational and music has to be eliminated. . . . The playing of music is an act of treason to this country and our youth; therefore, musical programs should be entirely stopped.[175]

On 24 July, the managing director of the Islamic Republic's radio and television declared that the broadcasting of music was prohibited according to the Imam's decree. He added that only Islamic and revolutionary martial music would be allowed. Later on, it was argued that classical music was acceptable while jazz, popular music and rock which excited individuals were unacceptable. Even though the Islamic government's policy towards music has gone through a number of alterations, the one principle that has constantly been abided by is the prohibition of female singers.

The cultural straitjacket that the Islamic leadership wished to impose led to the development of a cultural underground which flourished, despite the government's attempts to control and muzzle it. The government's imposition of a puritanical cultural life-style led to the proliferation of video recorders among urban middle-class Iranian households. While music lovers held private mini-concerts at home, youth kept in touch with the latest pop stars and fashion through their newly acquired video recorders. The elders used the same device to keep abreast with the latest original-version films and serials released in Hollywood, Paris and Rome. The acceptance of the duality between private and public life was implicitly condoned by Khomeini himself in his famous eight-point declaration of 16 December 1982, in which, contrary to his initial injunction, he prohibited the IRG from spying on people in the privacy of their homes and banned them from entering houses and conducting searches without authorization. The public and private dichotomy among a very large number of urban families was stark. Individuals adapted themselves to a pious life-style in public and with those they did not trust, while in private and among friends they led a cultural life similar to that led under the Shah. From the Islamic leadership's viewpoint, the public manifestation of piousness and righteousness was the real issue. Bani-Sadr recalls Khomeini's wife telling his wife that, according to Islam, the appearance and form of things were far more important than their content.[176] The clerical leadership realized that in spite of its desire to fill all the spare hours of its flock with Islamic issues, such as prayer, seminars or war, it was realistically impossible to do so. It gradually came to terms with the abandonment of the effective implementation of a thoroughly ascetic Islamic culture, especially in view of the rising social and political discontent in Iran, and contented itself with the maintenance of a dual culture: public piety and private laxity.

The cultural revolution

The revolution had united the high school and university students behind Khomeini in the struggle against the Shah. Yet after the victory of the revolution, Khomeini realized that a large majority of Iran's future experts, professionals and managers who would graduate from Iranian institutions of higher education were not only far from being his disciples, but were organizing themselves in opposition to him. Iranian universities which had always been at the foreground of the anti-dictatorial movement viewed the revolution as the liberating force which would allow them to experience the dynamic intellectual existence which was expected of universities in a newly won democracy. Iranian students were energetically participating in their newly gained experience of free exchange of ideas; social, political and philosophical inquisitiveness and, finally, the right to defy all authority. The spirit of intellectual liberation was shared by a large number of university professors who had been forced to communicate the politically unacceptable content of their lecturers in symbols and allegories under the *ancien régime*. Neither the large majority of university students nor their professors were supporters of Khomeini's vision of an ideal society. Politically, the universities were effectively divided between various student organizations of the left, such as the *Pishgaame* Organization of the Fadaian, the Student Organization of *Peykar*, the Democratic Students' Association of the Tudeh Party and the non-clerical Association of Islamic Students belonging to the People's *Mojahedeen*. The Islamic Association of Students (not to be confused with the *Mojahedeen*'s Association of Islamic Students) was made up of students loyal to Khomeini and was effectively controlled by the IRP. In all universities, both the students and professors affiliated with the IRP and the clerical leadership were in a minority and were thus marginalized. On the managing council of the universities, which were charged with administering the universities after the revolution, members representing the clerical leadership were always in a minority and, therefore, could not determine and control curricular and administrative decisions.

The clerical leadership viewed the situation in the universities as disastrous. The professors were by no means up to the establishment's required Islamic standards. They were, essentially, divided into three groups: leftists if not Marxists, liberals and non-clerical Islamic sympathizers of the National Front and Bazargan's Iran Freedom Movement and, finally, the non-politicized groups, some of whom were affiliated with the *ancien régime*. The majority of these professors were foreign trained and were adverse to the Islamization of education. Leaving the universities in the hands of such elements would have not produced the type of Islamic student that the régime desired.

The left student organizations had established their headquarters on university campuses from where they carried out a large part of their theoretical and propaganda work. Furthermore, under pressure from the left student organizations, Marxian-related courses began to proliferate during the first year of the revolution, while clerically approved Islamic courses were looked down upon by the majority of students. As political democracy in society came under attack from the IRP and its executive arms, the universities became the only democratic sanctuary for all those non-clerically approved political forces that were taking a beating from the Hezbollah. The universities provided space for thought provoking lectures, meetings of opposition groups and a free discussion zone which remained more or less out of the government's reach. This hegemony of non-clerically approved forces was clearly unacceptable to the authorities of the Islamic Republic. As did all other aspects of social and political life, the universities had to become Islamized. The process in other institutions would only have meant replacing those already employed with elements loyal to the 'Imam' and the IRP. In the universities, however, both professors and students had to be purged. The problem for the clerical leadership was finding a way to entirely remould the educational process so that it would produce obedient individuals subservient to Khomeini's vision of society as interpreted by the IRP. The call for a cultural revolution which would completely transform education and render it compatible with the needs of Iran's post-revolutionary Islamic state became a perfect excuse for closing and conducting a thorough purge in the universities.

Khomeini had often spoken about 'revolutionary culture' and had reiterated the need for 'a new culture which would rear our children as good Moslems'.[177] He had also, on numerous occasions, spoken on the subject of unity between the seminary schools and the universities, implying that the universities should take their lead from the seminary schools otherwise they would become isolated in Islamic society. The

IRP, who knew that any attempt on the part of the Hezbollah to wrest the universities out of the control of their student bodies would not be opposed by Khomeini, initiated isolated and sporadic attacks against Teheran University which was the stronghold of the non-IRP approved student association.

On 30 October 1979, a small group of the Hezbollah attacked the Department of Engineering of Teheran University ripping down posters and tearing up books belonging to anti-government Marxist-Leninist student organizations. This was the second attack in the space of two days; the first was carried out against the Department of Literature. Faced with vigilant students who reacted against such acts, the Hezbollah resorted to violence and attacked the students with knives. The assailants were finally overcome and six were arrested by the students, who interrogated them and discovered that they were workers in the major wholesale vegetable and fruit market of Teheran, a well-known source of lumpenproletarian manpower for the Hezbollah gangs. After a two-hour session in which the provisional president of Teheran University was also asked to attend, the students handed over their prisoners to the IRG.[178] In a meeting which followed the incident, the representative of the IRP-affiliated Islamic Association of Students condemned the arrest of the six members of the Hezbollah.[179] The IRP hoped to provoke a violent internal struggle which could then be used as a pretext for the IRG to enter and take over the university. The plan failed. The incident convinced the IRP that greater organizational preparation was needed to successfully evict the students from the university campus.

The preparations behind the scene for the second stage of the clerical leadership's attempt at occupying the universities is very well documented. A tape recording of Dr Hassan Ayat's conversation with a few IRP-affiliated student leaders, one of whom was an infiltrator who leaked the information to Bani-Sadr's paper, *Enqelab Islami*, revealed that Ayat and the IRP had prepared for the unleashing of the cultural revolution. Ayat, a key figure in the cultural revolution's launch, told pro-IRP students that:

> The murmur that un-Islamic professors should be purged has to come from the students who should make a fuss about it and the decision of what is to be done with the students once the universities are closed will be made by higher authorities. . . . The universities in their present state should be closed down. . . . but the Imam has to be informed before we put our plan into action.[180]

After informing student leaders of the plan to close the universities and of their assigned roles in the plot, Ayat explained that the IRP had established a closely knit operational network with the Islamic Association of Students and Professors, which connected the Teheran decision-making centre with Islamic associations across Iran. To obtain greater harmony and synchronization, Ayat spoke about a national congress of representatives of all Islamic associations of students, professors, staff and administrators in Teheran.[181] He stated that 'this new assault on the universities would start with such great intensity that no one would be able to stop it'.[182]

The Cultural Revolution was launched by a well-planned two-tier attack. Firstly, on 22 February 1980, a group of students affiliated with the pro-IRP Islamic Association of Students and Professors started a fight with Mashhad University's student council in the university canteen. The Islamic students, who had provoked the fight and were well known to the student body, were arrested by their peers and taken to the amphitheatre for questioning. According to a well-coordinated plan a large crowd of the Hezbollah forced its way into the university concurrently with the arrest of the Islamic students. In the fighting that ensued on the university campus, between students and the Hezbollah, ten people were injured.[183] In protest about the attacks against the university and the inability of the authorities to defend it, the managing council decided to provisionally suspend classes, thus falling into the trap set for them.

One day after the attack the People's Mojahedeen's meeting at Teheran University was attacked by the Hezbollah and 25 people were wounded.[184] The events in Mashhad and Teheran universities led to the resignation of the president of Mashhad University and the managing council of Teheran University. In their letter of protest, the managing council protested against the inability and lack of desire on the part of the forces of law and order to arrest the well-known group of 200 to 300 individuals who had repeatedly disturbed the 'peace and harassed students in the name of Islam and the "Imam"'. It was added that the IRG had immediately released the six individuals who were arrested and handed over to the IRG by students on 30 October. The letter stated that even though permission had been obtained from the ministry of the interior for the two separate meetings organized on the campus of Teheran University by the People's Mojahedeen and the People's Fadaian, both meetings were attacked by irresponsible groups of thugs, without there being any attempt on the part of the authorities to assure the safety of these meetings.[185]

As a part of the general plan to create tension in the universities, the University of Kashan was attacked on 4 March and several students were arrested. Three days later, the Islamic Association of Students and Professors attacked the president of Teheran's teacher training college and forced him to leave the college, arguing that the managing council which had appointed the president had been infiltrated by un-Islamic characters of whom it should have been purged. Tension and insecurity permeated Iranian universities and the stage was set for Khomeini to order the occupation of universities by the partisans of the 'Imam' and the IRP.

On 21 March 1980, five days after the election for the first parliament, Khomeini said:

all universities in Iran should be subjected to a proper revolution and all those professors who are connected with the West or East should be purged. The Universities should become a centre for the study of Islamic sciences. . . . Seminary and university students should pool their forces and study Islamic principles and teachings and replace the slogans of deviationist groups with thoughts of true Islam. . . . Our dear students should not follow the misleading footsteps of faithless university intellectuals.[186]

Khomeini's speech on the occasion of the Iranian new year gave Ayat and the IRP enough time to prepare for the final assault, since universities and schools in Iran close for the first thirteen days of the new year.

On the first Friday after the reopening of schools and universities, the speakers at Teheran's Friday congregational prayers attacked the universities and Iran's educational system as anti-Islamic, colonial and corrupt. One speaker who was introduced as a student at the Melli University said: 'if only people knew what is going on in our educational institutions and how the best years of our youth are being wasted, they would never tolerate such centres and would support any action which aimed at their Islamization'.[187] The rhetorical campaign reached its climax when Khamenei told his audience that the Moslem students of Iran were no longer willing to tolerate the un-Islamic universities. He said: 'the universities should be evacuated and returned to their true owners who are Moslem people'.[188] According to Ayat's plan, the clerical leadership acted as if it was responding to a need voiced by Islamic students. The IRP-organized attacks of late February and early March were used as evidence of such demands. Having completed their task of mobilizing and sensitizing the masses to the so-called needs of the Islamic students, the clerical leadership launched the final stage of this cultural revolution that had been completely engineered from above.

From 17 to 23 April 1980, all Iranian universities became the scenes of violent confrontations. Clashes in universities left at least two thousand injured and approximately twenty-eight dead.[189] The IRP's masterplan was being executed. At every institution of higher education, the buildings were surrounded by a combined force of Islamic Association of Students and Professors, Hezbollah and the revolutionary forces of law and order. All entrances and exits were prohibited and the offices of all left student associations were occupied. Bani-Sadr, who had been manoeuvred into endorsing the cleansing process of the universities, gave all political student associations a three-day deadline to evacuate the campuses. The Mojahedeen's Association of Islamic Students and the Tudeh Party's Democratic Students' Association evacuated their offices. The convulsions in all universities subsided after the initial day of crisis and bloodshed; it was only at the besieged Teheran University that the *Pisghaame*, the student organization of the People's Fadaian and the student supporters of *Peykar* and *Rahe Karegar* (Workers' Path) refused to evcuate their offices and resisted the IRG. The battle with stones, sticks, knives and guns lasted for eleven hours on 20 April 1980. By 22 April, all student associations had agreed to evacuate university premises and Bani-Sadr, along with members of the Revolutionary Council, entered the deserted Teheran University triumphantly, declaring that the occasion marked the establishment of the sovereignty of the government. Bani-Sadr had thought that the universities would be closed provisionally. He soon discovered that, having achieved their objective of closing the universities, the clerical leadership had no intention of reopening them without a thorough purge of students, staff and professors. In the aftermath of university closures, sixty research institutes were closed down and their employees were laid off.[190]

On 26 April 1980, Khomeini explained his reasons for the cultural revolution:

> When we speak of reform of universities, what we mean is that our universities are at present in a state of dependence, they are imperialist universities and those whom they educate and train are infatuated with the West.[191]

Khomeini went on to explain that after fifty years: 'we do not have doctors that can meet the needs of our people' and he added that 'we demand fundamental changes in our university system so that the universities come to serve the nation and its needs instead of serving foreigners'.[192]

On 13 June 1980, Khomeini appointed seven members to the newly created *Setade Enqelab-e Farhangi* (Headquarters of the Cultural Revolution, HCR) which was charged with the determination of appropriate cultural and educational policies for the country. The HCR was empowered to dissolve universities and determine the content of textbooks and university courses based on the principle of furthering the interests of the Islamic Republic; this was Article 4 of the HCR's goals. The main purpose of HCR was to draw up an Islamic educational system, compatible with other aspects of the Islamic state. The HCR relegated the responsibility of dealing with the real problems that resulted from closing the universities, such as what was to be done with the idle students, staff and professors, to a six-man team called the *Shoraye Aliye Jihad-e Daneshgahi* (Supreme Council of Academic Crusade – SCAC). The SCAC introduced the concept of devotion to the principles of the Islamic Republic as a criterion for access to university education.

In a revealing interview, Jalal-e-deen Farsi, a member of both HCR and SCAC, denied imposing an ideological criterion for entrance, but stressed the relevance of an applicant's 'degree of devotion to Islam'.[193] Critics of the SCAC accused it of imposing an inquisitional system, which purged university students on the basis of offences varying from ideological deviation to moral laxity and even excessive laughter in the case of girl students. New applicants, both as students and professors, were obliged to fill out questionnaires inquiring about their opinions on various religious decrees, their political views and their reflections on various governmental positions. In an open letter to the members of parliament, the general assembly of Teheran's Melli University pointed out that the educational policies pursued had led to a large-scale exodus of highly trained Iranians. Thirty doctors from the University's medical school were reported to have left, excluding those who were purged. From the Department of Sciences, more than one-third of the entire faculty was reported to have left. Altogether, 119 professors left the university due to the prevailing conditions. Again, this figure excludes those purged.[194]

After two academic years of closure, the universities were reopened in October 1982, without any great alterations in the structure of higher education. According to official government figures, during the academic year 1979 to 1980, the last year of what has become known as the old educational system, 175,675 students were enrolled in Iranian universities and 35,559 students graduated. During the first post-cultural-revolution academic year of 1982–3, only 117,148 students were enrolled and 5,793 graduated. Iran had a total of 16,222 teaching staff during the 1979-80 academic year and 9,042 during the 1982–3 academic year.[195] The clerical leadership's plan to close the universities and break the traditional stronghold of resistance to state autocracy in Iran was successful. While the destructive part of the cultural revolution proved relatively simple, though bloody, carrying out the second part of the plan, which according to the leadership was the main reason for the cultural revolution, proved more difficult. According to Khomeini, an independent Islamic system of education was to replace the dependent western system. The reopening of the universities, showed that cultural revolution simply meant the exercise of control over the ideological purity and dedication of the students and professors. The educational process remained the same. The content of the majority of courses was not changed, nor was the method of teaching.

The cultural revolution did succeed in imposing a culture of silence, which inevitably gives birth to violent resistance and struggle. In relation to the excesses committed by SCAC, Montazeri said:

> Maybe these people have good intentions, but the adverse effect of excesses such as accusing and harassing professors in universities is no less than the blows we receive from counter-revolutionaries. It would be far more beneficial if we were to use our own professors who are committed to the country and the revolution, instead of using foreign professors to educate our children.[196]

On 5 October 1983, Montazeri effectively announced the defeat of the cultural revolution's aim of freeing the universities of non-Islamic influences by purging them of all non-Islamic elements. He said:

> We are faced with a shortage of trained manpower, we should not delve into the past of those professors, students and civil servants who regret their past. Some of them believed that the Shah's regime would last forever and therefore collaborated with it, but now they have realised that there has been a revolution and they are willing to serve it. Providing they do not engage in counter-revolutionary and anti-

Islamic propaganda, they should not be put aside and excluded. We should use their skill, knowledge and experience to the benefit of our country.[197]

Between 1981 and 1984, disputes among the clergy damaged the bodies that Khomeini had created to deal with the Islamization of education. There were increasingly disagreements and accusations between the HCR, SCAC and the ministry of higher education. Khomeini responded by setting up a Supreme Council of the Cultural Revolution (SCCR) responsible for decision making in all aspects of higher education. The SCCR was given the power of drafting resolutions which would automatically become law without the parliament's approval. This resulted in a further concentration of power in the hands of classical figures close to Khomeini, since the council came to include Hashemi-Rafsanjani, Khamenei, Moussavi-Ardabilli and Mir-Hossein Moussavi.

Notes

1. *New York Times*, 25 September 1963.
2. Abol-Hassan Bani-Sadr, *Kianat be Omid* (Paris: n. p. 1982), p. 331.
3. Imam Khomeini, *Islam and Revolution*, op cit., pp. 63, 149
4. Ibid., p. 53.
5. Ibid., p. 79.
6. Ibid., p. 98.
7. *Ayandegan*, 27 Esfand, 1357.
8. Imam Khomeini, *Nedaye Haq* (Teheran: Entesharat Qalam, 1357), p. 42
9. Ibid., p. 44.
10. Ibid., p. 83.
11. Ibid., p. 40.
12. Ibid., p. 41.
13. *Keyhan*, 26 Dey, 1357.
14. Imam Khomeini, *Nedaye Haq*, op. cit., pp. 31, 77.
15. *Keyhan*, 26 Dey, 1357.
16. *Keyhan*, 2 Esfand, 1357.
17. Ibid.
18. *Keyhan*, 9 Esfand, 1357.
19. Bani-Sadr, *Kianat be Omid*, op. cit., p. 402.
20. Saeed Ahmadi, In *Aghazi-No Quarterly Review*, Winter-Spring 1986-7, p. 53.
21. Hossein Akhavan Towhidi, *Dar Passe Pardeh Tazvir*, op. cit., p. 300.
22. Saeed Ahmadi, op. cit., p. 54.
23. *Ayandegan*, 15 Farvardeen, 1358.
24. Ibid.
25. *Keyhan*, 27 Farvardeen, 1358.
26. *Keyhan*, 28 Farvardeen, 1358.
27. Ibid.
28. *Keyhan*, 30 Farvardeen, 1358.
29. *Ayandegan*, 28 Tir, 1358.
30. *Teheran Mosavar*, No. 22, 1 Tir, 1358.
31. *Ayandegan*, 14 Esfand, 1357.
32. *Ayandegan*, 28 Tir, 1358.
33. *Ayandegan*, 20 Ordibehesht, 1358.
34. Personal Interview, Teheran 1361.

35. *Ayandegan*, 6 May 1978.
36. *Keyhan*, 17 Ordibehest, 1358.
37. *Keyhan*, 15 Ordibehest, 1358.
38. *Keyhan*, 18 Ordibehest, 1358.
39. *Ayandegan*, 20 Ordibehest, 1358.
40. Ibid.
41. *Ayandegan*, 19 Ordibehest, 1358.
42. *Keyhan*, 20 Ordibehest, 1358.
43. *Ayandegan*, 22 Ordibehest, 1358.
44. *Teheran Mosavar*, No. 17, 28 Ordibehest, 1358.
45. *Ayandegan*, 31 Ordibehest, 1358.
46. Ibid.
47. *Keyhan*, 26 Ordibehest, 1358.
48. *Keyhan*, 11 Mordad, 1358.
49. *Keyhan*, 12 Mordad, 1358.
50. *Ayandegan*, 15 Mordad, 1358.
51. *Keyhan*, 17 Mordad, 1358.
52. *Teheran Mosavar*, No. 30, 26 Mordad, 1358.
53. *Keyhan*, 28 Mordad, 1358.
54. *Keyhan*, 30 Mordad, 1358.
55. *Keyhan*, 31 Mordad, 1358.
56. *Keyhan*, 4 Shahrivar, 1358.
57. *Dadgostare Jomhouri-e Islami-e Iran: Ghaeleh Chahardahome Esfand,* Teheran, 1359, p. 633.
58. Ibid., p. 679.
59. *Keyhan Saal*, Dooreh Jadid 1364, p 23.
60. Ibid.
61. *Keyhan*, 15 Esfand, 1357.
62. *Keyhan*, 19 Esfand, 1357.
63. *Keyhan*, 29 Esfand, 1357.
64. *Keyhan*, 29 Farvardeen, 1357.
65. *Keyhan*, 20 Farvardeen, 1358.
66. *Azadi*, No. 3, 22 Farvardeen, 1357.
67. *Keyhan*, 3 Ordibehest, 1358.
68. *Keyhan*, 28 Bahman, 1357 and 23 Farvardeen, 1358.
69. *Peygham-e Emrouz*, 2 Khordad, 1358.
70. *Keyhan*, 27 Ordibehest, 1358.
71. *Keyhan*, 30 Ordibehest, 1358. *Azadi*, Vol. 2, No. 3, Khordad-Shahrivar, 1366.
72. *Peygham-e Emrouz*, 30 Ordibehest, 1358.
73. *Keyhan*, 4 Khordad, 1358.
74. *Keyhan*, 5 Khordad, 1358.
75. *Keyhan*, 11 Mordad, 1358.
76. *Ayandegan*, 4 Mordad, 1358.
77. *Ayandegan*, 10 Mordad, 1358.
78. *Azadi*, Vol. 2, Bahman, 1364.
79. *Keyhan*, 20 Mordad, 1358.
80. *Keyhan*, op cit., *Ettelaat*, 20 Mordad, 1358.
81. *Ettelaat*, 21 Mordad, 1358.
82. *Keyhan*, 21 Mordad, 1358.
83. *Azadi*, Vol. 2, No. 3, Khordad-Shahrivar, 1366, p. 32.
84. *Keyhan*, 22 Mordad, 1358.
85. *Keyhan*, 31 Mordad, 1358.
86. *Keyhan*, 12 Esfand, 1357.
87. *Keyhan*, 29 Mordad, 1358.
88. *Keyhan*, 27 Mordad, 1358.
89. *Keyhan*, 28 Mordad, 1358.
90. Ibid.
91. *Keyhan*, 27 Mordad, 1358.

92. *Keyhan*, 25 Mordad, 1358.
93. Ibid.
94. *Teheran Mosavar*, No. 28. 28 Mordad, 1358.
95. *Keyhan*, 27 Mordad, 1358.
96. *Keyhan*, 28 Mordad, 1358.
97. Ibid.
98. *Keyhan*, 10 Shahrivar, 1358.
99. Sayyed Jalel-e-deen Madani, *Tarikh Siyasi Moasere Iran*. Jelde Dovoom (Teheran: Daftar Entesharat Islami, 1362), p. 56.
100. *Keyhan*, 20 Esfand, 1357.
101. Ibid.
102. *Keyhan*, 20 Khordad, 1358.
103. *Ayandegan*, 8 Khordad, 1358.
104. *Ettelaat*, 2 Mehr, 1358.
105. *Bamdad*, 16 Mehr, 1358.
106. *Bamdad*, 15 Azar, 1358.
107. *Khalq-e Mosalman*, 18 Azar, 1358.
108. Ibid.
109. *Keyhan*, 19 Azar, 1358.
110. *Ettelaat*, 20 Azar, 1358. Sepehr Zabih maintains that the IRPMPI had 9 million members while Shariatmadari puts the figure at 2-3 million. Zabih *Iran since the Revolution* (London: Croom Helm, 1982), p. 78.
111. *Keyhan*, 24 Azar, 1358.
112. Hamid Rouhani, *Shariatmadari Dar Dadgahe Tarikh* (Qum Daftar Entesharat Islami, 1361), p. 180.
113. *Keyhan*, 15 Dey, 1358.
114. *Keyhan*, 28 Esfand, 1358.
115. *Keyhan*, 29 Farvardeen, 1358.
116. *Peygham-e Emrouz*, 31 May 1979.
117. *Teheran Mosavar* No. 28, 12 Mordad, 1353.
118. *Payame Jebhe-e Melli*, 18 Farvardeen, 1360.
119. *Jomhouri-e Islami*, 31 Tir, 1359.
120. The People's Mojahedeen Telegram, 13 Aban, 1358.
121. *Keyhan*, 4 Esfand, 1358.
122. Ibid.
123. *Keyhan*, 7 Esfand, 1358.
124. *Keyhan*, 11 Esfand, 1358.
125. *Keyhan*, 28 Esfand, 1358.
126. *Barasi Mostanadi az Mavaze Gorooha Dar Qebale Enqelab-e Islami* (Teheran: Vezarate Ershad Islami, Bahman 1360), p. 176.
127. *Mojahed,* 13 Khordad, 1359.
128. *Enqelab-e Islami*, 16 Esfand, 1359.
129. Ibid.
130. *Enqelab-e Islami*, 13 Ordibehest, 1360.
131. Ibid.
132. Ghaeleh Chahardahome Esfand, op. cit., p. 657.
133. Ghaeleh Chahardahome Esfand, op. cit., p. 95.
134. Hashemi-Rafsanjani, *Notqehaye qabl-az-dastour* (Teheran: Ravabet Omoomi Majlis Shoura-e Islami, 1362), p. 29.
135. *Ettelaat*, 20 Mordad, 1360.
136. *Ettelaat*, 15 Ordibehest, 1363.
137. Ibid.
138. Interview with Masoud Rajavi, *Merip Reports* No. 104, March-April 1982.
139. People's Mojahedeen Organization of Iran: list of names and particulars of 14,208 victims of the Khomeini régime's executions, October 1987, p. 3.
140. *Ettelaat*, 15 Ordibehest, 1363.
141. Ibid.
142. Ibid.

143. J. A. Bill, *The Eagle and the Lion* (New Haven: Yale University Press, 1988), p. 272.

144. *Confessions of the Central Cadre of the Tudeh Party* (Teheran: Islamic Propagation Organization, 1985), pp. 19-20.

145. *Ettelaat*, 24 Mordad, 1362.

146. *Ettelaat*, 15 Mordad, 1362.

147. *Ettelaat*, 12 Mordad, 1362.

148. *Keyhan*, 6 Azar, 1368.

149. *Ettelaat*, 12 Mordad, 1362.

150. *Ettelaat*, 22 Tir, 1362.

151. *Ettelaat*, 12 Mordad, 1362.

152. *Ettelaat*, 13 Mordad, 1362.

153. *Ettelaat*, 15 Mordad, 1362.

154. The information in this section is largely based on an excellent article by Saeed Ahmadi, 'Dar Barehe Enhelal Sazmane Mojahedeen Enqelab-e Islami', *Aghazi-No Quarterly Review*, Winter-Spring 1986-7.

155. *Keyhan,* 14 Mehr, 1365.

156. Ibid.

157. *Keyhan*, 27 Bahman, 1358.

158. Bani-Sadr, *Khianat Be Omid*, op. cit., p. 103.

159. *Keyhan Chape Landan*, 25 June 1987.

160. *Jomhouri-e Islami*, 17 Ordibehest, 1362.

161. Saeed Ahmadi, 'Dar Barahe Enhelal Hezb Jomhouri-e Islami', *Aghazi-No Quarterly Review*, Double Issue. Summer-Autumn 1987.

162. *Keyhan*, 24 Esfand, 1365.

163. *Jomhouri-e Islami,* 12 Khordad, 1366.

164. Ibid.

165. Imam Khomeini, *Nedaye Haq*, vol. I (Teheran: Entesharat, Qalam 1357), p. 376.

166. *Kar* 67. Organ of the Fadaian Khalq (minority).

167. *Keyhan*, 16 Esfand, 1357.

168. *Keyhan*, 17 Esfand, 1357.

169. Ibid.

170. *Keyhan*, 18 Mordad, 1358.

171. *Ettelaat*, 3 Khordad, 1363.

172. *Ettelaat*, 26 Khordad, 1363.

173. *Ayandegan*, 13 Tir, 1358.

174. *Ayandegan*, 14 Tir, 1358.

175. *Ayandegan*, 1 Mordad, 1358.

176. Bani-Sadr, op. cit., p. 413.

177. Imam Khomeini: *Khate Imam, Kalam Imam*, op. cit., pp. 265-6.

178. *Keyhan*, 8 Aban, 1358.

179. *Keyhan*, 9 Aban, 1358.

180. Ghaeleh Chahardahome Esfand, op. cit., p. 341.

181. Ibid., p. 345.

182. Ibid., p. 346.

183. *Keyhan*, 2 Esfand, 1358.

184. *Keyhan*, 4 Esfand, 1358.

185. *Keyhan*, 6 Esfand, 1358.

186. *Keyhan*, 6 Farvardeen, 1359.

187. *Keyhan*, 16 Farvardeen, 1359.

188. *Keyhan*, 30 Farvardeen, 1359.

189. *Enqelab-e Islami*, 1 Ordibehest, 1360 and Ghaeleh Chahardah Esfand, op. cit., p. 292.

190. Imam Khomeini, *Writings and Declarations*, trans. Hamid Algar, op. cit., p. 295.

191. Ibid., p. 296.

192. *Enqelab-e Islami*, 3 Ordibehest, 1360.

193. *Enqelab-e Islami*, 6 Ordibehest, 1360.
194. *Enqelab-e Islami*, 20 Esfand, 1359.
195. *Salnameh Amari*, 1363, Jomhouri-e Islami Iran. Markaz Amar, p. 314.
196. *Jomhouri-e Islami*, 13 Esfand, 1362.
197. *Jomhouri-e Islami*, 14 Aban, 1362.

6. Post-Revolution Economic Measures, Reforms and Controversies

There follows an attempt to present the economic measures that have had an important effect on Iran's economic institutions. We will also examine the clergy's doctrinal disputes over domestic and foreign economic policies. There have been two main stages and the balance of power between the clergy and their allies changed, as different factions exercised different degrees of control. In the first stage, the clergy shared power with Bazargan and then with the Bani-Sadr faction under the indisputable leadership of Khomeini. Major economic measures were introduced and implemented to varying degrees. The dismissal of Bani-Sadr from the presidency marked the beginning of the second stage, full-fledged clerical rule and, paradoxically, a period of open dispute among clerical factions, generally manifested in economic controversies. In this second stage, no major economic measures were introduced and some of the previous ones were drastically modified or endlessly debated and disputed.

Khomeini's opposition to the Shah's economic strategy

In his *Islamic Government*, Khomeini presented a simplistic economic analysis of the Iranian economy in the 1960s and outlined the economic reforms that would be implemented under an Islamic government. He talked about: 'huge amounts of capital' that were 'being swallowed up', 'public funds' that were 'being embezzled' and oil that was 'being plundered'.[1] He emphasized that the country was being: 'turned into a market for expensive unnecessary goods by the representatives of foreign capitalists and their local agents, in order to pocket the people's money'.[2] Above all, what bothered him about the consumption pattern of the nation was: 'the veritable flood of forbidden consumption'.[3] He attacked the 'West and the East' and their 'agents' for the plunder of the economy in the following manner:

All this misappropriation of wealth goes on and on: in our foreign trade and in the contracts made for the exploitation of our mineral wealth, the utilisation of our forests and other natural resources, construction work, road building and the purchases of arms from the imperialists, both Western and Communist.[4]

His programme for solving all these problems was simply: 'to end all this plundering and usurpation of wealth' and 'to punish the embezzlers and traitors'.[5] On the whole, his ideal market-oriented Islamic economy was primarily based on self-sufficiency, autarky and agriculturally oriented small-scale commodity production that would have the least contact with the outside world's values, ideas, productive relations or technology. The apparatus for the implementation of this programme was 'a simple planning body' that was to replace the legislative assembly. This body was supposed to draw up: 'programmes for the different ministries, in the light of the ordinances of Islam and thereby determine how the public services are to be provided across the country'.[6] The Islamic government, under the leadership of the *faqih*, was to execute the *Shari'a*. Khomeini maintains that:'No one has the right to legislate and no law may be executed except the law of the Divine Legislator'.[7] By acknowledging the *Shari'a* as the sole source of legislation, Khomeini honoured the legitimacy of private property and implicitly limited the intervention of the government in public services and distributive activities. It is only later, in practice, that he extended the economic role of the government under the pretext that a strong Islamic government was indispensable for the defence and the expansion of Islam.

In the revolutionary period before the insurrection of 1979, Khomeini and the other clerical leaders of the revolution did not explicitly commit themselves to any economic reforms. Their economic rhetoric was ambiguous, simplistic and general. In his speech delivered on his first day in Teheran, Khomeini repeated his 1970 analysis of the state of the Iranian economy. He said that the economy had been disrupted and ruined by the *ancien régime* and that: 'years of continuous effort by the whole population will be needed to restore it; the efforts of the government alone, or a single segment of the population, will not be enough'.[8] He criticized the Shah's land reform by saying that it was enacted: 'in order to create markets for America', that it had resulted 'in the complete destruction of all forms of cultivation' and that it had left the country dependent 'on the outside world for all our essential needs'.[9] However, he did not advocate any Islamic land reform, but called on 'all' people to 'work hard, hand in hand' in the agricultural sector.[10]

As for the oil and gas industry, he said that: 'it was given away to America and the others', that oil reserves were spent on military bases and arms purchases and that the Shah's policy was 'to exhaust Iran's oil reserves in just the same way that it destroyed the agricultural sector'.[11]

History has shown that, despite the rhetoric, the Islamic Republic essentially followed the economic strategy of the former régime, but in a less coherent and a more roundabout manner. Khomeini never advocated a classless society and economic concerns were not at the top of his list of objectives. Although improvement in economic welfare was a matter of concern to the majority of Iranians who took part in the revolution, the clergy succeeded in turning the pressing demand of the people for political freedom, independence, economic well being and social justice into a campaign for an 'Islamic Republic' with no specific economic programme. The clergy avoided concrete and controversial economic programmes. In accordance with his ideas in the *Islamic Government*, Khomeini called on all classes to rise against the Shah. On a few occasions, he threw in populist slogans. For example, in his declaration from Neauphle-le-Chatêau on 23 November 1978, he asked all classes to become active in the struggle against the Shah's régime. At the same time, however, he told his followers to inform the people, especially the peasantry, that contrary to 'the poisonous propaganda of the Shah and his hangers-on . . . an Islamic state is not the protector of the capitalists and big landlords'.[12] Nevertheless, his attachment to the merchants of the bazaar and the traditional segment of the bourgeoisie is clearly expressed in his arrival speech in Teheran on 1 February 1979. Khomeini ranked the traditional bourgeoisie highly on his list of commendable social strata:

> I offer my thanks to all classes of the nation: to the religious scholars . . .; to the students, who have suffered heavily; to the merchants and traders, who have undergone hardship; to the youths in the bazaar, universities and *madrasas* of the country . . .; to the professors, judges and civil servants; to the workers and peasants . . .[13]

Bazargan and the clergy

Khomeini's appointment of Bazargan as prime minister, on 5 February 1979, was a step towards the realization of the Islamic Republic. Bazargan had the support of the majority of the liberal intelligentsia, the moderate left, the small and middle-rank entrepreneurs, the merchants, the state and private sector employees and the officers of the army, the police and the gendarmerie. The clerical leaders were aware that without the help of the technocracy they could not realize their objectives and gain immediate and complete control over the important levers of government. The clergy needed to restore law and order in the complex Iranian society after the fall of the Shah's régime. Despite their influence and connections among the masses, they had not created the necessary instruments of power that could guarantee their hold on the state apparatus and the destruction of existing and potential opposition. In fact, they were surprised by the speed with which the revolution brought them to power. They had to buy time.

Bazargan, too, wanted law and order, but for a different reason. Law and order for Bazargan was an objective in itself and not a means to the establishment of an absolute Islamic régime and he was very explicit about it. He, too, wanted the restoration of the army and security organs, the bureaucracy and, most important, the normal functioning of the economy.

Socially and economically, the clerical leadership and Bazargan's government shared numerous common viewpoints. Both had in mind the interests of small and medium-sized commercial and industrial capital. However, the clergy was more sensitive to the necessity of paying lip service to the demands of the dispossessed, who formed their principal political base in the struggle for the realization of an Islamic Republic. The economic objective of the Bazargan government was the restoration of the confidence of the owners of capital and economic reconstruction. After the victory of the revolution, the cabinet's spokesman announced that the revolution was over and the era of reconstruction had to begin.[14] Bazargan, himself an industrial entrepreneur, had always recognized the importance of the private sector as the agent of change and growth in the national economy. He argued for gradual reforms. However, the deteriorating state of the economy and the mood of the masses in the urban and rural areas did not lend themselves to gradualism and a time consuming policy of change. The clerical leadership, with its eye fixed on full-fledged clerical rule, was ready to react to the mood of the movement in a populistic manner.

The urban economy was in serious difficulties due to months of strikes or go-slows, raw material and intermediate goods shortages. In the spring and summer of 1979, industrial output had declined by 24 per cent and, in the same year, industrial units were only working at 58 per cent of their capacity.[15] The decline in sales disrupted output and cash flow. Many of the major owners and top managers of the very big industrial enterprises, the private banks and insurance companies had left the country and those who remained had lost confidence. According to Bazargan the: 'owners and shareholders have gone; they have taken the money and left us with a heritage of debts and difficulties'.[16] The banking system was facing a crisis due to massive withdrawals of money in the latter part of 1978. A further aggravating factor was the heavy debts of large industries to the banks.[17]

Immediately after the insurrection, white- and blue-collar workers were organizing employees' and workers' councils, demanding a purge of 'informers' and 'collaborators', higher wages and benefits and more control over the running of the factories and offices. They were supported in their demands by the leftist forces, certain young clerics and radical Moslems. As a result of increased lay-offs and lock-outs in industrial enterprises, demand for more control over managerial functions intensified.[18] Major government industrial complexes, such as steel mills, petrochemical plants, nuclear reactors, construction projects, ports and military bases that were incomplete were left idle. The workers who were employed by private contractors on government projects were losing their positions on a massive scale. According to the head of the central bank, the level of unemployment and underemployment increased to 3 million, or about 30 per cent of the labour force.[19]

The political organizations of the left and their cadres in factories, offices, educational institutions and the mass media were demanding nationalization of large industries, the banking system, arable and urban lands and empty dwellings. They were actively involved in the creation and consolidation of employees', and workers' and peasants' councils and even in leading squatters in the occupation of empty apartment complexes and hotels.

The rural sector was not affected by the political turmoil in the cities before the insurrection. However, after the insurrection, confrontation between landlords and peasants became widespread and violent. Some of the land seizures in rural areas were carried out by landlords who had lost land during the Shah's land reform, especially in the less developed provinces with their tribal traditions and semi-feudal relationships. In almost all provinces, in addition to the landlords, landless peasants and rural farm labourers participated in land seizures. In regions where the leftist forces were not strong, local Islamic revolutionary committees and courts also encouraged the seizure of lands of absentee landlords, or took over these lands themselves. In the Turkoman Plain, where mechanized cotton and wheat farms were extensively cultivated, peasants' councils were set up with the help of the People's Fadaian guerillas. In some regions, peasants prevented the landlords from coming to the villages, while in other villages, landlords' armed retainers intimidated peasants.[20]

The flight of capital was intensified in the second half of 1978 and in 1979, pushing up the price of foreign currencies against the rial in the black market. Of course, capital outflow had increased after the jump in oil revenues in 1973, mainly for the purchase of land and property and other investments abroad. Between 1973 and October 1978, a free market for foreign exchange transactions was established. The sale of foreign exchange for services to the private sector increased from $918 million in 1973 to $7.9 and $7.7 billion in 1977 and 1978 respectively. However, due to the increase in the outflow of capital, the central bank limited foreign exchange transactions for non-commercial activities in October 1978.[21]

Major economic measures in the first year of the revolution

Against such a background and in reaction to it, the Revolutionary Council and the provisional government moved slowly and cautiously, for a while. The leading clerics and the members of the cabinet simultaneously criticized both the 'bloated capitalists and feudal elements' and ordered the workers to return to work and observe work discipline. In fact, one of the first decisions of the Revolutionary Council concerned this issue.[22] At other times, members of the cabinet asked businessmen and industrialists to come back and start their activities and demanded 'revolutionary patience' from the masses.

The economic measures that were gradually approved by the Revolutionary Council and the government were a mixed bag of philanthropic and spontaneous populistic and radical measures. As long as the radical measures affected only the property of the royal family and the top echelons of the *ancien régime*, nobody objected. Trouble started when some of these measures touched the sensitive issue of property rights and property distribution.

On 28 February 1979, Khomeini authorized the Revolutionary Council

> to confiscate all the mobile and immobile properties of the Pahlavi dynasty and all those related to this dynasty . . . in favour of the needy, workers and lower echelon salaried people . . . to be used in the creation of housing, employment etc.[23]

The Foundation for the Disinherited was established to administer these properties. The immobile properties of the Pahlavi family included 200 large factories, farms, banks, hotels and trading companies.[24]

On 5 March 1979, the National Iranian Oil Company took over all the activities of the oil and gas industries. On 20 March 1979, the day of the nationalization of the oil industry in 1951, the government cancelled its agreements with the international consortium. The government also changed the oil-production target, reducing it from 6 million barrels a day (MBD) to 4 MBD, with an export target of 3.4 MBD.[25]

Certain routine and partly philanthropic measures were also introduced to reduce the problems of the industry and the banking system and to prevent economic stagnation intensifying. Thus, in April 1979, the central bank liberalized import regulations for raw materials and intermediate goods needed by industries and allocated 5 billion rials to the Chamber of Industries and Mines, to be distributed among industrial establishments with cash-flow problems. This sum was not enough and so 80 billion rials more was set aside by the banking system. However, private enterprises were reluctant to use the credit and, by the end of the winter of 1979, only 25 billion rials had been used.[26] More than 65 billion rials was authorized for the payment of outstanding claims to government contractors. It was also decided to defer current payments by importers for some customs charges. The government appointed managers for the major private industries whose owners had fled the country. Certain categories of unemployed people were granted short-term loans from a fund established for this purpose. To please employees, the National Bank set aside 115 billion rials for housing loans of which 97 billion rials were lent on very easy terms.[27] However, more substantial changes were inevitable. In the summer of 1979, certain important measures were approved by the Revolutionary Council that greatly increased the government's role and ownership in the crisis-ridden economy of the country.

Major nationalizations

On 7 June, the Revolutionary Council nationalized twenty-seven privately owned banks, of which thirteen were joint ventures with foreign share holdings and on 25 June, fifteen privately owned insurance companies were nationalized. According to the government, the justification for nationalization was the heavy domestic and foreign debts of some of the banks, especially the development banks, the possibility of bankruptcy of some others and the risk of outflow of funds to accounts abroad. In the Revolutionary Council's ruling, there was no reference to Islamic banking, but the head of the Planning and Budget Organization announced that the decision was an important step towards usury-free banking.[28] Four years later, in August 1983, a new Law of the Interest-free Banking System 'eliminated' interest and forbade banks to charge it. As early as 1979, the nationalized banks started to substitute the words 'service charge' and 'profit' for 'interest rate'.

At the end of the summer of 1979, thirty-six government and newly nationalized banks were reorganized and integrated into ten banks: the central bank; three specialized banks in the fields of industry and mines, housing and construction and agriculture and six commercial banks.[29]

In the large industrial establishments, government supervision became increasingly inevitable, due to the exodus of owners, managers and foreign technicians, outstanding debts and, after the insurrection, increasing dependence on government funds. On 14 June, the Revolutionary Council approved a measure for the appointment of one or more managers to all firms whose owners were absent. This also applied to firms which had closed or were unable to continue their operations and had asked for government help. The law also obliged the government to determine the ownership of those industries within the 'framework of Islamic law'.[30] These managers were to work with the representatives of post-revolution employees' councils. The employees' councils were effectively controlling many of these enterprises, but lost their power after the clergy's 1979 crackdown against the left, democrats and the nonconformist councils.

The next major step was taken in July. On 5 July, the Revolutionary Council approved the Law for the Protection and Expansion of Iranian Industry which nationalized three categories of private industries: strategic industries, such as metals, chemicals, ship building, aircraft manufacture and mining; industries belonging to fifty-three individuals and families whose owners 'had illegally . . . acquired their wealth through relations with the former régime',[31] industries whose liabilities exceeded their net assets and those which, despite their solvency, were indebted to the government. The latter clause explicitly protected the right of private ownership of enterprises excluded from the first three clauses. The enterprises in the last two categories were to be nationalized without compensation. The owners of enterprises in the first category could receive compensation according to their net assets, if their firms were not included in the other categories. The government was to part own enterprises whose assets were greater than their liabilities, in proportion to the value of their debts to the banking system. Originally the size of the government's stake in industries of this category was not adequately specified; a supplementary bill was, subsequently, approved. According to this bill, a board consisting of representatives of the president, parliament, public prosecutor, the enterprise and a religious judge was to determine the ownership stake of the shareholders of those enterprises placed under government supervision.

It is interesting to note that two days after the nationalization of large enterprises, Khomeini tried to reduce the worries of the merchants and traders of the bazaar about the security of private ownership. In an audience with them, he indicated that the Islamic economy's objective was not to eliminate private economic activity, but to reduce the concentration of wealth:

> [Iran] is not a communist country where the state can do whatever it wants. Islam is for moderation . . . , We must act according to Islam. As long as I am alive, I will not let the government deviate from the line of Islam.[32]

The collection of vast amounts of mobile and immobile assets under the control of the Foundation for the Disinherited, administered by friends and relatives of the clergy and people with little experience of management, led to numerous reports of embezzlement and corruption. In the early days of its establishment, the foundation remained unaccountable to higher authorities. No clear record was kept of the precious objects, carpets, antiques, foreign exchange and paintings that were confiscated on orders from the revolutionary courts. The absence of any proper bookkeeping created an atmosphere conducive to embezzlement and corruption. In the spring of 1980, Khomeini authorized an investigation into the matter. It uncovered 600 cases of embezzlement, but was soon dropped for unknown reasons. In 1983, another investigation, this time of 4,000 cases involving offences by the foundation, did not lead to any indictments.[33]

Urban and rural land measures

One of the spectacular and populistic moves of the clerical leadership in 1979 was a series of abortive housing measures that were introduced in the 1979–80 period. On 3 March 1979, Khomeini promised: 'homes for the poor across Iran'.[34] Thus, agitation for the seizure and distribution of empty houses, apartments, extra dwellings and urban land began. In June, the Housing Foundation was established and Khomeini appointed Ayatollah Khosrowshahi to its directorship. Khosrowshahi demanded the permission of the government to confiscate empty houses and apartments and to control rents and property transactions. His staff started a door-to-door survey on the number of residents and rooms in the well-to-do areas of Teheran and its suburbs. Based on these surveys, Khosrowshahi announced that 200,000 empty dwellings had been identified and would be either confiscated or bought. In the meantime, the leftist organizations encouraged poor families to occupy empty apartment buildings and hotels around the Teheran University campus. The revolutionary committees reacted and drove out the squatters, after several weeks of tension and dispute. No measure concerning the empty houses and apartments was officially approved until early 1980.

In June 1979, the council nationalized almost all dead lands (*mawat*) or undeveloped lands in urban areas. The Urban Land Development Organization was established to implement the law.[35] To circumvent the law, many landlords subdivided large holdings, backdated the deeds and sold off the property. Nevertheless, by early 1983, the organization had successfully transferred 20 million square metres of private urban land to government ownership.

With regard to rural land problems, the reactions of the Revolutionary Council and the provisional government were slower and more conservative, despite the violent confrontations that took place in virtually all provinces. Apart from the confiscations ordered by the revolutionary courts in Teheran and major cities, agricultural property was not officially subjected to nationalization or land reform. On the contrary, the provisional government tried to prevent forced seizure of arable lands by introducing a bill that was not enforced. Thus, in September 1979, the government brought in the Law for the Revival and Transfer of Arable Lands to the Revolutionary Council. The law envisaged the distribution of state arable lands, including cultivated lands confiscated from members of the *ancien régime* that were already under the control of the Foundation for the Disinherited and the dead lands (*mawat*). However, the peasants were not interested in dead lands and there was not enough state arable land to satisfy them all. The reclamation of dead lands was too costly for the landless peasants. The law allowed the government to set a ceiling on land ownership, but did not specify the limit. It also empowered the government to transfer dead and fallow lands, if these were left uncultivated for 2 and 3–5 years, respectively.[36]

The approval of this law did not bring peace to rural areas. Peasants in more agriculturally developed regions, such as the Turkoman Plain, were organizing themselves into rural peasant councils and were seizing land where they could. Landlords and commercial farmers took advantage of the law on agricultural councils, passed in April 1979, and used the councils for their own objectives which were, above all, to prevent land distribution. They actively lobbied religious leaders and government authorities.

The provisional government's land reform proposal was radicalized by the Revolutionary Council four months after the resignation of Bazargan on 6 November 1979. In September 1979, complaints about the 'non-revolutionary attitude' of the Bazargan government had become widespread among some followers of Khomeini and members of the Revolutionary Council. Bani-Sadr, as a member of the council, summed up the differences between the government and the council in the following manner:

I believe that Mr. Bazargan's government wants to keep the foundations of the former régime. [It] wants to reform it and this is the problem. The Revolutionary Council's problem is that it is compelled to work with this government.[37]

Ironically, Bani-Sadr found himself in the same position as the one he criticized Bazargan for, when he became president of the Islamic Republic. He found himself defending the major institutions of the former régime, the army and the bureaucracy, against the encroaching power of the parallel institutions under the control of the clergy and the Islamic Republic Party who wanted full-fledged clerical rule.

Bani-Sadr and the clergy

On 25 January 1980, Bani-Sadr was elected as the first president of the Islamic Republic. His ideological position was a mixture of Islamic pluralism and Islamic socio-economic views close to the ideas of Baqer Sadr, but with a greater usage of western analytical tools. In his book about Islamic economics published before the revolution, Bani-Sadr closely followed the conclusions drawn by Baqer Sadr. He believed in the uniqueness of Islamic economics and the possibility of an Islamic economic system based on social justice, the equitable distribution of wealth and state regulation of the economy.

Following the arguments of the Islamic jurists and especially Baqer Sadr, Bani-Sadr stated in his *Economics of Divine Unity* that 'absolute ownership belongs to God and that the only basis recognised in Islam for property ownership is labour'.[38] Therefore, according to Bani-Sadr (and for that matter, Baqer Sadr and most other jurisconsults), the individual has the right only to the fruits of her/his own labour. The 'surplus' earnings of each individual should be transferred to society, so as to eliminate the source of 'domination' and the 'exercise of force'. In fact, Bani-Sadr went so far as to state that Islam does not allow any inequality, since the slightest inequality would lead to an un-Islamic concentration and domination.[39] However, in his book, Bani-Sadr did not present a detailed and systematic argument for the way the Islamic economy functions or the laws governing its process of production, distribution and consumption. Furthermore his explanation did not rely heavily on the arguments of Islamic jurisconsults and was thus considered less authentic by the clergy.[40]

In his less doctrinal writings before and after the revolution, Bani-Sadr identified the Iranian economic and political relationships of the former régime as dependent on the West, especially on the United States. He is fond of numbering these dependencies and has identified fifty-seven types of dependency, fifteen of which were found in the agricultural sector. He believed that the nation's wealth was 'sucked' by the West and the multinational corporations through the channels of dependency. When he was in the Revolutionary Council, he criticized Bazargan's government for underestimating the dependent foundations of Iranian society. In his campaign for the presidency, he advocated the uprooting of Iran's dependent 'structure from its foundations to enable the establishment of the Islamic Republic'.[41] However, he never specified his economic programmes for doing this. Although he was not against the nationalization of the banking system and large dependent industries or land reform, he was, however, against any concentration of decision making in the hands either of the state or of an unspecified entity which he calls 'capital'. According to Bani-Sadr: 'what makes exploitation possible is the concentration of decision making'.[42] For him, 'capital' manifested itself in the form of ownership of 'instruments' of labour and was thus entitled to a rate of depreciation and not profit due to ownership.[43]

> Capital does not have any right over production. [Capital] does not have the right of management over production and [production] must be under the control of the labour force.[44]

Believing that a concentration of decision making was the source of all types of exploitation, Bani-Sadr was opposed to the idea of the absolute power of the *faqih* in the Constitution and was, consequently, averse to an authoritarian Islamic government and all 'official ideologies'. He spoke against the growing and monopolizing role of the clergy in state politics, calling them 'a fistful of Fascist clerics'. This explains the violent animosity between Bani-Sadr and the clerics who were gathered in the Islamic Republic Party under the leadership of Beheshti.

Bani-Sadr, as president, never sought to implement his egalitarian ideas. However, he did not oppose the passage of economic measures that adversely affected the interests of the bazaar people and undermined the confidence of the property owning classes. Apparently, his mind was fixed on the question of state power. Thus, in the period of his presidency, Bani-Sadr viewed law and order as a prerequisite for the elimination of the clergy's control of the state apparatus. He advocated a return to normality and a moderate central authority. Such a state of affairs required the repression of the Hezbollah which constantly threatened the social and political peace of the country. For the clerics, however, law and order was the continuation of the August 1979 crackdown on anything un-Islamic in the political, cultural and economic spheres. This included the left, liberals, national minorities, workers' and peasants' movements and their secular councils. Both tendencies tried to win Khomeini's favour and, for a while, Khomeini tried to keep the balance. Thus, both tendencies found their own imprints in Khomeini's new year message of March 1980. In that message, Khomeini reiterated his support for Islamic revolutionary institutions, but demanded the observance of law and order in factories and offices, along with the orderly implementation of Islamic laws and customs. Furthermore, Khomeini called for restraint and order in the 'Islamic' process of confiscation and land distribution. He warned those who incited disorder and did not obey government authorities. He advised workers to shun strikes and work go-slows. He asked the Hezbollah to go to the factories that were on strike, in order to investigate, identify and expose all counter-revolutionary forces. Khomeini exhorted: 'there is no reason for the people of Iran to pay wages to a handful of godless individuals'.[45] Demanding that the government severely punish workers who went on strike, Khomeini also warned the workers against the influence of the leftist forces that were tied 'to the aggressive East and the criminal West'.[46]

Major economic measures in the second year of the revolution

After the resignation of Bazargan, Beheshti promised that 'fundamental changes in the economic and social system' would be 'the priority of the Revolutionary Council's program'.[47] Two specific measures mentioned in the council's communiqué were aimed at solving the land and housing problems.[48] The radical mood of the country after the occupation of the US embassy and the approval of the Islamic Constitution hastened the approval of the economic bills of this period. The Islamic Constitution was approved in December 1979 and its articles on social and economic justice raised the expectations of the lower middle classes, peasants and the poor. In general, the economic and financial articles of the Constitution ruled out the 'exploitation of another's labour', 'infliction of harm and loss upon others, monopoly, hoarding and usury'.[49] It defined the forms of ownership of the economy as state, co-operative and private and stated that these sectors were 'to be based upon systematic and sound planning'.[50] The state sector included 'all large-scale and mother industries, foreign trade, major minerals, banking, insurance, power generation, dams and large-scale irrigation networks, radio and television, post, telegraph and telephone services, aviation, shipping, roads, railways and the like'.[51] Private ownership, 'legitimately acquired', was to be respected and the private sector could engage in all kinds of economic activities 'that supplement the economic activities of the state and co-operative sectors'.[52] However, there were also clauses concerning ownership that could lend themselves to different interpretations. Article 44 of the Constitution stipulated that:

> in each of these three sectors [ownership] is protected by the laws of the Islamic Republic, in so far as this ownership . . . does not go beyond the bounds of Islamic law, contributes to economic growth and progress . . . and does not harm society.[53]

Article 4 of the Constitution also had an important implication for future economic measures. It stated that all 'civil, penal, financial, economic, administrative, cultural, military, political and other laws and regulations must be based on Islamic criteria'.[54] This article made it clear that this principle 'applies absolutely and generally to all articles of the Constitution as well as to all other laws and regulations and the *Foqaha* [jurisconsults] of the Guardianship Council are judges in this matter'.[55]

The government became responsible for confiscating 'all wealth accumulated through usury, usurpation, bribery, embezzlement, theft, gambling, misuse of endowments, . . . the sale of uncultivated lands and other resources subject to public ownership . . . in accordance with the law of Islam'.[56]

Housing and rural land measures
In early 1980, due to rising housing shortages in Teheran, the Revolutionary Council approved the establishment of the Office for the Purchase and Transfer of Empty Dwellings. The council authorized the office to buy or lease empty dwellings in certain urban centres, with the consent of the owners, for rent or resale to the public. In April, the council went even further, allowing the government to house the shanty-town dwellers in empty houses and apartments with or without the consent of the owners. Based on these measures, in June, the government announced that all property transactions had to take place through the Office for the Purchase and Transfer of Empty Dwellings. The prices of property and rents were to be determined by this office. If owners were absent or unidentifiable, their property could be confiscated. The measure forbade purchases of a second residence and gave priority access to dwellings to tenants already residing in major cities, in order to reduce migration to the big cities.[57] However, from the outset, it was obvious that this undertaking was too difficult for the government and that the regulations could not be enforced. Circumvention of the regulations was widespread, by means of semi-formal documents and backdated deeds. Thus, by June 1981, most of the radical regulations were lifted and the director of the Housing Foundation, Khosrowshahi, who had incited much of the demand for the measures, was sent abroad as ambassador to the Vatican. The foundation was integrated into the ministry of housing and, by 1983, the government's control over housing transactions had ceased completely.[58]

Another important measure approved by the Revolutionary Council in the period of Bani-Sadr's presidency, was the land distribution bill in March 1980. The bill permitted the division of large estates, without compensation. However, the first draft of this bill provoked the stiff opposition of the prominent conservative ayatollahs, such as Qumi of Mashhad who condemned expropriation of private property as un-Islamic.[59] The council revised the law and, to appease the opposition of the conservative clergy, Khomeini asked ayatollahs Montazeri, Beheshti and Meshkini to judge whether the bill was according to Islamic law or not. They reviewed the bill and did not find anything un-Islamic in it. Nevertheless, they introduced minor changes to it. The bill approved the distribution of land to landless and land-poor peasants, high-school and agricultural-college graduates, civil servants and others who desired to cultivate the land. The size of each plot could not exceed three times the average that was considered enough in each district for the maintenance of one peasant family. Absentee landlords who had no other source of income were limited to twice this plot size. Mechanized farms were exempted from the break-up and were to join co-operatives. Landlords were to be compensated net of their debts to the government and outstanding religious dues. The distribution of land in the village was the responsibility of the seven-man local land transfer committees made up of government representatives, revolutionary agencies, the local religious judges and local villagers. These committees were authorized to determine the local ceiling on land-holding and to identify the properties that were to be distributed and those who were to receive land. Thirty-two of these committees took shape, confiscated cultivated land and transferred it to local peasants. In cases of dispute over the ownership of land, the committee temporarily solved the problem by leasing the disputed land to the peasants under rent or share-cropping contracts until the final owner could be determined.[60]

The committees presented themselves as the champions of the peasant cause. In response, the landlords became active, protesting against the work of the committees by lobbying members of parliament and religious leaders. They also managed to obtain some *fatvas* (formal religious proclamations) from cedrtain *mojtaheds* against land distribution. They even resorted to a *fatva* of Khomeini against the usurpation of private land. The formation and fate of the agricultural councils remain enigmatic. Even though they played an important role between 1979 and 1980, these organizations gradually withered away. Agricultural councils were organized by landlords in Teheran and other provinces according to the Revolutionary Council's law of April 1979 and protested actively while organizing campaigns against the land transfer committees.

In May 1980, an agricultural council published a resolution in which it drew the attention of the *mojtaheds* and Khomeini to the un-Islamic nature and the unconstitutionality of the denial of ownership and the violation of property rights. Ayatollah Golpayegani responded and formally declared the law un-Islamic. Ayatollah Rouhani sent a telegram to Bani-Sadr stating that the law was in gross violation of Islamic law and the Constitution and that it was not approved of by the newly created Guardianship Council. Others, such as ayatollahs Mahallati, Shirazi and Qumi, reiterated the same thing and, finally, the seminary teachers' society at Qum warned against bills that were presented in the name of Islam under the pretext of helping the oppressed and the ruinous effect of the land distribution law on agricultural output.[61] Finally, in November 1980, Khomeini ordered the suspension of articles 3 and 4 of the law concerning the distribution of private lands and, eventually, in 1981, left it to parliament to decide on land distribution and other property issues.[62] Peasants reacted in a defensive manner by sending their representatives and their petitions to parliament and the Teheran newspapers. Some of the clerics and members of the committees sided with them and accused the other clerics of being pro-landlord and following an 'American Islamic line'.[63] The dispute continued and the problem was left unresolved. After 1981, the struggle was mostly shifted to a debate among the members of parliament and Guardianship Council.

Islamization of the labour movement

If peasants veered towards a defensive struggle at the end of 1980, workers and salaried employees had been pushed in that direction after the first crackdown in August 1979. Workers and employees' organizations were steadily being purged of non-Islamic elements.[64] Workers were also threatened with the spectre of rising unemployment, as a result of the deteriorating economic situation. Nevertheless, after the fall of Bazargan's government, workers intensified their demands for control of the workplace and management. However, this new wave of struggle coincided with the intensification of the power struggle between Bani-Sadr and the clergy and later with the Iran-Iraq war. The clergy in the Islamic Republic Party and Prime Minister Rajaee transformed the *shuras* (councils) in to their own instruments in factories, offices and ministries. Gradually, Islamic associations were established in factories and governmental institutions and Islamic managers replaced the liberal managers of state-owned factories, most of whom had been appointed by the Bazargan government.

The clerics launched an anti-professional or anti-expert campaign, arguing that the country was in need of dedicated Islamic managers and not the western trained un-Islamic type of experts that Bani-Sadr supported. The political dispute which was being fought in the economic realm was gradually won by the clergy. Islamic associations and Islamic managers replaced the independent *shouras* and liberal managers. The major *shouras*, such as the *shouras* of the tool-making factories, Lift-Track, Pompiran and Kompidro in Tabriz, the Union of Workers' *shouras* of Gilan, the Union of Workers' *shouras* of western Teheran, *shouras* of the oil industry in Ahwaz and those of the railway workers were closed. Labour House, which was an independent headquarters for workers' assemblies, was turned into a centre for the pro-Islamic Republic *shouras* and Islamic associations.[65] In the same period, between August 1979 and the dismissal of Bani-Sadr in June 1981, labour unrest dropped mainly due to national campaigns of intimidation, repression and the cultural revolution, the forced establishment of the Islamic associations in factories and offices and the Iran-Iraq war. Labour's radical demands were reduced to immediate economic ones. No new labour law replaced the restrictive and undemocratic labour law of the *ancien régime* and even some of the perks of the profit-sharing scheme of the former régime were abolished.[66]

Foreign and domestic trade measures
In May 1980, the Revolutionary Council approved the implementation of a government monopoly over the importation of goods for which control was desirable. This was not really necessary, since a similar law had empowered the government with the same monopolistic right over foreign trade in 1930. However, the council, the left and the bazaar talked about the decision as if a new radical law had been approved.

Article 44 of the Constitution had explicitly stated that foreign trade was one of the activities of the state. The freeze on about $12 billion of Iranian assets, the trade sanctions against Iran by the US government during the hostage crisis and the subsequent rise in the prices of imported goods in the national market hastened the government's intervention in foreign trade. Nevertheless, the impracticality of complete nationalization of foreign trade in those days and the anticipated negative reaction of the merchants, who were regarded as an ally of the clergy, prevented the council from imposing a full government monopoly over foreign trade. Furthermore, the outbreak of war between Iraq and Iran, in September 1980, necessitated the extension of government control to domestic trade.

In 1980, the ministry of trade officially established a government monopoly over many imported goods, including machinery, metals, paper, wood, essential food and textiles. Thirteen procurement and distribution centres were set up to handle importation and domestic distribution of these goods. Very soon, these centres were handling 40 per cent of the value of imports.[67] Private traders could still import individually, but they were obliged to use a licensing system implemented by the *ancien régime*. However, since this type of activity was much more profitable than industrial activities, favouritism regarding the allocation of licences increased. Importers were also required to hand over 30 per cent of the volume of each consignment to the government and sell the goods at predetermined prices.

It is interesting to note that under the former régime, which was not known for its 'anti-capitalism', the government's share in the volume of total imports was 50.3 per cent. In the first four years of the revolution, this share dropped to 11 per cent,[68] mostly due to the decrease in government investment in those years. The size of the bureaucracy of the ministry of trade increased considerably, however.

The outbreak of war and the shortage of foreign exchange due to the decline in oil revenues forced the Islamic government to impose rationing on petrol and fuel. Bombing and shelling by Iraq destroyed 65 per cent of the Iranian refining capacity. Rationing was soon extended to essential goods, such as sugar, meat, vegetable oil and cloth. The Foundation for Economic Mobilization was established to administer the rationing and the local mosques distributed ration cards. This was one of the rare policies implemented by the Islamic régime that improved the distribution of essential goods.

In this period, the only notable economic measures that the Revolutionary Council passed in order to bring about 'fundamental changes in the economic and social system' were two abortive bills concerning rural land distribution and urban dwellings. Its performance was even more conservative than it had been during Bazargan's premiership. Nevertheless, the rhetoric used and the anarchy in decision making adversely affected the economic stability and confidence of businessmen and government managers. The rhetorical slogans were gradually abandoned as the period of full-fledged clerical rule imposing repressive political measures began in June 1981.

Foreign capital and the Islamic government

The Iranian revolution affected an important range of international economic relationships especially those between the United States and Iran. At the end of 1977, 315 companies with mixed ownership were operating in different branches of industry and 400 companies were officially trading. These were several joint-venture banks, associated mainly with US and Japanese banks and certain other commercial banks with mixed ownerships. Most of the major banks in the western world had some kind of presence in Iran. The government had large contracts and joint-venture agreements with foreign companies in small and big projects. Many of these investments were protected against nationalization and confiscation, according to the Law for Attraction and Protection of Foreign Investments that was passed in 1955. However, some investments were not registered and, therefore, were not covered by the law. Many Iranian companies were linked to foreign capital by agreements on licensing, supply and technical assistance. In 1977, the volume of US, Japanese, German and British investment in Iran was $700 million, $600 million, $220 million and $158 million, respectively.[69]

Most of the foreign exchange received from oil exports was spent on imports of primary, intermediate, capital and consumer goods that amounted to $18 billion in 1977. The major suppliers of these goods were West Germany, Japan and the United States. These countries were also the major investors in the Iranian economy. British and US banks held most of Iran's huge dollar deposits and were major lenders to Iran. The Iranian government had also granted loans and had invested abroad. In 1979, European and Asian countries owed Iran $7 billion. The United States was the main supplier of arms and military equipment and services. A large contract was concluded in 1971, amounting to $9 billion.[70]

After the revolution, the central banks in the major capital cities of the world, including the Federal Reserve Bank of New York, honoured payment instructions from the Central Bank of Iran and other western banks followed suit. However, some foreign economic contracts and agreements, such as the Consortium Agreement, were cancelled by the Iranian government. Some other contracts were hard to honour, under the circumstances, and others were not cancelled, but were officially stopped, such as the $9 billion contract for the purchase of armaments from the United States.[71] Foreign companies operating in Iran adopted a wait-and-see attitude. Iran honoured debt payments and the Law for Attraction and Protection of Foreign Investments was not rescinded. Nevertheless, the long-term security of such investments was uncertain. After the nationalization of all the private banking institutions and large industries, including those with mixed ownership, foreign owners started negotiations over compensation with the government authorities. The outcome of these negotiations has never been announced in Iran. However, considering the fact that trade between Iran and the rest of the world continues, the foreign owners of the nationalized banks and industries must have been compensated.[72]

Another major turning point in the strained economic relationship between Iran and the western world, particularly the United States, took place in the period after the occupation of the US embassy, in November 1978. In this period, the US government imposed its most comprehensive sanctions on a country in the twentieth century. A comprehensive trade embargo, banning the flow of physical goods between the United States and Iran, was imposed in April 1980. A ban on Iranian oil imports had been adopted immediately after the US embassy occupation in November 1979.[73] Before the embargo, Iran's oil exports to the United States had been 174,000 billion barrels per day (BPD) or only 5 per cent of total oil exports.[74] Every year, Iran was importing $2.7 billion worth of goods and services from the United States.[75] After April 1980, nearly all trade between the two countries stopped. The reaction of US allies to the US government's demand for the imposition of a similar embargo was not exactly wholehearted. In December 1979, these countries agreed to the following limited trade sanctions: a ban on military equipment sales to Iran (Iran bought military supplies on the black market at higher prices); a ban on paying premiums for Iranian oil (the increase to $45 per barrel made them reluctant to raise demands for this oil); a ban on opening new deposit facilities and a restriction on the increase in existing non-dollar balances, in order to reduce Iran's ability to transfer its revenues from dollar to non-dollar reserves and a ban on the extension of new credit (after the revolution no one was eager to grant any loans to Iran).

In order to prevent the development of a retaliatory mood, this agreement was not announced by US allies, but was, nevertheless, respected by them.[76] The whole plan only became public when the US government formally asked the reluctant European and Japanese governments to impose their own limited sanctions. Formally, they went along with the US decision to a limited extent.[77] The Iranian government had hoped they would not.[78] The effect on the Iranian economy of these trade sanctions was felt slowly, but surely. Initially, oil revenues did not drop, due to the increase in the price of oil. However, over time, oil revenues fell steadily, putting a strain on an economy much dependent on oil for its growth and development. Oil production, which was 3.1 million barrels per day (MBD) in 1979 declined to 1.5 MBD in 1980 and 1.3 MBD in 1981. Accordingly, government oil revenues decreased from 1,219.7 billion rials in 1979 to 888.8 billion rials in 1980 and increased to 937.9 billion rials in 1981.[79] The start of the Iran-Iraq war, in October 1980, undoubtedly exacerbated the situation. It forced the closure of some oil fields and facilities and scared-off prospective buyers. The combined effect of the sanctions and the war increased the cost of imports and changed import routes and foreign countries' shares in Iranian foreign trade. The largest Iranian port, Khoramshahr, was lost early in the Iran-Iraq war and this forced a rerouting of imports through overland routes via Turkey and the Soviet Union. In 1980, foreign-exchange shortages led to increases in barter trade with neighbouring countries like Turkey and Pakistan and the East bloc countries, especially the Soviet Union and

Bulgaria. North Korea became an important arms supplier to Iran and South Korea became the sixth-largest exporter to Iran in 1981. West Germany, Japan and the United Kingdom retained their share of Iran's foreign trade in 1980–1.[80] On the whole, in 1980–1, more than 50 per cent of Iran's imports was from the western European countries and Japan.[81]

By late autumn of 1980, the Iranian government was hard pressed for foreign exchange. Reserves were falling, due to the decline in oil revenues and non-oil exports and foreign military purchases were rising. The only source of relief was the unblocking of $12 billion of Iranian-government assets by the US government. In fact, the most effective US sanction was the financial freeze of the Iranian assets which was imposed on 14 November 1979. All holders of Iranian-government assets in the United States, or of those under the control of US entities overseas, were instructed to hold them as they then were. Any form of disposition was prohibited, unless permission was received from the US government. The blocked assets were held at the Federal Reserve Bank of New York ($2.358 billion), at overseas offices of US banks ($5.579 billion), at domestic branches of US banks (exclusive of accrued interest, $2.05 billion) and by US corporations and individuals ($2.1 billion).[82] These assets were owned or controlled mostly by the Central Bank of Iran and the National Iranian Oil Company. The US order, however, did not apply to the assets of private Iranian nationals and the former royal family. Most of the bank deposits were time deposits that could not be withdrawn immediately and could not be used as a means to threaten US financial institutions and the dollar. Nevertheless, an announcement by the then acting minister of foreign affairs and finance, Bani-Sadr, in which he declared the government's intention to transfer its dollar deposits from US banks to Europe, hastened the US government's decision to freeze assets.[83]

The nationalized Iranian banks owed the US banks about $800 million and the Iranian government's debt was more than $2.5 billion.[84] However, as far as the US banks were concerned many of them had sufficient deposits to cover their direct loan exposures to Iran. Citibank seized all Iranian assets in its possession to cover its exposure immediately after the imposition of the freeze. Some of these loans were syndications with other banks and Citibank angered members of the syndicate by not consulting them. Consultation is normal before any syndicated loan is declared to be in default. Regional US and European banks were upset because Citibank essentially held all the assets. The day after the Citibank seizure, the Central Bank of Iran notified Chase Manhattan that it was to draw on its accounts with several US banks in London to pay interest on a loan syndicated by Chase. Chase, however, did not comply due to the freeze and, therefore, the loan fell into default, since the interest payment was not made. In this case, the US banks in the syndicate (the majority) approved the action by Chase, while all non-US banks disapproved. However, the pattern was set and everything Iranian was taken by banks, corporations and individuals as protection for claims against Iran. They all went to court with claims against Iran and received orders attaching all the assets of Iran in the United States.[85] This meant that in case of a settlement, Iran had to go to court in the United States to lift the attachments and settle with the claimants. However, most banks did not have to worry about defaults because the existing syndicated loan convenants protected them.

The Islamic government's reaction to the freeze was to start litigation or demand the intervention of local banking authorities in Europe, with the aim of getting its assets back. However, it did not succeed in recovering the blocked overseas assets until the final settlement. The Islamic government also boycotted the dollar as a form of payment converting its dollar reserves to non-dollars. Since most of the Iranian reserves were held in time deposits, this policy was carried out gradually. In addition, the Iranian government tried to sell oil at premium prices to reduce European support for the US policy. In response to these actions, the US government stepped up its pressure by extending the trade sanctions. In January 1981, the final settlement was reached. The Islamic government reduced its original $24 billion claim ($14 billion in frozen assets and a $10 billion cash guarantee to insure the return of the Shah's wealth to Iran), to $9.5 billion.[86]

The transfer of assets to Iran was to take place in stages. Some $4 billion held in the United States was to be transferred to the Bank of England within six months. It was to be placed in a trust account to satisfy legal disputes with Iran which were to be settled by arbitration. Another $7.9 billion was transferred to an escrow account with the Algerian Central Bank. When the balance reached $7.9 billion, hostages were released and the money was transferred to an Iranian account. The $7.9 billion was divided as follows: $3.67 billion in outstanding syndicated loans with United States and foreign banks which was entirely paid off, much to the surprise of the US government; $1.42 billion which was put in an escrow account to be used to pay off Iran's debts to the US banks and $2.88 billion which was sent to Iran.[87]

According to the United States officials who were involved in the negotiations, 'the financial settlement overall and in historical perspective was favourable to the United States claimants against Iran'.[88] The banks were particularly satisfied with the settlement, since the Iranian loans were paid off, in full, immediately. As for the other US claimants against Iran, $4 billion was deposited in the escrow fund to provide security for arbitral awards to satisfy legal disputes with Iran. In fact, due to all the above payments to US claimants and other foreign banks and corporations, in 1981 the capital account of Iran's balance of payments was in the red by $5.184 billion. In 1981 and 1982, $6.295 billion was paid to foreign banks and companies.[89] As far as international arbitration is concerned, 4,000 US litigations, amounting to $15 billion and 470 Iranian litigations, amounting to $30 billion have been filed.[90] By September 1987, more than 3,800 litigations had been presented in the international court of The Hague, of which 905 were resolved by mutual agreement of the claimants or the verdict of the court. In these cases, the United States received $862 million (excluding interest payments to US banks) and Iran obtained only $41.3 million.[91]

In sum, during the hostage-crisis period, Iran suffered from its loss of access to about $12 billion in assets, it paid off its outstanding debts to the US banks and accepted a claim settlement procedure that favoured the claimants. The assets of the Shah and his family were not returned to Iran and the cost of imported goods greatly increased due to black-market purchases and the increased role of middlemen.

The clergy versus the clergy

After the dismissal of Bani-Sadr, the Islamic Republic Party (IRP), under the control of the clergy, emerged stronger than ever. In the second half of 1981, all the important governmental positions were either held by the clergy or their secular followers, representing different factions of the clerical leadership. To preserve its power, the clergy adopted heavily repressive measures. The Iran-Iraq war and the armed reaction of the Mojahedeen to the clergy's monopolistic rule provided the main excuses. Populist slogans concerning Islamic social justice were toned down for a relatively long period of time. A new mood of Islamic pragmatism set in, a pragmatism that did not mean civil and political liberalism or tolerance. It was a return to economic and administrative normality which was further manifested in a conditional reconciliation with Iran's European and Japanese trade partners.

Pragmatice clerical rule

By the end of 1982, the armed activities of the Mojahedeen and the Kurds had been curbed. Massive purges had been more or less completed. However, it became clear that even the supporters of the Islamic Republic had become exhausted by the scope and the intensity of the régime's violence and repression. Participation in the election of the second Assembly of Experts, which was to elect Khomeini's successor, was alarmingly low. Encouraged by the relative upturn in the level of economic activity in 1981–2 and the position of the Guardianship Council against any economic measures that tampered with the institution of private property and trade, representatives of the bazaar demanded more security and further expansion of private economic activity. The government was plagued by absence of discipline and unco-ordinated decision making in various institutions. The Hezbollah's intimidation campaign against experts had added to the paucity of trained technocrats, the majority of whom had emigrated. These conditions led to the remaining efficiency-conscious technocrats and government managers becoming demoralized. In December 1982, the ruling clerical coalition received an eight-point decree from Khomeini, ordering them to curb the excesses and semi-anarchy of the Islamic courts, committees and the IRG. The stated objective was to make people believe that they were 'under the protection of the laws of Islamic justice' and that 'their life, property and honour were secure'.[92] The decree ignored the subject of economic reforms and shelved any discussion of Islamic economic justice. Later, the revolutionary committees were placed under the ministry of the interior and the financial operations of the IRG became the responsibility of the newly created minister of the revolutionary guards. This move made both organizations more accountable to government and parliament, at least in terms of their budgets and programmes. Later, the purge committees in the government organizations and ministries were dissolved and the courts curbed their activities.

The eight-point decree strengthened the position of the pragmatic clergy and those government members who were conscious of the importance of rebuilding the crisis-ridden economy. The decree's emphasis on the security of property and social peace provided the pragmatists with a justification to call for an improvement in the Islamic Republic's relations with Europe and Japan. Teheran's empty hotels were gradually being filled with foreign businessmen and journalists. Nabavi, the minister of heavy industries and a former Islamic populist, reflected the new pragmatic mood. He criticized himself and others for being under the spell of the left in adhering to 'anti-dependency' and 'isolationist' economic policies, for underestimating the importance of managerial skills in factories and plants and for undermining the role of the private sector.[93] Hashemi-Rafsanjani, the powerful patron of the pragmatic faction, referred to those who had left the country and announced that 'people are prepared to forgive the fugitives' past record'.[94]

Cracks in the unity of the 'Government of God'

In February 1984, on the fifth anniversary of the revolution, Khomeini pointed out three crucial problems facing the Islamic Republic: the war with Iraq, the deepening of economic crisis and the rising and now open factional disputes among the ruling clerics.[95] All these problems had weakened the unity and stability of the Islamic régime. To solve the first problem, Khomeini stubbornly insisted on 'war, war, till victory'. He did not propose any concrete solutions for the second problem, but he did invite all factions to come to their senses and realize the threat their infighting posed to the preservation of the régime.

Historically, one can identify two principal factions with respect to economic issues: the interventionists and the non-interventionists. The advocates of intervention were of the opinion that the Islamic government should play a greater role in the market economy of Iran, in order to improve the economy's crisis-ridden performance. They argued for the preservation of the government sector, more government control over foreign trade, income policies, including price and wage control, and more government planning. They believed that 'traditional Islamic jurisprudence' was outdated and unable to provide all the answers to the complex problems of the present. Therefore, they insisted that the jurisconsult, in other words, Khomeini, should introduce new rulings or overrule former ones, as he saw fit. They referred to their ideal economic system as a 'mixed Islamic economy' and insisted that it was quite different from either capitalism or socialism.

The non-interventionist view was that: an unregulated 'Islamic' market economy, relying almost entirely on the private sector, could best achieve the goals of growth, employment, price stability and economic justice; government intervention should only be necessary under abnormal conditions as a temporary measure and minimal direct intervention should be the rule. They called for a strong Islamic government, but only in political and ideological areas. For them, the Islamic government should only supervise the functioning of the market, ensuring that Islamic economic regulations are observed and providing a stable and secure environment in which the private sector can function. They criticized the interventionists for ignorance of 'traditional jurisprudence' and for not adhering strongly enough to Islamic principles on the functioning of the economy. They called the other faction 'leftist', 'eclecticist' and 'statist'.

The interventionist faction argued that such an approach was at best naïve in face of war, deep recession and the existing profiteering attitude of merchants and traders. They dubbed the supporters of the non-interventionist view 'capitalist roaders' and 'reactionaries'.[96]

Hashemi-Rafsanjani, as speaker of parliament, acknowledged the existence of rival factions and summed up their differences in the following manner:

> Of course, in Iran, as in many other countries, there are disagreements. Specifically, there are now two relatively powerful factions in our country which disagree on how to run the government and on the role of state and private sectors. These two are present in the parliament and in the Cabinet. They are present among the clergy and even in the Islamic Republic Party. There are two approaches and two factions, always confronting each other, on the formation of the Cabinet, on the appointment of ministers and other authorities.[97]

Mir-Hossein Moussavi, who was prime minister from 1981–9, essentially represented the 'statist' faction. This faction claimed that it represented the general interest of the régime. While it called itself 'the protector of the three sectors',[98] that is the state, the co-operative and the private sectors, and reiterated that it was 'not against the growth of the private sector's investment', it criticized 'the excessive investment of the private sector in distributive and unnecessary middlemanship'.[99] It also found it necessary to impose some state control over the country's crisis-ridden war economy. It insisted that 'in this framework the government welcomes the co-operation of all the religious people of the bazaar for the realisation of the ideals and goals of the Islamic revolution'.[100] However, whenever the infighting intensified, some radical populists among the leadership raised the tone of their rhetoric which caused great concern among merchants and businessmen and widened the gap between the two factions.[101]

In 1982–3, Moussavi's cabinet consisted of a coalition of outspoken non-interventionist, pro-bazaar ministers and advocates of a mixed

Islamic economy. Following months of behind-the-scenes intra-government disputes, the cabinet was finally reshuffled in the summer of 1983 and two important pro-bazaar ministers (who presently contribute editorial articles to *Resalat*), Asgaroladi and Tavakoli, were dismissed.

There were two main reasons for the reshuffle: the heterogeneous character of the cabinet and the struggles arising from it and the people's dissatisfaction with the existing situation. Continued disregard for the demands of the poor, on the one hand, and the enrichment of merchants, on the other hand, was demoralizing Khomeini's poor followers.

The minister of labour, Tavakoli, and the minister of trade, Asgaroladi, became targets of criticism. Tavakoli was responsible for the dissolution of the workers' councils and suppression of workers' organizations. His proposed arch-reactionary Moslem Labour Law angered even the devoted followers of the Islamic Republic.[102] The minister of trade's nepotism and his 'sabotage' of the system of distribution of basic goods were disclosed and caused a tide of discontent.[103] The other ministers who were dropped, the minister of education and the minister of post, telegraph and telephone, had connections with the ultra-conservative *Hojatieh*, an Islamic secret society. However, some ministers who represented the contending faction within the government kept their posts.

The non-interventionist faction waited until early 1984 to attack the government. This time, the conflict shifted to parliament and spread to Friday congregational prayers and Islamic newspapers. In the debate over the government budget, the non-interventionist tendency criticized the wastefulness, inefficient policies and eclectic views of the Moussavi government. They blamed it for inflation and recession and the expanded bureaucracy. The government faction responded by accusing the Guardianship Council of being obstructive.

In autumn of 1985, the internal power struggle centred on the choice of a new prime minister and the issue was resolved by Khomeini's personal intervention in favour of Moussavi and against President Khamenei. This was an important boost for the interventionist faction. After Khomeini's endorsement of Moussavi, one of the deputies in the Moussavi faction declared that the 'Hezbollah became alive again' and another called the newspaper *Resalat* the paper of the 'bazaar merchants' and accused it of calling for the rehabilitation of rich people linked to the former régime.[104] The supporters of 'traditional jurisprudence', however, argued that:

> The great leader of the revolution, his excellency the Grand Ayatollah Montazeri and the President have many times stated that we should free the private sector so that Muslims are not in difficulties regarding their livelihoods. His excellency the Grand Ayatollah Golpayegani has told one of the government authorities to enrich all the people, not to make them all equal in poverty. The Government can be a good controller, but it is not a good merchant. When someone says let people earn their living [the government faction] responds by saying that you

are supporters of capitalism. Is it not true that the religious seminaries are supported by the money of those religious people and legitimate businesses?[105]

Khomeini's position on the issue of a mixed economy was more moderate than the interventionists. In a meeting with the president and Moussavi's cabinet, after reiterating the importance of Islamic unity, he said:

> Do not follow the policy of turning everything into state [control and ownership]. No, this has its limits . . . let people and the bazaar participate [in economic activity].[106]

However, much to his dislike, Khomeini was forced to take sides. More and more, on different occasions, he supported the Moussavi government.[107] Khomeini's conditional support can be explained by three principal considerations. Firstly, he wanted a strong and stable Islamic government and he found the views and policies of the interventionist faction better suited to the pursuit of a prolonged war with Iraq. In those days, the retention of nationalized industries, government control of the transportation services, distribution of basic necessities and control of foreign trade (considering Iran's current shortage of foreign currency) allowed for a more effective mobilization of resources for the war effort, which was very dear to Khomeini. Secondly, Khomeini had become apprehensive about the excessive demands of the merchants, their loyalty to his pan-Islamic objectives and their distaste for his political populism. Thirdly, to continue the war he had to be sensitive to the mood and morale of 'the downtrodden' who had become alarmingly disappointed with the ability of the Islamic government to solve the problems of inflation, unemployment, housing and so on. He would have preferred a peaceful coalition of the rival factions, an obedient clergy to act as the cadres of the state and an obedient bourgeoisie. However, given the way things had developed since the dismissal of Bani-Sadr, the realization of all those objectives had become exceedingly difficult.

It is interesting to note that the followers of 'traditional jurisprudence' took advantage of the religious nature of the state and reminded the interventionists that the government must obey the ordinances of the 'Imam' and 'traditional jurisprudence'. In November 1985, a member of parliament summed up the problem during the debate on the limits of the private sector's economic activity:

> We can not say we accept the governance of the jurisconsult while we differentiate between [Khomeini's] ordinances before and after the revolution. . . . This has to be done by the Imam himself and it is the Imam who must change his ordinances. As long as these ordinances [have not been changed], our responsibility is to obey them.[108]

Before Khomeini's ordinance of 7 December 1987, that reiterated his power to change his own ordinances in favour of new ones, the supporters of the Moussavi faction could only try to intimidate the others by accusing them of being 'employees of the Godless capitalists and millionaires'.[109] However, the prominent advocates of 'traditional juris-prudence' who considered themselves authorities on Islam were not intimidated by such name calling. For example, Khazali, an outspoken clergyman in the Guardianship Council and an appointee of Khomeini, in a speech for the bazaar supporters, reminded the other faction that they must follow the orthodox and conservative rulings of Khomeini in *Tahrir al-Vasileh*:

> I hereby announce that whenever the Guardianship Council rejects a bill passed by parliament, God is disapproving it and as long as you [deputies] have not submitted [to God's will], we [the Council] will not retreat. God's ordinances must be executed.[110]

Apparently, he was ignoring the fact that in the 'Government of God' interpreted by Khomeini, the grand jurisconsult could overrule the council when he found it necessary, despite his occasional support for the council. By late 1987, the council was taking its role all too seriously and its veto of important economic bills proposed by the 'statist' controlled parliament had made parliament look a barren institution in the eyes of the devoted followers of the Islamic Republic. A pro-Moussavi deputy explained the situation:

> Unfortunately the way things are going, Parliament will effectively loose its responsibility and will busy itself with petty chores. The Parliament has been effectively stripped of its prerogatives in policy making due to different interpretations and conceptions about the Constitution. . . . We must directly ask for the Imam's rulings on society's problems such as housing, pricing and the government's control and supervision.[111]

In fact, this was what the ministers of the Moussavi government started to do in late 1987. Their questions finally led to Khomeini's now famous reiteration of the idea of 'absolute power of the government of the Prophet of Allah' and to the curbing of the power of the Guardianship Council.

The enactment and rejection of major economic measures since 1981

In autumn 1981, the Islamic parliament was expected to discuss certain unresolved questions such as land reform, price control and nationaliza-tion of foreign trade. However, the interventionist faction of the Islamic Republic anticipated the opposition of the majority of the Guardianship Council and the other *mojtaheds* to those bills which entailed an expansionist role for the government in the economy. Thus, according to a prearranged procedure, in October 1981, Hashemi-Rafsanjani appealed to Khomeini to help parliament and government to solve the potential stalemate.[112] According to the Islamic Constitution, the council had the right to judge whether all 'civil, penal, financial, administrative, cultural, military, political and other laws and regulations' were based on the *Shari'a* or not. [113] To veto the council's decision, the parliament sought to obtain special religious powers not foreseen in the Constitution.

Khomeini's decree of 1981

In his letter to Khomeini, Rafsanjani asked him to exercise his unique authority as *Vali-e Faqih* in rulings where parliament did not have the authority to do so. Hashemi-Rafsanjani reiterated Khomeini's power to make decisions where 'overriding necessity' required them. The *Vali-e Faqih's* rulings in such situations were necessary because laws that tampered with the issues of property and freedom of trade were only within his authority. Non-compliance with the *faqih's* rulings in such cases was tantamount to religious disobedience to God's 'primary rulings'.[114]

According to this doctrine, the *faqih*, as the vicegerent of God and the Prophet, can offer rulings where decisions are required to protect the interests of the Islamic society. In response to Hashemi-Rafsanjani's appeal, Khomeini delegated part of his authority to the Islamic parliament, under certain conditions. He authorized their enactment of laws where 'overriding necessity' required them, on the condition that these laws be temporary in nature and that any officials who acted beyond their rights be punished. He later required a two-thirds majority in the parliament for such decisions and restricted them to 'secondary rulings'.[115] Khomeini, once again, avoided taking position on controversial issues, like land reform.

The advocates of a 'mixed economy' praised Khomeini's decree and thought that it would solve all the problems faced by parliament and government. However, practically all the major laws that were approved by parliament in the 1981–8 period were either rejected or modified considerably by the Guardianship Council. The council usually rejected or modified such laws for three general reasons: the laws were not really in response to 'overriding necessary conditions'; they were encroaching on the 'sphere of primary rulings' which did not come under parliament's authority and the laws had a universal bearing, whereas only a limited application was necessary. It is also worth noting that the council's reasons for rejecting these bills have not usually been announced in detail. One reason, according to Azari-Qumi, is that the *mojtaheds* of the council, like the *faqih*, 'do not have to provide any reason for their rulings'.[116]

The Guardianship Council uses Khomeini's decree against the interventionists

Two weeks after Khomeini's 1981 decree, the Guardianship Council rejected a bill approved by parliament. The bill was to postpone, for a year, the judicial eviction of tenants from rented houses and apartments. The council found the legislation contrary to the *Shari'a* and the Islamic Constitution. They had already opposed the government's control over the price of property and the forced rental of empty dwellings in June 1981.[117] In early 1982, parliament approved a bill on full nationalization of foreign trade. The bill made exports and imports of goods and services the monopoly of the government. This monopoly was to be established within five years. According to the bill, centres were to be set up for the import and export of goods, based on the nature of the goods involved. These centres were to control foreign trade under the supervision of the ministry of trade. The bill also provided for the establishment of centres for trade services that could buy the goods from foreign suppliers and control their transportation and wholesale distribution through public, private or co-operative distribution networks.[118]

When the first round of debates on the bill was taking place, Ayatollah Golpayegani sent a letter to members of parliament in oppostion to the bill. In this letter, he declared that monopolization of foreign trade was only legitimate in times of famine and emergency.[119] The response of the majority of deputies was that Article 44 of the Constitution approved the nationalization of foreign trade. However, the Guardianship Council immediately vetoed the bill, on the grounds that it was universal in scope and was, thus, contrary to the *Shari'a*'s rulings on free trade.[120] Since then, the government has not presented any other bill on foreign trade to parliament.

In 1985, according to the classification of imports by the ministry of trade, only fifty 'strategic goods', such as wheat, were imported solely by the government. About two hundred items previously imported by the government were now imported by the government and the private sector and the rest were left to the private sector. Non-oil exports, moreover, were mostly under the control of the private sector.[121] In May 1982, parliament passed another nationalization measure. It approved the nationalization of mines and placed the exploration and excavations of mines in the hands of government. This bill allowed private exploration and excavations of salt and construction materials, but explicitly outlawed private ownership of mines.[122]

The Guardianship Council refused to ratify the bill and sent it back to parliament for amendments. The important change demanded by the council concerned the exploration and excavation of mines in private lands and religious endowments. Parliament changed the relevant articles. However, the council rejected the bill again, twice demanding further changes that would increase the role of the private sector in government mining activities.[123] Finally, in 1985, the government presented a modified bill to parliament that allowed private partnership with government in mining activities. The share of the private sector in this partnership was to be up to 45 per cent.[124]

In May 1982, parliament extended the nationalization of urban dead lands (*mavat*) to *bayer* lands (lands once utilized). The ministry of housing was made responsible for the execution of the law. The Organization of Urban Lands was to buy the *bayer* lands from their owners and distribute the *mavat* and *bayer* lands among the applicants for construction of new dwellings. However, the Guardianship Council objected to all the articles that increased the role of the ministry of housing in the execution of the bill and reduced the rights of the owners of these lands, especially the beneficiaries of endowment lands.[125] By the end of 1984, the Organization of Urban Lands had nationalized 370 million square metres of land with compensation. However, less than one-seventh of it was resold, this was to 145,229 private applicants and 2,605 government institutions.[126]

In October 1982, President Kahmenei formally asked the opinion of the Guardianship Council about the interpretation of Article C of the Law for the Protection and Expansion of Iranian Industry, approved in 1979. This article did not clearly define the fate of the shareholders of industries that were indebted to the banking system. A board was set up to determine the shareholders' rights. Subsequently, the interpretation of the article proved to be controversial and became a source of dispute between the contending factions. The response of the Guardianship Council to the president's question was that the content of Article C of the law was not according to the *Shari'a*. Khamenei promptly stopped the activities of the board. This caused uproar in the interventionist faction and, finally, in 1984, the board resumed its work. However, this time, it had to have the approval of the council for all of its rulings.[127]

By March 1983, 580 large industrial establishments and mines were nationalized. The management of most of these units was divided between three ministries: the ministry of industry; the ministry of mines and metals; and the ministry of heavy industry.[128] All kinds of Islamic foundations created after the revolution were also controlling the management of the confiscated industries and mines. By 1985, for example, the Foundation for the Disinherited controlled 140 industrial units and 11 mines, with a labour force of 34,000. The Foundation of Martyrs owned 141 industrial, trading and service enterprises, with a labour force of 7,600.[129]

Every year, billions of rials worth of goods are declared abandoned since their owners, for different reasons, do not get them released from customs. In the summer of 1982, the government proposed a bill that would enable it to sell the abandoned goods and collect the proceeds. In July 1982, parliament authorized the government to establish a board comprising of representatives of different ministries and the general prosecutor's office for the execution of the bill. According to the bill, the board could administer the sale of these goods, giving priority to government institutions.[130] However, the Guardianship Council declared that according to the *Shari'a*, the government could not receive 'the proceeds from the sale of non-government goods'.[131]

Another bill that was rejected by the Guardianship Council dealt with the provision and distribution of certain necessities. According to the bill, certain essential goods were to be distributed under the supervision of the government.[132] The bill was rejected by the council, in May 1985, on the ground that it was not according to the *Shari'a* and the Constitution.[133]

Another sensitive issue of Islamic jurisprudence rose over a bill on direct taxes – income, inheritance and capital-gains taxes. The bill, which was presented to parliament in 1984, increased the share of business taxes in total direct taxes and imposed certain restrictions on tax avoidance. Encouraged by the Guardianship Council's successive vetoes of the economic bills, non-interventionist deputies opposed it on Islamic grounds. One of the deputies declared that parliament should not approve a bill that would obviously be rejected by the council. Another deputy stated that, if the government wanted to levy a tax on the basis of the *faqih's* order, it did not have to present the bill to parliament. Rabbani-Amlashi, a major conservative *mojtahed*, claimed that the bill was an imitation of western laws and, since taxes in Islam were limited to *khums* and zakat, the bill was un-Islamic.[134] Hashemi-Rafsanjani defended the bill and reiterated that there was no difference between the taxes discussed in the bill and *khums*. Hashemi-Rafsanjani added: 'those who do not pay taxes are just like those who don't pay *khums*'.[135] Based on Khomeini's rulings in *Tahrir al-Vasileh*, Azari-Qumi argued that any tax besides *khums* and zakat must meet the following criterion: it must prove that it is an 'overriding necessity'; it must be temporary and it must have the approval of a two-thirds majority of parliament.[136] The problem was left unresolved for a long time. In the meantime, the economic and financial committee of parliament asked Khomeini whether the Islamic government could levy taxes besides *khums* and zakat. Khomeini's answer was that the principle of taxation 'is part of the primary rulings' and, therefore, as in the case of a political ruling it was the prerogative of the Islamic government.[137] This verdict made the discussion of the bill in parliament possible and the bill was, finally, tabled before parliament in December 1987.

One of the most controversial measures in the Islamic Republic has been the abortive land reform bill. In the last ten years, several bills have been presented, debated on, partially implemented, delayed and, finally, rejected by the Guardianship Council. After Khomeini had delegated part of his power as the *faqih* to parliament in October 1981, the ministry of agriculture introduced an amended version of the suspended law of 1980 to Moussavi's cabinet. According to this bill, landlords could be compensated for the lands that were to be distributed. Fallow lands were also liable to distribution, if their owners did not cultivate them within a grace period. Since the cabinet could not reach a consensus, due to the active presence of the non-interventionists, the bill failed to attain sufficient support to be sent to parliament. This encouraged sixteen of the non-interventionist members of parliament to introduce a conservative bill before parliament. The sponsors of the bill tried 'to restore respect for legitimate private property' and justified their argument on the basis of Khomeini's ruling that legally acquired property must not be tampered with.[138] Thus, the bill allowed unlimited land-ownership, if the legitimacy of ownership could be established. The major criterion used for proving the legitimacy of ownership was the payment of Islamic dues and taxes by landlords. In March 1982, the Agricultural Committee of parliament amended certain points of the original bill, especially the point on the legitimacy of ownership, for which the size of the land became a criterion.

When the bill was presented to parliament, it was further watered down and then approved. The final version of the bill set an upper limit on arable landholdings for absentee and active landlords which was two and three times the size of an average local family farm, respectively. The excess land was to be leased to peasants under the traditional Islamic arrangements such as *muzara'a*, *ijara* and other Islamic partnership contracts. However, the bill allowed landlords to give priority in leasing land to their own children. Besides, mechanized farms, orchards, livestock and dairy farms were exempted from the bill and the owners of fallow land received a one-year grace period.

According to this bill, only 1 to 2 million hectares could be leased to peasants, rather than distributed. Nevertheless, the bill was dismissed by the Guardianship Council on the grounds that it was contrary to the *Shari'a* and the Constitution. In a rare detailed announcement, the council stated that 'considering all the articles, notes, stipulations and conditions, the whole scheme . . . is contrary to article 44 of the Constitution because it finally places agriculture under the domination of the government and since it leads to the domination of the Ministry of Agriculture over farmers, it is contrary to . . . the second article of the Constitution which negates any kind of domination'.[139] In addition, inasmuch as parliament had justified the implementation of the bill on the basis of Khomeini's decree of 1981, the council denied the relevance of the decree to the bill. It claimed that the objectives of agricultural self-reliance, elimination of poverty and scientific exploitation of land, as stated in the bill 'are not temporary necessities'.[140] The council ruled that in this case conditions of 'overriding necessity' did not exist, since the transfer of titles did not constitute a 'temporary remedy'.[141]

After the rejection of the law by the council, given the mood of moderation that was created following Khomeini's eight-point decree, some of the land transfer committees that were set up in 1979 to carry out land distribution in villages were liquidated. Encouraged by these events, religious courts favoured landlords in their rulings. However, peasants reacted, too, and, finally, the Supreme Judicial Council decided to stop the rulings of the courts against peasants who were cultivating the lands of the landlords provisionally.[142] In fact, 800,000 hectares of land were provisionally being cultivated by 120,000 peasant households, with the backing of the land transfer committees.[143]

Finally, in early 1985, parliament approved another bill that required landlords to cultivate, lease (on the basis of *muzara'a* or *ijara*) or sell their *bayer* (previously utilized) lands. Landlords had to choose one of the above alternatives, within one year. After that period, the land transfer committees could sell the land to peasants on behalf of landlords. According to the bill, those arable lands already distributed among villagers before 20 March 1980 and before 20 March 1984, in Kurdistan, for 'provisional cultivation', remained the property of the peasants who had received them. The landlords of these arable lands were to receive a 'just price' for their land. The rest of the arable lands that, at the time of the approval of the law, were under the control of their owners, could remain as the landlord's property.[144] The bill would have affected 800,000 hectares of disputed land had it been implemented.[145] However, the Guardianship Council vetoed the proposal and declared it contrary to the *Shari'a*. Then, in October 1986, the article of the bill about the transfer of lands with 'provisional cultivation' was approved by parliament in a joint session with the council. Such lands are now supposed to be transferred within three years. If the original owners of the land do not have any job other than farming, they can keep part of the land – three times the size of an average local family farm. If legitimacy of ownership is established, landlords can receive the price of the expropriated lands.[146]

The council's rejection of numerous economic measures did not imply its systematic aversion to economically related bills. For example, in January 1984, it approved a bill passed by parliament according to which all the religious land endowments that were distributed among peasants during the Shah's land reform were taken back. Peasants were to lease these lands from the Office of Endowments. This law affected 28,519 endowments, 6,989 farms and small villages and 6,082 parcels of land.[147] It was one of the rare examples of the Islamic Republic's 'efficiency' in the implementation of a law.

By 1988, 50,000 hectares of arable land had been confiscated and leased out to villagers. Furthermore, 600,000 hectares of dead land (*mavat*) and 150,000 hectares of barren land (*bayer*) had been distributed among villagers by the land transfer committees. The committees also transferred 60,000 hectares of barren land to government organizations. The agricultural corporations and co-operatives that were established during the Shah's land reform were liquidated and the original peasant owners of such lands received deeds to 515,000 hectares of land.[148] It it is worth noting that the Islamic Republic's land distribution schemes distributed far less land among peasants than the former régime had done in the 1960s.

Governmental ordinances: bypassing the Guardianship Council

In 1986 and 1987, price increases and shortages of many commodities intensified. The government was forced to impose control over the price of some goods and services. In the past, government attempts to impose controls over prices and the distribution of goods had been obstructed by the Guardianship Council. In the spring of 1987, the council had rejected a bill on 'the Provision and Distribution of Goods' and government itself withdrew its bill from parliament in despair.[149] In the summer of 1986, the council and the advocates of the non-interventionist view started a discussion about whether the concept of speculation and hoarding covered only 'date, wheat, barley, raisin and fat' or could also extend to other goods.[150] To bypass parliament and the council, the government addressed Khomeini directly, asking for a religious ruling on this matter. In the summer of 1987, Khomeini granted the government the right to execute the 'Law of Governmental Punishments' against speculation and hoarding and allowed the government to impose a limited price-control scheme over twenty-two commodities and to fine merchants and private and public enterprises or, in extreme cases, to nullify their work permits.[151] The government drafted a regulation for the implementation of the ordinance and engaged 12,000 officials for this purpose.[152] However, like other major government projects, Khomeini's ruling and the government's efforts to implement it gave rise only to populist phrasemongering, the expansion of bureaucracy and the spread of corruption, with little effective outcome.

The next round of disputes between the government and the council was also resolved by Khomeini's intervention. In October 1987, parliament sent a bill to the council concerning the government's ownership of oil wells. Knowing that years before the revolution, Khomeini had positively responded to the possibility of private use of oil wells, the council, for the first time, asked him directly about the possibility of government exploitation of oil wells on private lands. Khomeini responded by ruling that: 'the Islamic Government' can exploit oil on private properties, 'but must pay the rent of the land used or its price . . . to the owners of the property'.[153] In fact, this was a synthesis of the extreme positions of the two factions.

The point of greatest intensity in the economic dispute between the two factions was reached in December 1987. After several years of debate over the Islamic interpretation of labour codes in parliament and even within the government of Moussavi in 1982, parliament approved a labour law. The new law was similar to that of the former régime's. Nevertheless, it had to be justified within the framework of Islamic jurisprudence and there were articles of the law which could be problematic. One of the major articles provided an Islamic justification for government intervention in 'Islamic contracts' between employers and employees. It stated that, since the Islamic government provided private firms with services such as electricity, running water, foreign exchange and loans, it could bind the firms to observe regulations concerning insurance, minimum working age, hours of work and so on. The law justified these regulations by referring to the concept of 'obligatory conditions' in Islamic jurisprudence. The Guardianship Council found more than 100 articles of the 200 articles of the law un-Islamic and unconstitutional and rejected the law. The council's argument was strictly based on the *Shari'a* and scholastic arguments concerning 'Islamic contracts' between labourers and owners of means of production. It declared that such contracts were voluntary bonds between individuals and that a third partner, such as the government, had no right to impose conditions.[154] In the meantime, anticipating the council's argument and encouraged by Khomeini's recent ruling, the minister of labour sent a letter to the 'vicegerent of God', asking about the legitimacy of the 'obligatory conditions' specified in the labour law. Khomeini issued a religious ruling granting the government the right to legislate on such matters.[155] The council was faced with an embarrassing situation and sent a letter to Khomeini expressing its worries about the danger of un-Islamic interpretations of different forms of Islamic contracts. It noted that 'Islamic systems such as *muzara'a*, *ijara*, commerce and marriage [might] gradually be forbidden or reinterpreted and changed'.[156] It added that certain individuals and groups 'might take advantage of the ordinance for imposing [their ideal] socio-economic system'.[157] In addition, the council reminded Khomeini that the use of 'obligatory conditions' for the imposition of the 'universal' or general government policies was not Islamic. The reason provided was that, in such situations, 'people are rendered helpless (*muztarr*)' given that people have no choice but to use the monopolistic services provided to them by the government.[158] Khomeini angrily replied saying that: 'the Islamic government can receive the price of the services rendered . . . from the beneficiaries of services, in the form of Islamic conditions and even without conditions and that this is true in all cases that are within the government's jurisdiction.'[159] He also told the council to 'ignore the rumours spread by the . . . enemies of the Islamic Republic.'[160]

Naturally, the interventionist faction welcomed the 'Imam's commandments' with joy. Hashemi-Rafsanjani stated that Khomeini's 'word as the vice-gerent is the final word' and that:

> We must be obedient to the explicit views of the Imam and listen to him and . . . others [who] are experts. We must maintain our unity. . . . We must obey him and violation of this order is against piety, justice and is a great social sin.[161]

Moussavi called the 'Imam's' ordinances 'one of the fundamental pillars necessary for the realisation of the ideals of the Islamic Revolution'.[162] Some deputies and high-ranking officials called the new ordinances a revolution, solving all stalemates in the legislative and the executive.[163]

ıThe rival faction, however, tried to play down the importance of the rulings, by claiming that there was nothing new in them and that these ideas and concepts had been expressed by the 'imam' in his discussion in the *Islamic Government* in 1971. They went on as usual, debating the role of the government sector and criticizing its limitations and its inefficiency. Azari-Qumi, a professor at the Qum seminary and the founder of *Resalat*, continued his criticism of the government's excessive intervention in distributive and productive activities in a series of articles. He emphasized the conditional and temporary nature of the 'governmental ordinances' in *Shi'i* jurisprudence.[164] In contrast, Montazeri's reaction was conciliatory and he tried to calm the infighting. In his talk with the members of the Guardianship Council he advised them to take into consideration 'the realities' of the Islamic Republic and to adopt a pragmatic approach.[165]

To resolve the problem, Khomeini created a new institution, which was later incorporated into the Constitution, comprising the clerical members of the Guardianship Council, certain other ruling clerics and the prime minister.[166] This board is supposed to identify urgent matters of state and reduce the obstrucive role of the council. However, despite the rhetoric and promises concerning the end of the stalemate and the implementation of reforms and economic measures, no important break-through has occurred so far. Any one of the unresolved economic and political problems facing the Islamic Republic could start another internal crisis and intra-governmental conflict. Infighting has been endemic to the Islamic Republic in the process of its formation and establishment and it has its roots in the different politico-economic interests of the clergy and the realities of a crisis-ridden Iranian society. *Ad hoc* decision making and reaction to short-run economic events, political conflicts, rhetoric and phrasemongering, confusion and uncertainty and the existence of semi-anarchic decision-making centres prevented the implementation of a stable and consistent programme of economic reform betwen 1979 and 1989. Measures that have been implemented have not been sufficient or efficient enough to check the disastrous economic downturn which has characterized this period. In 1984, a clerical member of the second Islamic parliament summarized the fate of the economic institutions and policies of the Islamic Republic:

> Islam has a definite economic system [but] since it has not been fully compiled, everyone pulls it in a different direction according to taste.[167]

This situation has resulted in a severe and protracted economic crisis and a lower standard of living for the Iranian people.

Notes

1. Islamic Government, in *Writings and Declarations of Imam Khomeini*, translated and annotated by Hamid Algar (Berkeley: Mizan Press, 1981), p. 115. Hereafter cited as *Writings and Declarations*.
2. Ibid.
3. Ibid., p. 116.
4. Ibid.
5. Ibid.
6. Ibid., pp. 55–6.
7. Ibid., p. 55.
8. Ibid., p. 257.
9. Ibid.,
10. Ibid.
11. Ibid., p. 258.
12. Ibid., p. 244.
13. Ibid., pp. 252–3.
14. Shaul Bakhash, *The Reign of the Ayatollahs* (London: I. B. Tauris & Co. Ltd., 1985), p. 66. Hereafter cited as Bakhash.
15. Bank-e Markazi-e Jomhouri-e Islami-e Iran, *Barreci-e Eqtesadi-e Keshvar Ba'd az Enqelab* (Teheran, 1363), pp. 161–2 and 172. Hereafter cited as *Barreci-e Eqtesadi*.
16. *Keyhan*, 26 Farvardin, 1358.
17. *Barreci-e Eqtesadi, op. cit.*, pp. 394–5.
18. Assef Bayat, *Workers and Revolution in Iran* (London: Zed Books Ltd., 1987), pp. 103–6. Herafter cited as Bayat.
19. *Keyhan*, 26 Esfand, 1357.
20. *Keyhan,* 19 Ordibehesht, 1358 and *Kar*, 22 Mordad, 1359.

270 *The Secular Miracle*

21. *Barreci-e Eqtesadi, op. cit.,* p. 325.
22. *Kar*, 23 and 30 Farvardin, 1358.
23. Cited in Bahram Tehrani, *Pejooheshi dar Eqtesad-e Iran: 1354–64*, Vol. I (Paris: Khavaran, 1365), p. 454. Hereafter cited as *Tehrani*, Vol. I or Vol. II.
24. Tehrani, Vol., p. 457.
25. *Barreci-e Eqtesadi, op. cit.,* pp. 73–4. See also *Keyhan*, 26 Khordad, 1358.
26. *Keyhan*, 6 Ordibehesht, 1358 and *Barreci-e Eqtesadi, op. cit.,* pp. 162–3.
27. *Barreci-e Eqtesadi, op. cit.,* pp. 197–8.
28. *Keyhan*, 18 Khordad, 1358.
29. *Barreci-e Eqtesadi, op. cit.,* pp. 393–403.
30. Tehrani, Vol. II, *op. cit.,* p. 427.
31. *Keyhan*, 14 Tir, 1358.
32. *Keyhan.,*16 Tir, 1358.
33. Tehrani, Vol. II, *op. cit.,* pp. 456–62.
34. *Ettelaat*, 12 Esfand, 1357 and *Keyhan*, 26 Farvardin, 1358.
35. *Kar*, 18 Tir, 1359, *Keyhan*, 20 Mordad, 1358 and 4 Day, 1358.
36. *Kar*, 15 Esfand, 1358.
37. *Keyhan*, 24 Shahrivar, 1358.
38. Abol-Hassan Bani-Sadr, *Eqtesad-e Towhidi* (n.p., 1357), p. 113.
39. Ibid, p. 114.
40. See Ibid, pp. 132–4 and 50–1.
41. *Keyhan*, 27 Bahman, 1358.
42. *Keyhan*, 30 Farvardin, 1358.
43. Ibid.
44. Ibid.
45. *Writings and Declarations, op. cit.,* p. 290.
46. Ibid.
47. *Keyhan*, 16 Aban, 1358.
48. Ibid.
49. *The Constitution, op. cit.,* Article 43.
50. Ibid., Article 44.
51. Ibid.
52. Ibid.
53. Ibid.
54. Ibid., Article 4.
55. Ibid.
56. Ibid., Article 49.
57. *Barreci-e Eqtesadi, op. cit.,* p. 190.
58. Ibid.
59. *Kar*, 8 Mordad, 1359 and Bakhash, *op. cit.* p. 194.
60. *Barreci-e Eqtesadi, op. cit.,* pp. 29 and 44–6, *Kar*, 27 Esfand, 1359 and 21 Mordad, 1360.
61. *Kar*, 29 Esfand, 1358 and Bakhash, *op. cit.,* p. 204.
62. *Kar*, 12 Azar, 1359.
63. *Kar*, 6 and 13 Esfand, 1359.
64. *Kar*, 19 Azar, 1359.
65. Bayat, *op. cit.,* p. 102.
66. Ibid., pp. 107–9.
67. Bakhash, *op. cit.,* p. 193.
68. Tehrani, Vol. II., *op. cit.,* p. 363.
69. *Keyhan*, 16 Tir, 1358.
70. *Keyhan,* 19 Mehr, 1358.
71. *Keyhan,* 10 Ordibehesht, 1358.
72. Tehrani, Vol. I., *op. cit.,* pp. 301–5.
73. Warren Christopher, *et al, American Hostages in Iran* (New Haven: Yale University Press, 1985), p. 354. Hereafter cited as Christopher.
74. *Keyhan*, 13 Aban, 1358.
75. *Keyhan*, 19 Farvardin, 1359.

76. Christopher, *op. cit.*, p. 195.
77. Ibid., pp. 140–1 and 153–4.
78. *Keyhan*, 21 and 23 Farvardin, 1359.
79. Tehrani, Vol. I., *op. cit.*, pp. 62–3.
80. Tehrani, Vol. II, pp. 338–54.
81. Ibid., pp. 340–1.
82. Christopher, *op. cit.*, p. 205.
83. Christopher, *op. cit.*, pp. 176–7 and *Keyhan*, 24 Aban, 1358.
84. *Keyhan*, 19 Farvardin, 1359.
85. Christopher, *op. cit.*, pp. 192–3.
86. Ibid., p. 310.
87. Ibid., p. 228.
88. Ibid., p. 231.
89. Tehrani, Vol. I, *op. cit.*, p. 298.
90. *Keyhan*, 29 Ordibehesht, 1963.
91. *Sana'te Haml-oNaghl*, Khordad, 1367.
92. *Keyhan*, 25 Aban, 1361.
93. *Ettelaat*, 22 Farvardin, 1364.
94. Cited in Bakhash, *op. cit.*, p. 231.
95. *Keyhan*, 23 Bahman, 1363.
96. See for example *Jomhouri-e Islami* 20 and 29 Aban, 1364, *Resalat*, 19 Ordibehesht, 1367 and *Keyhan*, 9 Esfand, 1366.
97. Cited in *Fadai*, Tir, 1365.
98. *Ettelaat*, 7 Azar, 1363.
99. *Ettelaat*, 4 Day, 1363.
100. *Ettelaat*, 7 Azar, 1363.
101. See for example the populist statements of Khoainiha in *Keyhan*, 27 Day, 1364.
102. *Kar*, 9 Day, 1360 and *Bulletin-e Siyasi* (*Fadaian*), 17 Shahrivar, 1361.
103. *Kar*, 22 Ordibehesht, 1361.
104. *Jomhouri-e Islami*, 20 and 29 Aban, 1364.
105. *Jomhouri-e Islami*, 14 Day, 1364.
106. *Keyhan*, 11 Aban. 1364.
107. See for example *Jomhouri-e Islami*, 10 Khordad, 1363 and *Keyhan*, 3 Day, 1366.
108. *Keyhan,* (airmail weekly), 6 Azar, 1364.
109. Ibid.
110. *Resalat*, 27 Khordad, 1366.
111. *Keyhan*, 16 Khordad, 1366.
112. *Keyhan*, 20 Ahan, 1360.
113. Constitution, *op. cit.*, Article 4.
114. Primary rulings, principles or laws are the *Sharia's* immutable principles. In *Shi'i* Islam, the institution of the rule of vicegerent of the Prophet is one of these principles. Secondary rulings are applicable to cases where 'necessity' temporarily requires them.
115. *Keyhan*, 20 Aban, 1360.
116. *Resalat*, 29 Shahrivar, 1366.
117. *Kar*, 4 Azar, 1360.
118. *Kar,* 29 Ordibehesht, 1361.
119. *Kar*, 19 Khordad, 1361.
120. Ibid.
121. *Ettelaat*, 21 Ordibehesht, 1364.
122. *Kar*, 5 Khordad, 1361.
123. *Bulletin-e Siyasi* (*Fadaian*), 6 Esfand, 1361 and *Ettelaat*, 18 Ordibehesht, 1364.
124. *Ettelaat*, 1 Tir, 1364.
125. *Bulletin-e Siyasi* (*Fadaian*), 15 Day, 1361 and *Ettelaat*, 20 Day, 1363.
126. Ibid.
127. Tehrani, Vol. II, *op. cit.*, pp. 431–2.
128. *Barreci-e Eqtesadi*, *op. cit.*, p. 166.

129. *Keyhan*, 14 and 15 Esfand, 1364.
130. *Keyhan*, 28 Tir, 1361.
131. *Keyhan*, 29 Tir, 1361.
132. *Ettelaat*, 22 Farvardin, 1364.
133. *Ettelaat*, 17 Ordibehesht, 1364.
134. *Ettelaat*, 29 Azar, 1363.
135. *Ettelaat*, 25 Day, 1363.
136. *Ettelaat*, 29 Azar, 1363.
137. *Keyhan*, 4 Bahman, 1366.
138. *Ettelaat*, 1 Azar, 1361.
139. *Ettelaat*, 29 Day, 1361.
140. Ibid.
141. Ibid.
142. The agricultural contracts for the cultivation of these lands are renewed annually by the land transfer committees.
143. *Keyhan*, 24 Farvardin, 1367.
144. *Ettelaat*, 25 and 29 Ordibehesht, 1364.
145. *Keyhan*, 24 Farvardin, 1367.
146. *Keyhan*, 9 Aban, 1365.
147. *Ettelaat*, 23 Ordibehesht, 1363.
148. *Keyhan*, 13 Day, 1359 and 24 Farvardin, 1367. In 1982, total land under cultivation was about 9 million hectares.
149. *Keyhan*, 26 Farvardin, 1366.
150. *Keyhan*, 12 Mordad, 1365.
151. *Keyhan*, 13 Mordad, 1366.
152. *Keyhan*, 20 Mordad, 1366.
153. *Keyhan*, 4 Aban, 1366.
154. *Keyhan*, 16 Day, 1366.
155. *Keyhan*, 17 Day, 1366.
156. *Keyhan*, 19 Day, 1366.
157. Ibid.
158. *Keyhan*, 23 Day, 1366.
159. Ibid.
160. Ibid.
161. *Keyhan*, 5 Day, 1366.
162. *Keyhan*, 6 Day, 1366.
163. *Keyhan*, 17 Day, 1366.
164. *Keyhan*, 15 Day, 1366.
165. *Keyhan*, 19 Day, 1366.
166. *Resalat*, 18 Bahman, 1366.
167. *Keyhan*, 30 Aban, 1363.

7. Post-Revolution Economic Structure, Institutions and Performance

The economic structure and institutions in the Islamic Republic

The present economic structure and its institutions provide the framework within which business, labour, peasants, farmers and the government operate. They are the end product of many years' evolution and, to some extent, of the institutional changes since the revolution.

Population structure
According to the population census, in 1986 Iran had a population of 49.8 million, compared with 33.7 million in 1976. The rate of population growth in 1976-86 was, on average, 3.55 per cent per annum, compared with 3 per cent in 1966-76, which is one of the highest rates in the world. This rate, however, included 2.6 million refugees and their offspring from Iraq and especially Afghanistan, in the past nine years.[1] Iran's rapid demographic growth was due to a high birthrate and decreasing deathrate. This combination produced a very youthful population, 45 per cent being under 15 years of age (half of which are under 6), about 50 per cent being between 15 and 65 and less than 5 per cent being over 65.[2] With such an age structure, the proportion of youth (under 10 years of age) to economically active adults was high. In 1986, 11.1 million, or 22.3 per cent of the population, were employed (this figure includes those employed in the armed forces, IRG and the war draftees). This work-force had to support the rest of the population. Of the labour force, 20 per cent consisted of women, mostly employed in civil services. The high percentage of young people and the restricted role of women in economic activity kept the ratio of the sum of the employed and unemployed labour force over 10 years of age to total population at the low level of 26 per cent.

In 1986, about two out of nine people were employed. In every nine households, averaging 5.1 people, only ten people were employed.[3] Considering that the economy has been in crisis since 1976 and the proportion of dependent population has increased in the last decade it will be more difficult for those who are working to support those who are not. This is a handicap that will not be overcome easily. Nevertheless, before the cease-fire the reaction of the authorities of the Islamic Republic to these facts was amazingly militaristic: more people meant that more could be mobilized for the war effort. The response of the prime minister to the latest census data was that with more people the Islamic Republic would 'have one of the most important weapons' and the president boasted about 'the army of 30 million'.[4]

Of the population of 49.8 million, 17.5 per cent resided in the province of Teheran, of which more than 6 million lived in the city of Teheran. The same province, excluding the city of Teheran, had the highest growth rate of population due to the high level of migration into the province, which was 8.7 per cent anually in 1986. The share of the urban population, that is those who lived in towns with more than 5,000 inhabitants, in the total rose from 47.2 per cent in 1976 to 54.2 in 1986. However, 36.2 per cent of the population resided in 40 cities with a population of more than 100,000. A recorded 73.1 per cent of the population over 6 years of age in urban areas and 48.2 per cent of the population in rural areas was considered literate and 1.6 million households had only one literate person.[5]

The labour force, its welfare and its institutions
The 11.1 million people who were considered as employed in the 1986 population census were members of 5.6 million urban households and 4.2 million rural households.[6] The breakdown of the employed labour force indicates a relative decline in agricultural and industrial employment and a very rapid growth in the service-oriented work-force. The rapid increase in the labour force occupied in services is mainly due to the prolonged economic crisis that has pushed the work-force to less productive employment. In 1986, the employed labour force was distributed in different economic sectors as follows: 30 per cent in agriculture, 26.5 per cent in industry and 43.5 per cent in services (see Table 1). In the urban community, 56.5 per cent of the employed work-force was in the private sector and 43.5 per cent in the public sector. In the rural community 82 per cent was employed in the private sector and 18 per cent in the public sector.[7]

The spectre of cyclical unemployment haunts the employed labour force, especially the semi-skilled and unskilled, the young and women. In 1982, the skilled labour force, such as engineers, medical personnel, teachers, economists, lawyers and technicians, accounted for only 7.4 per cent of the employed labour force which is less than the pre-revolution figure. The situation is not improving. In 1985, the number of students in vocational training and higher education was about 330,000, compared with 452,400 in 1976.[8] In 1984, 65,133 Iranian students were studying abroad, 45 per cent of them in the United States. Only about 5 per cent of the students studying abroad have returned to Iran each year, which is lower than the pre-revolution rate.[9]

Table 1
Active labour force in different economic sectors

	1959		1977		1986
	(1,000s)	**(%)**	**(1,000s)**	**(%)**	**(%)**
Agriculture	3,280	52.0	2,966	32.1	30.0
Industries and mines	1,317	20.9	3,085	33.4	) 26.5
Oil and gas	30	0.5	56	0.6	)
Services	1,502	23.8	2,867	31.0	43.5
Employed population	6,129	97.2	8,974	97.1	
Unemployed population	179	2.8	270	2.9	
Active population	6,308	100.0	9,244	100.0	

Sources: Bank-e Markazi-e Iran, *Hesabhay-e Melli-e Iran: 1338–56* (Teheran, 1360) and *Keyhan*, 28 Khordad, 1367.

In 1982, 4.34 million urban households lived in 3.17 million residential units.[10] The shortage of housing has been estimated at 2.5 million dwellings, which means that about 2.5 million households, mostly residing in urban areas, with 700,000 of them in Teheran, do not own a housing unit. Of these families 90 per cent are living in rented residential units.[11] In 1976, 9.7 per cent of dwelling units in urban areas and 78.5 per cent of dwellings in rural areas were without tap water and 9.8 per cent and 85.8 per cent of them, respectively, were without electricity.[12]

In 1981, 3.5 per cent of the employed labour force benefited from retirement pay, compared with 45 per cent in West Germany and 20 per cent in the United States. At present, 2.5 million wage-earners and civil servants and 8.5 million of their relatives are insured. Of 2.5 million insured employees, only 125,00 are women and more than 1.8 million of them work in the private sector. The social security system is not something that was established during the Islamic Republic period; the whole scheme was put into effect in the mid-1970s. The social security scheme covers accidents and sickness, disability, retirement, and death, pregnancy and family allowances. Most of those covered by social security schemes contribute insurance premiums, representing 27 per cent of their salary –20 per cent paid by the employer and 7 per cent by the employees – and the rest contribute premiums representing 18 per cent of their salary –13 per cent paid by the employer and 5 per cent by the employees. Only a few thousand are voluntarily insured for social security benefits.[13] There are various organizations that to some extent help the needy, orphans, the old and the disabled. The Foundation for the Refugees of the Imposed War takes care of the Iran-Iraq war refugees.[14]

Unemployment benefit did not exist in Iran before 1987. In July 1987, in response to the rising rate of unemployment, the Unemployment Benefit Act was approved by parliament. According to the act, workers who lose their employment and report their unemployment within fifteen days of the day of unemployment can ask for unemployment benefits, provided that they have paid unemployment premiums for six months prior to their lay-off. They are entitled to a benefit corresponding to the minimum wage for a period of one year for single workers and two years for married workers (the present minimum wage is 760 rials per day).[15] However, given the conditions attached to payment of unemployment benefits, the majority of the labour force will not qualify for the benefits for a long time. A further problem arises from the shortage of health services and institutions and the small number of medical personnel. In 1984, 501 hospitals (387 public and 114 private) had 70,152 beds, which meant one bed for about every 650 people.[16]

In 1981, there was one physician for every 2,554 people and one dentist for every 17,485 people.[17] In addition, hospital facilities and medical people are mostly concentrated in big cities, especially in Teheran. In 1984, 34.2 per cent of the hospital beds were in Teheran province which accounted for only 16 per cent of the total population.[18]

Despite the long history of labour union movements in Iran and labour's relatively significant proportion in the labour force since the 1960s, labour does not have its independent union. Anti-labour and anti-union policies implemented by the Iranian governments since the Constitutional Revolution of 1906, along with the peasant origin of a high portion of workers and their youth, have adversely affected the continuity and militancy of the union movement. The main feature of the Iranian working class is that it is based on migration, especially migration to Teheran Province and that most workers are young. In addition, a relatively important proportion of workers is employed in traditional small industries.[19] At present, the only organizations allowed are the state-run Islamic labour councils and Islamic societies. All the non-Islamic unions and councils which were created by workers before and immediately after the revolution have been banned and liquidated.

Islamic associations were established under the auspices of the clergy after the revolution. Their main function was to intimidate and suppress any non-Islamic tendencies in factories, offices and the other institutions and to consolidate the clergy's power. Once full-fledged clerical rule was established, the power of these associations to interfere in the affairs of managers and administrators of factories and governmental departments was curbed. Islamic labour councils gradually substituted for the workers' councils that were set up during the revolutionary period and after February 1979. However, their legal status was finally approved by the Islamic parliament in 1984. These councils include 'representatives' of the workers, other employees and management, but only have consultative function with regard to management of the factories, wages, working hours and so on.

After five years of disputes between the two major factions in the Islamic parliament, the Islamic Labour Law was approved in November 1987. As we have seen, the law was vetoed by the Guardianship Council, but Khomeini overruled the council's decision. According to the law, workers are denied the right to join any unions except the Islamic labour

Table 2
Gross domestic expenditure in current prices (1984) (Billions of rials)

Private consumption expenditure	8,129.6
Government consumption expenditure	2,143.0
Gross fixed capital formation	2,884.1
Private	(1,816.2)
Government	(867.9)
Increase in stocks	1,929.0
Net exports of goods and services	–37.0
Statistical discrepancies	–19.1
Gross domestic expenditure	15,029.6

Source: Vezarat-e Barnameh va Budgeh, *Faslnameh-e Amari: 1364* (Teheran, 1365).

councils. They do not have the right to strike either. The law prohibits the employment of persons under 15 years of age and the employment of female workers for night shifts. Working hours are set at 44 per 6-day week and 7 hours 20 minutes per day for adult workers. Young workers between 15 and 18 years of age, and those employed for hard work, work 38 hours a week. Per day, 40 minutes is allowed for meals and religious rituals. The law stipulates 30 days of annual leave and the reinstatement of sacked workers, if they are acquitted by the appropriate courts. It also provides for a sliding scale of wages, according to the official rate of inflation. In order to enforce the articles of the law, the government can impose fines and compulsory conditions on the employees, in exchange for providing them with basic services and utilities.[20] The Islamic Law is not much different from the Labour Law of 1959 of the former régime, except there are some improvements in the provisions for paid leave and the reinstatement of sacked workers and there are some restrictions imposed on women's work and the weekly working hours. The Islamic Law, like its predecessor, applies only to large workshops which employ ten or more workers in the urban areas.

Resource allocation by private firms and government

The government has played an important role in the economy of Iran since the 1930s. Nevertheless, the share of the private sector in economic activities has been substantial. This is in spite of the relative insecurity of private ownership of the means of production, which has been an important feature of the pre-capitalist and capitalist economic history of Iran.[21] The private sector's share of aggregate demand exceeds that of the government. In 1984, the latest year for which national income accounts are available, private consumption of goods and services accounted for 54.1 per cent of nominal Gross National Expenditure. The private sector's demand for investment goods – inventories and fixed investment in plants, equipment and residential construction – made up 12.1 per cent of nominal GNE. In the same year, the government's consumption of goods and services constituted 14.3 per cent and government goods made up 7 per cent of nominal GNE (see Table 2).

According to official statistics, in the first four years after the revolution, the private sector and the government's shares in the total value of imports were 59 and 41 per cent, respectively, compared with 49.7 and 50.3 per cent in the last four years of the former régime.[22] The government share in foreign trade may have increased in the past five years. However, inasmuch as the private sector controls non-oil exports and the value of this category has increased since 1983, the role of the private sector in foreign trade is still considerable. The government share of aggregate supply has increased since 1979, due to nationalization and confiscation of industries and farms once owned by the royal family and business people closely associated with the former régime. In 1986, 68.4 per cent of the employed population were working in the private sector and the rest in the public sector.[23]

In the 1984 industrial sector, 6,596 workshops were active. They were considered as 'large' enterprises because each one of them employed more than 10 people.[24] However, the majority of these 'large' enterprises were actually quite small. Of 6,596 large enterprises, 2,939 had fewer than 20 employees, 757 had between 20 and 29 employees and 815 had between 30 and 49 employees. Thus, 68.5 per cent of the large enterprises employed fewer than 50 people. Only 4.3 per cent of these establishments (285 units) employed more than 500 people, 11.1 per cent (735 units) had between 100 and 499 employees and 16.1 per cent (1,065) had between 50 and 99 employees.[25]

Large enterprises employed 593,000 people, of whom 519,000 were wage-earners and 75,000 were salary-earners. Only 6.2 per cent, or 37,000, of the labour force in large enterprises were women, compared with 6.8 per cent in 1976.[26] Teheran Province alone accounted for 43.7 per cent of the value added produced by large enterprises. The same province employed 39.7 per cent of the large enterprises' labour force.[27] In 1983, 986 industrial establishments (excluding the oil and gas industries) were owned by the Islamic government. These enterprises produced 68.8 per cent of the value added, employed 67.2 per cent of the employees and provided for 55.5 per cent of the wage and salary payments of large enterprises.[28] The very large enterprises made up the modern industrial sector of the economy. Most were established before the revolution, mainly through licensing agreements and, to some extent, through foreign investment.

Due to the nature of licensing agreements and direct foreign investment in the pre-revolution period, on the one hand, and the weak inter-sector and intra-industry linkages and the continuation of the industrial strategy of the former régime by the Islamic government, on the other hand, a large portion of industrial inputs was imported. In 1984, 53.9 per cent of the input used in large enterprises was imported. The dependence of the heavy engineering, light engineering and chemical industries on imported input was the heaviest. The same industries imported 73.4, 73.1 and 63.5 per cent of their input, respectively.[29] These rates are higher than the pre-revolution rates.

Of large enterprises, 31 per cent (2,060 units) were considered sole proprietorships, 39 per cent (2,543 units) as registered partnerships, 27 per cent (1,796 units) were operating as unregistered partnerships and 3 per cent (197 units) as co-operatives.[30] The figure for small enterprises (employing less than 10 people) in urban areas after the revolution is not available. However, in 1976 there were about 330,000 small industrial workshops, employing about 630,000 mostly unpaid family workers, producing a variety of traditional items, such as woven goods and floor coverings. Value added generated by small enterprises came to 28 per cent of the value added generated by large enterprises.[31] Most of these workshops used primitive technology and, therefore, had a very low productivity rate.

The service sector, private and public, modern and traditional, grew to be the largest economic sector in the Islamic Republic era. In 1984, it accounted for about 55 per cent of the constant Gross Domestic Product and about 45 per cent of the labour force, compared with 31 per cent in 1977 (see Tables 1 and 3).

In 1984, public services accounted for 13.8 per cent of the total value added of the services sector, compared with 17.9 per cent in 1977. In fact, the value of the public services in constant rials has declined since 1979 (see Table 3). The private sector in services, mainly trade, absorbs a major part of the Iranian liquidity (money and quasi-money) which itself has been unprecedentedly high in the past nine years. In 1984, the value added of trade, property and personal services constituted 32.3 per cent of the current GDP. According to the minister of planning and budget, 90 per cent of this value added was profit.[32] In other words 29.2 per cent of the curent GDP was the profit accumulated by a very small portion of the population engaged in three subsectors of the services group. In the same year, the value added from oil, gas and manufacturing made up 10.3 per cent and 17.4 per cent of the current GDP, respectively.[33]

Despite the expansion of the Islamic government's role in domestic trade, the private-sector's role prevails in services. After the revolution, the government's role in domestic trade expanded in reaction to the US embargo of 1980 and the disrupting effect of the Iran-Iraq war in September 1980, which gave rise to shortages of foreign-exchange reserves, shortages of imported commodities, rising prices and hoarding. However, the government expanded its role in domestic trade, mainly by supervising the distributuion of staple commodities through a limited number of co-operatives and procurement and distribution centres. Coupon rationing was imposed on five commodities: sugar, rice, ghee, meat and kerosene. Chicken, eggs, butter, cheese, detergent materials, soap and petrol and bottled natural gas have all been rationed at times. As one would expect, a thriving black market has developed. The Islamic government has allowed this market to flourish and, in fact, part of it is an 'official' black market, sanctioning a system which supplies high-income groups with goods unavailable to the rest of the population and which reduces the supply of goods in the officially rationed market. Thus,

Table 3
Gross domestic product in constant 1974 prices (Billions of rials)

	1959	1977	1978	1979	1980	1981	1982	1983	1984
Agriculture	161.0	340.9	352.6	356.3	362.9	404.0	436.0	429.0	446.7
Oil and gas	264.7	1,363.4	929.8	767.6	330.5	273.6	526.8	531.1	452.5
Industries and mines	53.4	645.6	553.9	511.9	520.2	534.5	590.7	683.1	705.1
Services	192.3	1,753.8	1,620.4	1,560.7	1,475.6	1,504.1	1,546.2	1,833.7	1,871.8
(Trade, restaurants and hotels)	(73.4)	(486.3)	(420.1)	(345)	(310.5)	(436.5)	(487.3)	(725.3)	(747.4)
(Real estate and business services)	(39.3)	(350.9)	(308.4)	(241.8)	(287.5)	(310)	(335)	(359.1)	(376)
(Public services)	(24.1)	(313)	(354.1)	(463.8)	(309.8)	(279.9)	(292.9)	(281.2)	(257.6)
Less: Imputed bank service charge	5.7	181.4	189.8	126.0	121.2	76.8	59.4	59.1	54.8
Gross domestic product	665.7	3,922.3	3,266.9	3,070.5	2,568.0	2,639.4	3,040.3	3,417.8	3,421.3
Per capita GDP (1000 rials)	31.4	112.97	91.32	83.25	67.53	67.31	75.17	81.98	80.0

Sources: For 1959, Bank-e Markazi-e Iran, *Hesabhay-e Melli Iran: 1338–56* (Teheran, 1360).
For 1977–83, Vezarat-e Barnameh va Budgeh, *Gozaresh-e Eqtesadi-e Sal-e: 1363* (Teheran, 1364).
For 1984, Vezarat-e Barnameh va Budgeh, *Fashnameh-e Amari: 1364* (Teheran, 1365).

while there are continuous shortages of some goods in the official market, the black market always seems generously supplied.

The Islamic banking system, insurance and financial markets

Contrary to the noticeable growth of wholesale and retail trade, in the 1977–84 period the share of financial and monetary institutions in the service group has continuously declined. In 1984, the value added of the financial and monetary subsector, of which banking and insurance are the two major activities, represented two per cent of real GDP.[34] The banking system and insurance companies were nationalized in 1979 and the Law of Usury-Free Banking was approved by parliament in August 1983. According to the law, banks can accept two kinds of deposits: *gharz al-hassaneh* deposits (current and savings) and term-investment deposits. A *gharz al-hassaneh* current account is similar to conventional current accounts. *Gharz al-hassaneh* savings accounts are the same as conventional savings accounts, except that the former would not formally pay interest on deposits. However, banks can attract and mobilize deposits by one or all of the following: non-fixed bonuses in cash; exempting depositors from payment of commissions and fees; and granting priority to depositors in the use of banking facilities.

Term-investment deposits are of two kinds: short-term (3 months) with a minimum amount of 2,000 rials and long-term (1 year) with a minimum amoung of 50,000 rials. Banks can use their resources in investment projects, sharing the profit with the term-investment depositors. They can also act as the trustee of depositors by investing the depositors' funds, in which case a commission will be charged by the banks. In principal, the profits earned as a result of the banks' investment are to be divided among depositors, after the deduction of the banks' fees. The return is calculated in proportion to the total value of investment deposits, excluding the required reserves. In any case, the return of the principal of these deposits is guaranteed by the banks. According to the law, banks must announce their profit rates every six months, when the depositors' share of profits is to be paid into each account. Of course, if deposits are withdrawn before the minimum time required or reduced below the required minimum, no profit will be earned. Term-investment funds can be used by banks in accordance with Islamic contracts, such as *muzaraba*, *muzara'a*, partnership, direct investment forward transactions, hire purchase and *ja'ala* (see Table 4).[35]

The implementation of the law has been mainly limited to the liabilities of the banks. So far, banks have been able to convert their liabilities into Islamic deposits, but have not had much success in converting their assets into Islamic contracts. According to the balance sheet of the banking system, in March 1985, the first year of operation of the new system, 39.2 per cent of private-sector deposits had been transferred into *gharz al-hassaneh* and term-investment deposits; the rest were in the form of sight, non-sight, savings and time deposits. On the asset side, only 16.8 per cent of the new credits to the private sector were in new Islamic facilities, of which 78.4 per cent were allocated from term-investment deposits and the rest from *gharz al-hassaneh* deposits. In the same year, the commercial banks' share in the new banking facilities, that is the Islamic contracts and *gharz al-hassaneh* loans, was 73.3 per cent of the total, indicating the concentration of financial resources in commercial short-run activities, rather than in the kind of long-term productive investment that can be financed by investment banks.[36]

At present, the rate of profit on term-investment accounts is determined by the Central Bank on the basis of the overall profits of the banking system. In 1985-7, the official 'rates of profit' (or interest rates) for the short and long-term investment accounts were 6 per cent and 8.5 per cent, respectively. In 1987, the cash bonus, or prize, on *gharz al-hassaneh* savings accounts was 1.5 to 2 per cent of the value of deposits.[37] Banks charge a commission fee on the loans granted to borrowers. The lowest rate is charged on housing loans. Moreover, some of the banks have been ordered by the Central Bank to finance government projects, such as the Teheran underground train system, by investing in them.

It is also interesting to note that the 'purchase of debt' or discounting is legitimate in the Islamic banking law, since it is consistent with the *Shari'a* Whatever one calls the discount rate, the difference between the purchase price and the redemption value of a financial document represents an interest return on the purchase. It is expected that in the future the Central Bank will use this instrument a lot as a policy weapon and that banks will take advantage of the instrument in their relations with commercial and industrial firms.[38]

Table 4
Islamic contracts used by the banks in different fields of activity

Type of Activity	Islamic Contract
Production (industrial, mining and agricultural)	Credit sale, hire-purchase, forward transaction, partnership, direct investment, *muzara'a*, *musaqat* and *ja'ala*
Commercial	*muzaraba*, partnership, *ja'ala*
Housing	Hire-purchase, credit sale, *gharz-al-hassaneh*, *ja'ala*
Service	Hire-purchase, credit sale, *ja'ala*
Consumption	Credit sale, *gharz al-hassaneh*

Source: *Iran: Yearbook 88* (Bonn: Moini-Biontino Verlagsgesellschaft mbH, 1988), p. 259. (See footnote 35.

Of course, interest is charged in the large, but amorphous, uncontrolled money markets of the bazaar, catering to the financial needs of small and middle-sized firms and individuals. In this market, interest rates are very high. Attempts to increase the number of small private *gharz al-hassaneh* funds, in order to cut down these usurious practices, have not been promising. Many of the small 'interest free' funds have become bankrupt or their managers have embezzled funds. In fact, litigations against such establishments have been increasing and, in May 1988, the establishment of new private *gharz al-hassaneh* funds was forbidden.[39]

In 1979, ten private insurance companies were nationalized and two foreign insurance offices were closed down. Up until 1988, of the twelve nationalized Iranian insurance companies and the Iran Insurance Company (IIC) which was always state owned, only three, the IIC and two formerly private companies, have been able to expand and continue their operation.

After the revolution, transactions in corporate shares and government bonds on the Tehran Stock Exchange came to a standstill. The private banks, insurance companies and industries nationalized in 1979 were no longer quoted. However, by 1984, the total value of transactions in company shares and government bonds had slowly climbed back to one-fourth of the value of transactions in 1977.[40]

The agricultural sector, which includes fisheries and forestry, employs 30 per cent of the labour force most of whom work on nearly 3 million small and large plots of arable land. Nevertheless, in 1984 the contribution of the marketed output of the agricultural sector to nominal GDP was only 13.1 per cent, indicating a low productivity. Over half of the country's land is uncultivable. Nineteen per cent of the total could be reclaimed and developed. The land area is made up of 6 per cent of natural pasture and another 11 to 12 per cent of natural forests. Land under cultivation constitutes no more than 12 per cent of the country's land area.

In the 1960s, all the forests and pastures were nationalized by the Shah's government and 40 per cent of the very large land-holdings was sold to 53 per cent of the peasants who worked on these lands. After the revolution, the Islamic government and government-related institutions confiscated the farms, orchards and gardens of the royal family and their associates. However, most of the rural land used for irrigated or dry-farming cultivation is still privately owned.

According to the latest agricultural statistics covering all provinces except Kurdistan and Western Azerbaijan, in 1982, 2.7 million farmers owned their land and about 500,000 worked on the land of others as tenants. There were 1.2 million who were considered as agricultural labourers; they either owned nothing or a small plot of land. Of those who owned their lands, 71.3 per cent held less than 5 hectares and possessed only 21.7 per cent of the lands under cultivation or fallow lands. About 40 per cent of these holdings were operating at subsistence and produced nothing for the market. An estimated 0.6 per cent of the farmers owned 13.2 per cent of the agricultural lands, operating on farms over 50 hectares. It was mainly due to the 1960s land reform and the subsequent differentiation process taking place in the agricultural sector, that medium-sized holdings constituted 28.1 per cent of the total. These villagers owned 65.1 per cent of the arable land and worked on lands over 5 and less than 50 hectares. Over 30 per cent of these holdings did not produce for the market.

In 1982, of Iran's 13.1 million hectares of arable land 77.9 per cent belonged to 2.6 million sole proprietors, 19.1 per cent was owned by about 300,000 in partnership, 1.1 per cent was owned by 700 government institutions, including the Office of Endowments and 1.9 per cent was owned by 1,100 enterprises.[41]

The private sector's associations include the legal organizations and associations defending the rights and interests of the private sector, such as the Chamber of Commerce, Industry and Mines (CCIM) and the guild unions. The CCIM goes back to the 1920s. At present, it is a legal entity with 22 branches across Iran and about 17,000 members. It includes construction material producers' syndicates and 19 non-oil goods export unions. After the revolution, it has mainly been active in arranging contacts between foreign and Iranian businessmen and marketing Iranian goods in foreign markets, participating in price determination by the Exports Promotion Centre and in the Customs Revision Commission. The CCIM actively lobbies parliamentary committees. It presents and defends anti-interventionist views in its journal called the *Weekly Journal of the Chamber of Commerce, Industries and Mines of Iran*.[42] It has discreetly and sometimes overtly backed the position of Khamenei against the 'statists' and has advocated more private economic activities and less government control over foreign trade and domestic distribution of goods. It has always espoused the views of the non-interventionist clergy, inviting them to the CCIM's seminars and meetings.[43] For this reason, in 1987, parliament rescinded the chamber's right to issue trade cards to businessmen and industrialists, granting the right to the ministry of commerce. It was no longer necessary to be a member of the chamber to be able to issue a trade card.[44]

The guild unions form another important private network. These regional organizations represent trade guilds and issue vocational licences in co-ordination with government organizations and municipalities. They protect the interests of their members against government interference, help their members procure basic materials and means of work and lobby the government on the pricing of goods and services. In 1986, the guilds forced the government to agree to consult them before levying tax on members. They also espoused the non-interventionist approach and for this reason, their relationship with the government has not been good.

In a meeting with President Khamenei, the representative of Teheran's guilds complained that some authorities 'disturb the guilds on the pretext of supporting the *mostazafin* and even obstruct the guilds' efforts in the collection of financial aids' for the fronts. In response, Khamenei stated that 'bazaar and business are misunderstood in non-Islamic thoughts . . . [and] those who follow these non-Islamic thoughts . . . are not aware of realities; guilds and the bazaar people are the noble friends of the revolution'.[45] The government is trying to limit the guilds' role in issuing vocational licences. However, despite some moves in this direction, the guilds have, so far, successfully resisted the government's efforts.[46]

It is noteworthy that the largest and economically most powerful private enterprise in Iran at present is the Islamic Economic Organization (IEO). The IEO was originally established under the auspices of Ayatollahs Beheshti and Ardebili, immediately after the revolution, to work as an interest-free loan fund, accepting deposits and granting loans to borrowers. Initially, therefore, it was called the Islamic Bank. After the nationalization of all private banks, Khomeini personally exempted this institution from nationalization.[47] Nevertheless, very soon the Islamic Bank changed its name to IEO to avoid controversy. Ever since, it has extended its banking activities and, at present, has more than eight hundred affiliated funds and controls more than 2 per cent of the private sector's liquidity.[48] The IEO, as a 'non-profit'-oriented enterprise, is not under the control of the Central Bank and, in fact, competes with the nationalized banking system and does not always co-ordinate its policy with the government's monetary policy.[49] It has expanded its activity to cover trade, construction, imports and exports, in order to increase its capital. Recently, alarmed by the IEO's growing economic power, the interventionist faction has intensified criticism of its activities, but has not yet been able to curb its expansion.

Planning, monetary and fiscal policy instruments

Planning, monetary and fiscal policies were used by the former régime to affect both the supply and demand sides of the economy, according to its long-run and short-run objectives. Monetary and fiscal policies are also used by the Islamic government. However, despite the experience gained in planning in Iran, since the 1950s, the Islamic government has been unable to come up with and implement a medium-term and long-term economic plan. This is mainly due to factional disputes concerning the economic orientation of the 'Islamic economy' among the rulers of the Islamic Republic. In 1982, a five-year plan was tabled before parliament for approval. This plan envisaged a parallel growth and development in both the agricultural and industrial sectors, emphasizing economic independence, inter-sectoral linkages, the growth of capital goods industries at the expense of consumer goods industries and self-sufficiency. However, the plan was, at best, unrealistic; it assumed that the oil sector would expand by 16 per cent annually and that the price of oil would be $33.25 per barrel in constant 1982–3 prices, with exports rising from 2 million BPD in 1983, to a little less than 3 million BPD in 1987. Moreover, it did not take into consideration the effect of the war on the economy.

An intense dispute over the plan's objectives, the long-term economic orientation of the Islamic Republic, the government's sources of income, the plan's unrealistic assumptions about oil export revenues and over the need for a plan at all led to the plan being crossed off the parliamentary agenda in early 1983.[50] The government greatly modified the plan and presented a revised version to parliament in January 1986. This time, the plan emphasized war mobilization. It did not set any growth targets or promise any structural and institutional changes. The indefinite objectives of the plan were to be achieved 'gradually' by utilizing the existing 'capacities and capabilities' and 'organizational' changes. In fact, this plan was little more than an annual government budget bill. It allocated more than 30 per cent of total expenditure to the war effort. It also envisaged the encouragement of the private-sector's involvement in non-service oriented activities, including construction of housing, by means of credit policies and tax relief programmes. The plan avoided new major investments by the government and emphasized the policy of finishing existing projects. In short, the plan avoided controversy and was approved by parliament in January 1986.[51]

All the conventional instruments of monetary and fiscal policy are used to influence the performance of the economy according to the objectives of the Islamic government. Fiscal policy is reflected in the government's budgetary policy. Monetary policy is formally the responsibility of the Central Bank of the Islamic Republic of Iran. In accordance with the Islamic principle that precludes the use of interest rates by the Central Bank, monetary policy cannot formally use instruments that involve the application of fixed interest rates. However, reserve requirements for various types of bank deposits, direct credit control (bank-by-bank credit ceilings on aggregate and sectoral credit), moral suasion, a limited buying and selling of government bonds and re-discounting financial documents are used to determine the level of liquidity. In addition, the Central Bank intervenes in and supervises the banking system's operation in various ways. It fixes a minimum and maximum ratio of profit for banks in their joint venture and *muzaraba* contracts that can vary for different types of activity, a minimum expected rate of return for various investment and partnership projects that may vary for different fields of activity and a minimum and maximum margin of profit, calculated as a proportion of cost price of the goods transacted for banks in instalment and hire-purchase transactions. It determines the maximum and minimum rates of commission for banking services and the fees charged for investment accounts. It determines the types, amounts, minimum and maximum bonuses paid to depositors, the minimum and maximum ratios in all kinds of Islamic investments and contracts, such as joint venture, *muzaraba*, hire-purchase, forward transaction (*salaf*), *muzara'a*, credit sale or sale by instalment and *gharz al-hassaneh* ('interest-free loans') for banks in different kinds of activities.[52]

The government budget is presented to parliament in January each year for the following Iranian year, which begins on 21 March. It reflects the intended fiscal policy of the government. Government receipts include income taxes, such as salary taxes, business and government firms taxes, inheritance and capital gains taxes, indirect taxes (import taxes, sale and consumption taxes) and oil revenues. The government's expenditures are divided into development and current expenditures, including expenditures for the war effort.

There are certain structural constraints that greatly reduce the effectiveness of monetary and fiscal policies. The Iranian economy is a fragmented market economy with modern and traditional structures and institutions coexisting with each other. It depends heavily on oil export revenues as a source of capital and foreign exchange for growth. The oil industry is owned by the government and, therefore, fluctuations in oil export revenues strongly affect the level and composition of the government's expenditures and receipts. Since 1982, whenever oil revenues have fallen, the government has decreased its development expenditure and has raised sales and consumption taxes and, to some extent, business taxes. At the same time, it has increased expenditures for the war effort. On balance, the budget deficit has been high and has been financed by borrowing from the Central Bank.

In 1983–5, oil revenues accounted for 48.2 per cent of total government revenues. With the fall of oil revenues since 1984, the ratio has fallen to about 21 per cent. In 1982, sales and consumption taxes accounted for 16.4 per cent of total receipts. In 1983-6, this share steadily increased and in 1986 reached 30.7 per cent. The ratio of government borrowing to total receipts, which was 17.6 per cent, 9 per cent and 9.8 per cent in 1983, 1984 and 1985, respectively, rose to 34.6 per cent in 1986.

Table 5
Oil exports and revenues

	Exports (million barrels/day)	Revenues (billion $)
1981	0.79	11.9
1982	1.69	18.6
1983	2.04	20.2
1984	1.61	15.7
1985	1.56	13.12
1986	1.45	6.6

Source: Based on *Iran: Yearbook 88* (Bonn: Moini-Biontino Verlagsgesellschaft mbH, 1988), p. 388.

The ups and downs of oil revenues not only affect the level and composition of government revenues, expenditures and deficit, but together with the budgetary deficit, determine the monetary base of the economy. In 1984, the three components of the monetary base, that is net foreign assets, Central Bank claims against the government and the nationalized banking system, were 19.5 per cent, 68.1 per cent and 12.4 per cent, respectively, compared to 54.6, 28.3 and 17.2 per cent respectively, in 1973.[53] Increasing reliance on Central Bank credits for financing the deficit has overwhelmed the conduct of monetary policy for macroeconomic and microeconomic objectives. In fact, in spite of the decline of real GDP since 1984, the growth of private-sector liquidity (sum of money and quasi-money) has always been higher than that intended by the government. In 1974-86, the volume of liquidity grew thirteen fold, with the major part of the growth taking place since 1979. Moreover, despite the government's official policy of restricting the growth of commercial credit in favour of industrial and agricultural credit, granted by nationalized banks to private and state firms, it is commercial credit that has enjoyed the highest growth.[54] In addition, poor management, the absence of intermediate and capital goods which are usually imported and, in general, the overall lack of interdependence within the industrial sector give rise to structural supply constraints, such as low elasticity of supply. Budgetary deficits that increase demand for goods and services, combined with structural supply rigidities, lead to a chronic excess demand that merely knocks up prices, leads to higher inflation and inhibits the expansion of output. In the past ten years, this problem has been aggravated by the fall in output which has given rise to an unprecedented stagflation. Nevertheless, the rate of inflation, as we will see in the next section, has been lower than in other underdeveloped economies, mainly due to the fact that the increase in the level of liquidity has been partly held back by the private sector under recessionary conditions. The high level of liquidity does, however, indicate a high inflationary potential during the recovery and reconstruction period now that the Iran-Iraq war is over.

Conclusion

What conclusions are to be drawn from this review of the economic structure and institutions of the post-revolution period? The first is that there has been no fundamental change in the dependent and fragmented economic structure of Iran's economy. The Iranian economy is still composed of three sectors: the oil sector and the modern and traditional sectors in industry, agriculture and services. The oil industry mainly produces crude oil for the world market and provides part of the capital and a major part of the foreign exchange for the modern sector, both private and public. The oil industry's linkages to other economic sectors are limited, due to its capital-intensive nature and the underdeveloped state of the modern sector in Iran's capital goods industries. The modern sector relies on the traditional sector for labour and part of its raw material and sells much of its output to the traditional sector and the rest to itself. Of course, the relative importance of the traditional sector is bound to decline due to migration to towns and the expansion of the modern sector. However, since 1979, due to the unprecedented duration and the amplitude of the economic depression, its transformation has slowed down.

The second conclusion is that, despite significant nationalization, mainly in the first year after the revolution, the scope of the private sector's activity is substantial: private ownership of land and capital prevails and the private sector employs the majority of the labour force. Private enterprise accounts for most of the value added in agriculture and services and the vast traditional industries. On the whole, the share of the private sector in aggregate supply prevails over that of the government sector. Besides, one can safely predict that the share of the private sector in the post-war reconstruction period will increase due to the government's political and economic inability to face up to the task alone.

The economy's macro performance is strongly affected by the fluctuation of oil export revenues which are under government control. However, the allocation of resources in the process of production, distribution and consumption is to a great extent determined by national and international market forces. The scope for government planning is minimal and incomparably less than during the pre-revolution period. The Islamic government has imposed certain religious injunctions against certain practices, but their real effects have been undermined in practice. For example, alcoholic beverages and pork are forbidden goods and interest payment speculation and lotteries are considered against the *Shari'a*. Nevertheless, alcoholic beverages are produced in the underground economy, interest is charged in the uncontrolled financial markets of the bazaar and fees, bonuses, prizes and discount rates have replaced the interest rate in the controlled and nationalized banking system. What is new in the economy is the coupon-rationing system for certain staple goods, the increased role of the government in foreign trade (mainly imports) and the extensive black market for many goods which are in short supply. An important reason for the initial imposition of government direct and indirect control was the shortage of foreign exchange and constraints created by the US embargo in 1980 and the Iran-Iraq war which consumed an increasing part of the falling foreign-exchange receipts, rather than fundamental distrust of market resource allocation. Besides, government control and intervention, but not the provision of public services, have always been a characteristic feature of capitalism in Iran and many of the less developed economies.

Macroeconomic performance after the revolution

Far from being resolved, the most fundamental structural problems of the Iranian economy and the economic crisis which formed the backdrop to the revolution have steadily intensified since 1979. The stagnation in production of many agricultural and industrial goods, the disruption of the distribution process, rising inflation and unemployment, the decline in the real wages and salaries of a large part of the working population, the accelerating deterioration of the standard of living of the population, in general, and the growing poverty, are stark indicators of the economic crisis.

During the last three years of the Shah's régime, the economy's structural crisis was manifested in an inflationary gap and then in stagflation. This crisis, drastically compounded by the revolutionary situation, had its base in the economy's structural one-sided dependence upon the world-market system and in the distorted and fragmentary nature of the Iranian economy. There has been no fundamental change in these characteristics, since the revolution.[55] The main structural causes of the economic crisis have remained intact. Moreover, political crisis, the government's inability to execute a definite economic policy due to intra-governmental conflicts, the disastrous Iran-Iraq war and the fluctuation of oil-export revenues have all aggravated the economic crisis.

The Iran-Iraq War

The Iran-Iraq war had disastrous consequences for the people and economies of these two countries. In addition to the loss of more than 300,000 lives, there has been the mental and physical crippling of several hundreds of thousands of young Iranians and the brain-drain loss of more than 300,000 young Iranians who have gone into hiding or exile to avoid the draft or repression. There have been large economic costs in the form of large-scale destruction of assets, cities and infrastructure (including roads, harbours, transportation and communications), inflation, higher import costs, lost output due to redirection of labour away from civilian production, lost oil markets and revenues and loss of foreign-exchange reserves. The escalation of the war put severe constraints on the already ailing Iranian economy, decreased the potential for growth in the industrial and agricultural sectors and in investment and development programmes and created serious internal refugee problems.

In March 1984, the ministry of planning and budget estimated the opportunity cost of the war for the first time.[56] The estimate set the total damage at about $190 billion. The direct and indirect loss of oil exporting capacity, due to the destruction of loading facilities, pumping stations, refineries, terminals and pipelines in the war zone, has been one of the most costly consequences of the war. In 1984, the damage to the oil sector was estimated to be more than $65 billion, or about 35 per cent of the total damage to the economy.

In addition to the costly destruction of port facilities, the routing of imports from the Persian Gulf ports to routes through the Soviet Union and Turkey raised the delivered prices of imports and exports. The reallocation of resources in favour of the war increased Iran's dependence on foreign suppliers. Several important industrial, commercial and populous cities, such as Abadan, Khoramshahr, Ahwaz, Dezful and Bakhtaran, were totally or partially devastated and an estimated 2 million people became internal refugees.

From 1963 to 1978, the Shah's régime spent a large portion of the GNP on military build-up. In the period 1968-78, military expenditures absorbed from 11 to 16 per cent of the GNP. After the revolution, the military burden was reduced by half, falling to 8.5 per cent of GNP in 1980. However, it began climbing again soon afterwards, reaching 9.5 per cent in 1981 and 10 per cent in 1982.

Official figures indicate that military imports fell after the revolution, then rose again, and accounted for 13.4 per cent of total imports in 1982.[57] The war effort consumed over 30 per cent of annual government expenditure. In 1983, 11 out of every hundred people were enlisted in the armed forces, excluding several hundred thousand in the Mobilization Corps, the *Pasdaran* (Guardians) Corps and the other paramilitary forces.

The total cost of the war for both Iran and Iraq reached $416.2 billion by 1985, or $52 billion more than the total oil revenues of both countries since 1919. In short, the average annual cost of the war in Iran absorbed 54 per cent of the GNP.[58] The war heavily and irreparably taxed the Iranian economy, setting back the prospects for its economic development over the next few decades.

Macroeconomic trends

A review of macroeconomic trends in the years for which data have been available have provides a clear picture of the depth of the economic crisis in the post-revolution period.[59] The most important trends follow.

Output, income and expenditure

During the period 1977–80, real GDP decreased by 34.5 per cent. It fell by 16.7 per cent in 1978, 6 per cent in 1979 and 16.4 per cent in 1980. From 1981 to 1984, real GDP increased by 29.6 per cent. However, the absolute level of real GDP in 1984 was still 12.8 per cent lower than the real GDP in 1977. The decline in real GDP during 1977–80 was basically due to the decline in oil revenues and then to declines in industry and mining, utilities, construction, trade, transportation and financial services. The increase in real GDP during 1981–3 was again mainly due to rising oil revenues linked to fluctuations in the price of crude, although there was some growth in trade and industry (see Table 3).

In 1984, the economy's growth rate dropped sharply to 0.1 per cent. All sectors, except the agricultural sector, experienced a slow down in their rates of growth (see Table 3). Again, the decline in oil revenues was the major factor in the decline in the growth of real GDP. Moreover, due to the government's anti-inflationary credit policies and the imposition of restrictions on foreign-exchange appropriations, the levels of investment and employment declined, decreasing the growth of liquidity and aggregate demand. All these factors reduced the rate of inflation to some extent. In 1985, a further drop in the price of oil on the international market reduced oil revenues (see Table 5). The impact of fluctuating oil revenues on the volume of imports of capital and intermediate goods which are necessary to industry was such that the value of GDP declined by 1.1 per cent. The drop in the level of aggregate demand led to a slowdown in the growth of inflation and to a decline in the level of output.[60]

Ever since 1986, due to the decline in the price of oil, combined with the reduced volume of exports, war damage and the continuous decline in government development investment, GDP has been falling. In 1986, current GDP declined by 8 per cent. According to the minister of planning and budget, in 1988, all sectors except the agricultural sector were expected to have negative growth rates. What is worse is that, for the first time after twenty years of economic change, value added produced in the agricultural sector has been higher than the value added produced in mining and industry (manufacturing, construction, electricity, gas and water) for three consecutive years, from 1986–8.[61] The trend of real GDP composition reveals a dangerous shrinkage of the industrial sector and the swollen nature of services, especially trade.

Economic crisis and the large population growth have decreased the level of real per capita income between 1977 and 1987. Real per capita GDP, which was 112,970 rials in 1977, had fallen to 67,310 rials by 1981. During 1982–3 it increased but fell again to 80,000 rials in 1984. Therefore, real per capita GDP in 1984 was still about 30 per cent lower than in 1977 and 3 per cent lower in 1972.

From 1977–84, the share of the real value added of trade (including restaurants and hotels), housing and rental services, as well as professional and specialized services in real GDP increased from 21.34 per cent in 1977 to 32.8 per cent in 1984. The ratio of value added in the above service categories to their total value has increased rapidly, indicating rising profit margins. A small percentage (about 100,000 households) of the labour force is active in these kinds of service, of which only a small minority are wage and salary earners. One can conclude that an important part of the national income is earned by merchants of the bazaar, who are engaged in national and international trade. Moreover, government and private expenditure on goods and services in 1983 accounted for only 69.3 per cent of the GDP, indicating a 30.7 per cent saving ratio.[62] However, since the saving level for the lower income groups has been negative in recent years, this saving is concentrated in high-income groups – among them ruling clerics, merchants, high-level bureaucrats, big industrialists, landlords and professionals – who constitute a small percentage of society. In contrast, per capita wages and salaries in 'large' enterprises decreased from 291,000 to 210,000 rials from 1980 to 1983.[63]

Investment

Another disturbing trend of the economic crisis in Iran has been the catastrophic decline in investment, both public and private, during the postrevolution period. The level of investment declined between 1976 and 1981, went up in the 1981–2 period and dropped again in 1984–7. In 1984, the level of real gross fixed capital formation was 34.8 per cent lower than that of 1976.[64] The shares of the government and the private sector in total investment for the period 1971–7 were 56 and 46 per cent, respectively. The government's share in total investment decreased to 53 per cent in the 1979–83 period, despite extensive nationalization and the overwhelming government share in the ownership of very large industries.

While in the period 1971–7, 63 per cent of investment was in construction and the remainder in machinery and equipment, the share of these investments changed to 66 and 34 per cent, respectively, during 1978–83.[65] In fact, a steady and dangerous increase in the incremental capital-output ratio has emerged due to the following factors: the decline in real GDP, unemployment, the Iran-Iraq war and its catastrophic consequences, unsatisfactory use of the existing financial and productive capacities, the waste and mismanagement of existing resources, the exodus of technical and professional expertise and a lack of motivation on the part of workers and skilled people because of political, economic and civil oppression. In addition, this trend clearly shows the effects of Iran's dependent and distorted economic structure. The weakness of inter-sector and intra-sectoral linkages and the continuation of the industrial strategy used during the Shah's régime mean that the required goods and services are not provided to the productive sectors. The great majority of large industries are dependent on imported inputs and managerial and technical expertise. A lack of these resources, due to the US economic embargo of 1980 and the inability to import resulting from a decline in the oil revenues which provide the foreign exchange for exports, plunged the economy into depression.

In 1981, the rates of unused productive capacity in agriculture or farming, industry and electricity were 46, 39 and 36.2 per cent, respectively. A breakdown of the data on the rates of unused productive capacity shows that these rates increase with the level of dependence on imported input and technology.[66] In fact the dependency ratio, or the ratio of imported inputs to total inputs, has increased on the average in the last decade, requiring up to $15 billion worth of raw materials and intermediate capital goods to keep the level of output at that of 1982. This explains the drastic rise of the real incremental capital-output ratio, from 2.9 in the 1973–7 period to 21 for 1979–83. This ratio was 2.09 in 1977; it had increased to 4.3 by 1983.[67]

This unfortunate state of affairs has led, on the one hand, to the increased importation of many kinds of commodities especially agricultural goods and foodstuffs and, on the other hand, to an increase in factory closures, large-scale lay-offs, part-time work and unemployment. Since 1979, the proportion of imported consumer goods relative to the total value of imports has doubled. Thus, consumer goods which constituted 11.7 per cent of total imports in 1971, had risen to 22 per cent by 1982.[68] Moreover, because of the large and unusual profit in trade, a major part of financial and non-financial resources has been diverted to this unproductive sector, aggravating the bleak economic prospects.

Employment and unemployment

In 1984, 12.3 million people, or 28.6 per cent of the total population, made up the labour force. In the same year, 350,000 entered the labour market, a figure surpassing the natural increases which could be expected on the basis of trends in the previous decade. This increase was due to the economic crisis, the decline in real income among the lower social classes, the absence of opportunity for higher education (universities were closed down in 1980–82 and many students were ousted from their schools or banned altogether from higher educational institutions) and to the rising cost of living. About 40 per cent of those who entered the labour market in 1984 could not find employment and were forced to join the already substantial ranks of the unemployed, increasing the level of open unemployment to more than 2.4 million, or 19 per cent of the labour force. Moreover, it is estimated that some 20 per cent of the employed population does not contribute to changes in the GNP, since these workers are engaged in peddling and other non-productive activities. In 1984, about 40 per cent of the labour force were unemployed and underemployed.[69]

Of the total employed labour force in 1986, 30 per cent were employed in agriculture, 26.5 per cent in industry (including the oil industry) and 43.5 per cent in services - indicating an increase in the absolute number and in the share of the labour force in the agriculture and service sectors since 1977. In view of the downward trend in the level of real GDP, one can safely state that in 1988, at least 40 per cent of the labour force was unemployed and underemployed. The 1986 census data on unemployment have not been published. However, in March 1987, a member of parliament announced that the census results indicated that 3.8 million were unemployed.[70]

Inflation
Another manifestation of the economic crisis in Iran is the growing inflation of the post-revolution period which has greatly reduced the purchasing power of Iranians. Prices of basic goods and services such as food, clothing, tobacco, transportation, health services and so on have been greatly increased. Nevertheless, staple commodities and public transportation are subsidized. Certain staple goods, such as sugar, are distributed through a controlled ration-coupon system, but the government has allowed an 'official' black market to exist alongside it, thus sanctioning a system which supplies the rich with goods that are unavailable to the remaining population and which siphons off goods from the official market. This results in chronic shortages of some goods on the official market, while the black market remains, for the most part, well supplied.

Official Central Bank figures for the consumer price index, which relies partly on official prices, underestimate the real rate of inflation. However, this index increased by an average 19.2 per cent annually from 1977 to 1982.[71] In 1983, due to a short-term improvement in the economy's macroeconomic performance, the rate of inflation slowed down. Also in 1984, the rate of inflation was reduced to some extent, but this time it was due to an anti-inflationary credit policy of the government and the decline of aggregate demand. Since 1985, aggregate supply has also decreased, increasing rates of inflation and unemployment. The government has not published the price indexes since 1985, when the rate of inflation was officially announced to be more than 20 per cent. However, certain members of parliament with access to unpublished statistics put the rate of inflation at 47 per cent. Naturally, government authorities promptly denied this claim.[72]

There are structural and cyclical reasons for the continuing price increases: the dependence of output on imported goods and services, the wide gap between the official foreign-exchange rate and the free-market rate, the lopsided increase in the services' GNP share and the increasing number of hands involved in the process of distribution. Moreover, the unprecedented and steady increase in the government-budget deficit has resulted in a rise in its debt to the banking system, from 1,000 billion rials in 1977 to 9,743 billion rials in 1987. The rise in the government deficit, given inelasticity of aggregate supply at less than full-employment level of output, has been inflationary and has led to an alarming liquidity in the private sector. In fact, the private sector's liquidity increased sixfold from 1978 to 1987, while in the same period, real GDP decreased.[73]

Foreign-exchange gap

Since 1979, the Iranian currency has continuously depreciated in the black market for foreign exchange. In 1978, the official and unofficial exchange rate in relation to the dollar was $1 for 70.4 rials; in March 1988, 1,155 rials could be exchanged for $1, as against an official rate of 66.7 rials.[74] This is a result of the decline in the foreign-exchange revenues along with the high initial surge of capital flight in 1978–81 and its continuation, although at a lower rate, ever since. Since 1984, oil revenues have fallen due to the decline in oil prices and the volume of oil exports (see Table 5).

The decline in foreign-exchange revenues has forced the government to draw on reserves held in foreign banks. The present amount of foreign reserves is kept secret. However, officials of the Islamic Republic have quoted foreign journals' estimates from time to time, suggesting that these reserves fell from about $7.5 billion in 1985 to $5.1 billion in March 1987. Since 1987, it is claimed that Iran's foreign reserves have increased due to the government's effort to stop withdrawals from them.[75] In 1988, other countries' debts to Iran amounted to $3.7 billion and the sum of Iran's investment in other countries was $779 million.[76]

Since 1982, faced with a rising foreign-exchange gap, the government devalued the rial in order to encourage exports and discourage imports and, at the same time, imposed controls on the foreign-exchange expenditure of private and public sectors, firms and individuals. However, after successful lobbying by merchant exporters, the Central Bank liberalized its exchange control on their foreign-currency earnings. Exporters were allowed to use their exchange earnings for importing goods or to sell them to importers. Private owners of foreign exchange abroad were also allowed to sell their foreign currencies at free-market prices.[77]

In 1988, there were at least five exchange rates in operation: a free exchange rate, which was fifteen times the official exchange rate; an export exchange rate for foreign currency earned by exporters, which was six times the official rate; the rate of exchange offered to exporters at preferential rates which varied for various commodities exported; the rate of exchange for tourists and students abroad, and the official rate of exchange for certain rare instances.

In 1986–9, the government continued its policy of severe controls on foreign-exchange expenditure. The government drastically lowered the foreign-exchange appropriations to the service, agricultural and industrial sectors, both public and private, in order not to decrease its foreign reserves and to match receipts with expenditures on foreign exchange. At the same time, the government continued its policy of promoting private and non-oil exports. In 1987, only $400 million was allocated for the importation of goods required by all industries, while they needed $4 billion for their reproduction at the level of 1983.[78]

This disturbing state of affairs has seriously disrupted the process of production, distribution and consumption, intensifying the already critical state of the economy with its declining output, income and consumption, rising prices, shortages and bottlenecks. This situation was, in fact, an important reason for the abandonment of the dogmatic policy of 'war, war, till victory'.

In the early days of the post-revolution period, Khomeini said that concern for economic well being was worthy of donkeys and other animals. The majority of the Iranian people can expect to suffer the profound and disastrous consequences of this approach, as implemented in the 1980s, for decades to come.

Notes

1. *Resalat*, 1 Ordibehesht, 1367.
2. *Ibid* and *Keyhan*, 28 Khordad, 1367.
3. *Ettelaat*, 10 Day, 1365.
4. *Keyhan*, 13 Azar, 1365.
5. *Resalat*, 1 Ordibehesht, 1367.
6. *Ibid*.
7. Markaz-e Amar-e Iran, *Gozideh-e Natayej-e Tafsili-e Sarshomari*, 1365 (Teheran, 1367).
8. Anjoman-e Modiran-e Sanaye-e Jomhouri-e Islami-e Iran, *Estrategeihaye Tose'-e Sanay'-e Iran* (Teheran, 1363), p. 21. Hereafter cited as Anjoman-e Modiran.
9. *Ibid*.
10. *Ibid*., pp. 27–8.
11. *Iran: 88, op. cit.*, pp. 196.
12. Anjoman-e Modiran, *op. cit.*, pp. 27–8.
13. *Iran: Yearbook 88*, (Bonn: Moini-Biontino Verlagsgesellschaft mbH, 1988), pp. 189–92. Hereafter cited as *Iran: 88*.
14. *Ibid*.
15. *Ibid*., p. 478.
16. Vezarat-e Barnameh va Budgeh, *Faslnameh-e Amari: 1364* (Teheran, 1365). Hereafter cited as *Faslnameh-e Amari: 1364*.
17. Anjoman-e Modiran, *op. cit.*, p. 31.
18. *Faslnameh-e Amari: 1364, op. cit.*
19. For example see Bayat, *op. cit.*, Habib Ladjevardi, *Labour Unions and Autocracy in Iran*, (Syracuse: Syracuse University Press, 1985) and Fred Halliday, *Iran: Dictatorship and Development* (Harmondsworth: Penguin Books, Ltd., 1979), pp. 173–210.
20. *Iran: 88, op. cit.*, pp. 478–81.
21. For example see Nomani, *Feudalism, op. cit.*
22. Tehrani, Vol II, *op. cit.* p. 393.
23. Markaz-e Amar-e Iran, *Khososiat-e Omdeh-e Jame'iati-e Manategh-e Keshvar: 1365* (Teheran).
24. The data does not include the workshops that have been destroyed or have been inactive due to the Iran-Iraq war.
25. Markaz-e Amar-e Iran, *Amar-e Kargahay-e Bozorg-e Sana'ti: 1364* (Teheran, 1365). Hereafter cited as *Amar-e Kargahay-e Bozorg: 1364*.
26. *Ibid* and *Amar-e Kargahay-e Bozorg: 1355, op. cit.*
27. *Amar-e Kargahay-e Bozorg: 1364, op. cit.*
28. Markaz-e Amar-e Iran, *Amar-e Kargahay-e Bozorg-e Sana'ti Taht-e Modiriat-e Bakhsh-e Dolati: 1362* (Teheran, 1364). Hereafter cited as *Amar-e Bakhsh-e Dolati*.
29. *Amar-e Kargahay-e Bozorg: 1364, op. cit.*

30. *Ibid.*

31. Markaz-e Amar Iran, *Amar-e Kargahay-e Kouchak-e Sana'ti-e Shahri: 1355* (Teheran, 1359).

32. *Keyhan*, 6 Shahrivar, 1364.

33. *Faslnameh-e Amari: 1364, op. cit.*

34. *Ibid.*

35. According to the Law for Usury-Free Banking, some of the Islamic contracts used in the banking system are the following:

1) *muzaraba* 'is a contract wherein the bank undertakes to provide the cash capital and other party (the *amel* or agent) undertakes to use the capital for commercial purposes and divide the profit at a specified ratio between the two parties at the end of the term of the contract'.

2) *muzara'a* 'is a contract wherein the bank turns over a specified plot of land for a specified period of time to another party (*amel*) for the purpose of farming the land and dividing the harvest between the two parties at a specified ratio'.

3) *salaf* (forward transaction) 'is defined as the cash purchase of products beforehand at a fixed price. In order to provide the necessary facilities to raise working capital for the productive units, the banks are authorized, solely on the request of such units, to buy their products in advance'.

4) *Gharz al-hassaneh* 'is a contract according to which one of the two parties (the lender) gives possession of a specified amount of his wealth to another party (the borrower), on the understanding that the borrower will return it in kind or, if not possible, its price to the lender'.

5) hire-purchase 'is defined as a leasing contract. . . . In order to provide the necessary facilities for the expansion of service, agricultural, industrial and mining activities, banks, as the hirer, may participate in hire-purchase transactions'.

6) *ja'ala* 'is the undertaking by one party (the *ja'el*, bank or employer) to pay a specified amount of money (*ja'al*) to another party in return for rendering a specified service in accordance with the terms of the contract. . . . The banks are authorized to engage in *ja'ala* as *amel* or, if necessary, as *ja'el*'.

7) sale by instalment (credit sale) 'is defined as the surrender of existing property to someone else at an identifiable value in such a way that all or part of the mentioned value is received in equal or unequal instalments at a fixed date or dates. . . . The banks may acquire the raw materials, spare parts, working tools and other preliminary requirements of [producing] units, solely upon the written request and undertaking of the applicants to purchase and use the mentioned items and to sell them to applicants on instalments. . . . For the expansion in housing activities, the banks are empowered to construct low cost housing units and sell them to applicants under the above mentioned conditions'.

8) *musaqat* 'is a contract between the owner of an orchard or garden with another party . . . for the purpose of gathering the harvest of the orchard or garden and dividing it, in a specified ratio, between the two parties. . . . The banks are authorized to put to *musaqat* the orchards and useful trees that they either own or in any way are entitled to their possession and utilization'. See the Bank of the Islamic Republic of Iran, *Economic Report and Balance Sheet: 1362* (Teheran, 1364), pp. 68–73. Hereafter cited as *Economic Report and Balance Sheet: 1362.*

9) *kharid-e dain* is the discounting of financial documents by the Central Bank, banks and any other firm or individual (*Ettelaat*, 10 Shahrivar, 1365).

36. *Iran: 88, op. cit.*, pp. 260–62.

37. *Keyhan*, 8 Khordad, 1367.

38. *Ettelaat*, 10 Shahrivar, 1365.

39. *Keyhan*, 3 Khordad, 1367 and *Resalat*, 23 Tir, 1367.

40. *Iran: 88, op. cit.*, pp. 269–73.

41. Markaz-e Amar-e Iran, *Natayej-e Amargiri-e Keshavarzi: 1361* (Teheran, 1363).

42. For example, see *Hafteh-nameh-e Otagh-e Bazargani, Sanaye' va Ma'aden*, 16 Shahrivar, 1364.

43. For example see *Ibid*, 7 Day, 1364.

44. *Iran: 88, op. cit.*, pp. 235–7.

45. *Resalat*, 23 Esfand, 1366.

46. *Resalat*, 16 Tir, 1367.

47. *Keyhan*, 24 Khordad, 1358.

48. *Iran: 88, op. cit.*, p. 239.

49. For example see *Jomhouri-e Islami*, 9 Day, 1364 and *Keyhan*, 12 Khordad, 1366.

50. *Iran: 88, op. cit.*, p. 210.

51. *Ettelaat*, 17 Day, 1364.

52. *Economic Report and Balance Sheet: 1362, op. cit.*, pp. 72–3.

53. *Iran: 88, op. cit.*, pp. 251 and 264 and *Fadai*.

54. *Jomhouri-e Islami*, 12 Mordad, 1365 and *Keyhan*, 28 Khordad, 1366.

55. Farhad Nomani, 'Macroeconomic Trends in the Economic Crisis of Iran', *Mondes en Developpement*, Vol. 15, No. 58–9, pp. 38–52.

56. *Iran: 88, op. cit.*, p. 141.

57. A. Alnassrawi, 'Economic Consequences of the Iran-Iraq War', *Third World Quarterly*, Vol. 8, No. 3, pp. 881–2.

58. *Ibid.*, pp. 883–6.

59. The Central Bank has not published the national income accounts since 1983. However, the data for 1983 and 1984 are reported in the statistical abstract of the ministry of planning and budget.

60. *Iran: 88, op. cit.*, pp. 202–5.

61. *Keyhan* (airmail edition), 29 Tir, 1367.

62. Vezarat-e Barnameh, *Gozaresh-e Eqtesadi-e Sal-e 1363* (Teheran, 1364). p. 111. Hereafter cited as Vezarat-e Barnameh for the relevant year.

63. Markaz-e Amar-e Iran, *Amar-e Kargahay-e Bozorg-e Keshvar: 1358–62* (Teheran, 1363).

64. Vezarat-e Barnameh: 1362, *op. cit.*, p. 26 and *Ibid.*, 1363, p. 111.

65. *Ibid*, pp. 46–7.

66. *Ibid.*, p. 108.

67. *Ibid.* pp.39-40 and 107.

68. *Ibid.*

69. *Ibid.*, pp. 49–51.

70. *Iran: 88, op. cit.*, p. 477.

71. Vezarat-e Barnameh: 1363, *op. cit.*, pp. 53–4 and 114.

72. *Ettelaat*, 2 Ordibehesht, 1366 and *Keyhan*, 26 Ordibehesht, 1366.

73. Vezarat-e Barnameh: 1363, *op. cit.*, pp. 52–3 and *Iran: 88, op. cit.*, p. 251.

74. *Resalat*, 25 Farvardin, 1367.

75. *Iran: 88, op. cit.*, p. 249.

76. *Ettelaat*, 21 Khordad, 1367.

77. Sohrab Behdad, 'Foreign Exchange Gap, Structural Constraints and the Political Economy of Exchange Rate Determination in Iran', *International Journal of Middle East Studies*, Vol. 20, 1988, pp. 5 and 19.

78. *Fadai*, Tir, 1367.

8. The Islamic Republic's foreign policy

Revolutionary Iran's foreign policy was initially conducted on the basis of a single rule of thumb, befriending those governments which had opposed the Shah and supported the revolution, rupturing relations with those governments which were viewed as 'illegitimate' or racist by the Islamic or revolutionary community and withdrawing from all US-sponsored military and economic pacts. The absence of any clearly formulated Islamic theory of foreign policy led to *ad hoc* decisions which were improvised on a day-to-day basis in the face of newly emerging circumstances. Given the multiplicity of decision-making centres in the early days of the Islamic Republic, foreign policy positions and statements were, at best, contradictory and confused. Iran's position *vis-à-vis* western powers differed in relation to individual countries. The French embassy in Teheran was showered with flowers for the French hospitality that was accorded to Khomeini at Neauph Le Chateau, while relations with the United States, understandably, lost their pre-revolutionary fervour and sunk to a minimum, yet acceptable, diplomatic level.

As the clerical leadership gradually imposed its monolithic rule at home, it sought to formulate a distinctively Islamic theory of foreign policy. The most important characteristic of this policy was its fundamental incompatibility with the conventional definition, content and practice of foreign policy. Let us start from the orthodox premise that the objective of foreign policy is the defence and enhancement of all aspects of the national interest, economic, political and strategic, in relations with other nation states. The interaction of nation states in the pursuit of their national interests is governed and limited by the international code of conduct embodied in the UN Charter. International recognition and respectability flow from the degree to which nation states abide by the rules and laws established by the international bodies representing the world community.

In an enlightening article, Seyyed Ali Qaderi argues that a theoretical basis for an Islamic foreign policy can be constructed around three principles, all of which are well rooted in *Fiqh* or Islamic jurisprudence.[1] These principles are: the defence and maintenance of the abode of Islam; invitation, and rejection of all other paths. The application of each of these principles leads to a rejection of the mainstream definition of foreign policy.

The notion of nation states demarcated by boundaries has no place in Islam. In the *Shari'a*, reference is made to the *ummah* or the Islamic community. The *Dar al-Islam* (Abode of Islam) is viewed 'as one vast homogeneous commonwealth of people who have a common goal and a common destiny and who are guided by a common ideology in all matters both spiritual and temporal'.[2] The Moslem *ummah*, living within the Abode of Islam, is governed by the *Shari'a*, according to which sovereignty belongs to God alone. Therefore, the interests of Islam cannot be national, but collective and supranational. The defence of the Abode of Islam against the *Dar al-Kufr* (Abode of Disbelievers) concerns the interests of Islamic countries as one unit, set against the interests of the rest of the world. The reality of nationally divided Islamic nation states imposes the primary task of unifying all Islamic countries into a single Islamic community. This approach clearly qualifies as expansionist, according to conventional foreign policy standards. It was on this basis that Khomeini said: 'Moslems have to form a single unit, they have to become one and should not separate themselves from each other. They should not view boundaries as lines which divide their hearts. United, Moslems possess immense power'.[3]

The second principle involves the concept of invitation. Just as the Prophet was asked in the Qur'an to spread the religion, 'the Abode of Islam' is also charged with the responsibility of inviting all non-Moslems to join the faith. The growth and security of the faith depends on the effectiveness of invitation. While the principle of invitation can operate in practice through the use of propaganda and military and economic aid, some types of invitation in Islam can also undermine the mainstream definition of foreign policy. Motahhari argues that invitation has two stages, first wise counsel and good admonition, then, if this method does not attain the expected objective, struggle, *jihad* and the exercise of power.[4]

The familiar concept of 'exporting the revolution', which was invoked by all leaders of the Islamic Republic, was only a reaffirmation of this second principle of Islamic foreign policy. Even among the clerical leadership, differences existed concerning the correct determination of the stage of invitation. The export of revolution was defined by some as the establishment of an ideal model in Iran, that other countries would take as an example. This group believed that exporting the revolution could only be achieved through education and propaganda work. A second group of clerical leaders believed in exporting the revolution by force. According to this group, invitation, as a principle of foreign policy rooted in the *Shari'a*, necessitated bloody confrontation to expand the *Dar al-Islam* and to weaken the *Dar al-Kufr*. Generally, Khomeini's exhortations to export the revolution refer to the necessity of the expansion of the *Dar al-Islam* but leave the nature and manner of this exportation open. On the occasion of the Iranian new year on 21 March 1980, Khomeini said: 'We have to try hard to export our revolution and we should abandon the idea of not exporting our revolution . . . all the superpowers and all the powers are committed to our destruction and if we remain in a confined and enclosed environment we shall definitely face defeat'.[5]

According to the third principle of Islamic foreign policy, the Islamic community has to reject all deviationary paths, or all those trajectories that are not based on Islam. The famous slogan of 'Neither the East, nor the West' is based on this principle. The rejection of all other paths includes any institutions and relations that are based on anything other than Islamic precepts. Participation in any relation in which the rules, procedures and objectives are dictated by non-Islamic powers is, consequently, unacceptable. Qaderi argues that, according to this principle, even the prevalent world balance of power counts as something that is imposed on Islamic countries, as does the acceptance of arbitration and judgement by international courts and institutions.[6] Even the acceptance of veto power in the Security Council is argued to be problematic if one wishes to uphold the principle of rejecting the hegemony of others in all aspects of international activity. Compromise and concession, which constitute the most important tools of conflict resolution on the international scene, are simply not available to practitioners of an Islamic foreign policy.

Theoretically, therefore, a genuinely Islamic foreign policy would have to be Islamocentric with universalist aspirations, aggressive and expansionist, seeking to export its revolution either by example or by force. It would have to be inflexible and intransigent in relation to the institutions and rules of the non-Islamic international community. Clearly the exercise of this kind of foreign policy is likely to lead to a loss of respectability for the practising country. From an Islamic position, however, it is 'the abode of disbelievers' or the non-Islamic world community which has rebelled against the government of God and imposed an unjust and, therefore, illegal system.

In 1943, Khomeini wrote that:

> the only government that reason accepts as legitimate and welcomes freely and happily is the government of God, Whose every act is just and Whose right it is to rule over the whole world and all the particles of existence. Whatever He makes use of is His own property and whatever He takes, from whomever he takes, is again His own property. No one can deny this except the mentally disturbed. It is in contrast with the government of God that the nature of all existing governments becomes clear. It is on the basis of this comparison that the Islamic government can be considered as the only legitimate one.[7]

A foreign policy based on the three principles discussed provides a fairly predictable pattern of positions, statements and activities on the international political scene. It would be incorrect to say that the Islamic government has entirely based its own foreign policy on the theoretical construction presented above. Even though it has generously used religious justifications in supporting its acts, Iran's foreign policy has been more cyclical and unpredictable than a strict observance of the theory would allow for.

Iran's post-revolutionary foreign policy has been essentially conditioned by four factors. First, the different interpretations of the international role and obligations that Islam as an ideology imposes on a practising country. Second, the domestic political environment and national rather than international considerations. Third, influential historical factors that have left an imprint on the political consciousness of the people. Fourth, a realistic sense of survival. The flexibility of Islam allows Islamic leaders to find some Islamic justification for all their positions and subsequent changes in them. As Dr Ali-Akbar Velayati, the minister of foreign affairs, told his audience on 25 November 1986, 'Islamic ideology is a rich and fertile ideology and we shall find whatever we want in it'.[8]

Khomeini's foreign policy positions, before he became a serious contender for power in 1978, were essentially based on his dislike of foreigners. Foreign ideas posed a threat to traditionalism in general. He viewed the love for westernization which motivated Mustafa Kemal (Ataturk) in Turkey and Reza Shah in Iran to embark on modernization campaigns as synonymous with anti-clerical movements. A conscious policy of expunging society of all its religious traditions was seen by Khomeini as the natural consequence of foreign penetration in Islamic lands. His xenophobia was thus essentially a response to the weakening political position of the clergy in the face of modernization.

Khomeini's initial public disagreement with the Shah was over the reforms known as the White Revolution, which included land reform, the nationalization of forests, the privatization of nationalized industries, workers sharing profits in factories, women's suffrage and the creation of a literacy corps. Khomeini lashed out at the concept of women's suffrage 'as unacceptable from a religious point of view' and considered it as a step towards 'the spread of corruption and prostitution among women'.[9] The wide support that both the United States and the Soviet Union gave to these reforms undoubtedly left a mark on Khomeini. While Radio Moscow labelled the opponents of the White Revolution as 'reactionaries' and 'agents of the West', the British, American and German press referred to them only as 'reactionaries'.[10] It was common knowledge that the Shah's reform programme was at the behest of Kennedy and under pressure from the United States. Correctly viewing the White Revolution as a US concoction, which would lead to even greater westernization as a result of Iran's further integration in the world capitalist system, Khomeini started to capitalize on Iranian anti-colonial sentiments which had developed during the Mossadeq period. By unleashing an essentially anti-western movement under the guise of an anti-imperialist struggle, Khomeini successfully co-opted nationalist and left forces.

On 13 October 1964, the *Majlis* approved a law which came to be known as the Capitulation Agreement in Iran. According to this law, US military personnel and their dependants were no longer held accountable in Iranian courts for crimes committed in Iran. The extension of full diplomatic immunity to US military personnel effectively undermined Iran's claim to national sovereignty and exposed its increasing subservience to and dependence on the United States. The humiliation of the Capitulation Agreement was deepened by the US's curt offer of a $200 million tied loan to Iran. When the receipt of what was commonly believed to be blood money was officially recognized by parliament, Khomeini responded with an indignant speech. he said:

> If an American servant or an American cook assassinates your *marja* [source of religious imitation] in the middle of the bazaar or runs him over, the Iranian police do not have the right to stop him! Iranian courts do not have the right to try him! The files must be sent to America! And there the masters will decide what is to be done![11]

Khomeini pointed out that the acceptance of the Capitulation Agreement

> has reduced the status of the Iranian people to a level lower than that of an American dog. If some one runs over a dog belonging to an American, he will be interrogated. Even if the Shah of Iran were to run over a dog belonging to an American, he would be interrogated, but if an American cook runs over the Shah, no one will have the right to object.[12]

Khomeini had chosen the correct moment to attack all foreign influences and push himself forward as the leader of the anti-imperialist cause in Iran. Khomeini's words that were often repeated after the victory of the revolution were:

> Are we to be trampled upon by American boots just because we are a weak nation and have no dollars? America is worse than Britain; Britain is worse than America; the Soviet Union is worse than both of them. Each is worse and more vile than the other, but today our business is with the Americans. . . . Today the source of all our problems is America and Israel, however the source of all Israel's problems is America too, our members of parliament and our ministers are stooges of America, all are American stooges.[13]

The great majority of politicized Iranians who longed for an anti-imperialist and anti-monarchist leader only heard Khomeini's anti-American discourse, completely ignoring his real concern which he never concealed. In the same speech, Khomeini said: 'They wish to destroy the influence of the clergy since they have realised that clerical influence will not permit them to do what they want to do' and he concluded with the ultimate invocation of all politicized clerics 'beware as Islam is on the verge of disappearance, Islam is in danger'.[14]

Once Khomeini became a real political alternative to the Shah's régime and came to view his own rule and that of the clergy as a reality, he modified his tactics concerning foreign-affairs issues. In his speeches to the Iranian people which were circulated on cassettes on a wide scale in Iran, Khomeini kept on attacking the United States as 'evil' and responsible for the pillage of Iran's wealth.[15] Khomeini resorted to his regular attacks against the United States for its support of the Shah's régime, the Soviet Union for its plunder of Iranian gas, Britain for imposing Reza Shah on Iran and China for its support of the Shah's government during the revolution.

> From that end it is the British that take away our wealth, from this end it is others. The Americans are worst of all and so are the Soviets. They have all attacked our people and have united to keep this man [the Shah] in power and to plunder us.[16]

While the intensity of attacks against foreigners was maintained at a high level for domestic consumption, Khomeini's position on foreign-affairs issues became refined and moderate when he responded to foreign journalists. In response to the regular question posed to him on Iran's policy towards foreign powers after the victory of the revolution, Khomeini repeatedly provided the answer that: 'Our relation with foreigners will be based on mutual respect'.[17] On relations with the United States he told CBS correspondents that 'if the U.S. respects the future Iranian government, we will in turn base our position on mutual respect'.[18] Yet Khomeini explained the basis of his opposition to westernization and told foreign correspondents that 'the desire of the Islamic government and our people is to put an end to Western and all foreign penetration and influence in Iran'.[19] This dual approach to the West, moderation for foreign consumption and intransigence for domestic consumption, makes sense in terms of the increasing role of pragmatic *real politik* and the importance of the domestic political scene.

During the revolution and after victory, clerical leaders met and discussed issues with US officials. It is reported that William Sullivan, the US ambassador to Iran, and other embassy officers established contacts with and met Ayatollah Beheshti.[20] Negotiations between Sullivan and Beheshti are said to have led to the evacuation of the American embassy after its first occupation on 14 February 1979 by an armed group.[21] Henry Precht, Iran desk officer at the State Department and Bruce Laingen, the US chargé d'affaires after Sullivan's departure, are reported also to have met Beheshti. Precht recalls that he even met Ayatollah Montazeri after he attended his Friday congregational prayers in October 1979.[22]

The meetings between US and non-clerical Iranian revolutionary officials were more regular. According to James Bill, such direct contacts started in May 1978 when Mohammed Tavassoli, a prominent member Bazargan's Iran Freedom Movement, met US embassy officials.[23] Bazargan recalls that he and a clerical member of the Revolutionary Council met ambassador Sullivan during the latter half of

January 1979.[24] It is reported that on two occasions, American officials of the State Department and the CIA briefed Prime Minister Bazargan, Foreign Minister Yazdi and Deputy Prime Minister Amir-Entezam on the political situation in Iraq, the Palestinians, Afghanistan, the Soviet Union and the energy situation in the Soviet Union.[25]

By the autumn of 1979, the French and Soviet ambassadors had met Khomeini. The US still refused to establish such direct contact. Although there is no indication that Khomeini would have agreed to such an encounter, it was clear that the US posture towards Khomeini and the Iranian revolution remained reticent and ambivalent. It was only on 5 September 1979 that, according to a memorandum entitled *Policy Towards Iran*, the US decided to approach Khomeini and signal the US's definite acceptance of the revolution.[26] This was two months before Iranian students took over the US embassy. Expressing Khomeini's often repeated desire for mutual respect between the US and Iran, in early October 1979, Deputy Prime Minister Amir-Entezam criticized the 'U.S. failure to convey those signals which indicate U.S. acceptance of the Iranian revolution and a willingness to come to terms with the revolution on the basis of equality and respect'.[27] The US remained insensitive to the fact that on the domestic scene Khomeini had whipped up considerable anti-US sentiments to attract as wide a following as possible and unless the United States were to provide an excuse for Khomeini to 'forgive' them, he was obliged to act radically if he were to maintain his revolutionary image. As Amir-Entezam had requested, a strong state-ment of support or a message heralding a new chapter in Iran-US relations by US officials might have provided a face-saving pretext allowing for a reconciliatory posture. Such a signal never materialized. Khomeini thus reserved the right to deliver his anti-US promises when he deemed politically expedient.

The hostage crisis: foreign policy in the service of domestic expediency

On 24 October 1979, Iranian newspapers reported that the Shah had entered the US and had been hospitalized immediately. The spokesman of the ministry of foreign affairs expressed Iran's dissatisfaction with the Shah's trip to the United States but announced that in view of the fact that the Shah was being treated for cancer, Iran had been assured by the United States that he would not engage in political activities.[28] In a rally organized by the IRP on 26 October in support of the Constitution which was being drafted in the Assembly of Experts and was encountering stiff opposition by non-clerically supported organizations, Beheshti pointed out that Iran wished to have friendly and humane relations with all countries, but he warned the United States to clarify its position in relation to Iran. The greatest headache of the clerical leadership at this time was to get the Constitution which legitimized the governance of the jurisconsult ratified as smoothly as possible in a referendum. On 28

October, Khomeini said: 'we are confronted with despicable creatures in the U.S. . . . The U.S. is the source of all our problems. The U.S. is the source of all problems that Moslems face'.[29] The speech was clearly intended to unleash an anti-US crusade with Khomeini at the helm. The deflection of public attention from pressing internal problems to an external issue such as the United States mobilized and unified the people behind a common cause and catapulted Khomeini into the limelight as undisputable leader, just as his role as the governing jurisconsult was under attack. By admitting the Shah and remaining ambiguous towards the revolution, the United States facilitated Khomeini's task of rekindling popular anti-US feeling.

On 1 November 1979, as Prime Minister Bazargan, Foreign Minister Yazdi and Defence Minister Mustafa Chamran left for Algiers to attend the celebrations marking the twenty-fifth anniversary of the Algerian revolution, Khomeini sent a message inviting Iranian students to attack the United States and Israel. He said:

> our enemies are determined to conspire against us and these days they are intensifying their efforts to disturb the peace. Our high school, university and seminary students are obliged to concentrate all their attacks against the U.S. to extradite the murderous Shah, while they should themselves remain united and supportive of the Islamic Revolution.[30]

Khomeini's words were timed to set the tone for a huge student rally, to be held on 4 November. In Algiers, the national security adviser, Zbigniew Brzezinski, met Bazargan, Yazdi and Chamran. Bazargan recalls that Turkey's chargé d'affaires in Teheran informed him that Brzezinski was going to be in Algiers and would, therefore, probably come to meet him.[31] According to Bazargan, before leaving for Algiers, Yazdi had sought the 'Imam's' opinion on relations with the United States and its prospects. Yazdi was reported to have also discussed the provisional government's views on the matter.[32] News of the one-and-a-half-hour-long meeting was reported in Iranian newspapers as an important event; it was emphasized that it took place at Bazargan's residence in Algiers.[33] The Islamic Republic Party (IRP) published a letter questioning Bazargan's meeting with Brzezinski at a time when Khomeini was assailing the United States. The IRP demanded that Bazargan should provide a fully detailed report of his meeting to the 'Imam' and the Revolutionary Council. On 4 November, the same day that the IRP published its letter, the student rally was held. It led to the occupation of the US embassy and the 444-day-long hostage crisis.

Bruce Laingen, who had left the embassy early in the morning to pay a visit to the ministry of foreign affairs, was informed by the embassy security officer of the occupation of the embassy. Yazdi, who had just arrived from Algiers, was on his way from the airport to his office. At the ministry, Laingen was initially told that the students intended to stage a peaceful demonstration and that Khomeini would soon be on the radio ordering them to evacuate the embassy.[34] On his arrival at the embassy, Yazdi is reported to have assured Laingen that 'the events at the embassy were comparable to a sit-in at a US university and that the situation would be resolved within 48 hours'.[35] Yazdi's promise to Laingen indicates that the provisional government was not informed of the embassy occupation and that Yazdi believed that Khomeini was unaware of the events and that, once informed, he would order the evacuation of the embassy. The provisional government was kept in the dark, because it was going to become a very timely sacrificial lamb.

Less than a month before the referendum on the controversial Constitution, a second revolution was desperately needed. This second revolution was to be against US imperialism. The resignation of the provisional government would be presented as the end of liberalism and moderation and the Islamic Republic could, subsequently, lay claim to the leadership of the Third World's anti-imperialist movement. All members of the opposition, especially the left and the nationalist elements, would be forced to support such a movement and Khomeini would emerge as the great anti-imperialist leader. The hysteria and mass excitement created by the unprecedented act of taking US diplomats hostage would distract the public for at least one month from all domestic problems. This was all the time the clerical leadership needed for the Constitution to become officially and legally binding. Bazargan repeatedly pointed to the fact that he had presented his resignation to the Revolutionary Council on 23 October (two weeks before the embassy occupation) and that it was only accepted on 6 November (two days after the occupation). Yet the clerical leadership felt that it was important to present Bazargan's resignation as a consequence not only of his bourgeois liberal domestic policy, but also of his compromising and reconciliatory foreign policy.

The hostage crisis, which constituted an important aspect of Iran's post-revolution foreign policy, was essentially an outcome of growing internal problems. The step by step unfolding of events indicates a well-planned operation, similar to that which led to the cultural revolution. James Bill maintains that 'Ayatollah Khomeini himself at first quietly expressed disapproval of the move but later became a strong supporter when he realised the overwhelming popularity of the act among the Iranian masses'.[36] Furthermore, Bill believes that 'IRP leaders such as Mohammed Beheshti were initally ambivalent about the action',[37] although he does recognize that

> it now seems certain that the militants had plans to move on the American Embassy long before 4 November and that they put their plans into action when anti-American rhetoric and feeling began to peak in the first three days of that month.[38]

In fact, circumstantial evidence indicates not only that Khomeini and the top IRP leaders were aware of the students decision to occupy the embassy, but that Khomeini inspired and directed the take over through well-timed and targeted speeches and that once the operation succeeded, he masterfully used the situation to further his political objectives. Bani-Sadr's recollection concurs with the theory that Khomeini was directly responsible for the hostage crisis. According to Bani-Sadr, Khomeini had told him:

> We will keep the hostages and once we have successfully completed our domestic tasks we well release them. Today the hostage issue has united the people, the opposition does not dare to oppose us and we will easily be able to get the new Constitution ratified. Once we conclude the Presidential and Parliamentary elections we will release them.[39]

In their first public statement, the students who had occupied the embassy called themselves 'the Islamic students following the Imam's line' and assailed US imperialism's destructive role in the region.[40] A crucial aspect of Shariati's subsystem was being used and the masses were being told that Islam was synonymous with anti-imperialism. Mass mobilization centred on daily anti-US and anti-Israel sloganeering and speech making followed by a barrage of information on US interventionist policies and atrocities in the Third World. The Islamic Republic's anti-US campaign politicized a hard core of dedicated Moslem youth whose love for Islam and the 'Imam' could not be divided from their hatred for the United States and Israel. At least for the young Islamic zealots who came to constitute the large majority of the IRG certain precedents were set, deviation from which was heretical. Compromise, conciliation, negotiation and, finally, behind-the-scenes deals with imperialists and Zionists became forbidden and unforgivable acts in the ideology of these militant Moslems.

The self-righteous and intransigent and revolutionary image which Khomeini wished to portray to the world was well described in the nineteenth proclamation of the Moslem students following the 'Imam's line':

> It is surpising that Carter and his detested agents wish to enter into negotiations with Iran over the hostages and overall U.S.-Iran relations . . . Haven't we already said that negotiation is impossible and all we are asking for is the extradition of the Shah? Shall we ever forget that all U.S. agents are amongst the worst anti-God and anti-people murderers? . . . Who does America want to negotiate with? With Khomeini, the great leader of the revolution? How simplistic can one be? Do they not know that the spirit of God, Imam Khomeini, embodies the consciousness of our people . . . and is never prepared to negotiate with treacherous leaders? Who else remains? Do they wish to negotiate with the head of the Revolutionary Council? Do they forget that the Iranian people never forgave their Prime Minister who met with one of these murderers?[41]

Faced with an unprecedented situation and a government whose arguments and actions were totally incomprehensible by conventional foreign-policy standards, the Carter administration embarked on numerous strategies to bring pressure on Iran and secure the release of the hostages. On 12 November, President Carter ordered US oil purchasers to stop all transactions with Iran.[42] Two days later, Carter ordered a freeze on all Iranian assets, including deposits in US banks and their foreign branches and subsidiaries.[43] Having considered military options from the second day of the crisis, the White House released a statement on 20 November, suggesting the possibility of US military action. The statement was in response to the mounting rhetoric from Teheran that the hostages would be put on trial.[44] The United States backed up its threat with the dispatch of the aircraft carrier USS *Kitty Hawk* from the Pacific to the Arabian Sea. According to Gary Sick, on 23 November, Carter sent an unpublicized blunt message to Iranian leaders 'warning them of the US intention to respond militarily if the hostages were harmed or subjected to trials'.[45] On the Iranian side, Khomeini kept up a systematic virulent verbal bombardment of the United States. As US pressure increased, Khomeini's defiant and bombastic tone hardened. Having assured the Iranians that 'the Americans cannot do a damn thing', Khomeini escalated the propaganda war by responding to the possibility of US military intervention in Iran on 21 November. Khomeini said: 'we shall not retreat a step . . . we would welcome martyrdom . . . since this is no longer a struggle between Iran and the US but one between Islam and blasphemy'.[46] Even before the UN Security Council passed Resolution 457 demanding the release of the hostages and a settlement of differences between Iran and the United States on 4 December, Khomeini condemned its decision. On 28 November, Khomeini attacked the council for being a US puppet and said 'our people will not accept the verdict of the UN Security Council whose policies are dictated by the US'.[47]

Efforts by Secretary-General Waldheim on 1 January 1980, the UN Commission on 23 February and Qotbzadeh and Bani-Sadr on 1 April 1980 all failed because of Khomeini's refusal to show any flexibility. He refused to meet any of the foreign intermediaries and continued to assert that: 'we shall fight with the US till the end of our life'.[48] Even the initial step of transferring the hostages from the custody of the Islamic students who followed the 'Imam's' line to the Revolutionary Council was blocked by Khomeini. It is reported that after the Revolutionary Council voted 8–3 in favour of the transfer, the issue was taken to Khomeini who refused to approve the council's recommendation once he was told that Beheshti and two other clerics had disagreed with the transfer.[49] Khomeini maintained that the hostage crisis had to be resolved by Majlis, the parliament. After the transfer of the hostages to the Revolutionary Council failed to materialize, the United States broke off diplomatic relations with Iran on 7 April. Subsequently, Algeria served as Iran's diplomatic agent.

Frustrated at the breakdown of all attempts at negotiation and humiliated by Iran's refusal to release the hostages, the Carter administration came under even greater public pressure for some kind of effective action. Against Secretary of State Cyrus Vance's suggestion that the United

States should continue to exercise restraint, since the hostages would soon lose their value for Khomeini, Carter chose to launch a rescue mission.[50] At 7.30 pm on 24 April 1980, the rescue operation named Eagle Claw was launched. The rescue mission was planned in five stages.[51] First, eight Sea Stallion RH–53D helicopters and six C–130 aircraft were to fly into Iran and meet at a remote landing strip called Desert One, near the small town of Tabas. Second, after having refuelled and loaded, the helicopters were to fly under cover of darkness to a remote site in the mountains above Teheran, where they were to be camouflaged. Third, on the following night the rescue team was to drive to Teheran, rescue the hostages and get picked up by the helicopters. Fourth, the helicopters were to fly to Desert Two, an abandoned airfield close to Teheran where the rescue team and the hostages would board the C–130 transport planes. Fifth, abandoning the helicopters, the C–130 planes would leave the country under heavy US cover.

By the time the Sea Stallions met at Desert One, helicopter six had been abandoned somewhere in Iran, due to impending rotor-blade failure. Helicopter five experienced malfunction of essential flight instruments and returned to the aircraft carrier *Nimitz* in the Arabian Sea. Helicopter two experienced hydraulic problems, but proceded to Desert One, where it was discovered that the malfunction could not be repaired, and it had to be abandoned there. Since the prerequisite of advancing to stage two of the mission required the minimum of six helicopters, the mission commander decided to abort the operation. He demanded and received approval from the president. While the helicopters were refuelling for the withdrawal, one helicopter collided with the C–130 refuelling plane, setting both craft aflame. The rescue group left behind the remaining helicopters and eight dead servicemen. At 1.00 am on 25 April, the White House issued an announcement that a rescue mission had been attempted and that it had failed.

The failure of the rescue operation was heralded in Iran as a proof of God's love and support for the Islamic Republic's just position. The defeat of US might and technology by natural calamities, such as the sandstorm which helped cripple the rescue mission, was referred to as a miracle by God. Khomeini's image and position as a religious leader favoured and even aided by God were enhanced among the masses. Furthermore, he was placed in a position to point to the rescue mission as a proof of his assurance to the Iranian people that 'the U.S. cannot do a damn thing'.

Once the Constitution was ratified, the presidential and parliamentary elections successfully concluded, the cultural revolution implemented and the US elections were drawing closer, the Islamic government signalled its desire to commence the process of releasing the hostages. On 9 September 1980, the West German embassy in Teheran informed Bonn that a high-ranking Iranian official wished to meet secretly with a high-ranking American official to discuss the settlement of the hostage crisis.[52] The high-ranking Iranian official was neither a member of the government, the parliament nor a high-ranking clergyman. He was Sadeq

Tabatabai, the former spokesman of the provisional government, whose only credential at the time was his family linkage with Khomeini. Tabatabai, Ahmad Khomeini's brother-in-law, met a high-ranking American group in the presence of the West German Foreign Minister Hans-Deitrich Genscher in Bonn on 15 September 1980.[53] In this meeting, the two parties came close to a mutually acceptable set of principles which could have led to the release of hostages had not the Iran-Iraq war broken out on 22 September. According to Robert Owen, the legal adviser to the secretary of state, who was present at the meeting, the second issue raised by Tabatabai was whether the US 'would be prepared to supply Iran with the spare parts it needed for its vast arsenal of American military equipment' following the release of the hostages.[54] Tabatabai's enquiry must have been previously cleared by Khomeini, which indicates that in spite of his anti-US stance and self-sufficiency rhetoric, even before the outbreak of the Iran-Iraq war, Khomeini's sense of pragmatism clearly prevailed over the domestically emphasized ideology and Islamic purity.

On 2 November 1980 the Majlis, which had been made responsible for the fate of the hostages, sent a lengthy resolution to the State Department through Reza Malek, the Algerian ambassador.[55] The Majlis resolution was a complicated version of Khomeini's four conditions for the release of the hostages. According to Khomeini, the United States would have to: pledge that it would not intervene in the internal affairs of Iran; return all frozen assets to Iran; cancel all US claims against Iran; and return the wealth of the Shah.[56] On 19 January 1981, approximately four months after the meeting between Khomeini's envoy, Tabatabai, and the representatives of the US State Department, an agreement was reached between the 'Great Satan' and the Islamic Republic, securing the release of all US hostages. On 20 January 1981, the Islamic government freed the 52 US hostages whom it had held for 444 days. According to Robert Owen:

> in response to the four Iranian demands, we gave away nothing of value that was ours; we simply returned a relatively small part of what was theirs and the balance held back to pay off much of what Iran owed to our claimants. . . Arguably, therefore, if substantial concessions were made by anyone during the negotiation process, virtually all were made by Iran.[57]

In Iran, President Bani-Sadr criticized the process through which the hostages were released. He argued that none of the four conditions set for the release of the hostages had been met and proceeded to call for the prosecution of Prime Minister Rajaee, and the prime minister's adviser and head of the Iranian negotiation team, Behzad Nabavi. Bani-Sadr maintained that in releasing the hostages, the Rajaee government had violated the Constitution and embezzled public funds.[58] Bani-Sadr knew that the Rajaee government and Behzad Nabavi were only cogs in a larger wheel, but did not wish to attack the real decision maker. Khomeini turned a blind eye to the release of the hostages, but continued with his

domestic rhetoric against the United States, declaiming that: 'the worldmon-
gering U.S. should know that the dear people of Iran and Khomeini will
not give up until we have thoroughly destroyed all her interests'.[59]

The expansion and containment of Iran's revolutionary Islam

The fall of a régime which had become a reliable junior partner in the US
defence strategy in the region was an important initial setback for US
interests. Iran benefited from exceptional arrangements with the Nixon
administration, which allowed it to purchase any conventional weapon it
desired from the US arsenal. Iran was thus exempt from the 'arms-sales
review process in the State and Defense Departments'.[60] The Shah's
staunch anti-communism and his concern for containing the spread of
revolutionary movements, combined with Iran's military and financial
might, provided the right mix for the emergence of Iran as a sub-
imperialist power in the region. Between 1972 and 1977, the value of US
military sales to Iran amounted to $16.2 billion.[61] In early 1972, Iran
deployed its forces to Oman in order to crush the Marxist Popular Front
for the Liberation of Oman. Iranian troops stayed in Oman until 1978 to
obliterate the 'subversive communist threat' to the region. The Shah
continued to provide military aid to Pakistan in its struggle against the
Baluchi Popular Front for Armed Resistance and to the Somalian
government which was fighting against the Ethiopian Marxist-Leninist
government. The Shah's anti-subversion policy in the Persian Gulf and
beyond earned him the tacit approval and respect of the conservative Arab
states and the animosity of the radical ones. Iran and Israel, who had
excellent political, economic, military and intelligence relationships
with one another, constituted the United States' main political outposts
in the region. The two collaborated with each other in keeping at bay any
challenge to the balance of power which had been established to the
benefit of the United States in the Middle East.

On 18 February 1979, a week after the victory of the revolution, Yasser
Arafat arrived in Teheran and was given an official welcome befitting a
head of state. Two days after his arrival, the building which housed the
unofficial Israeli diplomatic mission in Iran was turned over to Arafat and
the Palestinian flag was hoisted. Arafat welcomed the Iranian revolution
as one which broke the encirclement of the Palestinian movement. He
said: 'this is not Iran's revolution and it is not a revolution which should
remain confined to Iran. This is an Islamic revolution and will expand to
the whole region'.[62] Asked whether he expected the Iranian army and,
especially, the air force to help the Palestinians in their struggle, Arafat
answered: 'we have said that we are two revolutions in one and two people
in one, I will leave the rest to U.S. computers to analyse'.[63]

The Shah's identification with US interests naturally led to the
assumption that an anti-Shah revolution would be an anti-imperialist
revolution and could, consequently, become a source of diplomatic,
economic and military aid to all liberation movements. Iran's revolution

led to a rising tide of expectation among anti-imperialist, anti-Zionist and Third Worldist movements. Khomeini played a decisive role in presenting Iran as a dynamic power which intended to usher in a new balance of international power. Initially addressing the Islamic states, Khomeini encouraged them to set aside their differences emphasizing that: 'once a great Islamic government was established, such a government would be able to prevail over the whole world'.[64] Invoking the Islamic principle of inviting all to join the cause of Islam, Khomeini presented himself as the leader of a world revolutionary Islamic movement which aimed at liberating the world and reconstructing it on the basis of a new Islamic world order. As the leader of Iran's revolution against a strongly US-backed régime, Khomeini could lay claim to the mantle of a successful anti-imperialist prophet, with at least the possibility of implementing his alternative model. The revolutionary agents of Khomeini's strategy were, naturally, the disinherited and the discontent. Yet Khomeini wished to apply his domestic methodology of gaining the support of different social classes, by promising each what they wanted, to the world at large. If Islam could give all the politically discontented in the world, in all their diversity, something to struggle for, then a well-concerted intentional Islamic movement could be launched. It seemed that, initially at least, such a naïve global design did indeed preoccupy the clerical leaders.

The development of the Islamic Republic's foreign policy in practice, however, went through three different broad stages. The first stage was characterized by the provisional government's attempt to conduct a mainstream foreign policy based on mutual respect and non-interference in the affairs of other countries. The provisional government demonstrated its 'revolutionary fervour' by withdrawing from the pro-western Central Treaty Organization (CENTO) and joining the Non-Aligned Movement which was, theoretically, very close to the centrepiece of Mossadeq's foreign policy, namely 'negative equilibrium' (*movazeneh manfī*). Bazargan's government intended to contain the over-zealous passion for internationalizing the revolution. He saw the main concern of the revolution as presenting a model Islamic Iran worthy of imitation by other Islamic states. Following the principles of his own subsystem, invitation to Islam according to Bazargan was only possible and desirable through the setting of an example and not through force. While revolutionary rhetoric could not be controlled at home, Ibrahim Yazdi who was the provisional government's second minister of foreign affairs tried hard to assure all Islamic countries, especially the Persian Gulf states, that Iran had no expansionist ambitions. Yazdi and Tabatabai, the government spokesman, travelled extensively abroad spreading the message that Iran's Islamic foreign policy was based on peaceful coexistence with all countries that accepted, basing their relations on mutual respect and the principle of non-intervention. At home, Bazargan's government sought to neutralize and counter statements that antagonized and alienated other countries.

The provisional government's conduct of foreign policy was greatly hampered by the unofficial foreign-policy statements of the clergy. Clerical statements and activities, especially in relation to the Persian Gulf states, frequently placed the provisional government in an embarrassing diplomatic situation. The provisional government had to forcefully deny Ayatollah Rouhani's claim that Iran would annex Bahrain unless it adopted Iran's Islamic model. Nevertheless, Abu Mohsen, one of the leaders of the Party of Bahrain's Disinherited which was created at the time of Khomeini's arrival in Teheran and claimed 1,600 members, was allowed to give a press conference in Teheran and announce that his movement was preparing for armed struggle in Bahrain to create an Islamic Republic.[65]

On 28 August 1979, Modaressi, who was Khomeini's representative in Bahrain, was arrested for anti-state activities. Modaressi went to Dubai where he was again arrested and finally forced to return to Iran on 23 September. On his arrival in Teheran, Modaressi accused the Persian Gulf states of placing a cultural and political quarantine on the Islamic revolution because they feared the ripple effect of Iran's authentic Islamic ideology. He explained that books printed in the Islamic Republic were banned and posters of 'Imam' Khomeini were torn down by the government authorities in Bahrain and the United Arab Emeritates.[66] Three days after the expulsion of Modaressi, Khomeini's representative in Kuwait was also sent back to Iran for disturbing public peace. Sayyed Abbas Mohri and his entire family were expelled from Kuwait after forty years of residency there.[67] This wave of expulsion came after Khomeini declared that the Islamic Republic's flag would be hoisted all over the world and that 'Islam based on Qur'anic principles should prevail in all countries'.[68]

As tension between Iran and the Arab states in the Persian Gulf rose, Bazargan's government took the initiative of minimizing the damage and normalizing relations. Tabatabai was dispatched on a tour of all Arab states, especially Kuwait and Bahrain, to reassure these countries that the government was resolutely committed to a policy of non-intervention and that, in future, it would control the activities of the clerics in matters of foreign policy. As a result of Tabatabai's goodwill tour, Kuwaiti newspapers announced a new phase of *rapprochement* and co-operation between Iran and the Arab states in the Persian Gulf.[69] At home, Bazargan met Bahrain's ambassador to dispel all doubts about the Iranian government's good intentions. However, while the provisional government tried hard to abide by the legal and diplomatic conventions of international relations, its efforts were being continuously undermined by various political groups in Iran who believed that Iran had to become actively involved in supporting radical and revolutionary causes.

Relations with Libya constituted a major issue on which the provisional government came under considerable pressure from pro-Libyan clerical groups. Sayyed Mohammed Montazeri, Ayatollah Montazeri's son, who later died in the bomb explosion which killed 72 members of the IRP, was the most prominent and active figure among the pro-Libyan groups. Montazeri wished to arrange a meeting between Khomeini and

Qadaffi in Iran to force the provisional government to establish diplomatic relations with Libya. Bazargan's government, however, held Qadaffi directly responsible for the disappearance of Imam Musa Sadr. Musa Sadr was born in Iran and became the leader of *Shi'i* Moslems in Lebanon and the founder of the Movement of the Deprived (*Harakat al-Mahruminn*) which was launched on 17 March 1974, in the city of Ba'albak. The movement later became known as AMAL, the acronym of its military wing *Afwaj al-Maqawama al-Lubnnaniya* (Lebanese Resistance Detachments). AMAL also means hope.[70] Many of the revolution's dignitaries, such as Mustafa Chamran, the deputy prime minister and later minister of defence, Saddeq Qotbzadeh, the first director of the Islamic Republic's Radio and Television Services, and Ahmad Khomeini, had received military training in AMAL camps and were closely attached to Musa Sadr.

Mohammed Montazeri's plan to bring Qadaffi to Teheran failed, but Abdul-Salaam Jaloud, Qadaffi's right-hand man, arrived in Teheran discreetly on 22 April 1979. In the meeting that was arranged between Jaloud and Khomeini, Jaloud was told how important the disappearance of Musa Sadr was to the Iranian clergy and people. Although Jaloud presented the official Libyan line that Sadr left Libya and was in Rome when he disappeared, Khomeini called on Qadaffi to solve the Sadr mystery.[71] It was in Qum that Jaloud revealed that Musa Sadr had been assassinated and he blamed 'Zionists and colonialists' for his murder.[72] The provisional government's position on Libya's involvement in the murder of Sadr remained cautious and reserved. Bazargan suggested dispatching an Iranian inquiry commission to Libya and stated that his government would not establish diplomatic relations with Libya until the commission was received. Only after the fall of the provisional government were diplomatic relations established with Libya.

The occupation of the US embassy and the resignation of the provisional government marked the beginning of the second stage in Iran's foreign policy. With the removal of the tendency within the leadership that aspired to gain international respect and recognition for Iran, within the established framework of international law, the views of Khomeini on restructuring international relations on an Islamic basis came to prevail. The main pillar of such a system was the acceptance of Iran's Islamic model, by other countries, as the only authentic and viable version of Islamic government. Khomeini wished to make Iran the motherland of the Islamic revolution to which all members of the Islamic community would look for guidance and leadership. The practical realization of an Islamic world order required effective control over as many liberation movements as possible. Such a control could, in turn, be obtained only through the provision of financial and military aid. On the propaganda front, the Islamic Republic had to launch a massive information campaign to win the hearts and minds of the world's disinherited and disenchanted to the cause of Islam.

On 6 May 1979, the statutes of the Corps of the Islamic Revolutionary Guards established by Khomeini's direct orders were published. The objective of the CIRG was 'to defend the Islamic Revolution in Iran and to expand it worldwide on the basis of an authentic Islamic ideology'.[73] Article 2 of the statutes stated that the CIRG was responsible for 'the support of just liberation movements of the world's dispossessed, under the supervision of the Revolution's leader and in consultation with the government'.[74] The dual identity of the CIRG, the purpose of which was both defensive and offensive, was a clear reflection of how the clerical leadership viewed the position of the Islamic Republic in relation to the rest of the world. As long as the birthplace of the Islamic government, Iran, was threatened internally or externally, the prime objective of the leadership was naturally the defence of the republic. However, once internal or external threats were repelled, then the Islamic Republic had an expansionist role to play.

Released from the legalistic mould that the provisional government had imposed, the clerical leadership set out to hoist the Islamic Republic's flag all over the world. Playing down the share of nationalism in Iran's revolution, Ayatollah Montazeri announced that: 'Iran's revolution is not essentially Iranian but Islamic and as long as the Moslem people of the world are enchained by colonialism, injustice and despotism, we believe it to be our responsibility to support all liberation movements of the world'.[75] Speaking at the Friday congregational prayers, Khamenei, who later became president, outlined the new official foreign policy. He said:

> After the victory of the revolution we abandoned our offensive posture and became introverted, this was the start of our erroneous path. . . . Some repeatedly said that revolutions are not for export and we do not wish to export our revolution. . . . But once again our brothers and sisters occupied the American embassy, they once again proved that they wish to universalise our revolution and that this is the correct path.[76]

The Islamic Republic's new approach to foreign policy was evinced by a series of spectacular events on the heels of the US embassy's occupation. During November and December of 1979, Mohammed Montazeri organized a camp close to Teheran, for all volunteers who wished to join the Palestinians fighting in southern Lebanon. On 19 December 1979, in spite of strong resistance from the Lebanese authorities and *Shi'i* Lebanese clergy, who labelled the arrival of Iranian volunteers as a second occupation of their land, the first group of volunteers were flown to Syria and given training in a PLO camp near Damascus.[77] By 30 December 1979, Mohammed Montazeri announced that approximately four hundred volunteers had arrived in Syria from where they would enter southern Lebanon.[78]

The export of the Islamic revolution also involved propagating Islamic ideas and winning revolutionary and liberation movements to the cause of Islam. Consequently, on 6 January 1980, the Islamic Students that followed the 'Imam's line' officially opened an impressive gathering of sixteen essentially non-communist international liberation movements, attended by several prominent revolutionary figures.[79] The Islamic students anounced that they felt the necessity for such a meeting since the provisional government had totally neglected the important tasks of supporting revolutionary movements and of internationalizing the revolution. In his message to the Gathering of Liberation Movements, Khomeini urged the participants to 'invite the people of the world to Islam and Islamic fraternity'.[80] The participation of representatives of the Front for the Liberation of Saudi Arabia (FLSA) and that of Iraq, who attended with their faces masked, caused some alarm among the more mainstream liberation movements, especially the PLO, who maintained close relations with both Saudi Arabia and Iraq. The Islamic Republic's attempt to seat the representative of FLSA on the executive committee of the gathering was blocked by the PLO; Abu Jihad, the PLO's number two man, and Hani al Hassan, the PLO ambassador to Iran, threatened to leave the conference.[81] After five assembly meetings and three committee meetings, the gathering issued a resolution which condemned US imperialism and labelled the United States the number one enemy of all the dispossessed people of the world, in its Articles 1 and 2. Article 7 of the resolution declared that: 'we unanimously support Iran's Islamic revolution under Imam Khomeini's leadership and consider our affiliation with it as fraternal. We recognise Iran's Islamic revolution as ours and that of the World's dispossessed'.[82]

Once a basic network of liberation movements had been established Iran's relations with them had to be cemented with concrete financial aid. On 17 February 1980, the Revolutionary Council, who had taken charge of the government after the fall of Bazargan, ratified a decree earmarking 1 billion rials for financial aid to liberation movements. The sum was placed at the disposition of a three-man team composed of Hojatolislam Khameini, Ali-Akbar Moinfar and Qotbzadeh.[83]

The government's open acknowledgement that a fund for the export of the revolution had been established cleared the way for the creation of an official institution with the purpose of fomenting Islamic revolution abroad. In September 1981, the 'Council of the Islamic Revolution' (CIR) was announced in Teheran under the leadership of an 11-man clerical group. The council was charged with the supervision and co-ordination of all activities and programmes of revolutionary forces in Arab and Islamic countries.[84] The CIR co-ordinated the activities of the Five Supreme Revolutionary Assemblies, each of which managed the revolutionary activities of specific areas. The most famous of these assemblies was that of the Supreme Assembly of the Islamic Revolution in Iraq (SAIRI) under the leadership of Hojatolislam Baqir al-Hakim. The SAIRI benefited from the close collaboration of the Iraqi *Da'wa* Party and the Iraqi Islamic AMAL Party, both of which are pro-Khomeini. The Iraqi Islamic AMAL Party has accepted responsibility for numerous attacks against Iraqi interests in Iraq and abroad. In Baghdad, the AMAL attacked the officers of the Iraqi airline and the security police headquarters in 1983. The attacks on the Iraqi embassy in Paris and Rome in 1980 and 1982 were also claimed by the organization. The clerical leadership

was initially convinced that the *Shi'i* population of Iraq, which constitutes 60 per cent of the total population, would revolt against Saddam
Hossein's Bathist rule. This prediction, however, proved unfounded,
despite the Islamic Republic's moral and material support for Iraq's pro-
Iranian liberation movements.

The Assembly of the Islamic Revolution in Lebanon (AIRL) occupies
a position as prominent as the SAIRI in the Council of the Islamic
Revolution since it co-ordinates and directs Iranian interests and designs
in Lebanon. In the July of 1982, Hossein Moussavi, a prominent figure
in Imam Mussa Sadr's Lebanese AMAL movement, allied himself with
the Islamic Republic of Iran. Splitting from the mainstream AMAL,
which was under Nabih Berri's control, Moussavi accused the movement's leaders of collaboration with the Israelis and formed the Lebanese
Islamic AMAL Movement (IAM).[85] In 1983, Moussavi's cousin became
the Iranian chargé d'affaires in Beirut. The IAM constitutes one of the
main forces of the AIRL. Moussavi's Islamic AMAL has been implicated
in a number of violent political acts against western interests. On 18 April
1983, the Islamic *Jihad* organization accepted responsibility for the
bombing of the US embassy in Beirut. According to the Beirut daily
newspaper *Al-Liwa*, an anonymous telephone call explained that the
attack was 'part of the Iranian Revolution's campaign against imperialist
targets throughout the World'.[86] It was generally assumed that Islamic
Jihad was a front name for Hossein Moussavi's AMAL.[87]

Moussavi's Islamic AMAL was also suspected of involvement in the
car-bomb attacks on US and French military installations in Beirut on 23
October 1983, which led to the death of 243 American soldiers and 50
French soldiers. Citing the Qur'an and the teachings of Imam Ali,
Moussavi declared that 'it is right to fight evil with evil'.[88] While
Hashemi-Rafsanjani denied that Iran had been involved in the bombing
incidents, Moussavi-Ardabili, chief of the supreme court, declared that
the Moslem people of Lebanon had learnt 'the lesson of revolution from
Iran' and that the Iranian example taught the United States and France
'not to embark on acts of aggression and attacks against oppressed
nations'.[89]

Another important political force in AIRL was the Lebanese Hezbollah (Party of God). The leadership of the Hezbollah is composed of four
young clerics. Shaykh Subhi Tufaili is known as its political leader;
Shaykh Abbas Moussavi, Hossein Moussavi's brother, is director of the
religious school in Ba'albak and responsible for military and security
affairs; Shaykh Ibrahim Amin, the spokesman of the party; and Shaykh
Hassan Nasrollah, the liaison person between Iran and its forces in
Lebanon.[90] The Hezbollah's close collaboration with the Islamic government is well reflected in the party's ideological statements and the aid
which it receives from Iran. In an open letter addressed by the Hezbollah
to the downtrodden in Lebanon, the political position of the party in
relation to Iran is clearly outlined. The letter says:

We ... abide by the orders of a single wise and just command currently embodied in the supreme Ayatollah Ruhollah al-Moussavi al-Khomeini, the rightly guided Imam who combines all the qualities of the total Imam, who has detonated the Islamic revolution and who is bringing about the glorious Islamic renaisance.[91]

Iran not only provides operating expenses, but based on the model adopted in Iran according to which families of the martyrs of war are compensated in both cash and kind, families of martyred members of the Lebanese Hezbollah are provided with a pension. Approximately US $225,000 is distributed monthly to the families of those martyred in the cause of the Lebanese Hezbollah.[92] The Hezbollah's ability to recruit full-time gunmen thanks to the aid that it receives from Iran has been put forward as one reason for its growing military strength. According to one report, Hezbollah militiamen are hired with an offer of 2,500 Lebanese pounds ($160) a month just for part-time service.[93] It is reported that Iran spent $30 million during 1985 and more than $64 million during 1987 in Lebanon.[94]

The Hezbollah's activities started in earnest in 1982, when, as a reaction to the possibility of an AMAL *rapprochement* with the United States, Syria sought to buttress pro-Iranian *Shi'i* groups as a countervailing *Shi'i* power in the region. In July 1982, Syria permitted 1,000 CIRGs, who had been dispatched to Syria to fight the Israeli invasion of southern Lebanon, to establish a base in Ba'albak. These revolutionary guards never actually fought against Israel during that summer, but outlawed the consumption of alcoholic beverages, enforced the veil on the women and trained the young and angry Lebanese who wished to do something against the invading Israelis. Subsequently, Ba'albak became the zone of influence of the Hezbollah and the Islamic AMAL.

Nabih Berri, who witnessed the weakening of his political organization at the hands of the Islamic Republic of Iran and believed that the Islamic AMAL and the Hezbollah pursued the interests of Iran and not that of the Lebanese *Shi'i*, never shied away from confronting his new challengers. Accompanied by Shaykh Abd al-Amir Qublan, one of the leading *Shi'i* clerics of Lebanon and a member of the AMAL Presidential Council, Berri made a moving speech before thousands of *Shi'i* in the historical fortress of Ba'albak, the stronghold of the pro-Iranian forces. In August of 1986, speaking in a melancholic voice, Berri said:

Imam Sadr, my absent leader . . . before you came we were a dagger in the hands of others, before you, we were part of geography and those who sat in Beirut wrote history. . . . Where should I start from . . . You are always before me, I see you in the memory of Mustafa Chamran, whom the deceitful *parvenu* revolutionaries murdered from behind, just as the madman of Libya trapped you in the guise of a friend. My master, I am sorrowed by Imam Khomeini and the rest, all those charlatans who now pose as Moslems. Imam Khomeini, is it just that all those who are kidnappers, murderers, smugglers and terrorists should be close allies of your Islamic government and those who have been subjected to torture, harassment and death be considered as your enemies? Today a bunch of corrupt bandits confront the dispossessed with your poster in their hands and with your money in their pockets and they wish to create a republic of terror called the Islamic Republic in Lebanon. . . . Where are you Imam Sadr?[95]

Even though Berri came to be considered as an arch enemy and a corruptor on earth by the Islamic Republic, Syria gradually came to realize that Berri's friendship in the region was far more important than that of his rivals. It was not until April 1988 that pro-Iranian forces lost their stronghold in that region and moved to Beirut. Their presence in Beirut prompted Syria to send 5,000 armed men into Beirut to prevent the pro-Iranian forces from waging war against the mainstream AMAL. Syria rapidly moved towards direct confrontation with the pro-Iranian forces. Skirmishes led to the death of 23 members of the Hezbollah during February 1987.

The Assembly of the Islamic Revolution in the Arabian Peninsula (AIRAP), which is led by Hojatolislam Mohammed-Taqi Modaressi, co-ordinates pro-Iranian Islamic activities in the three geopolitically sensitive countries of Saudi Arabia, Kuwait and Bahrain. The Islamic AMAL for the Liberation of Bahrain which was founded in 1979 and the Kuwaiti Islamic *Jihad* organization are affiliated with AIRAP.

The major bone of contention between Iran's brand of *Shi'i* Islam and Saudi Arabia's brand of Sunni Islam surfaced in the manner in which each perceived the proper manner of performing the *hadj* pilgrimage. The guardianship of the holy sites of Mecca and Medina, which attract some 2 million pilgrims annually, provides Saudi Arabia with a unique and exalted status among all Moslem nations. The guardianship of the holiest sites is internationally viewed as the guardianship of Islam. Consequently, even the most radical Arab and Moslem countries try to maintain friendly diplomatic relations with Saudi Arabia.

Khomeini's basis of dispute with the House of Saud was not over the Saudis' negligence in imposing Islamic laws, since the Saudis remained a model in terms of strict observance and the imposition of the *Shari'a* on their people. Khomeini, however, reproached the Saudis for their perfect integration within the western camp and their complaisance in relation to the 'Great Satan'. Saudi Arabia's foreign policy was viewed by Teheran as pro-United States and the Saudis' massive arms buildup, the presence of US AWACS aircraft and the Saudis' military dependence on the United States were offered as proof. The Islamic image which the Saudis presented on the international scene was sacrilegious to Khomeini, since it complied with the international rules which Khomeini believed to have been established by oppressive western countries. The Saudis refusal to politicize Islam enraged Khomeini who had always fought against those members of the clergy who believed that religion had to be separated from politics. The Saudis believed that the *hadj* pilgrimage was solely a religious act, during which the pilgrims had to devote all their time, thought and energy to the spiritual aspects of the faith. Adopting Shariati's subsystem, Khomeini believed that the *hadj* pilgrimage provided the ideal occasion for Moslems to condemn the blasphemous powers and invite everyone to the faith. For Khomeini, the *hadj* was an opportunity to put the three principles of Islamic foreign affairs into practice: announcing the resolute defence of the abode of Islam, inviting to the cause of Islam and renouncing all paths other than Islam. The Saudis viewed the Islamic Republic's position and arguments as simply an excuse to destabilize the Saudi régime.

On 10 October 1981, King Khaled of Saudi Arabia criticized Khomeini for the political demonstrations that were organized against the United States and Israel by the Iranian pilgrims during that year's *hadj*. Khaled wrote: 'in activities in your name which were not only contrary to your aims but were also contrary to the aims of pilgrimage and the honour of holy places', Iranian pilgrims shouted slogans which 'disturbed and disgusted other pilgrims to the holy house of God'.[96] Khomeini's response in this ideological duel was predictable. The real purpose of the *hadj* pilgrimage, Khomeini argued, was religio-political. Although the two men did not see eye to eye, Saudi Arabia continued to admit Iranian pilgrims until 1988.

In September 1982, the Saudi police broke up pro-Khomeini and anti-US demonstrations by Iranian pilgrims in the cities of Jedda and Medina. The reported number of Iranian pilgrims deported varied between 21 and 100.[97] The number of Iranian pilgrims increased each year and the intensity and scope of anti-US and pro-Khomeini demonstrations by Iranian pilgrims escalated in proportion. The clerical leadership continued to step up its anti-Saudi campaign by calling for the management and supervision of the holy precincts by an international Moslem committee. A two-day visit by Saudi Arabia's foreign minister, Prince Saud, on 18 May 1985 to Teheran, helped to temporarily reduce tension between the two countries. Ali Akbar Velayati's return visit as Iran's foreign minister to Riyadh was initially seen as marking a new phase of reconciliation between Iran and Saudi Arabia.

After revelations about the Islamic Republic's secret deals with the United States and the involvement of Israel in both the discussion and execution of these arrangements, the humiliated clerical leadership sought to salvage its revolutionary reputation by reverting to fiery rhetoric and propaganda. The document that came to be known as the *Manifesto of the Islamic Revolution* was Khomeini's address to the Iranian pilgrims. In his unprecedentedly long discourse, Khomeini called on Moslems to 'announce their opposition and disgust in the face of all the atrocities committed by the polytheists'. Khomeini wrote:

> Our cry of innocence is that of an Islamic community for the death of which blasphemy and the oppressors have been plotting. They have aimed their blows, arrows and spears at the Qur'an and the Islamic community. Alas that Mohammad's people . . . should concede to bondage by the East and the West. Alas that Khomeini should sit still

before the aggression of the beasts, polytheists and the blasphemous against the Qur'an, the children of the Prophet and the followers of Abraham and witness the misery and suffering of Moslems. I am prepared to sacrifice my worthless life in order to defend the Moslems and proclaim that which is just. I therefore await my martyrdom. The powers, superpowers and their servants must be assured that if Khomeini remains alone and isolated he will continue his path which is that of incessant battle against oppression, polytheism and idolatery. God willing, with the aid of the mobilised world of Islam, this army of the barefooted oppressed will deny the warmongers and perpetrators of injustice and oppression a moment of peaceful rest.[98]

Khomeini invited all Moslem pilgrims to join in a historic and passionate march against the oppressors and the polytheists and advised the participants to encourage bystanders and Saudi Arabian officials to join the march.

The bloody events of 31 July 1987, in Mecca, have become a source of controversy. According to official Saudi sources, 401 people were killed: 85 Saudi military and security personnel, 42 pilgrims of other countries and 274 Iranian pilgrims.[99] The Saudis maintain that the deaths occurred as a result of a stampede caused by rushing Iranian protestors and that the injuries were inflicted by the Iranians using knives, stones and sticks. The Iranian authorities maintain that during the mass demonstration, Iranian pilgrims were attacked by Saudi security forces using machine guns. The deaths were probably caused by a combination of all three factors. On Saturday 1 August the Saudi embassy in Teheran was occupied and sacked by Iranian demonstrators. The Saudi political attaché was seriously injured and died on Sunday. Saudi-Iranian relations fell to an unprecedented low as Khomeini announced that the liberation of the *Ka'ba* and other holy precincts in Saudi Arabia was far more important than the liberation of Karbala in Iraq, or even Jerusalem. He ordered Moslems all over the world to avenge the massacre of Iranian pilgrims.[100] Hashemi-Rafsanjani vowed that Iran would uproot the Saudi rulers.[101] Even though the events in Saudi Arabia succeeded in distracting Iranian zealots from the Iran-US negotiations, they were hardly effective as a propaganda campaign for the dissemination of Khomeini's brand of Islam among other Moslems. Internationally, Iran found itself even more isolated, since in addition to all major Moslem heads of state, President Assad of Syria, an ally of Iran, expressed his sympathy and support for Saudi Arabia's King Fahd.[102] On 27 April, Saudi Arabia officially severed diplomatic relations with Iran, citing Iran's threats and antagonistic position as the main reason for its decision. AIRAP failed to win any significant domestic support in Saudi Arabia and, subsequently, failed to destabilize the Saudi régime. AIRAP activities remained just as ineffective in triggering an Islamic revolution in Kuwait and Bahrain, although *Shi'i* constitute 25 per cent of the Kuwaiti population and 72 per cent of all Bahraini citizens.

On 12 December 1983, multiple explosions in Kuwait killed five and wounded 86 persons. Islamic *Jihad* claimed responsibility for the attacks on the US and French embassies, and Kuwaiti government offices and buildings of 'the American Raytheon Company which at the time was installing a Hawk missile system in Kuwait'.[103] Twenty-five men were arrested and accused of involvement in the bombing. Eighteen of those arrested were proven to be members of the Iraqi *Da'wa* Party which was an active member of the Iranian-supported Supreme Assembly of the Islamic Revolution in Iraq (SAIRI). The team of revolutionaries were revealed to have come to Kuwait by boat from Iran, carrying with them the explosives for the bombing, machine guns, rocket-launched grenades, rifles, pistols and detonators.[104] The planning and the execution order of the plot were reported to have originated in Iran.[105]

The Islamic *Jihad*'s prisoners became the source of future problems for Kuwait. On 4 December 1984, a Kuwaiti airliner was hijacked and forced to land in Teheran. The hijackers demanded the release of the *Shi'i* prisoners in Kuwait. After two US citizens were killed on board, Iranian soldiers stormed the plane, capturing the hijackers and releasing the passengers on 9 December. On 25 May 1985, an attempt was made on the life of Emir Shaykh Jaber al-Ahmad al-Sabbah of Kuwait. Islamic *Jihad* accepted responsibility for the suicide mission involving an explosive-loaded car which tried to hit the emir's car. The explosion killed three and wounded 11 people. Islamic *Jihad* announced that:

> we hope our message to the Emir will suffice. Ten days ago we warned that if our friends in Kuwait were not released all crowns and thrones in the Persian Gulf would be knocked down. . . . If our friends are not released the kings and the emirs of the Gulf will witness our future activities. . . . We shall continue our struggle until the final victory of the Islamic Revolution.[106]

Islamic *Jihad* kept its promise of attacking Kuwaiti interests. On 5 April 1988, a Kuwaiti jet was forced to land in Iran on its way home from Bangkok. The hijackers demanded the release of the 17 convicted members of Islamic *Jihad* in Kuwait. After 16 awesome days of captivity, having witnessed the murder of two Kuwaiti hostages, all the passengers were released in Algiers. As in 1985, the hijackers surrendered themselves to the authorities, never to be put on trial. The Kuwaiti authorities' resolute refusal to bargain with the hijackers won the small emirate considerable international recognition and respect. Since 1985, there have been almost no further actions by Islamic *Jihad* in Kuwait.

If the Islamic revolution was exportable, Bahrain, with its large majority of *Shi'i* citizens and its close traditional ties with Iran, constituted the ideal target. The ripple effect of the Iranian revolution in 1979 left its mark on Bahrain, as the country witnessed *Shi'i* unrest during which the leader of Bahrain's Islamic movement, Mohammad Ali al-Akri, was arrested. In August 1979, Khomeini's representative, Modaressi, was arrested and expelled for fomenting unrest among the *Shi'i*. A second wave of *Shi'i* unrest during January 1980 followed the arrest and execution of Ayatollah Mohammad Baqer Sadr in Iraq. Anti-government demonstrations reached a new peak after the death in prison of a Bahraini *Shi'i* leader, whom the demonstrators believed to have been executed by the government.[107]

On 13 December 1981, the Bahraini goverment announced that it had uncovered a plot and arrested the members of a clandestine *Shi'i* group called the Islamic Front for the Liberation of Bahrain (IFLB). The 73-man group was said to have been trained and armed in Iran where it had its headquarters. According to the Bahraini minister of the interior, the group had planned to assassinate government officials and overthrow the government with the aim of establishing an Islamic government. Apparently, Bahrain was viewed as the first domino, the fall of which would result in a series of other plots which would spread the Islamic revolution throughout the Persian Gulf. Iran's role in the plot was undeniable, according to the Bahraini authorities who established a connection between the IFLB and Modaressi: 'The plotters were apparently "trained" in Iran's holy city of Qum by Hojatolislam Hadi al-Modaressi'.[108] The 1981 plot in Bahrain was seen by the Gulf states as a real Iranian threat against their national sovereignty. In February 1984, two leading members of Bahrain's *Shi'i* Islamic Guidance Society were arrested and their society was proclaimed illegal. The men were charged with storing and hiding arms and ammunition and one of them reportedly confessed to the possession of pistols, ammunition and a rocket-propelled grenade.[109] Apart from the main 1981 challenge to Bahrain's national security, the IFLB has not been very successful in popularizing the demand for an Islamic government. Bahrain sought and received co-operation from Saudi Arabia in structuring its internal-security apparatus and has maintained its low level of diplomatic relations with Iran.

The Supreme Assembly of the Islamic Revolution in Africa and the Arabian Maghreb (SAIRAAM) constitutes the fourth force in the Council of Islamic Revolution. SAIRAAM was charged with the supervision and control of the activities of pro-Iranian Islamic groups in North Africa, Nigeria, Senegal and Mauritania. In 1983, the government of Senegal broke off diplomatic relations with Teheran, after a clandestine Islamic group closely connected with the Iranian embassy in Dakar was discovered.[110] Mauritania, Tunisia and Morocco have also severed diplomatic relations with Iran, claiming Iranian intervention in their domestic affairs.

The Supreme Assembly of the Islamic Revolution in Asia (SAIRA) forms the last of such assemblies in the council. Iran's limited aid to pro-Iranian Islamic groups in Afghanistan is channelled through SAIRA. In May 1985, a member of Indonesia's Islamic Revival Party, which calls for the establishment of an Islamic Republic, was sentenced to death and executed. He was accused of attacking a police station and injuring two policemen. In his interrogations, he had reportedly admitted to having had contact with the Iranian embassy in Jakarta.[111] Seventeen other members of the Islamic Revival Party were sentenced to life imprisonment. The SAIRA, however, has concentrated its efforts in Afghanistan, the Philippines and Pakistan.

Apart from the activities of the Council of the Islamic Revolutions in exporting the revolution, the Office of the Islamic Liberation Movements, which initially formed an integral part of the CIRG and was later placed under the control of Mehdi Hashemi (the brother of Ayatollah Montazeri's son-in-law Hadi Hashemi), also conducted its own propaganda and military activities abroad. Parallel to the institutionalized channels, clerical dignitaries also established their own offices for the export of the Islamic revolution. In September 1984, for example, President Khamenei created a centre, the objective of which was to support 'the just struggle' of US blacks. The new organization was called the Coordinating Office of Oppressed Americans and came under the supervision of the President himself. Announcing the responsibilities of the organization, Khamenei pointed out that first, sufficient information should be gathered on the condition of US blacks and then regular contacts should be established with radical black organizations. The organization's budget was said to be allocated from the president's special account. Khamenei added that 'the oppressed American blacks are looking at Imam Khomeini with keen eyes and it is our Islamic revolution that must rescue them'.[112]

The second phase of the Islamic Republic's foreign policy was essentially characterized by open support for all types of destabilizing activities in the hope of exporting the Islamic revolution. Iran's bellicose international posture alienated her initial close friends, such as the PLO, engendered the alliance and animosity of her initially neutral neighbours and provided a pretext for the superpowers to become more actively and forcefully involved in the Persian Gulf. As long as the prevailing political mood in Teheran derided diplomacy, negotiation and compromise as blasphemous and un-Islamic, Iran denied itself the common international language without which it could not break out of a self-imposed international isolation.

The third stage of Iran's foreign policy which has been characterized by a cautious movement towards the recognition of the prevailing international system, along with its established rules of conduct and channels of communication, is a clear indication and recognition of the failure of her foreign policy during the second stage. The gradual return to the methodology and objectives prevalent during Bazargan's government cannot, however, completely undo the important international effects of Iran's unconventional foreign policy during the preceeding stage. The Gulf Cooperation Council (GCC) created on 25 May 1981, which allied Bahrain, Kuwait, Oman, Qatar and the United Arab Emirates with Saudi Arabia, was one such side effect. The subversive activities of Khomeini's representatives and his disciples in a number of these countries and the radical and revolutionary posture and rhetoric of the Islamic Republic created enough anguish and fear among the Gulf States to push them into each others' arms. The members of the GCC clearly sought strength and security in regional unity and co-operation. Saudi Interior Minister Prince Nayif articulated the GCC's concern. He said:

> We had hoped that Iran, our neighbour and friend, would not have such [conspirational] intentions. But after what happened in Bahrain, our hopes have unfortunately been dashed and it has become clear to us that Iran has become a source of danger and harm to the Gulf nations and their security.[113]

The fear and distrust which have been sown by the Islamic Republic among the Persian Gulf states can be gradually overcome, although it will require considerable effort on the part of the Iranian government to re-establish good relations. The damage done during the second stage will tarnish Iran's reputation for a long time to come.

The escalating military and naval presence of western powers in the Gulf can also be attributed to Iran's attempt at exporting her revolution. According to Professor Ramazani:

> it was the Iranian Revolution that gave rise to the early ideas and courses of action that finally led to the Carter Doctrine and the formation of a multiservice force, which has had a unified regional command as the United States Central Command since January 1, 1983 and on which the Reagan administration has spent billions of dollars each year.[114]

The US deterrent force in the region was 'to be directed more at containing revolutionism and the spread of war than at Soviet expansionism'.[115] The tanker war, which was unleashed by Iraq and continued by Iran, led to the increasing presence of western and even Soviet naval vessels in the region. On 5 May 1987, the United States accepted a request by the Kuwaiti government to reflag its tankers and escort them through the Persian Gulf. The Soviets had already agreed to a similar request. By September 1987, several members of NATO had dispatched naval forces to the Gulf. Approximately 70 western vessels ensured the proper implementation of the Reagan Doctrine which focused on assuring 'free navigation' in the Gulf. The end of the Iran-Iraq war has rendered the presence of foreign navies in the Persian Gulf redundant. However, revolutionary Iran's foreign policy has led to a return to direct military and naval involvement by NATO powers in the Persian Gulf. The precedent that has been set by inviting western powers to intervene in the region in the name of safeguarding the freedom of navigation may eventually be used as a pretext for other military intervention in the region.

The Iran-Iraq war

The border skirmishes, military intrusions, violations of aerial space, propaganda and psychological warfare between Iran and Iraq which erupted shortly after the victory of the revolution, culminated in a full-scale conventional war on 22 September 1980, following Iraq's attack on Iranian soil. On the ground, the Iraqi invasion of Iran with approximately 45,000 men was launched across a 450-mile-wide front and on four separate axes aimed at the Qasr-e-Shirin area, the Mehran area, the Southern Khuzestan Province especially Susangerd, Ahwaz and Dezful and, finally, the sensitive Khoramshahr and Abadan areas. On the same day, Saddam Hossein tried to imitate Israel's pre-emptive aerial strike against Egypt during the 1967 Arab-Israeli war. The Iraqi airforce attacked 10 major Iranian air bases and airfields including Teheran, with no serious consequences.

The Iraqi government used Iran's violent anti-Iraqi propaganda and *Shi'i* agitation as evidence of Iran's subversive activities. Iran's efforts to destabilize and overthrow the Iraqi government provided an ideal justification for a pre-emptive war. The Iraqis allege that a hand grenade was thrown by an Iranian student at Tariq Aziz, Iraq's powerful deputy premier, as a result of which two people were killed and Tariq Aziz was wounded. Non-Iraqi sources have reported that the student under consideration was not an Iranian, but an Iraqi called Samir Nour-Ali.[116] The Iraqi ministry of foreign affairs maintains that the Iraqi *Da'wa* Party, which was controlled and directed by Teheran, intended 'to overthrow the Iraqi Government, through subversion, sabotage and terrorism by the so-called *Jondi-el Imam*, i.e. the Imam's soldiers'.[117]

The escalation of Iran's propaganda warfare, as a part of which Khomeini called on the Iraqi people to overthrow Saddam Hossein's corrupt régime and advised the Iraqi army not to obey the orders of the foes of Islam and join the people, came only after three highly provocative steps were taken by the Iraqi government. First, the Iraqis embarked on an unprecedented mass deportation of Iraqis of Iranian origin, essentially because of their *Shi'i* religion. Iranian authorities claimed that between 16,000 and 17,000 Iraqi citizens were deported to Iran during April 1980.[118] A circular from the Iraqi ministry of the interior ordered the police and gendarmerie to open fire on any deported person who attempted to return to Iraq.[119] At the same time, Iraqi authorities clamped down on *Shi'i* leaders. On 9 April 1980, the prominent *Shi'i* scholar and religious leader, Ayatollah Mohammed Baqer Sadr, was arrested and executed by the Iraqi régime. Ayatollah Sadr's sister, Bint al-Huda, faced the same fate on the same day. A considerable number of *Shi'i ulama* residing in Iraq were also deported. The Iraqi government was adamant about uprooting any potential *Shi'i* threat. The execution of Ayatollah Sadr, the expulsion of *Shi'i* clergymen and *Shi'i* citizens of Iraq were felt as a direct affront by the Islamic Republic and its clerical leadership. Finally, in an official letter to Waldheim the UN secretary general, Iraq demanded the withdrawal of Iranian forces from the three Persian Gulf islands of Greater and Lesser Tomb and Abu-Musa, which Iran had occupied on 30 November 1971, after the departure of the British from the Gulf. On 15 April 1980, Saddam Hossein listed three conditions for ending tensions and border skirmishes between the two countries: the unconditional withdrawal of Iranian forces from the three Persian Gulf islands; the return of the Shatt al-Arab to Iraq and, consequently, the abrogation of the Algiers Agreement of 6 March 1975; and the official recognition of the fact that the people of Khuzistan are Arabs.[120] The conditions set by Saddam Hossein were clearly unacceptable to Iran.

Although Sadam Hossein unilaterally declared the abrogation of the Algiers Agreement on 17 September 1980, he had toyed with the idea since mid-April. The Algiers Agreement, signed by the Shah of Iran and Saddam Hossein, recognized the thalweg principle concerning sovereignty over the Shatt al-Arab (Arvand Roud). The thalweg principle states that the border of two states separated by a river should be drawn down the centre of the major navigable channel of the river. The border between the two countries thus passed through the middle of the river, removing Iraq's traditional control of the waterways all the way to the Iranian shoreline. Iraq's unilateral abrogation of the Algiers treaty was an aggressive act of provocation against Iran.

President Saddam Hossein hoped to obtain a swift victory over what seemed to be a disorganized, strife-ridden, defenceless Iran, whose army, airforce and navy had been weakened, humiliated and persecuted as the Shah's main pillar of support. Apart from the decapitation of the apex of the Iranian military hierarchy, the revolutionary government had continued to purge the armed forces. On 7 February 1980, only two months before the preliminary round of the Iran-Iraq conflict, Shaykh Khalkhali had purged the airforce of 145 officers. Three days later, the army was purged of 8,000 men.[121] The size of the military had also been considerably reduced from approximately 450,000 to 200,000.[122]

Iran's defeat would have left Iraq as the single most powerful force in the region and Saddam Hossein longed to become the new leader of a pan-Arab movement. The victory of Iraq under Saddam Hossein's leadership would have proved the superiority of Arabs over the Persians and Arabism as an ideology over Islam. The re-establishment of Iraqi control over the Shatt al-Arab, the return of the three Persian Gulf islands to Arab possession, possible annexation of Iran's Khuzistan Province, the containment of the expansionist Islamic revolution and the replacement of the Khomeini government with one friendly towards Iraq provided sufficient incentive for Iraq to attack Iran.

Saddam Hossein, however, committed the grave error of attacking a country which had had a recent revolution supported by religious zealots and militants whose ideology held martyrdom to be God's greatest reward and honour. Although enthusiasm for the revolution was waning among certain segments of the population with the rise of clerical dictatorship, the war was an ideal opportunity to once again unify and mobilize the people under the guidance and control of the clerical leadership. Khomeini correctly called the war 'a blessing', since the Iranian revolution was provided with a cause, in whose name the clerical leadership could renew its demand for unswerving support and obedience. The opposition was further muzzled under the pretext of unity in the face of foreign aggression. The nation was put on a war footing, a siege mentality developed and any shortcomings of the revolution were attributed to the war. Finally, the Islamic revolutionaries were presented with a chance to realize their dream of exporting the revolution of *Shi'i* Iraq, by defeating the aggressor. Khomeini announced that the war against Iran was a war against Islam, the Qur'an and the Prophet of God and thus invited all devoted Moslems to participate in a crusade against the blasphemous régime of Saddam Hossein.

On 22 September 1980, Saddam Hossein relied heavily on an element of surprise, hoping that an Iraqi blitzkrieg would lead to the immediate crumbling of Iran. The four-pronged attack on the aforementioned targets was successful during the first ten days of their thrust into Iranian territory. Qasr-e-Shirin fell quickly and the Iraqis moved to take over Sare-pole-Zahad, Gilane-Gharb and Sumar. On the Mehran front, the towns of Mehran and Dehloran were taken in the early hours of battle. On the two other axes, Iraq was less successful. By the end of September, neither Abadan nor Khoramshahr had been captured, while the thrusts towards the strategically sensitive cities of Dezful and Ahwaz were stopped 15 to 20 kilometres short of these important military objectives. It seemed as if the Iraqis were capable of thrusting quickly into open territory, but when faced with the task of taking cities, they proved less successful. Instead of opting for fierce hand-to-hand combat to capture Iranian cities defended primarily by courageous and dedicated revolutionaries with little military knowledge, the Iraqis chose to encircle the cities and force them to surrender through heavy artillery and rocket bombardments. Where such fire power was insufficient, the airforce was used to pound the encircled cities.[123] From the first days of fighting, Iraq was well aware of the fact that failure to win a quick victory would drag it into a war of attrition in which Iran's numerical superiority could turn the tide.

The battle for Khoramshahr became the real acid test for the Iraqi army's capacity to capture a significant Iranian city. Having shelled the city for seven consecutive days and still believing that the 'Arab' population of Khoramshahr would welcome the so-called liberating Iraqi forces with open arms, the Iraqis expected a smooth resistance-free entrance into Khoramshahr. Over 100 tanks and armoured vehicles aided by groups of infantry attacked the city on 28 September 1980 and it was not before 24 October that the whole of Khoramshahr was in Iraqi hands. Between 3 and 24 October, a bloody battle was conducted on a street-by-street and house-by-house basis. The capture of Khoramshahr which was renamed Khuninshahr or 'the blood-stained city' imposed heavy casualties on the Iraqis. The estimates vary between 6,000 and 7,000 killed and wounded.[124] Even though the Iraqi army crossed the Karun River and encircled the city of Abadan, the casualties experienced in the battle of Khoramshahr dissuaded Iraq from entering the city. Bombardment alone did not force the Iranians to capitulate. With the seige of Abadan, the major Iraqi military thrust came to a halt.

At the end of the first stage of the Iran-Iraq war during which Iraq was on the offensive, the Iraqis had failed to obtain several important strategic objectives: capturing Dezful, Ahwaz and Abadan; cutting off the oil pipelines and the railroad that ran north through Dezful; cutting off the Ahwaz to Dezful road and taking full control of Susangerd. Iraq failed to effectively capitalize on its initial favourable local superiority in troops and armoured vehicles and the absence of any proper military central command and organization on the Iranian side for at least the first six weeks of fighting.

On 13 October 1980, Khomeini took the first step towards co-ordinating Iranian forces and creating a central command by establishing a seven-man Supreme Defence Council to run the war. President Bani-Sadr, who had already been appointed commander in chief of the army by Khomeini, was named to head the council. The centralized military command sought to co-ordinate the activities of the professional regular army, the ideologically motivated CIRG (*Sepah-e Pasdaran e-Enqelab-e Islami*) and the Volunteers Corps of the Organization for the Mobilization of the Dispossessed (*Baseej-e Mostazafin*), through the establishment of joint commands on different fronts.

The second stage in the war broke the lull which followed the fall of Khoramshahr. During this stage, Iran gradually repulsed Iraq from the positions it had captured in the first stage. The Iranian army's first successful offensive was launched with approximately 30,000 men against the Iraqi forces encircling Abadan. On 27 September 1981, the year-long siege of Abadan was lifted and the Iraqis were forced to the northern side of the Karun River. The strategic Ahwaz to Abadan road was opened and the flow of Iranian reinforcements and armour to Abadan was resumed. The *Samen al A'emeh* (the Eighth Imam) counter-offensive was an important moral boost for the Iranian forces. In a string of successful counter-attacks, Bostan was freed on 29 November through Operation *Tariq al-Qods* (Path to Jerusalem) and 160 square kilometres of territory was recovered west of Gilane-Gharb on 11 December, through Operation *Matta al-Fajr* (Rise of Dawn). During 1981, even though the Iranians scored important victories, the scale of operations was small and the changes effected in the general military line up were minimal.

During the two consecutive campaigns, *Fath al-Mobin* (Decisive Victory) on 22 March 1982, and *Qods* (Jerusalem) on 30 April 1982, the Iranian armed forces dramatically transformed the tempo, scale and pattern of the war. Under the command of General Sayyad Shirazi, operation *Fath al-Mobin* was launched in Khuzestan Province, west of Shoosh and Dezful. The Iranians reportedly attacked with 100,000 men; 30,000 conscripts and regulars; 40,000 revolutionary guards (*Pasdarans*) and about 30,000 *Baseeji* volunteers.[125] *Baseeji* members were lightly armed and barely trained. The 'human wave' tactic was used effectively and successfully on a wide scale during the *Fath al-Mobin* campaign. It is reported that the *Pasdaran* formed into 1,000-man brigades and 'moved forward firing as they advanced, followed by other "brigades" at a distance of about half a mile'.[126] After eight days of fighting, which caught the Iraqi high command by surprise and crippled their rigidly centralized command structure, the Iranians recaptured approximately 2,000 square kilometres of their own territory, took 15,000 prisoners, among whom four were superior officers, and seized a sizeable amount of military hardware, tanks and armoured vehicles.

The momentum of Iran's mobilization efforts enabled her to launch the *Qods* operation within a month of the *Fath al-Mobin* campaign. The main objective was the recapture of Khoramshahr. First, Iranian troops succeeded in driving a wedge between the Iraqi forces, 35,000 of whom remained in the city of Khoramshahr cut off from 30,000 to the north in the regions of Hamid, Jofeir and Howeizeh.[127] In their attempt to rectify the situation and tighten their defence of Khoramshahr, Iraqi forces withdrew from Hamid and Jofeir. Recapturing the Ahwaz to Khoramshahr highway, the Iranians paused for about two weeks while they brought in reinforcements by road and rail. On 22 May, the Iranians cut off the main supply road along the Shatt al-Arab which connected Khoramshahr to Iraq. By 24 May, the Iraqi forces occupying Khoramshahr surrendered and Iran regained the 'blood stained city'. The recapture of Khoramshahr lifted the morale of the Iranians and increased their self-confidence. The Iraqis, who had turned Khoramshahr into an impenetrable fortress on whose defence they had staked their military honour, felt humiliated and disgraced. During the *Qods* operation, Iranian forces took 19,000 prisoners, 12,000 of whom surrendered in Khoramshahr. 3,500 square miles of Iranian territory was regained. According to American satellite-intelligence reports, an estimated 30,000 Iraqis and 90,000 Iranian soldiers were killed during the first half of 1982.[128]

Following the Israeli occupation of southern Lebanon in June 1982, Saddam Hossein announced the withdrawal of all Iraqi troops from Iran 'in order to fight against the Israelis'. The Iraqis hoped that Iran would follow suit and accept a ceasefire. Although certain clerical circles called on Iranians to go to Lebanon in order to confront the Israelis, Khomeini suddenly declared that the imperialists wished to save Saddam's neck by diverting the Moslems from the real war between Islam and blasphemy which was being fought with the Iraqis. He, therefore, launched the motto of 'Jerusalem via Karbala', legitimizing the switch from a defensive war to a war of aggression. From Khomeini's point of view, this was a punitive war which had to end in the defeat of the defender of blasphemy and the victory of Islam. Khomeini used the circumstances to justify Iran's invasion of Iraq. On 13 April 1982, General Zahir-Nejad, joint chief of staff, had stated that 'the Imam has ordered the army to be a defensive one' and that 'Iran has no intention of invading another country'. On 7 July 1982, Colonel Mohammad Salimi, the Iranian defence minister, echoed the clerical leadership's new position and stated that 'entry into Iraq is inevitable'.[129] Hashemi-Rafsanjani outlined Iran's conditions for a ceasefire, which included the removal of Saddam Hossein, the acceptance of blame by Iraq for having started the war, return of Iranian territory and the payment of reparations.

During the second half of 1982, Iranian forces launched three successive campaigns with the objective of piercing through Iraq and capturing

Basra. Dizzy with their success in repulsing the Iraqis from Khoramshahr and convinced that low Iraqi morale combined with the Iraqi *Shi'i* readiness to embrace an Islamic government would imminently lead to the fall of Saddam Hossein's régime, Phase I of Operation *Ramezan* was launched on 13 July. It was believed that the fall of Basra, along with widespread *Shi'i* uprisings across Iraq, would precipitate the fall of Saddam Hossein. During this campaign, the *Baseeji* (volunteers) moved through the minefields ahead of the Islamic Revolutionary Guards who attacked in human waves. The campaign proved to be far less successful for the Islamic Republic than had been expected. Although Iranian forces broke through the outer defences of Basra after initial heavy fighting, they were pushed back to their point of departure. During the second phase of Operation *Ramezan*, Iranian forces advanced towards the Iraqi border post of Zaid, about 10 miles from Basra, but they were stopped after 6 miles.[130] The Iranian forces gained approximately 80 square kilometres of Iraqi territory, but took heavy casualties. According to Iranian sources, Iran lost 10,000 men and the Iraqis 7,000.[131]

On 1 October 1982, Iran launched the *Moslem Ibn Aqil* operation with the objective of taking Mandali and gaining access to the road from Mandali to Baghdad. The operation proved that the human-wave tactics adopted by the Iranian forces were largely ineffective in the mountainous terrain around the Khoneh-Rig peaks. Even though some of the heights around Mandali were taken, Iran's gains were very small and neither primary objective was attained.

Operation *Moharram al-Haraam* was launched on 30 October 1982, with the objective of taking the Basra to Baghdad road. The Iranians succeeded in recapturing approximately 150 square kilometres of their own territory and approximately 150 square kilometres of Iraqi territory.[132] The operation placed the Iranian forces in a strong strategic position on the heights overlooking the Basra to Baghdad road, even though the actual road was not taken. An unsuccessful attempt was also made at Mandali. By the end of November, the weather forced both sides to dig in and wait.

Iran's operations during 1982 enabled it to enter Iraqi territory and establish small, but important, strategic pockets which could be used as springboards for future operations. The fact that major Iraqi towns like Basra and Baghdad were now respectively only about 30 and 80 kilometres away from Iranian forward positions placed the Iraqi government under great pressure. Iran's generally successful human-wave tactics and her ability to continue recruiting soldiers for the war effort made Iranian victory seem quite possible. Iraq stepped up her diplomatic efforts for a ceasefire and resorted to launching missile attacks against Iranian cities. It has to be pointed out that as early as 12 August 1981, Iran alleged for the first time that Baghdad had used chemical weapons,[133] an allegation that the western world really did not wish to spend too much attention on. Attempts by the Islamic Conference Organization, Olaf Palme on behalf of the United Nations, Algeria, and the Gulf Co-operation Council all failed to bring about a ceasefire. Iran's insistence on her unrealistic demands made a ceasefire essentially non-negotiable. Iran was now insisting on the creation of an Islamic Republic in Iraq.[134] Although the Arab League Conference at Fez proposed a ceasefire plan, according to which Iran's demand for evacuation of Iraqi forces from Iranian territory would have been satisfied and Iran would have received $40 billion compensation from the Islamic Reconstruction Fund, the Iranian government refused the plan on the basis that it did not satisfy all of its conditions. On 27 October, Saddam Hossein announced his acceptance of the Algiers Agreement of 1975, proclaimed a unilateral ceasefire and demanded the creation of a peacekeeping force, but Iran refused to accept anything less than total victory.

On the same day that Saddam Hossein re-affirmed the validity of the 1975 Algiers Agreement, the initial rejection of which paved the way for his attack on Iran, the Iraqis fired SCUD-B ground-to-ground missiles at Dezful, destroying 100 houses and shops, killing 21 people and injuring over 100. Speaking to the Majlis Hashemi-Rafsanjani referred to the Iraqi attack and said: 'We hope that this time our warriors will be able to put an end to these attacks. We cannot always maintain a defensive posture'.[135] On 18 December 1982, the Iraqis resumed their missile attacks with SCUD-Bs and FROG-7s. These were the first of numerous such attacks against Dezful during 1982 and 1983. During 1983, the Iraqis extended their missile attacks against Marivan, Andimeshk, Behbehan and Masjed-Suleiman. At Behbehan, a missile hit a school killing at least 38 children.

Operation *Val Fajr* (Dawn), was launched on 6 February 1983. Operation Dawn was dubbed the offensive which would determine the fate of the war. On 7 February 1983, Hashemi-Rafsanjani announced that 'we expect that this will be our final military operation and that it will determine the final destiny of the region'.[136] Contrary to the expectations of Iran's Supreme Defence Council, the *Val Fajr* operation during 1983, which aimed at settling the war in Iran's favour, met with serious setbacks. The Iranian forces, relying essentially on the IRG and *Baseeji* volunteers and employing human-wave tactics, were confronted with well-protected positions and superior Iraqi firepower both on land and in the air. At the end of the ten-day *Val Fajr* offensive, an Iranian communiqué claimed that Iran had 'regained 60 square miles of territory and completely annihilated one Iraqi battalion'.[137]

Val Fajr-2 was resumed in Kurdistan with the objective of destroying the headquarters of Qassemlou's Kurdish Democratic Party of Iran. The Iranians succeeded in capturing the town of Haj Omran and the KDPI headquarters, along with a few strategically important heights. The town of Haj Omran was placed at the disposal of the Supreme Assembly of the Islamic Revolution in Iraq (SAIRI) and Hojatolislam Baqir Hakim established his headquarters in 'Liberated Zone of the Iraqi Islamic Republic'. *Val Fajr-3* followed on 30 July 1983, with the reportedly real objective of 'breaking through Iraqi defences in the direction of Kut, on the Basra to Baghdad road, to the south-west'.[138] During this campaign, two Iraqi border towns were captured, one Iranian border post was recaptured and several strategic heights fell to the Iranians. In all, the Iranians captured 40 square miles of territory. Operation *Val Fajr-4* started on 20 October 1983, again in Kurdistan. The Iranians seized five military camps used by the KDPI and advanced along the Panjwein Valley. However, the town of Panjwein did not fall. Approximately 30 Iraqi villages were captured by the Iranians and were handed over to SAIRI to administer. In this operation, the Iranians recaptured 100 square kilometres of their own territory and reportedly 1,000 square kilometres of Iraqi territory.[139] Even though operations *Val Fajr* increased Iranian control over pockets of land in Iraq, they were unsuccessful in delivering a final blow. The Iraqi army had taken a beating, but it was far from defeated.

The Iranian offensive operations in 1983 convinced the clerical leadership that the fall of Saddam Hossein's régime was possible only if a more rigorous mobilization effort could provide Iran with overwhelming numerical superiority. On 31 December 1983, Rafsanjani said 'in order to win this war we have to continue our mobilization effort and depend on our self-sacrificing volunteers'.[140] From 15 January to 15 February 1984, the Iranian newspapers regularly reported on the dispatch of thousands of fresh volunteers to the fronts. The motto 'To conquer Karbala – Go to the fronts' (*Baraye Fathe Karbala Pish Besoye Jebheha*) became the battle cry of the many thousands that flocked to the fronts. On 31 January 1984, Ali Shame'khani, the deputy commander in chief of the IRG, announced that a large-scale military exercise called the Freedom of Qods Manoeuvre would be launched on 9 February. Shame'khani announced that more than 100 battalions were participating in the exercises and that the troops had been well trained and prepared in advance.[141] On 16 February, *Val Fajr-5*, which was immediately succeeded by *Val Fajr-6*, was launched. It was an operation on an unprecedented scale. Reportedly, Iran had amassed a force of 'at least 500,000–750,000 men along a broad 730-mile front'.[142] The large majority of the forces involved in the attack were either IRGs or *Baseeji* volunteers. The military objective of the attack was to cut off the Basra to Baghdad road, isolate Basra from Baghdad, surround Basra and, finally, take it.

The Iranian offensive was launched through the Howeizeh Marshes which were waterlogged and covered with reeds. Three targets were attacked through the marshes in an assortment of small boats. The Iranians initially took the marsh villages of Beida and Sakhra and some Iranian forces actually reached the Tigris river, only a few hundred yards away from the road. The subsequent Iraqi counter-attack with a concentration of heavy firepower drove back the Iranians. The second Iranian military target was the Ghuzail area, located about 25 miles from the outskirts of Basra and strongly defended.[143] The lightly armed *Baseeji* volunteers were thrown against tanks, artillery and helicopter gunships in continuous human waves. Even with fresh divisions of *Baseejis* brought into the battle area, the Iraqi defences held firm. Reportedly, in the Ghuzail battle alone, Iranians lost 'at least 14,500 men'.[144] The third target of the operation was the Majnoon Islands, which are man-made sand and mud mounds in the Howeizeh Marshes, about two miles inside Iraqi territory. The Majnoon Islands were built by the Iraqis when large oil reserves were discovered in the region. As a result of the war, the approximately 50 wells in the area were capped and abandoned. The reed-covered marshes provided the Iranian forces with sufficient cover to take the islands and consolidate their positions there. Despite Iraq's numerous counter-attacks, the Iranians remained well entrenched on the islands. By mid-March, the Iranian assault came to an end. Once again, Iran had failed to obtain her primary objectives, only succeeding in the capture of the Majnoon Islands. US estimates of casualties during this campaign, based on AWACS and satellite surveillance, indicated that 20,000 Iranians and 7,000 Iraqis had been killed.[145] Other sources have placed the figure of Iranians killed at 30,000 to 50,000.[146]

The *Val Fajr-5* and *-6* offensives clearly indicated that the Iranians could move rapidly during the initial stages of the campaign, often attaining their objectives, yet proved incapable of maintaining their newly obtained positions under heavy fire from Iraqi counter-attacks. Iranian human-wave tactics directed against well-entrenched heavy Iraqi firepower resulted in very heavy casualties for little military gain. The widespread use of chemical weapons by Iraq during these campaigns played an undeniable role in the Iranian reverses. The Iraqis made systematic use of such weapons. Iran complained to the UN Security Council that the Iraqis had used chemical bombs on 49 occasions between May 1981 and March 1984, killing 1,200 Iranians and injuring 5,000.[147] A team of experts dispatched by the United Nations to investigate the Iranian charges confirmed the use of mustard gas by the Iraqis, but the UN refused to name the guilty party.

To compensate for their defensive posture and the loss of effective initiative in land battles, the Iraqis tried to shift the theatre of war to those engagements in which they felt superior. Iraq believed that by attacking Iranian economic targets, especially her oil-export capability, it could bring sufficient pressure on the economy and, consequently, on the people to force the government to accept a ceasefire. During January and February of 1984, Iraq claimed to have destroyed 17 'enemy naval targets', and officially warned all oil tankers not to approach Iran's Kharg Oil Terminal or the important ports of Khomeini and Bushehr. On 27 March 1984, Iraq attacked a Greek tanker close to the Kharg Oil Terminal. The Iraqis declared that the ship had been hit by an Exocet missile fired from a Super Etendard aircraft. The 'Tanker War' was launched and continued by Iraq in order to force Iran to the negotiating table. Initially, Iranians who had focused all their attention on the *Val Fajr-5* and *-6* operations, hoping that they would result in the fall of Saddam Hossein's régime, refused to get entangled in the Tanker War. After the failure of the land operations, Iran decided to respond to the Iraqi attacks. On 13 May 1984, Iranian fighters hit a Kuwaiti tanker near Bahrain.[148] The Tanker War continued throughout 1984, reducing the volume of oil exports from Iran and Iraq's allies without ever actually halting the outflow of oil from the Persian Gulf.

As Iran was preparing for the *Val Fajr-5 and -6* operations, calling on fresh volunteers to go to the fronts, Iraq tried to pre-empt Iran's massive land operation by unleashing the 'War of the Cities'. The Soviet Union's sale of SS-12 ground-to-ground missiles to Iraq placed all Iranian cities 500 miles or less from Iraq's launching pads within Iraqi reach.[149] On 1 February 1984 Iraq threatened to attack the cities of Abadan, Ahwaz, Dezful, Ilam and Kermanshah and on 11 February Iraq fired SCUD-B missiles at the city of Dezful, killing 36 and wounding 140 people. Iran responded by shelling Khaneqein, Mandali and Basra the next day. The War of the Cities subsided during *Val Fajr-5* and -6, but picked up again in June of 1984, continuing until 12 June when a UN moratorium on shelling and bombing of cities was accepted by both countries.

Iran's heavy casualties and reverses during the *Val Fajr-5* and -6 campaigns clearly indicated that dependence on the IRG and the *Baseeji* volunteers was not an effective means of attaining victory. Even though Iranian troops still had the tenacity, courage and spirit of self-sacrifice that had resulted in their spectacular initial gains, the absence of heavy combat equipment, co-ordination and appropriate logistics and support denied the Iranians a major victory. The Iranians spent the latter half of 1984 improving the training of their manpower and strengthening the hands of the regular army and its commanders.

Concentrating their efforts on the capture of Basra and the cutting off of the Basra to Baghdad strategic road, the Iranians launched Operation *Badr* during the night of 11 March 1985. The offensive was launched in the Howeizeh Marshes with 53,000 to 100,000 men.[150] The Iranians were relying on their comparative military advantage in infantry and believed that by engaging the Iraqis in the marshes, where only infantry could be properly used, they would be able to reach the Basra to Baghdad road. The Iranians were now equipped with chemical-warfare masks and nerve-gas antidotes. Taking advantage of the dark and of the high reeds in the marsh, Iranian forces crossed the Tigris and by 14 March had cut off the Basra to Baghdad road for the first time. The Iraqis rushed in the élite Republican Guard Division, their mobile brigades and their helicopter gunships. By 18 March, the Iraqis had recovered the territory they had initially lost and Baghdad radio declared victory. The Iranians had once again failed to maintain their hold on the strategic highway. It was reported that Iran had lost 15,000 to 20,000 men and Iraq had lost 8,000 to 12,000 men.

Operation *Badr* was the only significant ground offensive of 1985 and its outcome further divided the professional military, who supported gradual small-scale and well-planned operations, from the zealous IRG commanders, who believed that the human-wave tactics would finally overpower the Iraqis. Both the Tanker War and the War of the Cities continued throughout 1985, without any decisive results. The battles on land, sea and in the air had wound down during the rest of the year as Iran started preparing for a new military offensive in early 1986. Based on their experiences in the Howeizeh Marshes, the military planners had become convinced that the most certain way of capturing Basra was through the marshes. During 1985, Iran embarked on strengthening and developing its amphibious capabilities. Amphibious commando and frogmen units were created and trained in the Caspian Sea and the Karaj Lake. The amphibious commando units were well equipped with small boats and pontoon bridges.

Through the latter part of 1985, Iran amassed a heavy concentration of 150,000 to 200,000 men on the front. On 10 February 1986, Iran launched a two-pronged operation called *Val Fajr-8* with the objective of approaching Basra from the far south sector of the front, close to the mouth of the Shatt al-Arab. A diversionary attack was launched in the north, across the marshes. Depending on US intelligence analysis, the Iraqis had prepared themselves for an Iranian attack north of Basra and were, therefore, successful in repulsing Iran's diversionary attack, thinking that it had been the major offensive. The major Iranian attack was, in fact, focused on the strategically important Iraqi port of Faw, some 50 miles from Basra. The Iranian forces first took the island of Umm al-Rass in the Shatt al-Arab and moved on to the mainland. Concurrently, the Iranians crossed the Shatt al-Arab at six points and moved forward towards Faw. It has been reported that 'Iran may have obtained US intelligence on the weaknesses in the Iraqi position from Colonel Oliver North of the National Security Council'.[151] On 14 February, having established complete control over Faw and its surroundings, the Iranian forces set their sights on the capture of Basra from the south. Iranian troops then moved westward towards the Iraqi naval base at Umm al-Qasr. The Iraqis were caught by surprise and their counter-attack was considerably delayed. It was not until 12 February that the Iraqi military command launched its counter-attack. The Iraqis succeeded in recapturing Umm al-Rass Island, but after seven days of heavy fighting the Iranians held their ground and repulsed Iraqi attempts to recapture Faw.

Val Fajr-8 was a successful operation for the Iranians. The victory at Faw cut off Iraq from the Gulf, it ruptured Iraq's supply and communication lines with Kuwait and it gave Iran a favourable bridgehead to launch her final attack against Basra.[152]

By March, Iran had occupied about 160 square miles of the Faw Peninsula.[153] Iraq lost her anti-aircraft missile base, as well as the main radar-surveillance and control centre in Faw. Despite the fact that the Iraqis had again used chemical weapons, Iranian gains were considerable enough to cause murmurs about Iran's inevitable victory. According to one account, up to 8,000 Iranian soldiers were affected by Iraqi chemical weapons, 700 of whom were killed or seriously wounded.[154]

On 14 May 1986, the Iraqis recaptured two important heights around Mehran and the city itself. The Iraqi operation was launched to block off any attempt by the Iranians to use the shortest 'invasion route to Baghdad which ran by way of Badra and Baguba'.[155] Iraq's success was short lived; the Iranians launched Operation *Karballa-1*, with the objective of recapturing Mehran. The Iraqis were not only forced out of Mehran, a severe blow to their morale, but they lost the strategic Height 233 overlooking Mehran. On 31 August and 1 September, the Iranians followed with the *Karballa-2* and *-3* offensives. During these limited operations, Iranian naval forces captured the Iraqi radar post on the Al-Omaye Oil Terminal Platform and set fire to the Al-Bakr Oil Platform. In the Mehran Axis, Iranian forces captured numerous heights overlooking Badra and Zurbatiya. Even though Khomeini had urged the Iranian military planners to accelerate the war and Hashemi-Rafsanjani had organized the mobilization effort to muster 500 new battalions of *Baseeji* volunteer forces, the long-awaited final offensive that the Iranian clerical leadership often spoke about never materialized in 1986.

On 2 December 1986, however, Iran launched *Karballa-4*, an operation that lasted only two days, during which the Iranian forces took heavy casualties. The operation had two objectives: to cross the Shatt al-Arab and dig in on the Iraqi side and to take Umm al-Rass Island. Iran's *Baseeji* volunteers and IRGs found themselves up against heavily defended Iraqi positions. The Iranians lost 10,000 to 12,000 men in the offensive, which had once again relied on human-wave tactics. The operation, which was said to have been planned, supported and directed by Hashemi-Rafsanjani, ended as a military setback. It was generally believed to be a political move to ease the pressure that was mounting against Hashemi-Rafsanjani for his role in the Irangate affair. *Karballa-4* demonstrated the limitations of human waves and courageous audacity in the face of heavy firepower and strongly defended positions. After four years of the human-wave tactic the clerical leadership was gradually realizing that their strategy, which minimized the importance of military hardware and exaggerated the role of dedicated manpower, was incapable of bringing about the fall of Saddam Hossein's régime. The admission that sheer zeal and voluntarism could not win the war strengthened the hand of the professional army and undermined the position of the IRG.

Operation *Karballa-5*, initiated by the Iranians on 6 January 1987, again sought to cross the Shatt al-Arab and lay seige to or capture Basra. The Iraqis had built five defensive arcs around Basra. A moat had been built and flooded parallel to the border opposite Basra and a large man-made lake called Fish Lake provided a second protective shield for the city.[156] The Iranians attacked with approximately 75,000 men, the majority of whom were *Baseeji* volunteers and IRGs. The first two Iraqi defensive arcs were broken through during the early hours of battle and Shalamcheh was taken. The Iraqis, who had not anticipated the scale of the attack, used poison gas in addition to their conventional heavy firepower. However, the Iranians succeeded in positioning themselves on both sides of Fish Lake pouring in at least 30,000 troops, to hold the territories gained. By 22 February, Iranian forces had broken through the fourth Iraqi defensive arc and were six miles away from the outskirts of Basra. Caught in a 'narrow strip between the Shatt and Fish Lake', the Iranian forces could not advance further towards Basra and on 26 February, the Iranians announced that the objectives of *Karballa-5* had been attained.[157] The campaign was viewed as a success, since the Iranians had occupied some 60 additional square miles of Iraqi territory, captured Shalamcheh, broken through numerous Iraqi defensive arcs and had secured positions approximately nine miles east of Basra. Despite the estimated 17,000 Iranians killed and 35,000 to 45,000 wounded, *Karballa-5* proved that in a war of attrition, as most western observers were pointing out, Iran could not lose and Iraq could not win. Iranian forces were gradually inching up closer and closer to Basra. Iraq's efforts to force out the Iranians failed and Saddam Hossein reacted by relieving a number of officers in the 3rd and 7th Corps from duty and shooting several others.[158]

While *Karballa-5* was still in process, the Iranians launched *Karballa-6*, in the central sector of the front, near Qasr-e-Shirin. The attack, on 13 January, lasted five days and was described by Iran as a 'limited operation'. The operation was said to have recaptured 100 square miles of Iranian territory.[159] On 4 March, Iran launched another limited operation called *Karballa-7* in the Haj-Omran region. The Iranian forces captured the Gerdmand Heights and the Iraqi town of Shuma Mustafa, maintaining their newly won positions, despite repeated Iraqi counter-attacks. After five days of fighting, Iran had advanced 12 miles and announced that it had successfully achieved the objectives of its operation. Operation *Karballa-8*, resumed on 6 April lasted three days, during which Iranian forces eliminated a small Iraqi salient in the defences around Basra and took heavy casualties.[160] On 9 April, the *Karballa-9* operation, which lasted two days, was launched in the Qasr-e-Shirin area. The Iranians claimed that the operation had succeeded in 'liberating three strategic heights in Iranian territory'.[161] Clearly, after Iran's main *Karballa-5* offensive, the other operations were essentially of a diversionary nature, at best intended to harass Iraqi forces along the long frontier in the hope that the Iraqi central command would move its forces away from the Basra region where the Iranians had concentrated their manpower.

On the first day of operation *Karballa-5*, the Iraqis resumed the war of the cities and the Iranians responded in kind. While Iraq carried out regular raids against 35 Iranian towns and cities, including Teheran, Iran attacked Baghdad and Basra with missiles. On 18 February, a two-week moratorium on the War of the Cities was accepted by both sides. Iran claimed between 3,000 and 4,000 killed and between 9,000 and 12,000 injured.[162] The Tanker War continued throughout 1987 and US satellite intelligence reports indicated that the Iranians had installed Chinese Silk Worm anti-ship missiles on Qeshm Island. These newly acquired missiles gave Iran the power to strike at and sink tankers in the Persian Gulf. The United States offered Kuwait US naval escorts to protect her ships, seizing on the escalation of the Tanker War as a pretext to become even more involved in the Persian Gulf.

On the home front, pro-war rhetoric was intensified. Khomeini reiterated his theme that the war should be continued until final victory, claiming that it was a divine cause and, therefore, deserved all the nation's effort and capability. The clerical leadership repeated Khomeini's position in unison, demanding the allocation of greater resources and the mobilization of greater numbers for the achievement of rapid victory. The mobilization effort had lost its past tempo and the Mohammed Mobilization Corps which was intended to attract half-a-million soldiers had barely attracted 200,000.[163] The conscription period was lengthened from 2 years to 28 months on 5 January, as draft dodging increased in Iran.[164] War weariness was gradually setting in. The secret political overtures of the clerical leadership to the west had sown confusion among the true believers. Increasing deployment of 12- to 16-year-old soldiers to the front showed that recruitment was becoming a real problem. Khomeini had already declared that children could go to the front without their parents' consent.

Bazargan's Iran Freedom Movement (IFM) had consistently called for an honourable peace and criticized the autocratic manner in which issues concerning the war were decided by the clerical leadership. Bazargan argued that Iran should not have embarked on an aggressive war against Iraq once the Iraqis were repelled from Iranian soil. The IFM pointed out that the eastern and western superpowers and Israel were the only beneficiaries of the lingering Iran-Iraq war and that Islam and the Islamic people of Iran and Iraq were the biggest losers.[165] This position was shared by a growing number, even among those who were loyal to the Islamic Republic. The futility of the war and the austerity and hardship that it had imposed on society led to increasing public dissatisfaction. Even prominent clerical figures wrote to Khomeini requesting an end to the war. Ayatollah Golpayegani and Marashi-Najafi demanded an end to the war, to which Khomeini responded 'if you wish to have peace, you should pray that I die sooner'.[166]

Iran's next major offensive was launched in mid-March of 1988. Contrary to all expectations, the attack was not in the Basra region, but in the northern sector of the front, to the west of Nowsud. Iranian forces occupied the Kurdish town of Halabja and came close to the Darbandikhan Reservoir. The turbines at the reservoir generated a considerable part of the electricity used in north-east Iraq and parts of Baghdad. Iran captured numerous prisoners and a significant amount of military hardware. Iraq, surprised by the loss of Halabja, responded by indiscriminate use of chemical weapons which killed 3,000 to 5,000 people, the majority of whom were Iraqis. Iran's invitation of foreign journalists and photographers to the area and their wide coverage of the Iraqi atrocity at Halabja brought the issue of Iraq's systematic use of chemical warfare into the headlines.

On 18 April 1988, the US navy attacked and destroyed the Iranian oil platforms of Sassan and Sirri in the Persian Gulf, alleging that the Iranians used Sassan as a base for speedboat attacks against vessels in the Gulf and Sirri as an information gathering base on traffic in the Gulf.[167] In the engagement that ensued, six Iranian boats and one US helicopter were reportedly put out of action.[168] In a concurrent operation, the Iraqi 7th Corps and the élite Republican Guard launched an attack on Iranian positions in Faw. It was reported that after 35 hours of fighting, the Iraqis took control of Faw and the Iranians were forced to retreat to their own side of the Shatt al-Arab. A month after their success in Faw, on 24 May, the Iraqis attacked the Iranian forces in Shalamcheh, south-east of Basra, which had been captured by Iran during the *Karballa-5* operation, and forced the Iranians to retreat. The Iraqis were reported to have gained 120 square kilometres of land.[169] In his address to the third Majlis, on 28 May, Khomeini announced that 'wars have their ups and downs but the fate of the war will not be determined behind negotiation tables but in the battlefields'.[170] Meanwhile Iranian forces were being driven back from positions it had taken them eight years to secure. In May 1988, Bazargan published an open letter accusing Khomeini of refusing to consult with anyone on the issue of the war and imposing his will on the people. Bazargan wrote:

> if you [Khomeini] think that we should sacrifice our lives and our rights in order to export and impose Islam by war . . . you are free to think this way . . . but not at the cost of the lives of all those who do not think this way and who have not said that they are ready to sacrifice their lives and homes.[171]

Bazargan reiterated his demand for an honourable peace.

On 2 June, Khomeini appointed Hashemi-Rafsanjani as the new commander in chief of the armed forces, a position which he had not delegated to anyone since Bani-Sadr held the post. Rafsanjani immediately announced that he would 'try to achieve all the objectives set by Imam Khomeini in the war'. He added that 'our success in the war depends on the degree to which we can mobilize our people'.[172] On the night of 19 June, the People's Mojahedeen's National Liberation Army captured the Iranian city of Mehran and then withdrew. The Majnoon Islands were recaptured by the Iraqis on 27 June and the Iranians withdrew their forces from Halabja in July.

On 3 July 1988, an Iran Air airbus on its way to Dubai from Bandar Abbas in Iran was shot down by the USS *Vincennes*, killing all 290 passengers on board. Montazeri demanded an all-out attack against US interests all over the world, but Khomeini advised him to calm down. Then, on 20 July, Iran officially accepted Security Council Resolution 598, which called for an immediate ceasefire and had already been accepted by Iraq. On 20 August 1988, a ceasefire between Iran and Iraq came into effect. UN observers were positioned on the front between the two countries, with each country behind its own borders.

A question of arms

One of the major factors determining the outcome of the war was the ability of each country to obtain the necessary military hardware. Iran's superiority in manpower could only have been offset if Iraq could have dealt an initial decisive blow before Iran could react. As the war dragged on, Iraq could only balance Iran's numerical superiority by maintaining a net superiority in terms of arms and technology. Even if Iraq were to kill three or four Iranians for every Iraqi, Iran could bear the manpower loss, while Iraq could not.[173] Given both countries' infant arms industry prior to the war, access to imported military hardware became a principal concern. Iran's anti-western foreign policy during this period, coupled with the US embargo on the sale of arms and spare parts, accentuated the problem and led to the deployment, and subsequent massacre, of tens of thousands of sparsely armed *Baseeji* volunteers. The shortage of US spare parts after the hostage crisis had caused the Islamic Republic such great anxiety that, even before the outbreak of the Iran-Iraq war, Tabatabai inquired about the resumption of US military supplies to Iran after the release of the hostages, when he met Warren Christopher in Bonn.[174] During the seven months between the outbreak of the war and the ousting of Bani-Sadr, Iran continued to be in desperate need of US arms supplies, but no one in the leadership dared to publicly establish relations with western countries with the object of obtaining arms. Each faction, Bani-Sadr and IRP, feared exposure by the other. On 5 November 1980, Hashemi-Rafsanjani declared that 'we have decided not to import weapons from the U.S.'.[175] Once, however, the IRP established its unchallenged rule, it had the opportunity to safely seek and obtain western military hardware to support the war effort.

Faced with a virtual embargo on the delivery of arms by western powers and being internally vulnerable to embarrassing revelations about contracts with 'big and small Satans', the Islamic Republic sought to obtain arms on the international market in whatever way possible. It is reported that Iran established a large logistics support centre in the Iranian National Oil Company building in London, through which Iran's efforts to purchase arms in Europe and elsewhere in the world were co-ordinated.[176] Iran was forced to depend on middlemen of varying shades of integrity, from Iranian expatriates to western and even Israeli military and intelligence officers. The price that the clerical leadership paid to maintain its revolutionary and anti-western rhetoric for domestic political purposes was staggering for a war economy under stress. Iran's clandestine deals often delivered 'less than a dollar's worth of arms for every three dollars Iran spent'.[177] In one case, Iran received a can of dog food instead of the F-5 parts it had ordered.[178]

The purchase of arms on the black market imposed further problems. Iran was never certain of receiving the whole range of necessary spare parts that rendered her weapons fully operational. The right mix of weapons, ammunition and spares, necessary for the success of a military operation, was not often available, given the high risk that such illegal transactions entailed. On 19 April 1986, 'Iran was caught in a two billion dollar U.S. customs "sting" operation that led to 17 indictments'.[179] Furthermore, the delivery date for the weapons, a crucial element in planning and launching offensives, was always precarious.

The unreliability of the black market and Iran's growing need for arms imports forced it to diversify its sources and purchase arms from countries such as the People's Republic of China and North Korea. In 1985, Iran imported $2.158 billion worth of arms, 43 per cent of which was supplied by North Korea and China; in 1986, North Korea and China provided 70 per cent of all Iranian military imports.[180] The switch away from US equipment created severe problems. Military personnel had to be retrained in the use of the new weapons systems. Furthermore, since the two weapons systems were not interoperable, the new ones required their own maintenance facilities, stocks and spare parts.

Preoccupied with winning the war at any cost, the clerical leadership gradually became convinced that the resumption of western arms deliveries was the best guarantee of success. However, secrecy was essential. The clerical leadership could not afford to jeopardize the zeal and faith of its IRGs, which had proved to be the most effective weapon in Iran's arsenal. The Islamic government had to maintain the staunch anti-western and self-sufficient Islamic image that it had created for itself at home. It was this self-righteous identity that motivated the fierce yet barely armed IRGs and the *Baseeji* volunteers to defy death and charge well-defended Iraqi positions. The slightest tampering with this clerically created edifice of unfaltering revolutionary virtuousness meant a disastrous credibility and sincerity gap.

Since 1981, the Islamic Republic had been a recipient of arms from Israel. It is reported that in July 1981, Yaakov Nimrodi, Israel's former military attaché to Teheran signed a $135.8 million contract with Iran.[181] Israel apparently delivered forty 155mm field guns, 68 Hawk missiles, M-48 tanks, possibly 50 Lance missiles and 3,730 Copperhead laser-guided 155mm artillery shells.[182] In May 1982, Israel's defence minister, Ariel Sharon, openly discussed the sale of military equipment to the Islamic Republic valued at $27 billion. Both Sharon and Moshe Arens, the Israeli ambassador to the United States at the time, confirmed that Israeli arms sales to Iran were taking place with the knowledge and consent of the US government.[183] In January 1983, another contract involving arms deliveries worth $21 million was signed between Israel and Iran. The clerical leadership viewed these secret deals with those labelled as the sworn enemies of Moslems as justifiable in terms of the long-run good of the cause. Everything was permissible for the maintenance and expansion of the Islamic order.

Iraq's ability to openly buy any amount of arms was seen as one of the major reasons for her ability to withstand Iran's numerous heavy offensives. The less ideologically oriented and more power-conscious elements in the clerical leadership believed that Iran had to break out of her self-imposed radical isolation in the international community. Iran had to buy the international respectability which she had considered unrevolutionary and unimportant when the US hostages were taken. The objective of creating a new Islamic international order was now secondary. After Genscher, the minister of foreign affairs of the Federal Republic of Germany, visited Teheran in July of 1984, he told reporters that 'the Islamic leadership is clearly in favour of a *rapprochement* with the West and we welcome such a move'.[184] Genscher's invitation to Teheran was a clear indication by the pragmatists in the leadership that the Islamic Republic wished to mend fences with the West. Reportedly, the leaders of the Islamic Republic did not exclude the possibility of resuming diplomatic relations with the United States, and Foreign

Minister Velayati is reported to have told Genscher that, 'It is still a bit early for resuming diplomatic relations with the U.S.'.[185] The tempo of the Islamic Republic's foreign policy was, however, set by Hashemi-Rafsanjani's statement to Genscher that 'We have been considerably hurt by the crisis that has developed in our relations with the West'.[186]

On 14 June 1985, Iran was given the chance to prove her good intentions towards the international community when TWA flight 847 was hijacked by two Lebanese. According to the CIA inspector general, Israeli officials asked an Iranian businessman, Manouchehr Qorbanifar, who was reported to have close links with Prime Minister Moussavi's office, to use his influence in Teheran to obtain the release of the hostages.[187] On 19 June, Iran assured the United States that it would do all that was in its power to obtain the release of the hostages.[188] On 24 June, Hashemi-Rafsanjani condemned the hijacking and five days later all the hostages were freed. Iran's helpful intervention was a clear signal to US policy makers.

Well before the TWA hijacking, the United States had been notified that Iran was interested in releasing kidnapped US citizens in Lebanon in exchange for weapons. Theodore Shackley, a former CIA officer, reported to the State Department that he had met Manouchehr Qorbanifar and General Manouchehr Hashemi, formerly head of SAVAK's counter-espionage department, on 19 to 21 November 1984, in Hamburg, West Germany. Qorbanifar, according to Shackley, was a SAVAK agent and reported to have 'fantastic' contacts in Iran. Qorbanifar made two proposals, which must have been cleared by the government in Teheran. He suggested that 'Iran would be willing to trade some Soviet equipment captured in Iraq for TOW missiles'.[189] Qorbanifar also suggested that a cash ransom could be paid to Iran for the release of the four kidnapped US citizens in Lebanon.[190] Although the State Department turned down Qorbanifar's suggestions, it was evident that the Iranians were trying hard to get the attention of highly placed US foreign-policy makers to convince them of their change in policy.

When the United States refused to respond to Teheran's message, the Israelis were approached by Qorbanifar to sell the idea of exchanging arms for hostages to the Americans. David Kimche, the number two in the Israeli foreign ministry and a former senior officer in Mossad, masterminded a simple arms-for-hostages deal in which Israel played the role of supplier of TOW anti-tank missiles to Iran.[191] According to this plan, the United States was to replenish the Israeli arsenal. On 3 July 1985, Kimche met Robert McFarlane, the national security adviser to the president, who informed President Reagan of his discussions three or four days after his meeting with Kimche.[192] On 13 July, McFarlane was approached by an emissary of Israeli Prime Minister Peres, a Mr Schwimmer, who informed him that 'others inside Iran were interested in more extensive relations with the West and particularly the United States'.[193] At the first stage in the opening up of Iran-US relations, the Iranian government asked for 100 TOW missiles to be delivered to Iran. Even though Secretary of State Schultz and Secretary of Defence Weinberger

vigorously opposed the Kimche plan, the president approved the shipment of arms to Israel and eventually to Iran sometime in August.

A post-dated check for $1 million was given to Adnan Khashoggi by
the Iranian contact, Qorbanifar, on 17 August 1985. Khashoggi deposited
the check in Yaakov Nimrodi's Swiss bank account. Nimrodi, an active
arms salesman since his retirement from government service, had been
in contact with the Iranians since 1981.[194] Upon notification of the receipt
of funds, the Israelis delivered 100 TOW anti-tank missiles to Iran on 30
August 1985. The second Israeli delivery, consisting of 408 TOW
missiles, took place on 14 September 1985, through the same channels.[195]
On 15 September, the first US hostage, Reverend Benjamin Weir, was
released. In four additional deliveries, most of them by CIA-owned
aircraft, Iran received 1,000 US TOW missiles, HAWK spare parts and
an additional delivery of another 500 TOW missiles. The US delivery of
30 October 1986 was followed by the release of David Jacobsen on 2
November 1986.

The receipt of US arms from the summer of 1985 to the winter of 1986
made a direct contribution to Iran's military capability in the war. Iran's
success in the *Val Fajr-8* and *Karballa-5* offensives which led to the
capture of Faw and the breakthrough in Basra's defensive arcs should be
seen in the light of Iran's receipt of TOW anti-tank missiles and the
HAWK surface-to-air missiles. In the *Val Fajr-8* operation, Iraq lost 15
to 30 aircraft.[196] The receipt of the TOW missiles provided Iran with a
defence against Iraq's clear superiority in armour. The clerical leadership
was encouraged by the performance of the Iranian military machine and
stepped up its call for the final battle, hoping that the efficient combination of US arms and the Islamic and anti-US fighting spirit of the Iranian
warriors would continue to achieve results.

The Israelis played the principal role in the arms-for-hostages deal.
They drew up the plan for action, contacted US policy makers, exerted
pressure on the US administration to take part in the deal and, finally,
accepted responsibility for the initial deliveries. In view of Iran's relentless anti-Israeli rhetoric, the Israeli government's motive in coming to
Iran's help seems enigmatic. In a discussion with McFarlane, Kimche
clearly outlined why Israel was interested in the deal. Kimche said 'Well,
we in Israel have our own interests. They are basically to ensure a
stalemate of the conflict with Iraq, but also to get the United States back
into Iran, and that helps us if the US position in the Middle East is
strengthened; and separately, to reduce the Iranian support for terrorism,
if that is feasible, is very much in our interests and so we might very well
do this as a matter of Israeli interest'.[197] Other reasons, such as securing
the position of Iranian Jews or easing Iranian hostility towards Israel,
have also been put forward, yet it seems that by prolonging the war, Israel
attained its primary objective of keeping the Arabs divided between the
Iraqi and Syrian camps, thus reducing the potential danger of a united
Arab or Islamic front against it.

An Israeli observer wrote 'Iran destabilises the Arab camp and
neutralises one of the strongest and most venomous of our potential

enemies, Iraq'.[198] Yet Israel was simply applying the old axiom of 'My enemy's enemy is my friend'. Iran was a potential strategic ally, irrespective of who ruled the country. In 1984, Schweitzer wrote

> There is truth in the laws of geopolitics: whoever rules Teheran becomes, willy-nilly, an ally of whoever rules Jerusalem. The rule has proven its validity since the days of Cyrus. . . . Israel and Iran need each other. That is the way it has been and that is the way it will be.[199]

According to Gary Sick, some 5,000 tons of arms worth $500 to 1,000 million and involving 9 to 12 shipments went from Israel to Iran by sea between May and November 1986.[200] Although the revelation of the arms-for-hostages deal put a temporary end to the US supply of arms, the Israelis continued to sell to Iran. Amiran Nir, a high ranking counter-terrorism agent of the Israeli government, reportedly met Iranian arms-purchasing agents in mid-March 1987.[201]

The secret US-Iranian-Israeli talks which had led to the delivery of US arms, and the clandestine arrival of McFarlane, Lieutenant-Colonel North, George Cove, a CIA official and the Israeli, Amiran Nir, in Teheran on 28 May 1986 could not have remained a secret among the members of the clerical leadership. Qorbanifar reports that he had been in contact with the Prime Minister Moussavi, Hashemi-Rafsanjani and Ahmad Khomeini, but others must also have known about Iran's new foreign-policy initiatives.[202] Even though the clerical leadership seem to have been unanimous in their support of the secret contacts in order to win the war, groups connected with the leadership yet less influential in day-to-day policy making and more concerned with the ideological purity of the Islamic Republic's policies remained unconvinced of the soundness of Iran's initiative. Furthermore, the power struggle which was being waged over economic issues tended to spill over into foreign policy as well, leaving the Iranian negotiators with the United States in a very vulnerable position. Since Bazargan's talk with Brzezinski in 1980 contacts with the United States had become an unforgivable political sin from the point of view of the supporters of the Islamic government. The clerical leadership had embarked on the third stage of its foreign policy, namely *rapprochement* with the West and the search for international respectability, but it shied away from informing the people that the time had come to pay proper respect to the once burnt and trampled upon US flag.

The event that triggered off the chain reaction leading to Iran's acceptance of a ceasefire in the Gulf war in August 1988 was the abduction of the Syrian chargé d'affaires, Ayad Mahmood, in Teheran. On 2 October 1986, Ayad Mahmood's car was intercepted by a BMW and an ambulance and he was taken away by force, only to be released a few hours later. Iran's official news agency announced that the kidnapping had been 'an act of terrorism committed by CIA agents'.[203] The Iranian government conveyed its apologies to Syria by sending the minister of the revolutionary guards to Damascus. The kidnapping was reported to have been planned and executed by Mehdi Hashemi's powerful group. Some observers believed that the abduction was in response to Hafez al-Assad's statement in early autumn of 1986 that 'Iraq is an Arabic country and Syria would not allow any country to occupy it'.[204]

Mehdi Hashemi was a well-known figure among clerical circles. He was the brother of Ayatollah Montazeri's son-in-law, Hadi Hashemi. He had embarked on his career of Islamic militancy in 1961, founding a group called the Society of the Final Objective.[205] Hashemi's brand of *Shi'i* Islam was similar to that of Shariati's in that he campaigned against the Islam of superstition and empty rituals and invited his followers to act against the oppressors. Like Shariati, Hashemi cited Imam Hossein as the perfect example of a *Shi'i* revolutionary who defied the power of Yazid and rebelled against him to take power. The voluntaristic image of Imam Hossein was descibed in a book that was written by Shaykh Nematollah Salehi-Najafabadi with an introduction by Montazeri, published by Hashemi's group in 1962. The conservative clergy, who took offence at what they considered to be a falsification of facts, reacted against the book, branded Shaykh Salehi-Najafabadi as crazy and banned him from all religous centres. When Ayatollah Abolhassan Moussavi Ale-Ras-soul, better known as Shamsabadi, who was well established in Hashemi's zone of influence in Qadirjan and Lanjan, started to denounce Hashemi and his followers, Hashemi ordered his death. Between September 1965 and April 1966, Hashemi and his followers executed seven and injured six people who had opposed them. Among the executed were Ayatollah Shamsabadi and another cleric called Shaykh Qanbar-Ali Safarzadeh. Subsequently, Hashemi and a number of his followers were put on trial in 1966 and sentenced to death, but the sentence was never carried out. During February of 1987, when all prisons were opened, Hashemi was released and received a 'royal welcome' as an old Islamic warrior.

After his release from prison, Hashemi became the head of an important unit in the CIRG which co-ordinated and controlled the Islamic Liberation Movements abroad. It was with Hashemi's close collaboration that in January 1980 the Islamic students following the 'Imam's' line organized the Gathering of Liberation Movements in Teheran. Reportedly, by early 1981, Hashemi was provided with a 600 million-rial-per annum secret budget for his office for the Islamic Liberation Movements, in addition to 500 million rials annually from Montazeri's office. He was also believed to administer two training camps for revolutionary guerillas, one in Manzarieh and the other in Saleh-abad.[206] Hashemi was very influential in the CIRG and many of his followers became commanders of various units of the corps.

Hashemi's real motive for the abduction of the Syrian chargé d'affaires remains unclear, though there has been speculation that he might have ordered the kidnapping after Syria confiscated a shipment of arms sent by Hashemi to the Hezbollah in Lebanon.[207] Approximately two weeks after the kidnapping affair, the minister of intelligence, Hojatolislam Mohammed Reyshahri, announced the arrest of Medhi Hashemi and a large number of his collaborators and followers, including Montazeri's son, his son-in-law, at least two members of the Islamic parliament and a number of influential figures in the CIRG. The chronology of events has usually been presented so that it seems as if it was only after the arrest of Hashemi that his followers retaliated by leaking the arms-for-hostages scandal to the Lebanese weekly *Al-Shera*.[208] Hassan Sabra, the editor of *Al-Shera*, however, recalls that it was three or four weeks before he first published the news about secret talks between Washington and Teheran, that Ayatollah Montazeri's representative in Lebanon, Shaykh Mohammed-Esmaeel Khaleq 'Razavi', went to see him and gave him a letter in which the whole story about the secret talks was revealed. Sheykh Khaleq had implicitly asked Sabra to publish the story and had conveyed to him the warmest wishes of Ayatollah Montazeri and Mehdi Hashemi.[209] Therefore, according to Sabra, Hashemi and Montazeri had decided to publicize the talks well before Hashemi's arrest. The Hashemi-Montazeri faction had hoped to pressure the clerical leadership into abandoning their policy of expediency and pragmatism in favour of ideological purity. An interesting twist in the whole episode is that Sabra conferred with Damascus on the publication of the story and only after getting the go-ahead did he proceed to publish, on 2 November 1986. Did the Syrians inform the clerical leadership that Hashemi was planning to sabotage their secret honeymoon with the United States and Israel? Could this have been the reason why Hashemi ordered the abduction of the Syrian chargé d'affaires?

Hashemi was condemned to death on charges of murder before and after the revolution, kidnapping, illegal possession and storing of arms and explosives, illegal possession of state documents, forgery of state documents, formation of armed groups and initiating ideological deviation in seminary schools. He and two of his associates were executed in October 1987. The damage had been done, however. The third stage of Iran's foreign policy was now public knowledge. The consequences of the revelations were far greater than the clerical leadership realized. It took about eighteen months before the real impact became apparent on the war front.

Iran's new foreign-policy position necessitated a new approach to diplomacy and a new vocabulary. On 25 November 1986, some twenty days after the revelation of Iran's involvement in two years of secret talks, the minister of foreign affairs set the tone for Iran's conduct of foreign policy in this third stage. In a speech at the University of *Elm va Sanat*, Velayati assailed rhetoric and empty slogans and pointed out that it is incorrect 'to endanger our proper base in the process of attaining our ideals'.[210] Velayati emphasized that 'they consider the establishment of relations with the world to be a principle' and proceeded to ask:

why should we be afraid of negotiating with someone from a foreign country? That which should be a sensitive issue is not the act of negotiation but the content. Who has said that we should not defend our rights through dialogue and negotiation?[211]

Velayati's words echoed those of Bazargan when he defended his decison to meet Brezinski. After nearly ten years, dialogue, negotiation and compromise were once again gaining respectability.

Notes

1. Tarhe Tahquiq Siyasat Khareji Islam, *Journal of Foreign Policy*, Vol. I, April–June 1987, No 2, pp. 225–30.
2. A. R. I. Doi, *Shariah: The Islamic Law*, op. cit., p. 5.
3. Khomeini, *Khate Imam, Kalame Imam*, op. cit., p. 98.
4. Motahhari, *Jamme-e va Tarikh* (Teheran: Entesharat Sadra), p. 194.
5. *Keyhan*, 6 Farvardeen, 1359.
6. *Journal of Foreign Policy*, op. cit., pp. 229–30.
7. Imam Khomeini, *Islam*, trans. by Hamid Algar, op. cit., p. 170.
8. Daftar Motaleaat Siyasi va Beinolmelali, *Gozaresh Seminar 6*, p. 20.
9. Rouhani, *Nehzate Imam Khomeini*, op. cit., pp. 300–130.
10. Ibid., pp. 274–5.
11. Ibid., p. 717.
12. Ibid.
13. Ibid., pp. 722 and 724.
14. Ibid., p. 722.
15. Imam Khomeini, *Nedaye haqh* (Teheran: Entesharat Qalam Jeld 1.), p. 120.
16. Ibid., p. 121.
17. Ibid., p. 41.
18. Ibid., p. 50.
19. Ibid., p. 83.
20. Michael Ledeen and William Lewis, *Debacle: The American Failure in Iran* (New York: Vintage Books, 1982), p. 157. Bill, *The Eagle and the Lion*, op. cit., p. 279.
21. Ledeen and Lewis, op. cit., p. 193.
22. Bill, op. cit., p. 279.
23. Bill, op. cit., p. 289.
24. *Keyhan*, Bahman, 1358.
25. Bill, op. cit., p. 291.
26. Ibid., p. 281.
27. *Asnad Laneh Jasousi* 10:25, 34, 35, 41, cited in Bill, p. 283.
28. *Keyhan*, 2 Aban, 1358.
29. *Keyhan*, 7 Aban, 1358.
30. *Keyhan*, 12 Aban, 1358.
31. Bazargan, *Moshkelaat va Masael Aval in Saal-e Enqelab* (Teheran, 1362), p. 290.
32. Ibid., p. 290.
33. *Keyhan*, 12 Aban, 1358.
34. Warren Christopher ed., *American Hostages in Iran* (New Haven: Yale University Press, 1985), p. 41.
35. Gary Sick, *All Fall Down* (London: I. B. Tauris, 1985), p. 196.
36. Bill, op. cit., p. 295.
37. Ibid., p. 296.
38. Ibid., p. 295.
39. Bani-Sadr, op. cit., p. 169.
40. *Keyhan*, 14 Aban, 1358.
41. *Keyhan*, 17 Aban, 1358.
42. Christopher, op. cit., p. 93.
43. Ibid., p. 94.
44. Ibid., p. 147.
45. Ibid., p. 148.
46. *Keyhan*, 30 Aban, 1358.

47. *Keyhan*, 7 Azar, 1358.
48. *Keyhan*, 21 Esfand, 1358.
49. Harold H. Saunders in Christopher, op. cit., p. 135.
50. Cyrus R. Vance, *Hard Choices: Critical Years in America's Foreign Policy* (New York: Simon and Schuster, 1983), p. 408.
51. The information in this section is based on Gary Sick's article in Christopher, op. cit.
52. Robert Owen in Christopher, op. cit., 297.
53. Ibid., p. 365.
54. Ibid.
55. Ibid., p. 307.
56. Ibid., p. 302.
57. Ibid., p. 324.
58. *Enqelab-e Islami*, 2 Khordad, 1360.
59. *Enqelab-e Islami*, 17 Khordad, 1360.
60. Bill, op. cit., p. 208.
61. Ibid., p. 202.
62. *Keyhan*, 3 Esfand, 1357.
63. *Keyhan*, 30 Bahman, 1357.
64. *Keyhan*, 7 Esfand, 1357.
65. *Keyhan*, 13 Shahrivar, 1357.
66. *Keyhan*, 1 Mehr, 1358.
67. *Keyhan*, 7 Mehr, 1357.
68. *Keyhan*, 25 Mordad, 1358.
69. *Keyhan*, 16 Mehr, 1358.
70. Augustus Richard Norton, *AMAL and the Shi'a* (Austin: University of Texas Press, 1987), p. 48.
71. *Keyhan*, 5 Ordibehesht, 1358.
72. *Keyhan*, 15 Ordibehesht, 1358.
73. *Keyhan*, 16 Ordibehesht, 1358.
74. Ibid.
75. *Keyhan*, 6 Khordad, 1358.
76. *Keyhan*, 22 Aban, 1358.
77. *Keyhan*, 19 Azar, 1358.
78. *Keyhan*, 9 Dey, 1358.
79. *Keyhan*, 16 Dey, 1358.
80. Ibid.
81. *Keyhan*, 16 Dey, 1358.
82. *Keyhan*, 22 Dey, 1358.
83. *Keyhan*, 28 Bahman, 1358.
84. *Keyhan Chape Landan*, 12 Mehr, 1363.
85. R. C. Norton, op. cit., p. 88.
86. *New York Times*, 19 April 1983.
87. R. K. Ramazani, *Revolutionary Iran* (Baltimore: The John Hopkins University Press, 1986), p. 189.
88. *New York Times*, 28 October 1983, cited in Ramazani, op. cit., p. 184.
89. Ramazain, op. cit., p. 198.
90. Norton, op. cit., p. 102.
91. Norton, op. cit., p. 165.
92. *Middle East Reporter*, 22 March 1986, cited in Norton, op. cit., p. 103.
93. *New York Times*, 26 January 1985, cited in Ramazani, p. 186.
94. Cited in *Enqelab-e Islami*, 6 June 1988. ;8.
95. *Rouzegar, E. Now*, 23 Aout–22 Septembre 1986.
96. Ramazani, op. cit., p. 94.
97. *The Economist* (London), 18 September 1982 and *Washington Post*, 25 November, 1982.
98. *Ettelaat*, 8 Mordad, 1366.
99. *Rouzegar, E. Now*, Aout–Septembre 1987.

100. Ibid.
101. *The Times*, 3 August 1987.
102. Ibid.
103. Ramazani, op. cit., p. 44.
104. *Washington Post*, 3 February 1984, cited in Ramazani, op. cit., p. 44.
105. Ibid.
106. *Keyhan Chape Landan*, 9 Khordad, 1364.
107. Ramazani, op. cit., p. 50.
108. Ramazani, op. cit., p. 51.
109. Ramazani, op. cit., p. 53.
110. *Keyhan Chape Landan*, 12 Mehr, 1363.
111. *Keyhan Chape Landan*, 16 Khordad, 1364.
112. *Keyhan Chape Landan*, 5 Mehr, 1363.
113. Ramazani, op. cit., p. 131.
114. Ramazani, op. cit., p. 240.
115. Ibid.
116. *Le Monde*, 3 Avril 1980. *Jeune Afrique*, 16 April 1980, cited in A. H. Trab Zemzemi, *The Iran-Iraq War* (San Clemente: UNited States Publishing Company, 1986), p. 40.
117. Ramazani, op. cit., p. 59.
118. *Keyhan*, 25 Farvardeen, 1359.
119. Zemzemi, op. cit., p. 47.
120. *Keyhan*, 27 Farvardeen, 1359.
121. *Keyhan*, 18 and 21 Bahman, 1358.
122. S. R. Grummon, *The Iran-Iraq War* (NY: Praeger Publishers, 1982), p. 20.
123. S. Tahir–Kheli, Ayubi, S. (ed.), *The Iran-Iraq War* (NY: Praeger Publishers, 1983), p. 38.
124. S. Tahir–Kheli, Ayubi, S. (ed.), op. cit., p. 38 and Edgar O'Ballance, *The Gulf War* (London: Brassey's Defence Publishers, 1988), p. 38. Although the military information in this book on the Iran-Iraq war is reliable, its account of internal Iranian politics is downright erroneous and false on more than one occasion.
125. O'Ballance, op. cit., p. 79.
126. Ibid.
127. Zemzemi, op. cit., p. 107.
128. O'Ballance, op. cit., p. 86.
129. O'Ballance, op. cit., pp. 82–93.
130. O'Ballance, op. cit., p. 96.
131. Ibid.
132. Zemzemi, op. cit., p. 114.
133. O'Ballance, op. cit., p. 77.
134. Nehzat-e Azadi Iran, *Tahlili Piramoon-e Jang va Solh* (Teheran, 1363), p. 60.
135. Hojatolislam Hashemi-Rafsanjani, *Notqehaye Qabl az dastour* (Teheran: Ravabet Omoomi Majlis Shoura-e Islami 1363), p. 47.
136. Hojatolislam Hashemi-Rafsanjani, op. cit., p. 52.
137. Cited in O'Ballance, op. cit., p.118.
138. O'Ballance, op. cit., p. 114.
139. Zemzemi, op. cit., p. 117.
140. *Ettelaat*, 10 Dey, 1362.
141. *Ettelaat*, 11 Bahman, 1362.
142. A. H. Cordesman, *The Iran-Iraq War* (London: The Royal United Services Institute, 1987), p. 61.
143. O'Ballance, op. cit., p. 145.
144. Ibid., p. 146.
145. O'Ballance, op. cit., p. 147.
146. Cordesman, op. cit., p. 69.
147. O'Ballance, op. cit., p. 149.
148. Cordesman, op. cit., p. 66.
149. O'Ballance, op. cit., p. 153.

150. O'Ballance, op. cit., p. 161 and Cordesman, op. cit., p. 73.
151. Cordesman, op. cit., p. 93.
152. Cordesman, op. cit., p. 92.
153. O'Ballance, op. cit., p. 179.
154. Cordesman, op. cit., p. 97.
155. O'Ballance, op. cit., p. 179.
156. Cordesman, op. cit., p. 126.
157. Cordesman, op. cit., p. 128.
158. *Washington Post*, 9 February 1987.
159. *The Economist*, 17 January 1987.
160. O'Ballance, op. cit., p. 203.
161. Ibid., p. 204.
162. O'Ballance, op. cit., p. 201 and Cordesman, op. cit., p. 136.
163. O'Ballance, op. cit., p. 198.
164. *The Economist*, 13 February 1988.
165. Nehzat-e Azadi Iran, *Mozakereh, Atashbas, Solh*, Tir 1364, p. 3.
166. *Enqelab-e Islami*, 22 May 1988.
167. *The Economist*, 23 April 1988.
168. Rouzegar, *E. Now*, Juillet–Aout 1988.
169. *Le Monde*, 30 Mai, 1988.
170. *Enqelab-e Islami*, 6 June 1988.
171. Nehzat-e Azadi, *Hoshdar*, Ordibehesht 1367, p. 7.
172. Le Monde, 5 Juin, 1988.
173. Cordesman, op. cit., p. 22.
174. Christopher, op. cit., p. 305.
175. Ibid., p. 167.
176. Cordesman, op. cit., p. 28.
177. Ibid.
178. Ibid.
179. Ibid.
180. Cordesman, op. cit., p. 27 and 29.
181. B Beit-Hallahmi, *The Israeli Connection* (London: I. B. Tauris, 1987), p. 14.
182. *The Observer*, 1 December 1986.
183. Beit-Hallahmi, op. cit., p. 14.
184. *Keyhan Chape Landan.*, 26 July 1984.
185. Ibid.
186. Ibid.
187. *The Tower Commission Report, The Full Text* (New York: Bantam Books and Time Books, 1987), p. 126. Hereafter referred to as Report.
188. Ibid.
189. Report, op. cit., p. 107.
190. Ibid.
191. B. Woodward, *Veil, The Secret Wars of the CIA* (New York: Pocket Books, 1987), p. 474.
192. Report, op. cit., p. 24.
193. Ibid., p. 25.
194. Beit-Hallahmi, op. cit., p. 14.
195. Report, op. cit., p. 441.
196. Cordesman, op. cit., p. 94.
197. Report, op. cit., p. 137.
198. Beit-Hallahmi, op. cit., p. 15.
199. Ibid.
200. Cordesman, op. cit., p. 31.
201. Ibid., p. 32.
202. Report, op. cit., p. 538.
203. *Rouzegar, E. Now*, 23 Septembre au 22 Octobre 1986.
204. Ibid.
205. The information in this section is based on Ali-Reza Nourizadeh's article in

Rouzegar, E. Now, 23 Octobre au 21 Novembre 1986.
206. *Rouzegar, E. Now*, op. cit., p. 51.
207. *Rouzegar, E. Now*, op. cit., p. 53.
208. See R. K. Ramazami's *Revolutionary Iran* (Baltimore: The John Hopkins University Press 1988), p. 264, for this type of analysis.
209. Ali Reza Nourizadeh's article in *Rouzegar, E. Now*, 22 Novembre au 21 Decembre 1986.
210. *Gozaresh Seminar*, Daftar Motaleaat Siyasi va Beinolmelade (Teheran, 1365), p. 17.
211. Ibid., p. 19.

Conclusion

Secularization of the miracle

The outcome of the Iran-Iraq war will continue to remain a controversial subject among strategists and historians for years to come. The facts indicate that once the Iraqis were repelled from Iranian territory, each subsequent year Iran's offensives brought the armed forces of that country closer to the capture of Basra. Iran's important military victories in Iraq started in 1985 and reached a peak in February 1987, when military observers were unanimous in their prediction that Iran could not lose and Iraq could not win. It was felt that Iran's 3–1 numerical superiority assured her success in the long run. In 1986, the French general, Claude Le Borgne, who had visited the front several times, commented on the future of the war and wrote: 'The marked superiority of Iraq in tanks is not enough to assure her supremacy on the battlefield . . . when faced with the kind of men who gave their lives in the muddy plains of Faw, modern arms do not carry much weight'.[1] The fixed coefficient of Iran's winning formula was devoted and self-sacrificing combatants. So long as Khomeini could keep the Islamic fire burning among the youth, it seemed as if Iran was destined to win the war. Khomeini believed this and that was why he refused to yield to the growing pressure for peace until after Iran faced consecutive defeats on the battlefield. So why did Iran's advancing military machine suddenly crumble, in spite of the fact that in terms of military hardware it had never been in a better position?

The Iraqi soldiers were always said to have low morale. They readily surrendered in the face of advancing Iranian soldiers. The usual argument was that the Iranians were fighting for Islam, which provided the most potent incentive to fight to the bitter end. For the Islamic zealots, combat was for a divine cause and death was the greatest reward. The Iranians had as their incentive the highest eternal recompense, reserved for martyrs (*shohada*), they were the ones chosen by God, who fought and died for God. The indoctrination of Iranian combatants had provided them with a rudimentary political consciousness. They had all been steeped in a combination of Shariati's anti-imperialism and Navab-Safavi's xeno-phobia. The driving force of the Iranian fighters was their identity as soldiers of God who fought western and western-supported heretics and infidels, in an age when all those powers that claimed to be Islamic compromised with the West and betrayed the authentic Islamic cause. The righteousness and infallibility of their leaders buttressed their resolution and vigour. The clerical leadership took this devotion for granted and failed to realize that the revelation of its secret negotiations and deals with the United States and Israel would shatter its image in the eyes of its warriors and would place it in the ranks of the other compromising and collaborationist Islamic powers. A large majority of the Islamic Revolutionary Guards and a good number of the *Baseeji* volunteers were genuinely convinced of the justness of their cause and believed that their leadership was truly concerned with the glory of Islam, irrespective of worldly calculations. They had been ideologically moulded, and the mould could not be changed without grave consequences. The rank and file, as well as the ideologically committed commanders of the IRG, were shocked and disoriented by the Irangate revelations. Their firm belief in the honesty of the régime which invited them to fight for the cause of Islam was irreparably damaged. Their faith in martyrdom had not wavered, but their trust in those who benefited from their victories dwindled. Questioning and doubt eroded their convictions and gradually paralysed their fighting spirit.

It would be too simplistic not to take account of other factors which played a role in the disintegration of Iran's war machine. Undoubtedly, Iraq's widespread use of chemical weapons and the fact that the international community turned a blind eye to this outrage demoralised the Iranians. However, Iraq's use of chemical weapons in the war was not a new fact. Iraq had used such weapons since 1981.

It is important to note that Iran's real problems with mobilization started in late 1986 and persisted through 1987 and 1988. The impact of the revelations on the volunteers, conscripts and the new IRGs was so significant that the government began to openly complain about the decrease in the people's interest in the war. On 12 November 1987, Khomeini had to order the creation of the Supreme Council for the War Effort to assemble and dispatch all able-bodied individuals to the fronts. In a ten-point declaration, the council called on all those capable of carrying a weapon to register. It instructed those who could not go to the fronts, such as women and the sick, to financially support one or more warriors for the minimum of three months. Despite the government's all-out effort to replenish the manpower at the fronts, analysts were unanimous that Iran's inability to launch its usual February offensive in 1988 was due to its inability to muster the 1 million men necessary to implement a siege of Suleimaniyeh in the north and Basra to the south.

It was possible for Khomeini to turn his back on the foreign policy tenets of Navab-Safavi and Shariati subsystems since he could draw on the more pragmatic subsystems of Motahhari and Bazargan, while still remaining loyal to the Islamic system. Yet each subsystem had its own specific social and class basis. When Khomeini moved against the Guardianship Council in January 1988, it was because he wished to appeal to the social base that had to be solicited if the mobilization target of 1 million fighters set in November 1987 was to be attained. Revelations about the Islamic Republic's deals with the United States and Israel eroded that social base. The government's acceptance of the ceasefire and Khomeini's approval of it dealt another serious blow to the devoted followers of the 'Imam's "traditional" line of thought'.

The disinherited, to whom Khomeini had given a new identity as the pillars of the new Islamic society after the Shah's fall, were once again denuded of their *raison d'être*. Clearly, in the age of reconstruction, the disinherited, who had become experts only at wielding guns, had no role to play. The dispossessed were used by the clerical leadership and, finally, abandoned. The problem, however, was that the new social class to which the clerical leadership now had to turn for support, namely the property-owning bourgeoisie, had never trusted nor supported the régime wholeheartedly. Even if the régime succeeded in assuring the bourgeoisie of financial gains, it could never convince them that they would be left free to reap the profits of their investments. The bourgeoisie and the professionals had turned against the Shah because the Shah could not give them the political freedoms which they sought. Clearly the Islamic Republic was even less likely to provide those democratic rights which it had taken 10 years to crush. Switching from one base of support to another introduced a destabilizing element in the Islamic political system. Having alienated, if not antagonized, its dispossessed or disinherited social base, the Islamic Republic had no sure means of obtaining the support of the professionals and the modern bourgeoisie which it now sought to rally to its cause. This loss of ideological support will, therefore, force the régime to depend on apolitical and opportunistic elements. Unless it moves rapidly towards the reforms necessary for the implementation of the Motahhari-Bazargan subsystem, the clerical leadership's fate could resemble that of the Shah, who was left with no active power base at the end of his rule.

The Corps of the Islamic Revolutionary Guards (CIRG) will remain the hard core of opposition to the Islamic Republic's westward leaning foreign policy. The weakening, bureaucratization or gradual dismantling of the CIRG will remove an important hurdle on the way to *rapprochement*, but will also disarm the devoted armed supporters of the Islamic régime, leaving the régime at the mercy of an army which has never identified with nor benefited from the revolution.

The disarray in the ranks of the opposition in exile and the Islamic Republic's defeat of the People's Mojahedeen National Liberation Army demonstrate the absence of any viable and militarily comparable political fighting force. On 26 July 1988, the National Liberation Army (NLA) launched an attack into Iran from its base in Iraq. The People's Mojahedeen crossed the border with an estimated 6,800 to 8,000-strong force, with the objective of rapidly reaching Kermanshah and subsequently moving on to Hamadan and Teheran. The Mojahedeen assumed that their compatriots would welcome them with open arms as liberators. The NLA was, in fact, routed somewhere between Islamabad and

Kermanshah, leaving behind well over 4,000 dead.[2] The defeat of the Mojahedeen's well-trained and well-equipped army which was reported to have advanced under heavy Iraqi air cover demonstrated that although the Mojahedeen's urban guerilla force could harass the Islamic Republic, they were not a real threat to the régime.

The ceasefire presented itself as an ideal occasion for the régime to exorcise the ghosts of past radicalism, consolidate its power at home and embark upon reconstruction. Such glaring change in policy necessitated its own vocabulary and tools. In an important article in the daily *Ettelaat* which was under the direct supervision of Khomeini's office, *Daftar Imam*, Hojatolislam Hojattee-e Kermani, a prominent member of the clergy who had been a representative to the Assembly of Experts and later to the first parliament, wrote a series of articles, explaining the necessities of the revolution's 'new age'. The most important characteristic of this age, he argued, was the supremacy of reason. Hojattee-e Kermani argued that in the new age of reason ushered in by the ceasefire, which he referred to as the revolution's phase of maturity, the tools of 'anger and rage' had to be replaced with 'wisdom and reason'.[3] The article generated important exchanges which explained the prevailing mood of moderation in foreign policy. Writers in *Ettelaat* argued that Iran's foreign policy towards the United States had to be established on the basis of 'mutual benefits' and pressed for the 'removal of political, mental, legal and economic hurdles on the way to normalising relations with the U.S.'.[4]

Post-war reconstruction rekindled the old feud between the statists and the supporters of *laissez-faire*. The general tendency of the leadership became very clear after an important speech by Khomeini. The Islamic Republic had embarked on the abandonment of the Shariati-Navab-Safavi subsystems. Even the rhetorical lip-service paid to egalitarian, anti-exploitative, anti-imperialist and autarkic principles was dropped. Prime Minister Moussavi, who had always been a staunch supporter of de-linking from the western economies, direct and active control of the economy by the government and self-reliance as the most suitable strategy for economic development, had to speak in favour of a *laissez-faire* economy. The Prime Minister's apparent change of heart occurred after Khomeini's intervention in favour of leaving economic activities to the private sector. Khomeini told the president, prime minister and members of the government that: 'the people should be allowed to participate in importation, while the government should only supervise'.[5] Khomeini's statement clearly endorsed the position of the pro-*laissez-faire* faction which had persistently fought against the encroachments of the government on the private sector. After the ceasefire, President Khamenei declared that, 'In the process of post-war reconstruction, it is impossible for a nation not to use know-how, expertise and capabilities of foreigners'.[6] Khamenei's statement was an attempt at pre-empting the statist faction and heralded the official switch to an open-door economic and foreign-policy position similar to that endorsed by Bazargan during the provisional government.

Yet there were still those in the leadership who wished to whip up xenophobic feeling to further their own factional interests. A week after Khamenei's statement, Hojatolislam Mohtashemi, the minister of the interior, responded to Khamenei and retorted that: 'there are those who repeatedly argue that we have to use the knowledge of foreigners in the process of reconstructing our country, these people are either ignorant or traitors'.[7] It took Khomeini's espousal of the *laissez-faire* position to silence the supporters of the Shariati subsystem, such as Mohtashemi and Khoeini, who hoped to obtain political power through Khomeini's grace. After Khomeini's intervention, Prime Minister Moussavi said 'we will undoubtedly use and benefit from the knowledge of foreigners and their technology. But this cooperation should not lure Iran into the trap of dependency and uproot the values of the Islamic Revolution'.[8] The prime minister announced the government's new modified position and said 'we do not intend to adopt a completely open-door policy and we will decide on the participation of foreign firms on a case to case basis'.[9] Moussavi went as far as saying 'we do not write-off the possibility of seeking foreign loans, but such loans would have to be earmarked for specific projects and the duration of the credit would not be for more than 2 or 3 years'.[10]

Post-war economic reconstruction based upon a *laissez-faire* model, which weakens the role and control of the government in domestic distribution and foreign trade, inevitably provides greater power to the commercial bourgeoisie, whose lucrative activities have always been the target of attack by those who consider themselves as the supporters of the disinherited. The industrial bourgeoisie who were harrassed and persecuted in the initial stage of the revolution, usually for their close relations with the imperial court, were later left more or less unmolested and were even encouraged to increase their investment. Behzad Nabavi who entered the Rajaee government as a radical, gradually lost his fire and as minister of heavy industries pleaded with private investors to invest in the industrial sector, rather than the commercial sector. The relative freedom of the bourgeoisie during the post-war reconstruction period will, inevitably, bring in foreign firms and foreigners along with them. The increasing economic prosperity of the bourgeoisie and its economic implications do not seem to be of great concern to the clerical leadership. The greatest problem for the régime is the effect of such widespread and unbridled interaction and cooperation with foreigners on the Islamic values and morals that have been so painfully imposed by the clerical leadership. The spectre of the westernization process that swept Iran after the increase in oil prices in 1973 still haunts the clerical leadership.

The Islamic Republic is confronted with the inevitable task of reconstruction, which means the expenditure of large sums of money. Iran can finance its reconstruction by increasing its oil exports, seeking new loans or obtaining war reparations from Iraq. In contrast to Iraq, which has some $70 billion of debts, Iran is creditworthy and benefits from a sound financial record. Iran is reported to have short-term debts of $6–8 billion, which are matched by its liquid overseas assets,[11] and so it could easily borrow money if it wished. The prime minister's statement indicates that it might well do so. Mr Tariq Aziz, Iraq's foreign minister, has perceptively pointed out that 'Iran may have no friends, but it has plenty of suitors'.[12]

The ceasefire generated a rush of diplomatic and commercial envoys to Teheran to negotiate future cooperation. Within weeks of the ceasefire, the Japanese offered to help rebuild Iran's war-ravaged areas, high-level diplomatic missions from Australia, Italy, Japan, Turkey, India, Pakistan and Kuwait arrived in Teheran and the Korean Institute for Economics and Technology estimated that South Korea alone might pick up $15–16 billion in construction contracts over the 1988–93 period.[13] Iran was also reported to have started negotiating a contract with America's Bechtel company and France's Spie-Batignolles company jointly to manage a new refinery at Arak, near Bandar Abbas.[14]

The final issue, which is of both practical and theoretical interest, is the degree to which the Islamic Republic can be categorized as totalitarian. The Islamic Republic's monopoly over all means of effective domestic mass communication and education, along with regular physical and psychological repression of any deviation from the state's version of Universal Truth, does indicate a totalitarian state. The Islamic Republic's position in terms of the inter-communal conflict between the abode of Islam and that of atheists and disbelievers, which can only be resolved through the victory of Islam, can be viewed as a theory of world domination derived from an official ideology. The selfless character of the adherents of a totalitarian system could also easily be detected in the fighting spirit of the Islamic soldiers during the Iran-Iraq war. The cases of zealot Islamic mothers proudly denouncing their politically deviationist children and rejoicing at the death sentences given to them are illustrations of a fanaticism which has left a deep imprint on the social history of contemporary Iran.

According to Hannah Arendt,

> Wherever totalitarianism rose to power, it developed entirely new political institutions and destroyed all social, legal and political traditions of the country. No matter what the specifically national tradition or the particular spiritual source of its ideology, totalitarian governments always transformed classes into masses, supplanted the party system not by one-party dictatorship, but by a mass movement, shifted the centre of power from the army to the police and established a foreign policy openly directed towards world domination.[15]

Arendt adds that 'If lawfulness is the essence of non-tyrannical governments and lawlessness is the essence of tyranny, then terror is the essence of totalitarian domination'.[16]

It seems that by all standards, the Islamic Republic does qualify as a totalitarian state, yet the clerical leadership has fallen prey to so much vacillation, pragmatism and back-peddling, that the aim of all totalitarian states, the creation of a New Man in the image of the state ideology, has become difficult, if not impossible, to achieve.

However, the existence of numerous Islamic subsystems and the effective use of each in times of need prevent the Islamic Republic from setting its targets on a specific model of a new Islamic Man. As long as the political system needs the competition of subsystems for its survival, it cannot even move towards becoming totalitarian. Whenever the Islamic Republic confronted challenges which questioned the leadership of Khomeini, it applied terror to obtain conformity, yet dissent among those who publicly announced their allegiance to Khomeini was left unmolested. All four subsystems with their different conceptions of the New Islamic Man were allowed the right of expression, even though some were subjected to periodic waves of repression.

Khomeini's dilemma was that he could not risk jeopardizing the image of infallibility, sagacity and justice associated with his position as jurisconsult by being proven wrong and unwise by the failures and shortcomings that are the natural consequences of the practical government of a state. His attempt to combine the positions of leader and jurisconsult forced him to tolerate the existence of different subsystems so that he could easily distance himself from any one of them, blaming the ideas and projects associated with that subsystem for any failures. Khomeini needed other subsystems to turn to and embrace, to preserve the notion of the infallibility of the Islam that he wished to symbolize. His Islam became an amorphous amalgam of all four subsystems. Khomeini did not take risks when survival of the Islamic Republic was at stake. He pushed no aspect of his ideology against domestic and foreign resistance without being sure that he would be able to prevail. Wherever resistance to his aspirations proved to destabilize or effectively threaten the Islamic Republic, he took a step backwards, reassessed the situation, modified his position and shifted the focus of attention.

Claiming that Islam had been endangered by the Shah's policies, on 5 June 1963, Komeini's followers heeded their leader's call and for the first time engaged the Pahlavi régime in a bloody confrontation. On 4 June 1989, while the Islamic Republic was preparing for the annual commemoration of this historic date, the death of Ayatollah Khomeini was announced. Within 26 years, Khomeini had made his spectacular political debut, been forced into exile, challenged and dismantled the mighty Pahlavi régime, established his vision of an Islamic state and adopted all possible measures to ensure the survival of the Islamic Republic after his own death.

Two months before his death, Khomeini had secured the resignation of his heir to the position of leader and supreme jurisconsult, Ayatollah Montazeri, who had been chosen by the second Assembly of Experts in 1985 to succeed Khomeini, resigned under pressure from Khomeini, who was increasingly irritated by Montazeri's outspoken criticism of the régime's policies and excesses. Montazeri's growing sympathy for the Bazargan subsystem and the political implications of such *rapprochement* disquieted Khomeini whose policies had long been the target of Bazargan's criticism. Since 1985, Montazeri, who had exemplary credentials as a combative political activist, had been groomed as a *marje-*

e taqlid (source of religious imitation). Realizing the theoretical and practical problems that Montazeri's dismissal could create in terms of finding a new successor, Khomeini ordered the separation of political leadership from supreme religious leadership.

Yet Article 107 of the Constitution clearly stated that the leader of the Islamic Republic had to be a *marja*. Khomeini therefore convened a council and charged it with reviewing and revising the Constitution. In 1979, Khomeini was concerned with democratic appearances and had therefore left the drafting of the Constitution to the Assembly of Experts. Even though the majority of the Assembly's members were clerics, they were still popularly elected representatives. Ten years later Khomeini felt confident enough to confer the responsibility of revising the Constitution to a handpicked few whom he trusted. The revised Constitution increased the powers of the governing jurisconsult, legalized the separation of the position of the leader from that of the highest religious authority, abolished the Supreme Judicial Council, increased the authority of the head of the judiciary and finally abolished the position of prime minister conferring his responsibilities upon the president.

The new turn of events further reduced the significance of supreme religious authority in the governing of the Islamic state. Anxious about the fate of the Islamic state under the leadership of apolitical religious authorities such as Ayatollah Golpayegani or Marashi-Najafi, Khomeini opted for lesser ranked yet politicized clergy who would continue his domestic and foreign policies.

On the same day that Khomeini's death was announced, the Assembly of Experts convened for an extraordinary session and elected Hojatolislam Khamenei, who had been Iran's president, as the new leader and governing jurisconsult. In Iran's religious hierarchy numerous clerics ranked higher than Khamenei, who was not a *marja*. Moslems therefore had to follow the religious edicts of a source of imitation other than their political leader. Ironically, Khomeini had initiated the process of separating religion from politics, a process he had fought against ever since he entered politics.

In the absence of Khomeini as the supreme religious and political authority of Iran and the guarantor of internal equilibrium, the subsystems would be forced to bring their conflict out into the open in order to obtain effective political power. Post-Khomeini Iran will witness a protracted power struggle between these subsystems. The rules governing this tug-of-war could vary from a peaceful and gradual process effectuated through elections to violent plots, conspiracies, arests and executions within the competing subsystems.

The central question which remains is whether the fragile Islamic system of values and life-style now in place will stand the pressure of the billions of dollars which will flow through the economy in times of peace. Will not the new social relations permeating the areas and sectors in which the money will be spent necessitate a cultural and value system different from that which the Islamic Republic has sought to impose? Will not post-war prosperity breed consumerism, idleness, moral laxity and a love for leisure? In sum, will not the Iranian bourgeoisie demand a value system compatible with that of their international counterparts? The embourgeoisification of even the devoted functionaries of the Islamic Republic, in the absence of excuses to mobilize people and create mass hysteria, could usher in a welfare-oriented society which would eagerly forget its revolutionary period of rage, self-sacrifice and instability. Should the clerical leadership become pragmatic enough to allow the re-emergence of a non-Islamic value system, while maintaining the 'Islamic Order' as the basis for their own power, a coalition of democratic social forces may well dethrone them and impose the sovereignty of the people – the as yet unfulfilled objective of the Iranian revolution.

Notes

1. *Stratégique,* Numero 31, June 1986.
2. The *Guardian* Weekly, 11 September 1988.
3. *Ettelaat*, 25 Mordad, 1367.
4. *Ettelaat* cited in *Enqelab-e Islami*, 12 September 1988.
5. *Enqelab-e Islami*, 12 September 1988.
6. *Keyhan*, 21 Shahrivar, 1367.
7. Ibid.
8. *Ettelaat*, 19 Shahrivar, 1367.
9. Ibid.
10. Ibid.
11. *The Economist*, 20 August 1988.
12. *The Economist*, 13 August 1988
13. *Far Eastern Economic Review*, 8 September 1988.
14. *The Economist*, 20 August 1988.
15. Hannah Arendt, *The Origins of Totalitarianism* (New York: Harcourt Brace Jovanovich, 1973), p. 460.
16. Ibid., p. 464.

Bibliography

Abrahamian, E. *Iran Between Two Revolutions* (Princeton, NJ: Princeton University Press, 1982).

Afrasiabi, B. and Deqan, S. *Taleqani Va Tarikh* (Teheran: Nagsh-e Jahan Press,1359).

Ahmad, K. (ed.) *Studies in Islamic Economics* (London: The Islamic Foundation, 1981).

Akhavan Towhidi, H. *Dar Passe Pardeh Tazvir* (Paris: n.p., n.d.).

Akhavi, S. *Religion and Politics in Contemporary Iran* (Albany, NY: State University of New York Press, 1980).

Algar, H. *The Islamic Revolution in Iran* (London: The Open Press, 1980).

Alnassrawi, A. 'Economic Consequences of the Iran-Iraq War', *Third World Quarterly*, Vol. 8, No. 3.

Anjoman-e Modiran-e Sanaye-e Jomhouri-e Islami-e Iran, *Estrategihaye Tose-e Sanaye-e Iran* (Teheran, n.p., 1363).

Arendt, H. *The Origins of Totalitarianism* (New York: Harcourt Brace Jovanovich, 1973).

Bakhash, S. *The Reign of the Ayatollahs* (London: I. B. Tauris, 1985).

Bani-Sadr, A-H. *Eqtesad-e Towhidi* (n.p., 1357).

Bani-Sadr, A-H. *Khianat be Omid* (Paris: n.p., 1982).

Bank-e Markazi-e Iran, *Hesabhay-e Melli-e Iran: 1338–56* (Teheran: Bank-e Markazi, 1360).

Bank-e Markazi-e Jomhouri-e Islami-e Iran, *Barrasi Eqtesadi-e Keshvar Ba'd az Enqelab* (Teheran: Bank-e Markazi, 1363).

Baqer Sadr, M. *Eqtesad-e Ma* trans. M-K. Bojnourdi (Teheran: Entesharat Bohran, 1350).

Baqir al-Sadr, *Islam and Schools of Economics*, trans. M. A. Ansari (Accra: Islamic Seminary Publications, 1982).

Bayat, A. *Workers and Revolution in Iran* (London: Zed Books, 1987).

Bazargan, A-A. *Moshkelaat va Masael Avalin Saal-e Engelab* (Teheran: n.p., 1362).

Bazargan, M. *Bazyabi-e Arzeshha* 3 vols (Teheran: n.p., 1361).

Bazargan, M. *Mazhab da Eurupa* (Teheran: Bongahe Matbuati Iran, 1344).

Bazargan, M. *Enqelab-e Iran dar do Harekat* (Teheran: n.p., 1363).

Bazargan, M. *Azadi az do Didgah* (Teheran: Nehzat-e Azadi Iran, 1362).

Behdad, S. 'Foreign Exchange Gap, Structural Constraints and the Political Economy of Exchange Rate Determination in Iran', *International Journal of Middle East Studies*, Vol. 20, 1988.

Beit-Hallahmi, B. *The Israeli Connection* (London: I. B. Tauris, 1987).

Bell, J. F. *A History of Economic Thought* (New York: The Ronald Press Co.,

1967).

Bernard, C. and Khalilzad, Z. *The Government of God – Iran's Islamic Republic* (New York: Columbia University Press, 1984).

Bharier, J. *Economic Development in Iran: 1900–1970* (New York: Oxford University Press, 1971).

Biazar-e Shirazi, A-K. (ed. and trans.) *Resaleh-e Novin: masael-e Eqtesadi, Vol. 2 (Teheran: Nashr-e Farhang-e Islami, 1362).*

Bill, J. A. *The Eagle and the Lion* (New Haven: Yale University Press, 1988).

Bill, J. A. 'Power and Religion in Revolutionary Iran', *The Middle East Journal* Vol. 36, No. 1, 1982.

Bottomore, T. *A Dictionary of Marxist Thought* (Oxford: Basil Blackwell, 1985).

Cordesman, A. H. *The Iran-Iraq War* (London: The Royal United Services Institute, 1987).

Christopher, W. *American Hostages in Iran* (New Haven: Yale University Press, 1985).

Dadgostaree-e Jomhouri-e Islami-e Iran, *Qaeleh Chahardahome Esfand* (Teheran: Dadgostare, 1359).

Daftar-e Hamkari-e Hozeh va Daneshgah, *Daramadi bar Eqtesad-e Islami* (Teheran: Salman Farsi, 1363).

Doi, A. R. *Shariah: The Islamic Law* (London: Tatta Publishers, 1984).

Enayat, H. *Modern Islamic Political Thought* (London: Macmillan Education Ltd., 1982).

Esposito, J. *Voices of Resurgent Islam* (Oxford: Oxford University Press, 1983).

Fischer, M. *Iran: From Religious Dispute to Revolution* (Cambridge, Mass: Harvard University Press, 1980).

Gandy, R. *Marx and History* (Austin: University of Texas Press, 1979).

Godelier, M., *Perspectives in Marxist Anthropology* (Cambridge: Cambridge University Press, 1977).

Grummon, S. R. *The Iran-Iraq War* (New York: Praeger Publishers, 1982).

Halliday, F. *Iran: Dictatorship and Development* (Harmondsworth: Penguin Books Ltd., 1979).

Hashemi-Rafsanjani, A-A. *Siasat-e Eqtesadi* (Teheran: Hezb-e Jomhouri-e Islami, 1362).

Hashemi-Rafsanjani, A-A. *Notgehaye qabl az Dastour* (Teheran: Ravabet Omoomi Majlis Shoura-e Islami, 1362 and 1363).

Hazrat-e Ali, *Nahjul Balagha* (Rome: European Islamic Cultural Center, 1984).

Hesamian, F., Etemad, G. and Haeree, M-R. *Shahr Neshini dar Iran* (Teheran: Agah,1363).

Iran: Yearbook 88 (Bonn: Moini-Biontino Verlagsgesellschaft mbH, 1988).

Irfani, S. *Revolutionary Islam in Iran* (London: Zed Books, 1983).

Kazemi, F. *Poverty and Revolution in Iran* (New York: New York University Press, 1980).

Keddie, N. R. (ed.) *Religion and Politics in Iran* (New Haven: Yale University Press, 1983).

Khalili, A. *Gam be Gam ba Enqelab* (Teheran: Soroosh, 1360).

Khavari, M. *Naqde ketabe kashf al-Asrar* (Paris: Alam Afrouz, 1364).

Khomeini, R. *Kashf al-Asrar* (n.p.: n.p., n.d.).

Khomeini, R. *Hokomat Islami* (n.p.: n.p., n.d.).

Khomeini, R. *Nedaye Haq* (Paris: n.p., 1357) selection of speeches and interviews.

Khomeini, R. *Nedaye Haq* (Teheran: Qalam Publishers, 1357).

Khomeini, R. *Kalam Imam. Shakhsiatha* (Teheran: Amir Kabir, 1361).

Khomeini, R. *Islam and Revolution*, trans H. Algar (London: Routledge & Kegan Paul, 1981).

Khoshneiyat, H. *Sayyed Mojtaba Navab-Safavi* (Teheran: Entesharat Manshoor-e Baradari, 1360).

Lajevardi, H. *Labour Unions and Autocracy in Iran* (Syracuse: Syracuse University Press, 1985).

Ledeen, M. and Lewis, W. *Debacle: The American Failure in Iran* (New York: Vintage Books, 1982).

Madani, J. *Tarikhe Siyasi Moasere Iran*, 2 vols. (Teheran: Daftar Entesharat Islami, 1361).

Mannan, M. A. *Islamic Economics: Theory and Practice* (Cambridge: The Islamic Academy, 1986).

Markaz-e Amar-e Iran, *Amar-e Kargahay-e Bozorg-e Keshvar: 1358–62* (Teheran: 1363).

Markaz-e Amar-e Iran, *Amar-e Kargahay-e Bozorg-e Sana'ti: 1355* (Teheran: 1364 and 1365).

Markaz-e Amar-e Iran, *Gozideh-e Natayej-e Tafsili-e Sarshomari, 1365* (Teheran: 1367).

Markaz-e Amar-e Iran, *Khososiat-e Omedh-e Jame'iati-e Mantageh-e Ke shvar: 1365* (Teheran: n.d.).

Markaz-e Amar-e Iran, *Amar-e Kargahay-e Bozorg-e Sana'ti Taht-e Modiriat-e Bakhsh-e Dolati: 1362* (Teheran, 1364).

Markaz-e Amar-e Iran, *Amare-e Kargahay-e Kouchak-e Sana'ti Shahri: 1355* (Teheran, 1359).

Markaz-e Amar-e Iran, *Natayej-e Amargiri-e Keshavarzi: 1361* (Teheran, 1363).

Markaz-e Amar-e Iran, *Salnameh Amari: 1363* (Teheran, 1364).

Marx, K. *Surveys from Exile* (London: Penguin Books, 1977).

Marx, K. *The Class Struggle in France: 1848–1850* (New York: International Publishers, 1972).

Mawdudi, A. *Islamic Law and Constitution* (Lahore: Islamic Publications, 1967).

Mazrui, A. 'Ideological Encounters of the Third World', *Third World Book Review*, Vol. 7, No. 6, 1986.

Motahhari, M. *Adl Elahi* (Teheran: Entesharat Sadr, n.d.).

Motahhari, M. *Piramoone Enqelab-e Islami* (Teheran: Entesharat Sadra, n.d.).

Motahhari, M. *Naqdi bar Marxism* (Teheran: Entesharat Sadra, 1363).

Motahhari, M. *Moshkelaat Assasi dar Sazemane Ruhaniyat* (Teheran: n.p., n.d.).

Motahhari, M. *Nehzathaye Islami dar sad Saleh Akhir* (Teheran: Entesharat Sadra, n.d.).

Motahhari, M. *Dah Goftar* (Teheran: Entesharat Hekmat, n.d.).

Motahhari, M. *Jamme va Tarikh* (Teheran: Entesharat Sadra, n.d.).

Navab-Safavi, M. *Barnameh Enqelabi-e Fadaian-e Islam* (Teheran: n.p., n.d.).

Nehzat-e Azadi Iran, *Asnade Nehzat-e Moqavemat-e Melli* (Teheran: Nehzate Azadi Iran, 1938).

Nehzat-e Azadi Iran, M. *Bohran, Tahlili az Vekhamat ozae Keshvar* (Teheran: Nehzat-e Azadi Iran, 1361).

Nehzat-e Azadi Iran, *Piramoone Dastgirie Sarane Hezbe Khaeen Tudeh* (Teheran: Nehzat-e Azadi Iran, 1362).

Nehzat-e Azadi Iran, *Sheh Nameh-e Sar Goshadeh* (Teheran: Nehzat-e Azadi Iran, 1362).

Nehzat-e Azadi Iran, *Tahlili Piramoone Jang va Solh* (Teheran: Nehzat-e Azadi Iran, 1363).

Nehzat-e Azadi Iran, *Mozakeveh, Atashbas, Solh* (Teheran: Nehzat-e Azadi Iran, 1364).

Nehzat-e Azadi Iran, *Hoshdar* (Teheran: Nehzate Azadi Iran, 1367).

Nehzat-e Zanane Mosalman, *Mavazee Nehzat-e Azadi dar Barbare Enqelab-e Islami* (Teheran: Nehzate Zanan-e Mosalman, 1361).

Nomani, F. 'Macroeconomic Trends in the Economic Crisis of Iran', *Mondes en Developpement*, Vol. 15, No. 58–9.

Nomani, F. *Takamol-e Feudalism dar Iran*, Vol. 1 (Teheran: Kharazmi, 1358).

Norton, R. A., *Amal and the Shi'a* (Austin: University of Texas Press, 1987).

O'Ballance, E. *The Gulf War* (London: Brassey's Defence Publishers, 1988).

Parsons, A. *The Pride and the Fall* (London: Jonathan Cape, 1984).

Piscatori, J. (ed.) *Islam in the Political Process* (Cambridge: Cambridge University Press, 1983).

Rahnema, Z. *Qur'an Majid Tarjomeh va Tafseer* (Teheran: n.p., 1348).

Rahnema, Z. *Payambar* (Teheran: Amir-Kabir, 2536).

Rajaee, M-A. *Gozideh Sokhanan Raies Jomhoor* (Teheran: Nashr Saberin, 1360).

Ramazani, R. K. *Revolutionary Iran* (Baltimore: The Johns Hopkins University Press, 1986).

Rouhani, H. *Shariatmadari dar Dadgahe Tarikh* (Qum: Daftar Entesherat Islami, 1361).

Rouhani, H. *Barrasi va Tahlil Nehzate Imam Khomeini* (Teheran: n.p., 1361).

Saikal, A. *The Rise and Fall of the Shah* (New Jersey: Princeton University Press, 1980).

Schumpeter, J. A. *History of Economic Analysis* (London: George Allen & Unwin, 1963).

Shariati, A. *Collected Works* (Teheran: Entesharat Niloufar, 1362).

Shariati, A. *Pedar, Madar, ma Motahamim* (Teheran: Hosseinieh-e Irshad, 1350).

Shariati, A. *Martyrdom* (Teheran: Abu Dharr Foundation, n.d.)

Shariati, A. *Hajj* (Houston: Free Islamic Literature Inc., 1980).

Shariati, A. *Mazhab Alieh Mazhab* (n.p.: n.p., n.d.).

Shariati, A. *Tarikh Adyan* (Teheran: Entesharat Taheri, n.d.).

Sick, G. *All Fall Down* (London: I. B. Tauris, 1985).

Soroosh, A. (ed.) *Yad nameh ostad shaheed Morteza Motahhari* (Teheran: Sazeman Entesharat va Amoozesh Enqelab-e Islami, 1360).

Taheri, A. *The Spirit of Allah* (London: Hutchinson, 1985).

Tahir-keli, S. and Ayubi, S. (eds.) *The Iran-Iraq War* (New York: Praeger Publishers, 1983).

Taleghani, M. *Society and Economics in Islam*, trans. R. Campbell (Berkeley: Mizan Press, 1982).

Tehrani, B. *Pejooheshi dar Eqtesad-e Iran: 1354–64* 2 vols (Paris: Khavaran, 1365).

The Bank of the Islamic Republic of Iran, *Economic Report Sheet: 1362* (Teheran: n.p., 1364).

The Tower Commission Report, the Full Text (New York: Bantam Books and Time Books, 1987).

The Constitution of the Islamic Republic of Iran (Teheran: Islamic Propagation Organisation, n.d.).

Vance, C. R. *Hard Choices: Critical Years in America's Foreign Policy* (New York: Simon & Schuster, 1983).

Vezarat-e Barnameh va Budget, *Faslnameh-e Amari: 1364* (Teheran, 1365).

Vezarat-e Barnameh va Budget, *Gozaresh-e Eqtesadi-e Sal-e 1362* (Teheran, 1364).

Vezarat-e Barnameh va Budget, *Gozaresh-e Eqtesadi-e Sal-e 1363* (Teheran, 1364).

Vezarat-e Barnameh va Budget, *Gozaresh-e Eqtesadi-e sal-e 1364* (Teheran, 1365).

Vezarat-e Ershad Islami, *Barrasi Mostanadi az Mavazee Gorouhha dar Qebale Enqelab-e Islami* (Teheran: Vezarate Ershad Islami, 1360).

Woodward, B. *Veil: The Secret Wars of the CIA* (New York: Harcourt Brace Jovanovich, 1973).

Writings and Declarations of Imam Khomeini, trans. and annotated H. Algar (Berkeley: Mizan Press, 1981).

Zabih, S. *Iran since the Revolution* (London: Croom Helm, 1982).

Zemzemi, A. H. T. *The Iran-Iraq War* (San Clemente: United States Publishing Company, 1986).

Iranian newspapers and periodicals

Aghazi-no
Ayandegan
Azadi
Bamdad
Bulletin-e Siyasi (Fadaian)
Enqelab-e Islami
Enqelab-e Islami dar Hejrat
Ettelaat
Fadai
Gozaresh seminar
Hafteh-nameh-e Otag-e Bazargani, Sanaye'va Ma'aden
Jomhouri-e Islami
Journal of Foreign Policy
Kar
Keyhan
Keyhan Chape Landan
Keyhan Hava'ee (air mail edition)
Keyhan Saal
Khalq-e Mosalman
Mojahed
Payame Jebhe-e Melli
Peygham-e Emrouz
Resalat
Rouzegar, E. Now
Sana't-e Haml-o Naql
Teheran Mosavar

Index